# GLOBAL STUDIES

## A Historical and Contemporary Reader

**Kendall Hunt**
publishing company

## Giles Gunn

*University of California Santa Barbara*

# Kendall Hunt

publishing company

Copyright © 2003, 2018 by Giles Gunn

ISBN 978-1-5249-4674-6

Published in the United States of America

# Contents

## Chapter 5: The Scientific Revolutions in Global Perspective........... 81

## Chapter 6: The Enlightenment Project and the Liberal Agenda .... 103

## Chapter 7: Capitalism and the Industrial Revolution.................... 121

## Chapter 8: Liberalism and the Democratic Revolutions................ 145

## Chapter 9: Nationalism and Imperialism..................................... 159

## Chapter 10: Global War in the Twentieth Century ..................... 183

## Chapter 11: Marxism and the Socialist Revolutions..................... 197

# *Acknowledgments*

For this substantially revised edition of *Global Studies 1* under the new title *Global Studies: A Historical and Contemporary Reader*, I am grateful to my colleague, Esther Lezra, for her advise and support. I also wish to thank Taylor Knuckey of Kendall Hunt Publishing for her warm response to the idea of putting together a new edition of this reader and to Beverly Kraus for her enthusiastic and professional coordination of this project.

The image on the cover of this book is the photograph of planet earth known as "Blue Marble" taken by astronaut Harrison Schmitt of the crew of *Apollo 17*. As one of the first unobstructed images of the earth, the publication of this photograph and others like it is a global event in itself because it, or rather they, mark the first time that humankind has had an opportunity to see in full view the place of its own habitation in the universe.

# *Introduction*

This reader is designed to introduce students to some of the ways that the world has been woven into a system of interrelated but far from completely integrated processes, interactions, and transformations since long before the beginning of the Common Era. We will be concentrating on patterns of transmission, dispersion, exchange, and interconnection throughout the world that are primarily historical, ideological, or cultural. But even as we examine the historical emergence and consequences of global belief systems and cultural forms and practices, we will also need to look at important changes in global politics, sociology, and economics. Our aim will be to see how global formations, de-formations, and re-formations, at even the most ideational and subjective levels, have altered the way the world is now assumed to function as some kind of coordinated, or at least concatenated, system. We will also be interested in how scholars analyze and evaluate such phenomena.

The terms "global" and "globalization" are fraught with so many complications and discontents that one almost wishes one could substitute others in their place. As now used, globalization conjures up in many minds a spectacle of instantaneous electronic financial transfers, the amoral operations of the capitalist free-market, the erasure of local cultural differences, and the expansion of Western, but most especially American, power. This is hardly an attractive prospect, and when it is coupled with the world-wide evidence of increasing economic inequality, worsening degradation of the environment, heightened rivalry among ethnic groups, spreading militarism, the expansion of religious nationalism, normalization of the use of terror, and the proliferation of weapons of mass destruction, globalization becomes associated in many minds with some of the most destructive forces on the planet.

In the face of such a specter, it is small comfort to learn that globalizing trends have, since World War II, also made possible a threefold increase in the world's per capita income, reduced by half the number of people living in direst poverty, reinforced the desire to work for nuclear disarmament, lent support to the war against terror, helped expand the environmental movement, and encouraged the organization of literally thousands of international groups and non-governmental organizations

(NGOs) devoted to addressing various social, political, and economic grievances and the relief of human suffering generally.[1] Yet despite such developments (and sometimes, paradoxically, even because of them), the gap between rich and poor in the world is being widened still further by the forces of economic as well as political and cultural globalization, and these forces need to be thoroughly and rapidly reorganized, as the United Nations has stated repeatedly, if this gap is not to reach catastrophic proportions. Global governance will have to be restructured to ensure massive and efficient debt relief for insolvent nations, to redirect aid to the poorest countries, to reform the allocation of the world's limited resources, to curtail corruption in those countries where mismanagement discourages foreign investment, to redress the continual violation of human rights, to ensure that all counties in the world submit to the rule of international law, to restrict the spread of international terrorism, and to reduce the spread and number, as well as improve the security, of weapons of mass destruction. But the restructuring of global governance will also have to include reforms far more subtle, such as an alteration of the lenses by which cultures perceive and assess one another and an enhancement of opportunities for more and more of the world's people, as well as of sovereign states, to shape their own destinies.

However, before we venture too many generalizations about a worldwide process that in its latest phases is changing at a pace rapidly approaching what feels like warp speed, it is important to dispel a few myths about the words "globalization" and the "global" themselves. We can begin by conceding that the term "globalization" is commonly used to refer to the widening and deepening and speeding up of the interconnectedness of the world in many of its aspects, from the economic to the ecological, the cultural to the criminal, the social to the spiritual, but there are still vigorous disputes with very large consequences about just when globalization began, how it is best conceptualized, what its causal dynamics and structural features are, and whether it has, or has not, been good for the world and its peoples. About the only thing on which most students of the term "globalization" are agreed is that it refers to a set of processes by which the world is being threaded ever more tightly together, a process by which the world is becoming, if not a single place with systematic properties, then an interdependent system of localities whose fate is even more complexly, if also unpredictably, intertwined.[2]

But this in turn suggests that the corollary term "global" should not be assumed to represent some seamless whole or unified totality. The term "global" functions merely to suggest the reach and resonance of those processes by which the world is continuously being reconceived and remade as an almost infinitely intricate, but at the same time ever more interactive, organism that continues to remain something more than the simple sum of its parts. The term "global" did not achieve its meteoric rise until the mid-1980s, when it began to displace cognate terms like "international" and "international relations." Those earlier terms had come into usage toward the end of the eighteenth century and signaled the emergence of what in retrospect appears to have been a new world order, where territorial states now began to assume responsibility for organizing socio-political and cultural processes and the path was laid for the development of what, in the nineteenth century, became known as the era of European imperialism. But now at the end of the twentieth century and the beginning of the twenty-first, the ascendancy of the terms "global" and "globalization" seem to be auguries of the face that we are moving into still another world order, and this time one marked by a reduction rather than expansion of the power of "nation-states" as individuals and communities gain access to sources of information and power that are globally disseminated and thus bypass many of the traditional controls of the political state.

Yet this implies that the process of world-making, or re-making, known as globalization is a comparatively contemporary phenomenon which has accelerate to its present velocity only, perhaps, because of the collapse of the Soviet Union and hence the termination of the Cold War.[3] But a number of students of the subject push the date of this most recent and vigorous surge of globalization back a good many decades to the beginning of the modern era at the end of the nineteenth century, when industrial capitalism fueled the original expansion of European nation-states and those nation-states then undertook to acquire and consolidate colonial empires.[4] Other thinkers and scholars move the origins of the contemporary form of globalization back still further, to the inauguration of the Age of the Renaissance or, as it is often referred to, the Early Modern period, when Europe commenced its initial exploration of the rest of the globe and embarked simultaneously on the development of early world trade.[5]   *early 1600s*

Those who associate the origins of globalization with this first European Age of Exploration and Discovery are also likely to assume that when the "modern world system," as Immanuel Wallerstein has termed it, first took shape in the early 1600s, it was essentially an economic rather than political system and was built around a series of core states characterized by aggressive commercial growth, strong governmental structures, and a powerful sense of national identity, all of which permitted them to control, for their own benefit, the evolution of those weaker states and regions of the world that developed on their peripheries. Yet even then, in the seventeenth century, it was soon to become apparent that an emergent modern world system based on an extensive system of commodity exchanges was also becoming linked as well by systems of exchanges that were cultural and symbolic. Just as ideas and ideologies were being traded along with goods, so the new wealth thus accumulated was being defined not only by the size of capital reserves and sailing fleets but also by the production of commodities like buildings, monuments, and paintings reflective of new styles both of affluence and of taste. Commerce, in other words, was going cultural.

Earliest evidence on a global scale of these cultural and symbolic as well as commercial exchanges can, as a matter of fact, be detected more than two thousand years before the creation of the modern world system itself when, as historians like William H. McNeill and Marshall Hodgson have demonstrated, an Afro-Eurasian zone of civilization first came into existence over a period of something like a thousand years.[6] Stretching from the shores of the Atlantic to the waters of the Pacific, this zone of expanding interactions and transactions was organized by trade routes that served as a conduit not only for the passage of merchandise, services, and human beings but also for the slow but profound transmission—and transformation—of ideas, institutions, customs, diets, rituals, religions, and, perhaps above all, languages. Indeed, if this expanding zone of civilization, which still serves in certain respects as the prototype for the way globalization continues to operate today, reveals anything at all, it shows how cultural interactions have, throughout its long history, often proved as fateful, if not more fateful, than economic or political ones—if only because cultural transactions (and this can't be overemphasized) have so frequently determined the way economic and political transactions could be interpreted, evaluated, and even actualized.

As it happens, this history by which the world has, for several thousand years, been continuously woven and rewoven into an increasingly interlinked and interdependent assemblage of life-systems is not one to which, until very recently, the social sciences or in the humanities have paid very much attention. For all of our relatively recent interest, say, in the histories of slavery and racism, or of imperialism, colonialism, ethnicity, or even sexism, or of our earlier disciplinary involvements in such fields as comparative literature, world history, and the history of religions, or, for that matter, our pedagogical commitment to language programs (the latter of which deserve credit for keeping the possibility of globalism alive even if they could not provide a model for its full conceptualization), we still too often continue to view globalization merely as a temporary geopolitical and economic development or even as a passing academic fad and consequently fail respond to anything other than what we take to be its liabilities and banalities.

Thus while questions about globalization's evolution and subsequent historicization, or about its form and function in different locales, or about its association with other historical phenomena (such as the development of capitalism, or the democratic and, much later, socialist revolutions, or the rise of the nation-state, or the industrial revolution, or mass migration, or global war, or the transformations in communications and finance, or multiculturalism, or the World Wide Web) remain hotly debated issues both within universities and outside, globalization itself is clearly here to stay no matter how much its contemporary forms are certain to change. The challenge for higher education internationally, then, is not so much to decide whether globalization and the global deserve to be taken seriously but how best to engage them critically—how, in other words, to assess their implications and consequences without simply legitimating their most problematic features.

Needless to say, globalization has attracted its proponents and defenders as well as its skeptics and opponents. Among those who greet its features with some degree of enthusiasm, regarding globalization as essentially a positive development in a changing world that will lead to greater prosperity, peace, and freedom, one can distinguish between what David Held and his collaborators have described as "hyperglobalists" and "transformationalists."[7] "Hyperglobalists" are represented by those like the economist Kenichi Ohmae who believe that we have now entered a new era in the world's history in which most processes of human interaction and intervention are determined by the global marketplace.[8] In this new world, where economies have become denationalized, even as they have become more hegemonic, and the borders between nation-states have been rendered more fluid and porous, transnational class allegiances among elites and knowledge workers are displacing more traditional and territorialized ways of living and thinking and a new global civilization is evolving with its own mechanisms of world governance, such as the International Monetary Fund and the International World Court. "Transformationalists," on the other hand, like the sociologist Anthony Giddens, maintain that the unprecedented character of recent global change has produced a still more massive shakeout of institutions and societies that is by no means confined to economics alone and whose outcome still remains uncertain. New patterns of global stratification, together with an increased deterritorialization of economic enterprise, have seriously diminished the power once exercised by nation-states and, as a consequence, nation-states now find themselves increasingly subject to the jurisdiction, and sometimes the coercion, of international authorities and institutions.[9] Thus even if states retain a measure of authority and control over their own boundaries, those boundaries have become fragmented, viscous, and formless and what they enclose and keep out still more questionable and problematic.

Not surprisingly, these more enthusiastic proponents of globalization are countered by a large and growing body of skeptics, critics, and opponents of globalization. On one side are scholars like the historian Samuel P. Huntington who question the picture of a world dominated by a single global marketplace and challenge the idea that internationalization has now eroded the power of national governments to regulate their own affairs. Even more significant, Huntington disputes the claim made by its proponents that globalization has destroyed most traditional ways of thinking.[10] To the contrary, Huntington argues that the patterns of inequality, hierarchy, and hegemony that have always structured the world economy have in fact in fact strengthened rather than weakened the attraction of various national and religious orthodoxies, and he further maintains that these traditional orthodoxies and even fundamentalisms are now fracturing the world along ethnic and cultural lines that conform to civilizational differentiations and blocs. Such blocs or assemblages of tradition, Huntington maintains, are deeply resistant, often violently, to any notions of cultural homogenization and are almost inevitably bound to produce clashes, possibly cataclysmic, with other civilizational blocs. In the face of such possibilities and eventualities, Huntington counsels the need to recognize that the new world order that is emerging globally is civilization-based and that the only way to avoid a total war among civilizations like the West or Islam or China, all of which possess universalist pretentions, depends on convincing world leaders to accept the multicivilizational character of global politics and cooperate to maintain it.

At the other pole among skeptics and critics one finds a series of thinkers and actors (many of the latter having taken to the streets to protest the policies of the World Trade Organization, the International Monetary Fund, and the World Bank) who believe that globalization simply represents another form of domination by "First World" countries of "Third World" countries, a form of domination in which individual distinctions of culture and society are being erased and local economies are becoming more firmly coopted by or subsumed within a global system of capital expansion. This group of thinkers and activists is likely to associate globalization with everything from the destruction of local culture to the depletion and degradation of the biosphere, from the practice of an expansionist, multinational capitalism bent on controlling the world's oil reserves and even, as has been attempted, the world's water supply, to the creation of a new era of Western, but primarily American, imperialism where the United States will permit no other political entity to compete with it in power.

Such differences of opinion and perspective only point up the fact that the field of global studies is a site of contestation as well as consensus. As a field of inquiry as well as of agency, its object is not necessarily to resolve such disputes so much as to deepen understanding of them by placing them in a more complex historical and intra- as well as interdisciplinary perspective. The central questions to be asked, therefore, take a variety of different forms: What are the forces that have brought the world itself into being as an interactive, ever-changing structure of processes and practices? What forms has that densely concatenated, diversely elaborated structure taken over time? What fresh light do such forms, and the factors that bring them into being, throw on such issues as personal and cultural identity—formation, mass migration, international terrorism, practices of child rearing, religious violence, human rights reform, scientific and medical practice, stock market fluctuations, the digitalizatation of information, culinary and dietary habits, and the new ubiquity of the aesthetic? Is there such a thing as a global perspective? In this new, more global era, has humanity taken on new cosmopolitan forms of expression? To help humanize, manage, and regulate this new world order, can we develop something like a global ethics that emerges not, as it were, from above but rather from below?

The answers to such questions will not, and do not, and have not come easily, but the questions themselves become more pressing every day. To gain a critical purchase on them, much less to begin to formulate plausible answers to some of them, will require something more than an admission that the materials we study in the humanities and the social sciences—as well as in the life and physical sciences—are the product of globalizing forces. In addition, it will necessitate an acknowledgement that the methods by which we study our materials, no less than the disciplinary paradigms by which we organize and interpret those materials, will have to change as well. It is not enough to admit new materials into the curriculum. We shall have to develop new optics to bring them into focus.

Evidence of a new disposition in American higher education to begin to engage globalization critically can be seen in a number of places. Chief among them is the materialization over the last several decades of new transdisciplinary configurations such as Caribbean studies, inter-American studies, Atlantic studies, European studies, Iberian and Latin American studies, African, Sub-Saharan, East Asian, South Asian, Middle Eastern, Central Asian, and now Pacific Rim studies. Similar evidence can also be found in some of the exciting cross-cultural and transnational work associated with the assortment of practices known as "cultural studies." Yet despite the notoriety of some of these academic initiatives and the important scholarship associated with others, their achievements are still too frequently known only to a comparatively small circle of specialists and, as a consequence, they have had far less impact than they should have had on the way the rest of the humanities and the social sciences prioritize their questions and organize their research and, most especially, their teaching. Thus to enhance the possibility of engaging globalization critically, it will be necessary for students, particularly in the humanities and the social sciences, to relinquish some of their older intellectual habits and acquire some new ones.

The most debilitating among former intellectual habits that need to be abandoned is the maintenance of that barrier within the academy that currently divides the social sciences from the humanities. This barrier is not only anachronistic but in many ways indefensible, since its transgression, subversion, and reconstruction has been one of the central intellectual achievements on both sides of this disciplinary divide. During the last several decades, we have witnessed not only, as the anthropologist Clifford Geertz once famously termed it, "the humanistic refiguration of social thought" but also what might be described by the proponents of literary, historical, and religious studies as a sociopolitical refiguration of humanistic thought, and yet this important conceptual revisioning has done comparatively little, at least at the level of advanced scholarship, to change the way that knowledge is structured or pursued in most academic institutions.[11] In most institutions of higher learning, we still divide the College of Arts and Sciences, or its equivalent, into artificial compounds that wall off the so-called harder natural and physical sciences from so-called softer human sciences, like the humanities and the social sciences, and then segregate the latter two from each other on the pretext that the humanities deal with values, the social sciences with facts.

Next to go will have to be the practice of thinking primarily in terms of stable entities to be studied, whether they be traditions, periods, institutions, practices, texts, careers, genres, or what-have-you. Globalization, as its closest students have made abundantly clear, is about process, movement, flow, in manifold directions, at varying degrees of speed, with differing consequences, in specific sites and particular moments. Nothing can be studied any longer with any degree of accuracy that does not take account of at least these four variables. But this in turn suggests that our

—this & next basically saying everything is complex & unique procedures for mapping such developments and their interconnections, in truth our very methods of intellectual cartography themselves, must change. Where before it was assumed that flows, whether cultural, demographic, financial, or ideological were primarily linear, uniform, and mostly regular, we now realize that their operations are better understood on the model of a fractal whose patterns are irregular, haphazard, and multidirectional.[12] We have also come to appreciate that the arrangement of such processes can be overlapping or, as biologists say, polythetic. And, finally, we have come to realize that many changes historically seem to resemble what chaos theorists call "the butterfly effect," where infinitesimal alterations in complex structures can sometimes yield consequences all out of proportion to their initial causes.

Still a third habit that must be discarded in the social sciences as well as the humanities is our tendency to conceive of cultures, like identities, as homogenous, monolithic, and easily discriminable. Just as globalization has taught us about the capacity of cultures to move across national borders, to adapt to different local conditions, and to recombine, mutate, and recirculate in various ways, so we must learn that cultures, like the subjectivities they help organize and interpret, are not merely unstable but also mixed, hybrid, complex, diverse, and deterritorialized.

A fourth habit we must relinquish is the tendency to periodize by centuries, as though the life of time, if I may coin a phrase, can be measured everywhere and at all times in segments of one hundred years. Change occurs at different rates of speed in different cultures and at different moments; shifts in style as well as thought, like the movements of people and the development or reform of institutions sets—or finds—its own pace, not always according to the calendar but by means of temporal calculuses that are more unruly and diverse. The year 1789 when the French Revolution took place compresses time. The 250-year reign of the Tokugawa Shogunate in Japan that ended with such startling abruptness at the beginning of the Meiji Restoration when modern Japanese history was inaugurated attempted to extend time indefinitely. Various people in the Middle East organize time not in relation to decades or centuries, as we do in the United States but in relation to the collapse of the Caliphate or the end of the Ottoman Empire.

But if time in effect moves at different rates of speed in different places for different peoples in relation to different trajectories of hope, possibility, custom, and coercion, so place is also a more elastic and unwieldly category than we have acknowledged in much of our scholarship. If the city as center has always defined the sense of place in many historical communities throughout the world—this imagery is still used in world systems theory to describe the relations between core and periphery—the state and the nation more recently usurped it as the principal marker of space. This is again as a result of the weakening of state boundaries and the ever-shifting coordinates of spatial definition. Merely think of what was involved when the Soviet Union disintegrated and 27 states, along with hundreds of communities defining themselves as distinct nationalities, were set free of the imperial ligatures that for nearly half a century held them all together. Or, again, consider what is now happening to national identity on the Continent with the expansion of the European Union, the establishment of a common currency, and the development of a plethora of transnational agencies, institutions, and administrations with jurisdictions that can override the laws and procedures of individual states. But even here—and one could multiply examples ad infinitum in East Asia, the Indonesian archipelago, particular regions of the African continent— the topography of space conforms to large geopolitical entities. Yet space has not always been so conceived for people and cultures that have grown up along river systems or developed their lives in mountain, plain, desert, or forest regions. And then, too, there is the great company of nomadic peoples throughout history, or the equally large group of people in modern times who have been displaced by events beyond their own control and rendered refugees who simply migrate, if they are lucky, from one placeless locale, as it were, to another. While it becomes less and less likely that any people in the world now live utterly remote from, and untouched by, processes that are in some sense or other global, the fact remains that there are hundreds of millions of people in the world who go about their daily tasks with virtually no active conception of the geographies—urban, national, regional, continental, civilizational—by which we normally delineate space and place. Thus our maps, like our clocks, need to be recalibrated if we are to grasp the way time and space actually function in the life of many of the world's peoples.

Last but not least, we must acknowledge that if globalization has rendered cultures and the forms and practices that characterize them more mobile as well as socialized, enabling them to travel across traditional borders and help create and sustain new diasporic communities, it has also freed the faculty of the imagination, always a potent, if still too often undervalued, force in historical life, to become a principal agent in the construction and reconstruction of the global world itself. By this I mean that, we now think and feel in this new informational age as never before in forms whose origination is aesthetic and whose chief material is composed of symbols. Too often associated merely with escape, entertainment, or pure fantasy, the imagination now plays an even larger role in social construction, in productive work, than it has in the past. In addition to possessing the power it has always had in peoples' stories, dramas, dances, paintings, and constructions to help them make sense out of the sense of their lives, it has now come to acquire, with the increasingly instantaneous spread of mass culture, the power to influence, if not determine, the kinds of lives that make most sense to people. Hence we shall neither understand how in the past the global has lived its life through time, nor in the present how time itself has become ever more globalized, until we come to terms with the way the imagination has attempted, and continues to attempt, to turn life into the shape of its own desire.

After several chapters that seek to discuss some of the elemental terms that influence the debate about globalization, from notions of history, culture, and ideology to religion and empire as globalizing forces, the book is organized along a historical timeline of approximately one thousand years. Each chapter isolates some development along that timeline down to the present—the early modern oceanic discovery of the world, the scientific revolutions around the world, the rise of capitalisms and the industrial revolutions, the democratic and later socialist revolutions, colonialism, decolonization, and the postcolonial, global war, the international rights movement, the international women's movement—that essentially changed the coordinates of the global and thus altered the way its meaning could subsequently be recalculated. Such developments are followed down to the immediate present, where the world has again undergone global reconfigurations in relation to everything from the digitalization of culture, the spread of ethnic and religious violence, and the creation of global cities to the global endangerment of the planet itself.

# Footnotes

1. Several lines in this paragraph and elsewhere in the Introduction are drawn from my "Globalizing Literary Studies," Special Issue of *PMLA*, coordinated by Giles Gunn, 116/1 (January, 2001), 16–31.
2. For someone who favors the first view, see Barrie Axford, "Globalization," *Understanding Contemporary Society: Theories of the Present*, ed. Gary Browning, Abigail Halcli, Frank Webster (Thousand Oaks, Calif.: Sage Publications, 2000), 238–251; I am more inclined to the second in Giles Gunn, *Beyond Solidarity: Pragmatism and Difference in a Globalized World* (Chicago: University of Chicago Press, 2001).
3. For a defender of the first opinion, see Thomas Friedman, *The Lexus and the Olive Tree* (New York: Farrar, Straus, Giroux), 1999; for an advocate of the second, see David Harvey, *The Condition of Postmodernity: An Enquiry Into The Origins of Cultural Change* (New York: Blackwell, 1989).
4. This position is most often associated with Anthony Giddens, *The Consequences of Modernity* (London: Polity Press, 1990).
5. Immanuel Wallerstein, *The Modern World System* (New York: Academic Press, 1974).
6. William H. McNeill, *The Rise of the West; A History of the Human Community* (Chicago: University of Chicago Press, 1963); Marshall Hodgson, *Rethinking World History: Essays on Europe, Islam, and World History* (Cambridge: Cambridge University Press, 1993).
7. David Held and Anthony McGrew, David Goldblatt and Jonathan Perraton, *Global Transformations: Politics, Economics, and Culture* (Stanford, Ca.: Stanford University Press, 1999), 3–10.
8. Kenichi Ohmae, *The Evolving World Economy: Making Sense of the New World Order* (Boston: Harvard Business School, 1995).
9. Giddens, *The Consequences of Modernity.*
10. Samuel P. Huntington, *The Clash of Civilizations and the Remaking of World Order* (New York: Simon and Schuster, 1996).
11. Clifford Geertz, "Blurred Genres: The Refiguration of Social Thought," *Local Culture: Further Essays in Interpretive Anthropology* (New York: Basic Books, 1983), 19–35.
12. Arjun Appadurai, *Modernity At Large: Cultural Dimensions of Globalization.* Minneapolis: University of Minnesota Press, 1996.

# CHAPTER ONE

# *Thinking Globally About History and Culture*

The possibility of thinking globally about history and culture may, on the face of it, sound like an impossible task. Histories are always finite, cultures usually specific. Considering either of them in global terms may thus sound like a kind of contradiction, or at least a category mistake, unless we attempt to break it down. So let's us begin by what, more particularly, we mean by history and what we mean by culture.

There is a popular misconception that history simply includes all that happens, that it constitutes a record of everything that has occurred within a given span of time. However, this can't be true for several reasons. The first is because it is impossible to record everything that happens even within the briefest segments of time. The second is that even if that problem could be resolved, we would still be left with the issue of deciding whether all the occurrences within that multitude of events have equal weight or importance. It is sometimes countered that what matters is simply what we manage to remember, but the third problem is that memory is selective and thus much of what occurs in any sequence of events escapes our notice. And then there is the fourth problem that even if total recollection of everything were possible, there is always the possibility that new facts may, as we say, "come to light," which ultimately raises a fifth issue having to do with what we accept as evidence, as fact, in the first place.

Thus questions like the following begin to multiply: What does history, as we conceive it, include and not include (men's experience, women's experience, children's experience, the experience of ethnic and racial others)? Is there any driving source behind history that makes it proceed as it does (transcendental powers, the actions of elites, economic forces, accident, fate)? Which is the best measure of history's temporal movement (decades and centuries, dynastic reigns, ideological eras, geological changes?)? Does history have an end game or probable outcome (progressive change, social collapse, new tyrannies, planetary peril)? And what difference does history make, what lessons does it teach (what not to repeat, our inhumanity to one another, the inevitability of change, a tale told by an idiot full of sound and fury)?

Such questions are by no means inadvertent or arbitrary but constructive because they help us organize the otherwise disparate, multitudinous, random materials of the past into a meaningful pattern so that we can think about them. And we normally think about them in at least five different ways. Those ways constitute what are, in effect, five selective principles—conceptualization, causation, periodization, trajectory, and impact—that enable us to convert those materials from raw data into a form that will make them memorable. This form is usually narrative because its purpose is to help us find a significance in this pattern of events. In this sense, history is a kind of construct that isn't strictly or purely about the past as such but rather about the past that the present, in its efforts to define itself, needs for its own self-narration. In other words, the practice of history, of "historicizing" the past, derives from the needs of the present and constitutes the present's attempt to find in the past elements for the emplottment of what, in effect, is a meaningful future. As William Faulkner, the great modern American writer, once said: "The past is never dead. It is not even past."

Thinking about history globally would nonetheless still be impossible if it were not also for the existence of what we call cultures. Cultures are systems of meaning composed of symbols, gestures, rituals, performances, and other practices like story-telling that allow us both to make sense of the world and to share that sense, that knowledge, with others. These structures of signification, which are not inborn but rather inherited, are interpretive in two different but related senses. On the one hand, they provide models, blueprints, maps, templates of the world around us so that we can make sense of it. On the other, they furnish instruments, techniques, strategies for, so to speak, how to move about in it, how to negotiate its challenges. Cultural materials and systems perform this second function by operating like feedback loops that permit the networks of information, both cognitive and emotional, that are socially transmitted to us from families, friendships, school systems, work experience, and other sources to be modified and adapted by us not only across generations but also across other cultures.

The great danger is that such cultural systems of sense and sense-making can either become outdated, and thus less relevant, or ossified, and thus more rigid and inflexible, in which case they may become less useful in helping us adapt the lessons derived from past experience to the trials presented by new experience. And such difficulties as these only increase as we acknowledge that most people actually live in more than one culture at a time and that many of those cultures or cultural systems are often interlinked in unexpected or conflicting combinations. Here is where Eric R. Wolf's "Introduction" to his classic *Europe and the People Without History* is so instructive. One of the first scholars in the field of anthropology to argue that "the world of humankind constitutes a manifold . . . totality of interconnected processes," Wolf is deeply skeptical of any attempts to pull these processes apart for the sake of understanding them without reassembling them. Differentiating them into concepts like "society," "nation," "politics," or even "culture" itself runs the risk of turning such intricately related processes into inert things. This kind of objectification falsifies their actual reality as complex "bundles of relationship" that need to be re-embedded in the densely constructed fields from which they have been abstracted if they are actually to be understood.

If this kind of abstraction can be found everywhere—as in the European prejudice that informs Wolf's title, where "primitives" are defined as "people without history"—it may have something to do with the way Europeans and other Westerners have learned their history. That history has too often possessed a developmental form that specifically privileges Europe and then America by placing them in a narrative trajectory that situates the origins of "civilization" in the so-called "East," actually the "Middle East," and then follows its progression from Greece to Rome to Christian Europe and then on to the United States. Suppressing the contributions made to this historical chronicle by Chinese, Indian, Muslim, Byzantine, Minoan, and other civilizations, this "mainstream" Western narrative tends to turn history, Wolf argues, into a kind of "moral success story" and consequently treats all other developments either as a precursor—Native American agriculture, Arabic science, Chinese technology, Indian medicine—or as irrelevant—Africa, Latin America, Central Asia.

A second reason that the global reality of the world may have been missed is because of the way most of the world's people have learned their geography. While this is anything but an exclusive Western practice—the ancient Chinese perfected it several thousand years ago by thinking of themselves as inhabitants of earth's "Middle Kingdom"—nations, societies, and cultures have displayed a tendency to situate themselves at what the eminent scholar of Islam, Marshall G. S. Hodgon, once referred to as the "center of the map." In other words, space is just as effective a vehicle as is time for placing oneself at what Hodgson also called "the hub of history." Indeed, maps are a form of misreading (distortion or falsification, in Wolf's terms) that have encouraged the world to continue the late medieval practice of conferring on Europe the status of a continent while relegating the much larger land mass of India to the status of a subcontinent. This same bias was then inscribed in the first map capable of charting the correct angles for seaborne navigation known as the Mercator projection and continues down to the present to distort the size and shape of many of the entities it demarcates. Hence the representations of Greenland and North America are enlarged while those of India, Indonesia, and Africa are diminished, thus creating exaggerations of perspective above the 40th parallel so that more of the geographical details of Europe can be displayed than those not only of India but also of the Middle East and China.

These are precisely the kind of misrepresentations that Peter Frankopan wishes to expose and correct in his major new history of the world entitled *The Silk Roads*. What is remarkable is that his inspiration to do so dates back to his fourteenth birthday when, as a young child already obsessed with world maps, his parents actually gave him a copy of Eric Wolf's *Europe and the People Without History*! This birthday present, as he writes, "really lit the tinder" by helping him realize that the practice he had been taught in school of telling the story of the past from the perspective of "the winners of recent history," Wolf's "moral success story," was in need of revision. To accomplish this revision required, as he was much later to perceive, both a remapping and a re-narrativization of world history from its mid-point, so to speak, between the eastern shores of the Mediterranean and the Black Sea and the Himalayas. Repositioning the world along the pathways of commerce, culture, and conflict that lay between many of the emergent peoples, places, and civilizations of the East and West, as well as of the North and South, allows us to better understand how the world actually works and "why," as Frankopan says, "the cultures, cities, and peoples who lived along the Silk Roads developed and advanced: as they traded and exchanged ideas, they learnt and borrowed from each other, stimulating further advances in philosophy, the sciences, language, and religion." In this bold new history, the center of the world—and the cradle from which civilization essentially sprang and spread out in all directions—is neither China, nor what was once called the Near East or Fertile Crescent extending all the way to Iraq, nor even Europe; it is relocated still farther East where all their cultures crossed.

# Europe and the People Without History

 Eric R. Wolf

## Introduction

The central assertion of this book is that the world of humankind constitutes a manifold, a totality of interconnected processes, and inquiries that disassemble this totality into bits and then fail to reassemble it falsify reality. Concepts like "nation," "society," and "culture" name bits and threaten to turn names into things. Only by understanding these names as bundles of relationships, and by placing them back into the field from which they were abstracted, can we hope to avoid misleading inferences and increase our share of understanding.

On one level it has become a commonplace to say that we all inhabit "one world." There are ecological connections: New York suffers from the Hong Kong flu; the grapevines of Europe are destroyed by American plant lice. There are demographic connections: Jamaicans migrate to London; Chinese migrate to Singapore. There are economic connections: a shutdown of oil wells on the Persian Gulf halts generating plants in Ohio; a balance of payments unfavorable to the United States drains American dollars into bank accounts in Frankfurt or Yokohama; Italians produce Fiat automobiles in the Soviet Union; Japanese build a hydroelectric system in Ceylon. There are political connections: wars begun in Europe unleash reverberations around the globe; American troops intervene on the rim of Asia; Finns guard the border between Israel and Egypt.

This holds true not only of the present but also of the past. Diseases from Eurasia devastated the native population of America and Oceania. Syphilis moved from the New World to the Old. Europeans and their plants and animals invaded the Americas; the American potato, maize plant, and manioc spread throughout the Old World. Large numbers of Africans were transported forcibly to the New World; Chinese and Indian indentured laborers were shipped to Southeast Asia and the West Indies. Portugal created a Portuguese settlement in Macao off the coast of China. Dutchmen, using labor obtained in Bengal, constructed Batavia. Irish children were sold into servitude in the West Indies. Fugitive African slaves found sanctuary in the hills of Surinam. Europe learned to copy Indian textiles and Chinese porcelain, to drink native American chocolate, to smoke native American tobacco, to use Arabic numerals.

These are familiar facts. They indicate contact and connections, linkages and interrelationships. Yet the scholars to whom we turn in order to understand what we see largely persist in ignoring them. Historians, economists, and political scientists take separate nations as their basic framework of inquiry. Sociology continues to divide the world into separate societies. Even anthropology, once greatly concerned with how culture traits diffused around the world, divides its subject matter into distinctive cases: each society with its characteristic culture, conceived as an integrated and bounded system, set off against other equally bounded systems.

If social and cultural distinctiveness and mutual separation were a hallmark of humankind, one would expect to find it most easily among the so-called primitives, people "without history," supposedly isolated from the external world and from one another. On this presupposition, what would we make of the archaeological findings that European trade goods appear in sites on the Niagara frontier as early as early as 1570, and that by 1670 sites of the Onondaga subgroup of the Iroquois reveal almost no items of native manufacture except pipes? On the other side of the Atlantic, the organization and orientations of large African populations were transformed in major ways by the trade in slaves. Since the European slavers only moved the slaves from the African coast to their destination in the Americas, the supply side of the trade was entirely in African hands. This was the "African foundation" upon which was built, in the words of the British mercantilist Malachy Postlethwayt, "the magnificent superstructure of American commerce and naval power." From Senegambia in West Africa to Angola, population after population was drawn into this trade, which ramified far inland and affected people who had never even seen a European trader on the coast. Any account of Kru, Fanti, Asante, Ijaw, Igbo, Kongo, Luba, Lunda, or Ngola that treats each group as a "tribe" sufficient unto itself thus misreads the African past and the African present. Furthermore, trade with Iroquois and West Africa affected Europe in turn. Between 1670 and 1760 the Iroquois demanded dyed scarlet and blue cloth made in the Stroudwater Valley of Gloucestershire. This was also one of the first areas in which English weavers lost their autonomy and became hired factory hands. Perhaps there was an interconnection between the American trade and the onset of the industrial revolution in the valley of the Stroud. Conversely, the more than 5,500 muskets supplied to the Gold Coast in only three years (1658–1661) enriched the gunsmiths of Birmingham, where they were made (Jennings 1977: 99–100; Daaku 1970: 150–151).

If there are connections everywhere, why do we persist in turning dynamic, interconnected phenomena into static, disconnected things? Some of this is owing, perhaps, to the way we have learned our own history. We have been taught, inside the classroom and outside of it, that there exists an entity called the West, and that one can think of this West as a society and civilization independent of and in opposition to other societies and civilizations. Many of us even grew up believing that this West has a genealogy, according to which ancient Greece begat Rome, Rome begat Christian Europe, Christian Europe begat the Renaissance, the Renaissance the Enlightenment, the Enlightenment political democracy and the industrial revolution. Industry, crossed with democracy, in turn yielded the United States, embodying the rights to life, liberty, and the pursuit of happiness.

Such a developmental scheme is misleading. It is misleading, first, because it turns history into a moral success story, a race in time in which each runner of the race passes on the torch of liberty to the next relay. History is thus converted into a tale about the furtherance of virtue, about how the virtuous win out over the bad guys. Frequently, this turns into a story of how the winners prove that they are virtuous and good by winning. If history is the working out of a moral purpose in time, then those who lay claim to that purpose are by that fact the predilect agents of history.

The scheme misleads in a second sense as well. If history is but a tale of unfolding moral purpose, then each link in the genealogy, each runner in the race, is only a precursor of the final apotheosis and not a manifold of social and cultural processes at work in their own time and place. Yet what would we learn of ancient Greece, for example, if we interpreted it only as a prehistoric Miss Liberty, holding aloft the torch of moral purpose in the barbarian night? We would gain little sense of the class conflicts racking the Greek cities, or of the relation between freemen and their slaves. We would have no reason to ask why there were more Greeks fighting in the ranks of the Persian kings than in the ranks of the Hellenic Alliance against the Persians. It would be of no interest to us to know that more Greeks lived- in southern Italy and Sicily, then called Magna Graecia, than in Greece proper. Nor would we have any reason to ask why there were soon more Greek mercenaries in foreign armies than in the military bodies of their home cities. Greek settlers outside of Greece, Greek mercenaries in foreign armies, and slaves from Thrace, Phrygia, or Paphalagonia in Greek households all imply Hellenic relations with Greeks and non-Greeks outside of Greece. Yet our guiding scheme would not invite us to ask questions about these relationships.

Nowhere is this myth-making scheme more apparent than in schoolbook versions of the history of the United States. There, a complex orchestration of antagonistic forces is celebrated instead as the unfolding of a timeless essence. In this perspective, the ever-changing boundaries of the United States and the repeated involvements of the polity in internal and external wars, declared and undeclared, are telescoped together by the teleological understanding that thirteen colonies dinging to the eastern rim of the continent would, in less than a century, plant the American flag on the shores of the Pacific. Yet this final result was itself only the contested outcome of many contradictory relationships. The colonies declared their independence, even though a majority of their population—European settlers, native Americans, and African slaves—favored the Tories. The new republic nearly foundered on the issue of slavery, dealing with it, in a series of problematic compromises, by creating two federated countries, each with its own zone of expansion. There was surely land for the taking on the new continent, but it had to be taken first from the native Americans who inhabited it, and then converted into flamboyant real estate. Jefferson bought the Louisiana territory cheaply, but only after the revolt of the Haitian slaves against their French slave masters robbed the area of its importance in the French scheme of things as a source of food supply for the Caribbean plantations. The occupation of Florida closed off one of the main escape hatches from southern slavery. The war with Mexico made the Southwest safe for slavery and cotton. The Hispanic landowners who stood in the way of the American drive to the Pacific became "bandits" when they defended their own against the Anglophone newcomers. Then North and South—one country importing its working force from Europe, the other form Africa—fought one of the bloodiest wars in history. For a time the defeated South became a colony of the victorious North. Later, the alignment between regions changed, the "sunbelt" rising to predominance as the influence of the industrial Northeast declined. Clearly the republic was neither indivisible nor endowed with God-given boundaries.

It is conceivable that things might have been different. There could have arisen a polyglot Floridian Republic, a Francophone Mississippian America, a Hispanic New Biscay, a Republic of the Great Lakes, a Columbia—comprising the present Oregon, Washington, and British Columbia. Only if we assume a God-given drive toward geopolitical unity on the North American continent would this retrojection be meaningless. Instead, it invites us to account in material terms for what happened at each juncture, to account for how some relationships gained ascendancy over others.

Thus neither ancient Greece, Rome, Christian Europe, the Renaissance, the Enlightenment, the industrial revolution, democracy, nor even the United States was ever a thing propelled toward its unfolding goal by some immanent driving spring, but rather a temporally and spatially changing and changeable set of relationships, or relationships among sets of relationships.

The point is more than academic. By turning names into things we create false models of reality. By endowing nations, societies, or cultures with the qualities of internally homogeneous and externally distinctive and bounded objects, we create a model of the world as a global pool hall in which the entities spin off each other like so many hard and round billiard balls. Thus it becomes easy to sort the world into differently colored balls, to declare that "East is East, and West is West, and never the twain shall meet." In this way a quintessential West is counterposed to an equally quintessential East, where life was cheap and slavish multitudes groveled under a variety of despotisms. Later, as peoples in other climes began to assert their political and economic independence from both West and East, we assigned these new applicants for historical status to a Third World of underdevelopment—a residual category of conceptual billiard balls—as contrasted with the developed West and the developing East. Inevitably, perhaps, these reified categories became intellectual instruments in the prosecution of the Cold War. There was the "modern" world of the West. There was the world of the East, which had fallen prey to communism, a "disease of modernization" (Rostow 1960). There was, finally, the Third World, still bound up in "tradition" and strangled in its efforts toward modernization. If the West could only find ways of breaking that grip, it could perhaps save the victim from the infection incubated and spread by the East, and set that Third World upon the road to modernization—the road to life, liberty, and the pursuit of happiness of the West. The ghastly offspring of this way of thinking about the world was the theory of "forced draft urbanization" (Huntington 1968: 655), which held that the Vietnamese could be propelled toward modenization by driving them into the cities through aerial bombardment and defoliation of the countryside. Names thus become things, and things marked with an X can become targets of war.

# The Silk Roads

 Peter Frankopan

## Preface

As a child, one of my most prized possessions was a large map of the world. It was pinned on the wall by my bed, and I would stare at it every night before I went to sleep. Before long, I had memorised the names and locations of all the countries, noting their capital cities, as well as the oceans and seas, and the rivers that flowed in to them; the names of major mountain ranges and deserts, written in urgent italics, thrilled with adventure and danger.

By the time I was a teenager, I had become uneasy about the relentlessly narrow geographic focus of my classes at school, which concentrated solely on western Europe and the United States and left most of the rest of the world untouched. We had been taught about the Romans in Britain; the Norman conquest of 1066; Henry VIII and the Tudors; the American War of Independence; Victorian industrialisation; the battle of the Somme; and the rise and fall of Nazi Germany. I would look up at my map and see huge regions of the world that had been passed over in silence.

For my fourteenth birthday my parents gave me a book by the anthropologist Eric Wolf, which really lit the tinder. The accepted and lazy history of civilisation, wrote Wolf, is one where "Ancient Greece begat Rome, Rome begat Christian Europe, Christian Europe begat the Renaissance, the Renaissance the Enlightenment, the Enlightenment political democracy and the industrial revolution. Industry crossed with democracy in turn yielded the United States, embodying the rights to life, liberty and the pursuit of happiness." I immediately recognised that this was exactly the story that I had been told: the mantra of the political, cultural and moral triumph of the west. But this account was flawed; there were alternative ways of looking at history—ones that did not involve looking at the past from the perspective of the winners of recent history.

I was hooked. It was suddenly obvious that the regions we were not being taught about had become lost, suffocated by the insistent story of the rise of Europe. I begged my father to take me to see the Hereford Mappa Mundi, which located Jerusalem as its focus and mid-point, with England and other western countries placed off to one side, all but irrelevancies. When I read about Arab geographers whose works were accompanied by charts that seemed upside down and put the Caspian Sea at its centre, I was transfixed—as I was when I found out about an important medieval Turkish map in Istanbul that had at its heart a city called Balāsāghūn, which I had never even heard of, which did not appear on any maps, and whose very location was uncertain until recently, and yet was once considered the centre of the world.

I wanted to know more about Russia and Central Asia, about Persia and Mesopotamia. I wanted to understand the origins of Christianity when viewed from Asia; and how the Crusades looked to those living in the great cities of the Middle Ages—Constantinople, Jerusalem, Baghdad and Cairo, for example; I wanted to learn about the great empires of the east, about the Mongols and their conquests; and to understand how two world wars looked when viewed not from Flanders or the eastern front, but from Afghanistan and India.

It was extraordinarily fortunate therefore that I was able to learn Russian at school, where I was taught by Dick Haddon, a brilliant man who had served in Naval Intelligence and believed that the way to understand the Russian language and *dusha*, or soul, was through its sparkling literature and its peasant music. I was even more fortunate when he offered to give Arabic lessons to those who were interested, introducing half a dozen of us to Islamic culture and history, and immersing us in the beauty of classical Arabic. These languages helped unlock a world waiting to be discovered, or, as I soon realised, to be rediscovered by those of us in the west.

Today, much attention is devoted to assessing the likely impact of rapid economic growth in China, where demand for luxury goods is forecast to quadruple in the next decade, or to considering social change in India, where more people have access to a mobile phone than to a flushing toilet. But neither offers the best vantage point to view the world's past and its present. In fact, for millennia, it was the region lying between east and west, linking Europe with the Pacific Ocean, that was the axis on which the globe spun.

The halfway point between east and west, running broadly from the eastern shores of the Mediterranean and the Black Sea to the Himalayas, might seem an unpromising position from which to assess the world. This is a region that is now home to states that evoke the exotic and the peripheral, like Kazakhstan and Uzbekistan, Kyrgyzstan and Turkmenistan, Tajikistan and the countries of the Caucasus; it is a region associated with regimes that are unstable, violent and a threat to international security, like Afghanistan, Iran, Iraq and Syria, or ill versed in the best practices of democracy, like Russia and Azerbaijan. Overall, it appears to be a region that is home to a series of failed or failing states, led by dictators who win impossibly large majorities in national elections and whose families and friends control sprawling business interests, own vast assets and wield political power. They are places with poor records on human rights, where freedom of expression in matters of faith, conscience and sexuality is limited, and where control of the media dictates what does and what does not appear in the press.

While such countries may seem wild to us, these are no backwaters, no obscure wastelands. In fact the bridge between east and west is the very crossroads of civilisation. Far from being on the fringe of global affairs, these countries lie at its very centre—as they have done since the beginning of history. It was here that Civilisation was born, and where many believed Mankind had been created—in the Garden of Eden, "planted by the Lord God" with "every tree that is pleasant to the sight and good for food," which was widely thought to be located in the rich fields between the Tigris and Euphrates.

It was in this bridge between east and west that great metropolises were established nearly 5,000 years ago, where the cities of Harappa and Mohenjo-daro in the Indus valley were wonders of the ancient world, with populations numbering in the tens of thousands and streets connecting into a sophisticated sewage system that would not be rivalled in Europe for thousands of years. Other great centres of civilisation such as Babylon, Nineveh, Uruk and Akkad in Mesopotamia were famed for their grandeur and architectural innovation. One Chinese geographer, meanwhile, writing more than two millennia ago, noted that the inhabitants of Bactria, centred on the Oxus river and now located in northern Afghanistan, were legendary negotiators and traders; its capital city was home to a market where a huge range of products were bought and sold, carried from far and wide.

This region is where the world's great religions burst into life, where Judaism, Christianity, Islam, Buddhism and Hinduism jostled with each other. It is the cauldron where language groups competed, where Indo-European, Semitic and Sino-Tibetan tongues wagged alongside those speaking Altaic, Turkic and Caucasian. This is where great empires rose and fell, where the after-effects of dashes between cultures and rivals were felt thousands of miles away. Standing here opened up new ways to view the past and showed a world that was profoundly interconnected, where what happened on one continent had an impact on another, where the aftershocks of what happened on the steppes of Central Asia could be felt in North Africa, where events in Baghdad resonated in Scandinavia, where discoveries in the Americas altered the prices of goods in China and led to a surge in demand in the horse markets of northern India.

These tremors were carried along a network that fans out in every direction, routes along which pilgrims and warriors, nomads and merchants have travelled, goods and produce have been bought and sold, and ideas exchanged, adapted and refined. They have carried not only prosperity, but also death and violence, disease and disaster. In the late nineteenth century, this sprawling web of connections was given a name by an eminent German geologist, Ferdinand von Richthofen (uncle of the First World War flying ace the "Red Baron") that has stuck ever since: "Seidenstraßen"—the Silk Roads.

These pathways serve as the world's central nervous system, connecting peoples and places together, but lying beneath the skin, invisible to the naked eye. Just as anatomy explains how the body functions, understanding these connections allows us to understand how the world works. And yet, despite the importance of this part of the world, it has been forgotten by mainstream history. In part, this is because of what has been called "orientalism"—the strident and overwhelmingly negative view of the east as undeveloped and inferior to the west, and therefore unworthy of serious study. But it also stems from the fact that the narrative of the past has become so dominant and well established that there is no place for a region that has long been seen as peripheral to the story of the rise of Europe and of western society.

Today, Jalalabad and Herat in Afghanistan, Fallujah and Mosul in Iraq or Homs and Aleppo in Syria seem synonymous with religious fundamentalism and sectarian violence. The present has washed away the past: gone are the days when the name of Kabul conjured up images of the gardens planted and tended by the great Bābur, founder of the Mughal Empire in India. The Bagh-i-Wafa ("Garden of Fidelity") included a pool surrounded by orange and pomegranate trees and a clover meadow—of which Bābur was extremely proud: "This is the best part of the garden, a most beautiful sight when the oranges take colour. Truly that garden is admirably situated!"

In the same way, modern impressions about Iran have obscured the glories of its more distant history when its Persian predecessor was a byword for good taste in everything, from the fruit served at dinner, to the stunning miniature portraits produced by its legendary artists, to the paper that scholars wrote on. A beautifully considered work written by Simi Nīshāpūrī, a librarian from

Mashad in eastern Iran around 1400, records in careful detail the advice of a book lover who shared his passion. Anyone thinking of writing, he counsels solemnly, should be advised that the best paper for calligraphy is produced in Damascus, Baghdad or Samarkand. Paper from elsewhere "is generally rough, blotches and is impermanent." Bear in mind, he cautions, that it is worth giving paper a slight tint before committing ink to it, "because white is hard on the eyes and the master calligraphic specimens that have been observed have all been on tinted paper."

Places whose names are all but forgotten once dominated, such as Merv, described by one tenth-century geographer as a "delightful, fine, elegant, brilliant, extensive and pleasant city," and "the mother of the world"; or Rayy, not far from modern Teheran, which to another writer around the same time was so glorious as to be considered "the bridegroom of the earth" and the world's "most beautiful creation." Dotted across the spine of Asia, these cities were strung like pearls, linking the Pacific to the Mediterranean.

Urban centres spurred each other on, with rivalry between rulers and elites prompting ever more ambitious architecture and spectacular monuments. Libraries, places of worship, churches and observatories of immense scale and cultural influence dotted the region, connecting Constantinople to Damascus, Isfahan, Samarkand, Kabul and Kashgar. Cities such as these became home to brilliant scholars who advanced the frontiers of their subjects. The names of only a small handful are familiar today—men like Ibn Sīnā, better known as Avicenna, al-Bīrūnī and al-Khwārizmi—giants in the fields of astronomy and medicine; but there were many more besides. For centuries before the early modern era, the intellectual centres of excellence of the world, the Oxfords and Cambridges, the Harvards and Yales, were not located in Europe or the west, but in Baghdad and Balkh, Bukhara and Samarkand.

There was good reason why the cultures, cities and peoples who lived along the Silk Roads developed and advanced: as they traded and exchanged ideas, they learnt and borrowed from each other, stimulating further advances in philosophy, the sciences, language and religion. Progress was essential, as one of the rulers of the kingdom of Zhao in northeastern China at one extremity of Asia more than 2,000 years ago knew all too well. "A talent for following the ways of yesterday," declared King Wu-ling in 307 bc, "is not sufficient to improve the world of today." Leaders in the past understood how important it was to keep up with the times.

The mantle of progress shifted, however, in the early modern period as a result of two great maritime expeditions that took place at the end of the fifteenth century. In the course of six years in the 1490s, the foundations were laid for a major disruption to the rhythm of long-established systems of exchange. First Christopher Columbus crossed the Atlantic, paving the way for two great land masses that were hitherto untouched to connect to Europe and beyond; then, just a few years later, Vasco da Gama successfully navigated the southern tip of Africa, sailing on to India, opening new sea routes in the process. The discoveries changed patterns of interaction and trade, and effected a remarkable change in the world's political and economic centre of gravity. Suddenly, western Europe was transformed from its position as a regional backwater into the fulcrum of a sprawling communication, transportation and trading system: at a stroke, it became the new mid-point between east and west.

The rise of Europe sparked a fierce battle for power—and for control of the past. As rivals squared up to each other, history was reshaped to emphasise the events, themes and ideas that could be used in the ideological clashes that raged alongside the struggle for resources and for command of the sea lanes. Busts were made of leading politicians and generals wearing togas to make them look like Roman heroes of the past; magnificent new buildings were constructed in grand classical style that appropriated the glories of the ancient world as their own direct antecedents. History was twisted and manipulated to create an insistent narrative where the rise of the west was not only natural and inevitable, but a continuation of what had gone before.

Many stories set me on the path to looking at the world's past in a different way. But one stood out in particular. Greek mythology had it that Zeus, father of the gods, released two eagles, one at each end of the earth, and commanded them to fly towards each other. A sacred stone, the *omphalos*—the navel of the world—was placed where they met, to enable communication with the divine. I learnt later that the concept of this stone has long been a source of fascination for philosophers and psychoanalysts.

I remember gazing at my map when I first heard this tale, wondering where the eagles would have met. I imagined them taking off from the shores of the western Atlantic and the Pacific coast of China and heading inland. The precise position changed, depending where I placed my fingers to start measuring equal distances from east and west. But I always ended up somewhere between the Black Sea and the Himalayas. I would lie awake at night, pondering the map on my bedroom wall, Zeus' eagles and the history of a region that was never mentioned in the books that I read—and did not have a name.

Not so long ago, Europeans divided Asia into three broad zones—the Near, Middle and Far East. Yet whenever I heard or read about presentday problems as I was growing up, it seemed that the second of these, the Middle East, had shifted in meaning and even location, being used to refer to Israel, Palestine and the surrounding area, and occasionally to the Persian Gulf. And I could not understand why I kept being told of the importance of the Mediterranean as a cradle of civilisation, when it seemed so obvious that this was not where civilisation had really been forged. The real crucible, the "Mediterranean" in its literal meaning—the centre of the world—was not a sea separating Europe and North Africa, but right in the heart of Asia.

My hope is that I can embolden others to study peoples and places that have been ignored by scholars for generations by opening up new questions and new areas of research. I hope to prompt new questions to be asked about the past, and for truisms to be challenged and scrutinised. Above all, I hope to inspire those who read this book to look at history in a different way.

# CHAPTER TWO

# The Globalization Debate: The International vs. the Global

The debate about globalization has taken a number of different forms since it became a familiar term of reference in the 1980s. That debate has circulated around several different issues and moved in several different directions. Quite apart from disputes about the meaning of the term itself--how best to conceptualize it, when it began, what its causal dynamics are, how to measure its consequences, and in what ways it has or hasn't changed-- there is, first, a debate about whether such developments are the result of a world system that has been fundamentally altered globally in the latter half of the twentieth century or are simply the continuation of socio-economic and political trends long in process. Second, there is a debate about what, within its latest phase during the last third of the twentieth century and the first years of the twenty-first, it has or hasn't produced. Third, there is a debate about what difference there is between a world organized internationally around nation-states, and the institutions that manage the relations between and among them, and a world order organized as well around processes that go on above nation-states and below them and also within them. These are issues to which we will return throughout the course of this book, but it is important that we take an initial look at them as we set out on this journey.

To begin with the third debate first because it provides the background necessary to understand the other two debates, there is a divide between those who believe that the world is organized around institutions and practices that are principally, though not necessarily exclusively, geopolitical, and those who believe instead that the world is organized around institutions and practices that at least at times either transcend such factors or strongly, sometimes even definitively, shape their articulation. The first group includes those who assume that the world, or at least world order, is organized around, and driven by, territorially bounded states that are sovereign within their own realm and seek to govern themselves through processes of law-making and structures of law enforcement. The relations between states tend to be defined by concerns about security and status, but even when states act, as they always do, in their own self-interest, they tend to share a collective desire both to minimize impediments to state freedom and to maximize the scope of its exercise.

The problem with this system of governance, created as a result of Peace of Westphalia in 1648 designed to end the European wars of religion, is that the power of states is always unequal which makes the system itself unstable. This instability has become even more apparent during the several centuries it took for the Westphalian system to be established, when states have had to reinforce their own legitimacy by relying on the development of newer movements, such as nationalism, imperialism, colonialism, democracy, and socialism that are not only difficult to control but have also brought them into new kinds of conflicts, more ideological than geopolitical, both among themselves and also with their own people. As a result, a mode of governance that originally seemed to be defined by means of fixed boundaries and clear identities has never been able to sustain itself alone either by brute force or by legal distinctions but has instead always found itself dependent for its definition and defense on symbolic forms and practices that were more cultural than political.

Over against this seemingly internationalist way of mapping the world is the more trans-nationalist perspective of those who for the most part concede the existence of the state-based system of international order but also insist that there is much that goes on above and below as well as within nation-states that sometimes controls, but in any case influences, the kind of power they command and the way they seek to deploy that power. Such trans-nationalists, or globalists as they might be called, believe that the state is, at a minimum, influenced from above in one of several different ways: economically in the form of organizations like the World Trade Organization (WTE), the World Bank (WB), the International Monetary Fund (IMF), the Organization of Petroleum Exporting Countries (OPEC); politically by such institutions as the United Nations (UN), the North Atlantic Treaty Organization (NATO), or the New American Empire; and religiously through apocalyptic or jihadist organizations, whether they be Islamic, Hindu, Christian, or Jewish, or other faiths. Such globalists also believe that the international state-based system is influenced by globalization from below by such regional associations as the European Union (EU), the African Union (AU), the Arab League (AL), the Association of Southeast Asian Nations (ASEAN), and the Union of South American Nations (USAN), and by literally thousands of civic ones, such as the International Red Cross, Doctors Without Borders, Oxfam, Human Rights Watch, Islamic Relief International, and the Grameen Bank.

Yet this is only the tip of the iceberg. Just as globalization from above and below have influenced, and in some major respects reshaped, aspects of the Westphalian system, so the states that comprise that system are far from uniform—Russia is not Singapore, India not Norway—and they are constantly being altered, the better word sometimes is "assaulted," by global forces flowing through them that affect everything from notions of identity and belief to aesthetic styles and food preferences. Strong globalists like the theorist Barrie Axford, in the second selection of this chapter, actually go so far as to argue that the world is being made into one place, a map of variable tastes and temperaments, where whole cultures and identities are either being replaced by those less pure or traditional or are being hybridized and intermingled with them. This image of a world where, in Axford's language, the "local" can adapt the "global" to its own needs is probably more extreme than most students and interpreters of globalization would be prepared to endorse, but Axford is certainly correct in describing some of the chief properties of that world as multidimensional, complex, contradictory, and unpredictable. In his view, as in that of many proponents of the growing dominion of globalization, its largest effects are not reflected primarily in the fate of states and their continuing self-conceptions but rather in the spatial reordering of most social and cultural as well as political networks, the stretching of interpersonal relations, and the restructuring of the consciousness of consciousness itself.

This debate that puts someone like Barrie Axford on one side of the argument about globalization and on the other political "realists," as they are termed, who believe that the state-centric system of world order retains primacy, has been given further differentiation by David Held and his collaborators who, in the first selection in this chapter, distinguish between what he calls "Hyperglobalizers," "Skeptics," and "Transformationalists." "Hyperglobalizers" refer to those who have gone "all in" on globalization because of their belief that a single global economy has now subsumed all others as well as the world's major economic regions. This new global capitalism is usually identified with neoliberalism which tends to reduce the power of states by making them increasingly dependent on de-nationalized systems of corporate capital and global finance. When national boundaries provide no barriers to the instantaneous transfer of wealth, power is distributed more decisively by the operations of transnational banks and hedge funds than it is by international states.

But this hyperglobalist embrace of the new economic order that has replaced, or at any rate is outrunning, the old international political order has been disputed by "Skeptics." "Skeptics" believe that while much has changed in the world economy, that economy has not overthrown the ability of states to act on their own and in concert with others. If the world has broken up into a number of different economic blocs employing different forms of capitalism (market, finance, and state), the structures of power are still under the control of the most powerful states which use their new economic freedoms to consolidate their dominance.

To "Transformationalists," on the other hand, this skepticism appears slightly blinkered or narrow-minded. If there is no complete integration of the world's economy that has fundamentally challenged, if not hollowed out, the power of states, there is still abundant evidence of what Held and his other authors describe as a spatial re-organization and re-articulation of global power in all +inequality the major spheres of human experience, from politics and economics to culture and defense. While contemporary globalization is much too multidimensional to be reduced to any one of their individual logics, it is a process that has changed almost everything despite its uneven impacts across the globe.

So, what, then, are those impacts, those consequences, that this transformational process has had across the global? According to its initial critics at the end of the 1990s, it has produced everything from exploding economic inequalities, the erasure of local differences, the increase of Western, and particularly American, hegemony, the spread of militarism and weapons of mass destruction, "uneven increasing ethnic and religious hostilities and violence, the continued oppression of women and impacts" children, the displacement of whole populations often created by the collapse of states, and the degradation of the environment. When the anti-globalist movement initially erupted in 1999 in demonstrations like the one in Seattle against the World Trade Organization, its targets included specific practices such as sweat shops, free trade, environmental pollution, sex slavery, deforestation, and many others. The hope of its organizers and participants was, and remains, to remake the world in relation to such basic values as justice, equality, the rule of law, and humane global governance.

Since that period, however, a new and very different kind of anti-globalist movement has taken shape and is now challenging assumptions in various parts of the world. While many of the concerns of the two anti-globalist advocates remain similar—economic inequality, the loss of work, the fear of being left behind—most of the solutions they urge are strikingly different. In its latest forms, the anti-globalism spreading across the U.K., the U.S., parts of France, the Netherlands, Hungary, and elsewhere is not global at all but rather, in most cases, ultra-nationalist. Here the enemy is things like multiculturalism, or international cooperation, or foreign aid, or international treaties, or cosmopolitanism that put at risk narrowly defined state and national interests. In the Brexit movement in Great Britain, for instance, or the "America First" movement in the United States, people are not interested in building a fairer world but only a more self-protective one. The key is a reassertion of the primacy of national loyalty and reaffirmation of the potential supremacy of those individuals and groups tasked with creating and sustaining it. Ironically, such sentiments pose great risks not only to globalization itself but also to the state-based Westphalian order that, as such movements themself stridently allege, they are out to replace. What they want to replace it with varies from country to country, but it is an ultra-nationalism that is consistently authoritarian and racist.

# Introduction to Global Transformation

### DAVID HELD, ANTHONY MCGREW, DAVID GOLDBLATT AND JONATHAN PERRATON

Globalization is an idea whose time has come. From obscure origins in French and American writings in the 1960s, the concept of globalization finds expression today in all the world's major languages (cf. Modelski, 1972). Yet, it lacks precise definition. Indeed, globalization is in danger of becoming, if it has not already become, the cliché of our times: the big idea which encompasses everything from global financial markets to the Internet but which delivers little substantive insight into the contemporary human condition.

Clichés, nevertheless, often capture elements of the lived experience of an epoch. In this respect, globalization reflects a widespread perception that the world is rapidly being moulded into a shared social space by economic and technological forces and that developments in one region of the world can have profound consequences for the life chances of individuals or communities on the other side of the globe. For many, globalization is also associated with a sense of political fatalism and chronic insecurity in that the sheer scale of contemporary social and economic change appears to outstrip the capacity of national governments or citizens to control, contest or resist that change. The limits to national politics, in other words, are forcefully suggested by globalization.

Although the popular rhetoric of globalization may capture aspects of the contemporary zeitgeist, there is a burgeoning academic debate as to whether globalization, as an analytical construct, delivers any added value in the search for a coherent understanding of the historical forces which, at the dawn of the new millennium, are shaping the socio-political realities of everyday life. Despite a vast and expanding literature there is, somewhat surprisingly, no cogent theory of globalization nor even a systematic analysis of its primary features. Moreover, few studies of globalization proffer a coherent historical narrative which distinguishes between those events that are transitory or immediate and those developments that signal the emergence of a new conjuncture; that is, a transformation of the nature, form and prospects of human communities. In acknowledging the deficiencies of existing approaches, this volume seeks to develop a distinctive account of globalization which is both historically grounded and informed by a rigorous analytical framework. The framework is explicated in this introduction, while subsequent chapters use it to tell the story of globalization and to assess its implications for the governance and politics of nation-states today. In this respect, the introduction provides the intellectual foundation for addressing the central questions which animate the entire study:

- What is globalization? How should it be conceptualized?
- Does contemporary globalization represent a novel condition?

- Is globalization associated with the demise, the resurgence or the transformation of state power?
- Does contemporary globalization impose new limits to politics? How can globalization be 'civilized' and democratized?

As will soon become apparent, these questions are at the root of the many controversies and debates which find expression in contemporary discussions about globalization and its consequences. The subsequent pages offer a way of thinking about how these questions might be addressed.

## The Globalization Debate

Globalization may be thought of initially as the widening, deepening and speeding up of worldwide interconnectedness in all aspects of contemporary social life, from the cultural to the criminal, the financial to the spiritual. That computer programmers in India now deliver services in real time to their employers in Europe and the USA, while the cultivation of poppies in Burma can be linked to drug abuse in Berlin or Belfast, illustrate the ways in which contemporary globalization connects communities in one region of the world to developments in another continent. But beyond a general acknowledgement of a real or perceived intensification of global interconnectedness there is substantial disagreement as to how globalization is best conceptualized, how one should think about its causal dynamics, and how one should characterize its structural consequences, if any. A vibrant debate on these issues has developed in which it is possible to distinguish three broad schools of thought, which we will refer to as the *hyperglobalizers*, the *sceptics*, and the *transformationalists*. In essence each of these schools may be said to represent a distinctive account of globalization—an attempt to understand and explain this social phenomenon.

For the hyperglobalizers, such as Ohmae, contemporary globalization defines a new era in which peoples everywhere are increasingly subject to the disciplines of the global marketplace (1990; 1995). By contrast the sceptics, such as Hirst and Thompson, argue that globalization is essentially a myth which conceals the reality of an international economy increasingly segmented into three major regional blocs in which national governments remain very powerful (1996a; 1996b). Finally, for the transformationalists, chief among them being Rosenau and Giddens, contemporary patterns of globalization are conceived as historically unprecedented such that states and societies across the globe are experiencing a process of profound change as they try to adapt to a more interconnected but highly uncertain world (Giddens, 1990, 1996; Rosenau, 1997).

Interestingly, none of these three schools map directly on to traditional ideological positions or worldviews. Within the hyperglobalist's camp orthodox neoliberal accounts of globalization can be found alongside Marxist accounts, while among the sceptics conservative as well as radical accounts share similar conceptions of, and conclusions about, the nature of contemporary globalization. Moreover, none of the great traditions of social enquiry—liberal, conservative and Marxist—has an agreed perspective on globalization as a socio-economic phenomenon. Among Marxists globalization is understood in quite incompatible ways as, for instance, the extension of monopoly capitalist imperialism or, alternatively, as a radically new form of globalized capitalism (Callinicos et al., 1994; Gill, 1995; Amin, 1997). Similarly, despite their broadly orthodox neoliberal starting points,

Ohmae and Redwood produce very different accounts of, and conclusions about, the dynamics of contemporary globalization (Ohmae, 1995; Redwood, 1993). Among the hyperglobalizers, sceptics and transformationalists there is a rich diversity of intellectual approaches and normative convictions. Yet, despite this diversity, each of the perspectives reflects a general set of arguments and conclusions about globalization with respect to its

- globalization
- conceptualization
- causal dynamics
- socio-economic consequences
- implications for state power and governance
- and historical trajectory.

It is useful to dwell on the pattern of argument within and between approaches this will shed light on the fundamental issues at stake in the globalization debate.[1]

## The Hyperglobalist Thesis

For the hyperglobalizers, globalization defines a new epoch of human history in which 'traditional nation-states have become unnatural, even impossible business units in a global economy' (Ohmae, 1995, p. 5; cf. Wriston, 1992; Guéhenno, 1995). Such a view of globalization generally privileges an economic logic and, in its neoliberal variant, celebrates the emergence of a single global market and the principle of global competition as the harbingers of human progress. Hyperglobalizers argue that economic globalization is bringing about a 'denationalization' of economies through the establishment of transnational networks of production, trade and finance. In this 'borderless' economy, national governments are relegated to little more than transmission belts for global capital or, ultimately, simple intermediate institutions sandwiched between increasingly powerful local, regional and global mechanisms of governance. As Strange puts it, 'the impersonal forces of world markets . . . are now more powerful than the states to whom ultimate political authority over society and economy is supposed to belong . . . the declining authority of states is reflected in a growing diffusion of authority to other institutions and associations, and to local and regional bodies' (1996, p. 4; cf. Reich, 1991). In this respect, many hyperglobalizers share a conviction that economic globalization is constructing new forms of social organization that are supplanting, or that will eventually supplant, traditional nation-states as the primary economic and political units of world society.

Within this framework there is considerable normative divergence between, on the one hand, the neoliberals who welcome the triumph of individual autonomy and the market principle over state power, and the radicals or neo-Marxists for whom contemporary globalization represents the triumph of an oppressive global capitalism (cf. Ohmae, 1995; Greider, 1997). But despite divergent

---

[1] The approaches set out below present general summaries of different ways of thinking about globalization: they do not represent fully the particular positions and many differences among the individual theorists mentioned. The aim of the presentation is to highlight the main trends and faultlines in the current debate and literature.

ideological convictions, there exists a shared set of beliefs that globalization is primarily an economic phenomenon; that an increasingly integrated global economy exists today; that the needs of global capital impose a neoliberal economic discipline on all governments such that politics is no longer the 'art of the possible' but rather the practice of 'sound economic management'.

Furthermore, the hyperglobalizers claim that economic globalization is generating a new pattern of winners as well as losers in the global economy. The old North–South division is argued to be an increasing anachronism as a new global division of labour replaces the traditional core–periphery structure with a more complex architecture of economic power. Against this background, governments have to 'manage' the social consequences of globalization, or those who 'having been left behind, want not so much a chance to move forward as to hold others back' (Ohmae, 1995, p. 64). However, they also have to manage increasingly in a context in which the constraints of global financial and competitive disciplines make social democratic models of social protection untenable and spell the demise of associated welfare state policies (J. Gray, 1998). Globalization may be linked with a growing polarization between winners and losers in the global economy. But this need not be so, for, at least in the neoliberal view, global economic competition does not necessarily produce zero-sum outcomes. While particular groups within a country may be made worse off as a result of global competition, nearly all countries have a comparative advantage in producing certain goods which can be exploited in the long run. Neo-Marxists and radicals regard such an 'optimistic view' as unjustified, believing that global capitalism creates and reinforces structural patterns of inequality within and between countries. But they agree at least with their neoliberal counterparts that traditional welfare options for social protection are looking increasingly threadbare and difficult to sustain.

Among the elites and 'knowledge workers' of the new global economy tacit transnational 'class' allegiances have evolved, cemented by an ideological attachment to a neoliberal economic orthodoxy. For those who are currently marginalized, the worldwide diffusion of a consumerist ideology also imposes a new sense of identity, displacing traditional cultures and ways of life. The global spread of liberal democracy further reinforces the sense of an emerging global civilization defined by universal standards of economic and political organization. This 'global civilization' is also replete with its own mechanisms of global governance, whether it be the IMF or the disciplines of the world market, such that states and peoples are increasingly the subjects of new public and private global or regional authorities (Gill, 1995; Ohmae,1995; Strange, 1996; Cox, 1997). Accordingly, for many neoliberals, globalization is considered as the harbinger of the first truly global civilization, while for many radicals it represents the first global 'market civilization' (Perlmutter, 1991; Gill, 1995; Greider, 1997).

In this hyperglobalist account the rise of the global economy, the emergence of institutions of global governance, and the global diffusion and hybridization of cultures are interpreted as evidence of a radically new world order, an order which prefigures the demise of the nation-state (Luard, 1990; Ohmae, 1995; Albrow, 1996). Since the national economy is increasingly a site of transnational and global flows, as opposed to the primary container of national socio-economic activity, the authority and legitimacy of the nation-state are challenged: national governments become increasingly unable either to control what transpires within their own borders or to fulfil by themselves the demands of their own citizens. Moreover, as institutions of global and regional governance acquire a bigger role, the sovereignty and autonomy of the state are further eroded. On the other hand, the conditions facilitating transnational cooperation between peoples, given global infrastructures of communication and increasing awareness of many common interests, have never been so propitious. In this regard, there is evidence of an emerging 'global civil society'.

Economic power and political power, in this hyperglobalist view, are becoming effectively denationalized and diffused such that nation-states, whatever the claims of national politicians, are increasingly becoming 'a transitional mode of organization for managing economic affairs' (Ohmae, 1995, p. 149). Whether issuing from a liberal or radical/socialist perspective, the hyperglobalist thesis represents globalization as embodying nothing less than the fundamental reconfiguration of the 'framework of human action' (Albrow, 1996, p. 85).

## The Sceptical Thesis

By comparison the sceptics, drawing on statistical evidence of world flows of trade, investment and labour from the nineteenth century, maintain that contemporary levels of economic interdependence are by no means historically unprecedented. Rather than globalization, which to the sceptics necessarily implies a perfectly integrated worldwide economy in which the 'law of one price' prevails, the historical evidence at best confirms only heightened levels of internationalization, that is, interactions between predominantly national economies (Hirst and Thompson, 1996b). In arguing that globalization is a myth, the sceptics rely on a wholly economistic conception of globalization, equating it primarily with a perfectly integrated global market. By contending that levels of economic integration fall short of this 'ideal type' and that such integration as there is remains much less significant than in the late nineteenth century (the era of the classical Gold Standard), the sceptics are free to conclude that the extent of contemporary 'globalization' is wholly exaggerated (Hirst, 1997). In this respect, the sceptics consider the hyperglobalist thesis as fundamentally flawed and also politically naive since it underestimates the enduring power of national governments to regulate international economic activity. Rather than being out of control, the forces of internationalization themselves depend on the regulatory power of national governments to ensure continuing economic liberalization.

For most sceptics, if the current evidence demonstrates anything it is that economic activity is undergoing a significant 'regionalization' as the world economy evolves in the direction of three major financial and trading blocs, that is, Europe, Asia-Pacific and North America (Ruigrok and Tulder, 1995; Boyer and Drache, 1996; Hirst and Thompson, 1996b). In comparison with the classical Gold Standard era, the world economy is therefore significantly less integrated than it once was (Boyer and Drache, 1996; Hirst and Thompson,1996a). Among the sceptics, globalization and regionalization are conceived as contradictory tendencies. As both Gordon and Weiss conclude, in comparison with the age of world empires, the international economy has become considerably less global in its geographical embrace (Gordon, 1988; Weiss, 1998).

Sceptics tend also to discount the presumption that internationalization prefigures the emergence of a new, less state-centric world order. Far from considering national governments as becoming immobilized by international imperatives, they point to their growing centrality in the regulation and active promotion of cross-border economic activity. Governments are not the passive victims of internationalization but, on the contrary, its primary architects. Indeed, Gilpin considers internationalization largely a by-product of the US-initiated multilateral economic order which, in the aftermath of the Second World War, created the impetus for the liberalization of national economies (Gilpin, 1987). From a very different perspective, Callinicos and others explain the recent intensification of worldwide trade and foreign investment as a new phase of Western imperialism in which national governments, as the agents of monopoly capital, are deeply implicated (Callinicos et al., 1994).

However, despite such differences of emphasis, there is a convergence of opinion within the sceptical camp that, whatever its exact driving forces, internationalization has not been accompanied by an erosion of North–South inequalities but, on the contrary, by the growing economic marginalization of many 'Third World' states as trade and investment flows within the rich North intensify to the exclusion of much of the rest of the globe (Hirst and Thompson, 1996b). Moreover, Krugman questions the popular belief that a new international division of labour is emerging in which deindustrialization in the North can be traced to the operation of multinational corporations exporting jobs to the South (Krugman, 1996). Similarly Ruigrok and Tulder, and Thompson and Allen seek to demolish the 'myth' of the 'global corporation', highlighting the fact that foreign investment flows are concentrated among the advanced capitalist states and that most multinationals remain primarily creatures of their home states or regions (Ruigrok and Tulder, 1995; Thompson and Allen, 1997). Accordingly, the sceptical thesis is generally dismissive of the notion that internationalization is bringing about a profound or even significant restructuring of global economic relations. In this respect, the sceptical position is an acknowledgement of the deeply rooted patterns of inequality and hierarchy in the world economy, which in structural terms have changed only marginally over the last century.

Such inequality, in the view of many sceptics, contributes to the advance of both fundamentalism and aggressive nationalism such that rather than the emergence of a global civilization, as the hyperglobalizers predict, the world is fragmenting into civilizational blocs and cultural and ethnic enclaves (Huntington, 1996). The notion of cultural homogenization and a global culture are thus further myths which fall victim to the sceptical argument. In addition, the deepening of global inequalities, the realpolitik of international relations and the 'clash of civilizations' expose the illusory nature of 'global governance' in so far as the management of world order remains, as it has since the last century, overwhelmingly the preserve of Western states. In this respect, the sceptical argument tends to conceive of global governance and economic internationalization as primarily Western projects, the main object of which is to sustain the primacy of the West in world affairs. As E. H. Carr once observed: 'international order and "international solidarity" will always be slogans of those who feel strong enough to impose them on others' (1981, p. 87).

In general the sceptics take issue with all of the primary claims of the hyperglobalizers pointing to the comparatively greater levels of economic interdependence and the more extensive geographical reach of the world economy at the beginning of the twentieth century. They reject the popular 'myth' that the power of national governments or state sovereignty is being undermined today by economic internationalization or global governance (Krasner, 1993, 1995). Some argue that 'globalization' more often than not reflects a politically convenient rationale for implementing unpopular orthodox neoliberal economic strategies (Hirst, 1997). Weiss, Scharpf and Armingeon, among others, argue that the available evidence contradicts the popular belief that there has been a convergence of macroeconomic and welfare policies across the globe (Weiss, 1998; Scharpf, 1991; Armingeon, 1997). While international economic conditions may constrain what governments can do, governments are by no means immobilized. The internationalization of capital may, as Weiss argues, 'not merely restrict policy choices, but expand them as well' (1998, pp. 184ff.). Rather than the world becoming more interdependent, as the hyperglobalizers assume, the sceptics seek to expose the myths which sustain the globalization thesis.

## The Transformationalist Thesis

At the heart of the transformationalist thesis is a conviction that, at the dawn of a new millennium, globalization is a central driving force behind the rapid social, political and economic changes that are reshaping modern societies and world order (Giddens, 1990; Scholte, 1993; Castells, 1996). According to the proponents of this view, contemporary processes of globalization are historically unprecedented such that governments and societies across the globe are having to adjust to a world in which there is no longer a clear distinction between international and domestic, external and internal affairs (Rosenau, 1990; Cammilleri and Falk, 1992; Ruggie,1993; Linklater and MacMillan, 1995; Sassen, 1996). For Rosenau, the growth of 'intermestic' affairs define a 'new frontier', the expanding political, economic and social space in which the fate of societies and communities is decided (1997, pp. 4–5). In this respect, globalization is conceived as a powerful transformative force which is responsible for a 'massive shake-out' of societies, economies, institutions of governance and world order (Giddens, 1996).

In the transformationalist account, however, the direction of this 'shake-out' remains uncertain, since globalization is conceived as an essentially contingent historical process replete with contradictions (Mann, 1997). At issue is a dynamic and open-ended conception of where globalization might be leading and the kind of world order which it might prefigure. In comparison with the sceptical and hyperglobalist accounts, the transformationalists make no claims about the future trajectory of globalization; nor do they seek to evaluate the present in relation to some single, fixed ideal-type 'globalized world', whether a global market or a global civilization. Rather, transformationalist accounts emphasize globalization as a long-term historical process which is inscribed with contradictions and which is significantly shaped by conjunctural factors.

Such caution about the exact future of globalization is matched, nonetheless, by the conviction that contemporary patterns of global economic, military, technological, ecological, migratory, political and cultural flows are historically unprecedented. As Nierop puts it, 'virtually all countries in the world, if not all parts of their territory and all segments of their society, are now functionally part of that larger [global] system in one or more respects' (1994, p. 171). But the existence of a single global system is not taken as evidence of global convergence or of the arrival of single world society. On the contrary, for the transformationalists, globalization is associated with new patterns of global stratification in which some states, societies and communities are becoming increasingly enmeshed in the global order while others are becoming increasingly marginalized. A new configuration of global power relations is held to be crystallizing as the North–South division rapidly gives way to a new international division of labour such that the 'familiar pyramid of the core-periphery hierarchy is no longer a geographic but a social division of the world economy' (Hoogvelt, 1997,

p. xii). To talk of North and South, of First World and Third World, is to overlook the ways in which globalization has recast traditional patterns of inclusion and exclusion between countries by forging new hierarchies which cut across and penetrate all societies and regions of the world. North and South, First World and Third World, are no longer 'out there' but nestled together within all the world's major cities. Rather than the traditional pyramid analogy of the world social structure, with a tiny top echelon and spreading mass base, the global social structure can be envisaged as a three-tier arrangement of concentric circles, each cutting across national boundaries, representing respectively the elites, the contented and the marginalized (Hoogvelt, 1997).

The recasting of patterns of global stratification is linked with the growing deterritorialization of economic activity as production and finance increasingly acquire a global and transnational dimension. From somewhat different starting points, Castells and Ruggie, among others, argue that national economies are being reorganized by processes of economic globalization such that national economic space no longer coincides with national territorial borders (Castells, 1996; Ruggie,1996). In this globalizing economy, systems of transnational production, exchange and finance weave together ever more tightly the fortunes of communities and households on different continents.

At the core of the transformationalist case is a belief that contemporary globalization is reconstituting or 're-engineering' the power, functions and authority of national governments. While not disputing that states still retain the ultimate legal claim to 'effective supremacy over what occurs within their own territories', the transformationalists argue that this is juxtaposed, to varying degrees, with the expanding jurisdiction of institutions of international governance and the constraints of, as well as the obligations derived from, international law. This is especially evident in the EU, where sovereign power is divided between international, national and local authorities, but it is also evident in the operation of the World Trade Organization (WTO) (Goodman, 1997). However, even where sovereignty still appears intact, states no longer, if they ever did, retain sole command of what transpires within their own territorial boundaries. Complex global systems, from the financial to the ecological, connect the fate of communities in one locale to the fate of communities in distant regions of the world. Furthermore, global infrastructures of communication and transport support new forms of economic and social organization which transcend national boundaries without any consequent diminution of efficiency or control. Sites of power and the subjects of power may be literally, as well as metaphorically, oceans apart. In these circumstances, the notion of the nation-state as a self-governing, autonomous unit appears to be more a normative claim than a descriptive statement. The modern institution of territorially circumscribed sovereign rule appears somewhat anomalous juxtaposed with the transnational organization of many aspects of contemporary economic and social life (Sandel, 1996). Globalization, in this account, is therefore associated with a transformation or, to use Ruggie's term, an 'unbundling' of the relationship between sovereignty, territoriality and state power (Ruggie, 1993; Sassen, 1996).

Of course, few states have ever exercised complete or absolute sovereignty within their own territorial boundaries, as the practice of diplomatic immunity highlights (Sassen, 1996). Indeed the practice, as opposed to the doctrine, of sovereign statehood has always readily adapted to changing historical realities (Murphy, 1996). In arguing that globalization is transforming or reconstituting the power and authority of national governments, the transformationalists reject both the hyperglobalist rhetoric of the end of the sovereign nation-state and the sceptics' claim that 'nothing much has changed.' Instead, they assert that a new 'sovereignty regime' is displacing traditional conceptions of statehood as an absolute, indivisible, territorially exclusive and zero-sum form of public power (Held, 1991). Accordingly, sovereignty today is, they suggest, best understood 'less as a territorially defined barrier than a bargaining resource for a politics characterized by complex transnational networks' (Keohane, 1995).

This is not to argue that territorial boundaries retain no political, military or symbolic significance but rather to acknowledge that, conceived as the primary spatial markers of modern life, they have become increasingly problematic in an era of intensified globalization. Sovereignty, state power and territoriality thus stand today in a more complex relationship than in the epoch during which the modern nation-state was being forged. Indeed, the argument of the transformationalists is that globalization is associated not only with a new 'sovereignty regime' but also with the emergence of powerful new non-territorial forms of economic and political organization in the global domain, such as multinational corporations, transnational social movements, international regulatory agencies, etc. In this sense, world order can no longer be conceived as purely state-centric or even primarily state governed, as authority has become increasingly diffused among public and private agencies at the local, national, regional and global levels. Nation-states are no longer the sole centres or the principal forms of governance or authority in the world (Rosenau, 1997).

Given this changing global order, the form and functions of the state are having to adapt as governments seek coherent strategies of engaging with a globalizing world. Distinctive strategies are being followed from the model of the neoliberal minimal state to the models of the developmental state (government as the central promoter of economic expansion) and the catalytic state (government as facilitator of coordinated and collective action). In addition, governments have become increasingly outward looking as they seek to pursue cooperative strategies and to construct international regulatory regimes to manage more effectively the growing array of cross-border issues which regularly surface on national agendas. Rather than globalization bringing about the 'end of the state', it has encouraged a spectrum of adjustment strategies and, in certain respects, a more activist state. Accordingly, the power of national governments is not necessarily diminished by globalization but on the contrary is being reconstituted and restructured in response to the growing complexity of processes of governance in a more interconnected world (Rosenau, 1997).

The three dominant tendencies in the globalization debate are summarized in Table 2.1. To move beyond the debate between these three approaches requires a framework of enquiry through which the principal claims of each might be assessed. But to construct such a framework demands, as an initial condition, some understanding of the primary faultlines around which the debate itself revolves. Identifying the critical issues in the debate creates an intellectual foundation for thinking about how globalization might best be conceptualized and the particular grounds on which any assessment of competing claims about it might be pursued.

**TABLE 2.1** Conceptualizing Globalization: Three Tendencies

|  | *Hyperglobalists* | *Sceptics* | *Transformationalists* |
|---|---|---|---|
| **What's new?** | A global age | Trading blocs, weaker geogovernance than in earlier periods | Historically unprecedented levels of global interconnectedness |
| **Dominant features** | Global capitalism, global governance, global civil society | World less interdependent than in 1890s | "Thick" (intensive and extensive) globalization |
| **Power of national governments** | Declining or eroding | Reinforced or enhanced | Reconstituted, restructured |
| **Driving forces of globalization** | Capitalism and technology | States and markets | Combined forces of modernity |
| **Pattern of stratification** | Erosion of old hierarchies | Increased marginalization of South | New architecture of world order |
| **Dominant motif** | McDonalds, Madonna, etc. | National interest | Transformation of political community |
| **Conceptualization of globalization** | As a reordering of the framework of human action | As internationalization and regionalization | As the reordering of interregional relations and action at a distance |
| **Historical trajectory** | Global civilization | Regional blocs/clash of civilizations | Indeterminate: global integration and fragmentation |
| **Summary argument** | The end of the nation-state | Internationalization depends on state acquiescence and support | Globalization transforming state power and world politics |

# Globalization

BARRIE AXFORD

## Introduction

As the millennium approaches, globalization retains its allure as a designer concept of choice, despite conflicting claims that we now live in a postglobalized world, that the current frisson is only part of a 'recurrent tendency of world-capitalism since early modern times' (Arrighi, 1997: 1), or that there is no such beast anyway. While these are useful correctives to what one author has described as 'global-degook' (Freeman, 1995), such counterclaims are flawed because they oversimplify the nature, provenance and tenacity of globalization as an historical process which is redrawing the economic, political and cultural geographies of the world.

As part of a critical examination of the concept, I want to offer what might be called a 'strong' version of globalization, albeit one which draws attention to its complex, multidimensional character. While it is obvious that globalization is a fashionable term, it is often used just as a convenient rhetorical device. Debates on globalization show plenty of verve and commitment, but they are often under-theorized and conceptually naïve. Shortcomings include a failure to say what is global about globalization, an inattention to its multidimensional character and a reluctance to recognize the historicity of the process while remaining sensitive to the transformative qualities of particular moments of globalization. In the rest of this chapter I will write in more detail about each of these areas of neglect as a way of substantiating my 'strong' thesis. I will then discuss some of the fashionable strands of thinking which suggest that globalization is a myth, before concluding with brief remarks on why the study of globalization is important for any attempt to understand the present.

First, let me say a little more about my 'strong' version of globalization. It is strong primarily in the sense that it goes beyond anodyne definitions of globalization as growing interconnectedness. Instead this strong version has it that globalization is the historical process through which the world is being made into one place with systemic properties (Axford, 1995, 1997; Robertson, 1992). This is a fairly robust claim and I will return to it later in the chapter. In contrast to heavily normative positions and teleological accounts (for examples see Gray, 1998) I will argue that globalization is a complex, contradictory and multidimensional historical process. The historicity of the process does not, however, make the outcomes of this, or of any other moment of globalization, entirely predictable. Globalizing processes involve variable, but always significant, shifts in the spatial ordering and reach of networks (for example in trade, communications, finance, technology, migration, cultural goods and ideas) in the stretching of interpersonal and social relationships across time and space, and in organizational forms and functions (including the paradigm political forms of the modern territorial state and the international system of states). It is also a process which triggers important changes in consciousness, as individuals and collective actors embrace, oppose or in some way are 'constrained to identify' with the global condition (Robertson, 1992). The study of globalization requires attention both to material considerations such as the volume of goods traded, or the market penetration of 'global' products like Levi jeans, and to the meanings which attach to these 'transnational connections' (Hannerz, 1996). Only by examining the extent and intensity of global consciousness—in other words by seeing how agents actually experience and respond to globalizing pressures—is it possible to estimate the impact of global processes upon more or less sensitive and vulnerable actors (Keohane and Nye, 1977) and to assess the strength or fragility of global institutions.

My approach is multidimensional in that it does not privilege any one domain as providing the key to or essential dynamics of globalization, but addresses the complex and often contradictory interplay between economic, political and cultural forces, and between local agents and global forces in making the world one place. In this the approach differs from other 'strong' positions which traffic some version of a global entropic field where all differences between local structures are dissolved and individuals become interchangeable at an abstract global level.

## Global Speak

At the end of the 1990s globalization is a term found routinely across the social sciences, and one used promiscuously by all manner of folk, from politicians to media moguls. The word has become a paradigm for the allegedly uncertain and labile qualities of the times in which we live, an intimation of epochal changes in train, or a neat encapsulation of millenarian hopes and fears of the apocalypse. More prosaically, it is a convenient shorthand for a number of complex processes which, in David Harvey's felicitous expression, are serving to 'compress the world' in terms of time and space, and to redefine all sorts of borders—to taste and imagination as well as to territory and identities (Harvey, 1990).

Indeed, the burden of much global talk is that boundaries are vanishing, giving way to a world made up of more or less dense networks of communication and exchange and hybridized identities. In global talk it is quite common to hear about the demise of the territorial State, especially in its guise as the manager of economic affairs; about the 'borderless world' (Ohmae, 1989) of financial markets; and about all manner of cultural common denominators, from fast-food to faster entertainment, which pass for signifiers of a global culture. Taking all this on board, it will come as no surprise that global talk is also rife with conflicting interpretations. On the one hand, the processes which are making the world one place are seen as destructive—of localities, of 'real' cultures, of the environment—while on the other, they intimate a future rich in hope for humankind.

# So What Is Globalization?

To reiterate: globalization is the historical process whereby the world is being made into a single place with systemic properties. Historically, globalizing forces produced global systems which were of limited extent spatially, and in which the density of social relations across borders and time varied enormously. At the end of this century it is clear that through various media—the burgeoning capacity of electronic communications to compress both time and space, changes in technology which are allowing production and culture to be divorced from place, the pervasiveness of global ideologies on subjects such as the environment and human rights, and recent seismic shifts in the world's geopolitical balance—the world is now thoroughly globalized, a single place. What happens in one place routinely affects perceptions, attitudes and behaviour elsewhere. Indeed, because of technological innovations, this routine impact is almost instantaneous. Because social relations are being stretched across time and space the borders and walls which insulated and isolated individuals and collective actors in the past are being eroded. Gearoid O'Tuathail (1998: 6) says that 'territoriality is being eclipsed by telemetricality', where that refers to forms of electronic communications, and while this may strike us as too glib, even with a proper social scientific caution it deserves to be taken seriously.

Indeed the real charge in the concept of globalization, most poignantly observed in its current phase, is that conventional borders are becoming increasingly irrelevant to the actual patterns of much economic, cultural and even political activity. Translocal and transnational networks— of producers professionals, exchange students, commodity brokers and human rights activists— populate a truly global cultural economy, and territoriality as the organizational principle of the world polity is everywhere in retreat. The modern 'geopolitical imagination' (O'Tuathail, 1998), used to depicting the world in terms of spatial blocs, territory and the fixed identities usually attached to these, is now in some turmoil. Globalization presages a new geopolitics, and thus requires novel ways of imagining a global space increasingly made up of flows, networks and webs (Appadurai, 1990, 1996; Castells, 1996, 1997).

Of course, in quotidian reality it is all messier. Pretty much everywhere the space of flows of the global subsists with economic, cultural and political architectures characteristic of territorial spaces and the identities tied to them. It is true that global forms are all around us in the shape of transnational business organizations (Nestle, Nissan), transnational communities (New Age, fundamentalist, diasporic and virtual) and transnational structures (of production, finance, and also governance). But while the rise of transnational interest groups, like Friends of the Earth or Amnesty International, has created a politics which transcends particular boundaries, histories and cultures, and which is outside the remit of any one State, it is too easy to take these as modal phenomena, rather than just as intimations of what Ulrich Beck (1996: 121) has called a 'global sub-politics', one configured by connectivity among non-governmental actors and social movements, and not by space and territorial interests. Despite the claim made by Arjun Appadurai (1996: 46), 'boundaries, structures and regularities' are still very much in evidence. All of which is quite confusing, but does have the merit of focusing attention on what it means to describe the world as a single place.

## Treating the World as a Single Place:
## What Is Global about Globalization?

The idea of globalization creating a world which is a 'single place' should not be taken to imply complete homogeneity, despite the fact that it does produce 'an essential sameness' in the surface appearance of social and political life across the globe (McGrew, 1992). The relationships between situated actors and globalizing forces, or between lived localities and virtual communities, are rarely ones in which globalizing pressures are powerful enough simply to obliterate sub-global identities. Instead we see a global system which has a number of configurations, sometimes overlapping but often confronting each other.

The first, which perhaps comes closest to some notion of global homogeneity, has the globalized world as little more than a map of variable tastes. 'Glocal' consumer products produced and marketed by transnational corporations rely on the skills of designers and marketers to fashion a standard product which is sufficiently flexible to allow for local variation, or else can be packaged to appeal to local idiosyncrasies. This is the global system as McWorld (Barber, 1996), a world made up of MTV, McDonalds and M&Ms. The second configuration depicts a globalized world in which existing identities may be relativized or attenuated by globalizing processes, but where these same processes can be indigenized or used by local actors to meet their own needs (Hannerz, 1996). This sounds more grandiose and certainly more conscious than it is in practice. The point is that cultural commodities (both the material kind and cultural forms like movies which are created for a career as global commodities) are imbued with meaning in particular contexts and by specific agents or populations. In this configuration, the relationships between the local and the global are structured in and through what Zygmunt Bauman (1992: 190) has called 'habitats of meaning' which are produced by individuals as they go about their everyday lives. The local and the global are enmeshed at the intersection of different habitats of meaning—on the Internet, through the availability of fast or exotic foods in supermarkets, or by watching Blockbuster videos. At the same time quite scary brands of politics have been constructed around the claim that local culture has an authentic quality which must be protected, while global cultures are by definition protean and thus inauthentic.

So my third configuration has the globalized world as one which is characteristically, if uneasily, hybridized, and in which whole cultures and identities are being replaced by those which are, to borrow from Salman Rushdie (1991: 46), 'impure and intermingled'. If this sounds relatively benign, it still leaves some locals constrained to identify with the global condition through what they experience as a disabling loss of culture and identity. I am not suggesting that the outcome of hybridity is always, or even often, schizoid cultures and confused or pathological identities, although it can be (Axford, 1995: 167) but that the global 'organization of diversity' is often quite brutal, attesting to great asymmetries of power. Which leads to the last possible configuration, that of opposition to globalizing forces.

Global consciousness may lead actors to support or to oppose aspects of globalization. Local resistance to the homogenizing or hegemonic power of global products and institutions in the form of soft drinks, multimedia technologies or even secular values, often has an anti-American or anti-Western slant. For other actors whose concern is not the preservation of local identities, globalizing trends are to be resisted because they are all part of the 'endless accumulation of capital', the latest iteration of a world-historical process which now includes the entire world within its geography (Wallerstein, 1997). But opposition to globalization can also have a more particularistic slant, especially where borderless worlds and hybrid identities are seen to challenge or to defile more elemental or fundamental beliefs and identities. The emergence of post-national identities and practices in the guise of company cultures and networks of non-governmental organizations, and intimated in the multi-level polity of the European Union, vie with regional realignments and fracturings, nationalist and ethnic separatisms and all manner of fundamentalist credos.

So what sort of a system is this? Clearly it is not a unitary notion of the global. Rather, the process reveals contradictory tendencies towards increasing interconnectedness *and* greater fragmentation. Globalization creates various kinds of linkages, seen in the growing density and reach of networks and flows—of goods between nations, through migration, in business, tourism and knowledge— to create what Ulf Hannerz calls a 'global ecumene', a web of networks consisting of nodes of interaction, rather than centres and peripheries, and which is generally lacking in boundaries. The systemness or unity of the global system is thus a negotiated and contingent condition arising from the articulation of local subjects with global structures.

Today, nowhere is immune from these changes. Global processes affect the reproduction of locals and of localities. As a consequence, economic and probably political and cultural autarky are increasingly hard, if not impossible, to sustain in a globalized world, even taking into account the widespread evidence of resistance to globalization—in other words it is hard to opt out. Pol Pot's Cambodia, Iran under clerical rule, even Red China, have all been constrained to identify with the global system. The more mundane fact is that globalization is making it more difficult for social actors like nation-states, localities and individuals to sustain identity without reference to more encompassing global structures and flows. Interconnections globalize the world in a measurable, perhaps even an 'objective' way, but do so mainly because such forces are redefining the experiences and perceptions of more and more actors. So the global is now the cognitive frame of reference for many actors who are aware of global constraints, although it remains much less so in matters of culture and morality.

## Multidimensional Globalization

The dynamic and labile quality of globalization can only be studied by adopting an approach that abjures the conventional distinctions between levels of analysis (personal and global) as well as refusing to privilege the explanatory power of one domain of human activity over others (economics over politics, and both over culture). Yet one-dimensional accounts are legion. For example, many economists and management theorists view globalization as a recent phenomenon driven solely by the ideology and practice of neo-liberalism. Such positions are usually silent on the cultural and technological dimensions of globalization, and treat political questions as secondary. Instead globalization is reduced to a relatively simple affair involving an ever more integrated and unitary global trading and financial system, shaped, as Amin says (1997: 128), by bargaining coalitions among powerful nations, international regulatory institutions and global (or multinational) private corporations. In Kenichi

Ohmae's (1989) anthem to the borderless world, territorial states are seen as irrelevant to what he terms the 'real flows' of the world economy, while for Michael Porter (1990), more of an economic realist than Ohmae, they remain crucial to corporate and sectoral economic success, but only as the providers of the supply-side resources necessary in the global competitiveness stakes.

In each of these accounts of a globalizing world, as well as in others from opposite ideological perspectives, there is a common fault. Nowhere is it understood that the complex and contradictory relations of economy, politics and culture requires the observer to unravel the intertwinings of an economic system admittedly dependent on the principle of commodification and cultural terrains which are both determined by, and yet still manage to elude or even to subvert, that principle. Yet culture is an intriguing domain for the study of globalization because it affects the identity of people and provides them with meaning. The problem is that, apart from the more subtle interventions of cultural anthropologists (Appadurai,1996; Friedman, 1994; Hannerz, 1996) and some sociologists (Featherstone, 1990; Bauman, 1992; Robertson, 1992), culture is often reified as a kind of social cement, or as an ideological protection for dominant interests. For other writers, the very idea of global culture is an oxymoron (Smith, 1995). What such conceptions lack is any sense of culture being constructed rather than imposed, enacted by individuals in both stable and changing contexts. In other words they omit any developed sense of agency as an active component of globalization. Individuals and whole populations are constrained to identify with the global condition just by being there, through passively consuming global fare in one form or another. While this has to be true for some of the people some of the time, it is at best only part of the story. Users of the Internet are conscious and willing participants in the compression of the globe, as are governments and social movements which buy into globally sanctioned models of behaviour and development in areas such as the environment, gender equality and the treatment of refugees. And, as Ulf Hannerz (1996) says, although conscious and militant anti-globalism is itself part of the dialectic of globalization, at the very least it offers the possibility of alternative imagined worlds.

## Present and Past Globalizations

Globalization triggers changes in the scale of social organization and changes in consciousness of the world too. Understood in this way the process should not be seen as unique to one moment of world-historical time. As Hannerz (1996: 18) says with typical economy, 'different worlds, different globalizations'. For analysts the trick lies in avoiding the presentism found in those accounts which treat the current *frisson* as *sui generis*, as well as in being able to recognize the transformative potential of particular moments of globalization.

In a recent paper, Giovanni Arrighi (1997) sets down the case for treating current globalization as part of evolutionary changes in world capitalism. Transformations bruited as unique to current globalizing trends—the information revolution, the increased volume of trading in currencies, bonds and equities, the privatizing of key functions of governance—are novel only in terms of their 'scale, scope and complexity' (Arrighi, 1997: 2). Now this looks to me like turning a substantial mountain into a lowly molehill, and is sustainable only by reducing world-historical richness and complexity to an essential systemic identity, that of capitalism.

The notion that the only thing which is distinct about late twentieth-century globalization is its scope and scale is just a throwaway line. Arrighi mentions the evolutionary pattern 'that has enabled world capitalism and the underlying system of sovereign states to become a truly global system', implying a seamless functional transition (Arrighi, 1997: 5). But one of the things which is distinctive about late twentieth-century globalization, certainly when compared with the late nineteenth-century pattern, is that the former is not territorial or imperialistic in the classic sense (Pieterse, 1997: 373). While it might be appropriate to classify late nineteenth- and even midtwentieth-century globalization as the spread of the territorial state as a global standard, critically, late twentieth-century globalization owes less and less to this form of collective agency, and on some accounts is best characterized through its undoing. To argue that these differences are mere historical detail in a much larger canvas is at best poor social science, and at worst the sort of crude functionalism which has marred Marxist accounts of all large-scale, long-term social change. So that while Arrighi offers a strongly systemic view of world history, he does less than justice to the active version of systemness canvassed earlier, and largely ignores the plea for a multidimensional approach to globalization.

Yet his argument still has the signal virtue of reminding us that globalization is not brand new. Not only that, but that it is a force which ebbs and flows, takes on different appearances in different times, is characteristically uneven and strikes people in wildly different ways. How then to conceptualize and chart this historical variability and still be sensitive to the qualities of particular periods of globalization? I am drawn to the useful schema provided by Held *et al.* (1999). Their position is that globalization can be charted historically as a spatial phenomenon involving more or less extensive networks of economic, political and cultural activity, and one which increases the density of interactions between actors in states and societies. The upshot is a world of multiple interdependencies, which displays hierarchy (because of asymmetries in access to and control of global networks) as well as unevenness (because of the differential vulnerability of actors to global forces). Mapped in this way the contingent and variable nature of globalization can be studied over time. While such an approach presents major difficulties of research design, it is potentially a powerful corrective to one-dimensional and ahistorical accounts of globalization.

## The Myth of Globalization?

Let me just rehearse the strong position on globalization. Of late the boundaries between societies, cultures, polities and individuals are becoming increasingly fuzzy. Modern conceptions of space and of identity, which relied upon binary notions of the organization of space and time, like traditional/ modern and east/west, are giving way to post-spatial conceptions of the global order. Arjun Appadurai's allusive imagery of a highly contingent global order constructed at the intersection of various 'scapes'—*ethnoscapes* (migration), *finanscapes* (flows of money), *mediascapes* (flows of information and images), *ideoscapes* (the movement of ideas) and *technoscapes* (the realm of technological innovation)—is perhaps the best known example of this sort of thinking. But the starker dichotomy in Benjamin Barber's *Jihad vs McWorld* (1996) also paints a picture in which the world order of national and societal territories is increasingly moribund, and is being replaced by a glocalized networked cultural economy of production and consumption.

These are potent images, yet revisionism is now much in vogue. I want to talk at some length about one line of revisionist argument, the backlash against the 'myth' that globalization is the triumph of borderless capitalism. The revisionist thesis is exemplified most clearly in Paul Hirst and Grahame Thompson's tract *Globalization in Question* (1996). They argue the case against the marked and inevitable erosion of state power, and for new forms of international governance to combat the ideology of neo-liberalism and the practices of an unconstrained free market. For Hirst and Thompson what is often described as an economic system operating on a world scale is in fact little more than the intensification of trade and other sorts of flows within regional groupings which are still largely confined to the so-called 'Triad' economies of Europe, the Americas and parts of South-East Asia. They substantiate this argument by reference to what they see as the continued significance of national governments and economies in the regulation and successes of transnational business corporations (TNCs). At the same time, they admit that the regionalization of economic activity has made life more difficult for national regulatory regimes, thereby increasing the need for more effective forms of international governance. Moreover, Hirst and Thompson are at pains to show that truly global companies (that is, those which have broken free of any sort of national ties), are few and far between. Finally they go to some lengths to show that between 1878 and 1914, the *belle époque* of world capitalism, international flows of goods, investments and people exceeded current levels.

But globalization is not reducible to economic processes and certainly not just to neo-liberalism. Hirst and Thompson offer a detailed and wonderfully knockabout case, but it is based on a reading of globalization which is, to use Ash Amin's phrase, no more than 'a superficial quantitative evaluation of the phenomenon' (Amin, 1997: 128). Because of this a number of problems arise. The first is that because Hirst and Thompson want to cavil at whether there is a 'truly globalized economy', they trivialize the immense amount of transnational economic activity now in train. The phenomenal aspect of this activity consists of the massively extended circuits of production and exchange seen in recent years, largely under the auspices of TNCs. Perhaps more seminal is the spectacular expansion of world financial markets in the last few decades, and the general trend towards 'privatizing' key aspects of the management of economic policy.

But even for businesses this is only one side of the globalizing process. The other is rather more subjective, where this refers to the development of global 'mindsets' among managerial cadres who see the world as an operational whole. It might not be stretching the concept too far to suggest that the taxonomic status of a global company may lie as much in its management style and in how it perceives its market, as it does in more measurable criteria.

Second, Hirst and Thompson have scarcely anything to say about technological changes and how they accelerate globalization, and what they do say underestimates the transformative effects of recent innovations. Manuel Castells (1996), flirting with technological determinism, suggests a new configuration in what he is happy to call the global economy, based upon the role of informational labour, or what others have called knowledge work, in relation to other labour types. These labour types do not correspond to or coincide with particular countries, rather 'they are organised in networks and flows, using the technological infrastructure of the informational economy' (Castells, 1996: 91) to benefit particular companies and sectors. For Castells, the world economic order which is being formed is one in which the 'historically produced architecture' of economic governance, struggles with radically new forces of innovation and competition which do not acknowledge conventional boundaries.

Third, the continued vitality of the sovereign state against globalization is argued empirically and as an article of faith. It is, however, a weak reed upon which to tie a whole thesis. In the first place, as Jan Pieterse (1997: 373) points out, the modern nation-state as a global standard is itself a form of globalization, not a haven from it. While the world is fragmented because of its division into sovereign territorial units, they are themselves part of a constructed and conscious world order, with the policies of individual states often reliant upon prevailing models of national development found in global institutions and practices (Meyer *et al.*, 1997).

Of course, Hirst and Thompson are right to point to the continued vitality of states as players in the world economy and as the guardians of societal values, but in trying to rescue the State from the myth of its powerlessness, they are blind to some key considerations. Except in realist accounts of international relations where the ontology of every state is given, state power is always variable. Once this variability is admitted, it is no great step to acknowledge that globalization must empower some states at the same time as it disempowers others. For example, in East Asia some states have been able to attract and protect mobile capital rather than being supplicants for the largesse of TNCs in the form of direct investments. The whole basis of what has become known as 'Asian capitalism' lies in a much more state-centric model of global financial expansion, one which (up until recently at any rate) seemed to immunize its supporters against the kind of global pressures which have driven others to deregulate their domestic financial structures. At the end of the 1990s the fate of 'Asian capitalism' is still in the balance, but other examples provide evidence of the ubiquity of world-economic and world-polity constraints. The demise of the Soviet Union in 1991 shows how vulnerable even world-class states are to global economic forces, and the limited capacities of various 'quasi-states', most of them former colonial territories, to carry out basic governmental functions makes them especially vulnerable to these same forces. Even among the core states of the capitalist world, some of the most powerful, like Germany and Japan, have been described as only semi-sovereign (Cumings, 1997). Finally, the process of hollowing out state power from below (by regionalist and localist forces, and by various agencies, quangos and task forces) and from above (by various multilateral and supranational institutions) is transforming the architecture of statist governance. The overall message must be that it is not necessary to treat globalization as a myth in order to recognize the vitality of the State, and the more complex reality is that states and state policies have now to subsist in globalized contexts, which are neither illusory nor superficial.

## Conclusion

As a concept globalization belongs to no single branch of the social sciences. It is not, or not yet, a fully elaborated theory, but its value for the social sciences is that it directs attention to those processes which are making the world into a single place—a global system. The fact that the concept has been popularized through indiscriminate usage, or that it is viewed with suspicion by some strains of social science, should not blind us to its importance in this respect. The study of globalization is part of a wider social-scientific recognition that conventional units and levels of analysis—individual, local, societal, national and international—are not separate zones of experience and spheres of social organization, but entwined, and increasingly so. Having said this, my strong version of globalization is perhaps less systemic than proponents of world-systems analysis would find acceptable, in that it views the totality of the global system as a contingent and negotiated order arising from the articulation of economic, political and cultural domains and realized through the routine and dramatic practices of actors in their dealings with globalizing forces. The 'deeper meaning of globalization' spoken of by Alain Benoist (1997) lies in this understanding, and its revelation is possible only by careful attention to both patterns of interconnectedness and the twistings of consciousness.

## Summary

- Globolization is the process through which the world is being made into one place with systemic properties.
- This process is both historically variable and multidimensional.
- It involves interconnections across some boundaries and the dissolving of other boundaries.
- It also precipitates changes in consciousness and possibly in identity.
- To treat these profound changes simply as myth relies on a superficial and a historical understanding of globalization.
- The study of globalization and of the global system constitutes a potential revolution in the social sciences.

# CHAPTER THREE

# *Globalizing Forces: Religion and Empire*

Before setting out on a journey of more than 1,000 years, it is important to remember that many factors have contributed to the weaving and reweaving of the world into a set of interactive structures. They run the gamut from alterations in the world's climate and changing agricultural practices to new forms of social stratification, political organization, and advances in technology. Two among those principal structures that have shaped these and other factors are religion and empire. These factors have by no means been always present, much less related, in the formation of the global past, but their influence and effects can be recognized as persistent elements in human experience.

Religion is the much older of the two but eventually would come to be used as a supportive, indeed, legitimating force in the creation of empire. The origins of religion probably lie in the slow evolution of the human capacity to see life, or at least selected aspects of it, from a perspective removed from its daily immediacies, in terms of something at least sensed or imagined to be outside of, even beyond, them. This capacity for what might be called "beyonding" did not develop on its own; it required the human ability to project the mind beyond the field of the immediate present to a realm that seemed to exist, if not transcendent to it, at least different from or other than it. The potential for such an imaginative capacity, even the need for it, is easily to be explained by the fact that daily life for early human beings seemed continuously beset by forces that seemed to originate from elsewhere. Whether those supranatural forces took the familiar form of rain, wind, earthquakes, lightning, hostile creatures, blizzards, droughts, or other elements, our early ancestors were always faced with the necessity of trying to control such powers, or at any rate resist being destroyed by them. Hence it is no surprise that human beings would eventually seek to conjure with such transhuman forces, whether for the sake of protecting themselves against them, or propitiating them, or even allying themselves with their power. And thus was born the practice of seeking some relation either with natural forces themselves, or with the spirits assumed to inhabit them, or even with the gods alleged to have created them.

But in the long course of its evolution, religion has come to be associated with much more than the notion of deities assumed to exist above and beyond the self and has been identified with everything from stories or narratives about such beings, or the sets of feelings they inspire, or particular rituals designed to please them to the strategies of salvation they may provide, or the codes of conduct and forms of behavior they may prescribe. Religions have thus over thousands of years become many things to many people, some settling on the worship of a single divinity, some on many divinities, and some on none. It has long been held that there are at least eight major religions, which include Buddhism, Confucianism, Hinduism, Judaism, Christianity, Islam, Shinto, and Taoism, but along with these more highly organized religions that have existed for several millennia, there are thousands of other religions—tribal, folk, ethnic, vernacular—that have existed even longer, and often alongside, their better-known competitors.

It is often been asked if there is some essential human need, or set of needs, that all these religions address in their different ways. Is there something in the makeup of human beings for which religions furnish an answer or solution? There are no doubt as many responses to such questions as there are people asking them, but there is one family of problems that most human beings do confront, and not merely at one moment in their lives but in many. These are problems that have to do with the overall meaning of things, or rather with the necessity of finding some kind of inherent sense in them. The issue isn't whether things need to make the same kind of sense to all people but rather whether any people can survive for very long in the world where nothing makes any sense at all. The one experience that most people in the world, for seemingly most of human history, have been unable to cope with is the lack of meaning itself, the prospect lamented by Shakespeare's Macbeth that life "is a tale told by an idiot full of sound and fury, signifying nothing." This is the existential crisis that most human beings throughout history and across cultures cannot countenance, much less endure, and religions as they have evolved, and almost no matter how they have evolved, have offered themselves as a way of managing it.

This existential crisis of meaning can manifest itself in at least three different ways, and many people have experienced all three of them at one point or another in their lifetimes. The first of these ways is associated with the experience of utter bafflement, of complete uninterpretability, in the face of events such as death, or natural calamity, or obliterated expectations, where the need is not so much for satisfactory explanations of them as for the possibility of intelligibility itself. The second derives from the occurrence of overwhelming suffering or pain, where the need is less to terminate or avoid it—so many things in life simply cannot be—but to endure and cope with it. And the third is precipitated by exposure to genuine iniquity, true malice, radical evil, where the need, even if there is no possibility of overcoming or abolishing it, is still to believe that crimes against humanity are unacceptable, that the notion as opposed to the practice of justice is no mirage.

The scholar responsible for this existential interpretation of the purpose of religion is the cultural anthropologist Clifford Geertz. And he goes on in the selection in this chapter to discuss how religion manages to confront these universal threats to the meaningfulness of life by differentiating between what might be called the attributes of religion—the doctrines, rituals, salvational schemes, ethics, narratives, and emotions mentioned above—and the core or innermost feature or component of religion. Geertz identifies this core or innermost element of religion with a specific way of looking at things, a particular perspective on the nature of experience itself. This is a perspective which holds that there is a connection, no matter how indistinct to the uninitiated eye, between the way things "really are" in life, its inherent structure, and the way people ought to live. Whether one conceives of the source of this structure as God, or the Transcendent, or the Sacred, or the Ultimate, or the Open, those who view life religiously assume that there is, or should be, a congruence between this belief and how we act or behave in response.

For Geertz, then, religion possesses two structural components. On the one hand, it includes a worldview, or metaphysic, that expresses how the world essentially hangs together, that reflects, so it is assumed, the inherent architecture of the real. On the other, it includes a moral code of ethics that suggests or determines the way one should live in relation to this view of the whole. For the religious, however, the worldview and the code of behavior, the metaphysic and the ethic, cannot be dissociated from one another. Religion is neither philosophy nor ethics alone, by themselves. They become religious are only when they are construed as confirmations of one another. "What sacred symbols do for those to whom they are sacred is to formulate an image of the world's construction and a program for human conduct that are mere reflexes of one another."

The question then arises as to how religions spread; what enables them, as the reading in this chapter from David Held's *Global Transformations* puts it, "at certain historical moments to reach out from their place of origin and embrace, convert, and conquer other cultures and other religions." The key seems to be their ability to promote a sense of personal and social identity that is no longer local but, as it were, "translocal," that permits them to mobilize both extensively and intensively, as the historian Michael Mann once said, "on a scale sufficient to enter the historical record." Sometimes, as in the case of Christianity and Islam, the ability of religions to spread across vast geographical territories and absorb people of different faiths has been linked to military and cultural power. In other instances, as with Buddhism and Hinduism which have tended to remain associated with specific civilizational regions, their mobilizing power has had more to do with their ability to absorb indigenous faiths within their own systems of conviction. Nonetheless, in the case of all global religions, such mobility was facilitated by the development of writing and movable texts that enabled their interpreters in time to regularize systems of belief and practice so that they could be shared widely by different cultural networks. This process was further facilitated by the development of institutionalized clerical hierarchies, sometimes working in alliance with political and economic elites, who made possible the spread of religious systems across diverse societies and also by the development of such theological innovations as monotheism by Judaism and its subsequent adoption by Christianity and then Islam, which coupled a salvational scheme open to anyone with a moral code accessible to all.

One can thus see why religion was, or at least could be, so instrumental in the creation of empires. As a multiplicity of states and cultures unified under the domination a single government, empires face extraordinary problems of organization and centralization with which religion has often assisted. One of those ways has been by linking religion to a ruling class based on kinship or ethnicity that retains its power by means of the authority that some particular faith confers upon it. In this way empires, which are usually ruled from a metropolitan center, can extend their power throughout their domain because of the vertical stratification of classes rather than their horizontal dispersion to the periphery. And where this is not possible, as in the case of the Mongol Empire that at one point at the beginning of the 13th century extended all the way from Han China to the Russian steppes and the borders of what is now Hungary in the West and as far south as Persia, Mongol leaders, many of whom actually were Nestorian Christians, allowed those they conquered to keep their own faiths, and sometimes their own leaders, so long as they provided no resistance to their imperial overlords.

Religion and empire are therefore very different phenomena, but their spread and strength, and sometimes even their fate, have often gone hand in hand. This can be seen even now through the common practice of referring to various countries as Christian America, Hindu India, Buddhist Myanmar, Eastern Orthodox Russia, and Islamic Egypt. But one should not generalize. Christian America is in fact home to many faiths and contains historical traditions that forbid the confusion between church and state. Hindu India is a country that is home to 10% of the world's Muslims numbering 172 million, which makes it the third most popular Muslim nation in the world. And Egypt, which is 90% Muslim, has nonetheless been home for many centuries to Coptic Christians and other religious communities.

# The Struggle for the Real

 CLIFFORD GEERTZ

There has been, in short, a general shift in modern anthopological discussion of culture, and within it of religion as a part of culture, a shift from a concern with thought as an inner mental state or stream of such states to a concern with thought as the utilization by individuals in society of public, historically created vehicles of reasoning, perception, feeling, and understanding—symbols, in the broadest sense of the term. In the study of religion, this shift is in the process of altering our entire view of religious experience and its social and psychological impact. The focus is now neither on subjective life as such nor on outward behavior as such, but on the socially available "systems of significance"—beliefs, rites, meaningful objects—in terms of which subjective life is ordered and outward behavior guided.

Such an approach is neither introspectionist nor behaviorist; it is semantic. It is concerned with the collectively created patterns of meaning the individual uses to give form to experience and point to action, with conceptions embodied in symbols and clusters of symbols, and with the directive force of such conceptions in public and private life. So far as religion is concerned, the problem becomes one of a particular sort of perspective, a particular manner of interpreting experience, a certain way of going at the world as opposed to other ways, and the implications such a perspective has for conduct. The aim of the comparative study of religion is (or anyway, ought to be) the scientific characterization of this perspective: the description of the wide variety of forms in which it appears; the uncovering of the forces which bring these forms into existence, alter them, or destroy them; and the assessment of their influences, also various, upon the behavior of men in everyday life.

But how are we to isolate the religious perspective at all? Are we not thrown back once more upon the necessity of defining "religion," adding one more catch phrase—"the belief in spiritual beings," "morality touched with emotion," "ultimate concern"—to what is surely an endless catalog? Must we not go yet once more through the familiar exercise of sorting out "religion" from "superstition," "religion" from "magic," "religion" from "philosophy," "religion" from "custom," from "folklore," from "myth," from "ceremony"? Does not all understanding, or anyway all scientific understanding, depend upon an initial isolation, a laboratory preparation, so to speak, of what it is that one is trying to understand?

Well, no. One can begin in a fog and try to clear it. One can begin, as I have in this book, with an assortment of phenomena almost everyone but the professionally contrary will regard as having something vaguely to do with "religion" and seek for what it is that leads us to think so, what it is that leads us to think that these rather singular things certain people do, believe, feel, or say somehow belong together with sufficient intimacy to submit to a common name. This is, I admit, a definitional procedure also, but a definitional procedure of a more inductive sort, rather more comparable to noting the oblique resemblances in the way in which Dubliners talk or Parisians walk than to filtering out pure substances. We look not for a universal property—"sacredness" or "belief in the supernatural," for example—that divides religious phenomena off from nonreligious ones with Cartesian sharpness, but for a system of concepts that can sum up a set of inexact similarities, which are yet genuine similarities, we sense to inhere in a given body of material. We are attempting to articulate a way of looking at the world, not to describe an unusual object.

The heart of this way of looking at the world, that is, of the religious perspective, is, so I would like to argue, not the theory that beyond the visible world there lies an invisible one (though most religious men have indeed held, with differing degrees of sophistication, to some such theory ); not the doctrine that a divine presence broods over the world (though, in an extraordinary variety of forms, from animism to monotheism, that too has been a rather popular idea); not even the more diffident opinion that there are things in heaven and earth undreamt of in our philosophies. Rather, it is the conviction that the values one holds are grounded in the inherent structure of reality, that between the way one ought to live and the way things really are there is an unbreakable inner connection. What sacred symbols do for those to whom they are sacred is to formulate an image of the world's construction and a program for human conduct that are mere reflexes of one another.

In anthropology, it has become customary to refer to the collection of notions a people has of how reality is at base put together as their world view. Their general style of life, the way they do things and like to see things done, we usually call their ethos. It is the office of religious symbols, then, to link these in such a way that they mutually confirm one another. Such symbols render the world view believable and the ethos justifiable, and they do it by invoking each in support of the other. The world view is believable because the ethos, which grows out of it, is felt to be authoritative; the ethos is justifiable because the world view, upon which it rests, is held to be true. Seen from outside the religious perspective, this sort of hanging a picture from a nail driven into its frame appears as a kind of sleight of hand. Seen from inside, it appears as a simple fact.

Religious patterns such as those I have been discussing thus have a double aspect: they are frames of perception, symbolic screens through which experience is interpreted; and they are guides for action, blueprints for conduct. Indonesian illuminationism portrays reality as an aesthetic hierarchy culminating in a void, and it projects a style of life celebrating mental poise. Moroccan maraboutism portrays reality as a field of spiritual energies nucleating in the persons of individual men, and it projects a style of life celebrating moral passion. Kalidjaga in classical Morocco would not be heroic but unmanly; Lyusi in classical Java would not be a saint but a boor.

The world view side of the religious perspective centers, then, around the problem of belief, the ethos side around the problem of action. As I say, these are, within the confines of faith, not only inseparable, they are reflexes of one another. Yet for analytical purposes, I want to separate them here momentarily and, using the Moroccan and Indonesian cases as reference points, discuss them independently. Having done that, the general relevance of these particular cases for the understanding of religion as such should be more readily apparent, as should the usefulness (I would claim no more for it than that) of this whole approach to the comparative study of it.

# Global Transformations

David Held and Anthony McGrew, David Goldblatt and Jonathan Perraton

## World Religions

Paradoxically, none of the conventional list of world religions—Christianity, Islam. Confucianism, Hinduism, Judaism and Buddhism—is present in significant numbers in every continent or region, though Christianity and Judaism have spread their adherents to most corners of the globe. Hinduism, Buddhism and Confucianism are all more tightly concentrated in their regional strongholds—South Asia, East Asia and China. Islam occupies a middling position, strong in the Middle East and North Africa with significant numbers in the rest of Africa and East Asia. All, of course, have their small and not so small migratory or diaspora communities in the most unexpected of places: over a million Japanese Shintoists in Brazil; 4 million Turkish-German Muslims in the heart of Christian Europe; the Goan Catholic enclave on the west coast of India. The definition of a world religion is, in a sense, post hoc. For the faiths that are usually dubbed 'global' have only been described as such once the spatial extent of the faithful has already greatly exceeded its place of origin and creation. As Mann puts it, 'they became significant because of one shared characteristic: a translocal sense of personal and social identity that permitted extensive and intensive mobilization on a scale sufficient to enter the historical record' (1986, p. 363).

Thus it is their geographical extensity, albeit often a regionally focused one, and their social impact that truly mark out the world religions from the many faiths that did and do exist. They are systems of belief and ritual that have had the capacity at crucial historical moments to reach out from their place of origin and embrace, convert and conquer other cultures and other religions. Most clearly in the cases of Islam and Christianity, the mobilizing capacity of religion was coupled with the capacity to extend military power and cultural influence. Neither Chinese nor Indian civilization ever embarked on such bouts of conquest and thus their indigenous faiths remained within their own loosely defined borders, but it is worth remembering just how large these territories were themselves.

Applying our conceptual model of globalization to the world religions, we can argue that they have assumed an extraordinary extensity. Although the foundation of world religions stretches back over a number of millennia, we can compress their initial impact to around a thousand-year period between 300 bce and 700 ce. Buddhism and Hinduism assumed something like their contemporary form in the three centuries before Jesus's birth, while Islam had reached its core regions by about 700 ce. Over this thousand-year period the main agencies of religious expansion were organized clerical hierarchies. Sometimes they operated in alliance with dominant states and political and economic elites, at other times interstitially within and across the frame works set by states. The capacity of these religions to spread and to penetrate into the organization and beliefs of everyday life was facilitated by both theological and technological innovation. Buddhism and Hinduism, while remaining confined to South and East Asia, generated theological frameworks of sufficient complexity and adaptability that they could embrace and attract adherents across cultures and linguistic groups (Weber, 1951, 1958). The innovation of monotheism, although a Jewish creation, was multiplied in its potential reach and power by Christianity and Islam, both of which joined a singular moral code to a vision of salvation potentially open to all. Islam achieved a presence in diverse regions as early as the eighth century, a presence it has retained, although it remains thinly spread in many places (Gellner, 1981). Christianity would have to wait until the military and colonial expansion of Europe in the sixteenth and seventeenth centuries to acquire a global presence. The invention of writing allowed for the diffusion of a set of core texts which provided the infrastructure for establishing shared and stabilized beliefs and doctrines across large areas (Giddens, 1985; Goody, 1986). The development of writing and the movement of texts, as well as interpreters, made possible the development of cross-cultural networks of shared belief and behaviour with a systematization and routinization that was not possible in a preliterate world. It is this, combined with the development of institutionalized and .regularized clerical hierarchies—the key cultural infrastructure of world religions—that made possible the stretching and deepening of cultural relations between otherwise separate and different societies. That said, these processes of cultural globalization occurred slowly, taking decades to initiate and centuries to embed themselves.

Of course, world religions also display cultural hierarchy and unevenness in their spread. The religion of clerics and elites has rarely been identical to that of the mass of the population nor has the community of the faithful been particularly democratic in its regulation of belief and practice. Similarly, given the immense differences between adherents of these faiths across different societies it is little surprise that all show large geographical variations and complex mixtures with pre-existing cultures and religions. In terms of their impact, there is little doubt that the world religions are among humanity's most significant cultural innovations. World religions have furnished religious and political elites with immense power and resources, be it in their capacity to mobilize armies and peoples, in their development of transcultural senses of identity and allegiance or in their provision of the entrenched theological and legal infrastructure of societies. In these respects, world religions unquestionably constitute one of the most powerful and significant forms of the globalization of culture in the premodern era, indeed of all time.

## Empires

Alongside, and indeed often intimately intertwined with, the progress of the sacred realm on earth has followed the expansion of the secular realm of politics and military force, though in many ways the distinction is one that can only be drawn from the vantage point of a secularized later twentieth century. Empires have often been characterized by the attempt to impose centralized political authority over a loosely defined territory that is populated by a multiplicity of different social and ethnic groups. In this respect, empires and the process of empire building can be conceived as a form of political globalization stretching and deepening relationships of authority and control. Here our central concern is the role of cultural power in creating and maintaining political empires.

All empires inevitably face a series of interrelated structural problems or contradictions, particularly those that do not rely solely or predominantly on the repeated imposition of coercive force to obtain cooperation or subservience from their provinces (Eisenstadt, 1963; Mann, 1986). The essential problem is one of centralization and decentralization. For while empires are ruled from the centre, their capacity to enforce rule is often limited. Constantly imposing orders from the centre requires times, resources and effective infrastructures. Therefore empires need, as far as possible, to delegate power to the periphery. But in doing so, they threaten their own integrity. One way of partially circumventing this dilemma is cultural: an empire can try and create a universal ruling class bound by ties of kinship, belief and religion so that the essential political division in the imperium becomes vertical—between classes—rather than horizontal—between centre and periphery. Thus successful empires have inevitably been ones in which the extensive reach of military and political power has been reinforced by the reach of cultural power. Often cultural expansion arose interstitially, and unintentionally, between subaltern rather than ruling classes. The early expansion of Christianity within the Roman Empire is a good example of this. By contrast, cultural diffusion, emulation, stretching and deepening and the creation of cultural infrastructures can be part of an intentional strategy of rule.

# CHAPTER FOUR

# The Oceanic Discovery of the World and the Formation of Early World Trade in Goods and Bodies

Early world trade by ancient Mediterranean peoples began several thousand years before the age of European exploration and discovery that we associate with Christopher Columbus and Ferdinand Magellan. It was developed principally by the Phoenicians who were exploring the Mediterranean as early as 1500 B.C.E. and also by the Egyptians who sent explorations to Saudi Arabia around 1400 B.C.E. By 300 B.C.E. the Greeks had reached Britain, and not too much later by 100 B.C.E the Romans had extended their own empire to the British Isles and across Egypt to North Africa.

Such oceanic trade was inevitably coastal and confined to low-bulk, high-value merchandise, but all that began to change approximately one thousand years later when Portugal and Spain decided to embark on seaborne exploration. The motive remained the same—the pursuit of trade in spices and other exotics from the Near and Far East, but a new mode of transport was needed to allow ships to travel out of the sight of land for much greater distances. This required the development of everything from the creation of accurate navigational charts and the invention of new instruments to create them with, such as the astralobe and the quadrant, to the acquisition of new knowledge of winds and currents, to the design of different ships like the caravel, modeled after Arab vessels, with lateen sails that allowed ships to sail against the wind. The chief motivation for these nautical developments was the acquisition of trade routes to Asia that were not controlled by Muslims, but their chief result would be the discovery of the oceanic connection of all the continents on earth.

That discovery was indeed a world-transforming event. It meant that the earth itself was in fact more ocean than land or, as Greg Dening put it still more accurately, "the world is an ocean and all its continents islands." The American writer Herman Melville put the enormity of this discovery in perhaps richest symbolic perspective in his nineteenth-century epic novel Moby-Dick, when he has his narrator, Ishmael, remark in a chapter entitled "The Pacific":

To any meditative Magian rover, this serene Pacific, once beheld, must ever after be the sea of his adoption. It rolls the mid-most waters over the world, the Indian Ocean and Atlantic being but its arms. The same waves wash the moles of the new-built Californian towns, but yesterday planted by the recentest race of men, and lave the faded but still gorgeous skirts of Asiatic lands, older than Abraham; while all between float milky ways of coral isles, and low-lying, endless, unknown Archipelagoes, and impenetrable Japans. Thus this mysterious, divine Pacific zones the world's whole bulk about; makes all coasts one day to it; seems the tide beating heart of earth.

The era of early modern exploration and discovery redefined the entire notion of space as it was currently understood by enabling the oceanic world to enter history. As a result, the future of every continent would subsequently be shaped and reshaped by that history in a way that, if still not fully comprehended in the twenty-first century, could be potentially shared. The discovery of its oceanic connections opened the world to the creation of colonies by European powers. Created initially not only to obtain economic benefits such as land and materials and to expand trade and commerce, these colonies also provided Europe's emergent imperial states with the possibility of increasing their reputation among other nations, obtaining military advantages over their enemies, and spreading their religion to other peoples. Where the initial European colonies were established to facilitate trade, subsequent ones were eventually to morph into colonies of occupation, where a small number of Europeans could rule for the mother country as it mined precious metals or grew crops using native labor, then into plantation colonies, where a single crop like sugar or later cotton could be grown with imported slave labor on a large scale, and, finally, into colonies of settlement, where white settlers displaced native people in places as far afield as North America, South Africa, Australia, and New Zealand.

One of the most important commodities in foreign trade was to become silver as a result of the creation of Spain's land empire in Latin America and China's unquenchable thirst for this precious metal. A story told in fascinating detail in the first selection by Dennis Flynn and Arturo Giraldez titled "Born with a Silver Spoon: The Origin of World Trade in 1571," it began with the dissemination of Papal "bulls" or degrees issued by the Roman Catholic pontiff after Columbus's first voyage establishing a treaty that divided the entire "New World" between Spain and Portugal. This soon led to the creation of a Latin American Empire whose chief source of export would become silver and whose principal market would become China, which used silver both as a medium of exchange and as a monetary standard. The two transshipments points for this colossal commerce were to become Seville to Europe, the Middle East, and Asia, and Manila to China. It was this intercontinental trade network that for the first time in history linked America with Asia, where in the Far East it extended from Manila in the Philippines to Ming China and the Tokugawa Shogunate in Japan. Indeed, the extent of this trade network was so vast and its results so lucrative that that it forces one to question conventional assumptions. Although it has traditionally been believed by historians of early world trade that the West had a much greater economic impact on Asia than Asia did on the West, Flynn and Giraldez show that "the most powerful economic undercurrents ran in the opposite direction. If China had not opted for silver, the Spanish empire would have lost its greatest market." Thus China's monetary and fiscal conversion to silver reverberated on every continent. Inaugurating global trade on all five continents, it provided "a powerful force in shaping the modern world."

In time, however, silver was to be displaced as the most important commodity of foreign trade by the export of enslaved Africans to the New World. The source of their economic importance was closely related to the growing European demand for sugar, a crop that indigenous people were increasingly resistant to cultivate when it was first introduced in the Atlantic islands and then brought to the Americas because it too forbidding to work with. But this obstacle was overcome with the development of the African slave trade which suddenly began to provide an enormous supply of very cheap labor to produce a crop that could be raised and harvested only under the most inhuman conditions. Yet the African slave trade did much more than immediately enrich those who could profit from the agricultural product it yielded; the local capture of people from all over sub-Saharan Africa, their transport from the interior of the continent to the African coast, their incarceration sometimes for months awaiting transshipment, their lengthy transatlantic passage in utterly squalid conditions, and, finally the sale in the Americas and the Caribbean of the 14 million people who survived the horrors of this ordeal turned into an immensely lucrative practice of its own.

The story of this horrific practice is the subject of two further readings in this chapter. The first is an assessment by David Brion Davis, arguably the world's greatest modern historians of world slavery, of just how large a business slavery became between the 1490s and the 1830s. The second is an excerpt from the autobiography of a famous African slave whose "Interesting Narrative," as he called the story of his life, provides one of the earliest personal accounts of the experience of slavery itself. Captured at the age of 11, Olaudah Equiano's story is unusual because he was able to purchase his freedom only 11 years later. But this freedom was not purchased without compromise because he was later involved as a seaman in the Atlantic slave trade himself, for which he was roundly criticized and in partial expiation for which he decided to write his autobiography.

Among the two contributions to the chapter that detail how the trade in goods could become a traffic in bodies, David Brion Davis's has a special importance because he raises the kinds of moral questions that this monstrous practice has often begged. Those questions start with why so few representatives from so many of the world's religions failed to object to the buying, selling, and owning of human beings. But those unanswered, or barely considered, questions then multiply: Why did slavery spread into regions not organized agriculturally around plantations and the cultivation of such labor-intensive crops as sugar and later cotton, regions like New England, New York, and French Canada? Who was to blame for the sale of enslaved Africans if it was practiced by people of all races including Muslims from the Middle East and Africans themselves? How and why did Europeans so quickly began to use racism not only to dehumanize black people but to defend their own whiteness? Davis's belief is that while there is, and was, more than enough blame to go around to the "usual suspects"—popes, merchants, corrupt governments, and the like—the real blame may be more difficult to assign. Of all the culprits to be considered, Davis suggests that the greatest responsibility for the creation of the Atlantic slave trade, and the practices that followed in its wake, may have to be placed at the door of capitalism itself. Once unleashed and allowed to grow rampant, capitalism created an entirely new social, political and economic order that ultimately broke with traditional moral values. Carried to its extreme with the help of racism and imperialism, the logic of capitalism turned people of African descent into dehumanized commodities whose labor was to play a still insufficiently understood role both in the launching of the Industrial Revolution and in the birth of the modern age itself.

# Born with a "Silver Spoon": The Origin of World Trade in 1571

DENNIS O. FLYNN AND ARTURO GIRÁLDEZ

The birth of world trade has been described by C. R. Boxer (1969, p. 17) in the following terms: "Only after the Portuguese had worked their way down the West African coast, rounded the Cape of Good Hope, crossed the Indian Ocean and established themselves in the Spice Islands of Indonesia and on the shore of the South China Sea; only after the Spaniards had attained the same goal by way of Patagonia, the Pacific Ocean and the Philippines—then and only then was a regular and lasting maritime connection established between the four great continents."

Although Boxer does not pick a specific date for the birth of global trade, his logic leads us to choose 1571—the year the city of Manila was founded. Manila was the crucial entrepôt linking substantial, direct, and continuous trade between America and Asia for the first time in history.

For our purposes, global trade emerged when all important populated continents began to exchange products continuously—both with each other directly and indirectly via other continents—and in values sufficient to generate crucial impacts on all the trading partners. It is true that there was an important intercontinental trade before 1571, but there was no direct trade link between America and Asia, so the world market was not yet fully coherent or complete. To understand the global significance of the direct Pacific trade between America and Asia—international trade history's "missing link"—it is useful first to discuss the underlying economic forces that motivated profitable world trade in the early modern period. The singular product most responsible for the birth of world trade was silver.

## The Role of Silver in Creating a World Market

More than the market for any other commodity, the silver market explains the emergence of world trade. China was the dominant buyer of silver. On the supply side, Spanish America (Mexico and Peru) erupted with unprecedented production of the white metal. Conservative official estimates indicate that Latin America alone produced about 150,000 tons of silver between 1500 and 1800 (Barrett 1990, p. 237), perhaps exceeding 80% of the entire world production over that time span (Cross 1983, p. 397). Despite America's dominance in silver production over three centuries, Japan may have been the primary exporter of silver to China in the late sixteenth and early seventeenth centuries, shipping perhaps 200 tons per year at times. Japanese silver exports, however, fell off

*Born with a Silver Spoon*, Journal of World History, V1:2 (1995) pp 201-218. By permission of University of Hawai'i Press Journals.

dramatically in the second half of the seventeenth century (Innes 1980, chap. 6).[1] "The amount of Japanese silver poured into foreign trade in the heyday of Japan's overseas trade, 1615 to 1625, through Japanese, Chinese, Dutch, Portuguese and other ships, reached tremendous value, roughly estimated at 130,000–160,000 kilograms—equal to 30% or 40% of the total world silver production outside Japan. This explains why European and Asian merchants were so enthusiastic about developing trade with Japan" (Iwao 1976, p. 10). The central point is that all the great silver mines in both hemispheres sold ultimately to China.

We intentionally emphasize the role of China—and its tributary system (Hamashita 1988)—in the silver trade because the scholarly literature in general has neglected this pivotal country, certainly in terms of recognizing China as a prime causal actor. The literature on New World treasure is huge and multifaceted—sometimes focusing on sixteenth-century price inflation (the price revolution),[2] and/or the rise and fall of Spain,[3] and/or the transition from feudalism to capitalism,[4] and many other issues—but it is unified in one central respect: it focuses virtually exclusively on Europe as the fulcrum. Europe is considered the epicenter of early modern commercial activity. The sixteenth-century price revolution, for example, is mostly thought of in terms of European price inflation, when in reality it was a global phenomenon.[5] In a remarkably clear summary of China's participation in the global price revolution, Geiss (1979, p. 144) provides an exception to the normal Eurocentric focus: "In the late sixteenth century, however, when silver from Mexico and Japan entered the Ming empire in great quantity, the value of silver began to decline and inflation set in, for as the metal became more abundant its buying power diminished. This inflationary trend affected the values of all commodities; everything had been valued in silver and silver lost its value. Ramifications of this change touched the lives of almost everyone in the empire."

Europe's Dutch and English East India Companies are often viewed as prototypes of modern multinational corporations. The scholarly literature recognizes that huge quantities of silver flowed to Asia, but this phenomenon is considered a reflection of Europe's balance-of-trade deficit with east Asia; Europeans developed a far greater taste for Asian finery than the other way around, according to conventional wisdom, so treasure had to flow from west to east to pay for Europe's trade deficit. In short, all the key issues are normally framed in terms of European perspectives.

Acceptance of a global perspective instead of the predominant Eurocentric view outlined above yields a startlingly different view. It becomes clear that Europeans did indeed play an important role in the birth of world trade, but their role was as middlemen in the vast silver trade; they were prime movers on neither the supply side (except Spain in America) nor the demand side of the worldwide silver market. Europeans were intermediaries in the trade between the New World and China. Massive amounts of silver traversed the Atlantic. After it had reached European soil,

---

[1]  According to the calculations made by Barrett (1990, p. 225), Japan may have produced about 30% of the world's silver in the sixteenth century and around 16% in the seventeenth century.

[2]  For an overview of the main theoretical arguments of the price revolution literature, see Outhwaite 1969; Ramsey 1971; Flynn 1977, chap. 2; Flynn 1984a and 1984b.

[3]  See Hamilton 1937; Elliott 1961; Kamen 1964; Gordon 1975; Kamen 1978; Israel 1981; Kamen 1981; Flynn 1982.

[4]  Hamilton 1929; Keynes 1930, vol. 2; Neff 1936; Hamilton 1952; Felix 1956; Nadal 1959; Wallerstein 1974 and 1976; Brenner 1977; Hunt 1978; Flynn 1984.

[5]  For price inflation in China, see Cartier 1981 and Wilkinson 1980, for Japan, see Innes 1980; for Turkey, see Sahillioglu 1983; and for Russia, see Blum 1956.

the Portuguese in the sixteenth century and Dutch in the seventeenth century became dominant distributors of silver by a multitude of routes into Asia. Attman conservatively estimates that 150 tons of silver passed through Europe into Asia on an annual basis. "The country which reigned supreme in arranging solutions for the deficit problems in world trade was Holland, acting mainly on her own behalf in the Baltic area, the Levant and Asia, but also acting for other nations. . . . Even when other countries needed precious metals Holland acted in many cases as a clearing centre and in the final stage as an exporter of precious metals. . . . But the bulk of the precious metals required for the Asian trade came from Europe around the Cape" (Attman 1986, p. 6). It is worthwhile to reflect momentarily on Attman's estimate of 150 tons of silver exported each year from Europe to Asia. Attman emphasizes that his estimates include only specie shipments (i.e., bullion is excluded from consideration) and that he has studied only port records (i.e., overland trade is excluded). If Attman had included bullion shipments through ports, as well as specie and bullion shipments over land routes, his estimate of west-to-east silver flows would have been far greater. He warned readers of the conservative and partial nature of his estimates, but scholars rarely acknowledge this when citing his figures.

The Pacific leg of the China trade has not received the attention it deserves. Writing of the period 1571–1620, TePaske says that an enormous quantity of silver passed over the Pacific, especially out of Acapulco and through Manila on its way to China. "Mexican silver also flowed out to the islands in large sums, far exceeding the 500,000-peso limitation. In fact at the opening of the seventeenth century the drain of pesos from Mexico to the Orient through the Philippines was estimated at 5 million pesos [128 tons] annually, with a reported 12 million pesos [307 tons] being smuggled out in 1597" (TePaske 1981, p. 436). These are shocking figures because this alleged average of 5 million pesos (128 tons per year) over the Pacific, at the turn of the century, is only 15% less than the 150 tons minimum that Attman says Europe shipped to Asia on an annual basis. Moreover, the 12 million pesos (307 tons) in 1597 is more than double Attman's estimate of the entire European leg of the journey of silver to China. These may seem like fantastic figures to some, but Barrett 1990, p. 236) has pointed out a glaring discrepancy between Spanish American production figures and estimated exports to Europe: production seems to have exceeded exports to Europe by 5.5 million pesos (135 tons) per year. Barrett reasons that this 5.5 million pesos must have either remained in America or been exported through the Philippines.[6] It will become clear shortly that exportation of such a vast amount of silver through Manila makes sense in global terms, while its retention in the New World does not.

How has the Philippines trade been perceived by Asian scholars? Using the Blair and Robertson collection of primary sources, Chuan (1969, p. 79) estimates that at least 50 tons of silver (2 million pesos) passed over the Pacific annually throughout the seventeenth century; silver shipments did not decline slightly after 1620 and precipitously after 1640, as previously argued by Chaunu (1960, p. 250).[7]

---

[6] Cross 1983, p. 420, talks of a vast smuggling trade in the sixteenth century: "Quantities of silver left the New World through the ports of Buenos Aires and Sacramento and through the Manila Galleons. At the peak of these activities, perhaps as much as 6 million pesos per year (159,000 kg), or half the output of Peru, was diverted to these channels from the Seville trade."

[7] Pierre Chaunu's conclusions were based on study of the *almojarifazgo* duties, which covered only the taxed portion of the trade. It is widely known, however, that smuggling was rampant m the Manila trade, and sources from the Asian side of the Pacific provide estimates of silver exports far in excess of Chaunu's numbers (Flynn and Giráldez 1994a and 1995).

How significant is 50 tons in relative terms? Fifty tons of silver equals the average annual exports to Asia by Portugal plus the Dutch and English East India Companies combined in the seventeenth century (Flynn and Giraldez 1994a). Fifty tons of silver was also the amount that was shipped through the entire Baltic trade (the Russian and Polish-Lithuanian markets), according to Attman (1986, p. 81). It is interesting to contrast the historiographic notoriety of the Portuguese trade, in combination with that of the East India Companies, with the situation of the Manila galleons on the Pacific side; each may have shipped approximately equal quantities of silver annually, yet the Pacific trade is rarely mentioned.

Manila had no purpose other than the trade in silver and silk. The city contained 42,000 inhabitants in the middle of the seventeenth century (Wolf 1982, p. 153), approximately the same population as Barcelona, Danzig, Marseille, and other cities with more broadly based economies (Mols 1977, pp. 42–43; deVries 1984, app. I). Manila's population circa 1650 included about 15,000 Chinese, 7,350 Spaniards, and an estimated 20,124 Filipinos.[8] The Pacific route of silver to China was Spain's only avenue for entry into the lucrative Asian marketplace because the trade out of Europe in the sixteenth and seventeenth centuries was controlled first by the Portuguese and later by the Dutch. Spain's Manila galleons initiated the birth of Pacific rim trade more than 420 years ago.

Eurocentrism predisposes us to imagine that the East India Companies injected dynamism into backward Asian economies in the early modern period. Recent scholarship (Hamashita 1988, for example) suggests that the European companies simply plugged into the preexisting network of intra-Asian trade. The export of Japanese silver provides a good example of this process. As was the case in the west-to-east trade, first the Portuguese—in competition with Chinese junks and Japanese red-seal ships—and then (after 1639) the Dutch played the role of intermediaries in this crucial Sino-Japanese trade. Again within Asia's marketplace, the European role is most accurately portrayed as that of middlemen, not prime movers. Europeans were important, but potentially disposable, intermediaries who could be—and in the case of the expulsion of the Portuguese from Japan in 1637, were—replaced at the convenience of Asian trading partners.

## China: The World's Silver Sink

The early modern production and distribution of silver in the western hemisphere has been studied extensively, but the world's biggest end-customer, China, is routinely eliminated from the story. This is peculiar. Nobody would think of analyzing, say, the world oil industry today without paying considerable attention to the major oil-importing industrial regions; China's dominance as an importer of silver was arguably at least as pivotal during the birth of world trade as is the industrial world's dominance as importers of oil in today's global marketplace. Godinho (1963, 1:432–65) aptly describes China as a "suction pump" (*bomba aspirante*), a

---

[8]  Phelan (1959, p. 178). There were thousands of Japanese in Manila, too, including Japanese Catholics fleeing persecution at home. Spaniards feared a Japanese "fifth column" within the Philippines, however, and expelled large numbers of Japanese several times (Innes 1980, p. 59).

"vacuum cleaner" that attracted silver globally for centuries. Surprisingly, few scholars have continued to investigate the nature of China's metamorphosis into a seemingly bottomless silver sink; Atwell (1977, 1982, 1986, 1988) provides perhaps the most consistent exception to this bias.

The market value of silver in Ming territory was double its value elsewhere. This fact is reflected in the bimetallic ratios reported in Chuan (1969, p. 2): "From 1592 to the early seventeenth century gold was exchanged for silver in Canton at the rate of 1:5.5 to 1:7, while in Spain the exchange rate was 1:12.5 to 1:14, thus indicating that the value of silver was twice as high in China as in Spain." Divergent bimetallic ratios created tremendous prospects for profitable arbitrage trade. Economic theory predicts that gold should have flowed out of China, where it was undervalued relative to the rest of the world, in exchange for Japanese and Western silver, which was relatively overvalued in China compared with the rest of the world. This is precisely what happened from the middle of the fifteenth to the middle of the seventeenth century (Chaudhuri 1978 and 1986; Flynn 1986). It is crucial to focus on silver to understand the underlying motivation of world trade: it was the elevated value of silver inside China that created the opportunities for profit around the globe. Rather than see the west-to-east flow of silver as a reaction to Europe's trade deficit with Asia, we contend that the cause of the trade centered in China and its tributary system. Demand-side causation was of Asian origin, to which the rest of the world reacted.

How can we be confident that the arbitrage argument outlined above is superior to the traditional European trade-deficit hypothesis? The trade-deficit argument says that "money" would have to have been transshipped to Asia to cover the trade imbalance. "Money" here refers to all types of high-value coins containing internationally recognized intrinsic content, such as gold and silver. However, we have already established that gold and silver did not travel jointly into the Asian marketplace as a balancing item called "money." New World silver did indeed travel from Europe to Asia, but it crossed paths with gold coming in the opposite direction—out of Asia and into the West. Abstract "money" did not balance a trade deficit in the passive way commonly portrayed in the literature; rather, it was a specific commodity—silver—that traveled to Asia, not gold. Gold was one of the products for which silver was exchanged. The cause of this trade rests with developments endemic to the silver market, not with developments in nonsilver markets. Moreover, the exchange of silver for gold was not a Europe-versus-Asia issue in any case. Japanese silver also flowed to China in exchange for Chinese gold, which flowed into Japan, for exactly the same reasons that gold flowed to the West. In sum, Europe was not the causal center in early modern trade; moreover, the East-versus-West "trade imbalance" was not the mechanism driving world trade. There was no "trade imbalance" for which to compensate, so long as we recognize that silver itself was the key commodity distributed globally and that it was exchanged for items—mostly silk and porcelain but also gold—from the Asian mainland. Causation was located in the silver market itself, with America and Japan anchoring the supply side and China dominating the demand side.

China's metamorphosis from a paper-money system (dating from at least the eleventh century) to a silver-based economy was crucial. Overissue of paper money in China had reduced the value of this fiduciary medium to virtually nothing by the middle of the fifteenth century (Gernet 1982, p. 415). Daily commerce required a medium of exchange to replace the worthless paper money, and silver evolved as the metal of choice. Gold was too valuable for most ordinary transactions, but copper coinage was a candidate for monetary preeminence. Geiss (1979, p. 155) explains how silver defeated copper, in a passage worth quoting at length:

> The value of the coin lay in the metal, not in the mint. In that respect copper coins were hardly different from silver; each was valued as a piece of precious metal. While silver could, if necessary, be assayed for purity, copper coins could not. To assay a copper coin entailed its destruction. The only way to ascertain the copper content was to melt the coin, and this would defeat the purpose of coining money. But with coins of varying weight and metallic content in circulation, setting a price in copper coins became a tricky business. The rice merchant would have to specify what kind of copper coin he had in mind, each had a different value in the marketplace, and the price of the merchant's rice depended on the type of coin offered in payment. How much simpler to set the price in silver, and that in fact is what happened. Silver came to be the preferred medium of valuation and exchange.

Geiss's explanation is straightforward and compelling. Silver's gradual "conquest" of the Chinese economy may seem relatively innocuous to some at first glance—just another detail in "area studies"—but this development fundamentally altered the direction of international commerce. It also influenced the structure of power among nations throughout the world.

The Ming tried repeatedly to retard the intrusion of silver into (and from) the coastal centers of merchant power. Silver's penetration was irresistible, however, and local governments in maritime regions began specifying that taxes be paid in silver. Gradually Ming rulers abandoned their resistance to silver and implemented the Single-Whip tax system around the 1570s (Huang 1974; Liang 1970). The Single-Whip system specified two things: first, myriad existing national levies were consolidated into a single tax; second, all tax payments were to be made in the form of silver. Considering that China contained perhaps one-fourth of the earth's population by the seventeenth century, with urban centers of up to 1 million inhabitants (five to seven times greater than the largest cities in western Europe), the "silverization" of China inevitably had global ramifications.[9] China's tributary system also converted to silver, so we are talking about far more than one-quarter of the globe's population. Conversion of the world's largest economic entity to silver caused the metal's value to skyrocket in China relative to the rest of the world.

The early modern world silver trade involved structural transformations that penetrated much deeper than the mere movement of a couple of hundred thousand tons of the white metal to its most lucrative market. The process yielded prodigious profits for key individuals and institutions. From mines in the Andes and Japan to the streets of China, profit was the motive force at each stage of the trade. European middlemen profited mightily from intercontinental trade and perhaps even more from the inter-Asian trade linkages, but the truly grand profiteers in the silver saga were those entities that controlled the centers of its production: imperial Spain and the Tokugawa shogunate. Conversely and ironically, the silver trade may have contributed indirectly to the overthrow of the Ming dynasty.

---

[9] Demand for silver along China's coastal region alone must have been significant, considering that Nanjing contained more than 1 million inhabitants and Beijing around 660,000 in the late Ming period (Rodzinski 1979, p. 201).

# Silver and the Power Bases of Imperial Spain, the Tokugawa Shogunate, and Ming China

The richest silver mine in the history of the world was discovered at more than 15,000 feet altitude in the Andes in Potosí (present-day Bolivia), a one-way journey of two and one-half months via pack animal from Lima. Nothing grew at that altitude, so there was no population at the time silver was discovered in 1545. During the ensuing sixty years, Potosí's population swelled to 160,000, about equal to that of London or Paris.[10] This would be the modern-day equivalent of, say, 20 million people moving to a spot on Alaska's North Slope. Evidently something unusual was going on in Potosí.

Potosí's *cerro rico* (rich mountain) may have produced 60% of all the silver mined in the world in the second half of the sixteenth century.[11] Its veins were incredibly rich. In addition to naturally bountiful deposits, a series of new production technologies—the most famous being the mercury-amalgam "patio process"—combined to render Spanish American mines the world's lowest cost sources of silver (Jara 1966). This supply-side phenomenon was particularly fortuitous because it coincided chronologically with the extraordinary rise in the value of silver caused by the Chinese demand-side forces culminating in the Single-Whip tax reform. The combination of low supply-side production costs in Spanish America and Chinese-led demand-side elevation in silver's value in Asia generated probably the most spectacular mining boom in human history. This combination of supply-side and demand-side forces implied enormous profits.

No entity reaped greater rewards from the silver industry than the Spanish crown, which wisely allowed favored "private sector" entrepreneurs to operate New World mines, rather than attempting to do so itself.[12] Instead, the crown took a substantial fraction of mining profits through taxes. The most famous tax was the *quinto*, a 20% severance tax on gross value, but there were many indirect taxes as well.[13] According to Hamilton (1934, p. 34), 27.5% of total registered precious metals entering Seville between 1566 and 1645 belonged to the crown of Castile.[14] Revenues from overseas mines provided the fiscal foundation for the Spanish empire.

Spain was a small country of perhaps 7.5 million inhabitants by the middle of the sixteenth century, about half the population of France (Elliott 1961, p. 57). Elliott (1961, p. 62) has described Castile of 1600 as "an economy closer in many ways to that of an East European state like Poland, exporting basic raw materials and importing luxury products, than to the economies of West European states." Carande (1965, p. 340) and many others classify Spain as backward domestically, substantiating the observation that the financial foundation of the Spanish empire was based on

---

[10] DDeVries 1984, app. 1.

[11] Cross (1983, p. 404) states that "despite the decline of Potosí, beginning in the 1640s, the viceroyalty of Peru accounted for 60% of the world's silver production in the sixteenth and seventeenth centuries."

[12] The crown did directly control the famous mercury mines near Huancavelica on the Peruvian coast. Potosí's resurgence after 1573 was attributable to the reforms enacted by Toledo, which included successful adoption of the mercury-amalgam mining process (Cross 1983, p. 402).

[13] For discussion of the *quinto*, which frequently amounted to far less than 20% in reality, see Brading and Cross 1972.

[14] Note that the 27.5% of shipments belonging to the crown represents far more than 27.5% of the total profit. Much of the crown's revenues could be considered "profit," while huge costs had to be subtracted from private receipts before arriving at private net profit.

resources outside the Iberian peninsula.[15] Mine profits were enormous, and there was no comparable profit center elsewhere, so we conclude that the New World mines supported the Spanish empire (Flynn 1982).

This view of Spain leads to surprising but inevitable conclusions. We have already established that domestic developments inside China elevated the value of silver in world markets far beyond what it could have been otherwise. The largest beneficiary of silver's high value must have been the Spanish crown, the institution that reaped enormous profits by way of its control and taxation of the low-cost New World centers of production. Thus, the silver-industry profits that financed the Spanish empire were huge because China had become the world's dominant silver customer. This implies that ultimately China was responsible for a power shift within early modern Europe. In the absence of the "silverization" of China, it is hard to imagine how Castile could have financed simultaneous wars for generations against the Ottomans in the Mediterranean; Protestant England and Holland and the French in Europe, the New World, and Asia; and against indigenous peoples in the Philippines.

Even giant China could not prop up Spain indefinitely. As tens of thousands of tons of silver accumulated on the Asian mainland, its value gradually fell there (as it had already been doing in the West and Japan) toward its cost of production. Imports eventually glutted even China's vast silver market. We know that this portrayal of silver's loss of value is accurate because by about 1635 it took about 13 ounces of silver to buy an ounce of gold in China, while a half century earlier it took 6 ounces of silver (Geiss 1979, p. 165). The value of silver also fell relative to other things, not just gold, which is to say that price inflation occurred. "In the late sixteenth century . . . when silver from Mexico and Japan entered the Ming empire in great quantity, the value of silver began to decline and inflation set in, for as the metal became more abundant, its buying power diminished. This inflationary trend affected the value of all commodities; everything had been valued in silver and silver lost its value. Ramifications of this change touched the lives of almost everyone in the empire" (Geiss 1979, p.144). As silver lost value, more silver money was required to purchase items that had maintained their value. Price inflation is defined as the surrender of more pieces of money for a given set of items, so the descent of silver to its cost of production is what ultimately caused prices to inflate in China to about the same extent as in Europe and elsewhere (Cartier 1981, p. 464; Geiss 1979, pp. 159–64, 198; Goldstone 1991, p. 360).

The unavoidable fall in the value of silver is a crucial issue because each year as it descended closer to its cost of production in America, profit per unit of silver also shrank. Declining profits were not due to inefficient operations; rather, they were the inevitable result of the laws of demand and supply (Doherty and Flynn 1989). The existence of arbitrage profits motivated the trade, and the trade itself, in turn, led to the elimination of such profits. Faced with declining profits from its silver industry, Castile could no longer afford its vast empire. China contributed mightily to the duration of the Spanish empire, but even China's prodigious demand for silver could not prevent the eventual erosion of mine profits and therefore the decline of Spain. Spanish American silver production may

---

[15] Scholars such as Elliott (1961) and Lynch (1984, 2:i), have long emphasized both external and domestic foundations of the Spanish empire. For a more complete discussion of why we believe that the foundation of empire was external, not domestic, see Flynn and Giraldez 1995.

have peaked in the 1590s, but large production coupled with vanishing profits per ounce of silver still implied a vanishing overall profit level by this time (Flynn 1982, p. 142)

Historians tend to focus too much attention on the quantity of silver shipments, while the participants themselves cared only about the profits associated with the trade. In the words of an executive in a standard business joke today, "Since we are losing money on each item sold, we simply must make up for it in volume!" Spain experienced multiple bankruptcies in the late sixteenth and early seventeenth centuries, during a time of record silver production, because the value of each unit of silver continued to decline. When profit per unit of a product declines to zero, multiplication of zero per-unit profit times any quantity of output must yield zero total profit. Spanish American mines were not yet yielding zero profits per unit of product, but the trend was clearly in that direction. Silver's declining value affected the crown so profoundly that interest payments on Castile's federal debt alone—"the equivalent of at least ten years' revenue" by 1623 (Parker 1979, p. 188)—eventually exceeded total crown receipts. Spain vanished as a serious Western power as its silver basis eroded, but the Iberian surge to power had been lengthy and impressive. The fact that Spain's empire owed its financial foundation to distant Ming China is a forceful reminder that much of what passes for local history in the early modern period can only be understood in terms of world history.

Since China's hunger for silver altered the balance of power in the West by transferring huge profits to the Spanish crown, it is logical to suspect an Asian power shift as a result of the inter-Asian trade in silver. The laws of supply and demand apply on all continents. As noted earlier, China's primary source of silver in the late sixteenth and early seventeenth centuries was Japan, which shipped as much as 200 tons per year at times (Innes 1980, especially chap. 6; Tashiro 1986, p. 2). Contrast this figure to the conservative average estimated by Attman (1986, p. 78) of 150 tons of silver flowing annually through Europe and into Asia in the seventeenth century. Who captured the Japanese mine profits, and what became of them?

The Tokugawa shogunate provides an interesting example of East—West comparative history because, like the Spanish crown and its American mines, the shogunate gained control over Japanese silver mines (Tashiro 1986, p. 3) and sold to China. Flynn (1991) has argued that profits from silver mines financed the defeat of hundreds of rival feudal lords (*daimyo*), thereby permitting the consolidation of Japan. The shogun was forced to align himself with the merchant class, creating an indigenous market-based economy with Asian (not Western) roots. Unlike Spain, the Tokugawa invested heavily in agricultural and urban infrastructure. Japan succeeded in withdrawing from the Chinese tributary system and even sent hundreds of thousands of troops in an unsuccessful attempt to conquer China.

Europeans were important middlemen in the Sino-Japanese silver trade, with Japan as the dominant supplier and China the end-customer. It is ironic that China's demand for Japanese silver generated the profits used by the latter to withdraw from China's tributary system. With the help of profits from its silver mines, Japan established commercial capitalism in Asia at roughly the same time that capitalism was taking root in northwestern Europe. Capitalism's Japanese track evolved independently from, and almost simultaneously with, developments in northwestern Europe. But where Japan used mining profits to establish commercial capitalism in Asia, Spain used mining profits to attack the emerging capitalist powers of northwestern Europe. It is difficult to imagine how either one of these developments could have occurred in the absence of Chinese demand for silver.

What about the impact of silver on China itself? Atwell (1977, 1982, 1986, 1988) has long argued that American silver played a critical role in the commercial and political evolution of domestic China. Basing his argument on Geiss (1979), Goldstone (1991, p. 371) has challenged Atwell's emphasis on forces external to Asia (i.e., American treasure), insisting instead that intra-Asian factors explain structural changes within Ming and Qing China. Goldstone says that domestic price inflation in late sixteenth- and early seventeenth-century China destroyed the financial basis of the Ming dynasty. Taxes formerly paid in rice had been converted to payments in a fixed quantity of silver. But over a period of a century, silver itself had lost two-thirds of its value. Even if the quantity of silver collected had increased during the late Ming, it would still be true that the purchasing power of silver taxes definitely declined. The fiscal foundation of the Ming dynasty eroded because China's tax revenues declined continuously in terms of purchasing power. Institutionalization of fixed silver taxes during an era of global price inflation (in terms of silver) may have created a fiscal crisis on the Asian mainland that led inexorably to overthrow of the Ming (accomplished by the Manchus in 1644).

It appears that the core arguments of Atwell and Goldstone are not incompatible. Along with its Japanese counterpart, American silver contributed mightily to developments inside China. On the positive side, America and Japan were instrumental in the victory of a rising merchant class that succeeded in converting China to a silver zone. Unhappily for the Ming dynasty, however, fixing taxes in terms of silver may have created a fiscal crisis that led to the emergence of the Qing dynasty.

## Summary and Conclusion

Truly global trade dates from the founding of the city of Manila in 1571, which formed the first direct and permanent trade link between America and Asia. From this date forward, all heavily populated continents traded with each other directly and indirectly in substantial volumes. Silver was the sine qua non of this global trade. Spanish America was the source of an estimated 150,000 tons of silver between 1500 and 1800, comprising perhaps 80% of world production. The second-leading source of silver was Japan, responsible for around 30% of world output in the sixteenth century and perhaps 16% in the seventeenth century. Not coincidentally, entrepôt Nagasaki was founded at virtually the same time as Manila. Silver was shipped to China, the world's dominant end-customer, regardless of whether it was produced in Asia or in the West.

Much American silver traversed the Atlantic Ocean, passing through Europe on its journey to Asia. Europe exported at least 150 tons of silver annually to Asia, a significant portion of which passed through Amsterdam. Attman has been most vocal in calling attention to the Baltic route, which carried eastward at least 50 tons per year. Traditional Mediterranean-Levantine trade routes carried vast quantities of silver too, but the Cape route was biggest of the three. Direct trade out of Acapulco, through Manila, and onward to China has been mostly ignored in the scholarly literature, despite evidence that 128 tons annually may have been shipped through Manila in the late sixteenth and early seventeenth centuries (and 307 tons in 1597, according to a single source). Recent research seems to indicate that the Manila trade did not drop off after the 1620s or the 1640s, notwithstanding the claims of Chaunu (1960). The tremendous volume of unofficial trade (smuggling) rendered official figures misleading. Chuan (1969) indicates that the Pacific leg of silver's journey carried more than 50 tons of silver per year throughout the seventeenth century, equal to the combined European shipments of Portugal and the Dutch and English East Indies Companies.

The conventional explanation of this west-to-east flow of "money" is that Europe had to send treasure to Asia because the West had to settle its trade deficit with Asia. Europeans liked Asian silks, spices, and porcelain, but Asians had not yet developed an appreciation for European wares. This conventional view is flawed for at least three reasons. First, it was not "money" or "treasure" that flowed out of Europe, but silver. Silver, not gold, was attracted to Asia; Asian gold and sometimes copper (both "money" substances) flowed in the opposite direction, into Europe. It is best to look at factors affecting the supply and demand for silver in its own right, rather than confusing the issue by aggregating this unique substance with other metals as "money," which is alleged to have played a passive, reactive role. Second, the role of Japan needs to be considered. Japan was the Asian counterpart of America (site of production) and Spain (country controlling production) combined. We prefer to focus on the supply side and the demand side of the silver industry, irrespective of which hemisphere contained centers of production, rather than to visualize global trade as an abstract East-West issue. Third, there is a basic anomaly in the treatment of America in the conventional view. Since treasure is alleged to have flowed from Europe to Asia because of a European trade deficit, then why has the Pacific trade not been explained in the same terms? We know of no one who argues that the Manila galleons carried huge quantities of treasure to Asia because of America's insatiable appetite for Asian goods, which in turn caused an American trade deficit with Asia.

Depicting precious metals as passive "money" that adapts to trade imbalances diverts attention from the central issues. Silver was produced for profit. It migrated from points of production (Japan and America) to end-customers (mostly in China). Developments within China have been largely ignored in the diverse literatures dealing with global flows of precious metals and early modern price inflation, yet China was the pivotal country. International business entities would not have shipped tens of thousands of tons of silver to China unless significant profits induced that activity. Profits from the silver trade were immense for two reasons. First, on the demand side, China's monetary and fiscal systems had substantially converted from a paper-money system to silver by the time of the Single-Whip tax reform of the 1570s. Conversion of more than one-quarter of the world's population (and its government) to silver customers contributed to the rise in the price of silver in China. Second, on the supply side, extraordinarily rich silver mines were discovered in Japan and Spanish America, and new technologies reduced production costs. Supply and demand forces created disequilibrium: silver's value in China was double its value in the rest of the world. This is what drove the silver trade—the birth of world trade—and not some abstract notion of trade deficits.

Both the Spanish empire and Tokugawa shogunate captured a substantial portion of silver profits from mines they controlled. Spain's mines financed a century of multifaceted war and empire. The shogun (and his immediate predecessors) used mine profits to finance consolidation of Japan and withdrawal from the economic domination of China. Spain nearly crushed the emerging capitalistic powers of northwestern Europe, while a market-oriented economy was established within Japan. The laws of supply and demand guaranteed that the price of silver would slowly decline to its cost of production, which is what happened. A direct effect of this process is that profit per ounce of silver was steadily squeezed out. This caused the decline of Spain. Japanese silver-mine profits plummeted too, but gold and copper production soared in Japan in the second half of the seventeenth century. The shogun had also invested heavily in improvements in infrastructure, so there was no decline of Japan in the seventeenth century.

The worldwide decline in the value of silver in the early modern period translated directly into global price inflation. When money declines in value with respect to goods, the result is called price inflation. Geiss (1979, p. 158) explains this process clearly for late Ming China: "Such massive infusions of silver diminished the purchasing power of the metal. Silver, like any commodity, lost its high value when supply exceeded the usual demand. This in turn affected the prices of almost everything in the empire, for the structure of prices was tied to the value of silver." Transportation technology permitted connection of silver markets throughout the world. The interconnection of world markets guaranteed that the fall in silver's value was global, which in turn implies that price inflation was a global phenomenon in all areas on a silver standard.

We have consciously neglected any attempt to tie the African continent into the global trade of silver. Nonetheless, it seems that the Portuguese swapped huge numbers of (mostly smuggled) African slaves directly for (mostly smuggled) New World silver via the Rio Plata in Brazil:

> During the decade 1616–1625, recorded imports for Buenos Aires (the sum of legal and confiscated goods) were 7,957,579 pesos, while exports for the same period amounted to only 360,904 pesos. The annual trade deficit, which was met with smuggled silver from Upper Peru, amounted to at least three-quarters of a million pesos per year. Between 1619 and 1623, port officials seized a total of 3,656 slaves from illegally landing vessels; their market value in Lima would have approached two million pesos. These numbers do not include those slaves legally imported and those which evaded port officials. The size of these figures clearly indicates a flourishing and considerable illicit trade up the Rio Plata from the 1580s until probably the 1640s. During its most successful years, no less than 1–2 million pesos (roughly 25,000 to 50,000 kg) flowed illegally from the mines of Peru out through the port of Buenos Aires. These totals equalled from 15% to 30% of the silver output of Potosí. (Cross 1983, p. 414)

Not all the slaves remained in Brazil, nor were all of them plantation laborers. Palmer (1995) has provided demographic information suggesting that between 10,000 and 20,000 Africans were domestic slaves in Mexico City in the early seventeenth century. Since, as we have argued, the Spanish enterprise in America was financed by the world silver market (as were the activities of the Portuguese traders), and since China was the dominant factor in the global silver market, then it appears that the trans-Atlantic slave trade was heavily, though indirectly, influenced by monetary and fiscal developments in Ming China. In other words, end-customer China created profitable trade in the New World, and profitable trade in America created the demand for African slaves. Clearly, a global view of early modern trade may suggest many research topics that might otherwise be overlooked.

Scholars have long been interested in the impact of Europeans on Asia (and the rest of the world). The focus has shifted in recent years, however, especially among Asian scholars who increasingly emphasize the dominant historical role of the intra-Asian marketplace. These revisionists view Europeans as having participated in a vast and sophisticated existing Asian commercial network, rather than as having introduced modernization to backward Asia. This essay is in the revisionist camp; it even suggests a reversal of causality. The economic impact of China on the West was far greater than any European influence on Asia in the early modern period. We agree with the sentiments of Moloughney and Xia (1989, p. 68), who protest that "late Ming China was not an outpost of a Seville-centered world economy."[16] Perhaps a reversal of this logic would be more accurate: Seville was an outpost of a world economy that had not one center but three (Beijing on the demand side, and America and Japan on the supply side).

The physical presence of Europeans in Asia in early modern times—and the simultaneous physical absence of Asians in the West—has understandably led scholars to pay attention mostly to the impact of the West on Asia. Superior naval firepower may explain the presence of Europeans in Asia, but the most powerful economic undercurrents ran in the opposite direction. Without the Chinese demand for silver, there would have been no finance mechanism for the Spanish empire. Without China, there would have been no century-long price revolution. Without China, the birth of world trade would have been delayed to some unknowable extent. But China did convert, both monetarily and fiscally, to silver. This fact reverberated across all continents and gave birth to world trade in 1571, providing a powerful force in shaping the modern world.

# References

Attman, Artur. 1986. *American Bullion in the European World Trade,* 1600–1800. Göteborg.

Atwell, William S. 1977. "Notes on Silver, Foreign Trade, and the Late Ming Economy." *Ch'ing-shih ven-ti'i* 3/8:1–33.

———. 1982. "International Bullion Flows and the Chinese Economy circa 1530–1650." *Past and Present* 95:68–90.

———. 1986. "Some Observations on the 'Seventeenth-Century Crisis' in China and Japan." *Journal of Asian Studies* 45:223–44.

———. 1988. "Ming Observations of Ming Decline: Some Chinese Views on the 'Seventeenth Century Crisis' in Comparative Perspective." *Journal of the Royal Asiatic Society* 2:316–48.

Barrett, Ward. 1990. "World Bullion Flows, 1450–1800." In *The Rise of Merchant Empires: Long-Distance Trade in the Early Modern World*, 1350–1750, ed. James D. Tracy, pp. 224–54. Cambridge.

Blair, E. H., and J. A. Robertson. 1903–1909. *The Philippine Islands*. 55 vols. Cleveland.

Blum, Jerome. 1956. "Prices in Russia in the Sixteenth Century." *Journal of Economic History* 27:182–99.

Boxer, Charles R. 1969. *The Portuguese Seaborne Empire*, 1415–1825. New York.

---

[16] Moloughney and Xia (1989, pp. 67–68) have criticized Atwell for insisting on the importance of American silver in early modern Chinese history. The basis of the Moloughney-Xia counter argument is empirical: the influx of American silver peaked during rather than before the decline of the Ming in the 1640s. This essay is consistent with both sides of this debate. American silver may have been crucial in the decline of the Ming dynasty not because of its scarcity but precisely because its abundant accumulation depressed the value of silver. Views that are contradictory from the perspective of conventional macroeconomic logic become compatible in terms of our cost-of-production model.

Brading, D. A., and Harry E. Cross. 1972. "Colonial Silver Mining: Mexico and Peru." *The Hispanic American Historical Review* 52:545–79.

Brenner, Robert. 1977. "The Origins of Capitalist Development: A Critique of Neo-Smithian Marxism." *New Left Review* 104:25–92.

Cartier, Michel. 1981. "Les importations de métaux monétaires en Chine: Essai sur la conjoncture chinoise." *Annales E.S.C.* 36:454–66.

Chaudhuri, K. N. 1978. *The Trading World of Asia and the English East India Company, 1660–1760.* Cambridge.

———. 1986. "World Silver Flows and Monetary Factors as a Force of International Economic Integration, 1658–1758." In *The Emergence of a World Economy, 1500–1914: Papers of the IX International Congress of Economic History,* ed. W. Fisher, R. W. McInnis, and J. Schneider, 1:37–60. 2 vols. Stuttgart.

Chaunu, Pierre. 1960. *Les Philipines et le Pacifique des Ibériques (XVIe, XVIIe, XVIIIe siècles).* Paris.

Chuan, Hang-sheng. 1969. "The Inflow of American Silver into China from the Late Ming to the Mid-Ch'ing Period." *The Journal of the Institute of Chinese Studies of the Chinese University of Hong-Kong* 2:61–75.

Cross, Harry E. 1983. "South American Bullion Production and Export, 1550–1750." In *Precious Metals in the Later Medieval and Early Modern Worlds,* ed. J. F. Richards, pp. 397–424. Durham.

DeVries, Jan. 1984. *European Urbanization, 1500–1800.* Cambridge, Mass.

Doherty, Kerry W., and D. O. Flynn. 1989. "A Microeconomic Quantity Theory of Money and the Price Revolution." In *Precious Metals, Coinage and the Changes of Monetary Structures in Latin America, Europe and Asia,* ed. Eddy H. G. van Cauwenberghe, pp. 185–208. Leuven.

Elliott, John H. 1961. "The Decline of Spain." *Past and Present* 20:52–75.

Felix, David. 1956. "Profit Inflation and Industrial Growth: The Historic Record and Contemporary Analogies." *Quarterly Journal of Economics* 70:441–63

Flynn, Dennis O. 1977. "The Spanish Price Revolution and the Monetary Approach to the Balance of Payments." Ph.D. diss., University of Utah.

———. 1982. "Fiscal Crisis and the Decline of Spain (Castile)." *Journal of Economic History* 42:139–47.

———. 1984a. "Use and Mis-use of the Quantity Theory of Money in Early Modern Historiography." In *Munzpragung, Geldumlauf und Wechselkurse: Minting, Monetary Circulation and Exchange Rates: Akten des 8th International Economic History Congress, Section C7, Budapest, 1982,* ed. E. van Cauwenberghe and F. Irsigler, pp. 383–417. Trier.

———. 1984b. "The 'Population Thesis' View of Inflation versus Economics and History." In *Munzpragung, Geldumlauf und Wechselkurse: Minting, Monetary Circulation and Exchange Rates: Akten des 8th International Economic History Congress, Section C7,* Budapest, 1982, ed. E. van Cauwenberghe and F. Irsigler, pp. 361–82. Trier.

———. 1986. "The Microeconomics of Silver and East-West Trade in the Early Modern Period." In *The Emergence of a World Economy, 1500–1914: Papers of the IX International Congress of Economic History,* ed. W. Fisher, R. W. McInnis, and J. Schneider, I:37–60. 2 vols. Stuttgart.

———. 1991. "Comparing the Tokugawa Shogunate with Hapsburg Spain: Two Silver-Based Empires in a Global Setting." In *The Political Economy of Merchant Empires,* ed. James D. Tracy. Cambridge.

Flynn, Dennis O., and Arturo Giraldez. 1994a. "China and the Manila Galleons." In *Japanese Industrialization and the Asian Economy,* ed. A. J. H. Latham and H. Kawakatsu. London.

———. 1995. "Arbitrage, China, and World Trade in the Early Modern Period." *Journal of the Economic and Social History of the Orient.*

———. 1994b. "Silver and the Political Economy of the Spanish Empire." Paper presented before the Society for Spanish and Portuguese Historical Studies, Chicago.

Geiss, J. P. 1979. "Peking under the Ming, 1368–1644." Ph.D. diss., Princeton University.

Gernet, Jacques. 1982. *A History of Chinese Civilization.* Cambridge.

Godinho, V. Magalhaes. 1963. *Os descobrimientos e a economia mundial.* Lisbon.

Goldstone, Jack. 1991. *Revolution and Rebellion in the Early Modern World.* Berkeley.

Hamashita, Takeshi. 1988. *The Tribute System and Modern Asia.* Tokyo.

Hamilton, Earl J. 1929. "American Treasure and the Rise of Capitalism, 1500–1700." *Economica* 9:338–57.

———. 1934. *American Treasure and the Price Revolution in Spain, 1501–1650.* Cambridge, Mass.

———. 1937. "The Decline of Spain." *Economic History Review* 8:168–79.

———. 1952. "Prices as a Factor in Business Growth." *Journal of Economic History* 12:325–49.

Huang, Ray. 1974. *Taxation and Governmental Finance in Sixteenth-Century Ming China.* Cambridge, Mass.

Hunt, Verl F. 1978. "The Rise of Feudalism in Eastern Europe: A Critical Appraisal of the Wallerstein World-System Thesis." *Science and Society* 42:43–61.

Innes, R. L . 1980. "The Door Ajar: Japan's Foreign Trade in the Seventeenth Century." Ph.D. diss., University of Michigan.

Israel, Jonathan. 1981. "Debate: The Decline of Spain: A Historical Myth." *Past and Present* 91:170–80.

Iwao, Seiichi. 1959. "Japanese Gold and Silver in the World History." In *International Symposium on History of Eastern and Western Cultural Contacts.* Tokyo.

Jara, Alvaro. 1966. "Economia minera e historia economica hispano-americana." In *Tres ensayos sobre economia minera hispano-americana.* Santiago.

Kamen, Henry. 1964. "The Decline of Castile: The Last Crisis." *Economic History Review* 17:63–76.

———. 1978. "The Decline of Spain: A Historical Myth?" *Past and Present* 81:24–50.

———. 1981. "A Rejoinder." *Past and Present* 91:181–85.

Keynes, John Maynard. 1930. *A Treatise on Money.* 2 vols. New York.

Liang, Fang-chung. 1956. *The Single-whip Method of Taxation in China.* Cambridge, Mass.

Lynch, John. 1984. *Spain under the Habsburgs.* 2 vols. New York.

Moloughney, Brian, and Xia Weizhong. 1989. "Silver and the Fall of the Ming: A Reassessment." *Papers on Far Eastern History* (Canberra) 40:51–78.

Mols, Roger. 1977. "Population in Europe, 1500–1700." In *The Fontana Economic History of Europe,* ed. C. M. Cipolla. London.

Nadal, Oller Jorge. 1959. "La revolución de los precios en el siglo XVI." *Hispania* 19:503–29.

Nef, John U. 1934. "The Progress of Technology and the Growth of Large-Scale Industry in Great Britain, 1540–1640." *Economic History Review* 5:3–24.

Outhwaite, R. B. 1969. *Inflation in Tudor and Early Stuart England.* London.

Palmer, Colin. 1995. "From Africa to the Americas: Ethnicity in the Early Black Communities of the Americas." *Journal of World History* 6:223–36.

Parker, Geoffrey. 1979. "War and Economic Change: The Economic Costs of the Dutch Revolt." In *Spain and the Netherlands, 1559–1659: Ten Studies,* ed. G. Parker. Glasgow.

Phelan, John L. 1959. *The Hispanization of the Philippines: Spanish Aims and Filipino Responses.* Madison.

Ramsey, Peter. 1960. "The European Economy in the Sixteenth Century." *Economic History Review* 12:456–62.

Sahillioglu, H. 1983. "The Role of International Monetary and Metal Movements in Ottoman Monetary History, 1300–1750." In *Precious Metals in the Later Medieval and Early Modern World,* ed. J. F. Richards, pp. 269–304. Durham.

Tashiro, Kazui. 1982. "Foreign Relations during the Edo Period: Sakoku Reexamined." *Journal of Japanese Studies* 8:283–306.

TePaske, John J. 1983. "New World Silver, Castile and the Philippines, 1590–1800." In *Precious Metals in the Later Medieval and Early Modern Worlds,* ed. J. F. Richards, pp. 425–46. Durham.

Wallerstein, Immanuel. 1974. *The Modern World-System: Capitalist Agriculture and the Origins of the European World-Economy in the Sixteenth Century.* New York.

Wilkinson, Endymion P. 1980. *Studies in Chinese Price History.* New York.

Wolf, Eric. 1982. *Europe and the People without History.* Berkeley.

# A Big Business

DAVID BRION DAVIS

By limiting their attention to nation-states, especially the United States, historians have usually fragmented and obscured our understanding of the multinational Atlantic slave system. When most Americans hear the words "African-American slavery," they immediately think of the South and the Civil War. The story supposedly begins in Virginia, in 1619, when a colonist named John Rolfe casually noted that "a dutch man of warre... sold us twenty Negars." At best, the standard texts make only passing reference to the flow of African labor to the Caribbean, Spanish America, and Portuguese Brazil Even in US history, the subject of slavery has traditionally been given a marginal place—a chapter, as it were, in the history of the South (or recently a more prominent position in African-American studies). Even most American college graduates would probably be astonished to learn that Portugal began importing slaves from sub-Saharan Africa in the 1440s; that well before Columbus's famous voyages the Portuguese were exploiting black slave labor on sugar plantations in Madeira and Sao Tome, off the coast of West Africa; and that enslaved African migrants to the New World greatly outnumbered European immigrants in the first three hundred and twenty years of settlement.

An understanding of the phenomenon of racial slavery, even in a specific locale such as Virginia or Texas, requires some knowledge of what Robin Blackburn terms "The Old World Background of New World Slavery," as well as some knowledge of the *multinational* character of the Atlantic slave trade, the slave colonies, and the growing markets that absorbed the latter's produce.

Why did "white slavery" flourish in the early Middle Ages and then disappear and become morally repugnant in the very Northern European nations that became leaders in establishing plantation colonies and transporting millions of African workers to the New World? Why was it that African kings and merchants from the Senegambia region on down to the Niger delta, the Congo, and on south and eastward to Madagascar and Mozambique, continued to sell such staggering numbers of slaves, with only rare and brief protests, to Portuguese, Spanish, Italian, Dutch, English, French, Swedish, Danish, German, American, Cuban, and Brazilian traders?

Why did the representatives of so many different religions—Muslims, Catholics, Protestants, Jews, New Christians, even Moravians and for a time Quakers—express so few scruples about buying and selling human beings? How can we explain the diffusion of racial slavery into non-plantation regions, such as New England and French Canada, so that black slaves could be found by 1750 from the St. Lawrence to the Rio de la Plata, from Québec and Boston to Santiago? If American colonists like young John Adams could angrily claim in 1765 that the mother country was treating them like "Negroes," what does this say about the psychological influence of African-American slaves on the construction of white Creole, or American, identities? Finally, what was the relationship between

New World slavery, traditionally interpreted as a backward or regressive institution, and the much-debated industrial revolution and emergence of "modernity"?

Many thousands of scholarly works on New World slavery have appeared since the pioneering books in the 1940s and 1950s by Eric Williams, Frank Tannenbaum, Kenneth M. Stampp, and Stanley Elkins. Nevertheless, very few historians have succeeded in conveying the global dimensions of a ghastly system that first united five continents as Europeans traded Asian textiles, among other commodities, for African slaves who, after surviving the horrors of the Middle Passage to North or South America, were forced to produce the sugar, coffee, tobacco, rice, indigo, and cotton that helped to stimulate and sustain modern consumer economies. There are various reasons for this historical neglect, even apart from the racial myopia of white scholars and the parochial focus of histories limited to a particular nation-state. We are only beginning to discover the immense quantity and relative inaccessibility of many relevant records and sources. This problem is matched by the complexity and contentiousness of many issues, such as the effects within Africa of exporting millions of slaves for some twelve centuries to *Asia* (between 869 and 883 CE black slaves rebelled and fought Arab armies in the Tigris-Euphrates delta), and millions more for over four centuries to Portugal, Spain, and then the entire Western Hemisphere. Moreover, few historians today have a command of the nine or more languages needed to study the most important surviving records concerning the Atlantic slave trade.

There is a pressing need at the moment, however, for accurate and comprehensive syntheses of the specialized studies usually known only to specialists. It is remarkable that the two long and immensely ambitious books under review were both published in the same year, 1997, that both are the product of many years of extensive research (mostly in secondary sources), and that both are written by Englishmen. Perhaps Britons, drawing on their own traditions of imperial history, find it easier to take on such immense subjects as the making of New World slavery and 430 years of the Atlantic slave trade. As an unapologetic Marxist, editor of *The New Left Review*, and author of the outstanding book *The Overthrow of Colonial Slavery, 1776-1848*, Robin Blackburn writes in the great tradition of E.P. Thompson, Christopher Hill, and Eric Hobsbawm. Hugh Thomas, who was made a life peer in the House of Lords in 1981, has written more popular works on a variety of subjects including the Spanish Civil War and the conquest of Mexico, as well as *World History: The Story of Mankind from Prehistory to the Present*.

Thomas provides a straightforward narrative account of Muslim and Christian slave-making and how it was succeeded by the fifteenth-century Portuguese naval expeditions that first captured and then began purchasing slaves along Africa's western coast. Thomas is especially knowledgeable about Iberian history and presents much new personal detail regarding the early Portuguese and Spanish slave traders and the families who profited from the traffic. After moving on to the Dutch, English, and French internationalization of the Atlantic slave trade in the seventeenth centuiy, Thomas devotes eight chapters to the ways Africans were enslaved by other Africans and the stages of lethal transport from the interior of the continent to the putrid barracoons on the coast and on the tightly packed, stifling slave ships to their ultimate destinations in the New World. The last part of the book deals with the abolition movement, the nature of the slave trade in the nineteenth century, and Britain's aggressive measures to suppress it. One senses that Thomas would like to be regarded as a pure empiricist and storyteller. He shuns theories and theorizing, but deluges the reader with torrents of facts—facts which are often fascinating but which, as we shall see below, include a disturbing number of mistakes.

Although *The Making of New World Slavery* is less well-written than Thomas's book, it will have far greater appeal to scholars. Blackburn's introduction is dense and disjointed, and it contains obligatory quotations from Foucault and Baudrillard, and addresses such fashionable themes as "modernity," "identity," and "the dynamics of civil society." It was long reassuring, as Blackburn rightly suggests, "to identify slavery with traditionalism, patrimonialism and backwardness." This was the lesson of classical social science from the time of Adam Smith (Blackburn also mentions in this connection Auguste Comte, Max Weber, and Ludwig von Mises, but not Karl Marx). While Robert William Fogel, Stanley L. Engerman, Claudia Dale Goldin, and other "econometricians" have won much acclaim for documenting the productivity, profitability, and capitalist character of slavery in the American South, Blackburn is the first historian to explore at some length the role of the larger New World slave system in "the advent of modernity," by which he means the arrival of the modern industrial economy. After making tantalizing but undeveloped references to a kind of Darwinian "'natural selection' of social institutions and practices" that favored plantation slavery, he sensibly concludes that "slavery in the New World was above all a hybrid mixing ancient and modern, European business and African husbandry, American and Eastern plants and processes, elements of traditional patrimonialism with up-to-date bookkeeping and individual ownership." Blackburn's long chapters move from the Old World background and the uses of racial slavery in Portugal, Africa, and the various New World colonies to the eighteenth-century economic boom and British industrialization.

With respect to the Africans' part in selling as many as eleven or twelve million slaves to Europeans, nothing in either book rivals a succinct quotation from the late African-American scholar Nathan Huggins, which Blackburn uses as one of his first epigrams:

> The twentieth-century Western mind is frozen by the horror of men selling and buying others as slaves and even more stunned at the irony of black men serving as agents for the enslavement of blacks by whites.... The racial wrong was lost on African merchants, who saw themselves as selling people other than their own. The distinctions of tribe were more real to them than race, a concept that was yet to be refined by nineteenth- and twentieth-century Western rationalists.

Despite inevitable overlap and repetition when discussing slavery or the slave trade in the centuries from the 1440s to the 1770s, the new books by Thomas and Blackburn could hardly be more different. Thomas affirms at the outset that "historians should not look for villains," but 784 pages later he praises "the heroes"—the French, British, American, and Spanish writers and abolitionists who "achieved the abolition of the Atlantic slave trade and of slavery in the Americas." Very little is said in either book about slave heroes and slave resistance, though Blackburn discussed some slave resistance and especially the impact of the Haitian Revolution in his 1989 book.

Blackburn succeeds in conveying a deep sense of the "superexploitation" of millions of black slaves working millions of uncompensated hours to produce wealth that flowed into white industrial investment and conspicuous display. He shows no hesitation in identifying the historical villains: not the Baroque governments and popes that first authorized the African slave trade so much as the "civil society" that broke with the traditional "moral economy" and unleashed "rampant capitalism and the free market." While Blackburn's arguments regarding civil society and the transition "from baroque to modern" are difficult to follow, he reinforces the often forgotten point made by Robert William Fogel (and many others) that market forces and economic self-interest can produce the most immoral and humanly destructive institutions, epitomized historically by racial slavery in the New World. I should emphasize that Blackburn does not see the New World slave system as the necessary or optimum path to a modern society. But once chosen, because of its absolute centrality to the history of the past four hundred years it left a profound taint on the Western world we know.

Whereas Thomas totally rejects Eric Williams's "shocking argument" that profits from the slave trade financed the Industrial Revolution (Williams had not confined his argument to the slave trade, but had spoken of the larger and more ambiguous "triangular trade," which would presumably include the total profits from New World slavery),- Blackburn carefully considers the diverse views of various economic historians and concludes that while New World slavery did not produce capitalism, profits from the New World slave system made a significant contribution to British economic growth and investment in manufacturing.

In fact, Thomas provides telling examples that support this view, such as John Ashton, a Liverpool slave trader who helped finance the canal to Manchester; John Kennion and Brian Blundell, also of Liverpool, who turned to cotton manufacture and coal mining; and the great eighteenth-century French slave trader, René Montaudoin, who founded in Nantes "a factory in the modern sense of the word which made the first dyed cottons." And quite apart from the disputed question of profits and investment, Blackburn points to the slave system's neglected contribution to "the evolution of industrial discipline and principles of capitalist rationalization."

One thinks, for example, of Joseph J. Ellis's recent portrait of Thomas Jefferson as an efficiency expert, a kind of proto Frederick Winslow Taylor, personally enforcing "a rigid regimen" on the dozen or so young slave boys, "from 10 to 16 years of age," who worked long hours producing nails at the small factory at Monticello. Blackburn goes on to note the seeming paradox that "not by chance were prominent Abolitionists in the forefront of prison reform, factory legislation and the promotion of public education." He might have added that English and American Quakers, who were in the vanguard of the abolition movement, also led the way in devising and imposing new forms of labor discipline. There is a profound historical irony in the fact that "Speedy Fred" Taylor, our century's exponent of efficiency and the first to dispossess workers of all control of the workplace, was born of Quaker parents in Germantown, Pennsylvania, the site in 1688 of the world's first great petition against human bondage.

British and American abolitionists initiated a tradition of sharply differentiating New World and especially Anglo- American slavery from all previous forms of servitude. They were particularly intent on showing that modern plantation slavery was more inhumane and oppressive than the bondage recognized and sanctioned in the Bible or the servitude found in contemporary Africa. This line of argument later appealed to Marxists and other critics who were eager to demonize capitalism and market forces as the sources of the world's worst example of human exploitation. Blackburn is surely right when he insists that "the novelty of New World slavery resided in the scale and intensity of the slave traffic and the plantation trades." But because Blackburn desperately wants to see New

World slavery as a unique aberration, as a tragic choice dictated by capitalist greed when other choices were available, he tends to romanticize earlier forms of human bondage. He forgets that slaves in premodern societies have often been subject to cannibalism, torture, ritual sacrifice, sexual exploitation, and arbitrary death at the whim of an owner.

When Blackburn asserts that "the slavery of the Ancient World had not denied the basic humanity of the slave," he also forgets the appalling descriptions of slaves in the mine shafts at Laurium in ancient Attica and in Ptolemaic Egypt One need not dwell on the laws that sanctioned the Romans' pouring molten lead down the throats of slaves convicted of raping a virgin or crucifying four hundred household slaves after the murder of Pedanius Secundas, in 61 CE, in order to agree with the Quaker John Woolman that no human being is saintly enough to be entrusted with the power of owning a slave as a piece of property, a power which has always involved some degree of dehumanization. As Orlando Patterson and other scholars have demonstrated, while small numbers of highly privileged slaves can be found throughout history, even in nineteenth-century Mississippi, the institution of slavery has always depended on violent domination, dishonor, and a kind of "social death."

Hugh Thomas adopts an extremely effective literary device to convey the continuities between slavery in medieval Europe and the New World. His book begins with what seems to be a dramatic turning point in world history: Gomes Eannes de Zurara's vivid description of the sale, on August 8, 1444, in southwest Portugal, of 235 African slaves, "some white enough," some "like mulattoes," others "as black as Ethiops " This document has often been cited or reprinted to mark the beginning of Europe's exploitation of Africa. But Thomas proceeds to show that this sale of African slaves was part of a long sequence of events that included centuries of warfare and mutual enslavement between Christians and Muslims; the Christian reconquest of Portugal and Spain and the Portuguese capture of Ceuta, in North Africa, in 1415; the development of the Arab and Berber caravan trade in gold and slaves, which brought increasing numbers of black slaves (classified as *sclavi negri*) to Christian Sicily after the mid-1400s; and the westward shift in slave trading and sugar cultivation, which was hastened in 1453 by the Turkish conquest of Constantinople and the decline of the Venetian and Genoese trade in "Slavic slaves" from the Black Sea.

Neither Thomas nor Blackburn gives sufficient attention to the precedents set by Italian slave traders in the Black Sea and Mediterranean. As Stephen P. Bensch has pointed out, "Mediterranean slavery has frequently been brushed aside in synthetic treatments of Western servitude as a curious holdover, a peripheral phenomenon,... an unexpected detour on the road leading from servitude to freedom, all the more unsettling because it appeared in the sophisticated urban societies of Italy, Southern France, and Eastern Iberia." But Thomas does emphasize the direct continuities between medieval multiracial servitude and the kind of black bondage that first emerged on the sugar-producing Atlantic islands such as Madeira and São Tomé and then spread in the early sixteenth century to the New World. Blackburn provides much similar information, but by placing his brief discussion of the Atlantic islands *after* his chapter on "The Old World Background to New World Slavery," he reinforces his theme of discontinuity and distracts attention from the fact that when Columbus first entered the Caribbean, thousands of black slaves in the Old World were already producing sugar for a European market.

The most striking evidence of continuity can be seen in the great mercantile and banking families of the Italian Renaissance. The Marchionnis of Florence, for example, had long engaged in the Black Sea slave trade (Kaffa, their base in the Crimea, resembled in many respects the forts and trading posts Europeans would later establish along the West African coast). In 1470, after the Ottoman Turks had endangered the Italian colonies in the eastern Mediterranean and had diminished Europe's supply of both sugar and slaves, young Bartolommeo Marchionni moved to Lisbon, where he joined a growing community of Florentines. Bartolommeo soon owned sugar plantations in Madeira and purchased from the Portuguese king the right to trade in slaves from Guinea.

According to Thomas, Bartolommeo had ships in Vasco da Gama's expedition to India in 1498 and in Cabral's expedition of 1500 that discovered Brazil; he became "a monopoly trader in slaves from the Benin River in the 1490s, carrying captives not only to Portugal and Madeira but also to Elmina, on the Gold Coast, where he sold them to African merchants for gold." One might add that this friend of the Medicis and Amerigo Vespucci also sent African slaves back to Pisa and Tuscany. There were many other Florentines and Genoese who provided links from slave trading in the Mediterranean, which most people took for granted except when Muslim raiders enslaved Europeans, to the new social orders in Madeira, the Canary Islands, São Tomé, the Caribbean, and Brazil.

Judging whether enslavement was a continuous historical process or whether its American form was a historical exception is partly a matter of what historians choose to emphasize, and both Thomas and Blackburn recognize the multinational sponsorship of the early slave trade to the New World. In 1518 Spain's young King Charles, soon to be the Holy Roman Emperor Charles V, received fervent pleas from various Spanish colonists who were alarmed by the mortality and "weakness" of the Indians and who argued that only African slaves, like those in the Atlantic islands, could provide the labor needed to fulfill the New World's promise. King Charles agreed, and as Thomas puts it, the Flemish-born king awarded the coveted grant for supplying slaves to a Savoyard friend, the governor of Bresse in Burgundy. He in turn sold his rights, through a Castilian, to Genoese merchants—"who, in turn, would, of course, have to arrange for the Portuguese to deliver the slaves. For no Spanish ship could legally go to Guinea [according to the papal Treaty of Tordesillas], the in on arch s of the two countries were then allies, and anyway, only the Portuguese could supply slaves in that quantity."

Perhaps the most startling point that Hugh Thomas makes about the early Portuguese slave trade is the way it became dominated by New Christian or *converse* merchants. Fernão de Loronha, for example, an associate and successor of Marchionni, gained a temporary monopoly of trade in the Bight of Benin and supplied slaves and wine to Elmina (Africans in the Gold Coast region continued to buy slaves from the Portuguese in exchange for gold). José Rodrigues Mascarenhas and Fernando Jimenez were other sixteenth-century merchants of Jewish ancestry who gained control over large segments of the slave trade to the Americas. King Philip II of Spain awarded Portuguese New Christians with *asiento* contracts to supply the Spanish colonies with African slaves. Some of these merchants had relatives or close friends in Italy, Brazil, or Antwerp, long the major center for refining and marketing sugar.

Thomas, unlike Blackburn, avoids the error of thinking of these *converso* merchants as Jews. Since there has been recent controversy over the Jewish role in the Atlantic slave trade, it is important to be on guard against the Inquisition's or the Nazis' definition of Jewishness: that is, having the taint of Jewish ancestry. In 1492 many of the Jews expelled from Spain settled in Portugal, and in 1497 the Portuguese king banished all the Jews who refused to convert to Christianity. Given the frequency of intermarriage between New Christians and Old Christians, many of these New Christian families would have lost their *converso* identity and been assimilated if there had been no doctrine of "purity of blood" and if the Inquisition had not become obsessed with secret "judaizing" practices. Even so, with the passage of time, the great majority of New Christians became absorbed in the Iberian Catholic culture. As Seymour Drescher has pointed out, most of the New Christians who made their fortunes in Africa, Asia, or the Americas returned to Iberia and "were disinclined to resettle where they could openly practice Judaism or even syncretic brands of family religiosity."

But with respect to their participation in the slave trade, the genuineness of the *conversos'* Christian faith should be irrelevant. Neither Blackburn nor Thomas fully grasps the central point. The Church and the Catholic crowns prohibited Jews from owning baptized slaves or even traveling to the New World. What qualified men like Antônio Fernandes Elvas and Manuel Rodrigues Lamego to transport thousands of African slaves to the Spanish New world was their *convincing* Christian identity. According to Thomas, Pope Sixtus V thought so highly of Fernando Jiménez, despite his Jewish ancestry, that "he gave him the right to use his own surname, Peretti." When doubts arose that a *converso* merchant or planter was not a genuine Christian, he was often burned at the stake.

# from *The Interesting Narrative of the Life of Olaudah Equiano, or Gustavus Vassa, the African, Written by Himself* (1789)

 OLAUDAH EQUIANO

I hope the reader will not think I have trespassed on his patience in introducing myself to him, with some account of the manners and customs of my country. They had been implanted in me with great care, and made an impression on my mind, which time could not erase, and which all the adversity and variety of fortune I have since experienced, served only to rivet and record; for, whether the love of one's country be real or imaginary, or a lesson of reason, or an instinct of nature, I still look back with pleasure on the first scenes of my life, though that pleasure has been for the most part mingled with sorrow.

I have already acquainted the reader with the time and place of my birth. My father, besides many slaves, had a numerous family, of which seven lived to grow up, including myself and a sister, who was the only daughter. As I was the youngest of the sons, I became, of course, the greatest favorite with my mother, and was always with her; and she used to take particular pains to form my mind. I was trained up from my earliest years in the art of war: my daily exercise was shooting and throwing javelins; and my mother adorned me with emblems, after the manner of our greatest warriors. In this way I grew up till I was turned the age of eleven, when an end was put to my happiness in the following manner:—generally when the grown people in the neighborhood were gone far in the fields to labor, the children assembled together in some of the neighboring premises to play; and commonly some of us used to get up a tree to look out for any assailant, or kidnapper, that might come upon us—for they sometimes took those opportunities of our parents' absence, to attack and carry off as many as they could seize. One day as I was watching at the top of a tree in our yard, I saw one of those people come into the yard of our next neighbor but one to kidnap, there being many stout young people in it. Immediately on this I gave the alarm of the rogue, and he was surrounded by the stoutest of them, who entangled him with cords, so that he could not escape till some of the grown people came and secured him. But, alas! ere long it was my fate to be thus attacked, and to be carried off, when none of the grown people were nigh. One day, when all our people were gone out to their works as usual, and only I and my dear sister were left to mind the house, two men and a woman got over our walls, and in a moment seized us both, and, without giving us time to cry out, or make resistance, they stopped our mouths, and ran off with us into the nearest wood. Here they tied our hands, and continued to carry us as far as they could, till night came on, when we reached a small house, where the robbers halted for refreshment, and spent the night. We were then unbound, but were unable to take any food; and, being quite overpowered by fatigue and grief, our only relief was some sleep, which allayed our misfortune for a short time. The

From *The Interesting Narrative of the Life of Olaudah Equiano*, 1789.

next morning we left the house, and continued travelling all the day. For a long time we had kept the woods, but at last we came into a road which I believed I knew. I had now some hopes of being delivered; for we had advanced but a little way before I discovered some people at a distance, on which I began to cry out for their assistance; but my cries had no other effect than to make them tie me faster and stop my mouth, and then they put me into a large sack. They also stopped my sister's mouth, and tied her hands; and m this manner we proceeded till we were out of sight of these people. When we went to rest the following night, they offered us some victuals, but we refused it; and the only comfort we had was in being in one another's arms all that night, and bathing each other with our tears. But alas! we were soon deprived of even the small comfort of weeping together. The next day proved a day of greater sorrow than I had yet experienced; for my sister and I were then separated, while we lay clasped in each other's arms. It was in vain that we besought them not to part us; she was torn from me, and immediately carried away, while I was left in a state of distraction not to be described. I cried and grieved continually; and for several days did not eat any thing but what they forced into my mouth. At length, after many days travelling, during which I had often changed masters, I got into the hands of a chieftain, in a very pleasant country. This man had two wives and some children, and they all used me extremely well, and did all they could to comfort me; particularly the first wife, who was something like my mother. Although I was a great many days' journey from my father's house, yet these people spoke exactly the same language with us. This first master of mine, as I may call him, was a smith, and my principal employment was working his bellows, which were the same kind as I had seen in my vicinity. They were in some respects not unlike the stoves here in gentlemen's kitchens, and were covered over with leather; and in the middle of that leather a stick was fixed, and a person stood up, and worked it in the same manner as is done to pump water out of a cask with a hand pump. I believe it was gold he worked, for it was of a lovely bright yellow color, and was worn by the women on their wrists and ankles. I was there I suppose about a month, and they at last used to trust me some little distance from the house. This liberty I used in embracing every opportunity to inquire the way to my own home; and I also sometimes, for the same purpose, went with the maidens, in the cool of the evenings, to bring pitchers of water from the springs for the use of the house. I had also remarked where the sun rose in the morning, and set in the evening, as I had travelled along; and I had observed that my father's house was towards the rising of the sun. I therefore determined to seize the first opportunity of making my escape, and to shape my course for that quarter; for I was quite oppressed and weighed down by grief after my mother and friends; and my love of liberty, ever great, was strengthened by the mortifying circumstance of not daring to eat with the free-born children, although I was mostly their companion. While I was projecting my escape one day, an unlucky event happened, which quite disconcerted my plan, and put an end to my hopes. I used to be sometimes employed in assisting an elderly slave to cook and take care of the poultry; and one morning, while I was feeding some chickens I happened to toss a small pebble at one of them, which hit it on the middle, and directly killed it. The old slave, having soon after missed the chicken, inquired after it; and on my relating the accident, (for I told her the truth, for my mother would never suffer me to tell a lie,) she flew into a violent passion, and threatened that I should suffer for it; and, my master being out, she immediately went and told her mistress what I had done. This alarmed me very much, and I expected an instant flogging, which to me was uncommonly dreadful, for I had seldom been beaten at home. I therefore resolved to fly; and accordingly I ran into a thicket that was hard by, and hid myself in the bushes. Soon afterwards my mistress and the slave returned, and, not seeing me, they searched all the house, but not finding me, and I not making answer when they called to me, they thought I had run away, and the whole neighborhood was raised in the pursuit of me. In that part of the country, as in ours, the houses and villages were skirted with woods, or shrubberies, and the bushes were so thick that a man could readily conceal himself in them, so as to elude the strictest search. The neighbors continued the whole day looking for me, and several times many of them came within a few yards of the place where I lay hid. I expected every moment, when I heard a rustling among the trees, to be found out, and punished by my master; but they never discovered me, though they were often so near that I even heard their conjectures as they were looking about for me; and I now learned from them that any attempts to return home would be hopeless. Most of them supposed I had fled towards home; but the distance was so great and the way so intricate, that they thought I could never reach it, and that I should be lost in the woods. When I heard this I was seized with a violent panic, and abandoned myself to despair. Night, too, began to approach, and aggravated all my fears. I had before entertained hopes of getting home, and had determined when it should be dark to make the attempt; but I was now convinced it was fruitless, and began to consider that, if possibly I could escape all other animals, I could not those of the human kind; and that, not knowing the way, I must perish in the woods. Thus was I like the hunted deer—

—'Every leaf and every whisp'ring breath,
Convey'd a foe, and every foe a death.'

I heard frequent rustlings among the leaves, and being pretty sure they were snakes, I expected every instant to be stung by them. This increased my anguish, and the horror of my situation became now quite insupportable. I at length quitted the thicket, very faint and hungry, for I had not eaten or drank any thing all the day, and crept to my master's kitchen, from whence I set out at first, which was an open shed, and laid myself down in the ashes with an anxious wish for death, to relieve me from all my pains. I was scarcely awake m the morning, when the old woman slave, who was the first up, came to light the fire, and saw me in the fire place. She was very much surprised to see me, and could scarcely believe her own eyes. She now promised to intercede for me, and went for her master, who soon after came, and, having slightly reprimanded me, ordered me to be taken care of, and not ill treated.

Soon after this, my master's only daughter, and child by his first wife, sickened and died, which affected him so much that for some time he was almost frantic, and really would have killed himself, had he not been watched and prevented. However, in short time afterwards he recovered, and I was again sold. I was now carried to the left of the sun's rising, through many dreary wastes and dismal woods, amidst the hideous roarings of wild beasts. The people I was sold to used to carry me very often, when I was tired, either on their shoulders or on their backs. I saw many convenient well built sheds along the road, at proper distances, to accommodate the merchants and travellers, who lay in those buildings along with their wives, who often accompany them; and they always go well armed.

From the time I left my own nation, I always found somebody that understood me till I came to the sea coast. The languages of different nations did not totally differ, nor where they so copious as those of the Europeans, particularly the English. They were therefore, easily learned; and, while I was journeying thus through Africa, I acquired two or three different tongues. In this manner I had been travelling for a considerable time, when, one evening, to my great surprise, whom should I see brought to the house where I was but my dear sister! As soon as she saw me, she gave a loud shriek, and ran into my arms—I was quite overpowered: neither of us could speak; but, for a considerable time, clung to each other in mutual embraces, unable to do any thing but weep. Our meeting affected all who saw us and, indeed, I must acknowledge, in honor of those sable destroyers of human rights, that I never met with any ill treatment, or saw any offered to their slaves, except tying them, when necessary, to keep them from running away. When these people knew we were brother and sister, they indulged us to be together; and the man, to whom I supposed we belonged, lay with us, he in the middle, while she and I held one another by the hands across his breast all night; and thus for a while we forgot our misfortunes, in the joy of being together; but even this small comfort was soon to have an end; for scarcely had the fatal morning appeared when she was again torn from me forever! I was now more miserable, if possible, than before. The small relief which her presence gave me from pain, was gone, and the wretchedness of my situation was redoubled by my anxiety after her fate, and my apprehensions lest her sufferings should be greater than mine, when I could not be with her to alleviate them. Yes, thou dear partner of all my childish sports! thou sharer of my joys and sorrows! happy should I have ever esteemed myself to encounter every misery for you and to procure your freedom by the sacrifice of my own.—Though you were early forced from my arms, your image has been always rivetted in my heart, from which neither time nor fortune have been able to remove it; so that, while the thoughts of your sufferings have damped my prosperity, they have mingled with adversity and increased its bitterness. To that Heaven which protects the weak from the strong, I commit the care of your innocence and virtues, if they have not already received their full reward, and if your youth and delicacy have not long since fallen victims to the violence of the African trader, the pestilential stench of a Guinea ship, the seasoning in the European colonies, or the lash and lust of a brutal and and unrelenting overseer.

I did not long remain after my sister. I was again sold, and carried through a number of places, till after travelling a considerable time, I came to a town called Tinmah, in the most beautiful country I had yet seen in Africa. It was extremely rich, and there were many rivulets which flowed through it, and supplied a large pond in the centre of the town, where the people washed. Here I first saw and tasted cocoa nuts, which I thought superior to any nuts I had ever tasted before; and the trees which were loaded, were also interspersed among the houses, which had commodious shades adjoining, and were in the same manner as ours, the insides being neatly plastered and whitewashed. Here I also saw and tasted for the first time, sugar-cane. Their money consisted of little white shells, the size of the finger nail. I was sold here for one hundred and seventy-two of them, by a merchant who lived and brought me there. I had been about two or three days at his house, when a wealthy widow, a neighbor of his, came there one evening, and brought with her an only son, a young gentleman about my own age and size. Here they saw me; and, having taken a fancy to me, I was bought of the merchant, and went home with them. Her house and premises were situated close to one of those rivulets I have mentioned, and were the finest I ever saw in Africa: they were very extensive, and she had a number of slaves to attend her. The next day I was washed and perfumed, and when meal time came, I was led into the presence of my mistress, and ate and drank before her with her son. This filled me with astonishment; and I could scarce help expressing my surprise that the young gentleman should suffer me, who was bound, to eat with him who was free; and not only so, but that he would not at any time either eat or drink till I had taken first, because I was the eldest, which was agreeable to our custom. Indeed, every thing here, and all their treatment of me, made me forget that I was a slave. The language of these people resembled ours so nearly, that we understood each other perfectly. They had also the very same customs as we. There were likewise slaves daily to attend us, while my young master and I, with other boys, sported with our darts and bows and arrows, as I had been used to do at home. In this resemblance to my former happy state, I passed about two months; and I now began to think I was to be adopted into the family, and was beginning to be reconciled to my situation, and to forget by degrees my misfortunes, when all at once the delusion vanished; for, without the least previous knowledge, one morning early, while my dear master and companion was still asleep, I was awakened out of my reverie to fresh sorrow, and hurried away even amongst the uncircumcised.

Thus, at the very moment I dreamed of the greatest happiness, I found myself most miserable; and it seemed as if fortune wished to give me this taste of joy only to render the reverse more poignant.—The change I now experienced, was as painful as it was sudden and unexpected. It was a change indeed, from a state of bliss to a scene which is inexpressible by me, as it discovered to me an element I had never before beheld, and till then had no idea of, and wherein such instances of hardship and cruelty continually occurred, as I can never reflect on but with horror.

All the nations and people I had hitherto passed through, resembled our own in their manners, customs, and language: but I came at length to a country, the inhabitants of which differed from us in all those particulars. I was very much struck with this difference, especially when I came among a people who did not circumcise, and ate without washing their hands. They cooked also in iron pots, and had European cutlasses and cross bows, which were unknown to us, and fought with their fists among themselves. Their women were not so modest as ours, for they ate, and drank, and slept with their men. But above all, I was amazed to see no sacrifices or offerings among them. In some of those places the people ornamented themselves with scars, and likewise filed their teeth very sharp. They wanted sometimes to ornament me in the same manner, but I would not suffer them; hoping that I might some time be among a people who did not thus disfigure themselves, as I thought they did. At last I came to the banks of a large river which was covered with canoes, in which the people appeared to live with their household utensils, and provisions of all kinds. I was beyond measure astonished at this, as I had never before seen any water larger than a pond or a rivulet: and my surprise was mingled with no small fear when I was put into one of these canoes, and we began to paddle and move along the river. We continued going on thus till night, and when we came to land, and made fires on the banks each family by themselves; some dragged their canoes on shore, others stayed and cooked in theirs, and laid in them all night. Those on the land had mats, of which they made tents, some in the shape of little houses; in these we slept; and after the morning meal, we embarked again and proceeded as before. I was often very much astonished to see some of the women, as well as the men, jump into the water, dive to the bottom, come up again, and swim about.—Thus I continued to travel, sometimes by land, sometimes by water, through different countries and various nations, till, at the end of six or seven months after I had been kidnapped, I arrived at the sea coast. It would be tedious and uninteresting to relate all the incidents which befel me during this journey, and which I have not yet forgotten; of the various hands I passed through, and the manners and customs of all the different people among whom I lived—I shall therefore only observe, that in all the places where I was, the soil was exceedingly rich; the pumpkins, eadas, plaintains, yams, &c. &c. were in great abundance, and of incredible size. There were also vast quantities of different gums, though not used for any purpose, and every where a great deal of tobacco. The cotton even grew quite wild, and there was plenty of redwood. I saw no mechanics whatever in all the way, except such as I have mentioned. The chief employment in all these countries was agriculture, and both the males and females, as with us, were brought up to it, and trained in the arts of war.

The first object which saluted my eyes when I arrived on the coast, was the sea, and a slave ship, which was then riding at anchor, and waiting for its cargo. These filled me with astonishment, which was soon converted into terror, when I was carried on board. I was immediately handled, and tossed up to see if I were sound, by some of the crew; and I was now persuaded that I had gotten into a world of bad spirits, and that they were going to kill me. Their complexions, too, differing so much from ours, their long hair, and the language they spoke, (which was very different from any I had ever heard) united to confirm me in this belief. Indeed, such were the horrors of my views and fears at the moment, that, if ten thousand worlds had been my own, I would have freely parted with them all to have exchanged my condition with that of the meanest slave m my own country. When I looked round the ship too, and saw a large furnace of copper boiling, and a multitude of black people of every description chained together, every one of their countenances expressing dejection and sorrow, I no longer doubted of my fate; and, quite overpowered with horror and anguish, I fell motionless on the deck and fainted. When I recovered a little, I found some black people about me, who I believed were some of those who had brought me on board, and had been receiving their pay; they talked to me in order to cheer me, but all in vain. I asked them if we were not to be eaten by those white men with horrible looks, red faces, and long hair. They told me I was not: and one of the crew brought me a small portion of spirituous liquor in a wine glass, but, being afraid of him, I would not take it out of his hand. One of the blacks, therefore, took it from him and gave it to me, and I took a little down my palate, which, instead of reviving me, as they thought it would, threw me into the greatest consternation at the strange feeling it produced, having never tasted any such liquor before. Soon after this, the blacks who brought me on board went off, and left me abandoned to despair.

I now saw myself deprived of all chance of returning to my native country, or even the least glimpse of hope of gaining the shore, which I now considered as friendly; and I even wished for my former slavery in preference to my present situation, which was filled with horrors of every kind, still heightened by my ignorance of what I was to undergo. I was not long suffered to indulge my grief; I was soon put down under the decks, and there I received such a salutation in my nostrils as I had never experienced in my life: so that, with the loathsomeness of the stench, and crying together, I became so sick and low that I was not able to eat, nor had I the least desire to taste any thing. I now wished for the last friend, death, to relieve me; but soon, to my grief, two of the white men offered me eatables; and, on my refusing to eat, one of them held me fast by the hands, and laid me across, I think the windlass, and tied my feet, while the other flogged me severely. I had never experienced any thing of this kind before, and although not being used to the water, I naturally feared that element the first time I saw it, yet, nevertheless, could I have got over the nettings, I would have jumped over the side, but I could not; and besides, the crew used to watch us very closely who were not chained down to the decks, lest we should leap into the water; and I have seen some of these poor African prisoners most severely cut, for attempting to do so, and hourly whipped for not eating. This indeed was often the case with myself. In a little time after, amongst the poor chained men, I found some of my own nation, which in a small degree gave ease to my mind. I inquired of these what was to be done with us? they gave me to understand, we were to be carried to these white people's country to work for them. I then was a little revived, and thought, if it were no worse than working, my situation was not so desperate, but still I feared I should be put to death, the white people looked and acted, as I thought, in so savage a manner; for I had never seen among any people such instances of brutal cruelty; and this not only shown towards us blacks, but also to some of the whites themselves. One white man in particular I saw, when we were permitted to be on deck flogged so unmercifully with a large rope near the foremast, that he died in consequence of it; and they tossed him over the side as they would have done a brute. This made me fear these people the more; and I expected nothing less than to be treated in the same manner. I could not help expressing my fears and apprehensions to some of my countrymen; I asked them if these people had no country, but lived in this hollow place? (the ship) they told me they did not, but came from a distant one. 'Then,' said I, 'how comes it in all our country we never heard of them?' They told me because they lived so very far off. I then asked where were their women? had they any like themselves? I was told they had. 'And why,' said I, 'do we not see them?' They answered because they were left behind. I asked how the vessel could go? they told me they could not tell; but that there was cloth put upon the masts by the help of the ropes I saw, and then the vessel went on, and the white men had some spell or magic they put in the water when they liked, in order to stop the vessel. I was exceedingly amazed at this account, and really thought they were spirits. I therefore wished much to be from amongst them, for I expected they would sacrifice me; but my wishes were vain—for we were so quartered that it was impossible for any of us to make our escape.

While we stayed on the coast I was mostly on deck; and one day to my great astonishment, I saw one of these vessels coming in with the sails up. As soon as the whites saw it, they gave a great shout, at which we were amazed; and the more so, as the vessel appeared larger by approaching nearer. At last, she came to an anchor in my sight, and when the anchor was let go, I and my countrymen who saw it, were lost in astonishment to observe the vessel stop—and were now convinced it was done by magic. Soon after this the other ship got her boats out, and they came on board of us, and the people of both ships seemed very glad to see each other.—Several of the strangers also shook hands with us black people, and made motions with their hands, signifying I suppose, we were to go to their country, but we did not understand them.

At last, when the ship we were in, had got in all her cargo, they made ready with many fearful noises, and we were all put under deck, so that we could not see how they managed the vessel. But this disappointment was the least of my sorrow. The stench of the hold while we were on the coast was so intolerably loathsome, that it was dangerous to remain there for any time, and some of us had been permitted to stay on the deck for the fresh air; but now that the whole ship's cargo were confined together, it became absolutely pestilentail. The closeness of the place, and the heat of the climate, added to the number in the ship, which was so crowded that each had scarcely room to turn himself, almost suffocated us. This produced copious perspirations, so that the air soon became unfit for respiration, from a variety of loathsome smells, and brought on a sickness among the slaves, of which many died—thus falling victims to the improvident avarice, as I may call it, of their purchasers. This wretched situation was again aggravated by the galling of the chains, now became insupportable; and the filth of the necessary tubs, into which the children often fell, and were almost suffocated. The shrieks of the women, and the groans of the dying, rendered the whole a scene of horror almost inconceivable. Happily perhaps, for myself, I was soon reduced so low here that it was thought necessary to keep me almost always on deck; and from my extreme youth I was not put in fetters. In this situation I expected every hour to share the fate of my companions, some of whom were almost daily brought upon deck at the point of death, which I began to hope would soon put an end to my miseries. Often did I think many of the inhabitants of the deep much more happy than myself. I envied them the freedom they enjoyed, and as often wished I could change my condition for theirs. Every circumstance I met with, served only to render my state more painful, and heightened my apprehensions, and my opinion of the cruelty of the whites.

One day they had taken a number of fishes; and when they had killed and satisfied themselves with as many as they thought fit, to our astonishment who were on deck, rather than give any of them to us to eat, as we expected, they tossed the remaining fish into the sea again, although we begged and prayed for some as well as we could, but in vain; and some of my countrymen, being pressed by hunger, took an opportunity, when they thought no one saw them, of trying to get a little privately; but they were discovered, and the attempt procured them some very severe floggings. One day, when we had a smooth sea and moderate wind, two of my wearied countrymen who were chained together, (I was near them at the time,) preferring death to such a life of misery, somehow made through the nettings and jumped into the sea: immediately, another quite dejected fellow, who on account of his illness, was suffered to be out of irons, also followed their example; and I believe many more would very soon have done the same, if they had not been prevented by the ship's crew, who were instantly alarmed. Those of us that were the most active were in a moment put down under the deck, and there was such a noise and confusion amongst the people of the ship as I never heard before, to stop her, and get the boat out to go after the slaves. However, two of the wretches were drowned, but they got the other, and afterwards flogged him unmercifully, for thus attempting to prefer death to slavery. In this manner we continued to undergo more hardships than I can now relate, hardships which are inseparable from this accursed trade. Many a time we were near suffocation from the want of fresh air, which we were often without for whole days together. This, and the stench of the necessary tubs, carried off many.

During our passage, I first saw flying fishes, which surprised me very much; they used frequently to fly across the ship, and many of them fell on the deck. I also now first saw the use of the quadrant; I had often with astonishment seen the mariners make observations with it, and I could not think what it meant. They at last took notice of my surprise; and one of them, willing to increase it, as well as to gratify my curiosity, made me one day look through it. The clouds appeared to me to be land, which disappeared as they passed along. This heightened my wonder; and I was now more persuaded than ever, that I was in another world, and that every thing about me was magic. At last, we came in sight of the island of Barbadoes, at which the whites on board gave a great shout, and made many signs of joy to us. We did not know what to think of this; but as the vessel drew nearer, we plainly saw the harbor, and other ships of different kinds and sizes, and we soon anchored amongst them, off Bridgetown. Many merchants and planters now came on board, though it was in the evening. They put us in separate parcels, and examined us attentively. They also made us jump, and pointed to the land, signifying we were to go there. We thought by this, we should be eaten by these ugly men, as they appeared to us; and, when soon after we were all put down under the deck again, there was much dread and trembling among us, and nothing but bitter cries to be heard all the night from these apprehensions, insomuch, that at last the white people got some old slaves from the land to pacify us. They told us we were not to be eaten, but to work, and were soon to go on land, where we should see many of our country people. This report eased us much. And sure enough, soon after we were landed, there came to us Africans of all languages.

We were conducted immediately to the merchant's yard, where we were all pent up together, like so many sheep in a fold, without regard to sex or age. As every object was new to me, every thing I saw filled me with surprise. What struck me first, was, that the houses were built with bricks and stories, and in every other respect different from those I had seen in Africa; but I was still more astonished on seeing people on horseback. I did not know what this could mean; and, indeed, I thought these people were full of nothing but magical arts. While I was in this astonishment, one of my fellow-prisoners spoke to a countryman of his, about the horses, who said they were the same kind they had in their country. I understood them, though they were from a distant part of Africa; and I thought it odd I had not seen any horses there; but afterwards, when I came to converse with different Africans, I found they had many horses amongst them, and much larger than those I then saw.

We were not many days in the merchant's custody, before we were sold after their usual manner, which is this:—On a signal given, (as the beat of a drum,) the buyers rush at once into the yard where the slaves are confined, and make choice of that parcel they like best. The noise and clamor with which this is attended, and the eagerness visible in the countenances of the buyers, serve not a little to increase the apprehension of terrified Africans, who may well be supposed to consider them as the ministers of that destruction to which they think themselves devoted. In this manner, without scruple, are relations and friends separated, most of them never to see each other again. I remember, in the vessel in which I was brought over, in the men's apartment, there were several brothers, who, in the sale, were sold in different lots; and it was very moving on this occasion, to see and hear their cries at parting. O, ye nominal Christians! might not an African ask you—Learned you this from your God, who says unto you, Do unto all men as you would men should do unto you? Is it not enough that we are torn from our country and friends, to toil for your luxury and lust of gain? Must every tender feeling be likewise sacrificed to your avarice? Are the dearest friends and relations, now rendered more dear by their separation from their kindred, still to be parted from each other, and thus prevented from cheering the gloom of slavery, with the small comfort of being together, and mingling their sufferings and sorrows? Why are parents to lose their children, brothers their sisters, or husbands their wives? Surely, this is a new refinement in cruelty, which, while it has no advantage to atone for it, thus aggravates distress, and adds fresh horrors even to the wretchedness of slavery.

# CHAPTER FIVE

# The Scientific Revolutions in Global Perspective

The scientific revolution is often associated in the West with changing conceptions of the universe, the place of human beings in nature, new methods for acquiring knowledge, and social organizations that support scientific experiments. Assuming that this revolution began in the mid-16th century, it is widely believed that it led to the creation of what is now known as the scientific method. That method has at least four components that include the forming of hypotheses to explain things that are currently inexplicable or problematic, the collection of data through observations and measurements, the testing and validation of the hypothesis through the repetition of experiments, and, finally, the construction of theories that better explain what was initially held to be problematic or unknown in the first place.

As a description of the new set of conditions that precipitated the development of principles and methods of inquiry into the understanding of natural phenomena and the universe, this narrative is satisfactory as far as it goes, but it leaves a very great deal out of account. What it omits is the fact that the scientific revolution in the West had a great many precursors in Egyptian geometry, which developed to establish property lines and construction methods for building pyramids; Babylonian mathematics, which taught us to count in units of 60 for the sake of producing circles and understanding fractions, square roots, and eclipses; Chinese mathematics and medicine, which helped map major stars and developed the technique of acupuncture; Indian surgery and mathematics, which led to the development of preventive medicine, amputations, plastic surgery, and Hindu-Arabic numerals in use today; Amerindian astronomy, which studied the stars, developed calendars, and detected the motion of planets; and ancient Greek and Roman science, which de-coupled medicine from religion through the Hippocratic oath, produced Aristotle's theories of classification and reasoning, and led to Ptolemy's geocentric or earth-centered theory of the universe. There were, in addition, multiple specific achievements made by Arabic and Chinese science both before and during the period of the commencement of the Western scientific revolution which are discussed at length in the two selections by Jim al-Khalili and Joseph Needham.

Before introducing those, however, it is necessary to be reminded that narratives of the sort just created above tend to describe the breakout of the Western scientific revolution as kind of myth or origin story. By this the historian of science David J. Hess means that in using the term *science* to describe what in its own time was called *natural philosophy*, and suggesting that its development can be represented as a full-blown revolution rather than an evolution of what proceeded it, is to turn its history into something made up, a kind of fiction. The story this narrative is so often meant to tell isn't so much about the creation of new methods and techniques for understanding the natural world but about the triumph of reason that was accomplished essentially, no matter who its precursors were, by white men. Hess goes to considerable lengths to lay out the chief stages of this ethnocentric narrative about the triumphal creation of Western science before considering some of those other traditions of scientific advancement that complicate and complement it. The first is from China whose achievements in scientific and technological advancement considerably outpaced those of the West, and with whom it had frequent interchanges over the centuries, until the sixteenth century. The second is from the Arabic-Muslim world whose discoveries on so many fronts contributed to, or paralleled, breakthroughs in the West.

One result of this complication of the narrative has been to question the idea that the "scientific turn" in the West was all that radical in the first place. There were, to be sure, breakthroughs from the ancient world to the early modern but there were also consolidations, extensions, and above all borrowings. This has led Hess to propose that terms like "Western science" and "the scientific revolution" obscure or distort almost as much as they illumine. What they occlude or misrepresent are the initial as well as ongoing exchanges between Asia, Europe, the Middle East, and Africa that helped fuel and spread the advance of scientific inquiry in numerous fields. Rather than refer to "Western" scientific developments, Hess would rather think of them as "cosmopolitan" or "global" inasmuch as they occurred over a vast field of cultural networks and a vast expanse of time in which "different cultural systems still maintained their distinctive styles of scientific thought."

Therefore Jim al-Khali asserts in the title of his essay that the time has come "to herald the Arabic science that refigured Darwin and Newton." While his essay makes no attempt to be inclusive—Islamic science made significant achievements in fields as broadly dispersed as astronomy, mathematics, medicine, cartography, geography, chemistry, physics, botany, and others—he is particularly anxious to dissociate medieval Arabic science with any "Dark Age" of the sort that Europe experienced at least until the Mongol destruction of Baghdad in 1258 and the gradual deconstruction of the Abbasid Empire. His focus is particularly on exemplars, such as the Persian philosopher Avicenna, born in 980 C.E, who is known as the most famous physician of the Middle Ages but was actually preceded 600 years before by what al-Khali describes as the greatest scientist in Islam, Abu Rayhan al-Biruni. So great were al-Biruni's achievements as an astronomer, mathematician, geographer, pharmacologist, and physician, not to say geologist and anthropologist, that al-Khalili believes that al-Biruni's legacy, still little known in the Western world, is matched in Europe only by that of Leonardo da Vinci.

He also points out that Copernicus's work on the heliocentric or sun-centered model of the solar system was based on research conducted two centuries earlier by the Syrian astronomer, Ibn al-Shatir. Or, yet again, Sir Isaac Newton's work on optics, which it is assumed in the West that he invented, drew on the research 700 years before him of Ibn al-Haytham, an Abbasid scientist from the region known now as Iraq who is regarded in some circles "as the world's first physicist and as the father of the modern scientific method—long before Renaissance scholars such as Bacon and Descartes." While such claims can sometimes be disputed, they constitute impressive evidence of the scientific achievements of an Arabic, Muslim tradition that also discovered vision, invented the water clock, and produced surgical instruments some of which are still in use today.

In the "Introduction" to his classic *Science in Traditional China*," eminent historian of science Joseph Needham also seeks to amend the historical claim that the bases of modern science are Western. The Chinese had already made remarkable achievements in numerous fields before its science flowed, as Needham puts it, "like all other such rivers, into the larger Western sea." Needham notes exceptional advances from the first century of the Common Era to the Middle Ages in mathematics, astronomy, optics, acoustics, magnetism, mechanical, civil and hydraulic engineering, the invention of gunpowder, silk production, medicine, quantitative cartography, mechanical clock manufacture, the boot stirrup, efficient equine harnesses, and the list goes on. As Needham notes, China like the Middle Ages did not, as Europe did, undergo anything like a "Dark Ages" in the medieval period because its scientific experimentation and progress was both continuous and relentless. While the science of the ancient era and even the Middle Ages was often restricted to its regional setting, thus making it difficult for people to find a common basis for discourse, this did not deter inventions of great importance—think merely of gunpowder or the magnetic compass—from passing from one civilizational complex to another. Thus the story of the history of science, and even of its taking center stage in Europe after sixteenth century, is, as David Hess contends, a multicultural narrative.

# The Origins of Western Science: Technototems in the Scientific Revolution

DAVID S. HESS

Most stories about cosmopolitan science and technology begin with the scientific revolution, that is, the events in Western Europe between 1500 and 1700. Much of the science and technology practiced throughout the world today draws on the basic principles, formulas, and concepts that were elaborated if not developed, in Europe during that period. In this chapter I examine the cultural politics of narratives of the "scientific revolution" as a myth or origin story. In the process I provide one example of how to do reconstruction, in this case, the reconstruction of the history of the scientific revolution.

## What Was the Scientific Revolution?

### The Legacy of Ancient Science

Stories of the scientific revolution usually begin with the legacy of the ancient world. Ancient science is generally associated with the Greeks, although increasingly the Greeks are seen as the inheritors of scientific traditions from Babylonia, Egypt, and other cultures. Many of the ideas about the natural world that comprised the accepted worldview in Europe in 1500 can be traced to natural philosophers of the ancient world such as Ptolemy, Aristotle, and Galen. However, as historians now recognize, older stories of the "Dark Ages" in between tend to filter out Arab and non-Western influences on the inherited medieval worldview, just as they downplay the ferment and developments of medieval science in the centuries preceding 1500. Nevertheless, I shall begin with the ancient Creeks because their science is the usual starting point for discussions of the scientific revolution. Their "science" soon reveals itself to be very different from that of the modern period. As historians often say, the past is another culture.

In the ancient worldview the earth was at the center of the universe, and the sun, moon, planets, and stars all revolved around the earth. The view is an understandable conclusion that can be drawn from even a few quick looks at the sky, but it also rested on some very careful observations of the planets. For example, against the backdrop of the stars the path of Mercury or Mars engages in what is today called retrograde motion (see figure 5.1). At a certain point the planet appears to stop, go backward, and then zigzag forward. The Ptolomaic or geocentric theory assumed perfect circular motion of the planets and the sun around the earth. As a result, retrograde motion was explained by saying that a planet's orbit around the Earth is in the shape of a circle that contains a little circle known as an epicycle. One can achieve almost any kind of retrograde motion by combining epicycles with eccentrics and equants. Eccentrics are orbits around a point that is not centered on the earth, and equants are points around which the planet moves in uniform speed (see figure 5.1 again).

In today's sun-centered system, scientists explain retrograde motion as an optical illusion created by the relative movement of the orbits of the Earth and planets around the sun. As the planets move in their elliptical orbits, the relative movement of the Earth and either an inner planet such as Mercury or an outer planet such as Mars creates the effects of retrograde motion (see figures 5.2 and 5.3). The ancient Greeks and medieval philosophers were aware of alternative, sun-centered theories of what we call today the solar system. However, as long as they assumed that all orbits were circular (rather than elliptical, as Tycho Brahe later claimed), Ptolemy's system was the only one elaborated mathematically that fit the observations. His theory also fitted with common sense and the idea that heavenly bodies all took the shape of perfect circles.

Mercury          Mars

Seen against the backdrop of the stars, and over a period of days or weeks, the planet often moved in odd trajectories.

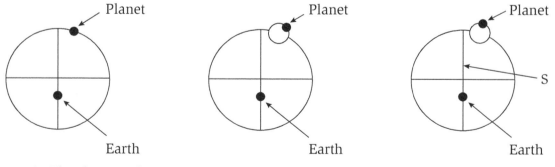

Eccentric. The planet's orbit is a circle around an "eccentric center, which is slightly off from Earth.

Eccentric with epicycle. The planet also moves in a small circle as it moves around the eccentric center.

System with equant. The planet now moves at a uniform rate around point S, rather than the eccentric center or Earth.

**FIGURE 5.1** Retrograde Motion and Geocentric Theory.

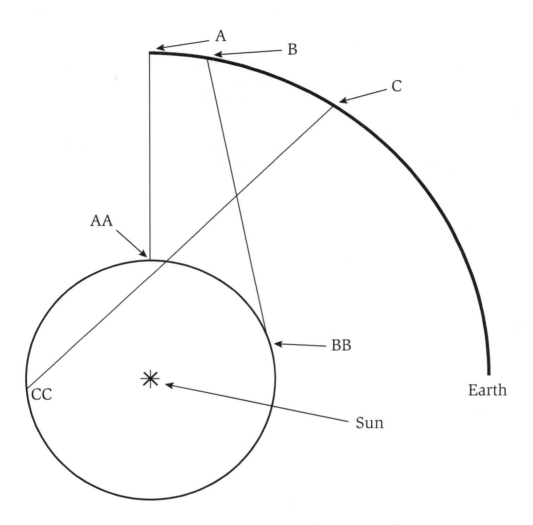

**FIGURE 5.2** Retrograde Motion for an Inner Planet.

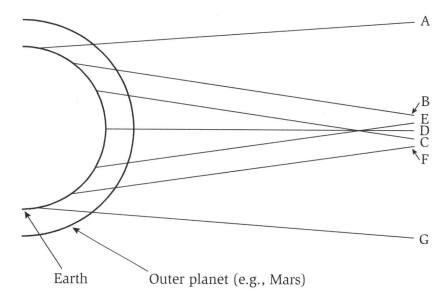

**FIGURE 5.3** Retrograde Motion for an Outer Planet.

A second argument in favor of the geocentric model had to do with motion and the behavior of objects on the surface of the earth. The ancient Greeks argued that if the earth rotated (which it would have to do in a heliocentric system), then there would be a tremendous wind and the birds would get left behind. Likewise, the water of the oceans would probably slurp over the shorelines. It made much more sense to assume that the world stayed put.

A whole science of natural motion was constructed around the idea that the earth was at the center of the universe. Aristotle's theory of natural motion was based on the assumption that all material in the universe was composed of four basic elements: earth, air, fire, and water. Materials composed of earth and water had a natural propensity to return to the earth and, therefore, to fall, whereas those composed of fire and air had the opposite tendency, to rise. Earthbound materials only moved if something propelled them, such as a horse pulling a cart. Once the horse or other force stopped propelling the object, it would come to rest or fall immediately to the ground. For apparent anomalies such as an arrow shot by a bow, Aristotle argued that the arrow pushed the air in front of it, which then rushed around the arrow to fill in the vacuum left behind it, thus propelling the arrow forward. Likewise, to explain why an object accelerates as it falls, Aristotle argued that objects rushed more quickly as they got closer to their natural resting place. He gave the rather implausible explanation that involved attributing to objects a desire to return to their natural resting place. His followers explained acceleration by arguing that there was a shorter column of air beneath the object, and as a result there was increasingly smaller air resistance. Thus, the theories of ancient physics were plausible and coherent, even if scientists today would consider them mistaken.

Ancient natural knowledge also had well-developed systems of medicine, physiology, and anatomy. For example, Galen practiced dissection and had a sophisticated sense of human anatomy. Questions of physiology such as the circulation of blood, however, remained more open to debate. Modern science has shown that blood circulates from the heart through the arteries and back to the heart through the veins. In contrast, Galen argued that there were two kinds of blood: one ran from the liver through the veins and provided nutrients to the organism; the other ran from the heart and contained a life-giving material called pneuma. For Galen circulation occurred independently in the two systems through an ebb and flow within each. The only interaction between the two systems was that the blood from the veins seeped through the dividing wall of the heart into the left ventricle, where it was purified to become part of the arterial blood. However, the heart did not pump blood; rather, it drew blood inward, and it also drew in air directly from the lungs.

## The Story of the Scientific Revolution

At the beginning of the sixteenth century ancient teachings such as those of Ptolemy on the planets, Aristotle on motion, and Galen on physiology constituted the basis of accepted wisdom. In schoolbook stories of the scientific revolution, a few bold and courageous thinkers in sixteenth- and seventeenth-century Europe rebuilt the entire edifice of ancient theories on nature and the universe. However, for some time now historians have questioned the extent to which there was really a "scientific revolution" rather than "evolution" of the ideas of previous thinkers. For example, in the centuries prior to the scientific "revolution," a number of scholars, particularly in Oxford and Paris, questioned central aspects of Aristotelian physics and began to develop a theory of what we would today call inertia.

The history of the scientific revolution is therefore a construction, as are all historical narratives. Yet, this particular history may have more fictive qualities to it than others. To begin, the title of the story is fictive. The term *science* is an anachronism, because the word *scientist* did not emerge in today's sense until the nineteenth century. The term used at the time was *natural philosophy*; however, the phrase "natural philosophy revolution" just does not seem to have the same ring to it. As for the word *revolution*, the plot of the story of the scientific revolution also has a fictive quality. Notwithstanding all the ferment that was going on prior to the sixteenth century, historians and scientists often give the story a clear beginning, such as the publication of Copernicus's *De Reuolutionibus Orbium*. In the manner of classic Aristotelian drama, the story has a phase of rising action (Brahe, Kepler), a climax (Galileo and his confrontation with the Catholic church hierarchy), and falling action (the codification of Western science by Bacon, Boyle, and Descartes). There is even a subplot: the story of William Harvey and the circulation of blood or Boyle's experimental demonstrations with the air pump. The ending varies a great deal, but often the last event in the story is Newton's *Principia*.

The story has been told and retold so many times that it has, to some extent, obtained some of the characteristics of a legend or myth. As with a legend, the story has a historical basis, but the protagonists have achieved a heroic, larger-than-life quality. As with many myths, the story has an etiological quality. In other words, it tells us how something came to be: it is about the origin of modern science and, to some extent, modern society. Like myths and legends, the story is no longer associated with a specific author but has, instead, passed into oral and popular tradition where, like a smooth pebble in a stream, it has become rounded over by the waters of popular consciousness. Rough edges—the historical details that do not fit—have been polished out of the story. What emerges in their place is a narrative of the triumph of reason, which, like a torch passed on from one runner to another in a relay race, is passed on from one heroic Great White Man to another.

Why tell the story one more time? Any understanding of modern science, technology, and culture requires a definition of the term *Western science*. Arguably a good way to begin to understand—and to interpret critically—the idea of *Western science* is to return to the origin tale. Keep in mind that there are many ways of telling the story. I could begin earlier, end later, add or cut characters, emphasize industry, deemphasize religion, make minor figures important and major figures unimportant, open up the story to the Muslims and other non-Western peoples, close the story in on England and Western Europe, and so on. The possibilities are endless. I give here something approximating the plot summary of what we might call the standard, Western textbook version of the story of the scientific revolution.

In 1543 Copernicus published *De Reuolutionibus Orbium*, in which he argued for a sun-centered theory of the universe. Copernicus's main achievement was to elaborate the heliocentric model mathematically; he introduced no new data and in fact relied on Ptolemy's data. Because Copernicus, like Ptolemy, assumed perfect circular orbits, he still had to use epicycles. Even though Copernicus's predictions were no better than those of Ptolemy, Copernicus's theory has generally been hailed as mathematically simpler and more elegant.

The transition to the Copernican system was a gradual one. One impetus for the transitions occurred in 1577, when a comet appeared and cut across the various celestial spheres that were supposed to be the provinces of the various planets. The Danish astronomer Tycho Brahe also developed a huge pool of new data, and he supported a compromise system in which some planets move around the sun while the sun and its satellites move around the earth. When examining Brahe's data on the motion of Mars, his student Johann Kepler came up with a theory of elliptical motion, and he proposed a series of laws of planetary motion. The transition from circles to ellipses made it much easier to accept the Copernican theory.

Galileo provided additional support for the Copernican theory when he trained his new telescope on Jupiter's moons, which revolved around the planet and therefore provided a suggestion of how the planets might revolve around the sun. He also showed how the moon had mountains and "seas," and was, therefore, far from the perfect celestial body described by Aristotle. Galileo published his results in 1610 in the book *The Starry Messenger,* which created a great stir. However, what caused his famous trial and imprisonment was the book he published in 1632 *Dialogue Concerning the Two Chief Systems of the World.* In the book he provided a detailed criticism of the fundamentals of the Aristotelian science of motion, and he introduced experiments to test many of Aristotle's ideas. For example, Galileo showed through experiment (sometimes he is said to have dropped a weight from the tower of Pisa) that both heavy and light bodies accelerated at the same rate, the opposite of what Aristotle had argued. Moreover, Galileo asserted that the movement of celestial and terrestrial bodies followed the same set of physical laws.

The great problem of the Copernican system was that without crystalline orbs to hold the planets in place, nothing seemed to prevent them from crashing into each other or falling into the sun. Isaac Newton suggested an answer in his book the *Principia*, which was published in 1687. Newton owes some debt to the work of William Gilbert, who in 1600 published a book on the magnet and suggested that the earth was itself a giant magnet. That idea became one of the sources for the theory of a gravitational force that could hold planets in their orbit. Gravity was required to balance out the opposing centrifugal force that would otherwise tend to make the planets fly off into outer space like rocks from a sling. Newton argued that the force of gravity acting on falling terrestrial bodies was roughly equivalent to the force required to keep a celestial body such as the moon in its orbital path.

The foundations of other branches of the modern sciences were also laid during this period. In chemistry Robert Boyle distinguished the element and the compound, defined chemical reaction and analysis, and developed the law stating that the volume of a confined gas at a constant temperature decreases with pressure. In medicine and biology in the middle and later decades of the sixteenth century, the Italians Vesalius, Colombo, and Fabricus took steps toward the theory of the circulation of blood, beginning with the idea that the blood does not cross the septum but instead circulates from the right side of the heart through the lungs and back to the left ventricle. The Englishman William Harvey studied at Padua and by the 1620s had developed his predecessors' ideas into a comprehensive theory that the blood circulates from the heart through the arteries and back through the veins to the heart.

In the early seventeenth century Bacon and Descartes provided a philosophical or methodological rationale for the growing movement of natural philosophers. Notwithstanding the differences discussed in the previous chapter, their work helped legitimate the subsequent founding of the first scientific societies, most notably the Royal Society of London in 1660 and the Académie Française in 1666. The two philosophers provided the first formulations of the scientific method, a term granted such status in the story that we might do better to capitalize it as the Scientific Method. In the past, historians and philosophers have argued that the Scientific Method eventually became a combination of deduction and empirical observation, a union of Descartes and Bacon. More recently, studies of scientists in practice reveal that they do not adhere to a single Scientific Method or a even a single set of scientific norms. Instead, they pursue their research in a flexible and opportunistic way. Thus, the divergence between Bacon and Descartes could be used to argue that the so-called Scientific Method was, even in its origins, more of a plurality of—and hack to the small letters—scientific methods.

## The Origin Story: Some Multicultural Questions

A conventional narrative about the scientific revolution has several common features. First, it tends to tell the story in intellectual terms. The social is filtered out, except when it is useful to construct science as a triumph over superstition. Society figures in the background as a source of secondary characters: enlightened princes who support science and dogmatic church leaders who oppose it. Second, the story focuses on Europe and it is told in the form of a dialogue between the Old Europe (ancient thinkers) and the New Europe (modern thinkers). What goes on during the time between the Old and New Europe, not to mention what happens before the Old Europe, is basically put into a black box. Exchanges between the West and the rest are written out of the narrative or relegated to secondary plot status. Third, the story is told as an event. A scientific revolution occurred. It is a dramatic change, not a gradual evolution.

Historians have long quarreled with each of the assumptions of the conventional narrative. Yet, the narrative continues to appear, especially in popular forums such as television programs. Told in conventional form, the narrative of the scientific revolution contributes to the ongoing ethnocentrism of West is best. In this sense the narrative can be seen as colonialist.

Let me begin my critique of the conventional scientific revolution narrative with a question: "How Western is 'Western' science and how revolutionary was the scientific 'revolution'?" One starting point for the answer to this question is the work of the scientist, historian, and sinologist Joseph Needham. Needham's studies of science in China were framed around the question, "Why did the scientific revolution not take place in China?" Although that question may seem to serve the West-is-best ideology, Needham documented the scientific and technical achievements of China, and in the process he helped erode the idea that other cultures are incapable of producing sophisticated scientific research.

Needham has also contributed to a critique of Western ethnocentrism by documenting the tremendous interchange between European and non-European cultures prior to the scientific revolution. He has argued that China was generally more advanced technologically than the West until about the sixteenth century. He has also shown that in many cases it is very likely that inventions and discoveries were made first in China and then transferred to Europe. Such innovations include, as Needham enumerates in one of his lists,

> magnetic science, equatorial celestial coordinates and the equatorial mounting of observational astronomical instruments, quantitative cartography, the technology of cast iron, essential components of the reciprocating steam-engine such as the double-acting principle and the standard interconversion of rotary and longitudinal motion, the mechanical clock, the boot stirrup and the efficient equine harnesses, to say nothing of gunpowder and all that followed therefrom. (1974:116)

Much of the technical infrastructure of what is considered to be Western science—including much of its mathematics—rests on borrowings from China and other non-Western cultures.

Other historians have begun to question the scientific revolution in a more profound way. They have increasingly looked back to earlier centuries and developed a more gradual narrative that shows ongoing developments in the centuries prior to the fifteenth century. Furthermore, by looking more carefully at medieval science and its achievements, historians are able to open up the complicated question of how Western science was deeply dependent on complex interchanges with non-Western sciences. As the historian Saleh Omar notes, extending the scientific revolution back to the thirteenth century

> gives fresh vigor to the question of Arab influence on medieval Latin science and, ultimately, on seventeenth-century European science. The revival of scientific activity in

Europe in the thirteenth century followed the translation into Latin of many Arabic works on optics, astronomy, mathematics, and medicine, as well as many of the Greek works, which were also translated from Arabic, toward the end of the twelfth century and the beginning of the thirteenth. (1979:68)

The conventional Western view of Arabic-Muslim science has tended to overlook its originality and its influence on the scientific revolution in Europe. For example, in a 1931 essay that reviewed the translation and transmission of Arabic-Muslim texts, the historian Max Meyerhof invoked the word *storehouse* to describe Arabic-Muslim science (Meyerhof 1931:344). Summarizing its role, he wrote:

Looking back we may say that Islamic medicine and science reflected the light of the Hellenic sun, when its day had fled, and that they shone like a moon, illuminating the darkest night of the European Middle Ages; that some bright stars lent their own light, and that moon and stars alike faded at the dawn of a new day—the Renaissance. (354)

Although an older generation of scholars recognized the achievements of Arabic-Muslim and other non-Western scientific traditions, many of those scholars also invoked the storehouse image and downplayed the direct influence of Arabic-Muslim science on the leaders of the "scientific revolution." One exception is the historian and medievalist Herbert Butterfield, who in *The Origins of Modern Science* noted that a thirteenth-century Muslim physician argued long before Harvey that the only way that the blood could go from the right to left ventricle of the heart was through the lungs (Butterfield 1957:55). Although Harvey's discovery of the circulation of the blood may be a case of rediscovery, the rediscovery itself was in part shaped by the Arabic-Muslim scientific tradition. The Arab philosopher Averroës (or Ibn Rushd) had a great influence on the university at Padua, where Harvey studied. In turn, Harvey's work owes a great deal to his teachers and predecessors at Padua, who nurtured experimental approaches in biology. Although Padua was an Aristotelian school, the university approached Aristotle from a relatively secular and therefore critical viewpoint. As Butterfield comments, "The Paduans were inclined to adopt this attitude because they were an Averroist university—seeing Aristotle in the light of the Arabian commentator, Averroës" (60).

Research on the Arabic-Muslim influence on early modern physics and optics has taken great strides in recent years. The historian George Saliba (1987) has put to rest the ethnocentric idea that Arabic-Muslim science served only as a storehouse of Greek science that was activated during the Renaissance. Saliba and other scholars have argued instead for a "scientific revolution" in Arabic-Muslim thought that took place during the thirteenth and fourteenth centuries and has become known as the Maraba school. Historians have demonstrated close parallels between Copernicus's work and that of the Arab astronomer Ibn al-Shatir of Damascus. The details of the transmission remain to be worked out, but it is now clear that Copernicus borrowed heavily from the developments achieved in the Arabic-Muslim school (Saliba 1991).

A similar argument may be possible to make for Galileo, who, like Harvey, was a student at Padua. Although by the 1620s the university had earned a reputation as a conservative place where peripatetic scholars defended Aristotelian physics against the new ideas of Galileo, Butterfield argues that Galileo himself may have been influenced by the general experimental approach to biology and the secular approach to Aristotle. It is also known that Galileo had a copy of the *Opticae Thesaurus* of Ibn al-Haytham (Alhazen), an Arab scientist who was known for his experimental method (Omar 1979:68). Galileo used Ibn al-Haytham's work to refute the theory that the moon was a polished mirror, and it is likely that the Muslim scientist may have had a more general impact on Galileo. Furthermore, Kepler also studied Alhazen's works, and the Arab optics specialist influenced a number of other Western scholars as well (ibid.).

The influence of Arabic-Muslim science on the leaders of the scientific revolution has clearly become a topic of serious scholarship. Similar work shows how a number of technological innovations in the West— weight-driven and water clocks, glass making, ogival (Gothic) architecture, water-raising machines, and paper making—were technology transfers from the Islamic world (Al-Hassan and Hill 1986:31–35). In turn, studies of the transmission of medieval Islamic science and technology to the West may lead to the recognition of other, more complex patterns of transmission.

One area of scholarship that is opening up the question of a multicultural history of science and technology is the history of mathematics. For example, in *The Crest of the Peacock* the historian of mathematics George Gheverghese Joseph argues that Eurocentric accounts tend to begin with classical Greek mathematics and to minimize the influence of Egyptian and Mesopotamian mathematics on the Greeks. Joseph shows how the pre-Greek mathematics of the Egyptians and Mesopotamians was considerably more sophisticated than previously understood, and those mathematical traditions may also have had more influence on the Greeks than previously recognized. He also opens the "black box"—or "multicolored box"—of the European Dark Ages to reveal a complex set of ongoing exchanges among Arab, Indian, Chinese, and other non-European mathematicians. For example, Joseph shows how the medieval Indian mathematicians in Kerala developed mathematics close to the calculus, and he opens up the still unanswered question of Indian influence on medieval Arab mathematicians and, through them, on modern European mathematics. Joseph also debunks the storehouse theory of medieval Islamic science by explaining the crucial role that Islamic mathematicians played in bringing the geometrical traditions of the Greeks together with the algebraic and arithmetic approaches of Babylonia, India, and China.

The careful work of scholars of medieval Arabic-Muslim science is also undermining the extent to which the scientific revolution was revolutionary. The very idea of the Scientific Revolution may someday come to be rejected as ethnocentric. Although the European natural philosophers of that period certainly deserve credit for their achievements, there is an ideological quality to a way of writing history around a great watershed, before which is prescience and after which is science. There were other revolutions, or dramatic shifts, of scientific and technical knowledge, especially outside the West, such as the Maraba school. To the extent that other developments are not given the label of the *scientific revolution*, the idea of a single scientific revolution tends to put the Great White Men of early modern Europe on a pedestal, and to relegate everyone else to a secondary status.

One of the implications of opening up the black box of the sources of the "scientific revolution" is that the very idea of "Western science" is becoming increasingly problematic and ethnocentric. Certainly it seems better to talk about modern or cosmopolitan science rather than Western science, because science is now practiced throughout the world just as it was during the period prior to the scientific revolution. What may be happening is that Europeans and European-descent populations are beginning to recognize that the tremendous international exchange that characterizes cosmopolitan science and technology today may not be unique to the nineteenth and twentieth centuries. Instead, even during the period of the "origins" of modern science, and before it, there were ongoing exchanges across Asia, Africa, and Europe. Unlike political institutions and forms of social organization, which travel slowly, scientific and technical ideas diffuse rapidly across cultural boundaries. They are carried around in people's heads and can often be adopted without threatening existing power structures. Thus, science and technology tend to travel lightly and quickly.

Thinking of science from a multicultural perspective can be distinguished from thinking about it from an international perspective. Although historical research is showing increasing evidence for connections among European and non-European mathematics, technology, and natural knowledge, a case can be made that different cultures still maintained their distinctive styles of scientific thought. The case of Greek geometry versus Near Eastern and Indian algebra is one example. In this sense the different mathematical and scientific traditions constitute streams of ethnomathematics and ethnoscience. The science of Copernicus, Kepler, Harvey, Bacon, Galileo, Descartes, and Newton might better be thought of not as a development of a transcendent international science but as a specifically early modern Western elaboration and development of a multicultural scientific and mathematical legacy.

# It's Time to Herald the Arabic Science That Prefigured Darwin and Newton

Jim Al-Khalili

Watching the daily news stories of never-ending troubles, hardship, misery and violence across the Arab world and central Asia, it is not surprising that many in the west view the culture of these countries as backward, and their religion as at best conservative and often as violent and extremist.

> I am on a mission to dismiss a crude and inaccurate historical hegemony and present the positive face of Islam. It has never been more timely or more resonant to explore the extent to which western cultural and scientific thought is indebted to the work, a thousand years ago, of Arab and Muslim thinkers.

What is remarkable, for instance, is that for over 700 years the international language of science was Arabic (which is why I describe it as "Arabic science"). More surprising, maybe, is the fact that one of the most fertile periods of scholarship and scientific progress in history would not have taken place without the spread of Islam across the Middle East, Persia, north Africa and Spain. I have no religious or political axe to grind. As the son of a Protestant Christian mother and a Shia Muslim father, I have nevertheless ended up without a religious bone in my body. However, having spent a happy and comfortable childhood in Iraq in the 60s and 70s, I confess to strong nostalgic motives for my fascination in the history of Arabic science.

If there is anything I truly believe, it is that progress through reason and rationality is a good thing —knowledge and enlightenment are always better than ignorance. I proudly share my worldview with one of the greatest rulers the Islamic world has ever seen: the ninth-century Abbasid caliph of Baghdad, Abu Ja'far Abdullah al-Ma'mun. Many in the west will know something of Ma'mun's more illustrious father, Harun al-Rashid, the caliph who is a central character in so many of the stories of the Arabian Nights. But it was Ma'mun, who came to power in AD813, who was to truly launch the golden age of Arabic science. His lifelong thirst for knowledge was such an obsession that he was to create in Baghdad the greatest centre of learning the world has ever seen, known throughout history simply as Bayt al-Hikma: the House of Wisdom.

We read in most accounts of the history of science that the contribution of the ancient Greeks would not be matched until the European Renaissance and the arrival of the likes of Copernicus and Galileo in the 16th century. The 1,000-year period sandwiched between the two is dismissed as the dark ages. But the scientists and philosophers whom Ma'mun brought together, and whom he entrusted with his dreams of scholarship and wisdom, sparked a period of scientific achievement that was just as important as the Greeks or Renaissance, and we cannot simply project the European dark ages on to the rest of the world.

Of course some Islamic scholars are well known in the west. The Persian philosopher Avicenna —born in AD980—is famous as the greatest physician of the middle ages. His Canon of Medicine was to remain the standard medical text in the Islamic world and across Europe until the 17th century, a period of more than 600 years. But Avicenna was also undoubtedly the greatest philosopher of Islam and one of the most important of all time. Avicenna's work stands as the pinnacle of medieval philosophy.

But Avicenna was not the greatest scientist in Islam. For he did not have the encyclopedic mind or make the breadth of impact across so many fields as a less famous Persian who seems to have lived in his shadow: Abu Rayhan al-Biruni. Not only did Biruni make significant breakthroughs as a brilliant philosopher, mathematician and astronomer, but he also left his mark as a theologian, encyclopedist, linguist, historian, geographer, pharmacist and physician. He is also considered to be the father of geology and anthropology. The only other figure in history whose legacy rivals the scope of his scholarship would be Leonardo da Vinci. And yet Biruni is hardly known in the western world.

Many of the achievements of Arabic science often come as a surprise. For instance, while no one can doubt the genius of Copernicus and his heliocentric model of the solar system in heralding the age of modern astronomy, it is not commonly known that he relied on work carried out by Arab astronomers many centuries earlier. Many of his diagrams and calculations were taken from manuscripts of the 14th-century Syrian astronomer Ibn al-Shatir. Why is he never mentioned in our textbooks? Likewise, we are taught that English physician William Harvey was the first to correctly describe blood circulation in 1616. He was not. The first to give the correct description was the 13th-century Andalucian physician Ibn al-Nafees.

And we are reliably informed at school that Newton is the undisputed father of modern optics. School science books abound with his famous experiments with lenses and prisms, his study of the nature of light and its reflection, and the refraction and decomposition of light into the colours of the rainbow. But Newton stood on the shoulders of a giant who lived 700 years earlier. For without doubt one of the greatest of the Abbasid scientists was the Iraqi Ibn al-Haytham (born in AD965), who is regarded as the world's first physicist and as the father of the modern scientific method—long before Renaissance scholars such as Bacon and Descartes.

But what surprises many even more is that a ninth-century Iraqi zoologist by the name of al-Jahith developed a rudimentary theory of natural selection a thousand years before Darwin. In his Book of Animals, Jahith speculates on how environmental factors can affect the characteristics of species, forcing them to adapt and then pass on those new traits to future generations.

Clearly, the scientific revolution of the Abbasids would not have taken place if not for Islam - in contrast to the spread of Christianity over the preceding centuries, which had nothing like the same effect in stimulating and encouraging original scientific thinking. The brand of Islam between the beginning of the ninth and the end of the 11th century was one that promoted a spirit of free thinking, tolerance and rationalism. The comfortable compatibility between science and religion in medieval

Baghdad contrasts starkly with the contradictions and conflict between rational science and many religious faiths in the world today.

The golden age of Arabic science slowed down after the 11th century. Many have speculated on the reason for this. Some blame the Mongols' destruction of Baghdad in 1258, others the change in attitude in Islamic theology towards science, and the lasting damage inflicted by religious conservatism upon the spirit of intellectual inquiry. But the real reason was simply the gradual fragmentation of the Abbasid empire and the indifference shown by weaker rulers towards science.

Why should this matter today? I would argue that, at a time of increased cultural and religious tensions, misunderstandings and intolerance, the west needs to see the Islamic world through new eyes. And, possibly more important, the Islamic world needs to see itself through new eyes and take pride in its rich and impressive heritage.

# Science in Traditional China: A Comparative Perspective

 Joseph Needham

## Introduction

When we say that modern science developed only in Western Europe in the time of Galileo during the Renaissance and during the scientific revolution, we mean, I think, that it was there alone that there developed the fundamental bases of *modern* science, such as the application of mathematical hypotheses to Nature, and the full understanding and use of the experimental method, the distinction between primary and secondary qualities, and the systematic accumulation of openly published scientific data. Indeed, it has been said that it was in the time of Galileo that the most effective method of discovery about Nature was itself, and I think that is still quite true.

Nevertheless, before the river of Chinese science flowed, like all other such rivers, into the sea of modern science, China had seen remarkable achievements in many directions. For example, take mathematics: decimal place value and a blank space for the zero had begun in the land of the Yellow River earlier than anywhere else, and a decimal metrology had gone along with it. By the −1st century, Chinese artisans were checking their work with sliding calipers decimally graduated. Chinese mathematical thought was always deeply algebraic, not geometrical, and in the Sung and Yüan the Chinese led the world in the solution of equations, so that the triangle called by the name of Blaise Pascal was already old in China in +1300. We often find examples of this sort. The system of linked and pivoted rings which we know as the Cardan suspension, after Jerome Cardan, really ought to be called Ting Huan's suspension because it had been used in China a whole thousand years before the time of Cardan. As for astronomy, we need only say that the Chinese were the most persistent and accurate observers of celestial phenomena anywhere before the Renaissance. Although geometrical planetary theory did not develop among them, they conceived an enlightened cosmology, mepped the heavens using our modern coordinates (and not the Greek ones), and kept records of eclipses, comets, novae, meteors, sun-spots, and so on that are used by radio astronomers down to this very day. A brilliant development of astronomical instruments also occurred, including the invention of the equatorial mounting and the clock drive, and this development was in close dependence on the contemporary capacities of Chinese engineers. I have already mentioned seismology as a case in point because the world's first seismograph was built by Chang Hêng, as we all know, probably in about +130.

Three branches of physics were particularly well developed in ancient and mediaeval China: optics, acoustics, and magnetism. This was in striking contrast with the West, where mechanics and dynamics were relatively advanced but magnetic phenomena almost unknown. Yet China and Europe differed most profoundly perhaps in the great debate between continuity and discontinuity; just as Chinese mathematics was always algebraic rather than geometrical, so Chinese physics was faithful to a prototypic wave theory and perennially averse to atoms. There is no doubt that the Buddhist philosophers were always bringing in knowledge of the Vai eshika theories about atoms, but nobody in China was willing to listen. The Chinese stuck to the ideas of universal motion in a continuous medium, action at a distance, and the wavelike motions of the Yin and Yang.

One most significant point is that although the Chinese of the Chou and Han, contemporary with the Greeks, probably did not rise to such heights as they, nevertheless in later centuries there was nothing at all in China corresponding to the Dark Ages in Europe. This fact is demonstrated well by the sciences of geography and cartography. Although the Chinese knew of discoidal cosmographic world maps, they were never dominated by them. Quantitative cartography began in China with Chang Hêng and P'ei Hsiu at about the time that Ptolemy's work was falling into oblivion in the West, indeed soon after his death, and it continued steadily with a consistent use of the rectangular grid right down to the coming of the Jesuits in the 17th century. Chinese geographers were also very advanced in the field of survey methods and the making of relief maps.

Mechanical engineering, and indeed engineering in general, were fields in which classical Chinese culture scored special triumphs. Both forms of efficient harness for equine animals, a problem of link-work essentially, originated in the Chinese culture area. There, too, water power was first used for industry, about the same time as in the West, in the + 1st or –1st century, not, however, for grinding cereals, but rather for the operation of metallurgical bellows. And that brings up something else, because the development of iron and steel technology in China constitutes a veritable epic, with the mastery of iron casing occurring some fifteen centuries before its achievement in Europe. Contrary to the usual ideas, mechanical clockwork began, not in early Renaissance Europe but in T'ang China, in spite of the highly agrarian character of East Asian civilisation. Civil engineering also shows many extraordinary achievements, notably iron-chain suspension bridges, and the first of all segmental-arch bridges, the magnificent one built by Li Ch'un in + 610. Hydraulic engineering was always prominent in China on account of the necessity to control waterways and to develop river conservation, defence against floods and drought, irrigation for agriculture, and the transport of tax grain.

In martial technology the Chinese people also showed notable inventiveness. The first appearance of gunpowder occurred in China in the + 9th century, and from + 1000 onward there was a vigorous development of explosive weapons some three centuries before they were known in the West. The first appearance of a cannon in Europe is the bombard depicted in the Bodleian Library manuscript of + 1327, but you have to go back a good three centuries before that to see the beginning of the affair in China. We know now that every single stage from the first development of the gunpowder formula to the development of the iron-barrel cannon, using the propellant force of gunpowder, was gone through in the Chinese culture area before it ever came to the Arabs or to Europe at all. Probably the key invention was that of the fire lance, the *huo ch'iang*, which we now know took place in the middle of the + 10th century. That was a device in which a rocket composition was enclosed in a bamboo tube and used as a dose-combat weapon. From this thing derived, we have no doubt, all subsequent rockets, barrel guns, and cannon of whatever material constructed.

Turning from the military to civilian, other aspects of technology have great importance, especially that of silk, in which the Chinese people excelled so early. Here the mastery of textile fibres of extremely long staple appears to have led to several fundamental engineering inventions, for example, the first development in any civilisation of the driving belt and the chain drive. It is also possible to say that the first appearance of the standard method of inter-conversion of rotary and longitudinal motion, which found its great use in the early steam engines in Europe, came up also in connection with the metallurgical blowing-engines referred to already. If one is going in for epigrams, I ought to have mentioned when speaking of magnetism and of the magnetic compass that in China people were worrying about the nature of the declination (why the needle does not usually point exactly to the north) before Europeans had even heard about the polarity.

Nor was there any backwardness in the biological field either, because we find many agricultural inventions arising form an early time. There are texts which parallel those of the Romans, like Varro and Columella from a similar period; and one could take a very remarkable example from the history of biological plant protection. I do not know how many of us are conscious of the fact that the first case of insects' being set to destroy other insects, and so work in the service of man, occurred in China: in the *Nan Fang Ts'ao Mu Chuang* written about + 340, there is a description of how the farmers in Kuangtung and the southern provinces in general who grow oranges in groves go to the marketplace at the right time of the year and purchase little bags containing a particular king of ant, which they then hang on the orange-trees. These ants completely keep down all the mites and spiders, and other insect pests, which would otherwise damage the orange crop. As a matter of fact, in China today very big things are going on in connection with biological plant protection. One of the experts in this field visited us in Cambridge the other day, and we could pick the *Nan Fang Ts'ao Mu Chuang* off the shelf and show her what her ancestors had done.

Medicine, again, is a field which it is rather absurd to bring up in a couple of minutes, because one could speak not for one hour, but many hours, on the subject of the history of medicine in China. It represents a field which aroused the intense interest of Chinese people all through the ages, and one which was developed by their special genius along lines perhaps more different from those of Europe than in any other case. I think one might just refer, as an example, to the fact that people in China were free form the prejudices against mineral remedies which were so striking in the West. They needed no Paracelsus to awaken them from their Galenical slumbers, because they never participated in such slumbers; in other words, the Pên Ts'ao books (the pharmaceutical natural histories) form the earliest times contained mineral and animal, as well as botanical, remedies. This was something that Europe did not have, bcause Galen laid such emphasis on plant drugs that people were rather afraid to use minerals or any animal substance. And then of course there was the development of acupuncture and moxa, which are the subjects of a special lecture later in this series.

Coming now to the further examination of some of the great contrasts between China and Europe, I would like to stress that the *philosophia parennis* of China was an organic materialism. You can illustrate this from the pronouncements of philosophers and scientific thinkers of every epoch. Metaphysical idealism was never dominant in China, nor did the mechanical view of the world exist in Chinese thought. The organicist conception in which every phenomenon was connected with every other according to a hierarchical order was universal among Chinese thinkers. In some respects this philosophy of Nature may have helped the development of Chinese scientific thinking. For example, that the lode stone should point to the north, to the North Star, the pole star, the *pei chi*, was not so surprising if one was already convinced that there was an organic wholeness in the cosmos itself. In other words, the Chinese were *a priori* inclined to field theories, and this might well account also for the fact that people in China arrived so early at correct ideas of the cause of the tides of the sea. As early as the San Kuo (Three Kingdoms, 220–265) period, one can find remarkable statements of action at a distance taking place without any physical contact across vast distances of space.

We mentioned before that Chinese mathematical thought and practice were invariably algebraic, not geometrical. No deductive Euclidean geometry developed spontaneously in Chinese culture, and that was, no doubt, somewhat inhibitory to the advances the Chinese were able to make in optics—in which study, on the other hand, they were never handicapped by the rather, absurd Greek idea that rays were sent forth by the eye. Euclidean geometry was probably brought to China in the Yuan period, but in did not take root until the arrival of the Jesuits. Nevertheless it is very remarkable that the lack of Euclidean geometry did not prevent the successful realisation of the great engineering inventions, including the highly complicated ones in which astronomical demonstrational and observational equipment was driven by water power through the use of elaborate gearing. Again, there was the interconversion of rotary and longitudinal motion already mentioned.

# The Enlightenment Project and the Liberal Agenda

The term "Enlightenment," when associated with a historical era, usually refers to the period between the late seventeenth century and the end of the eighteenth century when a small but influential number of men in Europe, England, and America took on the task of attempting philosophically to consolidate some of the intellectual meanings of the scientific advances of the seventeenth century. It is often assumed that their outlook was religiously skeptical and aggressively rationalistic, but this is to misinterpret not only their general intentions but also their way of thinking. Far from repudiating religion outright, they were more inclined to attempt to reconcile a "scientific" perspective with a loosely Christian one. Their enemies were theological dogma, religious absolutism, and ignorance, their allies open-mindedness, intellectual curiosity, and a commitment to critical reflection. It is also generally supposed that many of the intellectual values associated with this movement—belief in freedom, religious tolerance, respect for human rights, commitment to reason—were essentially Western as well as modern, but, as we shall see, this is far from the truth.

Immanuel Kant summarized the motto of the Enlightenment with the phrase "Dare to know." Daring to know required moral courage; it also reflected a willingness to put aside, or at least to suspend, prejudice for the sake of using reason to obtain knowledge. But faith in reason did not mean abandoning belief for the sake of thought, much less regarding thought as infallible. It simply meant that one should turn for whatever one believes not primarily to personal revelation, sacred scriptures, or ecclesiastical authorities but to the mind itself. The key to knowledge, as the French philosopher Rene Descartes put it, is not certainty but rather doubt. It also meant that in determining what should constitute the basis of one's beliefs, precedence should be given to those things that belong to the realm of experience, such as nature, history, and the world around us, and not to those, like mystery and superstition, that lie beyond it. As Voltaire, another French philosopher suggested, "those who can make you believe absurdities can make you commit atrocities." Finally, it meant that the critical use of reason, together with a willingness to learn from past experience, could produce progress across many spheres of life. Hence Thomas Jefferson's resistance in his draft of the American Declaration of Independence to "every form of tyranny over the mind of man."

The implications of the Enlightenment way of thinking were to have profound effects that extended far beyond the period associated with their development. Taken over particularly in the United States by the leaders of the American Revolution, such ideas encouraged a more democratic form of governance based in part on a more liberal conception of the individual and of the state. No one in the West was more responsible for linking these ideas than the English philosopher John Locke.

Locke's aim was to rethink the basis of political society by applying his theory of the mind to the construction of the state. According to Locke, there are no innate ideas already implanted in the brain, like the truths of revelation or the image of God, which can be awakened through the experience of salvation or regeneration. The human brain is instead a blank slate or *tabula rasa* on which experience writes the content derived from our senses. What is innate in the state of nature are merely certain rights to "life, health, liberty, and possessions," as Locke described them (Jefferson then modified in the Declaration of Independence to "life, liberty, and happiness"), and it is the responsibility of the state to protect them. But when the state fails to perform this function, as in the case of the British crown in the American colonies, it then becomes incumbent on the bearers of those rights to take matters into their own hands and overthrow that illegitimate government for the sake of achieving them.

Such liberal assumptions about the purpose of the state were subsequently to receive significant further support from the great Scottish political economist Adam Smith. Smith provided a rationale for linking political liberty with social and economic liberty by positing that Locke's reasoning defined individuals as "free agents." Agents or individuals could be defined as free because they were able, or should be able, to act in their own self-interest. But if individuals were free to act in their own self-interest, this should contribute, Smith reasoned, not merely to their own good but also to the public good. Smith was not interested in justifying selfishness for its own sake but rather in explaining how the public interest could be served even if individuals exercised their freedom to act in their own behalf. But when Smith added that self-interest would produce public and not just individual good "as if guided by an invisible hand," he opened the door to the later caricature of his entire theoretical attempt to show how the individual pursuit of wealth carefully managed could benefit everyone. Ever after his famous "invisible hand" theory could be used to justify subsequent arguments that have continued down to the present to justify claims about everything from the inherent beneficence of capitalism itself to the market's self-correcting ability to balance supply and demand.

And so was filled in the liberal agenda. The state essentially amounted to all the individuals who belonged to it—in Jefferson's time essentially propertied men, in ours all those citizens given the right to vote and presumably subject to taxes. All such individuals, being free agents, are held to be responsible for themselves. All restraints on their self-fulfillment, and particularly economic restraints, should be abolished because freedom and liberty are liberalism's classical ideals. And governmental powers should be employed wherever possible to prevent or inhibit governmental interference and regulation.

But wait just a moment! Don't these policies now sound like conservative rather than liberal ones? Isn't it now the case that conservatives and not liberals favor the restriction of governmental authority in behalf of protecting the rights of states and individuals? The story of how the liberal agenda became in the later nineteenth century a conservative agenda is a long one, but it turns on the way individualism and self-interest could become partisan, self-regarding, even predatory, leading almost a century and a half later to the socio-economic ideology now known as neo-liberalism. Neo-liberalism, at least in its more extreme forms, maps classic liberal ideals onto an economic program designed to deregulate the economy, liberalize trade and industry, privatize state-owned enterprises, provide massive tax cuts for the rich, reduce social welfare, and down-size government.

It is difficult to generalize about the European, and latterly American, Enlightenment without minimizing its various roots, its irregular progress, and its numerous controversies, but if there is one thing more than any other which accounted for its success as an intellectual enterprise, it is that it generalized, as the great British historian, J. M. Roberts, once said, "the critical attitude." Such an achievement is easy to underestimate because the Enlightenment has often been portrayed as a movement responsible for everything from instrumentalizing reason itself to using reason as a mask for power and domination. While it was certainly possible for Enlightenment thinkers to overstress the importance of critical reason, as in Pierre Bayle's insistence that all religious dogma not in accordance with reason should be refuted, the questioning of authority and the pursuit of intellectual and scientific curiosity were key elements of the Enlightenment's achievement. So, too, was the fact that it was the product not of "professionals" or of "experts" but for the most part of ordinary members of the thoughtful public. Calling themselves "philosophes" but working more often out of salons than of laboratories, they did as much of their mental labor by means of discussion as by means of experimentation. And thus was born our modern notion of the "intellectual" as someone obliged to put the mind in the service of constructive critique.

While John Locke and Alexander Newton were the presiding deities of the early Enlightenment, its greatest achievement by the mid-eighteenth century may have been the enormous compendium of knowledge it produced called simply *Encyclopedie* that was published in twenty-one volumes between 1751 and 1765 by Denis Diderot and Jon le Rond D'Alembert. Described by one of its authors as a "war machine" because of its ambition to convert the values of the Enlightenment into those of all civilized society, it held out the possibility of a genuine revolution. But the *Encyclopedie* was forced to operate within the restrictive structures of France's *ancient regime*, which meant that some of the Enlightenment's greatest accomplishments would have to await the future.

One of the questions this raises for Amartya Sen, the Nobel Prize winning economic theorist and moral philosopher, is whether the Enlightenment, in its promulgation of such values as tolerance, equality, and freedom, was a strictly European phenomenon. Whatever Westerners may believe, and against the arguments of Asians such as Singapore's former prime minister and defender of Asian values, Lee Kuan Yew, Sen is of the opinion that this is nonsense. As early as the third century B.C.E., the Indian emperor Ashoka, dismayed at the destruction he had perpetrated in one of his battles against an enemy, issued what deserve to be called Edits of Toleration. Discerning the necessity of standards for public ethics, he himself converted to Buddhism and championed forms of the good life that included egalitarianism and respect for the practices of others.

Another of Sen's witnesses is the Mogul Emperor Akbar who ruled from 1556 to 1605 C.E. and advocated various human rights including freedom of worship and religious practice. Sen's reference to these two Asian emperors who ruled nearly two thousand years apart is not intended to demonstrate that a concern with human dignity and rights existed long before the arrival of the Enlightenment but rather to show that components of these ideas were nonetheless widely respected in these distant ages and different cultures even if in different forms. Hence for Amartya Sen the essential issue related to the question of the Enlightenment's Eurocentricity is neither one of priority—which civilization got there first—or commitment—which civilization placed the strongest emphasis on these values—but cultural diversity—the recognition that many of these values belonged to various civilizations that came to affirm them in their own ways.

# Human Rights Asian Values

 Amartya Sen

## I.

In 1776, just when the Declaration of Independence was being adopted in this country, Thomas Paine complained, in Common Sense, that Asia had "long expelled" freedom. In this lament, Paine saw Asia in company with much of the rest of the world (America, he hoped, would be different): "Freedom hath been hunted round the globe. Asia and Africa have long expelled her. Europe regards her as a stranger and England hath given her freedom to depart." For Paine, political freedom and democracy were valuable anywhere, though they were being violated nearly everywhere.

The violation of freedom and democracy in different parts of the world continues today, if not as comprehensively as in Paine's time. There is a difference, though. A new class of arguments have emerged that deny the universal importance of these freedoms. The most prominent of these conventions is the claim that Asian values do not regard freedom to be important in the way that it is regarded in the West. Given this difference in value systems— the argument runs—Asia must be faithful to its own system of philosophical and political priorities.

Cultural differences and value differences between Asia and the West were stressed by several official delegations at the World Conference on Human Rights in Vienna in 1993. The foreign minister of Singapore warned that "universal recognition of the ideal of human rights can be harmful if universalism is used to deny or mask the reality of diversity." The Chinese delegation played a leading role in emphasizing the regional differences, and in making sure that the prescriptive framework adopted in the declarations made room for regional diversity. The Chinese foreign minister even put on record the proposition, apparently applicable in China and elsewhere, that "Individuals must put the states' rights before their own."

I want to examine the thesis that Asian values are less supportive of freedom and more concerned with order and discipline, and that the claims of human rights in the areas of political and civil liberties, therefore, are less relevant and less appropriate in Asia than in the West. The defense of authoritarianism in Asia on the grounds of the special nature of Asian values calls for historical scrutiny, to which I shall presently turn. But there is also a different justification of authoritarian governance in Asia that has received attention recently. It argues for authoritarian governance in

An earlier version of this essay was given as the Morganthau Memorial Lecture at the Carnegie Council on Ethics and International Affairs on May 1, 1997. © 1997 Carnegie Council on Ethics and International Affairs.

the interest of economic development. Lee Kuan Yew, the former prime minister of Singapore and a great champion of the idea of "Asian values," has defended authoritarian arrangements on the ground of their alleged effectiveness in promoting economic success.

Does authoritarianism really work so well? It is certainty true that some relatively authoritarian states (such as South Korea, Lee's Singapore, and post-reform China) have had faster rates of economic growth than many less authoritarian ones (such as India, Costa Rica or Jamaica). But the "Lee hypothesis" is based on very selective and limited information, rather than on any general statistical testing over the wide-ranging data that are available. We cannot really take the high economic growth of China or South Korea in Asia a "proof positive" that authoritarianism does better in promoting economic growth—any more than we can draw the opposite conclusion on the basis of the fact that Botswana, the fastest growing African country (and one of the fastest growing countries in the world), has been an oasis of democracy in that unhappy continent. Much depends on the precise circumstances.

There is little general evidence, in fact, that authoritarian governance and the suppression of political and civil rights are really beneficial in encouraging economic development. The statistical picture is much more complicated. Systematic empirical studies give no real support to the claim that there is a general conflict between political rights and economic performances. The directional linkage seems to depend on many other circumstances, and while some statistical investigations note a weakly negative relation, others find a strongly positive one. On balance, the hypothesis that there is no relation between freedom and prosperity in either direction is hard to reject. Since political liberty has a significance of its own, the case for it remains untarnished.

There is also a more basic issue of research methodology. We must not only look at statistical connections, we must examine also the causal processes that are involved in economic growth and development. The economic policies and circumstances that led to the success of east Asian economies are by now reasonably well understood. While different empirical studies have varied in emphasis, there is by now a fairly agreed-upon list of "helpful policies," and they include openness to competition, the use of international markets, a high level of literacy and education, successful land reforms, and public provision of incentives for investment, exporting, and industrialization. There is nothing whatsoever to indicate that any of these policies is inconsistent with greater democracy, that any one of them had to be sustained by the elements of authoritarianism that happened to be present in South Korea or Singapore or China. The recent Indian experience also shows that what is needed for generating faster economic growth is a friendlier economic climate rather than a harsher political system.

It is also important, in this context, to look at the connect on between political and civil rights, on the one hand, and the prevention of major disasters, on the other. Political and civil rights give people the opportunity to draw attention forcefully to general needs and to demand appropriate public action. The governmental response to acute suffering often depends on the pressure that is put on it, and this is where the exercise of political rights (voting, criticizing, protesting, and so on) can make a real difference. I have discussed (in these pages and in my book *Resources, Values, and Development*) the remarkable fact that, in the terrible history of famines in the world, no substantial famine has ever occurred in any independent and democratic country with a relatively free press. Whether we look at famines in Sudan, Ethiopia, Somalia, or other dictatorial regimes, or in the Soviet

Union in the 1930s, or in China from 1958 to 1961 (at the failure of the Great Leap Forward, when between 23 and 30 million people died), or currently in North Korea, we do not find exceptions to this rule. (It is true that Ireland was part of democratic Britain during its famine of the 1840s, but the extent of London's political dominance over the Irish was so strong—and the social distance so great and so old, as illustrated by Spenser's severely unfriendly description of the Irish in the sixteenth century—that the English rule over Ireland was, for all practical purposes, a colonial rule.)

While this connection is clearest in the case of famine prevention, the positive role of political and civil rights applies to the prevention of economic and social disasters generally. When things go fine and everything is routinely good, this consequence of democracy may not be sorely missed. But it comes into its own when things get fouled up, for one reason or another. Then the political incentives provided by democratic governance acquire great practical value. To concentrate only on economic incentives (which the market system provides) while ignoring political incentives (which democratic systems provide) is to opt for a deeply unbalanced set of ground rules.

## II.

I turn now to the nature and the relevance of Asian values. This is not an easy exercise, for various reasons. The size of Asia is itself a problem. Asia is where about 50 percent of the world's population lives. What can we take to be the values of so vast a region, with so much diversity? It is important to state at the outset that there are no quintessential values that separate the Asians as a group from people in the rest of the world and which fit all parts of this immensely large and heterogeneous population. The temptation to see Asia as a single unit reveals a distinctly Eurocentric perspective. Indeed, the term "the Orient," which was widely used for a long time to mean essentially what Asia means today, referred to the positional vision of Europe, as it contemplated the direction of the rising sun.

In practice, the advocates of "Asian values" have tended to look primarily at east Asia as the region of their particular applicability. The generalization about the contrast between the West and Asia often concentrates on the land to the east of Thailand, though there is an even more ambitious claim that the rest of Asia is rather "similar." Lee Kuan Yew outlines "the fundamental difference between Western concepts of society and government and East Asian concepts" by explaining that "when I say East Asians, I mean Korea, Japan, China, Vietnam, as distinct from Southeast Asia, which is a mix between the Sinic and the Indian, though Indian culture itself emphasizes similar values."

In fact, even east Asia itself has much diversity, and there are many variations to be found between Japan and China and Korea and other parts of east Asia. Various cultural influences from inside and outside this region have affected human lives over the history of this large territory. These influences still survive in a variety of ways. Thus, my copy of Houghton Mifflin's *Almanac* describes the region of the 124 million Japanese in the following way: 112 million Shintoist, 93 million Buddhist. Cultures and traditions overlap in regions such as east Asia and even within countries such as Japan or China or Korea, and attempts at generalization about "Asian values" (with forceful and often brutal implications for masses of people in this region with diverse faiths, convictions, and commitments) cannot but be extremely crude. Even the 2.8 million people of Singapore have vast variations of cultural and historical traditions, despite the fact that the conformism that characterizes its political leadership and the official interpretation of Asian values is very powerful at this time.

Still, the recognition of heterogeneity in the traditions of Asia does not settle the issue of the presence or the absence of a commitment to individual freedom and political liberty in Asian culture. The traditions extant in Asia differ among themselves, but they may share some common characteristics. It has been asserted, for example, that the treatment of elderly members of the family (say, aged parents) is more supportive in Asian countries than in the West. It is possible to argue about this claim, but there would be nothing very peculiar if some similarities of this kind or other kinds were to obtain across the diverse cultures of Asia. Diversities need not apply to every field. The question that has to be asked, rather, is whether Asian countries share the common feature of being skeptical of freedom and liberty, while emphasizing order and discipline. The advocates of Asian particularism allow internal heterogeneity within Asia, but in the context of a shared mistrust of the claims of political liberalism.

Authoritarian lines of reasoning often receive indirect backing from certain strains of thought in the West itself. There is clearly a tendency in America and Europe to assume, if only implicitly, the primacy of political freedom and democracy as a fundamental and ancient feature of Western culture—one not to be easily found in Asia. There is a contrast, it is alleged, between the authoritarianism implicit in, say, Confucianism and the respect for liberty and autonomy allegedly deeply rooted in Western liberal culture. Western promoters of personal and political freedom in the non-Western world often see such an analysis as a necessary preliminary to bringing Western values to Asia and Africa.

In all this, there is a substantial tendency to extrapolate backwards from the present. Values that the European enlightenment and other relatively recent developments have made Western heritage as it was experienced over millennia. In answer to the question, "at what date, in what circumstances, the notion of individual liberty . . . first became explicit in the West," Isaiah Berlin has noted: "I have found no convincing evidence of any clear formulation of it in the ancient world." This view has been disputed by Orlando Patterson among others. He points to particular features in Western culture, particularly in Greece and Rome and in the tradition of Christianity, which indicate the presence of selective championing of individual liberty.

The question that does not get adequately answered—it is scarcely even asked—is whether similar elements are absent in other cultures. Berlin's thesis concerns the notion of individual freedom as we now understand it, and the absence of "any clear formulation" of this can certainly co-exist with the advocacy of selected *components* of the comprehensive notion that makes up the contemporary idea of individual liberty. Such components are found in the Greco-Roman world and in the world of Jewish and Christian thought. But such an acknowledgment has to be followed up by examining whether these components are absent elsewhere—that is in non-Western cultures. We have to search for the parts rather than the whole in the West and in Asia and elsewhere.

To illustrate this point, consider the idea that personal freedom for all is important for a good society. This claim can be seen as being composed of two distinct elements: (1) the value of personal freedom: that personal freedom is important and should be guaranteed for those who "matter" in a good society and (2) the equality of freedom: that everyone matters and personal freedom should be guaranteed on a shared basis, for all. Aristotle wrote much in support of the former proposition, but in his exclusion of women and slaves he did little to defend the latter. Indeed, the championing of equality in this form is of quite recent origin. Even in a society stratified according to class and caste, freedom could be valued for the privileged—such as the Mandarins and the Brahmins—in much the same way that freedom was valued for non-slave men in corresponding Greek conceptions of a good society.

Or consider another useful distinction, between (1) the value of toleration: that there must be toleration of diverse beliefs, commitments and actions of different people; and (2) the equality of tolerance: that the toleration that is offered to some must be reasonably offered to all (except when tolerance of some will lead to intolerance for others). Again, arguments for some tolerance can be seen plentifully in earlier Western writings, without being supplemented by arguments for universal tolerance. The roots of modern democratic and liberal ideas can be sought in terms of constitutive elements, rather than as a whole.

In the terms of such an analysis, the question has to be asked whether these constitutive components can be found in Asian writings in the way they can be found in Western thought. The presence of these components must not be confused with the absence of the opposite, that is, with the presence of ideas and doctrines that clearly *do not* emphasize freedom and tolerance. The championing of order and discipline can be found in Western classics as well. Indeed, it is by no means clear to me that Confucius is more authoritarian than, say, Plato or Augustine. The real issue is not whether these non-freedom perspectives are present in Asian traditions, but whether the freedom-oriented perspectives are absent from them.

This is where the diversity of Asian value systems becomes quite central. An obvious example is the role of Buddhism, as a form of thought. In Buddhist tradition, great importance is attached to freedom, and the traditions of earlier Indian thinking to which Buddhist thoughts relate allow much room for volition and free choice. Nobility of conduct has to be achieved in freedom, and even the ideas of liberation (such as *moksha*) include this feature. The presence of these elements in Buddhist thought does not obliterate the importance of the discipline emphasized by Confucianism, but it would be a mistake to take Confucianism to be the only tradition in Asia—or in China. Since so much of the contemporary authoritarian interpretation of Asian values concentrates on Confucianism, this diversity is particularly worth emphasizing.

Indeed, the reading of Confucianism that is now standard among authoritarian champions of Asian values does less than justice to Confucius's own teachings, to which Simon Leys has recently drawn attention. Confucius did not recommend blind allegiance to the state. When Zilu asks him "how to serve a prince," Confucius replies: "Tell him the truth even if it offends him." The censors in Singapore or Beijing would take a very different view. Confucius is not averse to practical caution and tact, but he does not forgo the recommendation to oppose a bad government. "When the [good] way prevails in the state, speak boldly and act boldly. When the state has lost the way, act boldly and speak softly."

Indeed, Confucius clearly points to the fact that the two pillars of the imagined edifice of Asian values, loyalty to family and obedience to the state, can be severely in conflict with each other. The Governor of She told Confucius "Among my people, there is a man of unbending integrity: when his father stole a sheep, he denounced him." To this, Confucius replied: "Among my people, men of integrity do things differently: a father covers up for his son, a son covers up for his father—and there is integrity in what they do."

Elias Canetti observed that, in understanding the teachings of Confucius, we have to examine not only what he says, but what he does not say. The subtlety involved in what is often called "the silence of Confucius" seems to have escaped his austere modern interpreters who tend to assume that what is not explicitly supported must be implicitly forbidden. It is not my contention that Confucius was a democrat, or a great champion of freedom and dissent. Yet there is certainly good reason to question the monolithic image of an authoritarian Confucius that is championed by the contemporary advocates of Asian values.

# III

If we turn our attention from China to the Indian subcontinent, we are in no danger of running into a hard-to-interpret silence. It is difficult to out-do the Indian traditions in arguing endlessly and elaborately. India not only has the largest religious literature in the world, it also has the largest volume of atheistic and materialistic writings among the ancient civilizations. The Indian epic *Mahabharata*, which is often compared to the *Iliad* or the *Odyssey*, is in fact seven times as long as the *Iliad* and the *Odyssey* put together. In a well-known Bengali poem written in the nineteenth century by the religious and social leader Ram Mohan Ray, the horror of death is described thus: "Just imagine how terrible it will be on the day you die. Others will go on speaking, but you will not be able to respond."

This fondness for disputation, for discussing things at leisure and at length, is itself somewhat in tension with the order and discipline championed in allegedly Asian values. But the content of what has been written also displays a variety of views on freedom, tolerance, and equality. In many ways, the most interesting articulation of the need for tolerance on an egalitarian basis can be found in the writings of the emperor Ashoka in the third century B.C. Ashoka commanded a larger Indian empire than any other Indian king (including the Moghuls, and even the Raj, if we omit the native states that the British let be). He turned his attention to public ethics and enlightened politics after being horrified by the carnage that he witnessed in his own victorious battle against the king of Kalinga, in what is now Orissa.

The emperor converted to Buddhism. He helped to make it a world religion by sending emissaries abroad with the Buddhist message to East and West, and he covered the country with stone inscriptions describing forms of good life and the nature of good government. The inscriptions give a special importance to tolerance of diversity. The edict (now numbered XII) at Erragudi, for example, puts the issue thus:

. . . a man must not do reverence to his own sect or disparage that of another man without reason. Depreciation should be for specific reason only, because the sects of other people all deserve reverence for one reason or another.

By this acting, a man exalts his own sect, and at the same time does service to the sects of other people. By acting contrariwise, a man hurts his own sect, and does disservice to the sects of other people. For he who does reverence to his own sect while disparaging the sects of others wholly from attachment to his own, with intent to enhance the splendour of his own sect, in reality by such conduct inflicts the severest injury on his own sect.

The importance of tolerance is emphasized in these edicts from the third century B.C.—their importance as public policy by the government and as advice for the behavior of citizens toward each other.

About the domain and the jurisdiction of tolerance, Ashoka was a universalist. He demanded this for all, including those whom he described as "forest people," the tribal population living in pre-agricultural economic formations. Condemning his own conduct before his conversion, Ashoka notes that in the war in Kalinga "men and animals numbering one hundred and fifty thousands were carried away [captive] from that [defeated] kingdom." He goes on to state that the slaughter or the taking of prisoners of even a hundredth or thousandth part of all those people who were slain or died or were carried away [captive] at that time in Kalinga is now considered very deplorable" by him. Indeed, he proceeds to assert that now he believes that "even if [a person] should wrong him, that [offense] would be forgiven if it is possible to forgive it." The object of his government is described as "non-injury, restraint, impartiality, and mild behavior" applied "to all creatures."

Ashoka's championing of egalitarianism and universal tolerance may appear un-Asian to some commentators, but his views are firmly rooted in lines of analysis already in vogue in intellectual Buddhist circles in India in the preceding centuries. In this context, however, it is interesting to look at another author whose treatise on governance and political economy was also profoundly influential. I refer to Kautilya, the author of *Arthashastra*, which can be translated as "economic science," though it is at least as much concerned with practical politics as with economics. Kautilya was a contemporary of Aristotle. He lived in the fourth century B.C., and worked as a senior minister of emperor Chandragupta Maurya, Ashoka's grandfather, who had established the large Maurya empire across the subcontinent

Kautilya's writings are often cited as proof that freedom and tolerance were not valued in the Indian classical tradition. There are two aspects of the impressively detailed account of economics and politics to be found in *Arthashastra* that tend to suggest the view that there is no support here for a liberal democracy. First, Kautilya is a consequentialist of quite a narrow kind. While the objectives of promoting the happiness of the subjects and the order in the kingdom are strongly backed up by detailed policy advice, the king is seen as a benevolent autocrat, whose power, albeit to do good, is to be maximized through proper organization. Thus, *Arthashastra* presents ideas and suggestions on such practical subjects as famine prevention and administrative effectiveness that remain relevant even today—more than 2,000 years later—and at the same time it advises the king about how to get his way, if necessary through the violation of the freedom of his adversaries.

Second, Kautilya seems to attach little importance to political or economic equality, and his vision of the good society is strongly stratified according to lines of class and caste. Even though his objective of promoting happiness applies to all, his other objective clearly have an inegalitarian form and content. There is an obligation to provide the less fortunate members of society the support that they need for escaping misery and enjoying life—Kautilya specifically identifies as the duty of the king to "provide the orphans, the aged, the infirm, the afflicted, and the helpless with maintenance," along with providing "subsistence to helpless women when they are carrying and also to the [newborn] children they give birth to"; but this obligation is very far from valuing the freedom of these people to decide how they wish to live. The tolerance of heterodoxy is not to be found here. Indeed, there is very little tolerance in Kautilya, except tolerance for the upper sections of the community.

What, then, do we conclude from this? Certainly Kautilya is no democrat, no egalitarian, no general promoter of everyone's freedom. And yet, when it comes to the characterization of what the most favored people—the upper classes—should get, freedom figures quite prominently. The denial of personal liberty of the upper classes (the so-called "Ayra") is seen as unacceptable. Indeed, regular penalties, some of them heavy, are specified for the taking of such adults or children in indenture—even though the slavery of the existing slaves is seen as perfectly acceptable. To be sure, we do not find in Kautilya anything like Aristotle's clear articulation of the importance of free exercise of capability. But the focus on freedom is clear enough in Kautilya as far as the upper classes are concerned. It contrasts with the governmental duties to the lower orders, which take the paternalistic form of state assistance for the avoidance of acute deprivation and misery. Still, insofar as a view of the good life emerges in all this, it is an ideal that is entirely consistent with a freedom-valuing ethical system. Its domain is limited, to be sure; but this is not wildly different from the Greek concern with free men as opposed to slaves or women.

I have been discussing in some detail the political ideas and practical reason presented by two forceful, but very different, expositions in India respectively in the fourth and third centuries B.C., because their ideas have influenced later Indian writings. I do not want to give the impression that all Indian political commentators took lines of approach similar to Ashoka's or Kautilya's. Quite the contrary. There are many positions, before and after Kautilya and Ashoka, that contradict their respective claims, just as there are others that are more in line with Ashoka or Kautilya.

The importance of tolerance, even the need for its universality is eloquently expressed in different media: in Shudraka's drama, in Akbar's political pronouncements, and in Kabir's poetry, to name just a few examples. The presence of these contributions does not entail the absence of opposite arguments and recommendations. The point, rather, is that the heterogeneity of Indian traditions contains a variety of views and reasonings, and they include, in different ways, arguments in favor of tolerance, of freedom, and even (in the case of Ashoka) of equality at a very basic level.

Among the powerful expositors and practitioners of tolerance of diversity in India, of course, we must count the great Mogul, emperor Akbar, who reigned between 1556 and 1605. Again, we are not dealing here with a democrat. He was, instead, a powerful king who emphasized the acceptability of diverse forms of social and religious behavior, and who accepted human rights of various kinds, including freedom of worship and religious practice, that would not have been so easily tolerated in parts of Europe in Akbar's time.

Consider an example. As the year 1000 in the Muslim Hijra calendar was reached in 1591–92, there was excitement about it in Delhi and Agra (not unlike what is happening now, as the Christian year 2000 approaches). Akbar issued various enactments at this juncture of history, and these focused *inter alia* on religious tolerance, including the following:

> No man should be interfered with on account of religion. and anyone [is] to be allowed to go over to a religion he pleased. If a Hindu, when a child or otherwise, had been made a Muslim against his will, he is to be allowed, if he pleased, to go back to the religion of his fathers.

Again, the domain of tolerance, while neutral with respect to religion, was no universal in other respects—with respect to gender equality, or to equality between younger and older people. Akbar's enactment went on to argue for the forcible repatriation of a young Hindu woman to her father's family if she had abandoned it in pursuit of a Muslim lover. In the choice between supporting the young lovers and the young woman's Hindu father, old Akbar's sympathies are entirely with the father. Tolerance and equality at one level are combined with tolerance and inequality at another level. And yet the extent of general tolerance on matters of belief and practice is quite remarkable. It may not be irrelevant to note, especially in the light of the hard sell of "Western liberalism," that while Akbar was making these pronouncements on religious tolerance, the Inquisition was in full throttle in Europe.

## IV.

It is important to recognize that many of these historical leaders in Asia not only emphasized the importance of freedom and tolerance, they also had clear theories as to why this is the appropriate thing to do. This would apply very strongly to Ashoka and Akbar. Since the Islamic tradition is sometimes seen as being monolithic, this is particularly important to emphasize in the case of Akbar. Akbar was a Muslim emperor who was deeply interested in Hindu philosophy and culture, and he also took much interest in the beliefs and practices of other religions, including Christianity, Jainism and the Parsee faith. In fact, he also attempted to establish something of a synthetic religion for India, the *Din Nahi*, drawing on the different faiths in the country.

There is an interesting contrast here between Ashoka's and Akbar's forms of religious tolerance. Both stood for religious tolerance by the state, and both argued for tolerance as a virtue to be practiced by all. But Ashoka combined this with his own Buddhist pursuits (and tried to spread its "enlightenment" at home and abroad), while Akbar tried to combine the distinct religions of India, incorporating the "good points" of different religions. Akbar's court was filled with Hindu as well as Muslim intellectuals, artists, and musicians, and he tried in every way to be nonsectarian and fair in the treatment of his subjects.

It is also important to note that Akbar was not unique among the Moghul emperors in being tolerant. In many ways, the later Moghul emperor, the very intolerant Aurangzeb, who violated many of what we would now call the human rights of Hindus, was something of an exception to the Moghul rule. The exponents of Hindu politics in contemporary India often try to deny the tolerant nature of much of Moghul rule, but this tolerance was handsomely acknowledged by Hindu leaders of an earlier vintage. Sri Aurobindo, for example, who established the famous ashram in Pondicherry, specifically identified this aspect of the Moghul rule: "[T]he Mussulman domination ceased very rapidly to be a foreign rule. . . . The Moghul empire was a great and magnificent construction and an immense amount of political genius and talent was employed in its creation and maintenance. It was splendid, powerful and beneficent and it may be added, in spite of Aurangzeb's fanatical zeal, infinitely more liberal and tolerant in religion than any medieval or contemporary European kingdom or empire."

And, even in the case of Aurangzeb, it is useful to consider him not in isolation, but in his familial setting. For none of his immediate family seemed to have shared Aurangzeb's intolerance. Dara Shikoh, his elder brother, was much involved with Hindu philosophy and, with the help of some scholars, he prepared a Persian translation of some of the *Upanishads*, the ancient texts dating from about the eighth century B.C. In fact, Dara had much stronger claims to the Moghul throne than Aurangzeb, since he was the eldest and the favorite son of his father, the emperor Shah Jahan. Aurangzeb fought and killed his brother Dara, and imprisoned his father, Shah Jahan, for the rest of his life (leaving him, the builder of the Taj Mahal, to gaze at his creation in captivity).

Aurangzeb's son, also called Akbar, rebelled against his father in 1681 and joined hands in this enterprise with the Hindu kingdoms in Rajasthan and later the Marathas. (Akbar's rebellion was ultimately crushed by Aurangzeb.) While fighting from Rajasthan, Akbar wrote to his father, protesting his intolerance and his vilification of his Hindu friends. Indeed, the issue of the tolerance of differences was a subject of considerable discussion among the feuding parties. The father of the Maratha king, Raja Sambhaji, whom the young Akbar had joined, was none other than Shivaji, whom the present-day Hindu political activists treat as a super-hero, and after whom the intolerant Hindu party Shiv Sena is named.

Shivaji took quite a tolerant view of religious differences. As the Moghul historian Khafi Khan, no admirer of Shivaji in other respects, reports: "[Shivaji] made it a rule that wherever his followers were plundering, they should do no harm to the mosques, the book of God or the women of anyone. Whenever copy of the sacred Quran came into his hands, he treated it with respect, and gave it to some of his Mussulman followers." A very interesting letter to Aurangzeb on the subject of tolerance is attributed to Shivaji by some historians (such as Sir Jadunath Sarkar, the author of the classic *Shivaji and His Times*, published in 1919), though there are some doubts about this attribution. No matter who among Aurangzeb's Hindu contemporaries wrote this letter, the ideas in it are interesting. The text contrasts Aurangzeb's intolerance with the liberal policies of earlier Moghuls (Akbar, Jahangir, Shah Jahan), and then says: "If Your Majesty places any faith in those books by distinction called divine, you will there be instructed that God is the God of all mankind, not the God of Muslims alone. The Pagan and the Muslim are equally in His presence. . . . In fine, the tribute you demand from the Hindus is repugnant to justice."

The subject of tolerance was much discussed by many writers during this period of confrontation between the religious traditions and their associated politics. One of the earliest writers on this subject was the eleventh century Iranian writer Alberuni, who came to India with the invading army of Mahmood of Ghazni and recorded his revulsion at the atrocities committed by the invaders. He proceeded to study Indian society, culture, religion, and ideas (his translations of Indian mathematical and astronomical treatises were quite influential in the Arab world, which in turn was deeply influential on Western mathematics), and he also wrote on the subject of the intolerance of the unfamiliar.

> . . . in all manners and usages, [the Hindus] differ from us to such a degree as to frighten their children with us, with our dress, and our ways and customs, and as to declare us to be devil's breed, and our doings as the very opposite of all that is good and proper. By the bye, we must confess, in order to be just, that a similar depreciation of foreigners not only prevails among us and the Hindus, but is common to all nations towards each other.

The point of discussing all this now is to demonstrate the presence of conscious theorizing about tolerance and freedom in substantial and important parts of the Asian traditions. We could consider many more illustrations of this phenomenon from writings in early Arabic, Chinese, Indian and other cultures. Again, the championing of democracy and political freedom in the modern sense cannot be found in the pre-enlightenment tradition in any part of the world, West or East. What we have to investigate, instead, are the constitutes, the components, of this compound idea. It is the powerful presence of some of these elements—in non-Western as well as Western societies—that I have been emphasizing. It is hard to make sense of the view that the basic ideas underlying freedom and rights in a tolerant society are "Western" notions, and somehow alien to Asia, though that view has been championed by Asian authoritarians and Western chauvinists.

## V.

I would like to conclude with a rather different issue, which is sometimes linked to the debate about the nature and the reach of Asian values. The championing of Asian values is often associated with the need to resist Western hegemony. The linkage of the two issues, which has increasingly occurred in recent years, uses the political force of anticolonialism to buttress the assault on civil and political rights in post-colonial Asia.

This linkage, though quite artificial, can be rhetorically quite effective. Thus Lee Kuan Yew has emphasized the special nature of Asian values, and has made powerful use of the general case for resisting Western hegemony to bolster the argument for Asian particularism. The rhetoric has extended to the apparently defiant declaration that Singapore is "not a client state of America." This fact is certainly undeniable, and it is an excellent reason for cheer, but the question that has to be asked is what this has to do with the issue of human rights and political liberties in Singapore, or any other country in Asia.

The people whose political and other rights are involved in this debate are not citizens of the West, but of Asian countries. The fact that individual liberty may have been championed in Western writings, and even by some Western political leaders, can scarcely compromise the claim to liberty that people in Asia may otherwise possess. As a matter of fact, one may grumble, with reason, that the political leaders of Western countries take far too little interest in issues of freedom in the rest of the world. There is plenty of evidence that the Western governments have tended to give priority to the interest of their own citizens engaged in commerce with the Asian countries and to the pressures generated by business groups to be on good terms with the ruling governments in Asia. It is not that there has been more bark than bite; there has been very little bark, too. What Mao once described as a "paper tiger" looks increasingly like a paper mouse.

But even if this were not the case, and even if it were true that Western governments try to promote political and civil rights in Asia, how can that possibly compromise the status of the rights of Asians? In this context, the idea of "human rights" has to be properly understood. In the most general form, the notion of human rights builds on our shared humanity. These rights are not derived from citizenship in any country, or membership in any nation. They are taken as entitlements of every human being. These rights differ, therefore, from constitutionally created rights guaranteed for specified people (such as American citizens or French nationals). The human right of a person not to be tortured is affirmed independently of the country of which this person is a citizen, and also irrespective of what the government of that country—or any other country—wants to do. Of course, a government can dispute a person's legal right not to he tortured, but that will not amount to disputing what must be seen as the person's human right not to be tortured.

Since the conception of human rights transcends local legislation and the citizenship of the individual, the support for human rights can come from anyone—whether or not she is a citizen of the same country as the individual whose rights are threatened. A foreigner does not need the permission of a repressive government to try to help a person whose liberties are being violated. Indeed, insofar as human rights are seen as rights that any person has as a human being (and not as a citizen of any particular country), the reach of the corresponding duties can also include any human being (irrespective of citizenship).

This basic recognition does not suggest, of course, that everyone must intervene constantly in protecting and helping others. That may be both ineffective and unsettling. There is no escape from the need to employ practical reason in this field, any more than in any other field of human action. Ubiquitous interventionism is not particularly fruitful or attractive within a given nation, nor is it across national boundaries. There is no obligation to roam the four corners of the earth in search of liberties to protect. My claim is only that the barriers of nationality and citizenship do not preclude people from taking legitimate interest in the rights of others and even from assuming some duties related to them. The moral and political examination that is central to determining how one should act applies across national boundaries, and not merely within them.

To conclude, the so-called Asian values that are invoked to justify authoritarianism are not especially Asian in any significant sense. Nor is it easy to see how they could be made, by the mere force of rhetoric, into an Asian cause against the West. The people whose rights are being disputed are Asians, and,. no matter what the West's guilt may be (there are many skeletons in many closets throughout the world), the rights of Asians can scarcely be compromised on those grounds. The case for liberty and political rights turns ultimately on their basic importance and on their instrumental role. And this case is as strong in Asia as it is elsewhere.

There is a great deal that we can learn from studies of values in Asia and Europe, but they do not support or sustain the thesis of a grand dichotomy (or a "clash of civilizations"). Our ideas of political and personal rights have taken their particular form relatively recently, and it is hard to see them as "traditional" commitments of Western cultures. There are important antecedents of those commitments, but those antecedents can be found plentifully in Asian cultures as well as Western cultures.

The recognition of diversity within different cultures is extremely important in the contemporary world, since we are constantly bombarded by oversimple generalizations about "Western civilization," "Asian values," "African cultures," and so on. These unfounded readings of history and civilization are not only intellectually shallow, they also add to the divisiveness of the world in which we live. The authoritarian readings of Asian values that are increasingly championed in some quarters do not survive scrutiny. And the grand dichotomy between Asian values and European values adds little to our understanding, and much to the confounding of the normative basis of freedom and democracy.

# CHAPTER SEVEN

# *Capitalism and the Industrial Revolution*

Capitalism is a very broad term that can include societies as various as the United States, Japan, Sweden, France, the United Kingdom, France, Singapore, and many others. Though it encompasses a great many different practices, it reflects a general ideological preference for private property rather than communal or state ownership, free enterprise and individual entrepreneurship versus central planning and government control of the economy. Capitalist societies nonetheless generally reflect a mixture of public and private enterprise along with legal rules governing the pursuit of profit, an approved market structure, and limits on the amount of wealth accumulation. Capitalism has developed through several phases, from entrepreneurial capitalism between 1700 to the late 1800s, to international and then multinational capitalism between the late 1800s to the later 1900s, to the emergence of global capitalism from the 1970s to the present. In each of these phases, a different market structure required the creation of a different production structure, but it was the Industrial Revolution beginning in mid-1700s and accelerating into the mid-1800s that provided the key propellant.

From 1400 to 1700, major European powers used an economic system called mercantilism, a system where governments regulate economic activity in order to insure that exports always exceed imports. This is accomplished by placing high tariffs on goods brought in from abroad to protect the price of local goods at home, which then achieves the secondary effect of allowing local firms and industries at home to keep the prices of goods they export as low as possible in order to increase the volume of their sales abroad. When capitalism began to develop as an alternative system of commerce, it did so as a movement which sought to restrict the power of governments to interfere with trade. Inspired by the French physiocrats, its purpose was to encourage more freedom in the marketplace through the development of a policy to end, or at least to reduce, trade restrictions call *laissez-faire* (allowed to do). That policy gained important legitimation from the Scottish moral philosopher and political economist Adam Smith, who argued that individuals (and by implication larger commercial enterprises) should be recognized as "free agents" and left to pursue their own self-interest without intervention from the state. According to Smith, the expression of rational self-interest would encourage competition in the marketplace and thus function to keep prices low while increasing the production of goods and services for the masses. Hence left to itself, the market, and thus trade, could regulate itself and maintain a balance between supply and demand as if guided, as Smith added so famously, "by an invisible hand."

Karl Marx, the German political economist and father of Communism had a different understanding of how the market worked and the way that capitalist forces operated. As he explained in the first selection in this chapter from his book *Capital,* Vol. 1, capitalism is less a new mode of regulating state participation in the economy for the sake of achieving greater competition in the marketplace than a new mode of production in which monetary wealth is able to buy labor power for the purpose of enriching itself. Beginning in the seventeenth century, ordinary workers who had finally freed themselves from the soil as well as from slavery, serfdom, guilds, and other feudal arrangements lost their access to the means of production—tools, land, materials, resources, and social arrangements—and were forced to sell their labor power to those who could afford to purchase it. Those capable of purchasing that labor power used it to produce a surplus of goods for the sake of maximizing profits which in turn enabled them to acquire still more of the means of production for themselves and deny access to them to the workers. Hence commenced the cycle of capitalist enrichment: the wealthy became those who could use those surpluses of wealth produced by labor power to enrich themselves by means of a system now dedicated to ceaseless accumulation and advances in production that only further distanced laborers from the means of production themselves.

This whole process is reflected in the creation of the first Industrial Revolution which caused a massive expansion of capitalism and constituted a turning point, according to the global historian, Peter N. Stearns, in the history of the world. Harnessing some of the new knowledge made available by the scientific revolution in the West, it produced a transformation in the means, location, and form of production through mechanization and the concentration of both industry and population. Its original site of expansion was England, which possessed an abundance of natural energy in the form of coal, an industry of textile production open to technological improvements, an expanding system of transport built around numerous waterways, new roads, and the harnessing of steam to produce railroads, and, finally, a market that was not only national but, because of England's increasing colonial possessions, global.

The original benefactors of these developments were the industrial managers and owners of manufacturing facilities and all those who supported them. But the capital needed to expand these operations required the additional contribution of private investors and financiers who quickly became more important to the organization and control of manufacturing than the original entrepreneurs and owners who got the process moving. But the increasing dominance of banking and financial interests, in turn, only underlined how completely removed the laboring class had quickly become from the industrial revolution itself. Not only had machines changed the nature of work, but wages were purposely kept low to increase profits, housing and other services fell behind the rapid migration of labor from the country to the city, and workers were denied any voice in the improvement of their situation until the long-delayed and very uneven growth of labor unions.

Such conditions were to change because of the labor reform movements, sometimes inspired predominantly in Europe by the Socialist revolutions to be taken up later in this volume, but the plight of the laboring class, except in times of world war, would remain continually precarious, particularly at the lower levels, as industrial capitalism moved from the mid-nineteenth century to the late twentieth-century to international and multinational capitalism, and then from the late nineteenth century to the present to a more transnational or global capitalism. In the first, the rapid increase of resource-based wealth sought new markets through the creation of American and sometimes European cartels that increased economic imperialism though the expansion of multi-national corporations from the Ford Motor Company and the Coca-Cola Corporation to mining and construction conglomerates. In the second and latest phase of capitalism, resource-based, market-seeking international investment has become less important than the spatial optimization of production and profit that requires the outsourcing, off-shoring, and supply-chaining of production itself, the increase in world trade, the deregulation of economic and trade practices, the further privatization of the public enterprises, the downsizing of government, massive tax cuts to stimulate investment, and a number of other practices associated with what is now called neo-liberalism.

As the selection by the economic historian Jeremy Adelman emphasizes in this chapter, the narrative we have been tracing of the rise of capitalism favors the "West" as opposed to the "Rest." Nor is this any coincidence. As with the development of the scientific revolutions, the way you tell a story, how you remember history, matters greatly. Adelman seeks to demonstrate this by showing that the story of the rise of capitalism can be told in two different ways. The first is internal and follows the trajectory outlined above. It assumes that Europe's economic breakout from mercantilism was due to forces within the system itself. The West was in the process of rising, as many historians have depicted it, and capitalism's durability and superiority as an economic system was confirmed by its social, economic, and political success. The alternative narrative that is given far less space in Western histories of economic development argues instead that Europe's breakout depended not on its superiority over the rest so much as on its exploitation of them.

The chief example of this exploitation is to be found in the Atlantic slave trade, beginning by the middle of the 15th century and not ending until almost middle of the 19th century, which enabled economic development to be based on slave labor. More than that, this trade in persons, in bodies, which moved the West forward more rapidly than other parts of the world, required an empire, really several empires, to ground and support it. And thus were created imperial projects that moved from sugar to coal to cotton as part of what better deserves to be called the emergence of a kind of war capitalism. The West needed the rest for the sake of energizing and consolidating its imperial ambitions, subjugating entire peoples for the benefit of others.

This external narrative thus turns the traditional, altruistic history of capitalism on its head. It demonstrates that the narrative of heroic capitalism spreading its wings to foster economic well-being for all is as false as the narrative of capitalism as the machine that it created itself. What made economic breakouts possible but also difficult and tragic in the history of capitalism had to do with the interaction of the global and the local. Thus to tell the real history of the rise and development of capitalism in a global way requires thinking about it from multiple perspectives and, as Adelman insists, on multiple scales.

If this assessment is correct, so is the need to realize that the first Industrial Revolution from the late 1700s to the later 1800s was only one of several.  While the first Industrial Revolution was based on the mechanization of power through the use of steam and water, the second had to do with the electrification of power to create mass production and the third used electronics and information technology to automate production.  But now, since the latter part of the twentieth century and the beginning of the twenty-first, we are in the midst of a fourth Industrial Revolution, according to Klaus Schwab, that is essentially digital and blurs the lines between it and the realms of the physical and the biological.  What differentiates this revolution from the one that preceded it is the speed with which it is moving, the scope of its reach, and its impact on virtually every industrial or productive system on earth.  Though there is no way of determining in advance whether its outcome will ultimately be more beneficial to humankind than any of those which proceeded it—the fourth Industrial Revolution has obviously left hundreds of millions, if not billions, of people behind and countless others feeling that they will be left behind--Schwab is convinced that that we have no alternative but to try to use its inventions to further humanize it lest they use us.  Of no inventions created by this revolution is any more potentially consequential than artificial intelligence-- world renowned theoretical physicist Stephen Hawking has called it the most dangerous discovery ever made--but there are others like nuclear fission and climate change that we will also have to learn how to control, and perhaps the new instrumentalities of the fourth Industrial Revolution can help us.

# 2.4 The Transition from Feudalism to Capitalism

KARL MARX

The economic structure of capitalistic society has grown out of the economic structure of feudal society. The dissolution of the latter set free the elements of the former.

The immediate producer, the laborer, could only dispose of his own person after he had ceased to be attached to the soil and ceased to be the slave, serf, or bondman of another. To become a free seller of labor power, who carries his commodity wherever he finds a market, he must further have escaped from the regime of the guilds, their rules for apprentices and journeymen, and the impediments of their labor regulations. Hence, the historical movement which changes the producers into wage-workers, appears, on the one hand, as their emancipation from serfdom and from the fetters of the guilds, and this side alone exists for our bourgeois historians. But, on the other hand, these new freedmen became sellers of themselves only after they had been robbed of all their own means of production, and of all the guarantees of existence afforded by the old feudal arrangements. And the history of this, their expropriation, is written in the annals of mankind in letters of blood and fire.

The industrial capitalists, these new potentates, had on their part not only to displace the guild-masters of handicrafts, but also the feudal lords, the possessors of the sources of wealth. In this respect their conquest of social power appears as the fruit of a victorious struggle both against feudal lordship and its revolting prerogatives, and against the guilds and the fetters they laid on the free development of production and the free exploitation of man by man.

In the history of primitive accumulation, all revolutions are epoch-making that act as levers for the capitalist class in course of formation; but, above all, those moments when great masses of men are suddenly and forcibly torn from their means of subsistence, and hurled as free and "unattached" proletarians on the labor-market. The expropriation of the agricultural producer, of the peasant, from the soil, is the basis of the whole process. This history of this expropriation, in different countries, assumes different aspects, and runs through its various phases in different orders of succession, and at different periods. In England alone, which we take as our example, has it the classic form.

## The Expropriation of the Agricultural Population From the Land

In England, serfdom had practically disappeared in the last part of the 14th century. The immense majority of the population consisted then, and to a still larger extent, in the 15th century, of free peasant proprietors, whatever was the feudal title under which their right of property was hidden. In the larger seignorial domains, the old bailiff, himself a serf, was displaced by the free farmer.

From *Capital*, Volume 1 by Karl Marx, first published in 1867.

The wage-laborers of agriculture consisted partly of peasants, who utilized their leisure time by working on the large estates, partly of an independent special class of wage-laborers, relatively and absolutely few in numbers. The latter also were practically at the same time peasant farmers, since, besides their wages, they had allotted to them arable land to the extent of 4 or more acres, together with their cottages. Besides they, with the rest of the peasants, enjoyed the usufruct of the common land, which gave pasture to their cattle, furnished them with timber, fire-wood, turf, &c. . . .

The prelude of the revolution that laid the foundation of the capitalist mode of production, was played in the last third of the 15th, and the first decade of the 16th century. A mass of free proletarians was hurled on the labor-market by the breaking-up of the bands of feudal retainers, who, as Sir James Steuart well says, "everywhere uselessly filled house and castle." Although the royal power, itself a product of bourgeois development, in its strife after absolute sovereignty forcibly hastened on the dissolution of these bands of retainers, it was by no means the sole cause of it. In insolent conflict with king and parliament, the great feudal lords created an incomparably larger proletariat by the forcible driving of the peasantry from the land, to which the latter had the same feudal right as the lord himself, and by the usurpation of the common lands. The rapid rise of the Flemish wool manufacturers, and the corresponding rise in the price of wool in England, gave the direct impulse to these evictions. The old nobility had been devoured by the great feudal wars. The new nobility was the child of its time, for which money was the power of all powers. Transformation of arable land into sheep-walks was, therefore, its cry. Harrison, in his "Description of England, prefixed to Holinshed's Chronicles," describes how the expropriation of small peasants is ruining the country. "What care our great encroachers?" The dwellings of the peasants and the cottages of the laborers were razed to the ground or doomed to decay. "If," says Harrison, "the old records of euerie manour be sought . . . it will soon appear that in some manour seuenteene, eighteene, or twentie houses are shrunk . . . that England was never less furnished with people than at the present. . . . Of cities and townes either utterly decaied or more than a quarter or half diminished, though some one be a little increased here or there; of towns pulled downe for sheepewalks, and no more but the lordships now standing in them. . . . I could saie somewhat." The complaints of these old chroniclers are always exaggerated, but they reflect faithfully the impression made on contemporaries by the revolution in the conditions of producing.

The process of forcible expropriation of the people received in the 16th century a new and frightful impulse from the Reformation, and from the consequent colossal spoliation of the church property. The Catholic church was, at the time of the Reformation, feudal proprietor of a great part of the English land. The suppression of the monasteries, &c., hurled their inmates into the proletariat. The estates of the church were to a large extent given away to rapacious  royal favorites, or sold at a nominal price to speculating farmers and citizens, who drove out, en masse, the hereditary subtenants and threw their holdings into one. The legally guaranteed property of the poorer folk in a part of the church's tithes was tacitly confiscated. . . . These immediate results of the Reformation were not its most lasting ones. The property of the church formed the religious bulwark of the traditional conditions of landed property. With its fall these were no longer tenable.

After the restoration of the Stuarts, the landed proprietors carried, by legal means, an act of usurpation, effected everywhere on the Continent without any legal formality. They abolished the feudal tenure of land, i.e., they got rid of all its obligations to the State, "indemnified" the State by taxes on the peasantry and the rest of the mass of the people, vindicated for themselves the rights of modern private property in estates to which they had only a feudal title. . . .

The "glorious Revolution" brought into power, along with William of Orange, the landlord and capitalist appropriators of surplus-value. They inaugurated the new era by practicing on a colossal scale thefts of state lands, thefts that had been hitherto managed more modestly. These estates were given away, sold at a ridiculous figure, or even annexed to private estates by direct seizure. All this happened without the slightest observation of legal etiquette. The Crown lands thus fraudulently appropriated, together with the robbery of the Church estates, as far as these had not been lost again during the republican revolution, from the basis of the to-day princely domains of the English oligarchy. The bourgeois capitalists favored the operation with the view, among others, to promoting free trade in land, to extending the domain of modern agriculture on the large farm-system, and to increasing their supply of the free agricultural proletarians ready to hand. Besides, the new landed aristocracy was the natural ally of the new bankocracy, of the newly-hatched *haute finance*, and of the large manufacturers, then depending on protective duties.

The last process of wholesale expropriation of the agricultural population from the soil is, finally, the so-called clearing of estates, *i.e.*, the sweeping men off them. All the English methods hitherto considered culminated in "clearing." . . . Where there are no more independent peasants to get rid of, the "clearing" of cottages begins; so that the agricultural laborers do not find on the soil cultivated by them even the spot necessary for their own housing. But what "clearing of estates" really and properly signifies, we learn only in the promised land of modern romance, the Highlands of Scotland. There the process is distinguished by its systematic character, by the magnitude of the scale on which it is carried out at one blow (in Ireland landlords have gone to the length of sweeping away several villages at once; in Scotland areas as large as German principalities are dealt with), finally by the peculiar form of property, under which the embezzled lands were held.

The spoliation of the church's property, the fraudulent alienation of the State domains, the robbery of the common lands, the usurpation of feudal and clan property, and its transformation into modern private property under circumstances of reckless terrorism, were just so many idyllic methods of primitive accumulation. They conquered the field for capitalistic agriculture, made the soil part and parcel of capital, and created for the town industries the necessary supply of a "free" and outlawed proletariat.

## The Genesis of Industrial Capitalism

Now that we have considered the forcible creation of a class of outlawed proletarians, the bloody discipline that turned them into wage-laborers, the disgraceful action of the State which employed the police to accelerate the accumulation of capital by increasing the degree of exploitation of labor, the question remains: whence came the capitalists originally?

Doubtless many small guild-masters, and yet more independent small artisans, or even wage-laborers, transformed themselves into small capitalists, and (by gradually extending exploitation of wage-labor and corresponding accumulation) into full-blown capitalists. In the infancy of capitalist production, things often happened as in the infancy of mediaeval towns, where the question, which of the escaped serfs should be master and which servant, was in great part decided by the earlier or later date of their flight. The snail's pace of this method corresponded in no wise with the commercial requirements of the new world-market that the great discoveries of the end of the 15th century created.

The discovery of gold and silver in America, the extirpation, enslavement and entombment in mines of the aboriginal population, the beginning of the conquest and looting of the East Indies, the turning of Africa into a warren for the commercial hunting of blackskins, signalized the rosy dawn of the era of capitalist production. These idyllic proceedings are the chief momenta of primitive accumulation. On their heels treads the commercial war of the European nations, with the globe for a theatre. It begins with the revolt of the Netherlands from Spain, assumes giant dimensions in England's Anti-Jacobin War, and is still going on in the opium wars against China, etc.

The different momenta of primitive accumulation distribute themselves now, more or less, in chronological order, particularly over Spain, Portugal, Holland, France, and England. In England at the end of the 17th century, they arrive at a systematical combination, embracing the colonies, the nation, debt, the modern mode of taxation, and the protectionist system. These methods depend in part on brute force, *e.g.*, the colonial system. But they all employ the power of the State, the concentrated and organized force of society, to hasten, hothouse fashion, the process of transformation of the feudal mode of production into the capitalist mode, and to shorten the transition. Force is the mid-wife of every old society pregnant with a new one. It is itself an economic power. . . .

The history of the colonial administration of Holland—and Holland was the head capitalistic nation of the 17th century—"is on of the most extraordinary relations of treachery, bribery, massacre, and meanness." Nothing is more characteristic than their system of stealing men, to get slaves for Java. The men stealers were trained for this purpose. The thief, the interpreter, and the seller, were the chief agents in this trade, native princes the chief sellers. The young people stolen, were thrown into the secret dungeons of Celebes, until they were ready for sending to the slave-ships. An official report says: "This one town of Macassar, e.g., is full of secret prisons, one more horrible than the other, crammed with unfortunates, victims of greed and tyranny fettered in chains forcibly torn from their families." To secure Malacca, the Dutch corrupted the Portuguese governor. He let them into the town in 1641. They hurried at once to his house and assassinated him, to "abstain" from the payment of £21,875, the price of his treason. Wherever they set foot, devastation and de-population followed. Banjuwangi, a province of Java, in 1750 numbered over 80,000 inhabitants, in 1811 only 18,000. Sweet commerce!

The English East India Company, as is well known, obtained besides the political rule in India, the exclusive monopoly of the tea-trade, as well as of the Chinese trade in general, and of the transport of goods to and from Europe. But the coasting trade of India and between the islands, as well as the internal trade of India, were the monopoly of, the higher employes of the company. The monopolies of salt, opium, betel, and other commodities, were inexhaustible mines of wealth. The employes themselves fixed the price and plundered at will the unhappy Hindus. The Governor-General took part in this private traffic. His favorites received contracts under, conditions whereby they, cleverer than the alchemists, made gold out of nothing. Great fortunes sprang up like mushrooms in a day; primitive accumulation went on without the advance of a shilling. The trial of Warren Hastings swarms with such cases. Here is an instance. A contract for opium was given to a certain Sullivan at the moment of his departure on an official mission to a part of India far removed from the opium district. Sullivan sold his contract to one Binn for £40,000; Binn sold it the same day for £60,000, and the ultimate purchaser who carried out the contract declared that after all he realised an enormous gain. According to one of the lists laid before Parliament, the Company and its employes from 1757–1766 got £6,000,000 from the Indians as gifts. Between 1769 and 1770, the English manufactured a famine by buying up all the rice and refusing to sell it again, except at fabulous prices.

The treasures captured outside Europe by undisguised looting, enslavement, and murder, floated back to the mother-country and were there turned into capital. Holland, which first fully developed the colonial system, in 1648 stood already in the acme of its commercial greatness. It was "in almost exclusive possession of the East Indian trade and the commerce between the south-east and north west of Europe. Its fisheries, marine, manufactures, surpassed those of any other country. The total capital of the Republic was probably more important than that of all the rest of Europe put together." Gulich forgets to add that by 1648, the people of Holland were more over-worked, poorer and more brutally oppressed than those of all the rest of Europe put together.

To-day industrial supremacy implies commercial supremacy. In the period of manufacture properly so called, it is, on the other hand, the commercial supremacy that gives industrial predominance. Hence the preponderant role that the colonial system plays at that time.

The birth of Modern Industry is [also] heralded by a great slaughter of the innocents. Like the royal navy, the factories were recruited by means of the press-gang. Blasé as Sir F. M. Eden is as to the horrors of the expropriation of the agricultural population from the soil, from the last third of the 15th century to his own time; with all the self-satisfaction with which he rejoices in this process, "essential" for establishing capitalistic agriculture and "the due proportion between arable and pasture land"—he does not show, however, the same economic insight in respect to the necessity of child-stealing and child-slavery for the transformation of manufacturing exploitation into factory exploitation, and the establishment of the "true relation" between capital and labor-power. He says: "It may, perhaps, be worthy the attention of the public to consider, whether any manufacture, which, in order to be carried on successfully, requires that cottages and workhouses should be ransacked for poor children; that they should be employed by turns during the greater part of the night and robbed of that rest which, though indispensable to all, is most required by the young; and that numbers of both sexes, of different ages and disposition, should be collected together in such a manner that the contagion of example cannot but lead to profligacy and debauchery; will add to the sum of individual or national felicity?"

"In the counties of Derbyshire, Nottinghamshire, and more particularly in Lancashire," says Fielden, "the newly-invented machinery was used in large factories built on the sides of streams capable of turning the water-wheel. Thousands of hands were suddenly required in these places, remote from towns; and Lancashire, in particular, being, till then, comparatively thinly populated and barren, a population was all that she now wanted. The small and nimble fingers of little children being by very far the most in request, the custom instantly sprang up of procuring *apprentices* from the different parish workhouses of London, Birmingham, and elsewhere. Many, many thousands of these little, hapless creatures were sent down into the north, being from the age of 7 to the age of 13 or 14 years old. The custom was for the master to clothe his apprentices and to feed and lodge them in an 'apprentice house' near the factory; overseers were appointed to see to the works, whose interest it was to work the children to the utmost, because their pay was in proportion to the quantity of work that they could exact. Cruelty was, of course, the consequence. . . . In many of the manufacturing districts, but particularly, I am afraid, in the guilty county to which I belong [Lancashire], cruelties the most heart-rendering was practised upon the unoffending and friendless creatures who were thus consigned to the charge of master-manufacturers; they were harassed to the brink of death by excess of labor . . . were flogged, fettered and tortured in thee most exquisite refinement of cruelty; . . . they were in many cases starved to the bone while flogged to their work and . . . even in some instances . . . were driven to commit suicide. . . . The beautiful and romantic valleys of Derbyshire, Nottinghamshire and Lancashire, secluded from the public eye, became the dismal solitudes of torture, and of many a murder. The profits of manufacturers were enormous; but this only whetted the appetite that it should have satisfied, and therefore the manufacturers had recourse to an expedient that seemed to secure to them those profits without any possibility of limit; the began the practice of what is termed 'night-working,' that is, having tired one set of hands, by working them throughout the day they had another set ready to go on working throughout the night; the day-set getting into the beds that the night-set had just quitted, and in their turn again, the night-set getting into the beds that the day-set quitted in the morning. It is a common tradition in Lancashire, that the beds *never get cold*."

Such a task it was to establish the "eternal laws of Nature" of the capitalist mode of production, to complete the process of separation between laborers and conditions of labor, to transform, at one pole, the social means of production and subsistence into capital, at the opposite pole, the mass of the population into wage-laborers, into "free laboring poor," that artificial product of modern society. If money, according to Augier, "comes into the world with a congenital blood-stain on one cheek," capital comes dripping from head to foot, from every pore, with blood and dirt.

# What Caused Capitalism?
# Assessing the Roles of the West and the Rest

 Jeremy Adelman

Once upon a time, smart people thought the world was flat. As globalization took off, economists pointed to spreading market forces that allowed consumers to buy similar things for the same prices around the world. Others invoked the expansion of liberalism and democracy after the Cold War. For a while, it seemed as if the West's political and economic ways really had won out. But the euphoric days of flat talk now seem like a bygone era, replaced by gloom and anxiety. The economic shock of 2008, the United States' political paralysis, Europe's financial quagmires, the dashed dreams of the Arab Spring, and the specter of competition from illiberal capitalist countries such as China have doused enthusiasm about the West's destiny. Once seen as a model for "the rest," the West is now in question. Even the erstwhile booster Francis Fukuyama has seen the dark, warning in his recent two-volume history of political order that the future may not lie with the places that brought the world liberalism and democracy in the past. Recent bestsellers, such as Daron Acemoglu and James Robinson's *Why Nations Fail* and Thomas Piketty's *Capital in the Twenty-first Century*, capture the pessimistic Zeitgeist. So does a map produced in 2012 by the McKinsey Global Institute, which plots the movement of the world's economic center of gravity out of China in the year 1, barely reaching Greenland by 1950 (the closest it ever got to New York), and now veering back to where it began.

It was only a matter of time before this Sturm und Drang affected the genteel world of historians. Since the future seems up for grabs, so is the past. Chances are, if a historian's narrative of the European miracle and the rise of capitalism is upbeat, the prognosis for the West will be good, whereas if the tale is not so triumphal, the forecast will be more ominous. A recent spate of books about the history of global capitalism gives readers the spectrum. T*he Cambridge History of Capitalism*, a two-volume anthology edited by two distinguished economic historians, Larry Neal and Jeffrey Williamson, presents readers with a window into the deep origins of capitalism. Joel Mokyr's *The Enlightened Economy* explains how capitalism broke free in a remote corner of western Europe. And in *Empire of Cotton*, Sven Beckert, a leading global historian, offers a darker story of capitalism, born of worldwide empire and violence.

## WESTWARD HO!

The conventional narrative of the making of the world economy is internalist—that is, that it sprang up organically from within the West. The story goes like this: after the Neolithic Revolution, the global shift from hunting and gathering to agriculture that occurred around 10,000 BC, the various corners of the globe settled into roughly similar standards of living. From China to Mexico, the average person was more or less equal in height (five feet to five feet six inches) and life expectancy (30 to 35 years). Societies differed in their engineering feats, forms of rule, and belief systems. But on the economic front, they boasted common achievements: advanced metallurgy, big walls, and huge pyramids.

If there were tragedies, they entailed plagues and blights more than man-made catastrophes. This is not to say that the Mongol conquest of Baghdad in 1258 was polite; of the city's one million people, more than 200,000 were killed, and the Tigris is said to have run red with blood. But horrific episodes such as this did not determine social well-being, measured as income per person over the long run. That figure remained remarkably constant until about 1500. In this sense, the world was flat. About this portrait, there is consensus.

Where there is debate is over what came next. Some say that groups of Europeans, especially northern Protestants, began to be rewarded for the improved productivity that stemmed from their individualistic habits. Others argue that Europeans stumbled on the right balance of good governance and benevolent self-interest. Either way, late-medieval Europeans found the formula for success, banked on it, and turned it into what, by the nineteenth century, would be known as capitalism.

Internalists argue that capitalism was born European, or more specifically British, and then became global. A system of interconnected parts and peoples, it radiated out from a few original hot spots and over time replaced the "isms" it encountered elsewhere. "Replace" is actually a bland way of putting it. Champions of capitalism would say "liberate." Marxists would call it a "conquest." But the story line is the same: Europe exported its invention to the rest of the world and in so doing created globalization.

## CAPITALISM RISING

The internalist story remains the most familiar way of explaining the breakout from the long post-Neolithic *durée*. *The Cambridge History of Capitalism* goes so far as to argue that elements of capitalism have existed since prehistoric times and were scattered all over the planet; the traits of the individual optimizer were sown into our DNA. Clay tablets recording legal transactions with numbers offer proof of some Mesopotamian capitalist plying his wares. Relics of trading centers in Central Asia trace the primitive optimizer to the steppes. True, for millennia, capitalists were uncoordinated, fragile, and vulnerable. But the origins of capitalism go as far back as archeologists have found remnants of organized market activity. As Neal explains in his introduction, "The current world economy has been a long time in the making."

In this rendering, the survival of capitalists is a bit like that of early Christians: often in doubt. Just as Christians had to make Christendom, imperiled and scattered capitalists had to defeat predatory rulers and rent-seeking institutions in order to make capitalism. In *The Cambridge History of Capitalism*, it was the Italian city-states that first departed from the old order. Although they were vulnerable to rivals and tended to favor oligopolies, these polities laid the groundwork of institutions and norms that in the fifteenth century would pass to mercantile states of the Atlantic—Spain and

Portugal—and then the Netherlands, France, and England. Freed from a Mediterranean Sea crowded with Ottoman fleets and North African corsairs, the Atlantic upstarts unleashed themselves on the world's oceans. In the internalist account, what was important was getting a virtuous cycle going: creating institutions, such as the legal defense of private property, that rewarded entrepreneurial behavior and letting this profit seeking reinforce those institutions through people abiding by laws and paying taxes. The virtuous cycle lifted capitalists from trading with one another to coordinating with one another, thus creating a system of rules and norms to sustain the returns of profit-seeking pursuits. These moneymen put the "ism" in "capitalism."

Then came a second leap forward with the Industrial Revolution and the spread of the printed word, which, Neal writes, dissolved the "obstacles to imitation." European societies began to emulate one another. From pockets of accumulation and ingenuity emerged coordinated and, eventually, integrated processes. Coal, timber, draperies, and flatware filled European trade routes.

Afterward, according to this story, capitalism went global, as European actors and institutions fanned out to join forces with the huddled capitalists in Asia, Africa, and Latin America from the seventeenth to the nineteenth century. But here's the rub: beyond Europe, capitalism had weaker domestic roots, and so it yielded more conflict and tension in the periphery than in the heartland. Local societies resisted change and resented being viewed as backward, condemned as hewers of wood and drawers of water. The globalization of European capitalism has been an uneven and bitter process. Only a few in the periphery, such as Japan, got the mimicry right; these exceptions help confirm the norm that capitalism is best built from the inside out.

## FROM SCIENCE TO WEALTH

There are other ways of explaining how capitalism started in Europe and diffused. Mokyr, for instance, has championed the view that capitalism owes its existence to the cognitive, cultural, and intellectual breakthrough that came about as the scientific revolution swept Europe in the seventeenth and eighteenth centuries. More than any other scholar, he has connected the shifting attitudes to and uses of technology to economic change, crediting the rise of capitalism to an alliance of engineers and investors, tinkerers and moneymen. When those people finally joined forces in the middle of the eighteenth century, the obstacles to growth came crumbling down. In *The Enlightened Economy*, Mokyr goes further:

> A successful economy . . . needs not only rules that determine how the economic game is played, it needs rules to change the rules if necessary in a way that is as costless as possible. In other words, it needs meta-institutions that change the institutions, and whose changes will be accepted even by those who stand to lose from these changes. Institutions did not change just because it was efficient for them to do so. They changed because key peoples' ideas and beliefs that supported them changed.

This is a lot of entangled change and rules, and it's not easy to sort out the causality. The key to Mokyr's internalist argument is the emergence of what he calls "useful knowledge," which translated science into production. The process was far from simple. *The Enlightened Economy* charts the often imperceptible steps that rewarded intellectual innovators and aligned them with impresarios, to create circles of "fabricants" and "savants." "Interaction" is a key word in Mokyr's vocabulary; it's what conjugates curiosity and greed, ambition and altruism. The big breakout came with the Enlightenment, which gave birth to rational thought, the modern concept of good government, and scientific insights into what produced more wealth. After that, there was no looking back.

Internalist histories vary a lot. There are materialists, who see people responding to incentives and opportunities to pool their money. There are institutionalists, who insist on the primacy of property rights and constitutional constraints on greedy rulers. And there are idealists, who spotlight Europe's intellectual breakthroughs. Some combine elements. But internalist narratives also share a lot. Internalists argue that Europe's breakout was autopoietic—that is, that the causes can be found within the system itself, one capable of maintaining and reproducing success without depending on outside forces. In general, the internalist story is also a cheery one. It focuses on what went right, fits with a rise-of-the-West narrative, and tends to be confident of capitalism's durability. If the rest poses a threat, this is mainly because the rest seethes over lagging behind the West.

There are a couple of problems with this kind of history. The first is that what passes for capitalist behavior is so broad that it's no wonder one can find proof of *Homo economicus* from time immemorial. Charting the rise of capitalism can be like tracking the hedge fund manager from the hominids who marched out of Africa. Some internalist narratives rely so much on the capitalist as the maker of the system that they define the hero of the story in such a way that he is either unrecognizable to historians who see more in human behavior than material self-interest or so generic that he is hard to separate from the crowd.

The other problem involves the scale of analysis. "Britain," "Europe," and "the West" are notoriously imprecise and anachronistic terms. Why some city-states and not others? Why not Spain but France? Empires seem to drop out of Mokyr's story. When they do creep in, they play the role of agents nonprovocateurs, promoting greed of the wrong sort: Spain throttled capitalism because it acquired Aztec gold and then got conquistadors hooked on precious metals and not profits, and the United Kingdom acquired an empire in a fit of absent-mindedness—and that empire was merely an extension of the more important domestic market.

As for explaining the fate of the followers, the lesson of internalist theories has been "Replicate!" Catch up by copying. Borrow the script. Free markets; protect private property. But the problem has always been that the nature of catching up makes copying impossible. As the Russian-born economic historian Alexander Gerschenkron noted, "In several very important respects the development of a backward country may, by the very virtue of its backwardness, tend to differ fundamentally from that of an advanced country." Finally, as a new crop of global historians has been showing, it is not so easy to isolate the United Kingdom, Europe, or the West from the rest. When it comes to privileged internalist variables, such as scientific knowledge or the Enlightenment, a growing chorus of scholars is finding that West-rest interactions set the stage for the workings of impresarios, engineers, and philosophers. So what role did the rest play in the rise of the West?

# THE ROLE OF THE REST    *global injustice*

The internalist narrative has long been shadowed by an externalist rival, which sees Europe's leap forward as dependent on relations with places beyond Europe. Externalists summon a different battery of action verbs. Instead of "coordinating" or "interacting," the system favored "exploiting" and "submitting." The most recent externalist explanation of capitalism is Beckert's *Empire of Cotton.* The book is a triple threat: it insists that the Industrial Revolution would never have happened without external trade, that the rise of industrialism and factory labor would never have transpired without the spread of slave labor, and that cotton was a commodity that made an empire and thus the world economy. In other words, capitalism was born global because it required an empire to buoy it.

As is the case with Piketty's data-fueled bestseller, *Empire of Cotton* is modest only in style. A Harvard historian known for his legendary undergraduate course on the history of American capitalism, Beckert last wrote a penetrating history of the New York bourgeoisie in the Gilded Age, *The Monied Metropolis*, which described the immense concentration of power in a short period of time as the United States transformed from an agrarian society into an urban, cosmopolitan one. His newest book gives readers the global picture of which New York was a part. Collectively, historians have drawn up a shopping list of causal commodities. Sugar was once seen as the driver of the early modern triangle trade. Kenneth Pomeranz made coal famous, arguing in *The Great Divergence* that Europe succeeded because British mines were close to start-up factories, whereas China lagged behind because bituminous deposits there were out of reach. David Landes, in *The Unbound Prometheus*, made even the humble vat of grease a hidden hero of the Industrial Revolution. For Beckert, the globalizer is cotton.

In 1858, James Henry Hammond, a South Carolina planter-senator, thundered on the floor of the Senate, "Cotton is king." But cotton was not always king in the Atlantic world. For long stretches, it was a mere pawn. Where it was king was in India. At the start of Beckert's epic tale, in the early eighteenth century, India provided coveted muslins and calicoes for European markets. Its cotton was grown by peasants, along with their food crops, with enough supply to sustain an export boom until the nineteenth century. Europe was a growing, but fringe, market.

So how did India and Europe trade places as the center of the cotton industry? The key lies in the nature of the Atlantic trade. Beckert locates the preindustrial origins of that trade in what he calls "war capitalism." By this, he means the use of state power to wage war on rivals for markets and possessions and to shove native peoples off their land in the Americas and Africa. While Native Americans were dispossessed, Africans were shipped—about 12 million of them—from one side of the Atlantic to the other. Once American land, African labor, and European capital were bonded together on the cotton plantation, a new source of cotton could finally outmuscle the peasant household on the Indian subcontinent. It was not internalist factors, such as local property rights or useful knowledge, that punched through the capitalist transformation; "a wave of expropriation of labor and land characterized this moment, testifying to capitalism's illiberal origins," Beckert argues.

But this was not all. Manufacturers in Europe needed to keep out their Indian competitors and create new markets. Various kinds of protectionist policies came to the rescue, Beckert writes, "testifying . . . to the enormous importance of the state to the 'great divergence'" between industrializers and those that trailed behind. On the eve of the American Revolution, the British Parliament decreed that cotton cloth for sale at home could come only from cloth made in the United Kingdom. Other European governments did the same.

Even protectionism was not enough. Because European domestic markets alone could not sustain expanding factories, an export boom had to be manufactured. Europeans gave clothes to African traders in return for captives, pressured newly independent countries in Latin America to throw open their markets, and eventually introduced cheap, milled textiles to the bottom end of the Indian market. Thus subverted, Indian peasants became estate sharecroppers producing raw cotton for export to British mills. After the American Civil War, King Cotton fell on hard times, because Brazilian, Egyptian, and Indian estates could hire displaced peasants more cheaply than freed slaves. Once the traditional bond between peasants and land had been severed in Africa, Asia, and the Americas, cotton merchants were free to exploit the land as they saw fit. Beckert writes that from 1860 to 1920, 55 million acres of land in those regions were plowed for cotton. According to some estimates, by 1905, 15 million people made a living by growing cotton—about one percent of the world's population.

The cotton industry became so competitive that it attracted arrivistes. Japan, for example, replaced its imported textiles from British India and the United States with raw cotton from Korea in the early twentieth century and so became a new commercial empire in its own right. Belgium and Germany tried the same thing in Africa. Thus was born an imperial spasm in the name of free trade. The circle finally closed when India, too, tried to replace imports with domestic production and economic nationalists lobbied to free the colonial economy from British control. In the 1930s, the original textile manufacturers in the United Kingdom saw their business go overseas in response to labor costs and working-class militants. Mill towns hollowed out. By the 1960s, British cotton textile exports had shrunk to a sliver (2.8 percent) of what they once were. The American South saw its staple flee to Bangladesh. Eventually, Beckert writes, cotton mills in Europe and North America were refurbished as "artist studios, industrial-chic condos, or museums."

A narrative as capacious as this threatens to groan under the weight of heavy concepts. In fact, Beckert dodges and weaves between the big claims and great detail. His portrait of Liverpool, "the epicenter of a globe-spanning empire," puts readers on the wharves and behind the desks of the credit peddlers. His description of the American Civil War as "an acid test for the entire industrial order" is a brilliant example of how global historians might tackle events—as opposed to focusing on structures, processes, and networks—because he shows how the crisis of the U.S. cotton economy reverberated in Brazil, Egypt, and India. The scale of what Beckert has accomplished is astonishing.

Beckert turns the internalist argument on its head. He shows how the system started with disparate parts connected through horizontal exchanges. He describes how it transformed into integrated, hierarchical, and centralized structures—which laid the foundations for the Industrial Revolution and the beginnings of the great divergence between the West and the rest. Beckert's cotton empire more than defrocks the internalists' happy narrative of the West's self-made capitalist man. The rise of capitalism needed the rest, and getting the rest in line required coercion, violence, and the other instruments of imperialism. Cotton, "the fabric of our lives," as the jingle goes, remained an empire because it, like the capitalist system it produced, depended on the subjugation of some for the benefit of others.

# IMPERIAL DISCONTENTS

Like the heroic capitalist rising and spreading his wings in the internalist narrative, the distinctly unheroic empire in the externalist narrative functions as the machine that made itself. This raises all the same problems of circularity: empire becomes the cause and the effect of capitalism. It also raises problems of how to join inequality and integration, both of which lie at the heart of Beckert's book. Contrary to the externalist precept, coercion need not be the only binding force when power relations are asymmetric; global domination is not necessarily inherent to capitalism. Maybe it is because the English language lacks the right terms to describe a global order of uneven and asymmetric parts that externalists resort to shortcuts such as "empire" or "hegemony." Internalists, by contrast, offer a vocabulary that accents choices and strategies, such as "creating opportunities" and "maximizing returns."

Most historians side with a single narrative, captive to stories of capitalism as either liberating or satanic, springing from below or imposed from above. In order to plumb the past of global capitalism, however, they need a stock of global narratives that get beyond the dichotomies of force or free will, external or internal agents. To explain why some parts of the world struggled, one should not have to choose between externalist theories, which rely on global injustices, and internalist ones, which invoke local constraints.

Indeed, it's the interaction of the local and the global that makes breakouts so difficult—or creates the opportunity to escape. In between these scales are complex layers of policies and practices that defy either-or explanations. In 1521, the year the Spanish defeated the Aztec empire and laid claim to the wealth of the New World, few would have predicted that England would be an engine of progress two centuries later; even the English would have bet on Spain or the Ottoman Empire, which is why they were so committed to piracy and predation. Likewise, in 1989, as the Berlin Wall fell and Chinese tanks mowed through Tiananmen Square, "Made in China" was a rare sight. Who would have imagined double-digit growth from Maoist capitalism? Historians have trouble explaining success stories in places that were thought to lack the right ingredients. The same goes for the flops. In 1914, Argentina ranked among the wealthiest capitalist societies on the planet. Not only did no one predict its slow meltdown, but millions bet on Argentine success. To find clues to success or failure, then, historians should look not at either the world market or local initiatives but at the forces that combine them.

Alternative narratives may have to come from beyond the heartland of capitalism itself, the home of classical fables of modernization. In the nineteenth century, many liberals outside Europe struggled to find a different path, because copying the West was a hopeless pursuit. Since they could not claim histories of capitalism as their own but still believed in the credos of liberalism, they tried to think beyond the binary choice of coercion or free will. Juan Bautista Alberdi, the father of Argentina's 1853 constitution and a native of the country's cotton province of Tucumán, was devoted to free trade and opening up frontier lands for the production of commodities. Like many global liberals, he insisted that governments did not have to resort to coercion to integrate supply chains. Alberdi was a fierce critic of using war as a means to modernize, and he blasted Argentine and Brazilian elites for colluding during the Paraguayan War of 1864–70, the South American echo of the American Civil War. His work represents but one example of capitalist endeavors that were neither carbon-copied nor made out of the barrel of a gun.

The dichotomy between internalists and externalists is harmful because it creates a pressure to rely on just one of their heroic and unheroic duelers to explain capitalist development. In fact, the payoff from global history comes from thinking about capitalism in multiple ways and on multiple scales. Surely, the travails of the rest serve as a reminder that the isms of the West are neither as inevitable nor as durable as their chroniclers or critics believe.

# The Fourth Industrial Revolution: What It Means and How to Respond

 KLAUS SCHWAB

We stand on the brink of a technological revolution that will fundamentally alter the way we live, work, and relate to one another. In its scale, scope, and complexity, the transformation will be unlike anything humankind has experienced before. We do not yet know just how it will unfold, but one thing is clear: the response to it must be integrated and comprehensive, involving all stakeholders of the global polity, from the public and private sectors to academia and civil society.

The First Industrial Revolution used water and steam power to mechanize production. The Second used electric power to create mass production. The Third used electronics and information technology to automate production. Now a Fourth Industrial Revolution is building on the Third, the digital revolution that has been occurring since the middle of the last century. It is characterized by a fusion of technologies that is blurring the lines between the physical, digital, and biological spheres.

There are three reasons why today's transformations represent not merely a prolongation of the Third Industrial Revolution but rather the arrival of a Fourth and distinct one: velocity, scope, and systems impact. The speed of current breakthroughs has no historical precedent. When compared with previous industrial revolutions, the Fourth is evolving at an exponential rather than a linear pace. Moreover, it is disrupting almost every industry in every country. And the breadth and depth of these changes herald the transformation of entire systems of production, management, and governance.

The possibilities of billions of people connected by mobile devices, with unprecedented processing power, storage capacity, and access to knowledge, are unlimited. And these possibilities will be multiplied by emerging technology breakthroughs in fields such as artificial intelligence, robotics, the Internet of Things, autonomous vehicles, 3-D printing, nanotechnology, biotechnology, materials science, energy storage, and quantum computing.

Already, artificial intelligence is all around us, from self-driving cars and drones to virtual assistants and software that translate or invest. Impressive progress has been made in AI in recent years, driven by exponential increases in computing power and by the availability of vast amounts of data, from software used to discover new drugs to algorithms used to predict our cultural interests. Digital fabrication technologies, meanwhile, are interacting with the biological world on a daily basis. Engineers, designers, and architects are combining computational design, additive manufacturing, materials engineering, and synthetic biology to pioneer a symbiosis between microorganisms, our bodies, the products we consume, and even the buildings we inhabit.

## CHALLENGES AND OPPORTUNITIES

Like the revolutions that preceded it, the Fourth Industrial Revolution has the potential to raise global income levels and improve the quality of life for populations around the world. To date, those who have gained the most from it have been consumers able to afford and access the digital world; technology has made possible new products and services that increase the efficiency and pleasure of our personal lives. Ordering a cab, booking a flight, buying a product, making a payment, listening to music, watching a film, or playing a game—any of these can now be done remotely.

In the future, technological innovation will also lead to a supply-side miracle, with long-term gains in efficiency and productivity. Transportation and communication costs will drop, logistics and global supply chains will become more effective, and the cost of trade will diminish, all of which will open new markets and drive economic growth.

At the same time, as the economists Erik Brynjolfsson and Andrew McAfee have pointed out, the revolution could yield greater inequality, particularly in its potential to disrupt labor markets. As automation substitutes for labor across the entire economy, the net displacement of workers by machines might exacerbate the gap between returns to capital and returns to labor. On the other hand, it is also possible that the displacement of workers by technology will, in aggregate, result in a net increase in safe and rewarding jobs.

We cannot foresee at this point which scenario is likely to emerge, and history suggests that the outcome is likely to be some combination of the two. However, I am convinced of one thing—that in the future, talent, more than capital, will represent the critical factor of production. This will give rise to a job market increasingly segregated into "low-skill/low-pay" and "high-skill/high-pay" segments, which in turn will lead to an increase in social tensions.

In addition to being a key economic concern, inequality represents the greatest societal concern associated with the Fourth Industrial Revolution. The largest beneficiaries of innovation tend to be the providers of intellectual and physical capital—the innovators, shareholders, and investors— which explains the rising gap in wealth between those dependent on capital versus labor. Technology is therefore one of the main reasons why incomes have stagnated, or even decreased, for a majority of the population in high-income countries: the demand for highly skilled workers has increased while the demand for workers with less education and lower skills has decreased. The result is a job market with a strong demand at the high and low ends, but a hollowing out of the middle.

This helps explain why so many workers are disillusioned and fearful that their own real incomes and those of their children will continue to stagnate. It also helps explain why middle classes around the world are increasingly experiencing a pervasive sense of dissatisfaction and unfairness. A winner-takes-all economy that offers only limited access to the middle class is a recipe for democratic malaise and dereliction.

Discontent can also be fueled by the pervasiveness of digital technologies and the dynamics of information sharing typified by social media. More than 30 percent of the global population now uses social media platforms to connect, learn, and share information. In an ideal world, these interactions would provide an opportunity for cross-cultural understanding and cohesion. However, they can also create and propagate unrealistic expectations as to what constitutes success for an individual or a group, as well as offer opportunities for extreme ideas and ideologies to spread.

# THE IMPACT ON BUSINESS

An underlying theme in my conversations with global CEOs and senior business executives is that the acceleration of innovation and the velocity of disruption are hard to comprehend or anticipate and that these drivers constitute a source of constant surprise, even for the best connected and most well informed. Indeed, across all industries, there is clear evidence that the technologies that underpin the Fourth Industrial Revolution are having a major impact on businesses.

On the supply side, many industries are seeing the introduction of new technologies that create entirely new ways of serving existing needs and significantly disrupt existing industry value chains. Disruption is also flowing from agile, innovative competitors who, thanks to access to global digital platforms for research, development, marketing, sales, and distribution, can oust well-established incumbents faster than ever by improving the quality, speed, or price at which value is delivered.

Major shifts on the demand side are also occurring, as growing transparency, consumer engagement, and new patterns of consumer behavior (increasingly built upon access to mobile networks and data) force companies to adapt the way they design, market, and deliver products and services.

A key trend is the development of technology-enabled platforms that combine both demand and supply to disrupt existing industry structures, such as those we see within the "sharing" or "on demand" economy. These technology platforms, rendered easy to use by the smartphone, convene people, assets, and data—thus creating entirely new ways of consuming goods and services in the process. In addition, they lower the barriers for businesses and individuals to create wealth, altering the personal and professional environments of workers. These new platform businesses are rapidly multiplying into many new services, ranging from laundry to shopping, from chores to parking, from massages to travel.

On the whole, there are four main effects that the Fourth Industrial Revolution has on business—on customer expectations, on product enhancement, on collaborative innovation, and on organizational forms. Whether consumers or businesses, customers are increasingly at the epicenter of the economy, which is all about improving how customers are served. Physical products and services, moreover, can now be enhanced with digital capabilities that increase their value. New technologies make assets more durable and resilient, while data and analytics are transforming how they are maintained. A world of customer experiences, data-based services, and asset performance through analytics, meanwhile, requires new forms of collaboration, particularly given the speed at which innovation and disruption are taking place. And the emergence of global platforms and other new business models, finally, means that talent, culture, and organizational forms will have to be rethought.

Overall, the inexorable shift from simple digitization (the Third Industrial Revolution) to innovation based on combinations of technologies (the Fourth Industrial Revolution) is forcing companies to reexamine the way they do business. The bottom line, however, is the same: business leaders and senior executives need to understand their changing environment, challenge the assumptions of their operating teams, and relentlessly and continuously innovate.

# THE IMPACT ON GOVERNMENT

As the physical, digital, and biological worlds continue to converge, new technologies and platforms will increasingly enable citizens to engage with governments, voice their opinions, coordinate their efforts, and even circumvent the supervision of public authorities. Simultaneously, governments will gain new technological powers to increase their control over populations, based on pervasive surveillance systems and the ability to control digital infrastructure. On the whole, however, governments will increasingly face pressure to change their current approach to public engagement and policymaking, as their central role of conducting policy diminishes owing to new sources of competition and the redistribution and decentralization of power that new technologies make possible.

Ultimately, the ability of government systems and public authorities to adapt will determine their survival. If they prove capable of embracing a world of disruptive change, subjecting their structures to the levels of transparency and efficiency that will enable them to maintain their competitive edge, they will endure. If they cannot evolve, they will face increasing trouble.

This will be particularly true in the realm of regulation. Current systems of public policy and decision-making evolved alongside the Second Industrial Revolution, when decision-makers had time to study a specific issue and develop the necessary response or appropriate regulatory framework. The whole process was designed to be linear and mechanistic, following a strict "top down" approach.

But such an approach is no longer feasible. Given the Fourth Industrial Revolution's rapid pace of change and broad impacts, legislators and regulators are being challenged to an unprecedented degree and for the most part are proving unable to cope.

How, then, can they preserve the interest of the consumers and the public at large while continuing to support innovation and technological development? By embracing "agile" governance, just as the private sector has increasingly adopted agile responses to software development and business operations more generally. This means regulators must continuously adapt to a new, fast-changing environment, reinventing themselves so they can truly understand what it is they are regulating. To do so, governments and regulatory agencies will need to collaborate closely with business and civil society.

The Fourth Industrial Revolution will also profoundly impact the nature of national and international security, affecting both the probability and the nature of conflict. The history of warfare and international security is the history of technological innovation, and today is no exception. Modern conflicts involving states are increasingly "hybrid" in nature, combining traditional battlefield techniques with elements previously associated with nonstate actors. The distinction between war and peace, combatant and noncombatant, and even violence and nonviolence (think cyberwarfare) is becoming uncomfortably blurry.

As this process takes place and new technologies such as autonomous or biological weapons become easier to use, individuals and small groups will increasingly join states in being capable of causing mass harm. This new vulnerability will lead to new fears. But at the same time, advances in technology will create the potential to reduce the scale or impact of violence, through the development of new modes of protection, for example, or greater precision in targeting.

# THE IMPACT ON PEOPLE

The Fourth Industrial Revolution, finally, will change not only what we do but also who we are. It will affect our identity and all the issues associated with it: our sense of privacy, our notions of ownership, our consumption patterns, the time we devote to work and leisure, and how we develop our careers, cultivate our skills, meet people, and nurture relationships. It is already changing our health and leading to a "quantified" self, and sooner than we think it may lead to human augmentation. The list is endless because it is bound only by our imagination.

I am a great enthusiast and early adopter of technology, but sometimes I wonder whether the inexorable integration of technology in our lives could diminish some of our quintessential human capacities, such as compassion and cooperation. Our relationship with our smartphones is a case in point. Constant connection may deprive us of one of life's most important assets: the time to pause, reflect, and engage in meaningful conversation.

One of the greatest individual challenges posed by new information technologies is privacy. We instinctively understand why it is so essential, yet the tracking and sharing of information about us is a crucial part of the new connectivity. Debates about fundamental issues such as the impact on our inner lives of the loss of control over our data will only intensify in the years ahead. Similarly, the revolutions occurring in biotechnology and AI, which are redefining what it means to be human by pushing back the current thresholds of life span, health, cognition, and capabilities, will compel us to redefine our moral and ethical boundaries.

# SHAPING THE FUTURE

Neither technology nor the disruption that comes with it is an exogenous force over which humans have no control. All of us are responsible for guiding its evolution, in the decisions we make on a daily basis as citizens, consumers, and investors. We should thus grasp the opportunity and power we have to shape the Fourth Industrial Revolution and direct it toward a future that reflects our common objectives and values.

To do this, however, we must develop a comprehensive and globally shared view of how technology is affecting our lives and reshaping our economic, social, cultural, and human environments. There has never been a time of greater promise, or one of greater potential peril. Today's decision-makers, however, are too often trapped in traditional, linear thinking, or too absorbed by the multiple crises demanding their attention, to think strategically about the forces of disruption and innovation shaping our future.

In the end, it all comes down to people and values. We need to shape a future that works for all of us by putting people first and empowering them. In its most pessimistic, dehumanized form, the Fourth Industrial Revolution may indeed have the potential to "robotize" humanity and thus to deprive us of our heart and soul. But as a complement to the best parts of human nature—creativity, empathy, stewardship—it can also lift humanity into a new collective and moral consciousness based on a shared sense of destiny. It is incumbent on us all to make sure the latter prevails.

# CHAPTER EIGHT

# Liberalism and the Democratic Revolutions

The democratic revolutions of the later 1700s, particularly the American and French but also the Haitian as well as the Latin American, derived much of their ideological inspiration from the emergence of liberal thought that preceded them. That thought was itself a product of the French, English, and American Enlightenments. While its influence on economics was to lessen government interference in on trade and the marketplace on the assumption that any constraints on free competition would lead to social stagnation, state bureaucracies, and political corruption, its effects on politics were to be even more consequential. Defining individuals as self-responsible actors in the public sphere with innate rights to life, liberty, and (in John Locke's case) health, and possessions, (in Thomas Jefferson's case), life, liberty, and happiness, was only the beginning of these influences. If freedom and liberty were its fundamental ideals, not only should most, if not all, restraints on self-fulfillment be abolished, but the right to vote should be extended to all qualified to be citizens, and various freedoms should be protected pertaining to the press, free speech, assembly, religion, and the bearing of arms. Such rights and protections derived their legitimacy from the ethical emphasis that liberalism placed on the dignity of the individual as well as the legitimacy of minorities, and they were to go on to encourage constitutionalism, or the balancing of powers, and representative government. *of Enlightenment + liberal thought*

In America such rights and protections were also reinforced by political ideas going back far before the Enlightenment and the development of liberal thinking. Their origins lay in the classical age of the Roman republic and the writings of Cicero, Tacitus, and Plutarch who lived in the years of corruption and disorder following the empire's decline. For them, that decline could best be understood in contrast to an earlier world of rustic simplicity and pastoral virtue that represented an image of the good life, civic morality, and public well-being. Later reworked into a tradition of civic humanism by the Italian Renaissance philosopher Nicollo Machiavelli, these ideals became a kind of template to define the ideal society and successful politics, both dependent on independent citizens prepared to devote their service to their country in a disinterested manner. In England, this classical republican tradition had been passed on by writers like John Milton and James Harrington who then had a decisive effect on Benjamin Franklin, Thomas Jefferson, and other Founders.

What Republicanism gave to the Enlightenment and to Liberalism was an understanding of how best to serve one's fellow human being in a commonwealth. Republicanism supplemented the Enlightenment's reliance on the use of critical reason for the relief of the human estate with the belief that the governance of the social and political order could best be served by independent individuals whose worth is based on merit rather than birth and who are willing to sacrifice their own interests for those of the common good. Basing public order not on religious establishments, hereditary privilege, or bureaucratic patronage, but rather on the practice of civic virtue, was not, of course, without obvious risks. Despite competing interests and factions at stake in the creation of a new government, the American founders and leaders of other democratic revolutions hoped that Republican ideals, along with enlightened self-criticism and a healthy dose of skepticism about democratic politics, would help constrain partisan interests and personal selfishness. This, after all, was a leading rationale for the need for Constitutionalism and a government of checks and balances wherever liberal impulses combined with democratic aspirations in the early nineteenth century, but it was very difficult to hold together a politics of virtue in the midst of a world that was being taken over by more predatory impulses associated with a mixture of rampant individualism, expanding capitalism, divisive sectionalism, and nascent imperialism as the century progressed.

There were, moreover, other factors that impacted democratic revolutions in the late eighteenth and nineteenth centuries having to do with the development of modernization itself and the growth of secularism. While modernization is identified with movements of national unification and the cultivation of national identity, increased popular participation in political life, the spread of literacy, the development of public education, increased social mobility, urbanization, secularism adds to these processes a this-worldly outlook coupled together with a practical can-do way of thinking.

The marvel is that ideas and developments as mixed and volatile as these could produce revolutions not just in one country but in many. And these revolutions were by no means gradual but sudden and radical. It is often forgotten that the word "revolution" traditionally refers to turnings or rotations that interrupt an essential continuity or change the direction of an ongoing movement, but the democratic revolutions of the late eighteenth and nineteenth centuries were quite different. They represented radical upheavals and transformations of the entire political order that left almost no institutions unaffected. While such seismic shifts in the tectonic plates of governance were bound to generate considerable resistance that varied from country to country, their overall effect was not only eventually to transform the country into a nation but to normalize the idea of revolution itself by transforming the need for sweeping fundamental change into an inevitable and necessary feature of normal existence.

In no revolutions did this seem more the case, when they actually arrived, than the American and the French, but it could easily be argued that it was also true in different ways of the Haitian and the Latin American and even, in its own way, of the Japanese. In retrospect, it has sometimes been assumed that the American Revolution provided, with many modifications, the standard script for most democratic revolutions that followed, and that script was nowhere found in more succinct expression than the Declaration of Independence. This is a document that patiently outlines when it becomes necessary and legitimate, as its chief author, Thomas Jefferson, explained in the selection in this chapter drawn from his *Autobiography*, "for one people to dissolve the political bands which have connected them with another, and to assume among the powers of the earth the separate and equal station to which the laws of nature and of nature's God entitle them." Those powers permit them to overthrow any government that systematically deprives them of their inalienable rights as human beings. The Declaration bases this argument on an escalating series of offenses committed by the British crown that culminate (at least in the original version authored by Jefferson and indicated in the text by italics) in the outrage the Crown has committed against all humanity through its support of, profit from, and participation in the inhuman trafficking of African slaves.

While there is no small irony in the fact that this argument was authored by the owner of more than 300 slaves himself, there is equal irony in the fact that these specific offenses had to be removed from the Declaration's final text for it to be signed by South Carolina and Jefferson's own colony of Virginia. One can only wonder what the subsequent history of United States might have been like had these clauses and phrases not been struck to obtain the Declaration's final approval. The American patriots would not have been fighting for the freedom of some people and the enslavement or displacement of others but for the freedom of all people who belong to the human community.

There were many other reasons given for the necessity of revolution, none, perhaps, more effective as well as humorous than Thomas Paine's reminder of the absurdity of a continent being ruled by an island, but the American revolution was also based, like most such convulsions, on a series of negatives that included no established church or nobility or inherited system of manners, the abolition of primogeniture (inheritance only by the first-born son), the end of monarchy, the destruction of entrenched privilege, and, in the Bill of Rights (the first ten Amendments to the U.S. Constitution), the prevention of a number of forms of governmental abuse. Still more impressive, it led to a government of laws rather than men through the ratification of the U. S. Constitution, where powers were separated for the sake of being balanced and the collective identity of American citizens was memorialized and empowered by the phrase "We the people." While this phrase masked the fact that it extended only to those who were considered qualified to be citizens and that their rights applied exclusively to white males, it established the principle that all governments should derive their just powers from the consent of the governed and thus opened the way for federalism to become America's mode of governance and democracy its legitimate form.

The global effects of the American Revolution were, to be sure, immediate and long lasting. It altered the attitudes of great nations toward their colonies, ignited the desire for individual and civil rights all over Europe, clearly hastened the outbreak of the French Revolution, and decisively inspired the creation of the document that makes up the second selection in this chapter known as the French Declaration of the Rights of Man and Citizen. In some ways even more strongly influenced by the Enlightenment than the American Declaration of Independence, the French Declaration reaffirmed that human beings are born free and equal, but it then goes on to argue that this entitles them not only to the rights of liberty and property (actually its protection) but also to the rights of security and resistance to oppression. Other rights also, as in the American model and Constitution, protect freedom of thought and religion, due process by law, taxation by consent, and the separation of government powers.

Unfortunately, the rights of security and resistance to oppression were more difficult to achieve than the authors of the Declaration of the Rights of Man and Citizen may have imagined because the French Revolution itself turned almost immediately against many of its own people. During the 10-month Reign of Terror after the Jacobins seized control of the National Convention and, with Maximilien Robespierre installed as leader of the draconian Committee on Public Safety which suspended the institution of democratic practices, the Revolution began to devour its own, leading to 40,000 casualties, at least 70% of whom were peasants and workers. Caused not only by the cruelty of Robespierre but by the pressures of war and economic crisis, the Terror destroyed the illusion that democratic change is always peaceful and led to a restoration of a new dictatorial order when General Napoleon Bonaparte staged a coup d'etat that resulted in abolishing the Directory that had ruled France since the Reign of Terror. Bonaparte appointed himself "first Consul" from 1779 to 1804 and then crowned himself Emperor from 1804 to 1815.

Napoleon's rule ironically produced democratic revolutions in many other countries of Europe, from the Netherlands, Spain, Switzerland, and the many states of Germany to Milan and Naples. Inspired by the three great principles of the Revolution, "Liberty, Equality and Fraternity," all these revolutions that were fought in the name of liberty and freedom only succeeded in producing dictatorships. Yet these same dictatorships would in their turn inspire new nationalist movements to protest them.

In one of the further cruelties of the French Revolution, the creation of the Declaration inspired the hope among former slaves and mullatos living under French colonial rule across the Atlantic in Haiti to travel to France to secure their rights for themselves. But when they were rebuffed by the French government, a slave revolt followed, led by Toussaint l'Ouverture, that eventuated in the creation of a Haitian Constitution in 1801. The only slave rebellion leading to the creation of a state ruled by former slaves and blacks, the Haitian Revolution was then immediately betrayed tragically by the French under Napoleon when his invading army imprisoned Toussaint in 1802 and left him to die the next year. But by this time the French themselves had been overtaken by events and decided to withdraw from their New World Empire, allowing Haiti to gain its independence after all.

This is the story of French perfidy that is told with great feeling by Henri Christophe in his "Manifesto, 1814," but that narrative can in no way diminish the extraordinary achievement represented by the creation of Haitian independence. Not only did Haiti become the first state populated by former slaves to develop a Constitution and attain statehood; its resistance to Napoleon destroyed France's dream of an empire in the Americas and also encouraged France to relinquish its U.S. territorial possession known as the Louisiana Purchase by selling it in 1803 to the United States. Still more impressive, if Haiti's slave revolt spread fear throughout the Americas, helping to make U.S. slavery more restrictive than that of any other countries, it also shattered assumptions about black inferiority and became in time an inspiration for people the world over fighting for racial justice.

*Agree, great summary the only thing is I argue Haitian Revolution & its effects actually precedes/allowed French Rev/America Rev to happen.*

*Err.... in other words Haitian Rev fulfilled the failed promises of French & Ameri Rev, more significant in history but the narrative is SBM Eurocentric*

# Thomas Jefferson, The Framing of the Declaration of Independence from *Autobiography*

## *Autobiography*
## [THE FRAMING OF THE DECLARATION OF INDEPENDENCE, 1776]

It appearing in the course of these debates, that the colonies of New York, New Jersey, Pennsylvania, Delaware, Maryland, and South Carolina were not yet matured for falling from the parent stem, but that they were fast advancing to that state, it was thought most prudent to wait a while for them, and to postpone the final decision to July 1st; but, that this might occasion as little delay as possible, a committee was appointed to prepare a Declaration of Independence. The committee were John Adams, Dr. Franklin, Roger Sherman, Robert R. Livingston, and myself. Committees were also appointed, at the same time, to prepare a plan of confederation for the colonies, and to state the terms proper to be proposed for foreign alliance. The committee for drawing the Declaration of Independence, desired me to do it. It was accordingly done, and being approved by them, I reported it to the House on Friday, the 28th of June, when it was read, and ordered to lie on the table. On Monday, the 1st of July, the House resolved itself into a committee of the whole, and resumed the consideration of the original motion made by the delegates of Virginia, which, being again debated through the day, was carried in the affirmative by the votes of New Hampshire, Connecticut, Massachusetts, Rhode Island, New Jersey, Maryland, Virginia, North Carolina and Georgia. South Carolina and Pennsylvania voted against it. Delaware had but two members present, and they were divided. The delegates from New York declared they were for it themselves, and were assured their constituents were for it; but that their instructions having been drawn near a twelve-month before, when reconciliation was still the general object, they were enjoined by them to do nothing which should impede that object. They, therefore, thought themselves not justifiable in voting on either side, and asked leave to withdraw from the question; which was given them. The committee rose and reported their resolution to the House. Mr. Edward Rutledge, of South Carolina, then requested the determination might be put off to the next day, as he believed his colleagues, though they disapproved of the resolution, would then join in it for the sake of unanimity. The ultimate question, whether the House would agree to the resolution of the committee, was accordingly postponed to the next day, when it was again moved, and South Carolina concurred in voting for it. In the meantime, a third member had come post from the Delaware counties, and turned the vote of that colony in favor of the resolution. Members of a different sentiment attending that morning from Pennsylvania also, her vote was changed, so that the whole twelve colonies who were authorized to vote at all, gave their voices for it; and, within a few days, the convention of New York approved of it, and thus supplied the void occasioned by the withdrawing of her delegates from the vote.

Source: Henri Christophe, "Manifesto." 1814.

Congress proceeded the same day to consider the Declaration of Independence, which had been reported and lain on the table the Friday preceding, and on Monday referred to a committee of the whole. The pusillanimous idea that we had friends in England worth keeping terms with, still haunted the minds of many. For this reason, those passages which conveyed censures on the people of England were struck out, lest they should give them offence. The clause too, reprobating the enslaving the inhabitants of Africa, were struck out in complaisance to South Carolina and Georgia, who had never attempted to restrain the importation of slaves, and who, on the contrary, still wished to continue it. Our northern brethren also, I believe, felt a little tender under those censures; for though their people had very few slaves themselves, yet they had been pretty considerable carriers of them to others. The debates, having taken up the greater parts of the 2d, 3d, and 4th days of July, were, on the evening of the last, closed; the Declaration was reported by the committee, agreed to by the House, and signed by every member present, except Mr. Dickinson. As the sentiments of men are known not only by what they receive, but what they reject also, I will state the form of the Declaration as originally reported.

## A Declaration by the Representatives of the United States of America, in General Congress Assembled

When, in the course of human events, it becomes necessary for one people to dissolve the political bands which have connected them with another, and to assume among the powers of the earth the separate and equal station to which the laws of nature and of nature's God entitle them, a decent respect to the opinions of mankind requires that they should declare the causes which impel them to the separation.

We hold these truths to be self evident: that all men are created equal; that they are endowed by their Creator with CERTAIN [*inherent and*] inalienable rights; that among these are life, liberty, and the pursuit of happiness; that to secure these rights, governments are instituted among men, deriving their just powers from the consent of the governed; that whenever any form of government becomes destructive of these ends, it is the right of the people to alter or to abolish it, and to institute new government, laying its foundation on such principles, and organizing its powers in such form, as to them shall seem most likely to effect their safety and happiness. Prudence, indeed, will dictate that governments long established should not be changed for light and transient causes; and accordingly all experience hath shown that mankind are more disposed to suffer while evils are sufferable, than to right themselves by abolishing the forms to which they are accustomed. But when a long train of abuses and usurpations, [*begun at a distinguished period and*] pursuing invariably the same object, evinces a design to reduce them under absolute despotism, it is their right, it is their duty to throw off such government, and to provide such sufferance new guards for their future security. Such has been the patient sufferance of these colonies; and such is now the necessity which constrains them to ALTER [*expunge*] their former systems of government. The history of the present king of Great Britain is a history of REPEATED [*unremitting*] injuries and usurpations, ALL HAVING [*among which appears no solitary fact to contradict the uniform tenor of the rest, but all have*] in direct object the establishment of an absolute tyranny over these states. To prove this, let facts be submitted to a candid world [*for the truth of which we pledge a faith yet unsullied by falsehood*].

He has refused his assent to laws the most wholesome and necessary for the public good.

He has forbidden his governors to pass laws of immediate and pressing importance, unless suspended in their operation till his assent should be obtained; and, when so suspended, he has utterly neglected to attend to them.

He has refused to pass other laws for the accommodation of large districts of people, unless those people would relinquish the right of representation in the legislature, a right inestimable to them, and formidable to tyrants only.

He has called together legislative bodies at places unusual, uncomfortable, and distant from the depository of their public records, for the sole purpose of fatiguing them into compliance with his measures.

He has dissolved representative houses repeatedly [*and continually*] for opposing with manly firmness his invasions on the rights of the people.

He has refused for a long time after such dissolutions to cause others to be elected, whereby the legislative powers, incapable of annihilation, have returned to the people at large for their exercise, the state remaining, in the meantime, exposed to all the dangers of invasion form without and convulsions within.

He has endeavored to prevent the population of these states; for that purpose obstructing the laws for naturalization of foreigners, refusing to pass others to encourage their migrations hither, and raising the conditions of new appropriations of lands.

He has OBSTRUCTED [*suffered*] the administration of justice BY [*totally to cease in some of these states*] refusing his assent to laws for establishing judiciary powers.

He has made [*our*] judges dependent on his will alone for the tenure of their offices, and the amount and payment of their salaries.

He has erected a multitude of new offices [*by a self-assumed power*], and sent higher swarms of new officers to harass our people and eat out their substance.

He has kept among us in times of peace standing armies [*and ships of war*] without the consent of our legislatures.

He has affected to render the military independent of, and superior to, the civil power.

He has combined with others to subject us to a jurisdiction foreign to our constitutions and unacknowledged by our laws, giving his assent to their acts of pretended legislation for quartering large bodies of armed troops among us; for protecting them by a mock trial form punishment for any murders which they should commit on the inhabitants of these states; for cutting off our trade with all parts of the world; for imposing taxes on us without consent; for depriving us IN MANY CASES of the benefits of trial by jury; for transporting us beyond seas to be tried for pretended offences; for abolishing the free system of English laws in a neighboring province, establishing therein an arbitrary government, and enlarging its boundaries, so as to render it at once an example and fit instrument for introducing the same absolute rule into these COLONIES [*states*]; for taking away our charters, abolishing our most valuable laws, and altering fundamentally the forms of our governments; for suspending our own legislatures, and declaring themselves invested with power to legislate for us in all cases whatsoever.

He has abdicated government here BY DECLARING US OUT OF HIS PROTECTION, AND WAGING WAR AGAINST US [*withdrawing his governors, and declaring us out of his allegiance and protection*].

He has plundered oar seas, ravaged our coasts, burnt our towns, and destroyed the lives of our people.

He is at this time transporting large armies of foreign mercenaries to complete the works of death desolation and tyranny already begun with circumstances of cruelty and perfidy SCARCELY PARALLELED IN THE MOST BARBAROUS AGES, AND TOTALLY unworthy the head of a civilized nation.

He has constrained our fellow citizens taken captive on the high seas, to bear arms against their country, to become the executioners of their friends and brethren, or to fall themselves by their hands.

He has EXCITED DOMESTIC INSURRECTION AMONG US, AND HAS endeavored to bring on the inhabitants of our frontiers, the merciless Indian savages, whose known rule of warfare is an undistinguished destruction of all ages, sexes and conditions [of existence].

*[He has incited reasonable insurrections of our fellow citizens, with the allurements of forferiture and confiscation of our property.*

*He has waged cruel war against human nature itself, violating its most sacred rights of life and liberty in the persons of a distant people who never offended him, captivating and carrying them into slavery in another hemisphere, or to incur miserable death in their transportation hither. This piratical warfare, the opprobrium of INFIDEL powers, is the warfare of the CHRISTIAN king of Great Britain. Determined to keep open a market where MEN should be bought and sold, he has prostituted his negative for suppressing every legislative attempt to prohibit or to restrain this execrable commerce. And that this assemblage of horrors might want no fact of distinguished die, he is now exciting those very people to rise in arms among us, and to purchase that liberty of which he has deprived them, by murding the people on whom he also obtruded them: thus paying off former crimes committed against the LIBERTIES of one people, with crimes which he urges them to commit against the LIVES of another.]*

In every stage of these oppressions we have petitioned for redress in the most humble terms: our repeated petitions have been answered only by repeated injuries.

A prince whose character is thus marked by every act which may define a tyrant is unfit to be the ruler of a FREE people [*who mean to be free. Future ages will scarcely believe that the hardiness of one man adventured, within the short compass of twelve years only, to lay a foundation so broad and so undisguised for tyranny over a people fostered and fixed in principles of freedom.*]

Nor have we been wanting in attentions to oar British brethren. We have warned them from time to time of attempts by their legislature to extend AN UNWARRANTABLE [a] jurisdiction over us [*these our states*]. We have reminded them of the circumstances of our emigration and settlement here [*no one of which could warrant so strange a pretension: that these were effected at the expense of our own blood and treasure, unassisted by the wealth or the strength of Great Britain: that in constituting indeed our several forms of government, we bad adopted one common king, thereby laying a foundation for perpetual league and amity with them: but that submission to their parliament was no part of our constitution; nor ever in idea if history may be credited: and,*], we HAVE appealed to their native justice and magnanimity AND WE HAVE CONJURED THEM BY [*as Well as to*] the ties of our common kindred to disavow these usurpations which WOULD INEVITABLY [*were likely to*] interrupt our connection and correspondence, They too have been deaf to the voice of justice and of consanguinity. WE MUST THEREFORE [*and when occasions have been given them, by the regular course of their laws, of removing from their councils the disturbers of our harmony, they have, by their free election, re-established them in power. At this very time too, they are permitting their chief magistrate to send over not only soldiers of our common blood, but Scotch and foreign mercenaries to invade and destroy us. These facts have given the last stab to agonizing affection, and manly spirit bids us to renounce forever these unfeeling brethren. We must endeavor to forget our former love for them, and hold them as we hold the rest of mankind! enemies in war, in peace friends. We might have a free and a great people together; but a communication of grandeur and of freedom, it seems, is below their dignity. Be it so, since they will have it. The road to happiness and to glory is open to us, too. We will tred it apart from them, and*] acquiesce is the necessity which denounces our [*eternal*] separation AND HOLD THEM AS WE HOLD THE REST OF MANKIND, ENEMIES IN WAR, IN PEACE FRIENDS.

> We therefore the representatives of the United States of America in General Congress assembled, do in the name, and by the authority of the good people of these [*siates reject and renounce all allegiance and subjection to the kings of Great Britain and all others who may hereafter claim by, through or under them, we utterly dissolve all political connection which may heretofore have substituted between us and the people or parliament of Great Britain: and finally we do assert and declare these colonies to be free and independent states,*] and that as free and independent states, they have full power to levy war, conclude peace, contract alliances, establish commerce, and to do all other acts and things which independent states may of right do.
>
> And for the support of this declaration, we mutually pledge to each other our lives, our fortunes, and our sacred honor.

We, therefore, the representatives of the United States of America in General Congress assembled, appealing to the supreme judge of the world for the rectitude of our intentions, do in the name, and by the authority of the good people of these colonies, solemnly publish and declare, that these united colonies are, and of right ought to be free and independent states; that they are absolved from all allegiance to the British, crown, and that all political connection between them and the state of Great Britain is, and ought to be, totally dissolved; and that as free and independent states, they have full power to levy war, conclude peace, contract affiances, establish commerce, and to do all other acts and things which independent states may of right do.

And for the support of this declaration, with a firm reliance on the protection of divine providence, we mutually pledge to each other our lives, our fortunes, and our sacred honor.

# Declaration of the Rights of Man and Citizen

The representatives of the French people, organized in National Assembly, considering that ignorance, forgetfulness, or contempt of the rights of man are the sole causes of public misfortunes and of the corruption of governments, have resolved to set forth in a solemn declaration the natural, inalienable, and sacred rights of man, in order that such declaration, continually before all members of the social body, may be a perpetual reminder of their rights and duties; in order that the acts of the legislative power and those of the executive power may constantly be compared with the aim of every political institution and may accordingly be more respected; in order that the demands of the citizens, founded henceforth upon simple and incontestable principles, may always be directed towards the maintenance of the Constitution and the welfare of all.

Accordingly, the National Assembly recognizes and proclaims, in the presence and under the auspices of the Supreme Being, the following rights of man and citizen.

1. Men are born and remain free and equal in rights; social distinctions may be based only upon general usefulness.
2. The aim of every political association is the preservation of the natural and inalienable rights of man; these rights are liberty, property, security, and resistance to oppression.
3. The source of all sovereignty resides essentially in the nation; no group, no individual may exercise authority not emanating expressly therefrom.
4. Liberty consists of the power to do whatever is not injurious to others; thus the enjoyment of the natural rights of every man has for its limits only those that assure other members of society the enjoyment of those same rights; such limits may be determined only by law.
5. The law has the right to forbid only actions which are injurious to society. Whatever is not forbidden by law may not be prevented, and no one may be constrained to do what it does not prescribe.
6. Law is the expression of the general will; all citizens have the right to concur personally, or through their representatives, in its formation; it must be the same for all, whether it protects or punishes. All citizens, being equal before it, are equally admissible to all public offices, positions, and employments, according to their capacity, and without other distinction than that of virtues and talents.
7. No man may be accused, arrested, or detained except in the cases determined by law, and according to the forms prescribed thereby. Whoever solicit, expedite, or execute arbitrary orders, or have them executed, must be punished; but every citizen summoned or apprehended in pursuance of the law must obey immediately; he renders himself culpable by resistance.
8. The law is to establish only penalties that are absolutely and obviously necessary; and no one may be punished except by virtue of a law established and promulgated prior to the offence and legally applied.

From *The Declaration of the Rights of Man and of Citizens*, translated from the German by Max Farrand, 1901.

9. Since every man is presumed innocent until declared guilty, if arrest be deemed indispensable, all unnecessary severity for securing the person of the accused must be severely repressed by law.

10. No one is to be disquieted because of his opinions, even religious, provided their manifestation does not disturb the public order established by law.

11. Free communication of ideas and opinions is one of the most precious of the rights of man. Consequently, every citizen may speak, write, and print freely, subject to responsibility for the abuse of such liberty in the cases determined by law.

12. The guarantee of the rights of man and citizen necessitates a public force; such a force, therefore, is instituted for the advantage of all and not for the particular benefit of those to whom it is entrusted.

13. For the maintenance of the public force and for the expenses of administration a common tax is indispensable; it must be assessed equally on all citizens in proportion to their means.

14. Citizens have the right to ascertain, by themselves or through their representatives, the necessity of the public tax, to consent to it freely, to supervise its use, and to determine its quota, assessment, payment, and duration.

15. Society has the right to require of every public agent an accounting of his administration.

16. Every society in which the guarantee of rights is not assured or the separation of powers not determined has no constitution at all.

17. Since property is a sacred and inviolable right, no one may be deprived thereof unless a legally established public necessity obviously requires it, and upon condition of a just and previous indemnity.

# Henri Christophe, Manifesto, 1814

We have deserved the favors of liberty, by our indissoluble attachment to the mother country. We have proved to her our gratitude.

At the time when, reduced to our own private resources, cut off form all communication with France, we resisted every allurement; when, inflexible to menaces, deaf to proposals, inaccessible to artifice, we braved misery, famine, and privation of every kind, and finally triumphed over our enemies both within and without.

We were then far from perceiving that twelve years after, as the price of so much perseverance, sacrifice, and blood, France would deprive us in a most barbarous manner of the most precious of our possessions,—liberty.

Under the administration of Governor-General Toussaint L'Ouverture, Hayti arose from her ruins, and everything seemed to promise a happy future. The arrival of general Hédouville completely changed the aspect of affairs, and struck a deadly blow to public tranquility. We will not enter into the detail of his intrigues with the Haytian General, Rigaud, whom he persuaded to revolt against the legitimate chief. We will only say, that before leaving the island, Hédouville had put everything into confusion, by casting among us the firebrands of discord, and lighting the torch of civil war.

Ever zealous for the reëstablishment of order and of peace, Toussaint L'Ouverture, by a paternal government, restored their original energy to law, morality, religion, education, and industry. Agriculture and commerce were flourishing; he was favorable to white colonists, especially to those who occupied new possessions; and the care and partiality which he felt for them went so far that he was severely censured as being more attached to them than to people of his own color. This negro wall was not without reason; for some months previous to the arrival of the French, he put to death his own nephew, General Moise, for having disregarded his orders relative to the protection of the colonists. This act of the Governor, and the great confidence which he had in the French Government, were the chief causes of the weak resistance which the French met with in Hayti. In reality, his confidence in that Government was so grent, that the General had disbanded the greater part of the regular troops, and employed them in the cultivation of the ground.

Such was the state of affairs whilst the peace of Amiens was being negotiated; it was scarcely concluded, when a powerful armament landed on our coasts a large army, which, attacking us by surprise, when we thought ourselves perfectly secure, plunged us suddenly into an abyss of evils.

Posterity will find a difficulty in believing that, in so enlightened and philosophic an age, such an abominable enterprise could possibly have been conceived. In the midst of a civilized people, a horde of barbarians suddenly set out with the design of exterminating an innocent and peaceable nation, or at least of loading them anew with the chains of national slavery.

It was not enough that they employed violence; they also thought it necessary to use perfidy and villainy,—they were compelled to sow dissension among us, Every means was put in requisition to carry out this abominable scheme. The leaders of all political parties in France, even the sons of the Governor Tousaaint, were invited to take part in the expedition. They, as well as ourselves, were deceived by that *chef-d'oeuvre* of perfidy, the proclamation of the First Consul, in which he said to us, 'You are all equal and free before God and the Republic, such was his declaration, at the same time that his private instructions to General Leclerc were to reëstablish slavery.

The greater part of the population, deceived by these fallacious promises, and for a long time accustomed to consider itself as French, submitted without resistance. The Governor so little expected the appearance of an enemy that he had not even ordered his generals to resist in case of an attack being made; and, when the armament arrived, he himself was on a journey toward the eastern coast. If some few generals did resist, it was owing only to the hostile and menacing manner in which they were summoned to surrender, which compelled them to reapcct their duty, their honor, and the present circumstances.

After a resistance of some months, the Governor-General yielded to the pressing entreaties and the solemn protestations of Leclerc, 'that he intended to protect the liberties of every one, and that France would never destroy so noble a work.' On this footing, peace was negotiated with France; and the Governor Toussaint, laying aside his power, peaceably retired to the retreat he had prepared for himself.

Scarcely had the French extended their dominion over the whole island and that more by roguery and deceit than by force of arms, than they began to put in execution their horrible system of slavery and destruction.

To hasten the accomplishment of their projects, mercenary and Machiavellian writers fabricated fictitious narratives, and attributed to Toussaint designs that he had never entertained. While he was remaining peaceably at home, on the faith of solemn treaties, he was seized, loaded with irons, dragged away with the whole of his family, and transported to France. The whole of Europe knows how he ended his unfortunate career in torture and in prayer, in the dungeon of the Château de Joux.

Such was the recompense reserved for his attachment to France, and for the eminent services he had rendered to the colony.

At the same time, notice was given to arrest all suspected persons throughout the island. All those who had shown brave and enlightened souls, when we claimed for ourselves the rights of men, were the first to be seized. Even the traitors who had most contributed to the success of the French army, by serving as guides to their advanced guard, and by exciting their compatriots to take vengeance, were not spared. At first they desired to sell them into strange colonies; but, as this plan did not succeed, they resolved to transport them to France, where overpowering labor, the galleys, chains, and prisons, were awaiting them.

Then the white colonists, whose numbers have continually increased, seeing their power sufficiently established, discarded the mask of dissimulation, openly declared the reëstablishment of slavery, and acted in accordance with their declaration. They had the impudence to claim as their slaves men who had made themselves eminent by the most brilliant services to their country, in both the civil and military departments. Virtuous and honorable magistrates, warriors covered with wounds, whose blood had been poured out for France and for liberty, were compelled to fall back into the bonds of slavery. These colonists, scarcely established in the possession of their land, whose power was liable to be overthrown by the slightest cause, already marked out and chose in the distance those whom they determined should be the first victims of their vengeance.

The proud and liberty-hating faction of the colonists, of those traffickers in human flesh, who, since the commencement of the revolution, had not ceased to impregnate the successive Governments in France with their plans, their projects, their atrocious and extravagant memorials, and everything tending to our ruin,—these factious men, tormented by the recollection of the despotism which they had formerly exercised at Hayti, a prey to their low and cruel passions, exerted all. their efforts to repossess themselves of the prey which had escaped from their clutches. In favor of independence under the constitutional assembly, terrorists under the Jacobins, and finally, zealous Bonapartists, they knew how to assume the mask of any party, in order to obtain place and favor. It was thus, by their insidious counsels, they urged Bonaparte to undertake this iniquitous expedition to Hayti. It was this faction who, after having advised the expedition, furnished the pecuniary resources which were necessary, by means of subscriptions which were at this time commenced. In a word, it was this faction which caused the blood of our compatriots to flow in torrents,—which invented the exhausting tortures to which we were subjected; it is to these colonists that France owes the loss of a powerful army, which perished in the plains and marshes of Hayti. It is to them she owes the shame of an enterprise which has fixed an indelible stain on the French name. . . .

# *Nationalism and Imperialism*

Nationalism is an ideology that largely arose as a result of the Westphalian Peace of 1648 and the subsequent development over the next 150 years of the modern state system. Both a result as well as a cause of state formation, this ideology had less to do with the form or structure that states took for themselves than with the collective sense of identity on which they attempted to base it. That collective sense of identity transformed a term that in ancient times had been used pejoratively to refer to people born outside the empire and thus barbarian into a word that described what made the people belonging to state formations so unique and special. In its modern formulation, then, the state, or institutional structure of governance, and the nation, or sense of belonging it inspires and is based on, are ideally considered as a relationship that is or was preordained or fated, ideally allowing the state and the nation to feel to their citizens as mere reflections of one another.

However, there was nothing preordained or inevitable about it. If the world now contains as many as 5,000 nationalities, it possesses no more 195 independent, sovereign states, which suggests that the process of creating states out of deep senses of community and solidarity that express themselves as nations is a long and complicated one. Quite apart from the difficulty of creating states by themselves, the process by which they become bound to an ideology that legitimates them by defining that state's collective sense of shared identity takes a considerable amount of time to accomplish and an even greater amount of labor to maintain. In many instances, the first to develop is the formation of a mutual sense of identity among a particular people, whether due to shared ethnicity, religion, language, history, race, land, or customs, and then follows the desire to secure a territorial space where those bound by that collective sense of selfhood can live out their identity as a sovereign people. The ideology of nationalism thus provides a kind of adhesive that holds the two other components of state and nation together, eventually allowing nation-states to reach out beyond themselves to form empires.

It is important to remember, however, that this process of state-making required much more than mere force to allow states to establish and secure themselves and their societies. Even if the social theorist Max Weber once defined the state as no more than that agency within society which possesses a monopoly on the use of legitimate violence, they also had to employ various cultural as well as social, political, military, and legal instruments to consolidate their sovereignty and turn themselves into an object of supreme loyalty. Among such instruments, none was more important than the development of a narrative to explain the common history of the nation. But this creation or origin narrative then had to be linked to a still more elemental foundation myth both to elaborate the purpose of the nation itself and to define the national character thus achieved as in some sense ahistorical or timeless. Such cultural inventions would be impossible to sustain, however, if they had not also been reinforced by the construction of new patterns of ritual and symbolism to express and reinforce them and of new ceremonial occasions to memorialize them. What was being honored on such occasions was the sacred worldview of the nation itself, its place in the overall scheme of things, which helps explain why nationalism has often developed in close relationship with religion. For many citizens, nationalism can and does serve as a complement to religion, for others an alternative to religion, and for still others a compelling substitute for it.

The two readings for this chapter deal with different dimensions of nationalism and the nationalist imaginary. The anthropologist Benedict Anderson's classic study of nations is built on the somewhat startling assumption that before nations can be understood either as political or legal constructions, they need to be conceived as, in the title of his most famous book, "imagined communities." But the possibility of conceptualizing nations as "imagined" depended historically on the abandonment of several other conceptions. The first notion that had to be discarded was the belief that access to the truth is possible only through certain ancient, literary languages—Latin for Christians, Arabic for Muslims, Sanskrit for Hindus, Mandarin for Chinese, etc. The second was the dynastic assumption that society needs to be organized around monarchs who derive their right to rule, and by extension, their special access to the truth, by divine dispensation. And the third notion that had to be relinquished was the conviction that such a hierarchical order could only be guaranteed if time and thus history remained subject to divine or ecclesiastical calendars rather than ordinary temporal ones. Once these more traditional conceptions or imaginaries of world order collapsed, brought on as much as anything, Anderson believes, by the creation of print journalism and its reliance on the secular calendar of daily experience, the way was open to see what kind of fictive logics could be created to explain the nature of the nation-state itself.

Anderson conceives of nations as imagined in four different ways. First, they are imagined because they are "invisible," and they are invisible because no one has ever known or could know all of the individuals who make up the national collectivity they call their own. Second, they are "limited" because the boundaries other than geographical that define nations in the minds of their citizens are impossible to represent adequately even by legal instruments. Third, they are "sovereign" in the sense that they mark a value or significance that exceeds the possibilities of expression and can only be fully be felt both as a privilege and an entitlement. And, fourth and finally, they are "communal" in a way that is self-validating. That is, they express a sense of solidarity, what Anderson describes as "a deep, horizontal comradeship," that in times of national peril or pride can unify almost every citizen of the state.

This makes nations, with their semi-sacred ideology of nationhood and its implied ethic of heroic self-sacrifice, susceptible to two different kinds of pathologies. The first has been described by another eminent anthropologist included in this volume, Arjun Appadurai, as "vivisectionist" because it refers to the temptation to dismember parts of the body of the state itself, as in genocide, whenever citizens feel threatened by what they sense as different, or diseased, or treacherous. The second he calls "verificationist" in that it encourages the state to purge itself, as in racial profiling, of any element that is felt to be impure or incomplete. At its best, nationalism has provided many throughout the world with a system of beliefs to house their deepest needs for community and self-esteem; at its worst, it has fed the appetite for almost continuous violence and war throughout the nineteenth and twentieth-centuries and has led to unimaginable suffering and despair.

But some might well ask whether this seemingly Western notion of nationhood fits all the people of the world. While artifice and imagination play crucial roles in the construction of most national identities, it may be that for many non-Western and formerly colonized people some of their misery as citizens may have been caused by having to imagine their difference, even exclusion, from the image propagated by the West of a nationally coherent state. For many of those peoples who have had to wrest their sense of communal identity out of post-colonial struggles with foreign oppressors, their collective sense of themselves may well be derived from imagining their difference from the centralized forms of national identity propagated by the modernized West. At the same time, such invented identities can also operate at the transnational as well as the national level. For example, the regional entity now known as "Southeast Asia" did not even exist until after World War II, when the United States decided to turn an area that had never been conquered or unified before into a regional bulwark for the defense of democracy against Communist expansionism. This conversion of Southeast Asia into a new "imagined reality" was accomplished politically and militarily by the creation of the SEATO pact (Southeast Asia Treaty Organization), but in order for this new regional designation to gain credibility and validity, it subsequently required in addition the creation of a whole new academic field of study and research known as "Southeast Asian Studies," the renaming of thousands of formerly different peoples as "Southeast Asians," and the training of countless specialists called "Southeast Asianists" in the traditions, languages, and customs of these immensely varied peoples who over the centuries had populated this newly invented transnational region of the world.

The selection by Liah Greenfeld affords extraordinary insight into the special appeal of nationalism by exploring in further detail the historical development of the Western idea of "nation." As the Latin term for something born, the term "nation" was originally applied by ancient Romans to foreigners coming from the same region whose status was considered beneath their own. The association of the term "nation" with inferiors began to change when in the early Middle Ages when it was employed favorably to describe groups of students from similar regions coming to study at institutions like the University of Paris. Conferring on students a "national" identity had no other function than to indicate their place of origin and was immediately relinquished upon their return to their own homeland. Nonetheless, the term began to take on a second meaning when it became evident that students coming from the same region seemed to share similar opinions in scholastic debate and other student activities. Thus what was once a term employed to designate a community of origin now began to reflect something more like a community of opinion and shared ways of thinking. But it wasn't until students from the same nation were asked to serve as representatives at church councils and other ecclesiastical functions that these two notions of nation took a quantum leap forward. Suddenly national identity acquired a new hierarchical status conferring authority and prestige that allowed its bearers to be considered members of a special elite. But it was only when the term's new hierarchical status as referring to a special, prestigious elite was extended four centuries later in England and in Holland to the entire population of a country and identified with the word "people" that the modern transformation of the notion of the nation was ultimately complete. Now the "nation" became synonymous with all the citizens of a country and at the same time invested those same citizens with the privilege of representing symbolically the sovereignty associated with the state.

In time, the spread of nationalism in Europe was to produce a new age of imperialism based on the interest of states in extending their spheres of influence through the creation of colonies designed to rule over other people for the sake of exploiting their resources and labor. While colonialism in the West actually began as early as the 16th century with the formation of early world trade, it didn't achieve its fullest expression until the later nineteenth century and the beginning of the twentieth. Such nationalist expansionism, at least in Europe, was typically justified by the claim that the so-called mother country was motivated chiefly to extend the benefits of "civilization" to those who presumably lacked any, but this seemingly benign, even idealistic, presumption was simply a mask that concealed a reality that was very different.

Take Africa, for example, where few areas before 1880 were politically ruled by Europeans even if Europeans had made their commercial presence known centuries earlier. By 1913, however, just over 30 years later, Europeans ruled all but four of the forty territorial states in Africa, and by the 1930s colonial rule had spread to 84.6% of the world's population. Even if imperial rule may have had some beneficial effects in places like India under the British Commonwealth, it was based on monstrous hypocrisy and led to unspeakable suffering. The Polish writer, Joseph Conrad, got it right when he entitled his great novel of 1901 *Heart of Darkness*. Having experienced firsthand the horrors of colonialism in the Congo whose literal owner, King Leopold II of Belgium, had permitted the slaughter of literally half his subjects, the country's entire population, in a 20-year period, Conrad described imperialism as a crime: "It was just robbery with violence, aggravated murder on a grand scale. . . . The conquest of the earth, which mostly means taking it away from those who have a different complexion or flatter noses than ourselves, is not a pretty thing when you look into it too much. What redeems it is the idea only. An idea at the back of it; . . . and an unselfish belief in the idea – something you can set up, and bow down before, and offer a sacrifice to . . . ." This idea at the back imperialism that served as a justification, a rationalization, an excuse for whatever the colonizer wanted to do, possessed, Conrad added, "no more moral purpose at the back of it than there is in burglars breaking into a safe."

The potential for this same kind of hypocrisy lay at the heart of another ideological practice sponsored by Western imperialism known as "Orientalism." Originally created as a term to identify the professional and academic study of the culture, societies, and traditions of the so-called Orient, it soon came to be associated in a much more general way, as Edward W. Said points out in the final selection in this chapter, with the styles of thinking, feeling, and acting supposedly characteristic of the tens of millions of people who inhabited these enormous areas of the world with their thousands of cultures. But when this habit of simplification and stereotyping in turn gave way to discursive practices of describing, defining, dictating, and ruling over the Orient, then "Orientalism" itself was turned into an ideological instrument of domination and control that masked its motives under the disguise of altruism and cosmopolitanism.

The study of such discursive practices, in which Said's *Orientalism* played an important part, was associated with a kind of intellectual revolution that led to the study, as we shall see in Chapter 12, of colonialism and post-colonialism. This revolution was devoted to the attempt to bring the mind, so to speak, into the light by treating many of its operations as something accessible to investigation through study of the discursive or communicative modes by which the mind represents itself to itself. Examining the mind through the techniques by which it seeks to present itself as it wishes to be known, as it intends to be seen as much as understood, requires an interrogation of the assumptions and preconditions not of what people say but of what enables them to say it. The questions to be asked are what empowers their discourse, and how does it work in the interests of such goals as domination and subordination, subversion and containment, manipulation and disguise. Discourse analysis, as this kind of inquiry has come to be termed, and by means of which Said's *Orientalism* came to be viewed as a pioneering study not only in the history of Western imperialism but also of post-colonialism, thus focuses on the relationship between discourse, communication, power, inequality, and positionality.

# Introduction [Imagined Communities]

 BENEDICT ANDERSON

Perhaps without being much noticed yet, a fundamental transformation in the history of Marxism and Marxist movements is upon us. Its most visible signs are the recent wars between Vietnam, Cambodia and China. These wars are of world-historical importance because they are the first to occur between regimes whose independence and revolutionary credentials are undeniable, and because none of the belligerents has made more than the most perfunctory attempts to justify the bloodshed in-terms of a recognizable *Marxist* theoretical perspective. While it was still just possible to interpret the Sino-Soviet border clashes of 1969, and the Soviet military interventions in Germany (1953), Hungary (1956), Czechoslovakia (1968), and Afghanistan (1980) in terms of—according to taste—'social imperialism', 'defending socialism,' etc., no one, I imagine, seriously believes that such vocabularies have much bearing on what has occurred in Indochina.

If the Vietnamese invasion and occupation of Cambodia in December 1978 and January 1979 represented the first *large-scale conventional war* waged by one revolutionary Marxist regime against another,[1] China's assault on Vietnam in February rapidly confirmed the precedent. Only the most trusting would dare wager that in the declining years of this century any significant outbreak of inter-state hostilities will necessarily find the USSR and the PRC—let alone the smaller socialist states—supporting, or fighting on, the same side. Who can be confident that Yugoslavia and Albania will not one day come to blows? Those variegated groups who seek a withdrawal of the Red Army from its encampments in Eastern Europe should remind themselves of the degree to which its overwhelming presence has, since 1945, ruled out armed conflict between the region's Marxist regimes.

Such considerations serve to underline the fact that since World War II every successful revolution has defined itself in *national* terms—the Peoples Republic of China, the Socialist Republic of Vietnam, and so forth—and, in so doing, has grounded itself firmly in a territorial and social space inherited from the prerevolutionary past. Conversely, the fact that the Soviet Union shares with the

---

[1] This formulation is chosen simply to emphasize the scale and the style of the fighting, not to assign blame. To avoid possible misunderstanding, it should be said that the December 1978 invasion grew out of armed clashes between partisans of the two revolutionary movements going back possibly as far as 1971. After April 1977 border raids, initiated by the Cambodians, but quickly followed by the Vietnamese grew in size and scope, culminating in the major Vietnamese incursion of December 1977. None of these raids, however, aimed at overthrowing enemy regimes or occupying large territories, nor were the numbers of troops involved comparable to those deployed in December 1978. The controversy over the causes of the war is most thoughtfully pursued in: Stephen P. Heder, 'The Kampuchean-Vietnamese Conflict,' in David W. P. Elliott, ed., *The Third Indochina Conflict*, pp. 21–67; Anthony Barnett, 'Inter-Communist Conflicts and Vietnam,' *Bulletin of Concerned Asian of Scholars*, 11: 4 (October–December 1979), pp. 2–9; and Laura Summers, 'In Matters of War and Socialism Anthony Barnett would Shame and Honour Kampuchea Too Much,' ibid., pp. 10–18.

United Kingdom of Great Britain and Northern Ireland the rare distinction of refusing nationality in its naming suggests that it is as much the legatee of the prenational dynastic states of the nineteenth century as the precursor of a twenty-first century internationalist order.[2]

Eric Hobsbawm is perfectly correct in stating that Marxist movements and states have tended to become national not only in form but in substance, i.e., nationalist. There is nothing to suggest that this trend will not continue.[3] Nor is the tendency confined to the socialist world. Almost every year the United Nations admits new members. And many 'old nations,' once thought fully consolidated, find themselves challenged by 'sub'-nationalisms within their borders—nationalisms which, naturally, dream of shedding this subness one happy day. The reality is quite plain: the 'end of the era of nationalism', so long prophesied, is not remotely in sight. Indeed, nation-ness is the most universally legitimate value in the political life of our time.

But if the facts are clear, their explanation remains a matter of long-standing dispute. Nation, nationality, nationalism—all have proved notoriously difficult to define, let alone to analyse. In contrast to the immense influence that nationalism has exerted on the modern world, plausible theory about it is conspicuously meagre. Hugh Seton-Watson, author of far the best and most comprehensive English-language text on nationalism, and heir to a vast tradition of liberal historiography and social science, sadly observes: 'Thus I am driven to the conclusion that no "scientific definition" of the nation can be devised; yet the phenomenon has existed and exists.'[4] Tom Nairn, author of the path-breaking *The Break-up of Britain,* and heir to the scarcely less vast tradition of Marxist historiography and social science, candidly remarks: 'The theory of nationalism represents Marxism's great historical failure.'[5] But even this confession is somewhat misleading, insofar as it can be taken to imply the regrettable outcome of a long, self-conscious search for theoretical clarity. It would be more exact to say that nationalism has proved an uncomfortable *anomaly* for Marxist theory and, precisely for that reason, has been largely elided, rather than confronted. How else to explain Marx's failure to explicate the crucial adjective in his memorable formulation of 1848: 'The proletariat of each country must, of course, first of all settle matters with its own bourgeoisie'?[6] How else to account for the use, for over a century, of the concept 'national bourgeoisie' without any serious attempt to justify theoretically the relevance of the adjective? Why is *this* segmentation of the bourgeoisie—a world-class insofar as it is defined in terms of the relations of production—theoretically significant?

The aim of this book is to offer some tentative suggestions for a more satisfactory interpretation of the 'anomaly' of nationalism. My sense is that on this topic both Marxist and liberal theory have become etiolated in a late Ptolemaic effort to 'save the phenomena'; and that a reorientation of perspective in, as it were, a Copernican spirit is urgently required. My point of departure is

[2] Anyone who has doubts about the UK's claims to such parity with the USSR should ask himself what nationality its name denotes: Great Brito-Irish?

[3] Eric Hobsbawm, 'Some Reflections on "The Break-up of Britain"', *New Left Review,* 105 (September– October 1977), p. 13.

[4] See his *Nations and States,* p. 5. Emphasis added.

[5] See his 'The Modern Janus', *New Left Review,* 94 (November–December 1975), p. 3. This essay is included unchanged in *The Break-up of Britain* as chapter 9 (pp. 329–63).

[6] Karl Marx and Friedtich Engels, *The Communist Manifesto,* in the Selected Works, 1, p. 45. Emphasis added. In any theoretical exegesis, the words 'of course' should flash red lights before the transported reader.

that nationality or, as one might prefer to put it in view of that word's multiple significations, nation-ness, as well as nationalism, are cultural artefacts of a particular kind. To understand them properly we need to consider carefully how they have come into historical being, in what ways their meanings have changed over time, and why, today, they command such profound emotional legitimacy. I will be trying to argue that the creation of these artefacts towards the end of the eighteenth century[7] was the spontaneous distillation of a complex 'crossing' of discrete historical forces; but that, once created, they became 'modular,' capable of being transplanted, with varying degrees of self-consciousness, to a great variety of social terrains, to merge and be merged with a correspondingly wide variety of political and ideological constellations. I will also attempt to show why these particular cultural artefacts have aroused such deep attachments.

## Concepts and Definitions

Before addressing the questions raised above, it seems advisable to consider briefly the concept of 'nation' and offer a workable definition. Theorists of nationalism have often been perplexed, not to say irritated, by these three paradoxes: (1) The objective modernity of nations to the historian's eye vs. their subjective antiquity in the eyes of nationalists. (2) The formal universality of nationality as a socio-cultural concept—in the modern world everyone can, should, will 'have' a nationality, as he or she 'has' a gender—vs. the irremediable particularity of its concrete manifestations, such that, by definition, 'Greek' nationality is sui generis. (3) The 'political' power of nationalisms vs. their philosophical poverty and even incoherence. In other words, unlike most other isms, nationalism has never produced its own grand thinkers: no Hobbeses, Tocquevilles, Marxes, or Webers. This 'emptiness' easily gives rise, among cosmopolitan and polylingual intellectuals, to a certain condescension. Like Gertrude Stein in the face of Oakland, one can rather quickly conclude that there is 'no there there'. It is characteristic that even so sympathetic a student of nationalism as Tom Nairn can nonetheless write that: '"Nationalism" is the pathology of modern developmental history, as inescapable as "neurosis" in the individual, with much the same essential ambiguity attaching to it, a similar built-in capacity for descent into dementia, rooted in the dilemmas of helplessness thrust upon most of the world (the equivalent of infantilism for societies) and largely incurable.'[8]

Part of the difficulty is that one tends unconsciously to hypostasize the existence of Nationalism-with-a-big-N (rather as one might Age-with-a-capital-A) and then to classify 'it' as an ideology. (Note that if everyone has an age, Age is merely an analytical expression.) It would, I think, make things easier if one treated it as if it belonged with 'kinship' and 'religion', rather than with 'liberalism' or 'fascism'.

---

[7] As Aira Kemilainen notes, the twin 'founding fathers' of academic scholarship on nationalism, Hans Khon and Carleton Hayes, argued persuasively for this dating. Their conclusions have, I think, not been seriously disputed except by nationalist ideologues in particular countries. Kemilainen also observes that the word 'nationalism' did not come into wide general use until the end of the nineteenth century. It did not occur, for example, in many standard nineteenth century lexicons. If Adam Smith conjured with the wealth of 'nations,' he meant by the term no more than 'societies' or 'states.' Aira Kemiläinen, *Nationalism*, pp. 10, 33, and 48–49.

[8] *The Break-up of Britain*, p. 359.

In an anthropological spirit, then, I propose the following definition of the nation: it is an imagined political community—and imagined as both inherently limited and sovereign.

It is *imagined* because the members of even the smallest nation will never know most of their fellow-members, meet them, or even hear of them, yet in the minds of each lives the image of their communion.[9] Renan referred to this imagining in his suavely back-handed way when he wrote that 'Or l'essence d'une nation est que tous les individus aient beaucoup de choses en commun, et aussi que tous aient oublié bien des choses.'[10] With a certain ferocity Gellner makes a comparable point when he rules that 'Nationalism is not the awakening of nations to self-consciousness: it *invents* nations where they do not exist.'[11] The drawback to this formulation, however, is that Gellner is so anxious to show that nationalism masquerades under false pretences that he assimilates 'invention' to 'fabrication' and 'falsity', rather than to 'imagining' and 'creation'. In this way he implies that 'true' communities exist which can be advantageously juxtaposed to nations. In fact, all communities larger than primordial villages of face-to-face contact (and perhaps even these) are imagined. Communities are to be distinguished, not by their falsity/genuineness, but by the style in which they are imagined. Javanese villagers have always known that they are connected to people they have never seen, but these ties were once imagined particularistically—as indefinitely stretchable nets of kinship and clientship. Until quite recently, the Javanese language had no word meaning the abstraction 'society.' We may today think of the French aristocracy of the *ancien régime* as a class; but surely it was imagined this way only very late.[12] To the question 'Who is the Comte de X?' the normal answer would have been, not 'a member of the aristocracy,' but 'the lord of X,' 'the uncle of the Baronne de Y,' or 'a client of the Duc de Z.'

The nation is imagined as limited because even the largest of them, encompassing perhaps a billion living human beings, has finite, if elastic, boundaries, beyond which lie other nations. No nation imagines itself coterminous with mankind. The most messianic nationalists do not dream of a day when all the members of the human race will join their nation in the way that it was possible, in certain epochs, for, say, Christians to dream of a wholly Christian planet.

It is imagined as *sovereign* because the concept was born in an age in which Enlightenment and Revolution were destroying the legitimacy of the divinely-ordained, hierarchical dynastic realm. Coming to maturity at a stage of human history when even the most devout adherents of any universal religion were inescapably confronted with the living *pluralism* of such religions, and the allomorphism between each faith's ontological claims and territorial stretch, nations dream of being free, and, if under God, directly so. The gage and emblem of this freedom is the sovereign state.

Finally, it is imagined as a *community*, because, regardless of the actual inequality and exploitation that may prevail in each, the nation is always conceived as a deep, horizontal

---

[9]  Cf. Seton-Watson, *Nations and States*, p. 5: 'All that I can find to say is that a nation exists when a significant number of people in a community consider themselves to form a nation, or behave as if they formed one.' We may translate 'consider themselves' as 'imagine themselves.'

[10]  Ernest Renan, 'Qu'est-ce qu'une nation?' in *OEuvres Complètes*, 1, p. 892. He adds 'tout citoyen français doit avoir oublié la Saint-Barthélemy, les massacres due Miki an XIIIe siècle. Il n'y a pas en France dix familles qui puissent fournir la preuve d'une origine franque . . .'

[11]  Ernest Gellner, *Thought and Change*, p. 169. Emphasis added.

[12]  Hobsbawm, for example, 'fixes' it by saying that in 1789 it numbered about 400,000 in a population of 23,000,000. (See his *The Age of Revolution*, p. 78). But would this statistical picture of the noblesse have been imaginable under the ancien régime?

comradeship. Ultimately it is this fraternity that makes it possible, over the past two centuries, for so many millions of people, not so much to kill, as willingly to die for such limited imaginings.

These deaths bring us abruptly face to face with the central problem posed by nationalism: what makes the shrunken imaginings of recent history (scarcely more than two centuries) generate such colossal sacrifices? I believe that the beginnings of an answer lie in the cultural roots of nationalism.

# From Nationalism: Five Roads to Modernity

 LIAH GREENFELD

This book is an attempt to understand the world in which we live. Its fundamental premise is that nationalism lies at the basis of this world. To grasp its significance, one has to explain nationalism.

The word "nationalism" is used here as an umbrella term under which are subsumed the related phenomena of national identity (or nationality) and consciousness, and collectivities based on them—nations; occasionally it is employed to refer to the articulate ideology on which national identity and consciousness rest, though not—unless specified—to the politically activist, xenophobic variety of national patriotism, which it frequently designates.

The specific questions which the book addresses are why and how nationalism emerged, why and how it was transformed in the process of transfer from one society to another, and why and how different forms of national identity and consciousness became translated into institutional practices and patterns of culture, molding the social and political structures of societies which defined themselves as nations. To answer these questions, I focus on five major societies which were the first to do so: England, France, Russia, Germany, and the United States of America.

## The Definition of Nationalism

The specificity of nationalism, that which distinguishes nationality from other types of identity, derives from the fact that nationalism locates the source of individual identity within a "people," which is seen as the bearer of sovereignty, the central object of loyalty, and the basis of collective solidarity. The "people" is the mass of a population whose boundaries and nature are defined in various ways, but which is usually perceived as larger than any concrete community and always as fundamentally homogeneous, and only superficially divided by the lines of status, class, locality, and in some cases even ethnicity. This specificity is conceptual. The only foundation of nationalism as such, the only condition, that is, without which no nationalism is possible, is an idea; nationalism is a particular perspective or a style of thought. The idea which lies at the core of nationalism is the idea of the "nation."

## The Origins of the Idea of the "Nation"

To understand the nature of the idea of the "nation," it might be helpful to examine the semantic permutations which eventually resulted in it, as we follow the history of the word. The early stages of this history were traced by the Italian scholar Guido Zernatto. The origin of the word is to be found in the Latin *natio*—something born. The initial concept was derogatory: in Rome the name *natio* was reserved for groups of foreigners coming from the same geographical region, whose status—because they were foreigners—was below that of the Roman citizens. This concept was thus similar in meaning to the Greek *ta ethne*, also used to designate foreigners and, specifically, heathens, and to the Hebrew *amamim*, which referred to those who did not belong to the chosen monotheistic people. The word had other meanings as well, but they were less common, and this one—a group of foreigners united by place of origin—for a long time remained its primary implication.

In this sense, of a group of foreigners united by place of origin, the word "nation" was applied to the communities of students coming to several universities shared by Western Christendom from loosely—geographically or linguistically—related regions. For example, there were four nations in the University of Paris, the great center of theological learning: "l'honorable nation de France," "la fidèle nation de Picardie," "la vénérable nation de Normandie," and "la constante nation de Germanie." The "nation de France" included all students coming from France, Italy, and Spain; that of "Germanie," those from England and Germany; the Picard "nation" was reserved for the Dutch; and the Norman, for those from the Northeast. It is important to note that the students had a national identity only in their status as students (that is, in most cases, while residing abroad); this identity was immediately shed when their studies were completed and they returned home. While applied in this setting, the word "nation," on the one hand, lost its derogatory connotation, and on the other, acquired an additional meaning. Owing to the specific structure of university life at the time, the communities of students functioned as support groups or unions and, as they regularly took sides in scholastic disputations, also developed common opinions. As a result, the word "nation" came to mean more than a community of origin: it referred now to the community of opinion and purpose.

As universities sent representatives to adjudicate grave ecclesiastical questions at the Church Councils, the word underwent yet another transformation. Since the late thirteenth century, starting at the Council of Lyon in 1274, the new concept—"nation" as a community of opinion—was applied to the parties of the "ecclesiastical republic." But the individuals who composed them, the spokesmen of various intraecclesiastical approaches, were also representatives of secular and religious potentates. And so the word "nation" acquired another meaning, that of representatives of cultural and political authority, or a political, cultural, and then social elite. Zernatto cites Montesquieu, Joseph de Maistre, and Schopenhauer to demonstrate how late this was still the accepted significance of the word. It is impossible to mistake its meaning in the famous passage from *Esprit des lois*: "Sous les deux premières races on assembla souvent la nation, c'est à dire, les seigneurs et les évêques; il n'était point des communes."

## The Zigzag Pattern of Semantic Change

At this point, where Zernatto's story breaks off, we may pause to take a closer look at it. To an extent, the history of the word "nation" allows us to anticipate the analysis employed in much of the book. The successive changes in meaning combine into a pattern which, for the sake of formality, we shall call "the zigzag pattern of semantic change." At each stage of this development, the meaning of the word, which comes with a certain semantic baggage, evolves out of usage in a particular situation. The available conventional concept is applied within new circumstances, to certain aspects of which it corresponds. However, aspects of the new situation, which were absent in the situation in which the conventional concept evolved, become cognitively associated with it, resulting in a duality of meaning. The meaning of the original concept is gradually obscured, and the new one emerges as conventional. When the word is used again in a new situation, it is likely to be used in this new meaning, and so on and so forth. (This pattern is depicted in Figure 9.1.)

The process of semantic transformation is constantly redirected by structural (situational) constraints which form the new concepts (meanings of the word); at the same time, the structural constraints are conceptualized, interpreted, or defined in terms of the concepts (the definition of the situation changes as the concepts evolve), which thereby orient action. The social potency and psychological effects of this orientation vary in accordance with the sphere of the concept's applicability and its relative centrality in the actor's overall existence. A student in a medieval university, defined as a member of one or another nation, might derive therefrom an idea of the quarters he was supposed to be lodged in, people he was likely to associate with most closely, and some specific opinions he was expected to hold in the course of the few years his studies lasted. Otherwise his "national" identity, probably, did not have much impact on his self-image or behavior; outside the narrow sphere of the university, the concept had no applicability. The influence of the

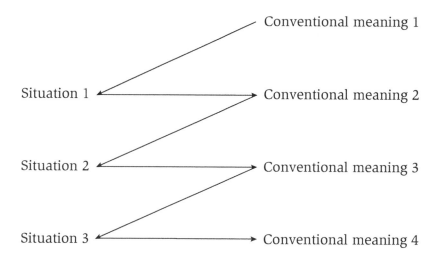

Etc.

**FIGURE 9.1** The zigzag pattern of semantic change.

equally transient "national" identity on a participant at a Church Council could be more profound. Membership in a nation defined him as a person of very high status, the impact of such definition on one's self-perception could be permanent, and the lingering memory of nationality could affect the person's conduct far beyond conciliar deliberations, even if his nation no longer existed.

## From "Rabble" to "Nation"

The applicability of the idea of the nation and its potency increased a thousandfold as the meaning of the word was transformed again. At a certain point in history—to be precise, in early sixteenth-century England—the word "nation" in its conciliar meaning of "an elite" was applied to the population of the country and made synonymous with the word "people." *This semantic transformation signaled the emergence of the first nation in the world, in the sense in which the word is understood today, and launched the era of nationalism.* The stark significance of this conceptual revolution was highlighted by the fact that, while the general referent of the word "people" prior to its nationalization was the population of a region, specifically it applied to the lower classes and was most frequently used in the sense of "rabble" or "plebs." The equation of the two concepts implied the elevation of the populace to the position of an (at first specifically political) elite. As a synonym of the "nation"—an elite—the "people" lost its derogatory connotation and, now denoting an eminently positive entity, acquired the meaning of the bearer of sovereignty, the basis of political solidarity, and the supreme object of loyalty. A tremendous change of attitude, which it later reinforced, had to precede such redefinition of the situation, for with it members of all orders of the society identified with the group, from which earlier the better placed of them could only wish to dissociate themselves. What brought this change about in the first place, and then again and again, as national identity replaced other types in one country after another, is, in every particular case, the first issue to be accounted for, and it will be the focus of discussion in several chapters of the book.

National identity in its distinctive modern sense is, therefore, an identity which derives from membership in a "people," the fundamental characteristic of which is that it is defined as a "nation." Every member of the "people" thus interpreted partakes in its superior, elite quality, and it is in consequence that a stratified national population is perceived as essentially homogeneous, and the lines of status and class as superficial. This principle lies at the basis of all nationalisms and justifies viewing them as expressions of the same general phenomenon. Apart from it, different nationalisms share little. The national populations—diversely termed "peoples," "nations," and "nationalities"— are defined in many ways, and the criteria of membership in them vary. The multiformity which results is the source of the conceptually evasive, Protean nature of nationalism and the cause of the perennial frustration of its students, vainly trying to define it with the help of one or another "objective" factor, all of which are rendered relevant to the problem only if the national principle happens to be applied to them. The definition of nationalism proposed here recognizes it as an "emergent phenomenon," that is, a phenomenon whose nature—as well as the possibilities of its development and the possibilities of the development of the elements of which it is composed—is determined not by the character of its elements, but by a certain organizing principle which makes these elements into a unity and imparts to them a special significance.

There are important exceptions to every relationship in terms of which nationalism has ever been interpreted—whether with common territory or common language, statehood or shared traditions, history or race. None of these relationships has proved inevitable. But from the definition proposed above, it follows not only that such exceptions are to be expected, but that nationalism does not have to be related to any of these factors, though as a rule it is related to at least some of them. In other words, *nationalism is not necessarily a form of particularism*. It is a political ideology (or a class of political ideologies deriving from the same basic principle), and as such it does not have to be identified with any particular community. A nation coextensive with humanity is in no way a contradiction in terms. The United States of the World, which will perhaps exist in the future, with sovereignty vested in the population, and the various segments of the latter regarded as equal, would be a nation in the strict sense of the word within the framework of nationalism. The United States of America represents an approximation to precisely this state of affairs.

## The Emergence of Particularistic Nationalisms

As it is, however, nationalism is the most common and salient form of particularism in the modern world. Moreover, if compared with the forms of particularism it has replaced, it is a particularly effective (or, depending on one's viewpoint, pernicious) form of particularism, because, as every individual derives his or her identity from membership in the community, the sense of commitment to it and its collective goals is much more widespread. In a world divided into particular communities, national identity tends to be associated and confounded with a community's sense of uniqueness and the qualities contributing to it. These qualities (social, political, cultural in the narrow sense, or ethnic) therefore acquire a great significance in the formation of every specific nationalism. The association between the nationality of a community and its uniqueness represents the next and last transformation in the meaning of the "nation" and may be deduced from the zigzag pattern of semantic (and by implication social) change.

The word "nation" which, in its conciliar and at the time prevalent meaning of an elite, was applied to the population of a specific country (England) became cognitively associated with the existing (political, territorial, and ethnic) connotations of a population and a country. While the interpretation of the latter in terms of the concept "nation" modified their significance, the concept "nation" was also transformed and—as it carried over the connotations of a population and a country, which were consistent with it—came to mean "a sovereign people." This new meaning replaced that of "an elite" initially only in England. As we may judge from Montesquieu's definition, elsewhere the older meaning long remained dominant, but it was, eventually, supplanted.

The word "nation," meaning "sovereign people," was now applied to other populations and countries which, like the first nation, naturally had some political, territorial, and/or ethnic qualities to distinguish them, and became associated with such geo-political and ethnic baggage. As a result of this association, "nation" changed its meaning once again, coming to signify "a unique sovereign people." (These changes are shown in Figure 9.2.) The last transformation may be considered responsible for the conceptual confusion reigning in the theories of nationalism. The new concept of the nation in most cases eclipsed the one immediately preceding it, as the latter eclipsed those from

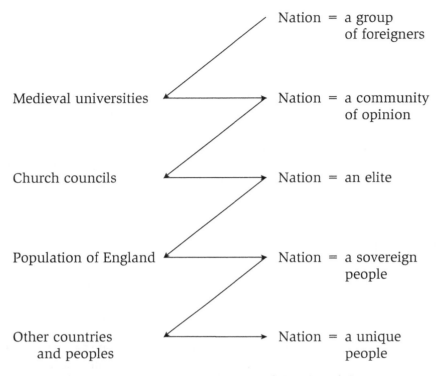

**FIGURE 9.2** The transformation of the idea of the nation.

which it descended, but, significantly, this did not happen everywhere. Because of the persistence and, as we shall see, in certain places development and extension of structural conditions responsible for the evolution of the original, non-particularistic idea of the nation, the two concepts now coexist.

The term "nation" applied to both conceals important differences. The emergence of the more recent concept signified a profound transformation in the nature of nationalism, and the two concepts under one name reflect two radically different forms of the phenomenon (which means both two radically different forms of national identity and consciousness, and two radically different types of national collectivities—nations).

## Types of Nationalism

The two branches of nationalism are obviously related in a significant way, but are grounded in different values and develop for different reasons. They also give rise to dissimilar patterns of social behavior, culture, and political institutions, often conceptualized as expressions of unlike "national characters."

Perhaps the most important difference concerns the relationship between *nationalism* and *democracy*. The location of sovereignty within the people and the recognition of the fundamental equality among its various strata, which constitute the essence of the modern national idea, are at the same time the basic tenets of democracy. Democracy was born with the sense of nationality. The two are inherently linked, and neither can be fully understood apart from this connection. Nationalism was the form in which democracy appeared in the world, contained in the idea of the nation as a butterfly in a cocoon. Originally, nationalism developed *as* democracy; where the conditions of such original development persisted, the identity between the two was maintained. But as nationalism spread in different conditions and the emphasis in the idea of the nation moved from the sovereign character to the uniqueness of the people, the original equivalence between it and democratic principles was lost. One implication of this, which should be emphasized, is that democracy may not be exportable. It may be an inherent predisposition in certain nations (inherent in their very definition as nations—that is, the original national concept), yet entirely alien to others, and the ability to adopt and develop it in the latter may require a change of identity.

The emergence of the original (in principle, non-particularistic) idea of the nation as a sovereign people was, evidently, predicated on a transformation in the character of the relevant population, which suggested the symbolic elevation of the "people" and its definition as a political elite, in other words, on a profound change in structural conditions. The emergence of the ensuing, particularistic, concept resulted from the application of the original idea to conditions which did not necessarily undergo such transformation. It was the other, in the original concept accidental, connotations of people and country which prompted and made possible such application. In both instances, the adoption of the idea of the nation implied symbolic elevation of the populace (and therefore the creation of a new social order, a new structural reality). But while in the former case the idea was inspired by the structural context which preceded its formation—the people acting in some way as a political elite, and actually exercising sovereignty—in the latter case the sequence of events was the opposite: the importation of the idea of popular sovereignty—as part and parcel of the idea of the nation—initiated the transformation in the social and political structure.

As it did so, the nature of sovereignty was inevitably reinterpreted. The *observable* sovereignty of the people (its nationality) in the former case could only mean that some individuals, who were *of* the people, exercised sovereignty. The idea of the nation (which implied sovereignty of the people) acknowledged this experience and rationalized it. The national principle that emerged was individualistic: sovereignty of the people was the implication of the actual sovereignty of individuals; it was because these individuals (of the people) actually exercised sovereignty that they were members of a nation. The theoretical *sovereignty* of the people in the latter case, by contrast, was an implication of the people's uniqueness, its very being a distinct people, because this was the meaning of the nation, and the nation was, by definition, sovereign. The national principle was collectivistic; it reflected the collective being. Collectivistic ideologies are inherently authoritarian, for, when the collectivity is seen in unitary terms, it tends to assume the character of a collective individual possessed of a single will, and someone is bound to be its interpreter. The reification of a community introduces (or preserves) fundamental inequality between those of its few members who are qualified to interpret the collective will and the many who have no such qualifications; the select few dictate to the masses who must obey.

These two dissimilar interpretations of popular sovereignty underlie the basic types of nationalism, which one may classify as individualistic-libertarian and collectivistic-authoritarian. In addition, nationalism may be distinguished according to criteria of membership in the national collectivity, which may be either "civic," that is, identical with citizenship, or "ethnic." In the former case, nationality is at least in principle open and voluntaristic; it can and sometimes must be acquired. In the latter, it is believed to be inherent—one can neither acquire it if one does not have it, nor change it if one does; it has nothing to do with individual will, but constitutes a genetic characteristic. Individualistic nationalism cannot be but civic, but civic nationalism can also be collectivistic. More often, though, collectivistic nationalism takes on the form of ethnic particularism, while ethnic nationalism is necessarily collectivistic. (These concepts are summarized in Figure 9.3.)

It must be kept in mind, of course, that these are only categories which serve to pinpoint certain characteristic tendencies within different—specific—nationalisms. They should be regarded as models which can be approximated, but are unlikely to be fully realized. In reality, obviously, the most common type is a mixed one. But the compositions of the mixtures vary significantly enough to justify their classification in these terms and render it a useful analytical tool.

|  | *Civic* | *Ethnic* |
|---|---|---|
| *Individualistic-libertarian* | Type I | Void |
| *Collectivistic-authoritarian* | Type II | Type III |

**FIGURE 9.3** Types of nationalism.

# Orientalism

## Introduction

### I.

On a visit to Beirut during the terrible civil war of 1975–1976 a French journalist wrote regretfully of the gutted downtown area that "it had once seemed to belong to . . . the Orient of Chateaubriand and Nerval." He was right about the place, of course, especially so far as a European was concerned. The Orient was almost a European invention, and had been since antiquity a place of romance, exotic beings, haunting memories and landscapes, remarkable experiences. Now it was disappearing; in a sense it had happened, its time was over. Perhaps it seemed irrelevant that Orientals themselves had something at stake in the process, that even in the time of Chateaubriand and Nerval Orientals had lived there, and that now it was they who were suffering; the main thing for the European visitor was a European representation of the Orient and its contemporary fate, both of which had a privileged communal significance for the journalist and his French readers.

Americans will not feel quite the same about the Orient, which for them is much more likely to be associated very differently with the Far East (China and Japan, mainly). Unlike the Americans, the French and the British—less so the Germans, Russians, Spanish, Portuguese, Italians, and Swiss—have had a long tradition of what I shall be calling Orientalism, a way of coming to terms with the Orient that is based on the Orient's special place in European Western experience. The Orient is not only adjacent to Europe; it is also the place of Europe's greatest and richest and oldest colonies, the source of its civilizations and languages, its cultural contestant, and one of its deepest and most recurring images of the Other. In addition, the Orient has helped to define Europe (or the West) as its contrasting image, idea, personality, experience. Yet none of this Orient is merely imaginative. The Orient is an integral part of European *material* civilization and culture. Orientalism expresses and represents that part culturally and even ideologically as a mode of discourse with supporting institutions, vocabulary, scholarship, imagery, doctrines, even colonial bureaucracies and colonial styles. In contrast, the American understanding of the Orient will seem considerably less dense, although our recent Japanese, Korean, and Indochinese adventures ought now to be creating a more sober, more realistic "Oriental" awareness. Moreover, the vastly expanded American political and economic role in the Near East (the Middle East) makes great claims on our understanding of that Orient.

It will be clear to the reader (and will become clearer still throughout the many pages that follow) that by Orientalism I mean several things, all of them, in my opinion, interdependent. The most readily accepted designation for Orientalism is an academic one, and indeed the label still serves in a number of academic institutions. Anyone who teaches, writes about, or researches the Orient—and this applies whether the person is an anthropologist, sociologist, historian, or philologist—either in its specific or its general aspects, is an Orientalist, and what he or she does is Orientalism. Compared with *Oriental studies* or *area studies*, it is true that the term *Orientalism* is less preferred by specialists today, both because it is too vague and general and because it connotes the high-handed executive attitude of nineteenth-century and early-twentieth-century European colonialism. Nevertheless books are written and congresses held with "the Orient" as their main focus, with the Orientalist in his new or old guise as their main authority. The point is that even if it does not survive as it once did, Orientalism lives on academically through its doctrines and theses about the Orient and the Oriental.

Related to this academic tradition, whose fortunes, transmigrations, specializations, and transmissions are in part the subject of this study, is a more general meaning for Orientalism. Orientalism is a style of thought based upon an ontological and epistemological t-"distinction made between "the Orient" and (most of the time) "the Occident." Thus a very large mass of writers, among whom are poets, novelists, philosophers, political theorists, economists, and imperial administrators, have accepted the basic distinction between East and West as the starting point for elaborate theories, epics, novels, social, descriptions, and political accounts concerning the Orient, its people, customs, "mind," destiny, and so on. *This* Orientalism can accommodate Aeschylus, say, and Victor Hugo, Dante and Karl Marx. A little later in this introduction I shall deal with the methodological problems one encounters in so broadly construed a "field" as this.

The interchange between the academic and the more or less imaginative meanings of Orientalism is a constant one, and since the late eighteenth century there has been a considerable, quite disciplined—perhaps even regulated—traffic between the two. Here I come to the third meaning of Orientalism, which is something more historically and materially defined than either of the other two. Taking the late eighteenth century as a very roughly defined starting point Orientalism can be discussed and analyzed as the corporate institution for dealing with the Orient—dealing with it by making statements about it, authorizing views of it, describing it, by teaching it, settling it, ruling over it: in short, Orientalism as a Western style for dominating, restructuring, and having authority over the Orient. I have found it useful here to employ Michel Foucault's notion of a discourse, as described by him in *The Archaeology of Knowledge* and in *Discipline and Punish,* to identify Orientalism. My contention is that without examining Orientalism as a discourse one cannot possibly understand the enormously systematic discipline by which European culture was able to manage—and even produce—the Orient politically, sociologically, militarily, ideologically, scientifically, and imaginatively during the post-Enlightenment period. Moreover, so authoritative a position did Orientalism have that I believe no one writing, thinking, or acting on the Orient could do so without taking account of the limitations on thought and action imposed by Orientalism. In brief, because of Orientalism the Orient was not (and is not) a free subject of thought or action. This is not to say that Orientalism unilaterally determines what can be said about the Orient, but that it is the whole network of interests inevitably brought to bear on (and therefore always involved in) any occasion when that peculiar entity "the Orient" is in question. How this happens is what this book tries to demonstrate. It also tries to show that European culture gained in strength and identity by setting itself off against the Orient as a sort of surrogate and even underground self.

Historically and culturally there is a quantitative as well as a qualitative difference between the Franco-British involvement in the Orient and—until the period of American ascendancy after World War II—the involvement of every other European and Atlantic power. To speak of Orientalism therefore is to speak mainly, although not exclusively, of a British and French cultural enterprise, a project whose dimensions take in such disparate realms as the imagination itself, the whole of India and the Levant, the Biblical texts and the Biblical lands, the spice trade, colonial armies and a long tradition of colonial administrators, a formidable scholarly corpus, innumerable Oriental "experts" and "hands," an Oriental professorate, a complex array of "Oriental" ideas (Oriental despotism, Oriental splendor, cruelty, sensuality), many Eastern sects, philosophies, and wisdoms domesticated for local European use—the list can be extended more or less indefinitely. My point is that Orientalism derives from a particular closeness experienced between Britain and France and the Orient, which until the early nineteenth century had really meant only India and the Bible lands. From the beginning of the nineteenth century until the end of World War II France and Britain dominated the Orient and Orientalism; since World War II America has dominated the Orient, and approaches it as France and Britain once did. Out of that closeness, whose dynamic is enormously productive even if it always demonstrates the comparatively greater strength of the Occident (British, French, or American), comes the large body of texts I call Orientalist.

It should be said at once that even with the generous number of books and authors that I examine, there is a much larger number that I simply have had to leave out. My argument, however, depends neither upon an exhaustive catalogue of texts dealing with the Orient nor upon a clearly delimited set of texts, authors, and ideas that together make up the Orientalist canon. I have depended instead upon a different methodological alternative—whose backbone in a sense is the set of historical generalizations I have so far been making in this Introduction—and it is these I want now to discuss in more analytical detail.

## II

I have begun with the assumption that the Orient is not an inert fact of nature. It is not merely *there*, just as the Occident itself is not just *there* either. We must take seriously Vico's great observation that men make their own history, that what they can know is what they have made, and extend it to geography: as both geographical and cultural entities—to say nothing of historical entities —such locales, regions, geographical sectors as "Orient" and "Occident" 'are man-made. Therefore as much as the West itself, the Orient is an idea that has a history and a tradition of thought, imagery, and vocabulary that have given it reality and presence in and for the West. The two geographical entities thus support and to an extent reflect each other.

Having said that, one must go on to state a number of reasonable qualifications. In the first place, it would be wrong to conclude that the Orient was *essentially* an idea, or a creation with no corresponding reality. When Disraeli said in his novel *Tancred* that the East was a career, he meant that to be interested in the East was something bright young Westerners would find to be an all- consuming passion; he should not be interpreted as saying that the East was *only* a career for Westerners. There were—and are— cultures and nations whose location is in the East, and their lives, histories, and customs have a brute reality obviously greater than anything that could be said about them in the West. About that fact this study of Orientalism has very little to contribute, except to acknowledge it tacitly. But the phenomenon of Orientalism as I study it here deals principally, not with a correspondence between Orientalism and Orient, but with the internal consistency of Orientalism and its ideas about the Orient (the East as career) despite or beyond any correspondence, or lack thereof, with a "real"' Orient. My point is that Disraeli's statement about the East refers mainly to that created consistency, that regular constellation of ideas as the pre-eminent thing about the Orient, and not to its mere being, as Wallace Stevens's phrase has it.

A second qualification is that ideas, cultures, and histories cannot seriously be understood or studied without their force, or more precisely their configurations of power, also being studied. To believe that the Orient was created—or, as I call it, "Orientalized"—and to believe that such things happen simply as a necessity of the imagination, is to be disingenuous. The relationship between Occident and Orient is a relationship of power, of domination, of varying degrees of a complex hegemony, and is quite accurately indicated in the title of K. M. Panikkar's classic *Asia and Western Dominance?* The Orient was Orientalized not only because it was discovered to be "Oriental" in all those ways considered commonplace by an average nineteenth-century European, but also because it *could be*—that is, submitted to being—*made* Oriental. There is very little consent to be found, for example, in the fact that Flaubert's encounter with an Egyptian courtesan produced a widely influential model of the Oriental woman; she never spoke of herself, she never represented her emotions, presence, or history. He spoke for and represented her. He was foreign, comparatively wealthy, male, and these were historical facts of domination that allowed him not only to possess Kuchuk Hanem physically but to speak for her and tell his readers in what way she was "typically Oriental." My argument is that Flaubert's situation of strength in relation to Kuchuk Hanem was not an isolated instance. It fairly stands for the pattern of relative strength between East and West, and the discourse about the Orient that it enabled.

This brings us to a third qualification. One ought never to assume that the structure of Orientalism is nothing more than a structure of lies or of myths which, were the truth about them to be told, would simply blow away. I myself believe that Orientalism is more particularly valuable as a sign of European-Atlantic power over the Orient than it is as a veridic discourse about the Orient (which is what, in its academic or scholarly form, it claims to be). Nevertheless, what we must respect and try to grasp is the sheer knitted-together strength of Orientalist discourse, its very close ties to the enabling socio-economic and political institutions, and its redoubtable durability. After all, any system of ideas that can remain unchanged as teachable wisdom (in academies, books, congresses, universities, foreign-service institutes) from the period of Ernest Renan in the late 1840s until the present in the United States must be something more formidable than a mere collection of lies. Orientalism, therefore, is not an airy European fantasy about the Orient, but a created body of theory and practice in which, for many generations, there has been a considerable material investment. Continued investment made Orientalism, as a system of knowledge about the Orient, an accepted grid for filtering through the Orient into Western consciousness, just as that same investment multiplied—indeed, made truly productive—the statements proliferating out from Orientalism into the general culture.

Gramsci has made the useful analytic distinction between civil and political society in which the former is made up of voluntary (or at least rational and noncoercive) affiliations like schools, families, and unions, the latter of state institutions (the army, the police, the central bureaucracy) whose role in the polity is direct domination. Culture, of course, is to be found operating within civil society, where the influence of ideas, of institutions, and of other persons works not through domination but by what Gramsci calls consent. In any society not totalitarian, then, certain cultural forms predominate over others, just as certain ideas are more influential than others; the form of this cultural leadership is what Gramsci has identified as *hegemony*, an indispensable concept for any understanding of cultural life in the industrial West. It is hegemony, or rather the result of cultural hegemony at work, that gives Orientalism the durability and the strength I have been speaking about so far. Orientalism is never far from what Denys Hay has called the idea of Europe, a collective notion identifying "us" Europeans as against all "those" non-Europeans, and indeed it can be argued that the major component in European culture is precisely what made that culture hegemonic both in and outside Europe: the idea of European identity as a superior one in comparison with all the non-European peoples and cultures. There is in addition the hegemony of European ideas about the Orient, themselves reiterating European superiority over Oriental backwardness, usually overriding the possibility that a more independent, or more skeptical, thinker might have had different views on the matter.

In a quite constant way, Orientalism depends for its strategy on this flexible *positional* superiority, which puts the Westerner in a whole series of possible relationships with the Orient without ever losing him the relative upper hand. And why should it have been otherwise, especially during the period of extraordinary European ascendancy from the late Renaissance to the present? The scientist, the scholar, the missionary, the trader, or the soldier was in, or thought about, the Orient because he *could be there*, or could think about it, with very little resistance on the Orient's part. Under the general heading of knowledge of the Orient, and within the umbrella of Western hegemony over the Orient during the period from the end of the eighteenth century, there emerged a complex Orient suitable for study in the academy, for display in the museum, for reconstruction in the colonial office, for theoretical illustration in anthropological, biological, linguistic, racial, and historical theses about mankind and the universe, for instances of economic and sociological theories of development, revolution, cultural personality, national or religious character. Additionally, the imaginative examination of things Oriental was based more or less exclusively upon a sovereign Western consciousness out of whose unchallenged centrality an Oriental world emerged, first according to general ideas about who or what was an Oriental, then according to a detailed logic governed not simply by empirical reality but by a battery of desires, repressions, investments, and projections. If we can point to great Orientalist works of genuine scholarship like Silvestre de Sacy's *Chrestomathie arabe* or Edward William Lane's *Account of the Manners and Customs of the Modern Egyptians*, we need also to note that Renan's and Gobineau's racial ideas came out of the same impulse, as did a great many Victorian pornographic novels (see the analysis by Steven Marcus of "The Lustful Turk").

And yet, one must repeatedly ask oneself whether what matters in Orientalism is the general group of ideas overriding the mass of material—about which who could deny that they were shot through with doctrines of European superiority, various kinds of racism, imperialism, and the like, dogmatic views of "the Oriental" as a kind of ideal and unchanging abstraction?—or the much more varied work produced by almost uncountable individual writers, whom one would take up as individual instances of authors dealing with the Orient. In a sense the two alternatives, general and particular, are really two perspectives on the same material: in both instances one would have to deal with pioneers in the field like William Jones, with great artists like Nerval or Flaubert. And why would it not be possible to employ both perspectives together, or one after the other? Isn't there an obvious danger of distortion (of precisely the kind that academic Orientalism has always been prone to) if either too general or too specific a level of description is maintained systematically?

My two fears are distortion and inaccuracy, or rather the kind of inaccuracy produced by too dogmatic a generality and too positivistic a localized focus. In trying to deal with these problems I have tried to deal with three main aspects of my own contemporary reality that seem to me to point the way out of the methodological or perspectival difficulties I have been discussing, difficulties that might force one, in the first instance, into writing a coarse polemic on so unacceptably general a level of description as not to be worth the effort, or in the second instance, into writing so detailed and atomistic a series of analyses as to lose all track of the general lines of force informing the field, giving it its special cogency. How then to recognize individuality and to reconcile it with its intelligent, and by no means passive or merely dictatorial, general and hegemonic context?

# CHAPTER TEN

# *Global War in the Twentieth Century*

If there is any certainty that unites most victims of war, and more specifically mass or total war, it is that no one who hasn't experienced it can possibly understand it. In its devastations and deprivations and degradations, it is simply incomparable. And so it has been for the two world wars of the twentieth century and their many offshoots. War on this scale does not end with the fatalities; in some ways, it just begins there. Apart from the ten empires that were destroyed by these two world wars and the more than 100 million deaths and nearly twice that number of wounded, there were many more millions of deaths caused by war-related famine and diseases, the tens of millions of refugees they generated and the populations they uprooted, along with the social and psychological violence inflicted on combatants and non-combatants alike.

But this is only the beginning of the catalogue of the casualties, casualties that have come from the conflicts generated by these wars. Think of how many hot wars followed in the wake of these two world wars—to name only the most obvious, the Korean War (1950-53), the Vietnam War (1954-1975), the Persian Gulf War (1990-91), the Afghan War (2001-present), and the Iraq War (2003-2011), and then couple that with the number of victims of the Communist and Socialist Revolutions (there are no figures for twentieth-century Democratic Revolutions) that estimates have put at close to another 100 million, and the list of casualties multiplies exponentially.

World War I (1914-1918) was the first mass war that was no longer confined to the battlefield and enlisted the energies of all the nations involved. It was caused by alliances generated by nationalism—Germany, Austria-Hungary, and Italy vs. Britain, France, Russia, and eventually the United States—and succeeded in destroying no less than seven empires. Nations were essentially fighting over their imperial roles that were defined by territorial shifts in boundaries, colonial possessions, and military power. Neither side sought massive consequences but both sides were devastated by a war of attrition. Defined by the double line of trenches that eventually extended from the Swiss border to the North Sea and that during three-and-a-half years never moved more than ten miles in either direction, World War I left 16 million dead and at least 21 million wounded. It moreover decimated an entire generation of young men on both sides and debased every abstraction that could have sustained and dignified their suffering. The American novelist Ernest Hemingway put it perfectly in the words of his protagonist, Fredric Henry, who confessed in *A Farewell to Arms*, "I was always embarrassed by the word sacred, glorious, and sacrifice. . . . I had seen nothing sacred, and the things that were glorious had no glory and the sacrifices were like the stockyards at Chicago if nothing was done with the meat but to bury it. There were many words that you could not stand to hear and finally only the names of places had dignity."

World War II (1941-1945) was another issue altogether. Though in some respects merely the continuation, after a 20-year suspension, of World War I, the Second World War was a struggle not merely over territory and resources but also over who should control them and at what price to others—political, economic, social, cultural, emotional. World War II was a conflict that sought the reordering of nearly the entire globe. It thus ranged over all the oceans and continents and caused catastrophic physical and human destruction, almost doubling the number of fatalities from World War I, bankrupting Germany, Japan, Italy, and England, driving the broken Soviet economy into a still more brutal dictatorship, and paving the way in 1949 for the Communist takeover in China. The only country that came out of the war stronger than before it began was the United States, which then set out to create a military empire of its own in the postwar era that now numbers nearly 800 overseas military bases. If the Japanese intention was to create an empire in East, Southeast, and South Asia that reached the Western Hemisphere, the German objective was to reorder demographically almost the entire Eurasian landmass by slaughtering, sterilizing, and enslaving tens, if not hundreds, of millions of people. This new empire was intended to extend across Europe to the Middle East as well as to Africa and the West.

Among many other developments, World War II reordered the theater of war itself by turning civilians rather than the military into its principal targets. This policy was first inaugurated by Germany during the Blitz beginning in September 1940, when German bombers raided London for 57 consecutive nights and continued this assault from the air until May of the next year. England was eventually to retaliate a year later, to be followed by the Americans, when it commenced the systematic bombing first of German industry and then of German cities to disable the economy and break civilian morale. But the Americans were to adopt this policy themselves with even greater zeal against the Japanese when, late in the war, they proceeded to firebomb with napalm no less than 67 cities.

Still more horrific damage was done to traditional, even military, values by the invention of two new forms of destruction in World War II. The first was the industrialization of murder known as the Holocaust that was directed against whole peoples simply as a punishment for in effect having been born. Its targets were principally Jews, some six million of whom either perished at the hands of firing squads, or in the ovens of the death camps, or were worked to death, but it should not be forgotten that the Germans also exterminated something on the order of another 10 million souls that included Roma (or gypsies), Ethnic Poles, Ukrainian and Belarusian Slavs, Soviet POWs, the disabled, Freemasons, Slovenes, homosexuals, and Jehovah's Witnesses. To many people around the world, this holocaust of merciless destruction—the Jews termed it the *Shoah*--seemed to augur the introduction of an entirely new kind of evil in the world that left virtually all of its survivors, as well as untold millions of its witnesses, wondering how such malevolence and cruelty could be countenanced by a just God or, in fact, any God at all.

But the Holocaust was not the only form of destruction introduced in World War II that seemed to redefine the terms of warfare and the scale of justice. This second source of evil was located in the power of the atom and its ability to be used not only to obliterate whole cities in the blink of an eye but to leave radioactive fallout that could keep killing and deforming people for generations. The atomic bomb that was detonated over Hiroshima, Japan on August 6, 1945 killed 90,000 people outright and another 200,000 within five years because of the lasting health effects of the radiation received by survivors. The atomic bomb dropped on Nagasaki, Japan three days later was actually intended to be 40% more destructive than the Hiroshima bomb because it was made of plutonium rather than uranium but, due to the fact that many school children had already been evaluated from the city before it was released, the initial blast killed only 40,000 people immediately and another 140,000 within five years. While such events as these produced psychological as well as physical aftereffects from which the Japanese people are still struggling to overcome, it should not be forgotten that nuclear power has now become hundreds of times more lethal than the destruction first visited on Japan, and the recent weaponization of still more unconventional arms like biological pathogens, chemical compounds, cyber warfare , and even nanotechnological devices have expanded the destructive geometry of warfare yet further.

The first reading in this chapter comes from one of the very best books written on World War I entitled *The Great War in Modern Memory* by Paul Fussell. The second comes from one of the very best books written on the entire twentieth century entitled *Age of Extremes* by Eric Hobsbawm. Fussell's aim in this selection is to explain how human memory could function at all in the face of scenes and experiences that expressed so vividly the ghastly disproportion between the altruistic ends for which World War I was supposedly fought and the horrific means that were employed to pursue them. His answer was that the only way that the human mind could recall such painful memories was by viewing them ironically, as Ernest Hemingway did in *A Farewell to Arms*. If Hemingway had just given way to his bitterness and disgust, it would simply have been swept up in the general sense of disbelief, horror, and despair that threatened to overwhelm anyone who tried to give vent to their feelings. But by relying instead on the understatement of irony, Hemingway was able not only to keep himself from being overwhelmed by these feelings but to find enough distance from them to render the monstrous spectacle of disproportion between means and ends that occasioned them. Not only was irony more capable of identifying, drawing forth, and lending significance to a perception that might otherwise simply have merged in the general stream of outrage; irony was also more capable at the same time of registering the sense of innocence and idealism that had been shattered in the process.

The selection from Eric Hobsbawm, drawn from his chapter on "The Age of Total War," seeks to assess the impact of this entire era on humanity itself. If the 20th century was, as Hobsbawm elsewhere describes in his book, "the cruelest, and most bestial, century in the history of human records," this was partly because total war was turned on all people, military and civilians alike. It was also partly because total war brought a new impersonality to killing itself by relying so completely on technology and thus enabling the war's greatest cruelties to be performed in the name of modern systems and mechanical routines rather of ancient enmities and traditional rivalries. Add to this the human displacements caused outside of Europe where, as in India alone, decolonization produced another 15 million refugees, or the Korean War, which left 5 million Koreans homeless, and one can begin to appreciate why war in the twentieth century has been so catastrophic.

Nor is it without significance that many of the twentieth century's wars involved terrible miscalculations. Germany, for example, never guessed that Britain would come to the defense of Belgium in 1914. Against overwhelming evidence, Stalin also kept himself in denial of the possibility that Hitler was preparing to invade Russia in 1941. In similar fashion, the Americans and the Japanese continuously misread each other's intentions and capacities before the beginning of the War in the Pacific and the U.S. never failed to anticipate that the Chinese would enter the Korean war in 1950, producing a dangerous stalemate that has now lasted more than 60 years.

The consequences of global war in the century just past were shattering enough in themselves, but they continue to reverberate in the present century. The destabilization of the Middle East is in no small measure due to the redrawing of the boundaries of regimes after World War I that left their people in arbitrarily contrived and deeply volatile autocratic state formations that paid no attention to the historic bonds or politics of religion, region, tribe, clan, or ethnicity. The breakup of the Soviet Union after the end of the Cold War left no less than 27 countries spanning its southern border to fend for themselves amidst feuds, hatreds, conflicts, and jealousies that go back centuries. And now, particularly as America has begun on a number of fronts to yield world leadership, great powers from China and Russia to India, Iran, and even Turkey are in the midst of reassessing their priorities and ambitions on a global scale. As a result, many of the countries of the world are like them turning themselves into giant security states designed essentially to protect themselves against adversaries of every kind, whether real or imagined.

# A Satire of Circumstance: Irony and Memory from The Great War and Modern Memory

 Paul Fussell

The innocent army fully attained the knowledge of good and evil at the Somme on July 1, 1916. That moment, one of the most interesting in the whole long history of human disillusion, can stand as the type of all the ironic actions of the war. What could remain of confidence in Divine assistance once it was known what Haig wrote his wife just before the attack: "I feel that every step in my plan has been taken with the Divine help"? "The wire has never been so well cut," he confided to his diary, "nor the artillery preparation so thorough." His hopes were those of every man. Private E. C. Stanley recalls: "I was very pleased when I heard that my battalion would be in the attack. I thought this would be the last battle of the war and I didn't want to miss it. I remember writing to my mother, telling her I would be home for the August Bank Holiday," Even the weather cooperated to intensify the irony, just as during the summer of 1914. "On the first of July," Sassoon says, "the weather, after an early morning mist, was of the kind commonly called heavenly." Thirteen years after that day Henry Williamson recalled it vividly:

> I see men arising and walking forward; and I go forward with them, in a glassy delirium wherein some seem to pause, with bowed heads, and sink carefully to their knees, and roll slowly over, and lie still. Others roll and roll, and scream and grip my legs in uttermost fear, and I have to struggle to break away, while the dust and earth on my tunic changes from grey to red.
>
> And I go on with aching feet, up and down across ground like a huge ruined honeycomb, and my wave melts away, and the second wave comes up, and also melts away, and then the third wave merges into the ruins of the first and second, and after a while the fourth blunders into the remnants of the others, and we begin to run forward to catch up with the barrage, gasping and sweating, in bunches, anyhow, every bit of the months of drill and rehearsal forgotten, for who could have imagined that the "Big Push" was going to be this?

What assists Williamson's recall is precisely the ironic pattern which subsequent vision has laid over the events. In reading memoirs of the war one notices the same phenomenon over and over. By applying to the past a paradigm of ironic action, a rememberer is enabled to locate, draw forth and finally shape into significance an event or a moment which otherwise would merge without meaning into the general undifferentiated stream.

This mechanism of irony-assisted recall is well illustrated by the writing of Private Alfred M. Hale. He was a genteel, delicate, monumentally incompetent middle-aged batman, known somewhat patronizingly as "our Mr. Hale" in the Royal Flying Corps installations where he served. Four years after the war, he composed a 658-page memoir of his agonies and humiliations, dwelling on his palpable unfitness for any kind of military life and on the constant ironic gap between what was expected of him and what he could perform. At one camp it was his job to heat water for the officers' ablutions. At the same time, he was strictly forbidden to gather fuel for heating water, since the only source of fuel was the lumber of numerous derelict barracks in the camp. Frustrated almost to madness by this conflict of obligations, by the abuse now from one set of officers for the insufficiently heated water, now from another for his tearing up and incinerating the barracks piece by piece, Hale confesses to an anxiety fully as agonizing as that faced by troops in an assault. "Heating water," he remembers, "was a sort of punishment for every sin I have ever committed, I should say." Writing his aggrieved memoir, he knows that he is dwelling excessively on his water-heating problems, incontinently returning to them again and again. He tries to break away and resume his narrative: "I said I was going to turn to other matters." But it is exactly the irony of his former situation that keeps calling him back: "In truth it is the irony of things, as they were in those days, that has forced me back on my tracks, as it has a habit of doing, whenever writing of what I then went through."

Another private, Gunner Charles Bricknall, recalling the war many years later, likewise behaves as if his understanding of the irony attending events is what enables him to recall them. He was in an artillery battery being relieved by a new unit fresh from England:

> There was a long road leading to the front line which the Germans occasionally shelled, and the shells used to drop plonk in the middle of it. This new unit assembled right by the wood ready to go into action in the night.

What rises to the surface of Bricknall's memory is the hopes and illusions of the newcomers:

> They was all spick and span, buttons polished and all the rest of it.

He tries to help:

> We spoke to a few of the chaps before going up and told them about the Germans shelling the road, but of course they was not in charge, so up they went and the result was they all got blown up.

Contemplating this ironic issue, Bricknall is moved to an almost Dickensian reiterative rhetoric:

> Ho, what a disaster! We had to go shooting lame horses, putting the dead to the side of the road, what a disaster, which could have been avoided if only the officers had gone into action the hard way [i.e., overland, avoiding the road]. That was something I shall never forget.

It is the *if only* rather than the slaughter that helps Bricknall "never forget" this. A slaughter by itself is too commonplace for notice. When it makes an ironic point it becomes memorable.

Bricknall was a simple man from Walsall, Staffordshire, who died in 1968 at the age of 76. He was, his son tells me, "a man; a real man; a real soldier from Walsall." Sir Geoffrey Keynes, on the other hand, John Maynard's brother, was a highly sophisticated scholar, surgeon, author, editor, book collector, and bibliographer, with honorary doctorates from Oxford, Cambridge, Edinburgh, Sheffield, Birmingham, and Reading. In 1968 he recalled an incident of January 26, 1916. A German shell landed near a British artillery battery and killed five officers, including the major commanding, who were standing in a group. "I attended as best I could to each of them," he remembers, "but all were terribly mutilated and were dead or dying." He then wonders why he remembers so clearly this relatively minor event: "Far greater tragedies were happening elsewhere all the time. The long, drawn-out horrors of Passchendaele were to take place not far away." It is, he concludes, the small ironic detail of the major's dead dog that enables him to "see these things as clearly today as if they had just happened": "The pattern of war is shaped in the individual mind by small individual experiences, and I can see these things as clearly today as if they had just happened, down to the body of the major's terrier bitch . . . lying near her master."

In gathering material for his book *The First Day on the Somme* in 1970, Martin Middlebrook took pains to interview as many of the survivors as he could find. They too use the pattern of irony to achieve their "strongest recollections." Thus Private E. T. Radband: "My strongest recollection: all those grand-looking cavalrymen, ready mounted to follow the breakthrough. What a hope!" And Corporal J. H. Tansley: "One's revulsion to the ghastly horrors of war was submerged in the belief that this war was to end all wars and Utopia would arise. What an illusion!"

"There are some contrasts war produces," says Hugh Quigley, "which art would esteem hackneyed or inherently false." And, we can add, which the art of memory organizes into little ironic vignettes, satires of circumstance more shocking, even, than Hardy's. Here is one from Blunden's *Undertones of War*:

> A young and cheerful lance-corporal of ours was making some tea [in the trench] as I passed one warm afternoon. Wishing him a good tea, I went along three fire bays; one shell dropped without warning behind me; I saw its smoke faint out, and I thought all was as lucky as it should be. Soon a cry from that place recalled me; the shell had burst all wrong. Its butting impression was black and stinking in the parados where three minutes ago the lance-corporal's mess-tin was bubbling over a little flame. For him, how could the gobbers of blackening flesh, the earth-wall sotted with blood, with flesh, the eye under the duckboard, the pulpy bone be the only answer?

And irony engenders worse irony:

> At this moment while he looked with dreadful fixity at so isolated a horror, the lance-corporal's brother came round the traverse.

Another example, again of an ironic family tragedy. Here the narrator is Max Plowman, author (under the pseudonym "Mark VII") of the memoir *A Subaltern on the Somme* (1928). The commanding officer of the front-line company in which Plowman is serving has received "a piteous appeal," a letter from "two or three influential people in a Northern town, setting forth the case of a mother nearly demented because she has had two of her three sons killed in the trenches since July 1 [1916], and is in mortal fear of what may happen to the sole surviving member of the family, a boy in our company named Stream." The authors of this letter ask if anything can be done. The company commander "is helpless at the moment, but he has shown the letter to the colonel, who promises to see what can be done next time we are out." The reader will be able to construct the rest of the episode himself. A few days later "Sergeant Brown . . . comes to the mouth of the dug-out to report that a big shell dropped right in the trench, killing one man, though who it was he doesn't yet know: the body was blown to pieces. No one else was hurt."

The irony which memory associates with the events, little as well as great, of the First World War has become an inseparable element of the general vision of war in our time. Sergeant Croft's ironic patrol in Mailer's *The Naked and the Dead* (1948) is one emblem of that vision. The unspeakable agonies endured by the patrol in order to win—as it imagines—the whole campaign take place while the battle is being easily won elsewhere. The patrol's contribution ("sacrifice," it would have been called thirty years earlier) has not been needed at all. As Polack puts it: "We broke our ass for nothin'."

There is continuity too in a favorite ironic scene which the Great War contributes to the Second. A terribly injured man is "comforted" by a friend unaware of the real ghastliness of the friend's wounds. The classic Great War scene of this kind is a real "scene": it is Scene 3, Act III, of R. C. Sherriff's play of 1928, *Journey's End*, which had the amazing run of 594 performances at the Savoy Theater. The dying young Second Lieutenant James Raleigh (played by the twenty-eight-year-old Maurice Evans) is carried down into the orderly-room dugout to be ministered to by his old public-school football idol, Captain Dennis Stanhope:

RALEIGH. Something—hit me in the back—knocked me clean over—sort of— winded me—
    I'm all right now. (*He tries to rise*)
STANHOPE. Steady, old boy. Just lie there quietly for a bit.
RALEIGH. I'll be better if I get up and walk about. It happened once before— I got kicked in
    just the same place at Rugger; it—it soon wore off. It—it just numbs you for a bit.
STANHOPE. I'm going to have you taken away.
RALEIGH. Away? Where?
STANHOPE. Down to the dressing-station—then hospital—then home. (*He smiles*) You've got
    a Blighty one, Jimmy.
(*There is quiet in the dug-out for a time. Stanhope sits with one hand on Raleigh's arm, and
Raleigh lies very still. Presently he speaks again—hardly above a whisper*)
    Dennis—
STANHOPE. Yes, old boy?
RALEIGH. Could we have a light? It's—it's so frightfully dark and cold.

STANHOPE. (rising) Sure! I'll bring a candle and get another blanket.

*(Stanhope goes out R, and Raleigh is alone, very still and quiet. . . . A tiny sound comes from where Raleigh is lying—something between a sob and a moan; his L hand drops to the floor. Stanhope comes back with a blanket. He takes a candle from the table and carries it to Raleigh's bed. He puts it on the box beside Raleigh and speaks cheerfully)*

Is that better, Jimmy? (Raleigh makes no sign) Jimmy—

The most conspicuous modern beneficiary of this memorable scene is Joseph Heller. Alfred Kazin has accurately distinguished the heart of *Catch-22* from the distracting vaudeville surrounding it: "The impressive emotion in *Catch-22*," he says, "is not 'black humor,' the 'totally absurd' . . . but horror. Whenever the book veers back to its primal scene, a bombardier's evisceration in a plane being smashed by flak, a scene given us directly and piteously, we recognize what makes *Catch-22* disturbing." What makes it disturbing, Kazin decides, is the book's implying, by its Absurd farce, that in the last third of the twentieth century, after the heaping of violence upon violence, it is no longer possible to " 'describe war' in traditional literary ways." But what is notable about Heller's "primal scene" is that it does "describe war" in exactly a traditional literary way. It replays Sherriff's scene and retains all its Great War irony.

Heller's unforgettable scene projects a terrible dynamics of horror, terrified tenderness, and irony. Yossarian has gone to the tail of the plane to help the wounded gunner, the "kid" Snowden: "Snowden was lying on his back on the floor with his legs stretched out, still burdened cumbersomely by his flak suit, his flak helmet, his parachute harness and his Mae West. . . . The wound Yossarian saw was in the outside of Snowden's thigh." It was "as large and deep as a football, it seemed." Yossarian masters his panic and revulsion and sets to work with a tourniquet. "He worked with simulated skill and composure, feeling Snowden's lack-luster gaze resting upon him." Cutting away Snowden's trouser-leg, Yossarian is pleased to discover that the wound "was not nearly as large as football, but as long and wide as his hand. . . . A long sigh of relief escaped slowly through Yossarian's mouth when he saw that Snowden was not in danger of dying. The blood was already coagulating inside the wound, and it was simply a matter of bandaging him up and keeping him calm until the plane landed."

Cheered by these hopes, Yossarian goes to work "with renewed confidence and optimism." He competently sprinkles sulfanilimide into the wound as he has been taught and binds it up, making "the whole thing fast with a tidy square knot. It was a good bandage, he knew, and he sat back on his heels with pride . . . and grinned at Snowden with spontaneous friendliness." It is time for ironic reversal to begin:

"I'm cold," Snowden moaned. "I'm cold."

You're going to be all right, kid," Yossatian assured him, patting his arm comfortingly. "Everything's under control."

Snowden shook his head feebly. "I'm cold," he repeated, with eyes as dull and blind as stone. "I'm cold."

"There, there," said Yossarian. . . . "There, there. . . ."

And soon everything proves to be not under control at all:

> Snowden kept shaking his head and pointed at last, with just the barest movement of his chin, down toward his armpit. . . . Yossarian ripped open the snaps of Snowden's flak suit and heard himself scream wildly as Snowden's insides slithered down to the floor in a soggy pile and just kept dripping out.

Yossarian "wondered how in the world to begin to save him."

> "I'm cold," Snowden whimpered. "I'm cold."
> "There, there," Yossarian mumbled mechanically in a voice too low to be heard. "There, there."

And the scene ends with Yossarian covering the still whimpering Snowden with the nearest thing he can find to a shroud:

> "I'm cold," Snowden said. "I'm cold."
> "There, there," said Yossarian. "There, there." He pulled the rip cord of Snowden's parachute and covered his body with the white nylon sheets.
> "I'm cold."
> "There, there."

This "primal scene" works because it is undeniably horrible, but its irony, its dynamics of hope abridged, is what makes it haunt the memory. It embodies the contemporary equivalent of the experience offered by the first day on the Somme, and like that archetypal original, it can stand as a virtual allegory of political and social cognition in our time. I am saying that there seems to be one dominating form of modern understanding; that it is essentially ironic; and that it originates largely in the application of mind and memory to the events of the Great War.

# The Age of Total War

 Eric Hobsbawm

It remains to assess the human impact of the era of wars, and its human costs. The sheer mass of casualties, to which we have already referred, are only one part of these. Curiously enough, except, for understandable reasons, in the USSR, the much smaller figures of the First World War were to make a much greater impact than the vast quantities of the Second World War, as witness the much greater prominence of memorials and the cult of the fallen of the First World War. The Second World War produced no equivalent to the monuments to 'the unknown soldier', and after it the celebration of 'armistice day' (the anniversary of 11 November 1918) gradually lost its inter-war solemnity. Perhaps ten million dead hit those who had never expected such sacrifice more brutally than fifty-four millions hit those who have already once experienced war as massacre.

Certainly both the totality of the war efforts and the determination on both sides to wage war without limit and at whatever cost, made its mark. Without it, the growing brutality and inhumanity of the twentieth century is difficult to explain. About this rising curve of barbarism after 1914 there is unfortunately, no serious doubt. By the early twentieth century, torture had officially been ended throughout Western Europe. Since 1945 we have once again accustomed ourselves, without much revulsion, to its use in at least one third of the member-states of the United nations, including some of the oldest and most civilized (Peters, 1985).

The growth of brutalization was due not so much to the release of the latent potential for cruelty and violence in the human being, which war naturally legitimizes, although this certainly emerged after the First World War among a certain type of ex-servicemen (veterans), especially in the strong-arm or killer squads and 'Free Corps' on the nationalist ultra-Right. Why should men who had killed and seen their friends killed and mangled, hesitate to kill and brutalize the enemies of a good cause?

One major reason was the strange democratisation of war. Total conflicts turned into 'people's wars', both because civilians and civilian life became the proper, and sometimes the main, targets of strategy, and because in democratic wars, as in democratic politics, adversaries are naturally demonized in order to make them properly hateful or at least despicable. Wars conducted on both sides by professionals, or specialists, especially those of similar social standing, do not exclude mutual respect and acceptance of rules, or even chivalry. Violence has its rules. This was still evident among fighter pilots in air forces in both wars, as witness Jean Renoir's pacifist film about the First World War, *La Grande Illusion*. Professionals of politics and diplomacy, when untrammeled by the demands of votes or newspapers, can declare war or negotiate peace with no hard feelings about the other side, like boxers who shake hands before they come out fighting, and drink with each other after the fight. But the total wars of our century were far removed from the Bismarckian or eighteenth-century pattern. No war in which mass national feelings are mobilized can be as limited as aristocratic wars. And, it must be said, in the Second World War the nature of Hitler's regime and the behaviour of the Germans, including the old non-Nazi German army, in eastern Europe, was such as to justify a good deal of demonization.

Another reason, however, was the new impersonality of warfare, which turned killing and maiming into the remote consequence of pushing a button or moving a lever. Technology made its victims invisible, as people eviscerated by bayonets, or seen through the sights of firearms could not be. Opposite the permanently fixed guns of the western front were not men but statistics not even real, but hypothetical statistics, as the 'body-counts' of enemy casualties during US Vietnam War showed. Far below the aerial bombers were not people about to be burned and eviscerated, but targets. Mild young men, who would certainly not have wished to plunge a bayonet in the belly of any pregnant village girl, could far more easily drop high explosive on London or Berlin, or nuclear bombs on Nagasaki. Hard-working German bureaucrats who would certainly have found it repugnant to drive starving Jews into abattoirs themselves, could work out the railway timetables for a regular supply of death-trains to Polish extermination camps with less sense of personal involvement. The greatest cruelties of our century have been the impersonal cruelties of remote decision, of system and routine, especially when they could be justified as regrettable operational necessities.

So the world accustomed itself to the compulsory expulsion and killing on an astronomic scale, phenomena so unfamiliar that new words had to be invented for them: 'stateless' ('apatride') or 'genocide'. The First World War led to the killing of an uncounted number of Armenians by Turkey the most usual figure is 1.5 millions which can count as the first modern attempt to eliminate an entire population. It was later followed by the belter-known Nazi mass-killing of about five million Jews the numbers remain in dispute. (Hilberg, 1985). One First World War and the Russian revolution forced millions to move as refugees, or by compulsory 'exchanges of populations' between states, which amounted to the same. A total of 1.3 million Greeks were repatriated to Greece, mainly from Turkey; 400,000 Turks were decanted into the state which claimed them; some 200,000 Bulgarians moved into the diminished territory bearing their national name; while 1.5 or perhaps 2 million Russian nationals, escaping from the Russian revolution or on the losing side of the Russian civil war, found themselves homeless. It was mainly for these rather than the 320,000 Armenians fleeing genocide, that a new document was invented for those who, in an increasingly bureaucratized world, had no bureaucratic existence in any state: the so-called Nansen passport of the League of Nations, named after the great Norwegian arctic explorer who made himself a second career as a friend to the friendless. At a rough guess the years 1914 22 generated between four and five million refugees.

This first flood of human jetsam was as nothing to that which followed the Second World War, or to the inhumanity with which they were treated. It has been estimated that by May 1945 there were perhaps 40.5 million uprooted people in Europe, excluding non-German forced labourers and Germans who fled before the advancing Soviet armies (Kulischer, 1948, pp. 253 73). About thirteen million Germans were expelled from the parts of Germany annexed by Poland and the USSR, from Czechoslovakia and parts of south-eastern Europe where they had long been settled (Holborn, p. 363). They were taken in by the new German Federal Republic, which offered a home and citizenship to any German who returned there, as the new state of Israel offered a 'right of return' to any Jew.

When, but in an epoch of mass flight, could such offers by states have been seriously made? Of the 11,332,700 'displaced persons' of various nationalities found in Germany by the victorious armies in 1945, ten millions soon returned to their homelands – but half of these were compelled to do so against their will (Jacobmeyer, 1986).

These were only the refugees of Europe. The decolonization of India in 1947 created fifteen million of them, forced to cross the new frontiers between India and Pakistan "(in both directions), without counting the two millions killed in the accompanying civil strife. The Korean War, another by-product of The Second World War, produced perhaps five million displaced Koreans. After the establishment of Israel – yet another of the war's after-effects — about 1.3 million Palestinians were registered with the United Nations Relief and Work Agency (UNWRA); conversely by the early 1960s 1.2 million Jews had migrated to Israel, the majority of these also as refugees. In short, the global human catastrophe unleashed by the Second World War is almost certainly the largest in human history. Not the least tragic aspect of this catastrophe is that humanity has learned to live in a world in which killing, torture and mass exile have become everyday experiences which we no longer notice.

Looking back on the thirty-one years from the assassination of the Austrian Archduke in Sarajevo to the unconditional surrender of Japan, they must be seen as an era of havoc comparable to the Thirty Years' War of the seventeenth century in German history. And Sarajevo – the first Sarajevo – certainly marked the beginning of a general age of catastrophe and crisis in the affairs of the world, which is the subject of this and the next four chapters. Nevertheless, in the memory of the generations after 1945, the Thirty-one Years' War did not leave behind the same sort of memory as its more localised seventeenth-century predecessor.

This is partly because it formed a single era of war only in the historians' perspective. For those who lived through it, it was experienced as two distinct though connected wars, separated by an 'inter-war' period without overt hostilities, ranging from thirteen years for Japan (whose second war began in Manchuria in 1931) to twenty-three years for the USA (which did not enter the Second World War until December 1941). However, it is also because each of these wars had its own historical character and profile. Both were episodes of carnage without parallel, leaving behind the technological nightmare images that haunted the nights and days of the next generation: poison gas and aerial bombardment after 1918, the mushroom cloud of nuclear destruction after 1945. Both ended in breakdown and – as we shall see in the next chapter — social revolution over large regions of Europe and Asia. Both left the belligerents exhausted and enfeebled, except for the USA, which emerged from both undamaged and enriched, as the economic lord of the world. And yet, how striking the differences! The First World War solved nothing. Such hopes as it generated – of a peaceful and democratic world of nationstates under the League of Nations; of a return to the world economy of 1913; even (among those who hailed the Russian Revolution) of world capitalism overthrown within years or months by a rising of the oppressed, I were soon disappointed. The past was beyond reach, the future postponed, the present bitter, except for a few fleeting years in the mid-1920s. The Second World War actually produced solutions, at least for decades. The dramatic social and economic problems of capitalism in its Age of entered its Golden Age; Western political democracy, backed by an extraordinary improvement in material life, was stable; war was banished to the Third World. On the other side, even revolution appeared to have found its way forward. The old colonial empires vanished or were shortly destined to go. A consortium of communist states, organized around the Soviet Union, now transformed into a superpower, seemed ready to compete in the race for economic growth with the West. This proved to be an illusion, but not until the 1960s did it begin to vanish. As we can now see, even the international scene was stabilized, though it did not seem so. Unlike after the Great War, the former enemies – Germany and Japan – reintegrated into the (Western) world economy, and the new enemies – the USA and the USSR – never actually came to blows.

Even the revolutions which ended both wars were quite different. Those after the First World War were, as we shall see, rooted in a revulsion against what most people who lived through it, had increasingly seen as a pointless slaughter. They were revolutions against the war. The revolutions after the Second World War grew out of the popular participation in a world struggle against enemies – Germany, Japan, more generally imperialism – which, however terrible, those who took part in it felt to be just. And yet, like the two World Wars, the two sorts of post-war revolution can be seen in the historian's perspective as a single process. To this we must now turn.

# CHAPTER ELEVEN

# Marxism and the Socialist Revolutions

As a theory of revolutionary power, Marxism is based on the work of Karl Marx and Friedrich Engels whose ideas were derived from German philosophy, French socialist thinking after the Revolution, and economic theory reflecting the Industrial Revolution. For Marxism, history is a natural process rooted in the material needs of human beings. From the Marxist perspective, all history is the history of class struggle, which the rise of capitalism has only increased. Just as capitalism replaced feudalism, Marx believed that socialism would eventually replace capitalism leading, after a transitional period called "the dictatorship of the proletariat," to a classless society that was communist in design.

While capitalism stimulates the development of productive forces, Marx also believed that it produces the conditions of its own collapse. Capitalism's chief aim is to accumulate wealth at the expense of impoverishing the masses. It impoverishes the masses by denying them access to the means of production. This then forces the masses to sell their labor as a commodity which consequently alienates them not only from the means of production themselves but from what they produce. Marx was convinced that once the workers of the world discovered their true condition, they would unite and throw off the chains of their oppression.

While Marx's predictions about the inevitability of revolution were mistaken, he was essentially correct about the historical cycle of capitalist exploitation and class struggle. His message that the bourgeois was creating its own gravediggers provided powerful inspiration to oppressed peoples all over the world. While Marx said that he wasn't a Marxist himself, his utopian analysis was quickly transformed into a worldview and, for many, a new religion in an increasingly secular age. It was also to lead not only to the communist revolution in Russia led by Vladimir Lenin and later, the communist revolution in China, under the inspiration of Mao Zedong, but also to the creation of the World Socialist movement.

Socialism is a theory of social organization that advocates the communal ownership and control of the means of production, capital, and land. It promotes their administration and distribution in the interests of all, believing that current political regimes represent the rule of dominant classes always seeking to exploit the classes beneath them. The industrial proletariat is the only class whose natural interests can be assumed to be socialist. But beliefs such as these were inevitably to raise almost as many questions as they answered. What is a community? How is ownership acquired? Does this happen by popular consensus? Who determines the "interests of all?" And how are common assets to be administered and distributed?

There were two quite distinct waves of socialist revolution. The first was European and centered around the Russian Revolution of 1917. It was the result of close relations between socialist political movements on the Continent and labor movements. The second wave of socialist revolution was trans-European and centered instead around the Chinese and then Cuban revolutions in 1949 and 1959, respectively. These later revolutions were the result of postwar decolonization and the Cold War division of the world into socialist and imperialist camps. There were, moreover, two kinds of trans-European ("Third World") socialism. One involved Independence movements built around political resistance to imperial power that that led to its withdrawal in countries such as India, Ghana, and Tanzania. The second involved National Liberation movements requiring armed struggle that led to some form of socialist transformation of society in places like Vietnam, Algeria, Angola, South Africa, Latin America, and Cuba. In the first wave, Russia served as the model because it presented itself with some exaggeration as an emergent industrial nation ripe for proletarian revolution. In the second wave, Russia's revolutionary experience proved irrelevant to non-industrial nations forced to escape foreign economic and colonial domination before they could begin to develop on their own. Here China and Cuba, with their large peasant populations, became the new revolutionary model instead.

In Europe, the international socialist movement gained considerable strength because most countries possessed urban labor parties with a base of support in the industrial working class. That support was significant enough in the long run to create partial, if not total, social welfare states out of countries as diverse as Germany, France, Great Britain, Sweden, Australia, and elsewhere, and had an indelible impact on raising consciousness about the socially oppressed everywhere. But the international socialist movement in Europe nonetheless suffered a shattering blow from which it never fully recovered with the outbreak of World War I, when transnational class identifications and socialist universalism found themselves suddenly in competition with the patriotic fervor and nationalism unleashed by global conflict.

Outside of Europe in the world that needed to be decolonized before it could be socialized, nationalist liberation movements gave the socialist revolution a different inflection. Reflecting a low level of urbanization, industrial development, and labor organization, these states needed to curb foreign penetration and encourage internal economic as well as political development. Thus revolutionary ideology for the new postcolonial state was generally provided by a small class of intellectuals like Vietnam's Ho Chi Min who had often been educated in Europe and were prepared, once the often armed struggle for independence succeeded, to combine socialism both with anti-imperialism and with the creation of a new nationalism.

While the world socialist revolution has now lost much of its former momentum even after initially producing significant reforms in countries that attempted to steer clear of its ideological politics, its decline has left world politics with some very serious issues. Who now speaks for the oppressed? Is there a revolutionary need for radical, continuous social change? Where does one find the sources for revolutionary change outside of ideology? And is violence the key to maintaining order or to stimulating change?

The first of the selections in this chapter is from Karl Marx's *The Communist Manifesto* and reveals how emphatically he wanted to place power in the hands of the proletariat. Insisting that the regularities of history result from the modes and relations of production, which in turn determine the nature of each historical epic, the specific forms of property prevailing in each, and the class structure in all, Marx believed that history is really the history of class struggle and that this struggle could lead to radical changes in production, property relations, and the distribution of goods. The power for change and thus for economic as well as political liberation lay in the hands of the working class, or proletariat as he called it, which would reorder society in terms of the new communist principal of "from each according to his ability to each according to his need."

The second selection in this chapter comes from Vladimir Lenin who had insisted fifteen years before the Bolshevik revolution of 1917, in his *What Is to Be Done* (1902), that socialism could not be produced by the working class itself but only by a disciplined party of professional revolutionaries. Called the "Soviet," this party of professional revolutionaries included the 240,000 Bolsheviks who were members of the Communist Party and in Lenin's view constituted the most class conscious, energetic, and progressive element of the proletariat.

It is worth noting that the Chinese Communist Revolution followed a different model. Because of the nature of its society, which was composed essentially of peasants rather than industrial workers, Mao Zedong, who founded the Chinese Communist Party in 1921 and became its leader from 1935 to 1976, assumed that while the Chinese revolution still depended on the Communist Party, its leadership could not be left, as Lenin believed, in the hands of the party itself, much less, as Marx believed, in the hands of the people. The responsibility for defining the aims and methods of China's war of liberation (1937-1949) and continuing revolution (1949-1976) could only be entrusted to the party's leaders, and so Mao took control of the revolution away from the workers and peasants as well as from the party itself and gave it to the leaders of what he called the People's Dictatorship.

The third selection in this chapter by Sheila Fitzpatrick who pulls all these lines of development together in a masterful survey of the relationship between Socialism and Communism. What she brings out is the variousness and diversity of these two great ideological movements that helped reorganize many social, economic, and political practices of the Western, or First, World, as it came to be called in Cold War parlance, and literally gave birth to so many of the new and diverse state formations and economic policies that came to be identified with the so-called Third World. First World Socialism was always more reformist in intent, Third World Socialism and Communism more revolutionary, but both were in time to become swept up in the superpower rivalries between the Soviet bloc and the Western bloc. These vast movements for social and economic and political change were in time to leave an indelible imprint on the societies and peoples they touched long after they began to be absorbed by the rampaging forces of globalization. Now that globalization is itself creating new axes of power that run not from North to South but from South to North, as well as from East to West and West to East, and now more recently from East to South and South to East, the legacies of Socialism and Communism will be with the world for generations, if not centuries, to come.

# The Communist Manifesto

KARL MARX

A spectre is haunting Europe—the spectre of communism. All the powers of old Europe have entered into a holy alliance to exorcise this spectre: Pope and Tsar, Metternich and Guizot, French Radicals and German police-spies.

Where is the party in opposition that has not been decried as communistic by its opponents in power? Where is the opposition that has not hurled back the branding reproach of communism, against the more advanced opposition parties, as well as against its reactionary adversaries?

Two things result from this fact:

I. Communism is already acknowledged by all European powers to be itself a power.
II. It is high time that Communists should openly, in the face of the whole world, publish their views, their aims, their tendencies, and meet this nursery tale of the spectre of communism with a manifesto of the party itself.

To this end, Communists of various nationalities have assembled in London and sketched the following manifesto, to be published in the English, French, German, Italian, Flemish and Danish languages.

## I. BOURGEOIS AND PROLETARIANS[1]

The history of all hitherto existing society[2] is the history of class struggles. Freeman and slave, patrician and plebian, lord and serf, guild-master[3] and journeyman, in a word, oppressor and oppressed, stood in constant opposition to one another, carried on an uninterrupted, now hidden, now open fight, a fight that each time ended, either in a revolutionary reconstitution of society at large, or in the common ruin of the contending classes.

In the earlier epochs of history, we find almost everywhere a complicated arrangement of society into various orders, a manifold gradation of social rank. In ancient Rome we have patricians, knights, plebians, slaves; in the Middle Ages, feudal lords, vassals, guild-masters, journeymen, apprentices, serfs; in almost all of these classes, again, subordinate gradations.

The modern bourgeois society that has sprouted from the ruins of feudal society has not done away with class antagonisms. It has but established new classes, new conditions of oppression, new forms of struggle in place of the old ones.

Our epoch, the epoch of the bourgeoisie, possesses, however, this distinct feature: it has simplified class antagonisms. Society as a whole is more and more splitting up into two great hostile camps, into two great classes directly facing each other—bourgeoisie and proletariat.

From the serfs of the Middle Ages sprang the chartered burghers of the earliest towns. From these burgesses the first elements of the bourgeoisie were developed.

The discovery of America, the rounding of the Cape, opened up fresh ground for the rising bourgeoisie. The East-Indian and Chinese markets, the colonisation of America, trade with the colonies, the increase in the means of exchange and in commodities generally, gave to commerce, to navigation, to industry, an impulse never before known, and thereby, to the revolutionary element in the tottering feudal society, a rapid development.

The feudal system of industry, in which industrial production was monopolized by closed guilds, now no longer suffices for the growing wants of the new markets. The manufacturing system took its place. The guild-masters were pushed aside by the manufacturing middle class; division of labor between the different corporate guilds vanished in the face of division of labor in each single workshop.

Meantime, the markets kept ever growing, the demand ever rising. Even manufacturers no longer sufficed. Thereupon, steam and machinery revolutionized industrial production. The place of manufacture was taken by the giant, MODERN INDUSTRY; the place of the industrial middle class by industrial millionaires, the leaders of the whole industrial armies, the modern bourgeois.

Modern industry has established the world market, for which the discovery of America paved the way. This market has given an immense development to commerce, to navigation, to communication by land. This development has, in turn, reacted on the extension of industry; and in proportion as industry, commerce, navigation, railways extended, in the same proportion the bourgeoisie developed, increased its capital, and pushed into the background every class handed down from the Middle Ages.

We see, therefore, how the modern bourgeoisie is itself the product of a long course of development, of a series of revolutions in the modes of production and of exchange. Each step in the development of the bourgeoisie was accompanied by a corresponding political advance in that class. An oppressed class under the sway of the feudal nobility, an armed and self-governing association of medieval commune[4]: here independent urban republic (as in Italy and Germany); there taxable "third estate" of the monarchy (as in France); afterward, in the period of manufacturing proper, serving either the semifeudal or the absolute monarchy as a counterpoise against the nobility, and, in fact, cornerstone of the great monarchies in general —the bourgeoisie has at last, since the establishment of Modern Industry and of the world market, conquered for itself, in the modern representative state, exclusive political sway. The executive of the modern state is but a committee for managing the common affairs of the whole bourgeoisie.

The bourgeoisie, historically, has played a most revolutionary part. The bourgeoisie, wherever it has got the upper hand, has put an end to all feudal, patriarchal, idyllic relations. It has pitilessly torn asunder the motley feudal ties that bound man to his "natural superiors," and has left no other nexus between man and man than naked self-interest, than callous "cash payment." It has drowned out the most heavenly ecstacies of religious fervor, of chivalrous enthusiasm, of philistine sentimentalism, in the icy water of egotistical calculation. It has resolved personal worth into exchange value, and in place of the numberless indefeasible chartered freedoms, has set up that single, unconscionable freedom—Free Trade. In one word, for exploitation, veiled by religious and political illusions, it has substituted naked, shameless, direct, brutal exploitation.

The bourgeoisie has stripped of its halo every occupation hitherto honored and looked up to with reverent awe. It has converted the physician, the lawyer, the priest, the poet, the man of science, into its paid wage laborers. The bourgeoisie has torn away from the family its sentimental veil, and has reduced the family relation into a mere money relation.

The bourgeoisie has disclosed how it came to pass that the brutal display of vigor in the Middle Ages, which reactionaries so much admire, found its fitting complement in the most slothful indolence. It has been the first to show what man's activity can bring about. It has accomplished wonders far surpassing Egyptian pyramids, Roman aqueducts, and Gothic cathedrals; it has conducted expeditions that put in the shade all former exoduses of nations and crusades.

The bourgeoisie cannot exist without constantly revolutionizing the instruments of production, and thereby the relations of production, and with them the whole relations of society. Conservation of the old modes of production in unaltered form, was, on the contrary, the first condition of existence for all earlier industrial classes. Constant revolutionizing of production, uninterrupted disturbance of all social conditions, everlasting uncertainty and agitation distinguish the bourgeois epoch from all earlier ones. All fixed, fast frozen relations, with their train of ancient and venerable prejudices and opinions, are swept away, all new-formed ones become antiquated before they can ossify. All that is solid melts into air, all that is holy is profaned, and man is at last compelled to face with sober senses his real condition of life and his relations with his kind.

The need of a constantly expanding market for its products chases the bourgeoisie over the entire surface of the globe. It must nestle everywhere, settle everywhere, establish connections everywhere.

The bourgeoisie has, through its exploitation of the world market, given a cosmopolitan character to production and consumption in every country. To the great chagrin of reactionaries, it has drawn from under the feet of industry the national ground on which it stood. All old-established national industries have been destroyed or are daily being destroyed. They are dislodged by new industries, whose introduction becomes a life and death question for all civilized nations, by industries that no longer work up indigenous raw material, but raw material drawn from the remotest zones; industries whose products are consumed, not only at home, but in every quarter of the globe. In place of the old wants, satisfied by the production of the country, we find new wants, requiring for their satisfaction the products of distant lands and climes. In place of the old local and national seclusion and self-sufficiency, we have intercourse in every direction, universal inter-dependence of nations. And as in material, so also in intellectual production. The intellectual creations of individual nations become common property. National one-sidedness and narrow-mindedness become more and more impossible, and from the numerous national and local literatures, there arises a world literature.

The bourgeoisie, by the rapid improvement of all instruments of production, by the immensely facilitated means of communication, draws all, even the most barbarian, nations into civilization. The cheap prices of commodities are the heavy artillery with which it forces the barbarians' intensely obstinate hatred of foreigners to capitulate. It compels all nations, on pain of extinction, to adopt the bourgeois mode of production; it compels them to introduce what it calls civilization into their midst, i.e., to become bourgeois themselves. In one word, it creates a world after its own image.

The bourgeoisie has subjected the country to the rule of the towns. It has created enormous cities, has greatly increased the urban population as compared with the rural, and has thus rescued a considerable part of the population from the idiocy of rural life. Just as it has made the country dependent on the towns, so it has made barbarian and semi-barbarian countries dependent on the civilized ones, nations of peasants on nations of bourgeois, the East on the West.

The bourgeoisie keeps more and more doing away with the scattered state of the population, of the means of production, and of property. It has agglomerated population, centralized the means of production, and has concentrated property in a few hands. The necessary consequence of this was political centralization. Independent, or but loosely connected provinces, with separate interests, laws, governments, and systems of taxation, became lumped together into one nation, with one government, one code of laws, one national class interest, one frontier, and one customs tariff.

The bourgeoisie, during its rule of scarce one hundred years, has created more massive and more colossal productive forces than have all preceding generations together. Subjection of nature's forces to man, machinery, application of chemistry to industry and agriculture, steam navigation, railways, electric telegraphs, clearing of whole continents for cultivation, canalization or rivers, whole populations conjured out of the ground—what earlier century had even a presentiment that such productive forces slumbered in the lap of social labor?

We see then: the means of production and of exchange, on whose foundation the bourgeoisie built itself up, were generated in feudal society. At a certain stage in the development of these means of production and of exchange, the conditions under which feudal society produced and exchanged, the feudal organization of agriculture and manufacturing industry, in one word, the feudal relations of property became no longer compatible with the already developed productive forces; they became so many fetters. They had to be burst asunder; they were burst asunder.

Into their place stepped free competition, accompanied by a social and political constitution adapted in it, and the economic and political sway of the bourgeois class. A similar movement is going on before our own eyes. Modern bourgeois society, with its relations of production, of exchange and of property, a society that has conjured up such gigantic means of production and of exchange, is like the sorcerer who is no longer able to control the powers of the nether world whom he has called up by his spells. For many a decade past, the history of industry and commerce is but the history of the revolt of modern productive forces against modern conditions of production, against the property relations that are the conditions for the existence of the bourgeois and of its rule. It is enough to mention the commercial crises that, by their periodical return, put the existence of the entire bourgeois society on its trial, each time more threateningly. In these crises, a great part not only of the existing products, but also of the previously created productive forces, are periodically destroyed. In these crises, there breaks out an epidemic that, in all earlier epochs, would have seemed an absurdity—the epidemic of over-production. Society suddenly finds itself put back into a state of momentary barbarism; it appears as if a famine, a universal war of devastation, had cut off the supply of every means of subsistence; industry and commerce seem to be destroyed. And why? Because there is too much civilization, too much means of subsistence, too much industry, too much commerce. The productive forces at the disposal of society no longer tend to further the development of the conditions of bourgeois property; on the contrary, they have become too powerful for these conditions, by which they are fettered, and so soon as they overcome these fetters, they bring disorder into the whole of bourgeois society, endanger the existence of bourgeois property. The conditions of bourgeois society are too narrow to comprise the wealth created by them. And how does the bourgeoisie get over these crises? One the one hand, by enforced destruction of a mass of productive forces; on the other, by the conquest of new markets, and by the more thorough exploitation of the old ones. That is to say, by paving the way for more extensive and more destructive crises, and by diminishing the means whereby crises are prevented.

The weapons with which the bourgeoisie felled feudalism to the ground are now turned against the bourgeoisie itself.

But not only has the bourgeoisie forged the weapons that bring death to itself; it has also called into existence the men who are to wield those weapons—the modern working class—the proletarians.

In proportion as the bourgeoisie, i.e., capital, is developed, in the same proportion is the proletariat, the modern working class, developed—a class of laborers, who live only so long as they find work, and who find work only so long as their labor increases capital. These laborers, who must sell themselves piecemeal, are a commodity, like every other article of commerce, and are consequently exposed to all the vicissitudes of competition, to all the fluctuations of the market.

Owing to the extensive use of machinery, and to the division of labor, the work of the proletarians has lost all individual character, and, consequently, all charm for the workman. He becomes an appendage of the machine, and it is only the most simple, most monotonous, and most easily acquired knack, that is required of him. Hence, the cost of production of a workman is restricted, almost entirely, to the means of subsistence that he requires for maintenance, and for the propagation of his race. But the price of a commodity, and therefore also of labor, is equal to its cost of production. In proportion, therefore, as the repulsiveness of the work increases, the wage decreases. What is more, in proportion as the use of machinery and division of labor increases, in the same proportion the burden of toil also increases, whether by prolongation of the working hours, by the increase of the work exacted in a given time, or by increased speed of machinery, etc.

Modern Industry has converted the little workshop of the patriarchal master into the great factory of the industrial capitalist. Masses of laborers, crowded into the factory, are organized like soldiers. As privates of the industrial army, they are placed under the command of a perfect hierarchy of officers and sergeants. Not only are they slaves of the bourgeois class, and of the bourgeois state; they are daily and hourly enslaved by the machine, by the overlooker, and, above all, in the individual bourgeois manufacturer himself. The more openly this despotism proclaims gain to be its end and aim, the more petty, the more hateful and the more embittering it is.

The less the skill and exertion of strength implied in manual labor, in other words, the more modern industry becomes developed, the more is the labor of men superseded by that of women. Differences of age and sex have no longer any distinctive social validity for the working class. All are instruments of labor, more or less expensive to use, according to their age and sex.

No sooner is the exploitation of the laborer by the manufacturer, so far at an end, that he receives his wages in cash, than he is set upon by the other portion of the bourgeoisie, the landlord, the shopkeeper, the pawnbroker, etc.

The lower strata of the middle class—the small tradespeople, shopkeepers, and retired tradesmen generally, the handicraftsmen and peasants—all these sink gradually into the proletariat, partly because their diminutive capital does not suffice for the scale on which Modern Industry is carried on, and is swamped in the competition with the large capitalists, partly because their specialized skill is rendered worthless by new methods of production. Thus, the proletariat is recruited from all classes of the population. The proletariat goes through various stages of development. With its birth begins its struggle with the bourgeoisie. At first, the contest is carried on by individual laborers, then by the work of people of a factory, then by the operative of one trade, in one locality, against the individual bourgeois who directly exploits them. They direct their attacks not against the bourgeois condition of production, but against the instruments of production themselves; they destroy imported wares that compete with their labor, they smash to pieces machinery, they set factories ablaze, they seek to restore by force the vanished status of the workman of the Middle Ages.

At this stage, the laborers still form an incoherent mass scattered over the whole country, and broken up by their mutual competition. If anywhere they unite to form more compact bodies, this is not yet the consequence of their own active union, but of the union of the bourgeoisie, which class, in order to attain its own political ends, is compelled to set the whole proletariat in motion, and is moreover yet, for a time, able to do so. At this stage, therefore, the proletarians do not fight their enemies, but the enemies of their enemies, the remnants of absolute monarchy, the landowners, the nonindustrial bourgeois, the petty bourgeois. Thus, the whole historical movement is concentrated in the hands of the bourgeoisie; every victory so obtained is a victory for the bourgeoisie.

But with the development of industry, the proletariat not only increases in number; it becomes concentrated in greater masses, its strength grows, and it feels that strength more. The various interests and conditions of life within the ranks of the proletariat are more and more equalized, in proportion as machinery obliterates all distinctions of labor, and nearly everywhere reduces wages to the same low level. The growing competition among the bourgeois, and the resulting commercial crises, make the wages of the workers ever more fluctuating. The increasing improvement of machinery, ever more rapidly developing, makes their livelihood more and more precarious; the collisions between individual workmen and individual bourgeois take more and more the character of collisions between two classes. Thereupon, the workers begin to form combinations (trade unions) against the bourgeois; they club together in order to keep up the rate of wages; they found permanent associations in order to make provision beforehand for these occasional revolts. Here and there, the contest breaks out into riots. Now and then the workers are victorious, but only for a time. The real fruit of their battles lie not in the immediate result, but in the ever expanding union of the workers. This union is helped on by the improved means of communication that are created by Modern Industry, and that place the workers of different localities in contact with one another. It was just this contact that was needed to centralize the numerous local struggles, all of the same character, into one national struggle between classes. But every class struggle is a political struggle. And that union, to attain which the burghers of the Middle Ages, with their miserable highways, required centuries, the modern proletarian, thanks to railways, achieve in a few years.

This organization of the proletarians into a class, and, consequently, into a political party, is continually being upset again by the competition between the workers themselves. But it ever rises up again, stronger, firmer, mightier. It compels legislative recognition of particular interests of the workers, by taking advantage of the divisions among the bourgeoisie itself. Thus, the Ten-Hours Bill in England was carried. Altogether, collisions between the classes of the old society further in many ways the course of development of the proletariat. The bourgeoisie finds itself involved in a constant battle. At first with the aristocracy; later on, with those portions of the bourgeoisie itself, whose interests have become antagonistic to the progress of industry; at all time with the bourgeoisie of foreign countries. In all these battles, it sees itself compelled to appeal to the proletariat, to ask for help, and thus to drag it into the political arena. The bourgeoisie itself, therefore, supplies the proletariat with its own elements of political and general education, in other words, it furnishes the proletariat with weapons for fighting the bourgeoisie.

Further, as we have already seen, entire sections of the ruling class are, by the advance of industry, precipitated into the proletariat, or are at least threatened in their conditions of existence. These also supply the proletariat with fresh elements of enlightenment and progress.

Finally, in times when the class struggle nears the decisive hour, the progress of dissolution going on within the ruling class, in fact within the whole range of old society, assumes such a violent, glaring character, that a small section of the ruling class cuts itself adrift, and joins the revolutionary class, the class that holds the future in its hands. Just as, therefore, at an earlier period, a section of the nobility went over to the bourgeoisie, so now a portion of the bourgeoisie goes over to the proletariat, and in particular, a portion of the bourgeois ideologists, who have raised themselves to the level of comprehending theoretically the historical movement as a whole.

Of all the classes that stand face to face with the bourgeoisie today, the proletariat alone is a genuinely revolutionary class. The other classes decay and finally disappear in the face of Modern Industry; the proletariat is its special and essential product. The lower middle class, the small manufacturer, the shopkeeper, the artisan, the peasant, all these fight against the bourgeoisie, to save from extinction their existence as fractions of the middle class. They are therefore not revolutionary, but conservative. Nay, more, they are reactionary, for they try to roll back the wheel of history. If, by chance, they are revolutionary, they are only so in view of their impending transfer into the proletariat; they thus defend not their present, but their future interests; they desert their own standpoint to place themselves at that of the proletariat.

The "dangerous class," the social scum, that passively rotting mass thrown off by the lowest layers of the old society, may, here and there, be swept into the movement by a proletarian revolution; its conditions of life, however, prepare it far more for the part of a bribed tool of reactionary intrigue.

In the condition of the proletariat, those of old society at large are already virtually swamped. The proletarian is without property; his relation to his wife and children has no longer anything in common with the bourgeois family relations; modern industry labor, modern subjection to capital, the same in England as in France, in America as in Germany, has stripped him of every trace of national character. Law, morality, religion, are to him so many bourgeois prejudices, behind which lurk in ambush just as many bourgeois interests.

All the preceding classes that got the upper hand sought to fortify their already acquired status by subjecting society at large to their conditions of appropriation. The proletarians cannot become masters of the productive forces of society, except by abolishing their own previous mode of appropriation, and thereby also every other previous mode of appropriation. They have nothing of their own to secure and to fortify; their mission is to destroy all previous securities for, and insurances of, individual property.

All previous historical movements were movements of minorities, or in the interest of minorities. The proletarian movement is the self-conscious, independent movement of the immense majority, in the interest of the immense majority. The proletariat, the lowest stratum of our present society, cannot stir, cannot raise itself up, without the whole superincumbent strata of official society being sprung into the air.

Though not in substance, yet in form, the struggle of the proletariat with the bourgeoisie is at first a national struggle. The proletariat of each country must, of course, first of all settle matters with its own bourgeoisie.

In depicting the most general phases of the development of the proletariat, we traced the more or less veiled civil war, raging within existing society, up to the point where that war breaks out into open revolution, and where the violent overthrow of the bourgeoisie lays the foundation for the sway of the proletariat.

Hitherto, every form of society has been based, as we have already seen, on the antagonism of oppressing and oppressed classes. But in order to oppress a class, certain conditions must be assured to it under which it can, at least, continue its slavish existence. The serf, in the period of serfdom, raised himself to membership in the commune, just as the petty bourgeois, under the yoke of the feudal absolutism, managed to develop into a bourgeois. The modern laborer, on the contrary, instead of rising with the process of industry, sinks deeper and deeper below the conditions of existence of his own class. He becomes a pauper, and pauperism develops more rapidly than population and wealth. And here it becomes evident that the bourgeoisie is unfit any longer to be the ruling class in society, and to impose its conditions of existence upon society as an overriding law. It is unfit to rule because it is incompetent to assure an existence to its slave within his slavery, because it cannot help letting him sink into such a state, that it has to feed him, instead of being fed by him. Society can no longer live under this bourgeoisie, in other words, its existence is no longer compatible with society.

The essential conditions for the existence and for the sway of the bourgeois class is the formation and augmentation of capital; the condition for capital is wage labor. Wage labor rests exclusively on competition between the laborers. The advance of industry, whose involuntary promoter is the bourgeoisie, replaces the isolation of the laborers, due to competition, by the revolutionary combination, due to association. The development of Modern Industry, therefore, cuts from under its feet the very foundation on which the bourgeoisie produces and appropriates products. What the bourgeoisie therefore produces, above all, are its own grave-diggers. Its fall and the victory of the proletariat are equally inevitable.

## Footnotes

[1]  By bourgeoisie is meant the class of modern capitalists, owners of the means of social production and employers of wage labor. By proletariat, the class of modern wage laborers who, having no means of production of their own, are reduced to selling their labor power in order to live. [*Note by Engels—1888 English edition*]

[2]   That is, all *written* history. In 1847, the pre-history of society, the social organization existing previous to recorded history, all but unknown. Since then, August von Haxthausen (1792–1866) discovered common ownership of land in Russia, Georg Ludwig von Maurer proved it to be the social foundation from which all Teutonic races started in history, and, by and by, village communities were found to be, or to have been, the primitive form of society everywhere from India to Ireland. The inner organization of this primitive communistic society was laid bare, in its typical form, by Lewis Henry Morgan's (1818–1861) crowning discovery of the true nature of the gens and its relation to the tribe. With the dissolution of the primeaval communities, society begins to be differentiated into separate and finally antagonistic classes. l have attempted to retrace this dissolution in *Der Ursprung der Familie, des Privateigenthumus und des Staats*, second edition, Stuttgart,1886. [Engels,1888 English edition]

[3]   Guild-master, that is, a full member of a guild, a master within, not a head of a guild. [*Engels: 1888 English edition*]

[4]   This was the name given their urban communities by the townsmen of Italy and France, after they had purchased or conquered their initial rights of self-government from their feudal lords. [*Engels: 1890 German edition*] "Commune" was the name taken in France by the nascent towns even before they had conquered from their feudal lords and masters local self-government and political rights as the "Third Estate." Generally speaking, for the economical development of the bourgeoisie, England is here taken as the typical country, for its political development, France. [*Engels: 1888 English edition*]

# Can the Bolsheviks Retain State Power?

 V. I. LENIN

The Soviets are a new state apparatus which, in the first place, provides an armed force of workers and peasants; and this force is not divorced from the people, as was the old standing army, but is very closely bound up with the people. From the military point of view this force is incomparably more powerful than previous forces; from the revolutionary point of view, it cannot be replaced by anything else. Secondly, this apparatus provides a bond with the people, with the majority of the people, so intimate, so indissoluble, so easily verifiable and renewable, that nothing even remotely like it existed in the previous state apparatus. Thirdly, this apparatus, by virtue of the fact that its personnel is elected and subject to recall at the people's will without any bureaucratic formalities, as far more democratic than any previous apparatus. Fourthly, it provides a close contact with the most varied professions, thereby facilitating the adoption of the most varied and most radical reforms without red tape. Fifthly, it provides an organisational form for the vanguard, i.e., for the most class-conscious, most energetic and most progressive section of the *oppressed* classes, the workers and peasants, and so constitutes an apparatus by means of which the vanguard of the oppressed classes can elevate, train, educate, and lead *the entire vast mass* of these classes, which has up to now stood completely outside of political life and history. Sixthly, it makes it possible to combine the advantages of the parliamentary system with those of immediate and direct democracy, i.e., to vest in the people's elected representatives both legislative and *executive* functions. Compared with the bourgeois parliamentary system, this is an advance in democracy's development which is of world-wide, historic significance.

In 1905, our Soviets existed only in embryo, so to speak, as they lived altogether only a few weeks. Clearly, under the conditions of that time, their comprehensive development was out of the question. It is still out of the question in the 1917 Revolution, for a few months is an extremely short period and—this is most important—the Socialist-Revolutionary and Menshevik leaders have *prostituted* the Soviets, have reduced their role to that of a talking-shop, of an accomplice in the compromising policy of the leaders. The Soviets have been rotting and decaying alive under the leadership of the Liebers, Dans, Tseretelis and Chernovs. The Soviets will be able to develop properly, to display their potentialities and capabilities to the full only by taking over *full* state power; for otherwise they have *nothing to do*, otherwise they are either simply embryos (and to remain an embryo too long is fatal), or playthings. "Dual power" means paralysis for the Soviets.

If the creative enthusiasm of the revolutionary classes had not given rise to the Soviets, the proletarian revolution in Russia would have been a hopeless cause, for the proletariat could certainly not retain power with the old state apparatus, and it is impossible to create a new apparatus immediately. The sad history of the prostitution of the Soviets by the Tseretelis and Chernovs, the

From *The Lenin Anthology*, New York: Norton, 1917.

history of the "coalition," is also the history of the liberation of the Soviets from petty-bourgeois illusions, of their passage through the "purgatory" of the practical experience of the utter abomination and filth of *all* and *sundry* bourgeois coalitions Let us hope that this "purgatory" has steeled rather than weakened the Soviets.

The chief difficulty facing the proletarian revolution is the establishment on a country-wide scale of the most precise and most conscientious accounting and control, of *workers' control* of the production and distribution of goods.

When the writers of *Novaya Zhizn* argued that in advancing the slogan "workers' control" we were slipping into syndicalism, this argument was an example of the stupid schoolboy method of applying "Marxism" without studying it, just *learning it by rote* in the Struve manner. Syndicalism either repudiates the revolutionary dictatorship of the proletariat, or else relegates it, as it does political power in general, to a back seat. We, however, put it in the forefront. * * *

This brings us to another aspect of the question of the state apparatus. In addition to the chiefly "oppressive" apparatus—the standing army, the police and the bureaucracy—the modern state possesses an apparatus which has extremely close connections with the banks and syndicates, an apparatus which performs an enormous amount of accounting and registration work, if it may be expressed this way. This apparatus must not, and should not, be smashed. It must be wrested from the control of the capitalists; the capitalists and the wires they pull must be *cut off, lopped off, chopped away* from this apparatus; it must be *subordinated* to the proletarian Soviets; it must be expanded, made more comprehensive, and nation-wide. And this *can* be done by utilising the achievements already made by large-scale capitalism (in the same way as the proletarian revolution can, in general, reach its goal only by utilising these achievements).

Capitalism has created an accounting *apparatus* in the shape of the banks, syndicates, postal service, consumers' societies, and office employees' unions. *Without big banks socialism would be impossible.*

The big banks are the "state apparatus" which we *need* to bring about socialism, and which we *take ready-made* from capitalism; our task here is merely to *lop off* what *capitalistically mutilates* this excellent apparatus, to make it even *bigger*, even more democratic, even more comprehensive. Quantity will be transformed into quality. A single State Bank, the biggest of the big, with branches in every rural district, every factory, will constitute as much as nine-tenths of the *socialist* apparatus. This will be country-wide *bookkeeping*, country-wide accounting of the production and distribution of goods, this will be, so to speak, something in the nature of the *skeleton* of socialist society.

We can "lay hold of" and "set in motion" this "state apparatus" (which is not fully a state apparatus under capitalism, but which will be so with us, under socialism) at one stroke, by a single decree, because the actual work of book-keeping, control, registering, accounting and counting is performed by *employees*, the majority of whom themselves lead a proletarian or semi-proletarian existence.

By a single decree of the proletarian government these employees can and must be transferred to the status of state employees, in the same way as the watchdogs of capitalism like Briand and other bourgeois ministers, by a single decree, transfer railwaymen on strike to the status of state employees. We shall need many more state employees of this kind, and more can be obtained, because capitalism has simplified the work of accounting and control, has reduced it to a comparatively simple system of *book-keeping,* which any literate person can do.

The conversion of the bank, syndicate, commercial, etc., etc., rank-and-file employees into state employees is quite feasible both technically (thanks to the preliminary work performed for us by capitalism, including finance capitalism) and politically provided the Soviets exercise control and supervision.

As for the higher officials, of whom there are very few, but who gravitate towards the capitalists, they will have to be dealt with in the same way as the capitalists, i.e., "severely." Like the capitalists, they will offer resistance. This *resistance* will have to be broken. * * *

We can do this, for it is merely a question of breaking the resistance of an insignificant minority of the population, literally a handful of people, over each of whom the employee's unions, the trade unions, the consumers' societies and the Soviets will institute such *supervision* that every Tit Titych[1] will be *surrounded* as the French were at Sedan. We know these Tit Tityches by name: we only have to consult the lists of directors, board members, large shareholders, etc. There are several hundred, at most several thousand of them in the *whole* of Russia, and the proletarian state, with the apparatus of the Soviets, of the employees' unions, etc., will be able to appoint ten or even a hundred supervisors to each of them, so that instead of "breaking resistance" it may even be possible, by means of workers' control (over the capitalists), to make all resistance impossible.

The important thing will not be even the confiscation of the capitalists' property, but country-wide, all-embracing workers' control over the capitalists and their possible supporters. Confiscation alone leads nowhere,' as it does not contain the element of organisation, of accounting for proper distribution. Instead of confiscation, we could easily impose a *fair* tax (even on the Shingyarov[2] scale, for instance), taking care, of course, to preclude the possibility of anyone evading assessment, concealing the truth, evading the law. And this possibility can be *eliminated only* by the workers, control of the *workers' state.*

*Compulsory syndication* i.e., compulsory amalgamation in associations under state control— this is what capitalism has prepared the way for, this is what has been carried out in Germany by the Junkers' state, this is what can be easily carried out in Russia by the Soviets, by the proletarian dictatorship, and this is what will *provide us with a state apparatus* that will be universal, up-to-date, and non-bureaucratic.

The proletariat, we are told, will not be able to set the state apparatus in motion.

Since the 1905 revolution, Russia has been governed by 130,000 landowners, who have perpetrated endless violence against 150,000,000 people, heaped unconstrained abuse upon them, and condemned the vast majority to inhuman toil and semi-starvation.

Yet we are told that the 240,000 members of the Bolshevik Party will not be able to govern Russia, govern her in the interests of the poor and against the rich. These 240,000 are already backed by no less than a million votes of the adult population, for this is precisely the proportion between the number of Party members and the number of votes cast for the Party that has been established by the experience of Europe and the experience of Russia as shown, for example, by the

---

[1]  A rich, tyrannical merchant in A. N. Ostrovsky's play *Shouldering Another's Troubles.*
[2]  A. I. Shingyarov (1869–1918) was minister of finance in the Provisional Government.

elections to the Petrograd City Council last August. We therefore already have a "state apparatus" of *one million* people devoted to the socialist state for the sake of high ideals and not for the sake of a fat sum received on the 20th of every month.

In addition to that we have a "magic way" to enlarge our state apparatus *tenfold* at once, at one stroke, a way which no capitalist state ever possessed or could possess. This magic way is to draw the working people, to draw the poor, into the daily work of state administration.

To explain how easy it will be to employ this magic way and how faultlessly it will operate, let us take the simplest and most striking example possible.

The state is to forcibly evict a certain family from a flat and move another in. This often happens in the capitalist state, and it will also happen in our proletarian or socialist state.

The capitalist state evicts a working-class family which has lost its breadwinner and cannot pay the rent. The bailiff appears with police, or militia, a whole squad of them. To effect an eviction in a working-class district a whole detachment of Cossacks is required. Why? Because the bailiff and the militiaman refuse to go without a very strong military guard. They know that the scene of an eviction arouses such fury among the neighbours, among thousands and thousands of people who have been driven to the verge of desperation, arouses such hatred towards the capitalists and the capitalist state, that the bailiff and the squad of militiamen run the risk of being torn to pieces at any minute. Large military forces are required, several regiments must be brought into a big city, and the troops must come from some distant, outlying region so that the soldiers will not be familiar with the life of the urban poor, so that the soldiers will not be "infected" with socialism.

The proletarian state has to forcibly move a very poor family into a rich man's flat. Let us suppose that our squad of workers' militia is fifteen strong; two sailors, two soldiers, two class-conscious workers (of whom, let us suppose, only one is a member of our Party, or a sympathiser), one intellectual, and eight from the poor working people, of whom at least five must be women, domestic servants, unskilled labourers, and so forth. The squad arrives at the rich man's flat, inspects it and finds that it consists of five rooms occupied by two men and two women—"You must squeeze up a bit into two rooms this winter, citizens, and prepare two rooms for two families now living in cellars. Until the time, with the aid of engineers (you are an engineer, aren't you?), we have built good dwellings for everybody, you will have to squeeze up a little. Your telephone will serve ten families. This will save a hundred hours of work wasted on shopping, and so forth. Now in your family there are two unemployed persons who can perform light work: a citizeness fifty-five years of age and a citizen fourteen years of age. They will be on duty for three hours a day supervising the proper distribution of provisions for ten families and keeping the necessary account of this. The student citizen in our squad will now write out this state order in two copies and you will be kind enough to give us a signed declaration that you will faithfully carry it out."

This, in my opinion, can illustrate how the distinction between the old bourgeois and the new socialist state apparatus and state administration could be illustrated.

We are not utopians. We know that an unskilled labourer or a cook cannot immediately get on with the job of state administration. In this we agree with the Cadets, with Breshkovskaya, and with Tsereteli. We differ, however, from these citizens in that we demand an immediate break with the prejudiced view that only the rich, or officials chosen from rich families, are capable of *administering* the state, of performing the ordinary, everyday work of administration. We demand that *training* in the work of state administration be conducted by class-conscious workers and soldiers and that this training be begun at once, i.e., that a *beginning* be made at once in training all the working people, all the poor, for this work.

We know that the Cadets are also willing to teach the people democracy. Cadet ladies are willing to deliver lectures to domestic servants on equal rights for women in accordance with the best English and French sources. And also, at the very next concert-meeting, before an audience of thousands, an exchange of kisses will be arranged on the platform: the Cadet lady lecturer will kiss Breshkovskaya, Breshkovskaya will kiss ex-Minister Tsereteli, and the grateful people will therefore receive an object-lesson in republican equality, liberty and fraternity. . . .

Yes, we agree that the Cadets, Breshkovskaya and Tsereteli are in their own way devoted to democracy and are propagating it among the people. But what is to be done if our conception of democracy is somewhat different from theirs?

In our opinion, to ease the incredible burdens and miseries of the war and also to heal the terrible wounds the war has inflicted on the people, *revolutionary* democracy is needed, *revolutionary* measures of the kind described in the example of the distribution of housing accommodation in the interests of the poor. *Exactly the same* procedure must be adopted in both town and country for the distribution of provisions, clothing, footwear, etc., in respect of the land in the rural districts, and so forth. For the administration of the state in *this* spirit we can *at once set in motion a state* apparatus consisting of ten if not twenty million people, an apparatus such as no capitalist state has ever known. We alone can create such an apparatus, for we are sure of the fullest and devoted sympathy of the vast majority of the population. We alone can create such an apparatus, because we have class-conscious workers disciplined by long capitalist "schooling" (it was not for nothing that we went to learn in the school of capitalism), workers who are capable of forming a workers' militia and of gradually expanding it (beginning to expand it at once) into a militia *embracing the whole people*. The class-conscious workers must lead, but for the work of administration they can enlist the vast mass of the working and oppressed people.

It goes without saying that this new apparatus is bound to make mistakes in taking its first steps. But did net the peasants make mistakes when they emerged from serfdom and began to manage their own affairs? Is there any way other than practice by which the people can learn to govern themselves and to avoid mistakes? Is there any way other than by proceeding immediately to genuine self-government by the people? The chief thing now is to abandon the prejudiced bourgeois-intellectualist view that only special officials, who by their very social position are entirely dependent upon capital, can administer the state. The chief thing is to put an end to the state of affairs in which bourgeois officials and "socialist" ministers are trying to govern in the old way, but are incapable of doing so and, after seven months, are faced with a peasant revolt in a peasant country! The chief thing is to imbue the oppressed and the working people with confidence in their own strength, to prove to them in practice that they can and must themselves ensure the *proper*, most strictly regulated and organised distribution of bread, all kinds of food, milk, clothing, housing, etc., *in the interests of the poor*. Unless this is done, Russia *cannot* be saved from collapse and ruin. The conscientious, bold, universal move to hand over administrative work to proletarians and semi-proletarians will, however, rouse such unprecedented revolutionary enthusiasm among the people, will so multiply the people's forces in combating distress, that much that seemed impossible to our narrow, old, bureaucratic forces will become possible for the millions, who will *begin to work for themselves* and not for the capitalists, the gentry, the bureaucrats, and not out of fear of punishment.

Ideas become a power when they grip the people. And precisely at the present time the Bolsheviks, i.e., the representatives of revolutionary proletarian internationalism, have embodied in their policy the idea that is motivating countless working people all over the world.

Justice alone, the mere anger of the people against exploitation, would never have brought them on to the true path of socialism. But now that, thanks to capitalism, the material apparatus of the big banks, syndicates, railways, and so forth, has grown, now that the immense experience of the advanced countries has accumulated a stock of engineering marvels, the employment of which is being *hindered* by capitalism, now that the class-conscious workers have built up a party of a quarter of a million members to systematically lay hold of this apparatus and set it in motion with the support of all the working and exploited people—now that these conditions exist, no power on earth can prevent the Bolsheviks, *if they do not allow themselves to be scared* and if they succeed in taking power, from retaining it until the triumph of the world socialist revolution.

# Socialism and Communism

 Shelia Fitzpatrick

S ocialism has many meanings. *The Oxford English Dictionary*[1] offers the following definition: "A theory or policy of social organization which aims at or advocates the ownership and control of the means of production, capital, land, property, etc., by the community as a whole, and their administration or distribution in the interests of all." But what is that "community" (a nation-state? a region or municipality? a self-selected group of like-minded persons?), and how does it attain ownership and control of the means of production? Is socialism a necessary stage in the development of human societies? Is it a free moral choice made by popular consensus, and if so, is that choice reversible? Who determines what "the interests of all" are, and who adjudicates claims arising from the conflicting interests of individuals and groups? How are the common assets "administered," and what control do other members of the socialist community have over the administrators? Socialists have given many different answers to these questions. Moreover, the answers given by socialist theory have often been different from the answers given by socialists' practice.

My task in this chapter will be to describe the variety of meanings that socialism as a practice has had throughout the world in the twentieth century.[2] Several aspects of this statement of intention need to be emphasized. In the first place, I am focusing on socialist practice, not socialist theory. The doctrinal disputes that so preoccupied many Marxist groups will receive little attention in this essay. In the second place, in writing of a "variety of meanings," I am taking the position that for the historian there is not and cannot be one "true" practice of socialism, by comparison to which all other practices of socialism deviate or fall short. For my purposes, there is no *Ur-Sozialismus*. The range of socialisms that will be discussed extends from German Social Democracy to Soviet Communism in the first half of the twentieth century and from the postwar British and Scandinavian "welfare states" to the Maoist-inspired national liberation movements in the Third World in the second half of the century.

This broad-church approach means that, generally speaking, I accept as socialist those social movements, political parties, and state regimes that describe themselves as socialist and are recognized as such by other (but not necessarily all other) socialist groups. Of course, recognition is not always a straightforward matter. It has been standard practice for Marxists to accuse each other of being "renegades," "apostates," "deviationists," or "capitalist-roaders" at the slightest provocation; but from my standpoint such accusations may be understood as a backhanded affirmation of kinship. The German National Socialists pose a more complex problem in terms of my criteria, as their name identified them as "socialist." I exclude them from consideration, however, since this claim was not seriously pursued by the Nazis themselves, and they were regarded as alien (not as apostates or deviationists) by socialists of virtually all persuasions. Regimes whose claims to a socialist identity appeared dubious or opportunistic to contemporaries, such as Nasser's in the United Arab Republic in the 1950s or Sukarno's in Indonesia in the 1960s, pose another problem. I grant them a place, but only a marginal one, in the history of socialist practice.

Another definitional question that must be dealt with before proceeding further is the relationship of "socialism" to "communism." Once again, I am not interested in essential meanings,[2] but in the meanings established by twentieth-century usage and practice. In some contexts, the two terms were used almost synonymously. In another established usage,the distinction between socialism and communism was a matter of degree, communism being considered a more extreme or advanced form of socialism. The most salient twentieth-century distinction between socialism and communism, however, was based simply on the existence in most European nations in the interwar period (and subsequently in many nations in other parts of the world) of two competing parties of the left, a Socialist Party (democratic, parliamentary-based, reformist) and a Communist Party (revolutionary at least in rhetoric, and affiliated with the Moscow-based Communist or Third International Party).

For all the variety of socialist theory and practice in the twentieth century, some generalizations may still be offered. It is notable, first of all, that, despite the internationalist principles of most socialists, the nation-state has almost always been central to the practice of socialism in the twentieth century. This is the "state power" that socialist parties have aspired to seize by revolution or win by parliamentary means. For the bureaucracy of the state (or, in the case of communist regimes, the party-state) has been the implementing mechanism of social change when power is won. In all socialist and communist regimes, branches of the central state bureaucracy have become the instruments of public ownership and management, economic planning, redistribution of wealth, and administration of social welfare.

Marxism (including derivatives such as Marxism-Leninism and Maoism) has unquestionably been the most influential form of socialism in the twentieth century. Of course, Marxism itself is far from a unitary phenomenon. Important traits of "classical" Marxism include:

1. understanding of socialism as the antithesis of capitalism (meaning that capitalism is "the other" for socialists),
2. a theory of history that holds that capitalism will inevitably collapse and be succeeded by socialism,
3. the belief that political regimes represent the rule of a dominant class and that conflict between exploited and exploiting classes provides the basic dynamics of politics,
4. the view that the industrial proletariat is the class whose natural interest is socialism.

Several of these traits have undergone radical metamorphosis in the course of the twentieth century. In the first place, the capitalist "other" of the era before the Second World War became the imperialist "other" of the postwar period, imperialism being understood by Marxists as an outgrowth or final stage of capitalism. This was part of a shift of the central arena of socialist contestation from the industrialized world to the economically backward, ex-colonial Third World. In the second place, as a consequence of the same shift, Marxist socialism lost the identification with a particular socioeconomic class—the industrial proletariat, and by extension the urban labor movement—that had been central to both its theory and its practice in Europe before the Second World War. In the third place, the idea of socialism as the designated heir of a collapsing capitalism, which was widely accepted during the Great Depression, lost credibility in the Western economic boom after the Second World War. By the 1990s, few socialists still held to the idea that history was on their side.

Socialism has been a dominant presence in the internal and international politics of the twentieth century. But in the understanding of most observers, it has not been *the* dominant presence. The twentieth century is rarely labeled "the age of socialism," on the pattern of the nineteenth-century "age of liberalism." This no doubt reflects the fact that, from a Western perspective, socialism/communism has characteristically been perceived less as an actuality than as a powerful *alternative*—externally, a threat or a model; internally, more often the party in opposition than the party in power. If there is something of an "always a bridesmaid, never a bride" flavor to the history of twentieth-century socialism, however, socialist rhetoric must bear part of the blame. Its insistent claim that the future belonged to socialism implied (perhaps incorrectly) that the present did not.

The drama that will be related in the following pages can be divided into two acts. In the first act, set in industrialized Europe, socialist movements develop in close association with labor movements, and the great events are the First World War and, arising out of it, the Russian Revolution of 1917. In the second act, for which the Second World War serves as prelude, much of the action takes place outside Europe in a context of postwar decolonization and the cold war division of the world into socialist and imperialist (or totalitarian and democratic) camps. Russia, representing itself at the beginning of act 1 as a developed nation ripe for proletarian revolution, appears in a different light in act 2, when its historical experience is reinterpreted in terms of its relevance to the general problem of underdeveloped nations, namely, how to escape foreign economic domination and catch up with the developed West. By the middle of the second act, however, the role of exemplar to the Third World is increasingly passing to China—communist since 1949, and a competing center of world Communist leadership since the late 1950s—and, in a different way, Cuba. The United States, almost absent from act 1, assumes a central role in act 2 as the chief enemy of socialism, leader a worldwide anticommunist crusade. The climax and finale of the play is the abrupt collapse of communist power in Eastern Europe in 1989 and the demise of the Soviet Union at the end of 1991, 74 years after Russia had experienced the world's "first socialist revolution" in October of 1917.

## Socialism in the Early Twentieth Century

At the beginning of the twentieth century, the socialist movement was gaining strength in Western Europe. Most countries had recently acquired or were in the process of acquiring socialist (labor) political parties with a base of support in the industrial working class and the trade unions. There was already an international organization, the Second International, espousing Marxist socialist principles (though the influence of Marxism on labor parties in the English-speaking world was much less than on the Continent). The German Social-Democratic Party dominated the International and was the most powerful in Europe, but in Britain and Sweden the labor (socialist) parties had also achieved a strong parliamentary presence. To be sure, none of the European socialist parties had yet won a parliamentary majority and set up a government. Only in distant Australia had a labor party won a national election and formed a government before 1914—and the Australian Labour Party had an even more ambiguous relationship to socialism than its relative, the Labour Party in Britain.

To many people within the socialist movement, and to an increasing number outside it in the years before the First World War, socialism seemed the wave of the future. This perception was related to the socialists' rapid rise to political prominence over the past decades, the strength in both numbers and resentment of the industrial workers who supported the socialist parties and trade unions, and the sense of impending crisis associated with the danger of a general European war. For socialism's supporters, its apparently inexorable advance demonstrated the simple justice of its cause: who but the privileged few could reject the argument that wealth, privilege, and opportunity were inequitably distributed in society, and that these wrongs should be righted? For the opponents of socialism, its organizational and parliamentary successes underlined a threat to the established order that was even greater than that of war—the threat of revolution.

In Marx's analysis, formulated half a century earlier, capitalism polarized society, generating an ever poorer and ever larger proletariat that would finally realize its strength and overthrow the capitalists in a socialist revolution. The necessity of workers' revolution remained an article of faith in the Second International in the early twentieth century, but at the same time the socialists' own successes were undermining it. If socialist parties could win power by parliamentary means, would it not be possible to use the existing governmental structure to redress social inequities? Was this not already happening in Germany and England, even before the socialist parties achieved a majority position? Were there not signs of improvement in the condition of the working class, rather than the progressive immiseration Marx had predicted? When Eduard Bernstein raised these questions in the 1890s, the German Socialists rejected them as heresy. All the same, as more and more evidence came in to support the "reformist" position, revolution became an increasingly abstract and remote concept for the leaders of European socialism.

In the early twentieth century, socialism was primarily a European phenomenon, though its members included parties from the United States, Japan, Australia, South Africa, and several Latin American countries. The Second International was predominantly an association of European socialist parties. Though in India, China, and elsewhere, a few intellectuals were becoming interested in socialism—which they often first encountered as students in Europe—this had no immediate practical consequences. Economic backwardness—the absence of industrial development, urbanization, a strong urban proletariat, labor organizations—seemed an insuperable obstacle to the development of socialism. There was, however, one partial exception to this rule: Russia, that slovenly giant on the fringe of Europe, which was still mainly a backward, peasant country, but from the 1890s had experienced rapid industrial growth in a few major cities and regions of the country.

Russian intellectuals, westward-looking, alienated, and inclined to socialism since the mid-nineteenth century, began reading Marx in the 1880s, before Russia had any of the prerequisites of the socialist revolution he described. A splinter group of Marxists detached itself from the populist mainstream of the Russian intelligentsia, arguing that capitalist industrialization was inevitable in Russia and that the peasant commune, on whose socialist potential the populists relied, was bound to disintegrate under its impact. No sooner had the Marxists made this prediction than it started to come true, albeit with a much larger dose of state sponsorship and foreign investment than the processes of capitalist industrialization observed by Marx in Western Europe. Industrialization generated a new class of urban industrial workers, volatile and uprooted, with which the Marxist intellectuals made tentative contact; its strength was manifested in the revolution that engulfed Russian towns and villages in 1905, almost but not quite overthrowing the old regime. The Russian Social-Democratic Labor Party, formed at the turn of the century, split into Menshevik and Bolshevik factions a few years later. Its leaders, including Trotsky (a Menshevik in the prewar period) and Lenin (leader of the intransigent Bolshevik party), were reasonably prominent participants in the politics of the Second International, though the turbulent and faction-prone Russians were treated with some condescension by the dominant German socialists.

In the context of international socialism, the United States was also an anomaly, though of the opposite kind from Russia. Here was a developed, industrialized society with powerful capitalists, a large urban working class, and even a trade-union movement—that is, a society possessing all the prerequisites for socialism—that yet stubbornly refused to move in a socialist direction. "Why is there no socialism in the United States?" was the title of a widely read study by the German sociologist Werner Sombart, published in 1906.[3] Sombart's answer was that workers in America, unlike those in Europe, were not attracted to socialism because of the greater flexibility of the class structure, the opportunities for upward mobility, the open frontier, and the greater material benefits available to workers under American capitalism. In addition, Sombart remarked in wonder, "I believe that emotionally the American worker has a share in capitalism: I believe that he loves it."[4]

## The First World War and the Russian Revolution

The outbreak of the First World War was an enormous blow to the international socialist movement. Instead of workers of different countries realizing their class solidarity and refusing to fire on each other, almost all were swept up in the waves of patriotism that engulfed the belligerent countries in August of 1914. The same thing happened to the major socialist parties, which abruptly abandoned their internationalist and antiwar positions and voted full support for their governments. Socialist leaders such as Jules Guesde in France, Emile Vandervelde in Belgium, and Arthur Henderson in Britain were co-opted into wartime cabinets. Some socialists whose countries were not yet involved in the war protested, but dissidents in the belligerent countries were exceedingly few. One of the few was Lenin, whose Bolshevik party not only opposed the war but also stated that it was in the interests of the Russian revolutionary movement that Russia be defeated.

The enormous carnage of the war and misery of the trenches produced great war-weariness in the soldiers and civilians of the belligerent countries. But it was Russia—"the weakest link in the capitalist chain," as Trotsky put it—that snapped. In March of 1917 (February, according to the old Julian calendar that remained in use in Russia until 1918), a revolution took place that led to the abdication of Emperor Nicholas II and the formation of a Provisional Government; initially led by liberals but supported by most socialists, it was hailed as a triumph for democracy in the Allied camp. This in turn survived only a few months until the Bolsheviks, acting with substantial support in the streets but virtually no support from other Russian socialist groups, overthrew it in the October Revolution and proclaimed a "dictatorship of the proletariat" that would lead the new Soviet Republic through the transitional period between capitalism and socialism.

The Bolshevik Revolution terrified Western governments, which feared that it would set off a string of mutinies and rebellions elsewhere as well as causing Russia's unilateral withdrawal from the war. The leaders of European socialism were scarcely less appalled, not only because of their commitment (on the Allied side) to the war effort and emotional stake in the Provisional Government, but also because they saw the Bolsheviks' action as an irresponsible putsch in a country still too undeveloped in orthodox Marxist terms to have earned a socialist revolution. Lenin and Trotsky (a recent convert to Bolshevism) naturally disputed this reading of Marxism. But the Bolsheviks nevertheless took for granted in the early years that the long-term survival of their revolution depended on its providing the spark to set off European social revolution. They attached particular importance to the success of revolution in Germany, the advanced, industrialized country that had historically provided the leadership of the international socialist movement.

In 1918–1919, it did indeed seem possible that, as in 1848, the flames of revolution would sweep all over Europe. As the European war ended with the defeat of Germany and Austria-Hungary, Kaiser Wilhelm and the new Hapsburg emperor, Karl, abdicated, and governmental order collapsed. Workers' and soldiers' councils, on the model of the Russian soviets, sprang up in many German cities; Bavaria for a few months proclaimed itself a Soviet Republic. The Austro-Hungarian Empire disintegrated into factious chaos as the newly independent states of Poland, Czechoslovakia, Austria, Hungary, and Yugoslavia struggled into being. In the Austrian capital of Vienna, socialists dominated; in Hungary, the left socialist Bela Kun headed a short-lived Soviet Republic. The victorious allies, Britain and France, never came so close to revolution, despite isolated mutinies in their armed forces, but the governments' fear of such an outcome was acute.

In the turmoil of these years, most of the leaders of the now-defunct Second International found that their instincts were overwhelmingly on the side of law and order and against "irresponsible" revolutionary attempts, despite the Marxist doctrine on socialist revolution to which they all, in principle, subscribed. This was particularly obvious in Germany, where the Social-Democratic Party was closely involved in the crushing of revolution and the establishment of a new parliamentary regime, the Weimar Republic.

The Bolsheviks, fighting for survival in a civil war in which the Western powers were actively supporting their opponents, observed this cutting of their revolutionary lifeline with horror. From their standpoint, the renegade leaders of the old Second International had betrayed the socialist cause and thrown in their lot with the capitalists. Their bitterness was intensified when the European socialist leaders accused them of betraying democracy by embracing dictatorship; Karl Kautsky's reproach that the Bolshevik terror of the civil war period represented a setback to the progress of world civilization brought an angry response from Trotsky. The capitalist bourgeoisie (or any other ruling class), Trotsky answered, would never relinquish power without a fight, and "history [shows] no other way of breaking the class will of the enemy except the systematic and energetic use of violence."[5]

After the events of 1917–1919, a lasting split between Europe's reformist and revolutionary socialists was almost inevitable. Still, the Bolsheviks did their best to facilitate it, first by creating a new Communist International, whose First Congress was held in Moscow in 1919, and then by demanding that any party desiring entry into the Comintern should demonstrate its revolutionary credentials by demonstratively splitting with or expelling its moderates. Almost no European socialist party escaped a traumatic and acrimonious breakup, which usually left a majority of members in a "reformist" Social-Democratic Party and a minority in a "revolutionary" Comintern-affiliated Communist Party. The reformist parties formed their own Labor and Socialist International, headquartered in London, but this never enjoyed the prestige or influence of the Second International. The Comintern, based in Moscow and dominated by the Soviet Communist Party,[6] provoked great fear in the governments of Europe but proved inept, and after a while uninterested, in fomenting revolution in the West.

## Third World Socialism and National Liberation Movements

For the great powers in the postwar world, socialism (communism) scarcely had meaning outside of their confrontation. But it was a different matter in the rest of the world, most dramatically in those countries emerging from colonial status with the collapse of the British, French, and Dutch empires in the wake of the Second World War. In almost all of these emerging countries in the Third World, a small class of native intellectuals, usually educated in the West, provided an ideology for the new postcolonial state regime that combined nationalism, anti-imperialism, and socialism. In this context, "socialism" meant primarily an anti-imperialist ideology for the independence struggle and, after independence, for extensive state control and intervention in the economy.

From the perspective of the decolonizing Third World, the value of Soviet socialism was primarily as a model for rapid economic modernization without dependence on foreign capital in a backward country. This was in many ways a more realistic interpretation of Soviet experience than the one prevalent in European socialist circles before the war, which treated the Russia of 1917 as roughly on a par with other modern, industrialized European states, and accepted at face value Bolshevik claims about the strength and so-called maturity of the Russian proletariat. To some Western scholars, it suggested a new reading of the historical significance of Marxism as an ideology of modernization.[7]

China, however, had an even greater appeal than the Soviet Union as a developmental model for the Third World. It was a more recent example of state-directed socialist modernization, and, unlike the Soviet Union, was neither integrated into a Euro-American geopolitical world nor bashful about acknowledging that it was a predominantly peasant country whose experience had much in common with that of colonial Asia and Africa. The Chinese Communists who took power in 1949 had just emerged from a national liberation struggle against the Japanese, in addition to the country's earlier experience of competing Western imperialisms at the turn of the century, and they were eager to encourage others on the same path.

The common context of Third World socialism may be summarized as follows: a colonial heritage; a low level of urbanization, industrial development, and labor organization (which made the classical Marxist emphasis on the proletariat irrelevant); and a small native elite, including some Western-educated intellectuals, that tended to view private entrepreneurship with suspicion and assumed that the state had to take the lead in economic life as well as in building a sense of nationhood.

For a large number of newly emergent nations after the Second World War, primarily those that had been under British rule, independence was achieved as a result of the imperial power's decision to depart. In this context—for example, India under Nehru, Sri Lanka (formerly Ceylon) under S.W.R.D. Bandaranaike, Ghana under Kwame Nkrumah, or Tanzania under Julius Nyerere— the socialism of the new regimes had little revolutionary content and focused on state economic planning, selective nationalization, control of foreign investment, and social welfare policies.

Where Third World countries had to fight for independence, socialism had a different meaning, with a much sharper anti-imperialist and revolutionary thrust. The most familiar example is Vietnam, where the Vietminh—led by Ho Chi Minh, whose Marxism went back to Paris circa 1920 and whose revolutionary experience started in the Comintern—fought first the French and then the Americans in a war that lasted three decades. The term "national liberation movement" came into use in the 1970s for independence movements emphasizing armed struggle, strongly hostile to the West and Western imperialism, using mobilization techniques similar to those of the Chinese Communist Party in its revolutionary struggle, and advocating some form of socialist transformation of society as a revolutionary goal. In addition to the Algerian FLN (one of the few national liberation movements that was not explicitly Marxist), such movements included the MPLA in Angola, FRELIMO in Mozambique, SWAPO in Southwest Africa, and the ANC in South Africa.

The same term came to be used for Latin American guerrilla movements in countries that already had political independence but sought both to overthrow a reactionary government at home and to escape from foreign economic imperialism. These movements espoused different variants of socialism, ranging from the Sandinistas in Nicaragua to the "Shining Path" in Peru, but hostility to "Yankee imperialism" was a common thread. Fidel Castro's Cuba was an inspiration for such movements (though Castro's socialist ideology and strong Soviet connections were acquired only *after* the 1959 Revolution), as was Che Guevara, the Argentine-born hero of the Cuban Revolution, who was killed in 1967 while leading a guerrilla movement in Bolivia.

Third World socialism, especially in its more revolutionary guise, became closely linked with the cold war rivalries of the superpowers. Its anti-imperialist component had a strongly anti-American tinge, since the United States was seen in the Third World as assuming the "white man's burden" laid down by the declining European powers; and the United States for many years saw national liberation movements purely as Moscow's (or possibly Beijing's) pawns in the global advance of world communism.

The Soviet Union, though not really very interested in national independence movements even after Stalin (who had ignored them almost completely), started trying to exploit the opportunities inherent in this situation in the second half of the 1950s. Two well-known early examples, the flirtation with Nasser in Egypt and Sukarno in Indonesia, ended badly and left the Soviet Union with a skeptical attitude to the socialist pretensions of Third World nationalist leaders. By the 1970s, however, the Soviet Union had acquired some enthusiasm for playing games with Third

World clients, not out of any belief in their socialist potential, but because it was felt to enhance the Soviet Union's status as a superpower. In most Third World conflicts of the 1970s and 1980s, the contending parties established themselves as clients of the two superpowers (for example, India/Pakistan; Somalia/Ethiopia; Israel/the Arab states of the Middle East), adopting a rhetoric of "socialism" or "democracy" that suited the patron but otherwise often had little relation to reality.[8]

More ideologically fervent support for national liberation movements came from China and Cuba, which helped to the best of their ability with men and matériel, especially in Africa. These countries, and the Soviet Union as well, also provided various forms of training, ranging from general education at institutions like the Lumumba "Friendship" University in Moscow to guerrilla warfare camps, for Third World sympathizers and revolutionaries.

## Endnotes

1. Second edition, 1989. My thanks to Jonathan Bone for his indefatigable and imaginative research assistance in the writing of this article.

2. The *Oxford English Dictionary*, 2d ed. (1989) gives the following definitions of communism:

   a. A theory which advocates a state of society in which there should be no private ownership, all property being vested in the community and labor being organized for the common benefit of all members; the professed principle being that each should work according to his capacity, and receive according to his needs.

   b. A political doctrine or movement based on Marxism and later developed by Lenin, seeking the overthrow of capitalism through a proletarian revolution.

3. W. Sombart,*Warton gibt es in den Vereinigten Staaten keinen Sozialismus?* (Tübingen: 1906). Translated by Patricia M. Hocking and C. T. Husbands as Why Is There No Socialism in the United States? (White Plains, N.Y.: International Arts and Sciences, 1976). This question has since been addressed by several generations of American sociologists and labor historians. See, for example, John M. Laslett and Seymour Martin Lipset, Failure of a Dream? Essays in the History of American Socialism (Garden City, N.Y.: Anchor Press, 1974).

4. Sombart, *Why Is There No Socialism*, p. 20.

5. Leon Trotsky, *Terrorism and Communism: A Reply to Karl Kautsky* (1920; reprint, Ann Arbor: University of Michigan Press, 1961), p. 55. Karl Kautsky's similarly titled work was written in 1918–1919.

6. The Bolsheviks adopted the name of the Russian (later Soviet) Communist Party in 1918.

7. See Adam B. Ulam, "The Historical Role of Marxism," in *The New Face of Soviet Totalitarianism* (Cambridge: Harvard University Press, 1963).

8. On Soviet attitudes to the Third World socialism, see Jerry F. Hough, *The Struggle of the Third World: Soviet Debates and American Options* (Washington, D.C.: Brookings Institution, 1986).

# CHAPTER TWELVE

# Colonialism, Postcolonialism, and the Global South

Colonialism is a specific form of imperialist exploitation that developed in the West as a result of the capitalist expansion of Europe over 400 years at the end of the fifteenth century. But colonialism did not begin in Europe and it did not end there. A practice that stretches around the globe and across time, colonialism was practiced by everyone from the ancient Hittites of Anatolia and the Mongols of northern China to the Incas of Peru and the British of England's green and verdant isle. It was employed in the early American colonies against the indigenous people or Native Americans, and it was utilized by the Japanese throughout the South Pacific in preparation for and during World War II. It is an institution that involves the rule of distant people from a mother country or metropole, and it often brings with it a set of attitudes about the superiority of the dominating power and the inferiority of those they seek to subjugate.

Those attitudes were, at least during the 400-period of European colonialism, eventually organized into an ideology that simultaneously reflected the attitudes, prejudices, and presumptions of the dominating metropolitan center and was crafted to ensure not just the physical but also the psychological governance and oppression of its subject peoples. This ideology was based on what might be called a hierarchy of difference. This hierarchy of difference was employed to prevent the possibility of fair or just exchanges—political, economic, social, cultural—between center and colony and was reinforced by a certain notion of "civilization." This idea of civilization was associated with system of stratification which assumed that civilization could be acquired in any one of at least several different ways—through blood, history, society, achievement, and wealth—and by the end of the 18th-century, the Western, or at least West European, conception of "civilization" had come to be further linked with notions of refinement and superiority. It was not until the nineteenth century, however, that these somewhat miscellaneous notions of civilization were finally codified by the English philosopher, John Stuart Mill, into a list of attributes that British and other elites could identify with themselves. These attributes included the multiplication of physical comforts, the advancement and diffusion of knowledge, the decay and disappearance of superstition, the softening of manners, the spread of social intercourse, the limitation of tyranny, the decline of war and conflict, and the creation of great works accomplished globally by people of distinction.

So conceived, the idea of "civilization" functioned as a social construct that could best be understood by contrast with its opposite. If "civilization" represented a stage of human development related to certain social advantages such as education, wealth, and leisure, the term "uncivilized" inevitably referred to a more rudimentary stage of human development wholly bereft of such benefits. This left its subjects not only "different," even "other," but also, from the perspective of those who assumed their own condition to be the converse of this, "primitive," "infantile," "barbaric," "savage." This disparity, really binary, was not only intended to denigrate and debase those "others" who were assumed to lack "civilization" but literally to dehumanize them. In the language of condescension that characterized the colonial relationship, such "unfortunates" were assumed to lack what any human being needed to rise above the level of other animals, and this implicit disdain on the part of colonizers left the colonized almost everywhere exposed to the most inhuman barbarities. But in Africa in particular, and with those tens of millions caught up in the net of slavery, it turned black people in particular into what Achille Mbembe accurately describes in the last selection of this chapter as "the most visible symbol of the possibility of violence without limits and of vulnerability without a safety net."

This ideology of difference could operate in a variety of hierarchical registers. If one of the most powerful was race, where differences in color were used to naturalize inequality by enabling subject people, even if they were the actual descendants of monarchs or held the status of royals in their own societies, to be situated or positioned outside of civilization, they were constantly exiled as well, as Eric Wolf maintains in Chapter 1, outside of history. Race was further naturalized by encouraging whites to view all people of color as inferior not just culturally but also, as the science developed, genetically. And when Social Darwinism arrived in the second half of the nineteenth century, whites were able to transfer the evolutionary idea of natural selection to human society by convincing themselves that the emergence of "civilization" merely confirmed Darwin's conclusion about "the survival of the fittest."

But if colonialism could support its hierarchy of difference by means of a manipulation of the concept of race, it could also do so by means of appropriation of the notion of gender. Indeed, this followed almost of necessity from the sexist exclusivity of so much colonial discourse that centered around theories of "man" or "mankind" and allied that discourse with practices that were exclusively patriarchal. The civilizing task of colonization was clearly the responsibility of males, but that chauvinistic bias was carried a good many steps further when the English writer, Rudyard Kipling, actually went so far as to describe the American attempt to colonize the Philippines as the "white man's burden." Gendering the responsibility of colonialism as male reinforced the view that "white men" are "born to rule," and this, in turn, reinforced the corollary belief that this capacity as well as responsibility for rule inevitably derives from the natural endowments and entitlements of "whiteness" itself. Such presumptions about "whiteness" as more than a marker of color but also as a designation of character, ability, and supremacy could then, of course, also be turned back on women to suggest that the female gender is, or should be, no less dependent on the theory of whiteness than men are because under colonialism women of all colors, both free and enslaved, were born to serve the mission of white males.

These terminological subtleties and conversions reflect the fact that colonial ideology was dependent on a kind of linguistic or discursive subterfuge (saying one thing but meaning another—"civilizing" for "plundering," "evangelization" for indoctrination," studying for manipulation, control, and coersion) that enabled violent and unjust practices to be hidden behind a smokescreen of deception and mystification. Such processes of masking motives and misrepresenting intentions, of what has been called "obfuscatory justification, are what Edward Said exposed, as was discussed in Chapter 9, in his book *Orientalism* and what made that book one of the founding texts in the field of what has come to be called post-colonial studies. It is also key to the intellectual methods employed by the two selections featured in this chapter.

The initial selection in this chapter is from Aime Cesaire's *Discourse on Colonialism*. First published in 1950, it helped initiate what has been called a "'tidal wave" of anti-colonial literature that followed World War II and helped spur de-colonization movements all over the world. Cesaire identifies Western civilization as one that has used its principles and its power for "trickery," "deceit," and "hypocrisy." Such treachery has produced the false equations by which colonialism justifies and perpetuates itself—"Christianity = civilization, paganism = savagery"—but this is by no means the worst of its offenses. "Europe," Cesaire contends, "is ultimately indefensible," and this is not, Cesaire goes on to insist, because of colonialism's effects on the colonized alone but rather because of what it has also done to the colonizer. Colonialism does not bring civilization to the colonized so much as it de-civilizes the colonizer. Cesaire thus anticipates the insight of Frantz Fanon and other spokespersons for those Fanon called, in the title of his famous book <u>The Wretched of the Earth</u>: "Europe," having founded itself colonially on the false binary of master and slave, "is literally the creation of the Third World."

That Third World has since been renamed the global South but now functions even more explicitly as a territorial as well as an ideological marker. On the one hand, it refers to all those societies, peoples, and countries that have been the object or subject of exploitation and control by the wealthier and more powerful nations of the north. On the other, it also refers in a much less specific but more critical manner to the way the binary distinctions created by this colonial opposition—rich vs. poor, developed vs. undeveloped, advanced vs. backward--are now in the process not simply of being reversed but of being transformed. What now identifies the global South, as Achille Mbembe clarifies in the second selection in this chapter, is its function as a window from, and through which, to better detect and interrogate the prospects—economic, social, political, ethical—for the world as a whole.

It is from and through this window, Mbembe reminds us, that the birth of the racial subject, and thus of blackness itself, is linked not to colonialism alone but instead, as was clarified in Chapter 4, to the history of capitalism that created it. To recall that history is to realize that we can only recover from its ravages by restoring a sense of what it has lost, or sacrificed, in the process. What was lost or forfeited was nothing less than a sense of the world as a whole, what Edward Glissant has described as "the *Tout-Monde*, or All-World." This notion is a way of speaking about the one world that all humans share, a world without meaning except in relation to the humanity of those who share it. For it is nothing less than all of humanity that gives the world its name, delegating to it, and receiving confirmation from it, that "its own" includes all those who, as human, possess a special relation to it, "single yet fragile, vulnerable yet partial," in terms of the other forces that make up the universe. To deny the sacred, ecumenical nature of this fact is therefore not only an offense against humanity but an offense against the world that belongs to all human beings if it can be said to belong to any. Thus to build a world that is sharable, Mbembe, argues, we must replace the abstraction and objectification that accompanied the capitalist revolution, and produced the systemic, world-denying racism of colonialism, with the restitution, reparation, and the reinvention of the human community itself. And the reinvention of that community will depend, in turn, on how we inhabit and care for what, following the French philosopher Jacques Derrida, Mbembe calls "the Open." The "Open" is that which is neither closed nor restricted but rather "in-common."

# Discourse on Colonialism

 Aimé Césaire

A civilization that proves incapable of solving the problems it creates is a decadent civilization.

A civilization that chooses to close its eyes to its most crucial problems is a stricken civilization.

A civilization that uses its principles for trickery and deceit is a dying civilization.

The fact is that the so-called European civilization—"Western" civilization—as it has been shaped by two centuries of bourgeois rule, is incapable of solving the two major problems to which its existence has given rise: the problem of the proletariat and the colonial problem; that Europe is unable to justify itself either before the bar of "reason" or before the bar of "conscience"; and that, increasingly, it takes refuge in a hypocrisy which is all the more odious because it is less and less likely to deceive.

*Europe is indefensible.*

Apparently that is what the American strategists are whispering to each other.

That in itself is not serious.

What is serious is that "Europe" is morally, spiritually indefensible.

And today the indictment is brought against it not by the European masses alone, but on a world scale, by tens and tens of millions of men who, from the depths of slavery, set themselves up as judges.

The colonialists may kill in Indochina, torture in Madagascar, imprison in Black Africa, crack down in the West Indies. Henceforth the colonized know that they have an advantage over them. They know that their temporary "masters" are lying.

Therefore that their masters are weak.

And since I have been asked to speak about colonization and civilization, let us go straight to the principal lie that is the source of all the others.

Colonization and civilization?

In dealing with this subject, the commonest curse is to be the dupe in good faith of a collective hypocrisy that cleverly misrepresents problems, the better to legitimize the hateful solutions provided for them.

In other words, the essential thing here is to see clearly, to think clearly—that is, dangerously—and to answer dearly the innocent first question: what, fundamentally, is colonization? To agree on what it is not: neither evangelization, nor a philanthropic enterprise, nor a desire to push back the frontiers of ignorance, disease, and tyranny, nor a project undertaken for the greater glory of God, nor an attempt to extend the rule of law. To admit once and for all, without flinching at the consequences, that the decisive actors here are the adventurer and the pirate, the wholesale grocer and the ship owner, the gold digger and the merchant, appetite and force, and behind them, the baleful projected shadow of a form of civilization which, at a certain point in its history, finds itself obliged, for internal reasons, to extend to a world scale the competition of its antagonistic economies.

Pursuing my analysis, I find that hypocrisy is of recent date; that neither Cortéz discovering Mexico from the top of the great teocalli, nor Pizzaro before Cuzco (much less Marco Polo before Cambuluc), claims that he is the harbinger of a superior order; that they kill; that they plunder; that they have helmets, lances, cupidities; that the slavering apologists came later; that the chief culprit in this domain is Christian pedantry, which laid down the dishonest equations *Christianity = civilization, paganism = savagery,* from which there could not but ensue abominable colonialist and racist consequences, whose victims were to be the Indians, the Yellow peoples, and the Negroes.

That being settled, I admit that it is a good thing to place different civilizations in contact with each other; that it is an excellent thing to blend different worlds; that whatever its own particular genius may be, a civilization that withdraws into itself atrophies; that for civilizations, exchange is oxygen; that the great good fortune of Europe is to have been a crossroads, and that because it was the locus of all ideas, the receptacle of all philosophies, the meeting place of all sentiments, it was the best center for the redistribution of energy.

But then I ask the following question: has colonization really *placed civilizations in contact*? Or, if you prefer, of all the ways of *establishing contact*, was it the best?

I answer *no*.

And I say that between *colonization* and *civilization* there is an infinite distance; that out of all the colonial expeditions that have been undertaken, out of all the colonial statutes that have been drawn up, out of all the memoranda that have been dispatched by all the ministries, there could not come a single human value.

# There Is Only One World

 Achille Mbembe

The birth of the racial subject—and therefore of Blackness—is linked to the history of capitalism. Capitalism emerged as a double impulse toward, on the one hand, the unlimited violation of all forms of prohibition and, on the other, the abolition of any distinction between ends and means. The Black slave, in his dark splendor, was the first racial subject: the product of the two impulses, the most visible symbol of the possibility of violence without limits and of vulnerability without a safety net

Capitalism is the power of capture, influence, and polarization, and it has always depended on *racial subsidies* to exploit the planet s resources. Such was the case yesterday. It is the case today, even as capitalism sets about recolonizing its own center. Never has the perspective of a *Becoming Black of the world* loomed more clearly.

No region of the world is spared from the logics of the distribution of violence on a planetary scale, or from the vast operation under way to devalue the forces of production.

But as long as the retreat from humanity is incomplete, there is a still a possibility of restitution, reparation, and justice. These are the conditions for the collective resurgence of humanity. Thinking through what must come will of necessity be a thinking through of life, of the reserves of life, of what must escape sacrifice. It will of necessity be a *thinking in circulation, a thinking of crossings, a world-thinking.*

The question of the world—what it is, what the relationship is between its various parts, what the extent of its resources is and to whom they belong, how to live in it, what moves and threatens it, where it is going, what its borders and limits, and its possible end, are—has been within us since a human being of bone, flesh, and spirit made its first appearance under the sign of the Black Man, as *human-merchandise, human-metal,* and human-money. Fundamentally, it was always our question. And it will stay that way as long as speaking the world is the same as declaring humanity, and vice versa.

For, in the end, there is only one world. It is composed of a totality of a thousand parts. Of everyone. Of all worlds.

Édourd Glissant gave this living entity with multiple facets a name: *Tour-Monde,* or *All-World.* It was a way of underscoring the fact that the concept of humanity itself is simultaneously an epiphany and an ecumenical gesture, and concept without which the world, in its thingness, would signify nothing.

It is therefore humanity as a whole that gives the world its name. In conferring its name on the world, it delegates to it and receives from it confirmation of its own position, singular yet fragile.

vnlnerable and partial, at least in relation to the other forces of the universe-animals and vegetables, objects, molecules divinities, techniques and raw materials, the earth trembling, volcanoes erupting, winds and storms, rising waters, the sun that explodes and burns, and all the rest of it: There is therefore no world except by way of naming, delegation, mutuality; and reciprocity.

But humanity as a whole delegates itself in the world and receives from the world confirmation of its own being as well as its fragility. And so the difference between the world of humans and the world of nonhumans is no longer an external one. In opposing itself to the world of nonhumans, humanity opposes itself. For, in the end, it is in the relationship that we maintain with the totality of the living world that the truth of who we are is made visible.

In ancient Africa the visible sign of the epiphany that is humanity was the seed that one placed in the soil. It dies, is reborn, and produces the tree, fruit, and life. It was to a large extent to celebrate the marriage of the seed and life that ancient Africans invented speech and language, objects and techniques, ceremonies and rituals, works of art-indeed, social and political institutions. The seed had to produce life in the fragile and hostile environment in the midst of which humanity also had to find space for work and rest—an environment that needed protection and repair. What made most vernacular knowledge useful was the part it played in the endless labor of reparation. It was understood that nature was a force in and of itself. One could not mold, transform, or control nature when not in harmony with it. And this double labor of transformation and regeneration was part of a cosmological assembly whose function was to consolidate the relationships between humans and the other living beings with which they shared the world.

Sharing the world with other beings was the ultimate debt. And it was, above all, the key to the survival of both humans and nonhumans. In this system of exchange, reciprocity, and mutuality, humans and nonhumans were silt for one another.

Glissant spoke of silt as the castoff of matter: a substance made up of seemingly dead elements, things apparently lost, debris stolen from the source, water laden. But he also saw silt as a residue deposited along the banks of rivers, in the midst of archipelagos, in the depths of oceans, along valleys and at the feet of cliffis—everywhere, and especially in those arid and deserted places where, through an unexpected reversal, fertilizer gave birth to new forms of life, labor, and language.

The durability of our world, he insisted, must be thought from the underside of our history, from the slave and the cannibal structures of our modernity, from all that was put in place at the time of the slave trade and fed on for centuries. The world that emerged from the cannibal structure is built on countless human bones buried under the ocean, bones that little by little transformed themselves into skeletons and endowed themselves with flesh. It is made up of tons of debris and stumps, of bits of words scattered and joined together, out of which—as if by a miracle—language is reconstituted in the place where the human being meets its own animal form. The durability of the world depends on our capacity to reanimate beings and things that seem lifeless—the dead man, turned to dust by the desiccated economy; an order poor in worldliness that traffics in bodies and life.

The world will not survive unless humanity devotes itself to the task of sustaining what can be called the *reservoirs of life*. The refusal to perish may yet turn us into historical beings and make it possible for the world to be a world. But our vocation to survive depends on making the desire for life the cornerstone of a new way of thinking about politics and culture.

Among the ancient Dogon people, the unending labor of reparation had a name: the dialectic of meat and seed. The work of social institutions was to fight the death of the human, to ward off corruption, that process of decay and rot. The mask was the ultimate symbol of the determination of the living to defend themselves against death. A simulacrum of a corpse and substitute for the perishable body, its function was not only to commemorate the dead but also to bear witness to the transfiguration of the body (the perishable envelope) and to the apotheosis of a rot-proof world. It was therefore a way of returning to the idea that, as long as the work of reparation continued, life was an imperishable form, one that could not decay.

In such conditions we create borders, build walls and fences, divide, classify, and make hierarchies. We try to exclude—from humanity itself— those who have been degraded, those whom we look down on or who do not look like us, those with whom we imagine never being able to get along. But there is only one world. We are all part of it, and we all have a right to it. The world belongs to all of us, equally, and we are all its coinheritors, even if our ways of living in it are not the same, hence the real pluralism of cultures and ways of being. To say this is not to deny the brutality and cynicism that still characterize the encounters between peoples and nations. It is simply to remind us of an immediate and unavoidable fact, one whose origins lie in the beginnings of modem times: that the processes of mixing and interlacing cultures, peoples, and nations are irreversible.

There is therefore only one world, at least for now, and that world is all there is. What we all therefore have in common is the feeling or desire that each of us must be a full human being. The desire for the fullness of humanity is something we all share. And, more and more, we also all share the proximity of the distant. Whether we want to or not, the fact remains that we all share this world. It is all that there is, and all that we have.

To build a world that we share, we must restore the humanity stolen from those who have historically been subjected to processes of abstraction and objectification. From this perspective, the concept of reparation is not only an economic project but also a process of reassembling amputated parts, repairing broken links, relaunching the forms of reciprocity without which there can be no progress for humanity.

Restitution and reparation, then, are at the heart of the very possibility of the construction of a common consciousness of the world, which is the basis for the fulfillment of universal justice. The two concepts of restitution and reparation are based on the idea that each person is a repository of a portion of intrinsic humanity. This irreducible share belongs to each of us. It makes each of us objectively both different from one another and similar to one another. The ethic of restitution and reparation implies the recognition of what we might call the other's share, which is not ours, but for which we are nevertheless the guarantor, whether we want to be or not. This share of the other cannot be monopolized without consequences with regard to how we think about ourselves, justice, law, or humanity itself, or indeed about the project of the universal, if that is in fact the final destination.

Reparation, moreover, is necessary because of the cuts and scars left by history. For much of humanity, history has been a process of habituating oneself to the deaths of others—slow death, death by asphyxiation, sudden death, delegated death. These accommodations with the deaths of others, of those with whom we imagine to have shared nothing, these many ways in which the springs of life are dried up in the name of race and difference, have all left deep traces in both imagination and culture and within social and economic relations. These cuts and scars prevent the realization of community. And the construction of the common is inseparable from the reinvention of community.

This question of universal community is therefore by definition posed in terms of how we inhabit the Open, how we care for the Open—which is completely different from an approach that would aim first to enclose, to stay within the enclosure of what we call our own kin. This form of *unkinning* is the opposite of difference. Difference is, in most cases, the result of the construction of desire. It is also the result of a work of abstraction, classification, division, and exclusion—a work of power that, afterward, is internalized and reproduced in the gestures of daily life, even by the excluded themselves. Often, the desire for difference emerges precisely where people experience intense exclusion. In these conditions the proclamation of difference is an inverted expression of the desire for recognition and inclusion.

But if, in fact, difference is constituted through desire (if not also envy), then desire is not necessarily a desire for power. It can also be a desire to be protected, spared, preserved from danger. And the desire for difference is not necessarily the opposite of the project of the *in-common*. In fact, for those who have been subjected to colonial domination, or for those whose share of humanity was stolen at a given moment in history, the recovery of that share often happens in part through the proclamation of difference. But as we can see within certain strains of modem Black criticism, the proclamation of difference is only one facet of a larger project—the project of a world that is coming, a world before us, one whose destination is universal, a world freed from the burden of race, from resentment, and from the desire for vengeance that all racism calls into being.

# CHAPTER THIRTEEN

# *The Globalization of Mass Culture*

If culture is defined as those systems of meaning by which we lend import and significance to everything else we experience, culture has been undergoing a process of globalization ever since people from different locales began to communicate with one another and become changed in the process. Its chief enabler in the past was long-distance interactions due to trade, war, migrations, and conversions, but it was given further momentum by the rise of civilizations when the creation of cities led to regional kingdoms, and beyond that to regional civilizations, and ultimately beyond that to fully articulated global orders. The rise of print capitalism provided new stimulation to this process, but this was then also carried forward by the transportation revolution associated with seaborne navigation and the new intermingling of peoples that it slowly but inevitably enabled. While that intermingling was often drastically one-sided, communication being defined by, and flowing typically from, the privileged and the powerful to the deprived and the dispossessed, it nonetheless opened channels of communication over time that would bring people into the orbit of each other's worlds of meaning. It would take the Industrial Revolution and urban migration to provide the tools and conditions for spreading culture to the masses and in turn putting those masses in touch with one another, but by the end of the nineteenth century and the beginning of the twentieth, such processes were vigorously underway.

The key to their expansion, as the selection in this chapter by David Held and his collaborators entitled "Historical Forms of Cultural Globalization" helps clarify, were a variety of quite specific technological advances that opened different cultural systems across the world to each other's informational networks, including the telegraph, the telephone, the radio, and then, in the immediate postwar period, television, cable and fiber optic transmission, digitalization, and satellite communication. Such innovations began to allow images and messages to move at greater and greater velocity across national and other boundaries, thanks to such instruments as radio broadcasting, commercial advertising, film exports, cellular telephones, video conferencing, and the Internet. Systems developed for business and commerce were then reappropriated for the production and transmission of popular culture, quickly dissolving the boundaries between elite or high culture and mass culture, and eventually enabling the business of culture to compete with the culture of business. If the new agents of cultural diffusion were no longer states and their intellectual elites but multinational corporations and publicly owned telecommunication giants, the field of communications itself became more quickly transnationalized. By 2009, the Indian film "Slumdog Millionaire" swept eight Oscars at the Academy Awards in Hollywood, including those for Best Picture and Best Director, while Facebook and Twitter began to foment political revolutions all over the world. In the course of these developments, the stratification of globalization itself began to change, with the U.S. replacing Europe in the West, and traffic beginning to shift from South to North and, for an even longer period of time, from East to West. If these reversals were due to the migration of people and ideas as well as of wealth and resources, they were also due to the international exchange in food, ideas, beliefs, literature, clothing, music, and many other things.

One of the great assets of Held's table is that it not only tracks the expansion of these processes, flows, and networks over a period of 1,000 years but measures them in relation to a variety of analytic categories that determine their global reach and articulation. Defining the global is not simply a matter of determining the spread of certain processes over time, which Held calls "extensivity," but of figuring out how deep they go and how intensive they are, which he describes as "density." But then there is also the issue of how fast they spread and with what speed they produce changes, which he defines as "velocity," and the consequences that they are likely to produce, which he describes as "impact propensity." What needs still further to be factored in are, as he puts it, the "trajectory," of these changes, and these trajectories can only be calculated in terms of the infrastructures, institutions, and modes of interaction involved, which Held calls "stratification." Only by considering all these variables can one obtain an accurate estimate of just what globalization in any given instance actually means and amounts to.

As the global anthropologist Arjun Appadurai demonstrates in his path-breaking essay on "Disjuncture and Difference in the Global Cultural Economy," which makes up the second selection in this chapter, many of these more recent changes are related to the way the imagination has broken out of the more traditional forms in which it was once sequestered—religion, myth, ritual, and high art—and now circulates, and has even undertaken new kinds of fantasy work, in the broader precincts of global life. Appadurai shows how this process actually operated in relation to two of the most highly publicized cultural processes of the late twentieth century.

The first had to do with the way England's Princess Diana was turned from an icon of the media into a global superstar in the twenty years between her marriage to Prince Charles, heir to the British crown, and her tragic death in an automobile crash in Paris after a high-speed chase by international paparazzi. While 250 million people watched Princess Diana's Cinderella-like wedding, no less than 2.5 billion people, close to half the people on earth, witnessed her funeral after she had transformed herself from the wronged woman abandoned by Prince Charles and single mother of two sons into a global citizen advocating for such unpopular causes as AIDs and the abolition of land mines.

The second concerned the way a Nobel-prizing winning world author named Salmon Rushdie was turned into a global pariah, at least in the Muslim world, because of a novel he published entitled *The Satanic Verses,* inspired in part by the life of the Prophet Muhammed. This novel, which made satirical comments about Islam, not only elicited a *fatwa* (literally, ruling based on Islamic law) from the Ayatollah Khomeini of Iran that included a death sentence for Rushdie but also resulted in numerous killings and bombings throughout the world. What made this fatwa against Rushdie so culturally explosive was both the death sentence itself and the violence which followed (requiring Rushdie to be placed under the protection of the British government for a number of years) and also because it seemed, at least in the West as well as elsewhere, to clash with so many international cultural pieties and taboos. On the one hand, it provoked an enormous debate about the politics of reading, the cultural relevance of censorship, the dignity of religion, the right of religious authorities to judge books, and the claim that there are universal standards of taste and aesthetics. On the other, it reflected the hazards of a text-in-motion crossing cultural, not to say as well, national and civilizational boundaries, boundaries where Western notions about artistic freedom have limited recognition and books and ideas can be banned by religious and political leaders who operate as they choose within their own transnational sphere.

Phenomena such as these have led Appadurai to rethink the territorial, which is to say the spatial, dimensions of the global itself. His new way of conceiving the global spatially is to think of it as being composed of different kinds of cultural processes or "scapes," as he calls them, continuously in motion. Appadurai has come up with at least five distinct processes or scapes that crisscross the world, but there could potentially be any number of others depending on how you believe the world of global flows can be mapped. Among these various flows or processes, Appadurai distinguishes between "ethnoscapes" (referring to people in motion), "technoscapes" (referring to technologies in motion), "financescapes" (referring to capital in motion), "mediascapes" (referring to images and information in motion), and "ideoscapes" (referring to ideas and ideologies in motion). Because such flows or "scapes" are rarely integrated or coordinated with one another, being more disjunctive than conjunctive, they describe a world that in fundamental ways has been essentially de-territorialized rather than re-territorialized. This is a world whose new geography of features requires, according to Appaduarai, nothing less than a complete rethinking of the way the world culturally now actually operates.

Appadurai therefore proposes the outline of a new general theory of the global cultural economy. What makes his theory of particular interest is that he turns neither to the social sciences nor to the humanities for metaphorical assistance to describe it but rather to the natural and physical sciences. For example, he borrows the term "fractal" from mathematics to define cultural processes that are now nonlinear, irregular, and infinitely complex, like clouds, mountain ranges, and coastlines. He borrows the term "polythetic" from biology to describe these same processes because they also share overlapping characteristics which commonly occur in members of a group but are not essential for membership in that group. And from physics he utilizes the term "chaos" to underline the uncertain, random behavior of such processes, likening them to the "butterfly effect," as it is known in Chaos Theory, where the sensitive dependence that certain processes exhibit on initial conditions can enable small disturbances to cascade catastrophically into great ones. This kind of borrowing of terms and frames of reference from one discipline or field to describe the behavior of phenomena usually associated with another is what is meant by interdisciplinary studies, and it has the effect not only of changing how one field or discipline, in this case cultural studies very broadly conceived, can make sense of itself with the help of another, such as physics, biology, or mathematics, but also how that same discipline can now represent its own knowledge to itself.

# Historical Forms of Cultural Globalization

 DAVID HELD, ANTHONY MCGREW, DAVID GOLDBLATT
AND JONATHAN PERRATON

**TABLE 13.1** Historical Forms of Cultural Globalization

| *Premodern* *Pre-1500* | *Early modern* *Approx. 1500–1850* | *Modern* *Approx. 1850–1945* | *Contemporary* *1945 on* |
|---|---|---|---|
| **EXTENSITY** | | | |
| All world religions and empires remain regional though stretching across many societies and cultures | Christianity expands to Americas on the back of demographic and military victory | Western global empires develop, creating thin inter-elite cultural connections. This provides part of the infrastructure for the diffusion of transnational secular ideologies and discourses to Asia, Africa, Latin America | Infrastructures of telecommunications, linguistic interaction and transport more extensive than ever before |
| Hinduism restricted to Indian subcontinent; Buddhism restricted to South and East Asia; Christianity restricted to Europe and Near East; Islam most global in the early phase of world religions, from South Asia to North and East Africa | Capacity of Western culture to penetrate and influence outside of the New World very limited | Western global empires develop early infrastructures of transcontinental and interregional telegraphic communications | Use of English as a global language unparalleled |
| Most successful enduring multicultural empires also regional: Roman Empire, Han China | | Western global empires embed European languages as key global lingua francas | Scale of corporate ownership, operations and reach of global markets in cultural products very extensive though highly uneven |
| Nomadic Mongol empires bigger but culturally weak | | Emergence of early international media corporations—news agencies | Global diffusion of new means of cultural reception and transmission (TV, radio, etc.) |
| | | Increasingly cultural institutions and flows organized at the level of emerging nation-states in West | Movement of popular cultural artefacts largely within West but also from North to the South |
| | | | A small but growing trend sees return of popular and literary cultural forms from South to North |

**TABLE 13.1** (continued)

| Premodern Pre-1500 | Early modern Approx. 1500–1850 | Modern Approx. 1850–1945 | Contemporary 1945 on |
|---|---|---|---|
| **DENSITY** | | | |
| Low | Low | Increasing at a global level compared to pre-modern era, but in relative terms becoming less important in West given rise of national cultures, institutions, circuits of communication and transport | Sheer volume of regularized movement and communications unparalleled within states and across regions<br><br>Digitization of all media |
| **VELOCITY** | | | |
| Negligible | Low | Increasing as modes of transport become faster and more reliable and early telecommunications makes simple text/voice instantaneous communication possible | Instantaneous communication possibilities, transport speeds incomparably faster and cheaper than ever before |
| **IMPACT PROPENSITY** | | | |
| Initial arrival of world religions and empires transforms cultural life of converts, often bringing literacy along with profound shifts in worldviews<br><br>Long-distance cultural flows and relationships within Eurasia provide key instruments of imperial cohesion, and possibility of diffuse peace and shared cross-community identities | Initial European expansion more powerful in extending military/environmental reach of Europe than cultural reach<br><br>Christianity established in Americas but only tiny outposts in Africa and Asia. Minimal impact on entrenched civilizations—Islamic, Indian, Chinese, etc. | Colonial communication infrastructures increase surveillance of colonies by metropolis<br><br>Nationalism achieves powerful if variable cultural influence on elite and mass audiences in Western nations<br><br>Nationalism has some impact on colonial elite cultures, less on popular cultures | Transformation of possibilities and costs of global cultural, economic and political interaction; aids establishment, operation of MNCs, INGOs, etc.<br><br>Increasing foreign component to national systems of ownership and control of media corporations, cultural product markets |

**TABLE 13.1** (continued)

| Premodern<br>Pre-1500 | Early modern<br>Approx. 1500–1850 | Modern<br>Approx. 1850–1945 | Contemporary<br>1945 on |
|---|---|---|---|
| | | **IMPACT PROPENSITY** (continued) | |
| Diffusion of new ideas, technologies across major civilizations within Eurasia and parts of Africa has important cumulative effects, e.g. diffusion of printing | Impact of encountering other cultures probably greater on European culture initially than vice versa | Other transnational ideologies and discourses predominantly impact at elite level. Marxism, through intellectuals and mass political movements, has major impact in Soviet Union, China, etc. Spread of science transforms context and status of many beliefs and practices outside of West | Increasing difficulties presented for totalitarian/authoritarian cultural projects and control of information |
| | | | Increasing difficulties presented for state-led nationalist cultural projects in the culture industries |
| | | | Localized but intense economic and cultural consequences from mass tourism |
| | | Rise of nations and nation-states has important impacts on organization and spatial extent of systems of communications, transport, education, cultural institutions of all sorts (national press, national media, etc.) | Transformation in the cultural context of national identity formation |
| | | **INFRASTRUCTURES** | |
| Reliable non-oceanic shipping | Reliable oceanic shipping | Railways | Telecommunications, cable, satellite, computing, Internet |
| Writing | Mechanized printing | Telegraphy | Radio, television |
| Imperial frameworks for safe and regular land/sea passage over long distances | Imperial frameworks for safe and regular land/sea passage over long distances | Steam-powered/ mechanized shipping | Jet airliners |
| | | Imperial systems of control | |

**TABLE 13.1** (continued)

| Premodern Pre-1500 | Early modern Approx. 1500–1850 | Modern Approx. 1850–1945 | Contemporary 1945 on |
|---|---|---|---|
| **INSTITUTIONALIZATION** | | | |
| No formal institutions exist for regulating or mediating intercivilizational encounters | No formal institutions exist for regulating or mediating intercivilizational encounters | Early international public unions begin to regulate cultural interactions—introducing standard time, early international copyright law, regulation of international telegraphy and postal services | International cultural interactions and infrastructures increasingly regulated—in part by corporate and trade law. Political organizations—like UNESCO—have weak regulatory capacity |
| **STRATIFICATION** | | | |
| Cultural flows dominated by imperial and theocratic bureaucracies and ruling classes<br><br>Scientific, literary, philosophical cultures and ideas have an elite and narrow audience, i.e. Hellenization of Near East after Alexander; spread of Islamic mathematics to medieval Europe | World religions enjoy mass audience—though often reliant on prior military conquest | Fundamental inequalities between metropoles and colonies in terms of control over cultural institutions, flows and messages grounded in fundamental military, political inequalities and domination<br><br>Elite audience for transnational discourses and ideologies<br><br>Predominantly elite audience in colonies for imperial communications<br><br>Mass audience for nationalism—though invariably elite dominated | Mass audience for popular culture, highly uneven within societies especially by generation<br><br>Mass consumption of tourism, mainly restricted to wealthy societies and wealthy social classes<br><br>Maintenance of elite intellectual, cultural power networks<br><br>Dominance of Western cultural flows but increasing diversity of flows |

# Disjuncture and Difference in the Global Cultural Economy

 Arjun Appadurai

It takes only the merest acquaintance with the facts of the modern world to note that it is now an interactive system in a sense that is strikingly new. Historians and sociologists, especially those concerned with translocal processes (Hodgson 1974) and the world systems associated with capitalism (Abu-Lughod 1989; Braudel 1981–84; Curtin 1984; Wallerstein 1974; Wolf 1982), have long been aware that the world has been a congeries of large-scale interactions for many centuries. Yet today's world involves interactions of a new order and intensity. Cultural transactions between social groups in the past have generally been restricted, sometimes by the facts of geography and ecology, and at other times by active resistance to interactions with the Other (as in China for much of its history and in Japan before the Meiji Restoration). Where there have been sustained cultural transactions across large parts of the globe, they have usually involved the long-distance journey of commodities (and of the merchants most concerned with them) and of travelers and explorers of every type (Helms 1988; Schafer 1963). The two main forces for sustained cultural interaction before this century have been warfare (and the large-scale political systems sometimes generated by it) and religions of conversion, which have sometimes, as in the case of Islam, taken warfare as one of the legitimate instruments of their expansion. Thus, between travelers and merchants, pilgrims and conquerors, the world has seen much long-distance (and long term) cultural traffic. This much seems self-evident.

But few will deny that given the problems of time, distance, and limited technologies for the command of resources across vast spaces, cultural dealings between socially and spatially separated groups have, until the past few centuries, been bridged at great cost and sustained over time only with great effort. The forces of cultural gravity seemed always to pull away from the formation of large-scale ecumenes, whether religious, commercial, or political, toward smaller-scale accretions of intimacy and interest.

Sometime in the past few centuries, the nature of this gravitational field seems to have changed. Partly because of the spirit of the expansion of Western maritime interests after 1500, and partly because of the relatively autonomous developments of large and aggressive social formations in the Americas (such as the Aztecs and the Incas), in Eurasia (such as the Mongols and their descendants, the Mughals and Ottomans), in island Southeast Asia (such as the Buginese), and in the kingdoms of precolonial Africa (such as Dahomey), an overlapping set of ecumenes began to emerge, in which congeries of money, commerce, conquest, and migration began to create durable cross-societal bonds. This process was accelerated by the technology transfers and innovations of the late eighteenth and nineteenth centuries (e.g., Bayly 1989), which created complex colonial orders centered on European capitals and spread throughout the non-European world. This intricate and overlapping set of Eurocolonial worlds (first Spanish and Portuguese, later principally English, French, and Dutch) set the basis for a permanent traffic in ideas of peoplehood and selfhood, which created the imagined communities (Anderson 1983) of recent nationalisms throughout the world.

With what Benedict Anderson has called "print capitalism," a new power was unleashed in the world, the power of mass literacy and its attendant large-scale production of projects of ethnic affinity that were remarkably free of the need for face-to-face communication or even of indirect communication between persons and groups. The act of reading things together set the stage for movements based on a paradox—the paradox of constructed primordialism. There is, of course, a great deal else that is involved in the story of colonialism and its dialectically generated nationalisms (Chatterjee 1986), but the issue of constructed ethnicities is surely a crucial strand in this tale.

But the revolution of print capitalism and the cultural affinities and dialogues unleashed by it were only modest precursors to the world we live in now. For in the past century, there has been a technological explosion, largely in the domain of transportation and information, that makes the interactions of a print-dominated world seem as hard-won and as easily erased as the print revolution made earlier forms of cultural traffic appear. For with the advent of the steamship, the automobile, the airplane, the camera, the computer, and the telephone, we have entered into an altogether new condition of neighborliness, even with those most distant from ourselves. Marshall McLuhan, among others, sought to theorize about this world as a "global village," but theories such as McLuhan's appear to have overestimated the communitarian implications of the new media order (McLuhan and Powers 1989). We are now aware that with media, each time we are tempted to speak of the global village, we must be reminded that media create communities with "no sense of place" (Meyrowitz 1985). The world we live in now seems rhizomic (Deleuze and Guattari 1987), even schizophrenic, calling for theories of rootlessness, alienation, and psychological distance between individuals and groups on the one hand, and fantasies (or nightmares) of electronic propinquity on the other. Here, we are close to the central problematic of cultural processes in today's world.

Thus, the curiosity that recently drove Pico Iyer to Asia (1988) is in some ways the product of a confusion between some ineffable McDonaldization of the world and the much subtler play of indigenous trajectories of desire and fear with global flows of people and things. Indeed, Iyer's own impressions are testimony to the fact that, if a global cultural system is emerging, it is filled with ironies and resistances, sometimes camouflaged as passivity and a bottomless appetite in the Asian world for things Western.

Iyer's own account of the uncanny Philippine affinity for American popular music is rich testimony to the global culture of the hyperreal, for somehow Philippine renditions of American popular songs are both more widespread in the Philippines, and more disturbingly faithful to their originals, than they are in the United States today. An entire nation seems to have learned to mimic Kenny Rogers and the Lennon sisters, like a vast Asian Motown chorus. But Americanization is certainly a pallid term to apply to such a situation, for not only are there more Filipinos singing perfect renditions of some American songs (often from the American past) than there are Americans doing so, there is also, of course, the fact that the rest of their lives is not in complete synchrony with the referential world that first gave birth to these songs.

In a further globalizing twist on what Fredric Jameson has recently called "nostalgia for the present" (1989), these Filipinos look back to a world they have never lost. This is one of the central ironies of the politics of global cultural flows, especially in the arena of entertainment and leisure. It plays havoc with the hegemony of Eurochronology. American nostalgia feeds on Filipino desire represented as a hypercompetent reproduction. Here, we have nostalgia without memory. The paradox, of course, has its explanations, and they are historical; unpacked, they lay bare the story of the American missionization and political rape of the Philippines, one result of which has been the creation of a nation of make-believe Americans, who tolerated for so long a leading lady who played the piano while the slums of Manila expanded and decayed. Perhaps the most radical postmodernists would argue that this is hardly surprising because in the peculiar chronicities of late capitalism, pastiche and nostalgia are central modes of image production and reception. Americans themselves are hardly in the present anymore as they stumble into the megatechnologies of the twenty-first century garbed in the film-noir scenarios of sixties' chills, fifties' diners, forties' clothing, thirties' houses, twenties' dances, and so on ad infinitum.

As far as the United States is concerned, one might suggest that the issue is no longer one of nostalgia but of a social *imaginaire* built largely around reruns Jameson was bold to link the polities of nostalgia to the postmodern commodity sensibility, and surely he was right (1983). The drug wars in Colombia recapitulate the tropical sweat of Vietnam, with Ollie North and his succession of masks—Jimmy Stewart concealing John Wayne concealing Spiro Agnew and all of them transmogrifying into Sylvester Stallone, who wins in Afghanistan—thus simultaneously fulfilling the secret American envy of Soviet imperialism and the rerun (this time with a happy ending) of the Vietnam War. The Rolling Stones, approaching their fifties, gyrate before eighteen-year-olds who do not appear to need the machinery of nostalgia to be sold on their parents' heroes. Paul McCartney is selling the Beatles to a new audience by hitching his oblique nostalgia to their desire for the new that smacks of the old. *Dragnet* is back in nineties' drag, and so is *Adam-12*, not to speak of *Batman* and *Mission Impossible*, all dressed up technologically but remarkably faithful to the atmospherics of their originals.

The past is now not a land to return to in a simple politics of memory. It has become a synchronic warehouse of cultural scenarios, a kind of temporal central casting, to which recourse can be taken as appropriate, depending on the movie to be made, the scene to be enacted, the hostages to be rescued. All this is par for the course, if you follow Jean Baudrillard or Jean-François Lyotard into a world of signs wholly unmoored from their social signifiers (all the world's a Disneyland). But I would like to suggest that the apparent increasing substitutability of whole periods and postures for one another, in the cultural styles of advanced capitalism, is tied to larger global forces, which have done much to show Americans that the past is usually another country. If your present is their future (as in much modernization theory and in many self-satisfied tourist fantasies), and their future is your past (as in the ease of the Filipino virtuosos of American popular music), then your own past can be made to appear as simply a normalized modality of your present. Thus, although some anthropologists may continue to relegate their Others to temporal spaces that they do not themselves occupy (Fabian 1983), postindustrial cultural productions have entered a postnostalgic phase.

The crucial point, however, is that the United States is no longer the puppeteer of a world system of images but is only one node of a complex transnational construction of imaginary landscapes. The world we live in today is characterized by a new role for the imagination in social life. To grasp this new role, we need to bring together the old idea of images, especially mechanically produced images (in the Frankfurt School sense); the idea of the imagined community (in Anderson's sense); and the French idea of the imaginary (*imaginaire*) as a constructed landscape of collective aspirations, which is no more and no less real than the collective representations of Emile Durkheim, now mediated through the complex prism of modern media.

The image, the imagined, the imaginary—these are all terms that direct us to something critical and new in global cultural processes: *the imagination as a social practice*. No longer mere fantasy (opium for the masses whose real work is elsewhere), no longer simple escape (from a world defined principally by more concrete purposes and structures), no longer elite pastime (thus not relevant to the lives of ordinary people), and no longer mere contemplation (irrelevant for new forms of desire and subjectivity), the imagination has become an organized field of social practices, a form of work (in the sense of both labor and culturally organized practice), and a form of negotiation between sites of agency (individuals) and globally defined fields of possibility. This unleashing of the imagination links the play of pastiche (in some settings) to the terror and coercion of states and their competitors. The imagination is now central to all forms of agency, is itself a social fact, and is the key component of the new global order. But to make this claim meaningful, we must address some other issues.

## Homogenization and Heterogenization

The central problem of today's global interactions is the tension between cultural homogenization and cultural heterogenization. A vast array of empirical facts could be brought to bear on the side of the homogenization argument, and much of it has come from the left end of the spectrum of media studies (Hamelink 1983; Mattelart 1983; Schiller 1976), and some from other perspectives (Gans 1985; Iyer 1988). Most often, the homogenization argument subspeciates into either an argument about Americanization or an argument about commoditization, and very often the two arguments are closely linked. What these arguments fail to consider is that at least as rapidly as forces from various metropolises are brought into new societies they tend to become indigenized in one or another way this is true of music and housing styles as much as it is true of science and terrorism, spectacles and constitutions. The dynamics of such indigenization have just begun to be explored systemically (Barber 1987; Feld 1988; Hannerz 1987, 1989; Ivy 1988; Nicoll 1989; Yoshimoto 1989), and much more needs to be done. But it is worth noticing that for the people of Irian Jaya, Indonesianization may be more worrisome than Americanization, as Japanization may be for Koreans, Indianization for Sri Lankans, Vietnamization for the Cambodians, and Russianization for the people of Soviet Armenia and the Baltic republics. Such a list of alternative fears to Americanization could be greatly expanded, but it is not a shapeless inventory for polities of smaller scale, there is always a fear of cultural absorption by polities of larger scale, especially those that are nearby. One man's imagined community is another man's political prison.

This scalar dynamic, which has widespread global manifestations, is also tied to the relationship between nations and states, to which I shall return later. For the moment let us note that the simplification of these many forces (and fears) of homogenization can also be exploited by nation-states in relation to their own minorities, by posing global commoditization (or capitalism, or some other such external enemy) as more real than the threat of its own hegemonic strategies.

The new global cultural economy has to be seen as a complex, overlapping, disjunctive order that cannot any longer be understood in terms of existing center-periphery models (even those that might account for multiple centers and peripheries). Nor is it susceptible to simple models of push and pull (in terms of migration theory), or of surpluses and deficits (as in traditional models of balance of trade), or of consumers and producers (as in most neo-Marxist theories of development). Even the most complex and flexible theories of global development that have come out of the Marxist tradition (Amin 1980; Mandel 1978; Wallerstein 1974; Wolf 1982) are inadequately quirky and have failed to come to terms with what Scott Lash and John Urry have called disorganized capitalism (1987). The complexity of the current global economy has to do with certain fundamental disjunctures between economy, culture, and politics that we have only begun to theorize.

I propose that an elementary framework for exploring such disjunctures is to look at the relationship among five dimensions of global cultural flows that can be termed (a) *enthnoscapes*, (b) *mediascapes*, (c) *technoscapes*, (d) *financescapes*, and (e) *ideoscapes*.[2] The suffix *-scape* allows us to point to the fluid, irregular shapes of these landscapes, shapes that characterize international capital as deeply as they do international clothing styles. These terms with the common suffix -scape also indicate that these are not objectively given relations that look the same from every angle of vision but, rather, that they are deeply perspectival constructs, inflected by the historical, linguistic, and political situatedness of different sorts of actors nation-states, multinationals, diasporic communities, as well as subnational groupings and movements (whether religious, political, or economic), and even intimate face-to-face groups, such as villages, neighborhoods, and families. Indeed, the individual actor is the last locus of this perspectival set of landscapes, for these landscapes are eventually navigated by agents who both experience and constitute larger formations, in part from their own sense of what these landscapes offer.

These landscapes thus are the building blocks of what (extending Benedict Anderson) I would like to call *imagined worlds*, that is, the multiple worlds that are constituted by the historically situated imaginations of persons and groups spread around the globe (chap. 1). An important fact of the world we live in today is that many persons on the globe live in such imagined worlds (and not just in imagined communities) and thus are able to contest and sometimes even subvert the imagined worlds of the official mind and of the entrepreneurial mentality that surround them.

By *ethnoscape*, I mean the landscape of persons who constitute the shifting world in which we live tourists, immigrants, refugees, exiles, guest workers, and other moving groups and individuals constitute an essential feature of the world and appear to affect the politics of (and between) nations to a hitherto unprecedented degree. This is not to say that there are no relatively stable communities and networks of kinship, friendship, work, and leisure, as well as of birth, residence, and other filial forms. But it is to say that the warp of these stabilities is everywhere shot through with the woof of human motion, as more persons and groups deal with the realities of having to move or the fantasies of wanting to move. What is more, both these realities and fantasies now function on larger scales, as men and women from villages in India think not just of moving to Poona or Madras but of moving to Dubai and Houston, and refugees from Sri Lanka find themselves in South India as well as in Switzerland, just as the Hmong are driven to London as well as to Philadelphia. And as international capital shifts its needs, as production and technology generate different needs, as nation-states shift their policies on refugee populations, these moving groups can never afford to let their imaginations rest too long, even if they wish to.

By *technoscape*, I mean the global configuration, also ever fluid, of technology and the fact that technology, both high and low, both mechanical and informational, now moves at high speeds across various kinds of previously impervious boundaries. Many countries now are the roots of multinational enterprise a huge steel complex in Libya may involve interests from India, China, Russia, and Japan, providing different components of new technological configurations. The odd distribution of technologies, and thus the peculiarities of these technoscapes, are increasingly driven not by any obvious economies of scale, of political control, or of market rationality but by increasingly complex relationships among money flows, political possibilities, and the availability of both un- and highly skilled labor. So, while India exports waiters and chauffeurs to Dubai and Sharjah, it also exports software engineers to the United States—indentured briefly to Tata-Burroughs or the World Bank, then laundered through the State Department to become wealthy resident aliens, who are in turn objects of seductive messages to invest their money and know-how in federal and state projects in India.

The global economy can still be described in terms of traditional indicators (as the World Bank continues to do) and studied in terms of traditional comparisons (as in Project Link at the University of Pennsylvania), but the complicated technoscapes (and the shifting ethno-scapes) that underlie these indicators and comparisons are further out of the reach of the queen of social sciences than ever before. How is one to make a meaningful comparison of wages in Japan and the United States or of real-estate costs in New York and Tokyo, without taking sophisticated account of the very complex fiscal and investment flows that link the two economies through a global grid of currency speculation and capital transfer?

Thus it is useful to speak as well of *financescapes*, as the disposition of global capital is now a more mysterious, rapid, and difficult landscape to follow than ever before, as currency markets, national stock exchanges, and commodity speculations move megamonies through national turnstiles at blinding speed, with vast, absolute implications for small differences in percentage points and time units. But the critical point is that the global relationship among ethnoscapes, technoscapes, and financescapes is deeply disjunctive and profoundly unpredictable because each of these landscapes is subject to its own constraints and incentives (some political, some informational, and some technoenvironmental), at the same time as each acts as a constraint and a parameter for movements in the others. Thus, even an elementary model of global political economy must take into account the deeply disjunctive relationships among human movement, technological flow, and financial transfers.

Further refracting these disjunctures (which hardly form a simple, mechanical global infrastructure in any case) are what I call *mediascapes* and *ideoscapes*, which are closely related landscapes of images. *Mediascapes* refer both to the distribution of the electronic capabilities to produce and disseminate information (newspapers, magazines, television stations, and film-production studios), which are now available to a growing number of private and public interests throughout the world, and to the images of the world created by these media. These images involve many complicated inflections, depending on their mode (documentary or entertainment), their hardware (electronic or preelectronic), their audiences (local, national, or transnational), and the interests of those who own and control them. What is most important about these mediascapes is that they provide (especially in their television, film, and cassette forms) large and complex repertoires of images, narratives, and ethnoscapes to viewers throughout the world, in which the world of commodities and the world of news and politics are profoundly mixed. What this means is that many audiences around the world experience the media themselves as a complicated and interconnected repertoire of print, celluloid, electronic screens, and billboards. The lines between the realistic and the fictional landscapes they see are blurred, so that the farther away these audiences are from the direct experiences of metropolitan life, the more likely they are to construct imagined worlds that are chimerical, aesthetic, even fantastic objects, particularly if assessed by the criteria of some other perspective, some other imagined world.

Mediascapes, whether produced by private or state interests, tend to be image-centered, narrative-based accounts of strips of reality, and what they offer to those who experience and transform them is a series of elements (such as characters, plots, and textual forms) out of which scripts can be formed of imagined lives, their own as well as those of others living in other places. These scripts can and do get disaggregated into complex sets of metaphors by which people live (Lakoff and Johnson 1980) as they help to constitute narratives of the Other and protonarratives of possible lives, fantasies that could become prolegomena to the desire for acquisition and movement.

*Ideoscapes* are also concatenations of images, but they are often directly political and frequently have to do with the ideologies of states and the counterideologies of movements explicitly oriented to capturing state power or a piece of it. These ideoscapes are composed of elements of the Enlightenment worldview, which consists of a chain of ideas, terms, and images, including *freedom, welfare, rights, sovereignty, representation,* and the master term *democracy.* The master narrative of the Enlightenment (and its many variants in Britain, France, and the United States) was constructed with a certain internal logic and presupposed a certain relationship between reading, representation, and the public sphere. (For the dynamics of this process in the early history of the United States, see Warner 1990.) But the diaspora of these terms and images across the world, especially since the nineteenth century, has loosened the internal coherence that held them together in a Euro-American master narrative and provided instead a loosely structured synopticon of politics, in which different nation-states, as part of their evolution, have organized their political cultures around different keywords (e.g., Williams 1976).

As a result of the differential diaspora of these keywords, the political narratives that govern communication between elites and followers in different parts of the world involve problems of both a semantic and pragmatic nature semantic to the extent that words (and their lexical equivalents) require careful translation from context to context in their global movements, and pragmatic to the extent that the use of these words by political actors and their audiences may be subject to very different sets of contextual conventions that mediate their translation into public politics. Such conventions are not only matters of the nature of political rhetoric for example, what does the aging Chinese leadership mean when it refers to the dangers of hooliganism? What does the South Korean leadership mean when it speaks of discipline as the key to democratic industrial growth?

These conventions also involve the far more subtle question of what sets of communicative genres are valued in what way (newspapers versus cinema, for example) and what sorts of pragmatic genre conventions govern the collective readings of different kinds of text. So, while an Indian audience may be attentive to the resonances of a political speech in terms of some keywords and phrases reminiscent of Hindi cinema, a Korean audience may respond to the subtle codings of Buddhist or neo-Confucian rhetoric encoded in a political document. The very relationship of reading to hearing and seeing may vary in important ways that determine the morphology of these different ideoscapes as they shape themselves in different national and transnational contexts. This globally variable synaesthesia has hardly even been noted, but it demands urgent analysis. Thus *democracy* has clearly become a master term, with powerful echoes from Haiti and Poland to the former Soviet Union and China, but it sits at the center of a variety of ideoscapes, composed of distinctive pragmatic configurations of rough translations of other central terms from the vocabulary of the Enlightenment. This creates ever new terminological kaleidoscopes, as states (and the groups that seek to capture them) seek to pacify populations whose own ethnoscapes are in motion and whose media-scapes may create severe problems for the ideoscapes with which they are presented. The fluidity of ideoscapes is complicated in particular by the growing diasporas (both voluntary and involuntary) of intellectuals who continuously inject new meaning-streams into the discourse of democracy in different parts of the world.

This extended terminological discussion of the five terms I have coined sets the basis for a tentative formulation about the conditions under which current global flows occur they occur in and through the growing disjunctures among ethnoscapes, technoscapes, finance-scapes, mediascapes, and ideoscapes. This formulation, the core of my model of global cultural flow, needs some explanation. First, people, machinery, money, images, and ideas now follow increasingly nonisomorphic paths; of course, at all periods in human history, there have been some disjunctures in the flows of these things, but the sheer speed, scale, and volume of each of these flows are now so great that the disjunctures have become central to the politics of global culture. The Japanese are notoriously hospitable to ideas and are stereotyped as inclined to export (all) and import (some) goods, but they are also notoriously closed to immigration, like the Swiss, the Swedes, and the Saudis. Yet the Swiss and the Saudis accept populations of guest workers, thus creating labor diasporas of Turks, Italians, and other circum-Mediterranean groups. Some such guest-worker groups maintain continuous contact with their home nations, like the Turks, but others, like high-level South Asian migrants, tend to desire lives in their new homes, raising anew the problem of reproduction in a deterritorialized context.

Deterritorialization, in general, is one of the central forces of the modern world because it brings laboring populations into the lower-class sectors and spaces of relatively wealthy societies, while sometimes creating exaggerated and intensified senses of criticism or attachment to politics in the home state. Deterritorialization, whether of Hindus, Sikhs, Palestinians, or Ukrainians, is now at the core of a variety of global fundamentalisms, including Islamic and Hindu fundamentalism. In the Hindu case, for example, it is clear that the overseas movement of Indians has been exploited by a variety of interests both within and outside India to create a complicated network of finances and religious identifications, by which the problem of cultural reproduction for Hindus abroad has become tied to the politics of Hindu fundamentalism at home.

At the same time, deterritorialization creates new markets for film companies, art impresarios, and travel agencies, which thrive on the need of the deterritorialized population for contact with its homeland. Naturally, these invented homelands, which constitute the mediascapes of deterritorialized groups, can often become sufficiently fantastic and one-sided that they provide the material for new ideoscapes in which ethnic conflicts can begin to erupt. The creation of Khalistan, an invented homeland of the deterritorialized Sikh population of England, Canada, and the United States, is one example of the bloody potential in such media-scapes as they interact with the internal colonialisms of the nation-state (e.g., Hechter 1975). The West Bank, Namibia, and Eritrea are other theaters for the enactment of the bloody negotiation between existing nation-states and various deterritorialized groupings.

It is in the fertile ground of deterritorialization, in which money, commodities, and persons are involved in ceaselessly chasing each other around the world, that the mediascapes and ideoscapes of the modern world find their fractured and fragmented counterpart. For the ideas and images produced by mass media often are only partial guides to the goods and experiences that deterritorialized populations transfer to one another. In Mira Nair's brilliant film India Cabaret, we see the multiple loops of this fractured deterritorialization as young women, barely competent in Bombay's metropolitan glitz, come to seek their fortunes as cabaret dancers and prostitutes in Bombay, entertaining men in clubs with dance formats derived wholly from the prurient dance sequences of Hindi films. These scenes in turn cater to ideas about Western and foreign women and their looseness, while they provide tawdry career alibis for these women. Some of these women come from Kerala, where cabaret clubs and the pornographic film industry have blossomed, partly in response to the purses and tastes of Keralites returned from the Middle East, where their diasporic lives away from women distort their very sense of what the relations between men and women might be. These tragedies of displacement could certainly be replayed in a more detailed analysis of the relations between the Japanese and German sex tours to Thailand and the tragedies of the sex trade in Bangkok, and in other similar loops that tie together fantasies about the Other, the conveniences and seductions of travel, the economics of global trade, and the brutal mobility fantasies that dominate gender politics in many parts of Asia and the world at large.

While far more could be said about the cultural politics of deterritorialization and the larger sociology of displacement that it expresses, it is appropriate at this juncture to bring in the role of the nation-state in the disjunctive global economy of culture today. The relationship between states and nations is everywhere an embattled one. It is possible to say that in many societies the nation and the state have become one another's projects. That is, while nations (or more properly groups with ideas about nationhood) seek to capture or co-opt states and state power, states simultaneously seek to capture and monopolize ideas about nationhood (Baruah 1986; Chatterjee 1986; Nandy 1989a). In general, separatist transnational movements, including those that have included terror in their methods, exemplify nations in search of states. Sikhs, Tamil Sri Lankans, Basques, Moros, Quebecois—each of these represents imagined communities that seek to create states of their own or carve pieces out of existing states. States, on the other hand, are everywhere seeking to monopolize the moral resources of community, either by flatly claiming perfect coevality between nation and state, or by systematically museumizing and representing all the groups within them in a variety of heritage politics that seems remarkably uniform throughout the world (Handler 1988; Herzfeld 1982; McQueen 1988).

Here, national and international mediascapes are exploited by nation-states to pacify separatists or even the potential fissiparousness of all ideas of difference. Typically, contemporary nation-states do this by exercising taxonomic control over difference, by creating various kinds of international spectacle to domesticate difference, and by seducing small groups with the fantasy of self-display on some sort of global or cosmopolitan stage. One important new feature of global cultural politics, tied to the disjunctive relationships among the various landscapes discussed earlier, is that state and nation are at each other's throats, and the hyphen that links them is now less an icon of conjuncture than an index of disjuncture. This disjunctive relationship between nation and state has two levels at the level of any given nation-state, it means that there is a battle of the imagination, with state and nation seeking to cannibalize one another. Here is the seedbed of brutal separatisms—majoritarianisms that seem to have appeared from nowhere and microidentities that have become political projects within the nation-state. At another level, this disjunctive relationship is deeply entangled with the global disjunctures discussed throughout this chapter: ideas of nationhood appear to be steadily increasing in scale and regularly crossing existing state boundaries, sometimes, as with the Kurds, because previous identities stretched across vast national spaces or, as with the Tamils in Sri Lanka, the dormant threads of a transnational diaspora have been activated to ignite the micropolitics of a nation-state.

In discussing the cultural politics that have subverted the hyphen that links the nation to the state, it is especially important not to forget the mooring of such politics in the irregularities that now characterize disorganized capital (Kothari 1989c; Lash and Urry 1987). Because labor, finance, and technology are now so widely separated, the volatilities that underlie movements for nationhood (as large as transnational Islam on the one hand, or as small as the movement of the Gurkhas for a separate state in Northeast India) grind against the vulnerabilities that characterize the relationships between states. States find themselves pressed to stay open by the forces of media, technology, and travel that have fueled consumerism throughout the world and have increased the craving, even in the non-Western world, for new commodities and spectacles. On the other hand, these very cravings can become caught up in new ethnoscapes, mediascapes, and, eventually, ideoscapes, such as democracy in China, that the state cannot tolerate as threats to its own control over ideas of nationhood and peoplehood. States throughout the world are under siege, especially where contests over the ideoscapes of democracy are fierce and fundamental, and where there are radical disjunctures between ideoscapes and technoscapes (as in the case of very small countries that lack contemporary technologies of production and information); or between ideoscapes and financescapes (as in countries such as Mexico or Brazil, where international lending influences national politics to a very large degree); or between ideoscapes and ethnoscapes as in Beirut, where diasporic, local, and translocal filiations are suicidally at battle); or between ideoscapes and mediascapes (as in many countries in the Middle East and Asia) where the lifestyles represented on both national and international TV and cinema completely overwhelm and undermine the rhetoric of national politics. In the Indian case, the myth of the law-breaking hero has emerged to mediate this naked struggle between the pieties and realities of Indian politics, which has grown increasingly brutalized and corrupt (Vachani 1989).

The transnational movement of the martial arts, particularly through Asia, as mediated by the Hollywood and Hong Kong film industries (Zarilli 1995) is a rich illustration of the ways in which long-standing martial arts traditions, reformulated to meet the fantasies of contemporary (sometimes lumpen) youth populations, create new cultures of masculinity and violence, which are in turn the fuel for increased violence in national and international politics. Such violence is in turn the spur to an increasingly rapid and amoral arms trade that penetrates the entire world. The worldwide spread of the AK-47 and the Uzi, in films, in corporate and state security, in terror, and in police and military activity, is a reminder that apparently simple technical uniformities often conceal an increasingly complex set of loops, linking images of violence to aspirations for community in some imagined world.

Returning then to the ethnoscapes with which I began, the central paradox of ethnic politics in today's world is that primordia (whether of language or skin color or neighborhood or kinship) have become globalized. That is, sentiments, whose greatest force is in their ability to ignite intimacy into a political state and turn locality into a staging ground for identity, have become spread over vast and irregular spaces as groups move yet stay linked to one another through sophisticated media capabilities. This is not to deny that such primordia are often the product of invented traditions (Hobsbawm and Ranger 1983) or retrospective affiliations, but to emphasize that because of the disjunctive and unstable interplay of commerce, media, national policies, and consumer fantasies, ethnicity, once a genie contained in the bottle of some sort of locality (however large), has now become a global force, forever slipping in and through the cracks between states and borders.

But the relationship between the cultural and economic levels of this new set of global disjunctures is not a simple one-way street in which the terms of global cultural politics are set wholly by, or confined wholly within, the vicissitudes of international flows of technology, labor, and finance, demanding only a modest modification of existing neo-Marxist models of uneven development and state formation. There is a deeper change, itself driven by the disjunctures among all the landscapes I have discussed and constituted by their continuously fluid and uncertain interplay, that concerns the relationship between production and consumption in today's global economy. Here, I begin with Marx's famous (and often mined) view of the fetishism of the commodity and suggest that this fetishism has been replaced in the world at large (now seeing the world as one large, interactive system, composed of many complex subsystems) by two mutually supportive descendants, the first of which I call production fetishism and the second, the fetishism of the consumer.

By *production fetishism* I mean an illusion created by contemporary transnational production loci that masks translocal capital, transnational earning flows, global management, and often faraway workers (engaged in various kinds of high-tech putting-out operations) in the idiom and spectacle of local (sometimes even worker) control, national productivity, and territorial sovereignty. To the extent that various kinds of free-trade zones have become the models for production at large, especially of high-tech commodities, production has itself become a fetish, obscuring not social relations as such but the relations of production, which are increasingly transnational. The locality (both in the sense of the local factory or site of production and in the extended sense of the nation-state) becomes a fetish that disguises the globally dispersed forces that actually drive the production process. This generates alienation (in Marx's sense) twice intensified, for its social sense is now compounded by a complicated spatial dynamic that is increasingly global.

As for the *fetishism of the consumer*, I mean to indicate here that the consumer has been transformed through commodity flows (and the mediascapes, especially of advertising, that accompany them) into a sign, both in Baudrillard's sense of a simulacrum that only asymptotically approaches the form of a real social agent, and in the sense of a mask for the real seat of agency, which is not the consumer but the producer and the many forces that constitute production. Global advertising is the key technology for the worldwide dissemination of a plethora of creative and culturally well-chosen ideas of consumer agency. These images of agency are increasingly distortions of a world of merchandising so subtle that the consumer's consistently helped to believe that he or she is an actor, where in fact he or she is at best a chooser.

The globalization of culture is not the same as its homogenization, but globalization involves the use of a variety of instruments of homogenization (armaments, advertising techniques, language hegemonies, and clothing styles) that are absorbed into local political and cultural economies, only to be repatriated as heterogeneous dialogues of national sovereignty, free enterprise, and fundamentalism in which the state plays an increasingly delicate role too much openness to global flows, and the nation-state is threatened by revolt, as in the China syndrome; too little, and the state exits the international stage, as Burma, Albania, and North Korea in various ways have done. In general, the state has become the arbitrageur of this *repatriation of difference* in the form of goods, signs, slogans, and styles). But this repatriation or export of the designs and commodities of difference continuously exacerbates the internal politics of majoritarianism and homogenization, which is most frequently played out in debates over heritage.

Thus the central feature of global culture today is the politics of the mutual effort of sameness and difference to cannibalize one another and thereby proclaim their successful hijacking of the twin Enlightenment ideas of the triumphantly universal and the resiliently particular. This mutual cannibalization shows its ugly face in riots, refugee flows, state-sponsored torture, and ethnocide (with or without state support). Its brighter side is in the expansion of many individual horizons of hope and fantasy, in the global spread of oral rehydration therapy and other low-tech instruments of well-being, in the susceptibility even of South Africa to the force of global opinion, in the inability of the Polish state to repress its own working classes, and in the growth of a wide range of progressive, transnational alliances. Examples of both sorts could be multiplied. The critical point is that both sides of the coin of global cultural process today are products of the infinitely varied mutual contest of sameness and difference on a stage characterized by radical disjunctures between different sorts of global flows and the uncertain landscapes created in and through these disjunctures.

## The Work of Reproduction in an Age of Mechanical Art

I have inverted the key terms of the title of Walter Benjamin's famous essay (1969) to return this rather high-flying discussion to a more manageable level. There is a classic human problem that will not disappear however much global cultural processes might change their dynamics, and this is the problem today typically discussed under the rubric of reproduction (and traditionally referred to in terms of the transmission of culture). In either case, the question is, how do small groups, especially families, the classical loci of socialization, deal with these new global realities as they seek to reproduce themselves and, in so doing, by accident reproduce cultural forms themselves? In traditional anthropological terms, this could be phrased as the problem of enculturation in a period of rapid culture change. So the problem is hardly novel. But it does take on some novel dimensions under the global conditions discussed so far in this chapter.

First, the sort of transgenerational stability of knowledge that was presupposed in most theories of enculturation (or, in slightly broader terms, of socialization) can no longer be assumed. As families move to new locations, or as children move before older generations, or as grown sons and daughters return from time spent in strange parts of the world, family relationships can become volatile; new commodity patterns are negotiated, debts and obligations are recalibrated, and rumors and fantasies about the new setting are maneuvered into existing repertoires of knowledge and practice. Often, global labor diasporas involve immense strains on marriages in general and on women in particular, as marriages become the meeting points of historical patterns of socialization and new ideas of proper behavior. Generations easily divide, as ideas about property, propriety, and collective obligation wither under the siege of distance and time. Most important, the work of cultural reproduction in new settings is profoundly complicated by the politics of representing a family as normal (particularly for the young) to neighbors and peers in the new locale. All this is, of course, not new to the cultural study of immigration.

What is new is that this is a world in which both points of departure and points of arrival are in cultural flux, and thus the search for steady points of reference, as critical life choices are made, can be very difficult. It is in this atmosphere that the invention of tradition (and of ethnicity, kinship, and other identity markers) can become slippery, as the search for certainties is regularly frustrated by the fluidities of transnational communication. As group pasts become increasingly parts of museums, exhibits, and collections, both in national and transnational spectacles, culture becomes less what Pierre Bourdieu would have called a habitus (a tacit realm of reproducible practices and dispositions) and more an arena for conscious choice, justification, and representation, the latter often to multiple and spatially dislocated audiences.

The task of cultural reproduction, even in its most intimate arenas, such as husband-wife and parent-child relations, becomes both politicized and exposed to the traumas of deterritorialization as family members pool and negotiate their mutual understandings and aspirations in sometimes fractured spatial arrangements. At larger levels, such as community, neighborhood, and territory, this politicization is often the emotional fuel for more explicitly violent politics of identity, just as these larger politics sometimes penetrate and ignite domestic politics. When, for example, two offspring in a household split with their father on a key matter of political identification in a transnational setting, preexisting localized norms carry little force. Thus a son who has joined the Hezbollah group in Lebanon may no longer get along with parents or siblings who are affiliated with Amal or some other branch of Shi'i ethnic political identity in Lebanon. Women in particular bear the brunt of this sort of friction, for they become pawns in the heritage politics of the household and are often subject to the abuse and violence of men who are themselves torn about the relation between heritage and opportunity in shifting spatial and political formations.

The pains of cultural reproduction in a disjunctive global world are, of course, not eased by the effects of mechanical art (or mass media), for these media afford powerful resources for counternodes of identity that youth can project against parental wishes or desires. At larger levels of organization, there can be many forms of cultural politics within displaced populations (whether of refugees or of voluntary immigrants), all of which are inflected in important ways by media (and the mediascapes and ideoscapes they offer). A central link between the fragilities of cultural reproduction and the role of the mass media in today's world is the politics of gender and violence. As fantasies of gendered violence dominate the B-grade film industries that blanket the world, they both reflect and refine gendered violence at home and in the streets, as young men (in particular) are swayed by the macho politics of self-assertion in contexts where they are frequently denied real agency, and women are forced to enter the labor force in new ways on the one hand, and continue the maintenance of familial heritage on the other. Thus the honor of women becomes not just an armature of stable (if inhuman) systems of cultural reproduction but a new arena for the formation of sexual identity and family politics, as men and women face new pressures at work and new fantasies of leisure.

Because both work and leisure have lost none of their gendered qualities in this new global order but have acquired ever subtler fetishized representations, the honor of women becomes increasingly a surrogate for the identity of embattled communities of males, while their women in reality have to negotiate increasingly harsh conditions of work at home and in the non-domestic workplace. In short, deterritorialized communities and displaced populations, however much they may enjoy the fruits of new kinds of earning and new dispositions of capital and technology, have to play out the desires and fantasies of these new ethnoscapes, while striving to reproduce the family-as-microcosm of culture. As the shapes of cultures grow less bounded and tacit, more fluid and politicized, the work of cultural reproduction becomes a daily hazard. Far more could, and should, be said about the work of reproduction in an age of mechanical art the preceding discussion is meant to indicate the contours of the problems that a new, globally informed theory of cultural reproduction will have to face.

## Shape and Process in Global Cultural Formations

The deliberations of the arguments that I have made so far constitute the bare bones of an approach to a general theory of global cultural processes. Focusing on disjunctures, I have employed a set of terms (*ethnoscape, financescape, technoscape, mediascape,* and *ideoscape*) to stress different streams or flows along which cultural material may be seen to be moving across national boundaries. I have also sought to exemplify the ways in which these various flows (or landscapes, from the stabilizing perspectives of any given imagined world) are in fundamental disjuncture with respect to one another. What further steps can we take toward a general theory of global cultural processes based on these proposals?

The first is to note that our very models of cultural shape will have to alter, as configurations of people, place, and heritage lose all semblance of isomorphism. Recent work in anthropology has done much to free us of the shackles of highly localized, boundary-oriented, holistic, primordialist images of cultural form and substance (Hannerz 1989; Marcus and Fischer 1986; Thornton 1988).

But not very much has been put in their place, except somewhat larger if less mechanical versions of these images, as in Eric Wolf's work on the relationship of Europe to the rest of the world (1982). What I would like to propose is that we begin to think of the configuration of cultural forms in today's world as fundamentally fractal, that is, as possessing no Euclidean boundaries, structures, or regularities. Second, I would suggest that these cultural forms, which we should strive to represent as fully fractal, are also overlapping in ways that have been discussed only in pure mathematics (in set theory, for example) and in biology (in the language of polythetic classifications). Thus we need to combine a fractal metaphor for the shape of cultures (in the plural) with a polythetic account of their overlaps and resemblances. Without this latter step, we shall remain mired in comparative work that relies on the clear separation of the entities to be compared before serious comparison can begin. How are we to compare fractally shaped cultural forms that are also polythetically overlapping in their coverage of terrestrial space?

Finally, in order for the theory of global cultural interactions predicated on disjunctive flows to have any force greater than that of a mechanical metaphor, it will have to move into something like a human version of the theory that some scientists are calling chaos theory. That is, we will need to ask not how these complex, overlapping, fractal shapes constitute a simple, stable (even if large-scale) system, but to ask what its dynamics are: Why do riots occur when and where they do? Why do states wither at greater rates in some places and times than in others? Why do some countries flout conventions of international debt repayment with so much less apparent worry than others? How are international arms flows driving ethnic battles and genocides? Why are some states exiting the global stage while others are clamoring to get in? Why do key events occur at a certain point in a certain place rather than in other? These are, of course, the great traditional questions of causality, contingency, and prediction in the human sciences, but in a world of disjunctive global flows, it is perhaps important to start asking them in a way that relies on images of flow and uncertainty, hence chaos, rather than on older images of order, stability, and systematicness. Otherwise, we will have gone far toward a theory of global cultural systems but thrown out process in the bargain. And that would make these notes part of a journey toward the kind of illusion of order that we can no longer afford to impose on a world that is so transparently volatile.

Whatever the directions in which we can push these macrometaphors (fractals, polythetic classifications, and chaos), we need to ask one other old-fashioned question out of the Marxist paradigm is there some pregiven order to the relative determining force of these global flows? Because I have postulated the dynamics of global cultural systems as driven by the relationships among flows of persons, technologies, finance, information, and ideology, can we speak of some structural-causal order linking these flows by analogy to the role of the economic order in one version of the Marxist paradigm? Can we speak of some of these flows as being, for a priori structural or historical reasons, always prior to and formative of other flows? My own hypothesis, which can only be tentative at this point, is that the relationship of these various flows to one another as they constellate into particular events and social forms will be radically context-dependent. Thus, while labor flows and their loops with financial flows between Kerala and the Middle East may account for the shape of media flows and ideoscapes in Kerala, the reverse may be true of Silicon Valley in California, where intense specialization in a single technological sector (computers) and particular flows of capital may well profoundly determine the shape that ethnoscapes, ideoscapes, and mediascapes may take.

This does not mean that the causal-historical relationship among these various flows is random or meaninglessly contingent but that our current theories of cultural chaos are insufficiently developed to be even parsimonious models at this point, much less to be predictive theories, the golden fleeces of one kind of social science. What I have sought to provide in this chapter is a reasonably economical technical vocabulary and a rudimentary model of disjunctive flows, from which something like a decent global analysis might emerge. Without some such analysis, it will be difficult to construct what John Hinkson calls a "social theory of postmodernity" that is adequately global (1990, 84).

# CHAPTER FOURTEEN

# *Feminisms and the International Women's Movements*

In 1900 women almost everywhere were living under patriarchal rule reinforced by religious sanctions. Almost everywhere they also suffered from domestic violence, lacked property or political rights, and were obliged to submit to arrange marriages often at an early age and in many instances to men with several wives. Inadequate sanitation or medical care and poverty kept child mortality extremely high and daughters in increased danger. Industrialization and urbanization were to bring improved standards of living to a small but growing number of women who would in time gain greater independence from traditional family structures. But at the same time such changes would create new forms of exploitation for the poor and everything from low wages and frequent unemployment to sexual harassment and increased challenges of abandonment for women. The conditions of women of color, at least everywhere color could be used as a mark of inferiority, were, of course, typically far worse, and the inability of white women of all classes to understand such differences would continue to shadow the long history of their struggle for emancipation as members of the same sex.

The traditional story of the woman's movement, which grew out of the Abolitionist Movement of the nineteenth century, usually dates its origin from a small convention held in upper state New York at Seneca Falls in 1848. Eight years before, one of its organizers, Lucretia Mott, had been refused a seat at the World Antislavery Convention in London, and she decided almost a decade later with her friend and collaborator, Elizabeth Stanton, to arrange the Seneca Falls convention for the explicit purpose of considering the condition of women. In preparation, Stanton drew up a Declaration of Sentiments to be deliberated by the convention and upon its conclusion all sentiments but the one on women's suffrage were unanimously adopted by its 300 participants. It was not without significance that 40 of those participants included men and that the Declaration's passage might not have occurred without the help of Frederick Douglass. A former escaped slave who had just published three years earlier his autobiography entitled *Narrative of the Life of Frederick Douglass*, Douglass's words at the convention were no less true for the world than they were for America itself: "In this denial of the right to participate in government, not merely the degradation of woman and the perpetuation of a great injustice happens, but the maiming and repudiation of one-half of the moral and intellectual power of the government of the world."

Nonetheless, it would be a gross misrepresentation to assume that Douglass's words implied that women couldn't speak for themselves, or that black women in particular were not advocates for members of their own sex. While the term "black feminism" was not used until the 1970s, its descriptive relevance goes all the way back to the mid-1800s and before, when free black women like Sojourner Truth, Harriet Tubman, and Francis E. W. Harper spoke out and acted in behalf of women's rights in the context of racism and slavery. Nevertheless, the differences between their situation racially and that of their white sisters would continue to surface throughout the history of the American women's movement, even when such events like the anti-lynching crusades of the 1890s led by Ida B. Wells helped unite women across the color line and encouraged them to fight together for women's suffrage which was still 30 years away.

The international women's movement went through several waves in the twentieth century, inspired in part by writers like the American Sarah Perkins Gilman, author of "The Yellow Wallpaper," which is the second selection in this chapter, and the English author, Virginia Woolf, who mounted her own feminist argument in her famous book entitled *A Room of One's Own*. Both were asking, as Woolf put it, "What happens to our lives if we let others run them for us?," and the answers were to come over the years from a vast company of articulate and committed women. But the answer was also in part to come from somewhat unexpected from sources, such as World War I (which gave women new roles in a wartime economy), postwar consumer culture (which gave those women who were better off new freedoms of choice), communist and socialist revolutions (which in many cases, though not consistently, gave new rights to all women), national liberation movements (whose rhetoric of self-determination could apply to members of both sexes), new theories about women's sexuality (which placed emphasis for the first time on the differences between men's and women's desire), and new social welfare policies developed after the war (which furnished new protection in particular of women and children). If such advances were then to be blocked or destroyed by the global depression of the 1930s and the sexist policies of authoritarian Fascist totalitarian regimes in the inter-war period, real changes had nonetheless already begun to occur in places like Latin America and particularly China, where the Communists gave women equal rights with men; bigamy, concubinage, and childbirth marriage were prohibited; and women were given the freedom to marry, divorce, and remarry. Significant as all these social and political movements were, none, however, were perhaps to make more difference in time than the arrival of the birth control pill.

If the first wave of the international women's movement carried all the way into the middle of the twentieth century, the first stirrings of the second wave of the women's movement could be detected in the United States at least in the American Civil Rights Movement, the Counter-cultural Revolution, and the Vietnam War Protest Movement, but movements of civil unrest generally broke out in France and then all over Europe in 1968, and they were complimented and augmented by the forces of women's liberation associated in particular with the second wave of trans-European liberation movements that enabled decolonization particularly after World War II.

What differentiated the second wave of the international women's movement from the first, at least in Europe and America, was epitomized by the claim made by the French thinker and writer, Simon de Beauvoir, in her book published in 1968 entitled *The Second Sex*, that "one is not born, but rather becomes, a woman." What she meant is not only that gender is culturally acquired but also that, like sexuality itself (as gays and lesbians asserted in a riot demanding their rights at Stonewall Inn in Greenwich Village, New York in 1969), it is far more diverse and varied than is publically acknowledged in most countries across the world. And so was launched what is now known, and too often dismissed or disparaged as, "identity politics," a movement that is far from being restricted to issues of gender, much less to those of race, class, sex, or even ethnicity, so much as to issues of intersectionality that determine the way that their various oppressions are expressed and experienced. A politics that is often attributed by its critics to the rich democracies of the West, identity politics has nonetheless been a particularly effective way within the West and outside it for racialized, gendered, and sexualized people to define the nature of their grievances and press for change. It has also helped generate yet a third wave of the international women's movement that has clearly gone still more global.

This third wave exhibits a new awareness of the intersections of race, gender, sexuality, nation, and economic exploitation on a world scale. It also includes new forms of resistance to neo-imperialism and neo-colonialism. Furthermore, it has inspired new critiques of the way Western feminisms in particular construct the category of "Third World" or "Southern" women and it resists the idea of a "global sisterhood" in favor of seeking more productive relations among women across cultural, political, economic, and national boundaries and specifically differences. Indeed, it reflects a deeper appreciation of the way that local and regional conditions so often determine the form that the global can take. Thus while women in Africa have had to cope so often with the overwhelming problems that colonialism and now neo-colonialism have left in their wake, women in the Middle East and elsewhere have experienced the enormous backlash by men against Western feminism because of the coupling of strict religious laws with the increasingly anti-Western politics of their own countries. Non-Western feminists tend to advocate a combination of social, economic, and legal reforms rather than identity claims, and in Latin America women often find themselves organizing around such explicitly non-feminist issues as healthcare, slums, electricity, and running water.

Thus the women's movement in the postcolonial world, unlike that in Western countries, has tended to be as much a product of modernization as of state control. Where feminists in the United States have focused their attention on domestic violence, rape, abortion, and sexual orientation, women's movements in places like Russia, China, and Eastern Europe concentrate on more public issues like employment, political representation, and social security contexts. Their success has not been dependent primarily on the activities of large national organizations so much as on those of small activist groups. Their interest has been less focused on changing consciousness that on reforming political structures and processes.

One example of such a focus is provided by the first reading in this chapter. The Beijing Conference of 1995, which drew 30,000 participants from around the world, was devoted to creating a platform of action based on "the goals of equality, development, and peace for all women everywhere," and, it significantly added, "in the interest of all humanity." The Declaration centers around the fact that the burden of poverty is felt disproportionately by women more than men. They suffer from the lack of equal access to education, health services, and legal protections. Hence the violence against them continues worldwide even though it is usually caused by an intimate male partner. The Declaration deplores the lack of respect for women's rights, identity, dignity, and representation, and notes specifically the discrimination against girls, including infanticide.

In the second selection in this chapter, Charlotte Perkins Gilman's story "The Yellow Wallpaper," the protagonist grapples with the experience of female entrapment. This experience is rendered through her perception of the figure of a woman encased within the wallpaper of her room who seems to be her ghostly double. A story of repressed desire and futile desperation, "The Yellow Wallpaper" turns on the conflict between the narrator's desire for liberation and her realization that she is imprisoned by patriarchal categories. An experience particularly familiar to Western women in the nineteenth century who could never escape the stereotypes with which they were bound, it also speaks to the condition of women everywhere when they are compelled to submit to a world defined and dominated by male power.

# "The Beijing Declaration and the Platform for Action"

*The United Nations Fourth World Conference on Women was held in Beijing, China, September 4–15, 1995, with over 30,000 women attending.\* This document was adopted by the 181 governments represented, which committed themselves to implementing the Platform for Action formulated there. In the context of an organization (the UN) that professes commitment to human rights, it is only proper that they did so. However, we must keep in mind the words of Boutros Boutros-Ghali, then Secretary General of the UN: "Despite the progress made since the First World Conference on Women, twenty years ago, women and men still live in an unequal world." He calls upon all governments that have not yet done so to "ratify UN human rights instruments and labour conventions," among them CEDAW, the Convention on the Elimination of Discrimination Against Women, which was drafted in Mexico City during the First World Conference, adopted by the UN General Assembly in 1979, and ratified by the membership in 1981. We must note that the United States is one of those governments that has never ratified it. It was signed by President Carter in 1980 and submitted to the Senate, where no action was taken. In 1995 it was placed before the Senate Foreign Relations Committee, but again no action was taken.† This could not simply be an oversight.*

## Part One
## Beijing Declaration

1. We, the Governments participating in the Fourth World Conference on Women,
2. Gathered here in Beijing in September 1995, the year of the fiftieth anniversary of the founding of the United Nations,
3. Determined to advance the goals of equality, development and peace for all women everywhere in the interest of all humanity,
4. Acknowledging the voices of all women everywhere and taking note of the diversity of women and their roles and circumstances, honouring the women who paved the way and inspired by the hope present in the world's youth,
5. Recognize that the status of women has advanced in some important respects in the past decade but that progress has been uneven, inequalities between women and men have persisted and major obstacles remain, with serious consequences for the well-being of all people,

\* The first was held in Mexico City in 1975, the second in Copenhagen in 1980, and the third in Nairobi in 1985.
† "The UN Fourth World Conference on Women," by Beatrice W. Dierks, *NWSA Journal*, Vol. 8, No. 2 (Summer 1996), provides an excellent history and description of the Beijing conference. Many of the facts reported in this note are found in that article.

6. Also recognize that this situation is exacerbated by the increasing poverty that is affecting the lives of the majority of the world's people, in particular women and children, with origins in both the national and international domains,

7. Dedicate ourselves unreservedly to addressing these constraints and obstacles and thus enhancing further the advancement and empowerment of women all over the world, and agree that this requires urgent action in the spirit of determination, hope, cooperation and solidarity, now and to carry us forward into the next century.

## We reaffirm our commitment to:

8. The equal rights and inherent human dignity of women and men and other purposes and principles enshrined in the Charter of the United Nations, to the Universal Declaration of Human Rights and other international human rights instruments, in particular the Convention on the Elimination of All Forms of Discrimination against Women and the Convention on the Rights of the Child, as well as the Declaration on the Elimination of Violence against Women and the Declaration on the Right to Development;

9. Ensure the full implementation of the human rights of women and of the girl child as an inalienable, integral and indivisible part of all human rights and fundamental freedoms;

10. Build on consensus and progress made at previous United Nations conferences and summits—on women in Nairobi in 1985, on children in New York in 1990, on environment and development in Rio de Janeiro in 1992, on human rights in Vienna in 1993, on population and development in Cairo in 1994 and on social development in Copenhagen in 1995 with the objective of achieving equality, development and peace;

11. Achieve the full and effective implementation of the Nairobi Forward-looking Strategies for the Advancement of Women;

12. The empowerment and advancement of women, including the right to freedom of thought, conscience, religion and belief, thus contributing to the moral, ethical, spiritual and intellectual needs of women and men, individually or in community with others and thereby guaranteeing them the possibility of realizing their full potential in society and shaping their lives in accordance with their own aspirations.

## We are convinced that:

13. Women's empowerment and their full participation on the basis of equality in all spheres of society, including participation in the decision-making process and access to power, are fundamental for the achievement of equality, development and peace;

14. Women's rights are human rights;

15. Equal rights, opportunities and access to resources, equal sharing of responsibilities for the family by men and women, and a harmonious partnership between them are critical to their well-being and that of their families as well as to the consolidation of democracy;

16. Eradication of poverty based on sustained economic growth, social development, environmental protection and social justice requires the involvement of women in economic

and social development, equal opportunities and the full and equal participation of women and men as agents and beneficiaries of people-centred sustainable development;

17. The explicit recognition and reaffirmation of the right of all women to control all aspects of their health, in particular their own fertility, is basic to their empowerment;

18. Local, national, regional and global peace is attainable and is inextricably linked with the advancement of women, who are a fundamental force for leadership, conflict resolution and the promotion of lasting peace at all levels;

19. It is essential to design, implement and monitor, with the full participation of women, effective, efficient and mutually reinforcing gender-sensitive policies and programmes, including development policies and programmes, at all levels that will foster the empowerment and advancement of women;

20. The participation and contribution of all actors of civil society, particularly women's groups and networks and other non-governmental organizations and community-based organizations, with full respect for their autonomy, in cooperation with Governments, are important to the effective implementation and follow-up of the Platform for Action;

21. The implementation of the Platform for Action requires commitment from Governments and the international community. By making national and international commitments for action, including those made at the Conference, Governments and the international community recognize the need to take priority action for the empowerment and advancement of women

## We are determined to:

22. Intensify efforts and actions to achieve the goals of the Nairobi Forward-looking Strategies for the Advancement of Women by the end of this century;

23. Ensure the full enjoyment by women and the girl child of all human rights and fundamental freedoms and take effective action against violations of these rights and freedoms;

24. Take all necessary measures to eliminate all forms of discrimination against women and the girl child and remove all obstacles to gender equality and the advancement and empowerment of women;

25. Encourage men to participate fully in all actions towards equality;

26. Promote women's economic independence, including employment, and eradicate the persistent and increasing burden of poverty on women by addressing the structural causes of poverty through changes in economic structures, ensuring equal access for all women, including those in rural areas, as vital development agents, to productive resources, opportunities and public services;

27. Promote people-centred sustainable development, including sustained economic growth, through the provision of basic education, lifelong education, literacy and training, and primary health care for girls and women;

28. Take positive steps to ensure peace for the advancement of women and, recognizing the leading role that women have played in the peace movement, work actively towards general and complete disarmament under strict and effective international control, and support negotiations on the conclusion, without delay, of a universal and multilaterally and

effectively verifiable comprehensive nuclear-test-ban treaty which contributes to nuclear disarmament and the prevention of the proliferation of nuclear weapons in all its aspects;

29. Prevent and eliminate all forms of violence against women and girls;

30. Ensure equal access to and equal treatment of women and men in education and health care and enhance women's sexual and reproductive health as well as education;

31. Promote and protect all human rights of women and girls;

32. Intensify efforts to ensure equal enjoyment of all human rights and fundamental freedoms for all women and girls who face multiple barriers to their empowerment and advancement because of such factors as their race, age, language, ethnicity, culture, religion, or disability, or because they are indigenous people;

33. Ensure respect for international law, including humanitarian law, in order to protect women and girls in particular;

34. Develop the fullest potential of girls and women of all ages, ensure their full and equal participation in building a better world for all and enhance their role in the development process.

## We are determined to:

35. Ensure women's equal access to economic resources, including land, credit, science and technology, vocational training, information, communication and markets, as a means to further the advancement and empowerment of women and girls, including through the enhancement of their capacities to enjoy the benefits of equal access to these resources, inter alia, by means of international cooperation;

36. Ensure the success of the Platform for Action, which will require a strong commitment on the part of Governments, international organizations and institutions at all levels. We are deeply convinced that economic development, social development and environmental protection are interdependent and mutually reinforcing components of sustainable development, which is the framework for our efforts to achieve a higher quality of life for all people. Equitable social development that recognizes empowering the poor, particularly women living in poverty, to utilize environmental resources sustainably is a necessary foundation for sustainable development. We also recognize that broad-based and sustained economic growth in the context of sustainable development is necessary to sustain social development and social justice. The success of the Platform for Action will also require adequate mobilization of resources at the national and international levels as well as new and additional resources to the developing countries from all available funding mechanisms, including multilateral, bilateral and private sources for the advancement of women; financial resources to strengthen the capacity of national, subregional, regional and international institutions; a commitment to equal rights, equal responsibilities and equal opportunities and to the equal participation of women and men in all national, regional and international bodies and policy-making processes; and the establishment or strengthening of mechanisms at all levels for accountability to the world's women;

37. Ensure also the success of the Platform for Action in countries with economies in transition, which will require continued international cooperation and assistance;

38. We hereby adopt and commit ourselves as Governments to implement the following Platform for Action, ensuring that a gender perspective is reflected in all our policies and programmes. We urge the United Nations system, regional and international financial institutions, other relevant regional and international institutions and all women and men, as well as non-governmental organizations, with full respect for their autonomy, and all sectors of civil society, in cooperation with Governments, to fully commit themselves and contribute to the implementation of this Platform for Action.

# Part Two
# Platform for Action

## *Mission Statement*

1. The Platform for Action is an agenda for women's empowerment. It aims at accelerating the implementation of the Nairobi Forward-looking Strategies for the Advancement of Women[1] and at removing all the obstacles to women's active participation in all spheres of public and private life through a full and equal share in economic, social, cultural and political decision-making. This means that the principle of shared power and responsibility should be established between women and men at home, in the workplace and in the wider national and international communities. Equality between women and men is a matter of human rights and a condition for social justice and is also a necessary and fundamental prerequisite for equality, development and peace. A transformed partnership based on equality between women and men is a condition for people-centred sustainable development. A sustained and long-term commitment is essential, so that women and men can work together for themselves, for their children and for society to meet the challenges of the twenty-first century.

2. The Platform for Action reaffirms the fundamental principle set forth in the Vienna Declaration and Programme of Action,[2] adopted by the World Conference on Human Rights, that the human rights of women and of the girl child are an inalienable, integral and indivisible part of universal human rights. As an agenda for action, the Platform seeks to promote and protect the full enjoyment of all human rights and the fundamental freedoms of all women throughout their life cycle.

3. The Platform for Action emphasizes that women share common concerns that can be addressed only by working together and in partnership with men towards the common goal of gender equality around the world. It respects and values the full diversity of women's situations and conditions and recognizes that some women face particular barriers to their empowerment.

4. The Platform for Action requires immediate and concerted action by all to create a peaceful, just and humane world based on human rights and fundamental freedoms, including the principle of equality for all people of all ages and from all walks of life, and to this end, recognizes that broadbased and sustained economic growth in the context of sustainable development is necessary to sustain social development and social justice.

5. The success of the Platform for Action will require a strong commitment on the part of Governments, international organizations and institutions at all levels. It will also require adequate mobilization of resources at the national and international levels as well as new and additional resources to the developing countries from all available funding mechanisms, including multilateral, bilateral and private sources for the advancement of women; financial resources to strengthen the capacity of national, subregional, regional and international institutions; a commitment to equal rights, equal responsibilities and equal opportunities and to the equal participation of women and men in all national, regional and international bodies and policy-making processes; and the establishment or strengthening of mechanisms at all levels for accountability to the world's women.

## Global Framework

6. The Fourth World Conference on Women is taking place as the world stands poised on the threshold of a new millennium.

7. The Platform for Action upholds the Convention on the Elimination of All Forms of Discrimination against Women[3] and builds upon the Nairobi Forward-looking Strategies for the Advancement of Women, as well as relevant resolutions adopted by the Economic and Social Council and the General Assembly. The formulation of the Platform for Action is aimed at establishing a basic group of priority actions that should be carried out during the next five years.

8. The Platform for Action recognizes the importance of the agreements reached at the World Summit for Children, the United Nations Conference on Environment and Development, the World Conference on Human Rights, the International Conference on Population and Development and the World Summit for Social Development, which set out specific approaches and commitments to fostering sustainable development and international cooperation and to strengthening the role of the United Nations to that end. Similarly, the Global Conference on the Sustainable Development of Small Island Developing States, the International Conference on Nutrition, the International Conference on Primary Health Care and the World Conference on Education for All have addressed the various facets of development and human rights, within their specific perspectives, paying significant attention to the role of women and girls. In addition, the International Year for the World's Indigenous People,[4] the International Year of the Family,[5] the United Nations Year for Tolerance,[6] the Geneva Declaration for Rural Women,[7] and the Declaration on the Elimination of Violence against Women[8] have also emphasized the issues of women's empowerment and equality.

9. The objective of the Platform for Action, which is in full conformity with the purposes and principles of the Charter of the United Nations and international law, is the empowerment of

all women. The full realization of all human rights and fundamental freedoms of all women is essential for the empowerment of women. While the significance of national and regional particularities and various historical, cultural and religious backgrounds must be borne in mind, it is the duty of States, regardless of their political, economic and cultural systems, to promote and protect all human rights and fundamental freedoms.[9] The implementation of this Platform, including through national laws and the formulation of strategies, policies, programmes and development priorities, is the sovereign responsibility of each State, in conformity with all human rights and fundamental freedoms, and the significance of and full respect for various religious and ethical values, cultural backgrounds and philosophical convictions of individuals and their communities should contribute to the full enjoyment by women of their human rights in order to achieve equality, development and peace.

10. Since the World Conference to Review and Appraise the Achievements of the United Nations Decade for Women: Equality, Development and Peace, held at Nairobi in 1985, and the adoption of the Nairobi Forward-looking Strategies for the Advancement of Women, the world has experienced profound political, economic, social and cultural changes, which have had both positive and negative effects on women. The World Conference on Human Rights recognized that the human rights of women and the girl-child are an inalienable, integral and indivisible part of universal human rights. The full and equal participation of women in political, civil, economic, social and cultural life at the national, regional and international levels, and the eradication of all forms of discrimination on the grounds of sex are priority objectives of the international community. The World Conference on Human Rights reaffirmed the solemn commitment of all States to fulfil their obligations to promote universal respect for, and observance and protection of, all human rights and fundamental freedoms for all in accordance with the Charter of the United Nations, other instruments related to human rights and international law. The universal nature of these rights and freedoms is beyond question.

11. The end of the cold war has resulted in international changes and diminished competition between the super-Powers. The threat of a global armed conflict has diminished, while international relations have improved and prospects for peace among nations have increased. Although the threat of global conflict has been reduced, wars of aggression, armed conflicts, colonial or other forms of alien domination and foreign occupation, civil wars and terrorism continue to plague many parts of the world. Grave violations of the human rights of women occur, particularly in times of armed conflict, and include murder, torture, systematic rape, forced pregnancy and forced abortion, in particular under policies of ethnic cleansing.

12. The maintenance of peace and security at the global, regional and local levels, together with the prevention of policies of aggression and ethnic cleansing and the resolution of armed conflict, is crucial for the protection of the human rights of women and girl children, as well as for the elimination of all forms of violence against them and of their use as a weapon of war.

13. Excessive military expenditures, including global military expenditures and arms trade or trafficking, and investments for arms production and acquisition have reduced the resources available for social development. As a result of the debt burden and other economic

difficulties, many developing countries have undertaken structural adjustment policies. Moreover, there are structural adjustment programmes that have been poorly designed and implemented, with resulting detrimental effects on social development. The number of people living in poverty has increased disproportionately in most developing countries, particularly the heavily indebted countries, during the past decade.

14. In this context, the social dimension of development should be emphasized. Accelerated economic growth, although necessary for social development, does not by itself improve the quality of life of the population. In some cases, conditions can arise which can aggravate social inequality and marginalization. Hence, it is indispensable to search for new alternatives that ensure that all members of society benefit from economic growth based on a holistic approach to all aspects of development: growth, equality between women and men, social justice, conservation and protection of the environment, sustainability, solidarity, participation, peace and respect for human rights.

15. A worldwide movement towards democratization has opened up the political process in many nations, but the popular participation of women in key decision-making as full and equal partners with men, particularly in politics, has not yet been achieved. South Africa's policy of institutionalized racism—apartheid—has been dismantled and a peaceful and democratic transfer of power has occurred. In Central and Eastern Europe the transition to parliamentary democracy has been rapid and has given rise to a variety of experiences, depending on the specific circumstances of each country. While the transition has been mostly peaceful, in some countries this process has been hindered by armed conflict that has resulted in grave violations of human rights.

16. Widespread economic recession, as well as political instability in some regions, has been responsible for setting back development goals in many countries. This has led to the expansion of unspeakable poverty. Of the more than 1 billion people living in abject poverty, women are an overwhelming majority. The rapid process of change and adjustment in all sectors has also led to increased unemployment and under-employment, with particular impact on women. In many cases, structural adjustment programmes have not been designed to minimize their negative effects on vulnerable and disadvantaged groups or on women, nor have they been designed to assure positive effects on those groups by preventing their marginalization in economic and social activities. The Final Act of the Uruguay Round of multilateral trade negotiations[10] underscored the increasing interdependence of national economies, as well as the importance of trade liberalization and access to open, dynamic markets. There has also been heavy military spending in some regions. Despite increases in official development assistance (ODA) by some countries, ODA has recently declined overall.

17. Absolute poverty and the feminization of poverty, unemployment, the increasing fragility of the environment, continued violence against women and the widespread exclusion of half of humanity from institutions of power and governance underscore the need to continue the search for development, peace and security and for ways of assuring people-centred sustainable development. The participation and leadership of the half of humanity that is

female is essential to the success of that search. Therefore, only a new era of international cooperation among Governments and peoples based on a spirit of partnership, an equitable, international social and economic environment, and a radical transformation of the relationship between women and men to one of full and equal partnership will enable the world to meet the challenges of the twenty-first century.

18. Recent international economic developments have had in many cases a disproportionate impact on women and children, the majority of whom live in developing countries. For those States that have carried a large burden of foreign debt, structural adjustment programmes and measures, though beneficial in the long term, have led to a reduction in social expenditures, thereby adversely affecting women, particularly in Africa and the least developed countries. This is exacerbated when responsibilities for basic social services have shifted from Governments to women.

19. Economic recession in many developed and developing countries, as well as ongoing restructuring in countries with economies in transition, have had a disproportionately negative impact on women's employment. Women often have no choice but to take employment that lacks long-term job security or involves dangerous working conditions, to work in unprotected home-based production or to be unemployed. Many women enter the labour market in under-remunerated and undervalued jobs, seeking to improve their household income; others decide to migrate for the same purpose. Without any reduction in their other responsibilities, this has increased the total burden of work for women.

20. Macro- and microeconomic policies and programmes, including structural adjustment, have not always been designed to take account of their impact on women and girl-children, especially those living in poverty. Poverty has increased in both absolute and relative terms, and the number of women living in poverty has increased in most regions. There are many urban women living in poverty; however, the plight of women living in rural and remote areas deserves special attention given the stagnation of development in such areas. In developing countries, even those in which national indicators have shown improvement, the majority of rural women continue to live in conditions of economic underdevelopment and social marginalization.

21. Women are key contributors to the economy and to combating poverty through both remunerated and unrenmunerated work at home, in the community and in the workplace. Growing numbers of women have achieved economic independence through gainful employment.

22. One fourth of all households worldwide are headed by women and many other households are dependent on female income even where men are present. Female-maintained households are very often among the poorest because of wage discrimination, occupational segregation patterns in the labour market and other gender-based barriers. Family disintegration, population movements between urban and rural areas within countries, international migration, war and internal displacements are factors contributing to the rise of female-headed households.

23. Recognizing that the achievement and maintenance of peace and security are a precondition for economic and social progress, women are increasingly establishing themselves as central actors in a variety of capacities in the movement of humanity for peace. Their full participation in decision-making, conflict prevention and resolution and all other peace initiatives is essential to the realization of lasting peace.

24. Religion, spirituality and belief play a central role in the lives of millions of women and men, in the way they live and in the aspirations they have for the future. The right to freedom of thought, conscience and religion is inalienable and must be universally enjoyed. This right includes the freedom to have or to adopt the religion or belief of their choice either individually or in community with others, in public or in private, and to manifest their religion or belief in worship, observance, practice and teaching. In order to realize equality, development and peace, there is a need to respect these rights and freedoms fully. Religion, thought, conscience and belief may, and can, contribute to fulfilling women's and men's moral, ethical and spiritual needs and to realizing their full potential in society. However, it is acknowledged that any form of extremism may have a negative impact on women and can lead to violence and discrimination.

25. The Fourth World Conference on Women should accelerate the process that formally began in 1975, which was proclaimed International Women's Year by the United Nations General Assembly. The Year was a turning-point in that it put women's issues on the agenda. The United Nations Decade for Women (1976–1985) was a worldwide effort to examine the status and rights of women and to bring women into decision-making at all levels. In 1979, the General Assembly adopted the Convention on the Elimination of All Forms of Discrimination against Women, which entered into force in 1981 and set an international standard for what was meant by equality between women and men. In 1985, the World Conference to Review and Appraise the Achievements of the United Nations Decade for Women: Equality, Development and Peace adopted the Nairobi Forward-looking Strategies for the Advancement of Women, to be implemented by the year 2000. There has been important progress in achieving equality between women and men. Many Governments have enacted legislation to promote equality between women and men and have established national machineries to ensure the mainstreaming of gender perspectives in all spheres of society. International agencies have focused greater attention on women's status and roles.

26. The growing strength of the non-governmental sector, particularly women's organizations and feminist groups, has become a driving force for change. Non-governmental organizations have played an important advocacy role in advancing legislation or mechanisms to ensure the promotion of women. They have also become catalysts for new approaches to development. Many Governments have increasingly recognized the important role that non-governmental organizations play and the importance of working with them for progress. Yet, in some countries, Governments continue to restrict the ability of non-governmental organizations to operate freely. Women, through non-governmental organizations, have participated in and strongly influenced community, national, regional and global forums and international debates.

27. Since 1975, knowledge of the status of women and men, respectively, has increased and is contributing to further actions aimed at promoting equality between women and men. In several countries, there have been important changes in the relationships between women and men, especially where there have been major advances in education for women and significant increases in their participation in the paid labour force. The boundaries of the gender division of labour between productive and reproductive roles are gradually being crossed as women have started to enter formerly male-dominated areas of work and men have started to accept greater responsibility for domestic tasks, including child care. However, changes in women's roles have been greater and much more rapid than changes in men's roles. In many countries, the differences between women's and men's achievements and activities are still not recognized as the consequences of socially constructed gender roles rather than immutable biological differences.

28. Moreover, 10 years after the Nairobi Conference, equality between women and men has still not been achieved. On average, women represent a mere 10 percent of all elected legislators worldwide and in most national and international administrative structures, both public and private, they remain underrepresented. The United Nations is no exception. Fifty years after its creation, the United Nations is continuing to deny itself the benefits of women's leadership by their underrepresentation at decision-making levels within the Secretariat and the specialized agencies.

29. Women play a critical role in the family. The family is the basic unit of society and as such should be strengthened. It is entitled to receive comprehensive protection and support. In different cultural, political and social systems, various forms of the family exist. The rights, capabilities and responsibilities of family members must be re-spected. Women make a great contribution to the welfare of the family and to the development of society, which is still not recognized or considered in its full importance. The social significance of maternity, motherhood and the role of parents in the family and in the upbringing of children should be acknowledged. The upbringing of children requires shared responsibility of parents, women and men and society as a whole. Maternity, motherhood, parenting and the role of women in procreation must not be a basis for discrimination nor restrict the full participation of women in society. Recognition should also be given to the important role often played by women in many countries in caring for other members of their family.

30. While the rate of growth of world population is on the decline, world population is at an all-time high in absolute numbers, with current increments approaching 86 million persons annually. Two other major demographic trends have had profound repercussions on the dependency ratio within families. In many developing countries, 45 to 50 percent of the population is less than 15 years old, while in industrialized nations both the number and proportion of elderly people are increasing. According to United Nations projections, 72 percent of the population over 60 years of age will be living in developing countries by the year 2025, and more than half of that population will be women. Care of children, the sick and the elderly is a responsibility that falls disproportionately on women, owing to lack of equality and the unbalanced distribution of remunerated and unremunerated work between women and men.

31. Many women face particular barriers because of various diverse factors in addition to their gender. Often these diverse factors isolate or marginalize such women. They are, inter alia, denied their human rights, they lack access or are denied access to education and vocational training, employment, housing and economic self-sufficiency and they are excluded from decision-making processes. Such women are often denied the opportunity to contribute to their communities as part of the mainstream.

32. The past decade has also witnessed a growing recognition of the distinct interests and concerns of indigenous women, whose identity, cultural traditions and forms of social organization enhance and strengthen the communities in which they live. Indigenous women often face barriers both as women and as members of indigenous communities.

33. In the past 20 years, the world has seen an explosion in the field of communications. With advances in computer technology and satellite and cable television, global access to information continues to increase and expand, creating new opportunities for the participation of women in communications and the mass media and for the dissemination of information about women. However, global communication networks have been used to spread stereotyped and demeaning images of women for narrow commercial and consumerist purposes. Until women participate equally in both the technical and decision-making areas of communications and the mass media, including the arts, they will continue to be misrepresented and awareness of the reality of women's lives will continue to be lacking. The media have a great potential to promote the advancement of women and the equality of women and men by portraying women and men in a nonstereotypical, diverse and balanced manner, and by respecting the dignity and worth of the human person.

34. The continuing environmental degradation that affects all human lives often has a more direct impact on women. Women's health and their livelihood are threatened by pollution and toxic wastes, large-scale deforestation, desertification, drought and depletion of the soil and of coastal and marine resources, with a rising incidence of environmentally related health problems and even death reported among women and girls. Those most affected are rural and indigenous women, whose livelihood and daily subsistence depends directly on sustainable ecosystems

35. Poverty and environmental degradation are closely interrelated. While poverty results in certain kinds of environmental stress, the major cause of the continued deterioration of the global environment is the unsustainable patterns of consumption and production, particularly in industrialized countries, which are a matter of grave concern and aggravate poverty and imbalances.

36. Global trends have brought profound changes in family survival strategies and structures. Rural to urban migration has increased substantially in all regions. The global urban population is projected to reach 47 percent of the total population by the year 2000. An estimated 125 million people are migrants, refugees and displaced persons, half of whom live in developing countries. These massive movements of people have profound consequences for family structures and well-being and have unequal consequences for women and men, including in many cases the sexual exploitation of women.

37. According to World Health Organization (WHO) estimates, by the beginning of 1995 the number of cumulative cases of acquired immunodeficiency syndrome (AIDS) was 4.5 million. An estimated 19.5 million men, women and children have been infected with the human immunodeficiency virus (HIV) since it was first diagnosed and it is projected that another 20 million will be infected by the end of the decade. Among new cases, women are twice as likely to be infected as men. In the early stage of the AIDS pandemic, women were not infected in large numbers; however, about 8 million women are now infected. Young women and adolescents are particularly vulnerable. It is estimated that by the year 2000 more than 13 million women will be infected and 4 million women will have died from AIDS-related conditions. In addition, about 250 million new cases of sexually transmitted diseases are estimated to occur every year. The rate of transmission of sexually transmitted diseases, including HIV/AIDS, is increasing at an alarming rate among women and girls, especially in developing countries.

38. Since 1975, significant knowledge and information have been generated about the status of women and the conditions in which they live. Throughout their entire life cycle, women's daily existence and long-term aspirations are restricted by discriminatory attitudes, unjust social and economic structures, and a lack of resources in most countries that prevent their full and equal participation. In a number of countries, the practice of prenatal sex selection, higher rates of mortality among very young girls and lower rates of school enrollment for girls as compared with boys suggest that son preference is curtailing the access of girl-children to food, education and health care and even life itself. Discrimination against women begins at the earliest stages of life and must therefore be addressed from then onwards.

39. The girl-child of today is the woman of tomorrow. The skills, ideas and energy of the girl-child are vital for full attainment of the goals of equality, development and peace. For the girl-child to develop her full potential she needs to be nurtured in an enabling environment, where her spiritual, intellectual and material needs for survival, protection and development are met and her equal rights safeguarded. If women are to be equal partners with men, in every aspect of life and development, now is the time to recognize the human dignity arid worth of the girl-child and to ensure the full enjoyment of her human rights and fundamental freedoms, including the rights assured by the Convention on the Rights of the Child,[11] universal ratification of which is strongly urged. Yet there exists worldwide evidence that discrimination and violence against girls begin at the earliest stages of life and continue unabated throughout their lives. They often have less access to nutrition, physical and mental health care and education and enjoy fewer rights, opportunities and benefits of childhood and adolescence than do boys. They are often subjected to various forms of sexual and economic exploitation, paedophilia, forced prostitution and possibly the sale of their organs and tissues, violence and harmful practices such as female infanticide and prenatal sex selection, incest, female genital mutilation and early marriage, including child marriage.

40. Half the world's population is under the age of 25 and most of the world's youth—more than 85 percent—live in developing countries. Policy makers must recognize the implications of

these demographic factors. Special measures must be taken to ensure that young women have the life skills necessary for active and effective participation in all levels of social, cultural, political and economic leadership. It will be critical for the international community to demonstrate a new commitment to the future—a commitment to inspiring a new generation of women and men to work together for a more just society. This new generation of leaders must accept and promote a world in which every child is free from injustice, oppression and inequality and free to develop her/his own potential. The principle of equality of women and men must therefore be integral to the socialization process.

## Critical Areas of Concern

41. The advancement of women and the achievement of equality between women and men are a matter of human rights and a condition for social justice and should not be seen in isolation as a women's issue. They are the only way to build a sustainable, just and developed society. Empowerment of women and equality between women and men are prerequisites for achieving political, social, economic, cultural and environmental security among all peoples.

42. Most of the goals set out in the Nairobi Forward-looking Strategies for the Advancement of Women have not been achieved. Barriers to women's empowerment remain, despite the efforts of Governments, as well as non-governmental organizations and women and men everywhere. Vast political, economic and ecological crises persist in many parts of the world. Among them are wars of aggression, armed conflicts, colonial or other forms of alien domination or foreign occupation, civil wars and terrorism. These situations, combined with systematic or de facto discrimination, violations of and failure to protect all human rights and fundamental freedoms of all women, and their civil, cultural, economic, political and social rights, including the right to development and ingrained prejudicial attitudes towards women and girls are but a few of the impediments encountered since the World Conference to Review and Appraise the Achievements of the United Nations Decade for Women: Equality, Development and Peace, in 1985.

43. A review of progress since the Nairobi Conference highlights special concerns—areas of particular urgency that stand out as priorities for action. All actors should focus action and resources on the strategic objectives relating to the critical areas of concern which are, necessarily, interrelated, interdependent and of high priority. There is a need for these actors to develop and implement mechanisms of accountability for all the areas of concern.

44. To this end, Governments, the international community and civil society, including non-governmental organizations and the private sector, are called upon to take strategic action in the following critical areas of concern:

    • The persistent and increasing burden of poverty on women
    • Inequalities and inadequacies in and unequal access to education and training
    • Inequalities and inadequacies in and unequal access to health care and related services
    • Violence against women

- The effects of armed or other kinds of conflict on women, including those living under foreign occupation
- Inequality in economic structures and policies, in all forms of productive activities and in access to resources
- Inequality between men and women in the sharing of power and decision-making at all levels
- Insufficient mechanisms at all levels to promote the advancement of women
- Lack of respect for and inadequate promotion and, protection of the human rights of women
- Stereotyping of women and inequality in women's access to and participation in all communication systems, especially in the media
- Gender inequalities in the management of natural resources and in the safeguarding of the environment
- Persistent discrimination against and violation of the rights of the girl-child

## Notes

1. *Report of the World Conference to Review and Appraise the Achievements of the United Nations Decade for Women: Equality, Development and Peace, Nairobi, 15–26 July 1985* (United Nations publication, Sales No. E.85.IV.10) chap. I, sect. A.
2. *Report of the World Conference on Human Rights, Vienna, 14–25 June 1993* (A/CONF.157/24 (Part I)), chap. III.
3. General Assembly resolution 34/180, annex.
4. General Assembly resolution 45/164.
5. General Assembly resolution 44/82.
6. General Assembly resolution 48/126.
7. A/47/308-E/1992/97, annex.
8. General Assembly resolution 48/104.
9. Vienna Declaration and Programme of Action, *Report of the World Conference on Human Rights* . . . , chap. III, para. 5.
10. See *The Results of the Uruguay Round of Multilateral Trade Negotiations: The Legal Texts* (Geneva, GATT secretariat, 1994).
11. General Assembly resolution 44/25, annex.

# The Yellow Wall-Paper

 CHARLOTTE PERKINS GILMAN

It is very seldom that mere ordinary people like John and myself secure ancestral halls for the summer. A colonial mansion, a hereditary estate, I would say a haunted house, and reach the height of romantic felicity—but that would be asking too much of fate!

Still I will proudly declare that there is something queer about it.

Else, why should it be let so cheaply? And why have stood so long untenanted?

John laughs at me, of course, but one expects that in marriage.

John is practical in the extreme. He has no patience with faith, an intense horror of superstition, and he scoffs openly at any talk of things not to be felt and seen and put down in figures.

John is a physician, and *perhaps*—(I would not say it to a living soul, of course, but this is dead paper and a great relief to my mind)—*perhaps* that is one reason I do not get well faster.

You see, he does not believe I am sick!

And what can one do?

If a physician of high standing, and one's own husband, assures friends and relatives that there is really nothing the matter with one but temporary nervous depression—a slight hysterical tendency—what is one to do?

My brother is also a physician, and also of high standing, and he says the same thing.

So I take phosphates or phosphites—whichever it is, and tonics, and journeys, and air, and exercise, and am absolutely forbidden to "work" until I am well again.

Personally, I disagree with their ideas.

Personally, I believe that congenial work, with excitement and change, would do me good.

But what is one to do?

I did write for a while in spite of them; but it *does* exhaust me a good deal—having to be so sly about it, or else meet with heavy opposition.

I sometimes fancy that in my condition if I had less opposition and more society and stimulus— but John says the very worst thing I can do is to think about my condition, and I confess it always makes me feel bad.

So I will let it alone and talk about the house.

The most beautiful place! It is quite alone, standing well back from the road, quite three miles from the village. It makes me think of English places that you read about, for there are hedges and walls and gates that lock, and lots of separate little houses for the gardeners and people.

There is a *delicious* garden! I never saw such a garden—large and shady, full of box-bordered paths, and lined with long grape-covered arbors with seats under them.

There were greenhouses, too, but they are all broken now.

There was some legal trouble, I believe, something about the heirs and co-heirs; anyhow, the place has been empty for years.

Source: Charlotte Perkins Gilman, "The Yellow Wall-Paper." 1892.

That spoils my ghostliness, I am afraid; but I don't care—there is something strange about the house—I can feel it.

I even said so to John one moonlight evening, but he said what I felt was a *draught*, and shut the window.

I get unreasonably angry with John sometimes. I'm sure I never used to be so sensitive. I think it is due to this nervous condition.

But John says if I feel so I shall neglect proper self-control; so I take pains to control myself,—before him, at least,—and that makes me very tired.

I don't like our room a bit. I wanted one downstairs that opened on the piazza and had roses all over the window, and such pretty old-fashioned chintz hangings! but John would not hear of it.

He said there was only one window and not room for two beds, and no near room for him if he took another.

He is very careful and loving, and hardly lets me stir without special direction.

I have a schedule prescription for each hour in the day; he takes all care from me, and so I feel basely ungrateful not to value it more.

He said we came here solely on my account, that I was to have perfect rest and all the air I could get. "Your exercise depends on your strength, my dear," said he, "and your food somewhat on your appetite; but air you can absorb all the time." So we took the nursery, at the top of the house.

It is a big, airy room, the whole floor nearly, with windows that look all ways, and air and sunshine galore. It was nursery first and then playground and gymnasium, I should judge; for the windows are barred for little children, and there are rings and things in the walls.

The paint and paper look as if a boys' school had used it. It is stripped off—the paper—in great patches all around the head of my bed, about as far as I can reach, and in a great place on the other side of the room low down. I never saw a worse paper in my life.

One of those sprawling flamboyant patterns committing every artistic sin.

It is dull enough to confuse the eye in following, pronounced enough to constantly irritate, and provoke study, and when you follow the lame, uncertain curves for a little distance they suddenly commit suicide—plunge off at outrageous angles, destroy themselves in unheard-of contradictions.

The color is repellant, almost revolting; a smouldering, unclean yellow, strangely faded by the slow-turning sunlight.

It is a dull yet lurid orange in some places, a sickly sulphur tint in others.

No wonder the children hated it! I should hate it myself if I had to live in this room long.

There comes John, and I must put this away,—he hates to have me write a word.

We have been here two weeks, and I haven't felt like writing before, since that first day.

I am sitting by the window now, up in this atrocious nursery, and there is nothing to hinder my writing as much as I please, save lack of strength.

John is away all day, and even some nights when his cases are serious.

I am glad my case is not serious!

But these nervous troubles are dreadfully depressing.

John does not know how much I really suffer. He knows there is no *reason* to suffer, and that satisfies him.

Of course it is only nervousness. It does weigh on me so not to do my duty in any way!

I meant to be such a help to John, such a real rest and comfort, and here I am a comparative burden already!

Nobody would believe what an effort it is to do what little I am able—to dress and entertain, and order things.

It is fortunate Mary is so good with the baby. Such a dear baby!

And yet I *cannot* be with him, it makes me so nervous.

I suppose John never was nervous in his life. He laughs at me so about this wall-paper!

At first he meant to repaper the room, but afterwards he said that I was letting it get the better of me, and that nothing was worse for a nervous patient than to give way to such fancies.

He said that after the wall-paper was changed it would be the heavy bedstead, and then the barred windows, and then that gate at the head of the stairs, and so on.

"You know the place is doing you good," he said, "and really, dear, I don't care to renovate the house just for a three months' rental."

"Then do let us go downstairs," I said, "there are such pretty rooms there."

Then he took me in his arms and called me a blessed little goose, and said he would go down cellar if I wished, and have it whitewashed into the bargain.

But he is right enough about the beds and windows and things.

It is as airy and comfortable a room as any one need wish, and, of course, I would not be so silly as to make him uncomfortable just for a whim.

I'm really getting quite fond of the big room, all but that horrid paper.

Out of one window I can see the garden, those mysterious deep-shaded arbors, the riotous old-fashioned flowers, and bushes and gnarly trees.

Out of another I get a lovely view of the bay and a little private wharf belonging to the estate. There is a beautiful shaded lane that runs down there from the house. I always fancy I see people walking in these numerous paths and arbors, but John has cautioned me not to give way to fancy in the least. He says that with my imaginative power and habit of story-making a nervous weakness like mine is sure to lead to all manner of excited fancies, and that I ought to use my will and good sense to check the tendency. So I try.

I think sometimes that if I were only well enough to write a little it would relieve the press of ideas and rest me.

But I find I get pretty tired when I try.

It is so discouraging not to have any advice and companionship about my work. When I get really well John says we will ask Cousin Henry and Julia down for a long visit; but he says he would as soon put fire-works in my pillow-case as to let me have those stimulating people about now.

I wish I could get well faster.

But I must not think about that. This paper looks to me as if it knew what a vicious influence it had!

There is a recurrent spot where the pattern lolls like a broken neck and two bulbous eyes stare at you upside-down.

I get positively angry with the impertinence of it and the everlastingness. Up and down and sideways they crawl, and those absurd, unblinking eyes are everywhere. There is one place where two breadths didn't match, and the eyes go all up and down the line, one a little higher than the other.

I never saw so much expression in an inanimate thing before, and we all know how much expression they have! I used to lie awake as a child and get more entertainment and terror out of blank walls and plain furniture than most children could find in a toy-store.

I remember what a kindly wink the knobs of our big old bureau used to have, and there was one chair that always seemed like a strong friend.

I used to feel that if any of the other things looked too fierce I could always hop into that chair and be safe.

The furniture in this room is no worse than inharmonious, however, for we had to bring it all from downstairs. I suppose when this was used as a playroom they had to take the nursery things out, and no wonder! I never saw such ravages as the children have made here.

The wall-paper, as I said before, is torn off in spots, and it sticketh closer than a brother—they must have had perseverance as well as hatred.

Then the floor is scratched and gouged and splintered, the plaster itself is dug out here and there, and this great heavy bed, which is all we found in the room, looks as if it had been through the wars.

But I don't mind it a bit—only the paper.

There comes John's sister. Such a dear girl as she is, and so careful of me! I must not let her find me writing.

She is a perfect and enthusiastic housekeeper, and hopes for no better profession. I verily believe she thinks it is the writing which made me sick!

But I can write when she is out, and see her a long way off from these windows.

There is one that commands the road, a lovely, shaded, winding road, and one that just looks off over the country. A lovely country, too, full of great elms and velvet meadows.

This wall-paper has a kind of sub-pattern in a different shade, a particularly irritating one, for you can only see it in certain lights, and not clearly then.

But in the places where it isn't faded, and where the sun is just so, I can see a strange, provoking, formless sort of figure, that seems to sulk about behind that silly and conspicuous front design.

There's sister on the stairs!

Well, the Fourth of July is over! The people are gone and I am tired out. John thought it might do me good to see a little company, so we just had mother and Nellie and the children down for a week.

Of course I didn't do a thing. Jennie sees to everything now.

But it tired me all the same.

John says if I don't pick up faster he shall send me to Weir Mitchell in the fall.

But I don't want to go there at all. I had a friend who was in his hands once, and she says he is just like John and my brother, only more so!

Besides, it is such an undertaking to go so far.

I don't feel as if it was worth while to turn my hand over for anything, and I'm getting dreadfully fretful and querulous.

I cry at nothing, and cry most of the time.

Of course I don't when John is here, or anybody else, but when I am alone.

And I am alone a good deal just now. John is kept in town very often by serious cases, and Jennie is good and lets me alone when I want her to.

So I walk a little in the garden or down that lovely lane, sit on the porch under the roses, and lie down up here a good deal.

I'm getting really fond of the room in spite of the wall-paper. Perhaps because of the wall-paper.

It dwells in my mind so!

I lie here on this great immovable bed—it is nailed down, I believe—and follow that pattern about by the hour. It is as good as gymnastics, I assure you. I start, we'll say, at the bottom, down in the corner over there where it has not been touched, and I determine for the thousandth time that I will follow that pointless pattern to some sort of a conclusion.

I know a little of the principle of design, and I know this thing was not arranged on any laws of radiation, or alternation, or repetition, or symmetry, or anything else that I ever heard of.

It is repeated, of course, by the breadths, but not otherwise.

Looked at in one way each breadth stands alone, the bloated curves and flourishes—a kind of "debased Romanesque" with *delirium tremens*—go waddling up and down in isolated columns of fatuity.

But, on the other hand, they connect diagonally, and the sprawling outlines run off in great slanting waves of optic horror, like a lot of wallowing seaweeds in full chase.

The whole thing goes horizontally, too, at least it seems so, and I exhaust myself in trying to distinguish the order of its going in that direction.

They have used a horizontal breadth for a frieze, and that adds wonderfully to the confusion.

There is one end of the room where it is almost intact, and there, when the cross-lights fade and the low sun shines directly upon it, I can almost fancy radiation after all,—the interminable grotesques seem to form around a common centre and rush off in headlong plunges of equal distraction.

It makes me tired to follow it. I will take a nap, I guess.

I don't know why I should write this.

I don't want to.

I don't feel able.

And I know John would think it absurd. But I must say what I feel and think in some way—it is such a relief!

But the effort is getting to be greater than the relief.

Half the time now I am awfully lazy, and lie down ever so much.

John says I musn't lose my strength, and has me take cod-liver oil and lots of tonics and things, to say nothing of ale and wine and rare meat.

Dear John! He loves me very dearly, and hates to have me sick. I tried to have a real earnest reasonable talk with him the other day, and tell him how I wish he would let me go and make a visit to Cousin Henry and Julia.

But he said I wasn't able to go, nor able to stand it after I got there; and I did not make out a very good case for myself, for I was crying before I had finished.

It is getting to be a great effort for me to think straight. Just this nervous weakness, I suppose.

And dear John gathered me up in his arms, and just carried me upstairs and laid me on the bed, and sat by me and read to me till it tired my head.

He said I was his darling and his comfort and all he had, and that I must take care of myself for his sake, and keep well.

He says no one but myself can help me out of it, that I must use my will and self-control and not let any silly fancies run away with me.

There's one comfort, the baby is well and happy, and does not have to occupy this nursery with the horrid wall-paper.

If we had not used it that blessed child would have! What a fortunate escape! Why, I wouldn't have a child of mine, an impressionable little thing, live in such a room for worlds.

I never thought of it before, but it is lucky that John kept me here after all. I can stand it so much easier than a baby, you see.

Of course I never mention it to them any more,—I am too wise,—but I keep watch of it all the same.

There are things in that paper that nobody knows but me, or ever will.

Behind that outside pattern the dim shapes get clearer every day.

It is always the same shape, only very numerous.

And it is like a woman stooping down and creeping about behind that pattern. I don't like it a bit. I wonder—I begin to think—I wish John would take me away from here!

It is so hard to talk with John about my case, because he is so wise, and because he loves me so.

But I tried it last night.

It was moonlight. The moon shines in all around, just as the sun does.

I hate to see it sometimes, it creeps so slowly, and always comes in by one window or another.

John was asleep and I hated to waken him, so I kept still and watched the moonlight on that undulating wall-paper till I felt creepy.

The faint figure behind seemed to shake the pattern, just as if she wanted to get out.

I got up softly and went to feel and see if the paper *did* move, and when I came back John was awake.

"What is it, little girl?" he said. "Don't go walking about like that—you'll get cold."

I thought it was a good time to talk, so I told him that I really was not gaining here, and that I wished he would take me away.

"Why darling!" said he, "our lease will be up in three weeks, and I can't see how to leave before.

"The repairs are not done at home, and I cannot possibly leave town just now. Of course if you were in any danger I could and would, but you really are better, dear, whether you can see it or not. I am a doctor, dear, and I know. You are gaining flesh and color, your appetite is better. I feel really much easier about you."

"I don't weigh a bit more," said I, "nor as much; and my appetite may be better in the evening, when you are here, but it is worse in the morning when you are away."

"Bless her little heart!" said he with a big hug; "she shall be as sick as she pleases! But now let's improve the shining hours by going to sleep, and talk about it in the morning!"

"And you won't go away?" I asked gloomily.

"Why, how can I, dear? It is only three weeks more and then we will take a nice little trip of a few days while Jennie is getting the house ready. Really, dear, you are better!"

"Better in body perhaps"—I began, and stopped short, for he sat up straight and looked at me with such a stern, reproachful look that I could not say another word.

"My darling," said he, "I beg of you, for my sake and for our child's sake, as well as for your own, that you will never for one instant let that idea enter your mind! There is nothing so dangerous, so fascinating, to a temperament like yours. It is a false and foolish fancy. Can you not trust me as a physician when I tell you so?"

So of course I said no more on that score, and we went to sleep before long. He thought I was asleep first, but I wasn't,—I lay there for hours trying to decide whether that front pattern and the back pattern really did move together or separately.

On a pattern like this, by daylight, there is a lack of sequence, a defiance of law, that is a constant irritant to a normal mind.

The color is hideous enough, and unreliable enough, and infuriating enough, but the pattern is torturing.

You think you have mastered it, but just as you get well under way in following, it turns a back somersault and there you are. It slaps you in the face, knocks you down, and tramples upon you. It is like a bad dream.

The outside pattern is a florid arabesque, reminding one of a fungus. If you can imagine a toadstool in joints, an interminable string of toadstools, budding and sprouting in endless convolutions,—why, that is something like it.

That is, sometimes!

There is one marked peculiarity about this paper, a thing nobody seems to notice but myself, and that is that it changes as the light changes.

When the sun shoots in through the east window—I always watch for that first long, straight ray—it changes so quickly that I never can quite believe it.

That is why I watch it always.

By moonlight—the moon shines in all night when there is a moon—I wouldn't know it was the same paper.

At night in any kind of light, in twilight, candlelight, lamplight, and worst of all by moonlight, it becomes bars! The outside pattern I mean, and the woman behind it is as plain as can be.

I didn't realize for a long time what the thing was that showed behind,—that dim sub-pattern,—but now I am quite sure it is a woman.

By daylight she is subdued, quiet. I fancy it is the pattern that keeps her so still. It is so puzzling. It keeps me quiet by the hour.

I lie down ever so much now. John says it is good for me, and to sleep all I can.

Indeed, he started the habit by making me lie down for an hour after each meal.

It is a very bad habit I am convinced, for, you see I don't sleep.

And that cultivates deceit, for I don't tell them I'm awake,—oh, no!

The fact is I am getting a little afraid of John.

He seems very queer sometimes, and even Jennie has an inexplicable look.

It strikes me occasionally, just as a scientific hypothesis, that perhaps it is the paper!

I have watched John when he did not know I was looking, and come into the room suddenly on the most innocent excuses, and I've caught him several times *looking at the paper*! And Jennie too. I caught Jennie with her hand on it once.

She didn't know I was in the room, and when I asked her in a quiet, a very quiet voice, with the most restrained manner possible, what she was doing with the paper she turned around as if she had been caught stealing, and looked quite angry—asked me why I should frighten her so!

Then she said that the paper stained everything it touched, that she had found yellow smooches on all my clothes and John's, and she wished we would be more careful!

Did not that sound innocent? But I know she was studying that pattern, and I am determined that nobody shall find it out but myself!

Life is very much more exciting now than it used to be. You see I have something more to expect, to look forward to, to watch. I really do eat better, and am more quiet than I was.

John is so pleased to see me improve! He laughed a little the other day, and said I seemed to be flourishing in spite of my wall-paper.

I turned it off with a laugh. I had no intention of telling him it was because of the wall-paper—he would make fun of me. He might even want to take me away.

I don't want to leave now until I have found it out. There is a week more, and I think that will be enough.

I'm feeling ever so much better! I don't sleep much at night, for it is so interesting to watch developments; but I sleep a good deal in the daytime.

In the daytime it is tiresome and perplexing.

There are always new shoots on the fungus, and new shades of yellow all over it. I cannot keep count of them, though I have tried conscientiously.

It is the strangest yellow, that wall-paper! It makes me think of all the yellow things I ever saw—not beautiful ones like buttercups, but old foul, bad yellow things.

But there is something else about that paper—the smell! I noticed it the moment we came into the room, but with so much air and sun it was not bad. Now we have had a week of fog and rain, and whether the windows are open or not, the smell is here.

It creeps all over the house.

I find it hovering in the dining-room, skulking in the parlor, hiding in the hall, lying in wait for me on the stairs.

It gets into my hair.

Even when I go to ride, if I turn my head suddenly and surprise it—there is that smell!

Such a peculiar odor, too! I have spent hours in trying to analyze it, to find what it smelled like.

It is not bad—at first, and very gentle, but quite the subtlest, most enduring odor I ever met.

In this damp weather it is awful. I wake up in the night and find it hanging over me.

It used to disturb me at first. I thought seriously of burning the house—to reach the smell.

But now I am used to it. The only thing I can think of that it is like is the *color* of the paper! A yellow smell.

There is a very funny mark on this wall, low down, near the mopboard. A streak that runs round the room. It goes behind every piece of furniture, except the bed, a long, straight, even *smooch*, as if it had been rubbed over and over.

I wonder how it was done and who did it, and what they did it for. Round and round and round—round and round and round—it makes me dizzy!

I really have discovered something at last.

Through watching so much at night, when it changes so, I have finally found out.

The front pattern *does* move—and no wonder! The woman behind shakes it!

Sometimes I think there are a great many women behind, and sometimes only one, and she crawls around fast, and her crawling shakes it all over.

Then in the very bright spots she keeps still, and in the very shady spots she just takes hold of the bars and shakes them hard.

And she is all the time trying to climb through. But nobody could climb through that pattern—it strangles so; I think that is why it has so many heads.

They get through, and then the pattern strangles them off and turns them upside-down, and makes their eyes white!

If those heads were covered or taken off it would not be half so bad.

I think that woman gets out in the daytime!

And I'll tell you why—privately—I've seen her!

I can see her out of every one of my windows!

It is the same woman, I know, for she is always creeping, and most women do not creep by daylight.

I see her on that long shaded lane, creeping up and down. I see her in those dark grape arbors, creeping all around the garden.

I see her on that long road under the trees, creeping along, and when a carriage comes she hides under the blackberry vines.

I don't blame her a bit. It must be very humiliating to be caught creeping by daylight!

I always lock the door when I creep by daylight. I can't do it at night, for I know John would suspect something at once.

And John is so queer now, that I don't want to irritate him. I wish he would take another room! Besides, I don't want anybody to get that woman out at night but myself.

I often wonder if I could see her out of all the windows at once.

But, turn as fast as I can, I can only see out of one at one time.

And though I always see her she *may* be able to creep faster than I can turn!

I have watched her sometimes away off in the open country, creeping as fast as a cloud shadow in a high wind.

If only that top pattern could be gotten off from the under one! I mean to try it, little by little.

I have found out another funny thing, but I shan't tell it this time! It does not do to trust people too much.

There are only two more days to get this paper off, and I believe John is beginning to notice. I don't like the look in his eyes.

And I heard him ask Jennie a lot of professional questions about me. She had a very good report to give.

She said I slept a good deal in the daytime.

John knows I don't sleep very well at night, for all I'm so quiet!

He asked me all sorts of questions, too, and pretended to be very loving and kind.

As if I couldn't see through him!

Still, I don't wonder he acts so, sleeping under this paper for three months.

It only interests me, but I feel sure John and Jennie are secretly affected by it.

Hurrah! This is the last day, but it is enough. John is to stay in town over night, and won't be out until this evening.

Jennie wanted to sleep with me—the sly thing! but I told her I should undoubtedly rest better for a night all alone.

That was clever, for really I wasn't alone a bit! As soon as it was moonlight, and that poor thing began to crawl and shake the pattern, I got up and ran to help her.

I pulled and she shook, I shook and she pulled, and before morning we had peeled off yards of that paper.

A strip about as high as my head and half around the room.

And then when the sun came and that awful pattern began to laugh at me I declared I would finish it to-day!

We go away to-morrow, and they are moving all my furniture down again to leave things as they were before.

Jennie looked at the wall in amazement, but I told her merrily that I did it out of pure spite at the vicious thing.

She laughed and said she wouldn't mind doing it herself, but I must not get tired.

How she betrayed herself that time!

But I am here, and no person touches this paper but me—not alive!

She tried to get me out of the room—it was too patent! But I said it was so quiet and empty and clean now that I believed I would lie down again and sleep all I could; and not to wake me even for dinner—I would call when I woke.

So now she is gone, and the servants are gone, and the things are gone, and there is nothing left but that great bedstead nailed down, with the canvas mattress we found on it.

We shall sleep downstairs to-night, and take the boat home to-morrow.

I quite enjoy the room, now it is bare again.

How those children did tear about here!

This bedstead is fairly gnawed!

But I must get to work.

I have locked the door and thrown the key down into the front path.

I don't want to go out, and I don't want to have anybody come in, till John comes.

I want to astonish him.

I've got a rope up here that even Jennie did not find. If that woman does get out, and tries to get away, I can tie her!

But I forgot I could not reach far without anything to stand on!

This bed will *not* move!

I tried to lift and push it until I was lame, and then I got so angry I bit off a little piece at one corner—but it hurt my teeth.

Then I peeled off all the paper I could reach standing on the floor. It sticks horribly and the pattern just enjoys it! All those strangled heads and bulbous eyes and waddling fungus growths just shriek with derision!

I am getting angry enough to do something desperate. To jump out of the window would be admirable exercise, but the bars are too strong even to try.

Besides I wouldn't do it. Of course not. I know well enough that a step like that is improper and might be misconstrued.

I don't like to *look* out of the windows even—there are so many of those creeping women, and they creep so fast.

I wonder if they all come out of that wall-paper as I did?

# CHAPTER FIFTEEN

# *International Human Rights and Global Ethics*

The charter for the United Nations was created in direct response to the mass slaughter of World War II. It's intent, as the Preamble of the UN Charter stated, was to save succeeding generations from the scourge of war by making war a political alternative of last resort. A secondary aim of the Charter was to assure that the United Nations itself be prevented from interfering in matters essentially belonging to the domestic jurisdiction of states. At the same time, it altered the conduct of states by extending human rights beyond the state itself to the individual. Its hope was to ensure that the people of the world never become a victim of the evils of which Europe itself as, to a lesser extent, Japan and, too many in the world, the United States, were themselves guilty. Thus the Preamble went on to reaffirm faith in the dignity and worth of the human person, the equal rights of men and women, and the responsibility of nations large and small to establish conditions under which justice and respect for the obligations arising from treaties and other sources of international law could be maintained.

In principle, then, neither the creation of the United Nations nor the establishment of international human rights were Eurocentric. They were part of the wider reordering of international relations after World War II. If they were paradoxically championed by Western nations like the United States that failed to practice what they preached—racial segregation, gender and job discrimination, housing restrictions, and the like were the rule in much of America in 1945—and never supposed that they would be held accountable for fully supporting their ideals, the founding of the United Nations and the broadcasting of rights claims all over the world not only helped fuel the anti-colonial revolutions in the postwar period abroad but also the civil rights revolution in the United States.

If European and American influence would nonetheless quickly intervene to control the structuring of the United Nations, particularly its Security Council, and the establishment of its agendas, and if numerous Conventions and Covenants would have to be established protecting against genocide, offering immunity to noncombatants, establishing rights for refugees, insuring economic, social, cultural, civil, and political rights, prohibiting torture, and protecting children, its achievements over the last 80 years are not without great significance. Most states ratified human rights conventions even when they didn't practice them and didn't believe those conventions would constrain them. Some new countries even incorporated such rights into their new constitutions without quite realizing what they were agreeing to. But no matter: the very fact of their publication, together with the slow evolution of their dissemination across the world, has led to the creation an international human rights culture itself and that culture, however imperfectly, has had more than a little to do with relieving, or at least addressing, many of the conditions that produce future wars. While it hasn't stopped those wars from occurring, or restrained the major powers of the world from imposing their will on those less powerful, the United Nations has provided a forum in which such issues can be debated and sometimes equitably resolved.

The key document is the first selection in this chapter, "The Universal Declaration of Human Rights." While biased in favor of the Western conception of the individual over against more Middle Eastern and Asian notions of the communal identity of the self, it urges recognition of the rights of all individuals without distinctions. It does so by insisting on the rights to life, liberty, and security of person before the law, protection against slavery, torture, degrading treatment, and discrimination, freedom of movement within one's own state and the right to leave and return, along with other rights to a nationality, to own property, to assemble with others, to exchange opinions freely, and to receive remedy for acts in violation of the law. "The Universal Declaration" is even more specific on the rights it seeks to establish for women, which include the right to marry and found a family regardless of race, nationality, or religion, to choose whom to marry, how to practice it, whether to dissolve it, and why marriage should be considered a natural and fundamental unit of society deserving the protection of the state.

The development of the human rights revolution has a long political history that begins in the West at the end of the Middle Ages and the beginning of the early modern period with the attempt by members of the nobility to protect themselves from abuse by monarchs, and then was quickly adopted by the emergent middling classes as a tactic that sought to insulate them both from government and from the masses. These tactics might have remained merely local were it not for the Enlightenment's eventual fascination with rights language, as in "rights of man," "natural rights," "rights of humanity," and the usage of "rights talk" in such unexpected artistic forms as the eighteenth-century "novel of letters" and the rise of the portraiture of non-royals. These new aesthetic forms helped foster a sense of individuality in their audience and a capacity for empathy toward their subjects because those subjects were increasingly drawn not from the ranks of the nobility or saints but rather from the ranks of more ordinary people. Such practices were then to be reinforced over the next 250 years by rights legislation that anticipated the International Declaration itself, from the French Revolution's Declaration of the Rights of Man and Citizen, to various anti-torture protests in nineteenth-century European literature and art, to twentieth-century campaigns against human rights violations.

The discussion of international human rights, as it has evolved through the second half of the twentieth century and the early years of the twenty-first, has been part of an even wider conversation about whether there are any more universal or global norms besides rights to which the people of the world should be accountable. Are there any values or principles on which the people of the world could agree, or is the diversity of cultures and the assumptions that define such values too varied? For some, it may be enough if there is at least disagreement about the same issues, the terms of the disagreements themselves thus defining the measure of consensus. For others, the key to what might be called a global ethics capable of being shared across vast cultural differences has less to do with the shared or shareable sense of the issues at stake than with a shared or shareable sense of the human that needs to be acknowledged, confronted, and engaged. In any case, there seems to be a difference, as the Canadian philosopher Charles Taylor has pointed out, between ethical norms themselves, the legal forms in which they are expressed and through which they are given force, and the philosophical systems by which they are justified. Taylor believes that an unforced consensus on certain norms might be achievable if we allow for, and make a concerted effort to understand, the two crucial legal and philosophical variables that determine their articulation and, to a considerable degree, their comprehension.

As Michael Ignatieff points out in the second selection of this chapter, what he calls "the cross-cultural validity—and hence legitimacy—of human rights norms" have been challenged from the very beginning not only by certain, but not necessarily all, sectors of Islam based on sharia law and patriarchal authority, but also by those countries in the West that do not see themselves as based on the ideology of liberal individualism, and East Asian countries that put family and community ahead of individualism and democracy. Ignatieff's defense of the principle of human rights and its reliance on a kind of individualism is based on the distinction between rights holders and rights withholders, and thus maintains that rights in the minimal human, rather than the radical liberal, sense "are worth having only if they can be enforced against institutions such as the family, the state, and the church." The crux of his argument is based on the notion of rights as protections rather than as permissions, "freedom from" as opposed to "freedom to or for." The philosopher Isaiah Berlin imagined this kind of freedom as a form of negative liberty, or "freedom from oppression, bondage, and gross physical harm," and Ignatieff maintains that this kind of liberty does not, or at least should not, oblige anyone to adopt a distinctively Western frame of values. All anyone needs to agree, Ignatieff insists, is that the definition of the human is in some sense, or at least at some level, independent of the forms in which it is permitted to express itself, that there are indeed crimes against the human which transcend any particular culture's or society's definition of itself.

As the selection by Giles Gunn explains, determining how societies and cultures define the self, and specifically how they go about answering the ethical question about "the better life for the self to be led," as the American philosopher John Dewey put it, is not as simple as it looks. What quickly becomes apparent is that most people do their ethical thinking about the better life to be led not simply with the help of the rational categories, theoretical concepts, or immutable laws that social, cultural, religious, and other normative institutions supply them but also, and often rather, with what might be called a repertoire of more figurative or symbolic instruments. These include what might be thought of as prototypical structures, semantic or linguistic frames of reference, conceptual metaphors, and basic elemental experiences that put great pressure on all the other imaginative components of moral reflection, including pain, bewilderment, fear, cruelty, and humiliation. Moreover, all of these less conceptual components are for most of us held together and organized not by means of argument so much as with the help of narratives, tales, stories, chronicles, proverbial lessons, and even tell-tale anecdotes.

This does not mean that ethical thinking can dispense with categories and concepts altogether; only that categories and concepts do not represent sets of properties that belong to actual structures or things in the world. Rather their purpose is to indicate resemblances between things in the world that seem to be of a particular type no matter what their properties or features. Thus our ethical thinking actually operates with the help of frames of thought—let's call them scaffoldings for ideas--that are less rigid or inelastic than strict categories and hence free us up to undertake more flexible mappings of the world with the help of metaphors. Metaphors are particularly indispensable to advancing ethical reflection because they suggest analogies between conventional cases and more atypical ones. New cases can, of course, conceivably lack any known prototypes or defy metaphorical comparisons, in which case more traditional schemes or frames of reference must then be revised and reorganized. But the key to the process of organizing any of these elements of analysis into a meaningful construction is usually to narrativize it.

Narratives, stories, tales, proverbs help us preserve insights in memorable form, render truths credible, and they do so by dispensing with the logic of arguments arranged around concepts in favor of employing what might be call a logic of plausibility pointing less in the direction of a set of certainties or convictions than a set of possibilities or probabilities. Whatever their terms of specific reference—Goldilocks and her three bears, the Brothers Grimm and their fairy tales, Scheherazade and her one thousand and one nights of stories—narratives of all kinds invite us to follow the arrow of sense projected by their unfolding plots, where meanings are not so much told or declared as suggested and dramatized. In this way, formal distinctions between the theoretical and the practical, the universal and the particular, the general and the specific, tend to melt away for the purpose of revealing the story, tale, or account as something that is intended to be taken or accepted less as conclusive or definitive than as typical exemplary, or archetypal. Ethical norms like human rights are thus difficult to fully inscribe in legal codes or doctrinal edicts; they gain credibility and traction as norms of accountability only as they become forms of embodied knowledge, modes of perception and structures of feelings.

# The Universal Declaration of Human Rights

## Preamble

Whereas recognition of the inherent dignity and of the equal and inalienable rights of all members of the human family is the foundation of freedom, justice and peace in the world,

Whereas disregard and contempt for human rights have resulted in barbarous acts which have outraged the conscience of mankind, and the advent of a world in which human beings shall enjoy freedom of speech and belief and freedom from fear and want has been proclaimed as the highest aspiration of the common people,

Whereas it is essential, if man is not to be compelled to have recourse, as a last resort, to rebellion against tyranny and oppression, that human rights should be protected by the rule of law,

Whereas it is essential to promote the development of friendly relations between nations,

Whereas the peoples of the United Nations have in the Charter reaffirmed their faith in fundamental human rights, in the dignity and worth of the human person and in the equal rights of men and women and have determined to promote social progress and better standards of life in larger freedom,

Whereas Member States have pledged themselves to achieve, in co-operation with the United Nations, the promotion of universal respect for and observance of human rights and fundamental freedoms,

Whereas a common understanding of these rights and freedoms is of the greatest importance for the full realization of this pledge,

Now, Therefore,

The General Assembly,

Proclaims this Universal Declaration of Human Rights as a common standard of achievement for all peoples and all nations, to the end that every individual and every organ of society, keeping this Declaration constantly in mind, shall strive by teaching and education to promote respect for these rights and freedoms and by progressive measures, national and international, to secure their universal and effective recognition and observance, both among the peoples of Member States themselves and among the peoples of territories under their jurisdiction.

## Article 1

All human beings are born free and equal in dignity and rights. They are endowed with reason and conscience and should act towards one another in a spirit of brotherhood.

# Article 2

Everyone is entitled to all the rights and freedoms set forth in this Declaration, without distinction of any kind, such as race, colour, sex, language, religion, political or other opinion, national or social origin, property, birth or other status. Furthermore, no distinction shall be made on the basis of the political, jurisdictional or international status of the country or territory to which a person belongs, whether it be independent, trust, non-self-governing or under any other limitation of sovereignty.

# Article 3

Everyone has the right to life, liberty and security of person.

# Article 4

No one shall be held in slavery or servitude; slavery and the slave trade shall be prohibited in all their forms.

# Article 5

No one shall be subjected to torture or to cruel, inhuman or degrading treatment or punishment.

# Article 6

Everyone has the right to recognition everywhere as a person before the law.

# Article 7

All are equal before the law and are entitled without any discrimination to equal protection of the law. All are entitled to equal protection against any discrimination in violation of this Declaration and against any incitement to such discrimination.

# Article 8

Everyone has the right to an effective remedy by the competent national tribunals for acts violating the fundamental rights granted him by the constitution or by law.

# Article 9

No one shall be subjected to arbitrary arrest, detention or exile.

# Article 10

Everyone is entitled in full equality to a fair and public hearing by an independent and impartial tribunal, in the determination of his rights and obligations and of any criminal charge against him.

# Article 11

1. Everyone charged with a penal offence has the right to be presumed innocent until proved guilty according to law in a public trial at which he has had all the guarantees necessary for his defence.
2. No one shall be held guilty of any penal offence on account of any act or omission which did not constitute a penal offence, under national or international law, at the time when it was committed. Nor shall a heavier penalty be imposed than the one that was applicable at the time the penal offence was committed.

# Article 12

No one shall be subjected to arbitrary interference with his privacy, family, home or correspondence, nor to attacks upon his honour and reputation. Everyone has the right to the protection of the law against such interference or attacks.

# Article 13

1. Everyone has the right to freedom of movement and residence within the borders of each state.
2. Everyone has the right to leave any country, including his own, and to return to his country.

# Article 14

1. Everyone has the right to seek and to enjoy in other countries asylum from persecution.
2. This right may not be invoked in the case of prosecutions genuinely arising from non-political crimes or from acts contrary to the purposes and principles of the United Nations.

# Article 15

1.  Everyone has the right to a nationality.
2.  No one shall be arbitrarily deprived of his nationality nor denied the right to change his nationality.

# Article 16

1.  Men and women of full age, without any limitation due to race, nationality or religion, have the right to marry and to found a family. They are entitled to equal rights as to marriage, during marriage and at its dissolution.
2.  Marriage shall be entered into only with the free and full consent of the intending spouses.
3.  The family is the natural and fundamental group unit of society and is entitled to protection by society and the State.

# Article 17

1.  Everyone has the right to own property alone as well as in association with others.
2.  No one shall be arbitrarily deprived of his property.

# Article 18

Everyone has the right to freedom of thought, conscience and religion; this right includes freedom to change his religion or belief, and freedom, either alone or in community with others and in public or private, to manifest his religion or belief in teaching, practice, worship and observance.

# Article 19

Everyone has the right to freedom of opinion and expression; this right includes freedom to hold opinions without interference and to seek, receive and impart information and ideas through any media and regardless of frontiers.

# Article 20

1.  Everyone has the right to freedom of peaceful assembly and association.
2.  No one may be compelled to belong to an association.

# Article 21

1. Everyone has the right to take part in the government of his country, directly or through freely chosen representatives.
2. Everyone has the right of equal access to public service in his country.
3. The will of the people shall be the basis of the authority of government; this will shall be expressed in periodic and genuine elections which shall be by universal and equal suffrage and shall be held by secret vote or by equivalent free voting procedures.

# Article 22

Everyone, as a member of society, has the right to social security and is entitled to realization, through national effort and international co-operation and in accordance with the organization and resources of each State, of the economic, social and cultural rights indispensable for his dignity and the free development of his personality.

# Article 23

1. Everyone has the right to work, to free choice of employment, to just and favourable conditions of work and to protection against unemployment.
2. Everyone, without any discrimination, has the right to equal pay for equal work.
3. Everyone who works has the right to just and favourable remuneration ensuring for himself and his family an existence worthy of human dignity, and supplemented, if necessary, by other means of social protection.
4. Everyone has the right to form and to join trade unions for the protection of his interests.

# Article 24

Everyone has the right to rest and leisure, including reasonable limitation of working hours and periodic holidays with pay.

# Article 25

1. Everyone has the right to a standard of living adequate for the health and well-being of himself and of his family, including food, clothing, housing and medical care and necessary social services, and the right to security in the event of unemployment, sickness, disability, widowhood, old age or other lack of livelihood in circumstances beyond his control.
2. Motherhood and childhood are entitled to special care and assistance. All children, whether born in or out of wedlock, shall enjoy the same social protection.

# Article 26

1. Everyone has the right to education. Education shall be free, at least in the elementary and fundamental stages. Elementary education shall be compulsory. Technical and professional education shall be made generally available and higher education shall be equally accessible to all on the basis of merit.
2. Education shall be directed to the full development of the human personality and to the strengthening of respect for human rights and fundamental freedoms. It shall promote understanding, tolerance and friendship among all nations, racial or religious groups, and shall further the activities of the United Nations for the maintenance of peace.
3. Parents have a prior right to choose the kind of education that shall be given to their children.

# Article 27

1. Everyone has the right freely to participate in the cultural life of the community, to enjoy the arts and to share in scientific advancement and its benefits.
2. Everyone has the right to the protection of the moral and material interests resulting from any scientific, literary or artistic production of which he is the author.

# Article 28

Everyone is entitled to a social and international order in which the rights and freedoms set forth in this Declaration can be fully realized.

# Article 29

1. Everyone has duties to the community in which alone the free and full development of his personality is possible.
2. In the exercise of his rights and freedoms, everyone shall be subject only to such limitations as are determined by law solely for the purpose of securing due recognition and respect for the rights and freedoms of others and of meeting the just requirements of morality, public order and the general welfare in a democratic society.
3. These rights and freedoms may in no case be exercised contrary to the purposes and principles of the United Nations.

# Article 30

Nothing in this Declaration may be interpreted as implying for any State, group or person any right to engage in any activity or to perform any act aimed at the destruction of any of the rights and freedoms set forth herein.

# The Attack on Human Rights

 Michael Ignatieff

## From Within and Without

Since 1945, human rights language has become a source of power and authority. Inevitably, power invites challenge. Human rights doctrine is now so powerful, but also so unthinkingly imperialist in its claim to universality, that it has exposed itself to serious intellectual attack. These challenges have raised important questions about whether human rights norms deserve the authority they have acquired: whether their claims to universality are justified, or whether they are just another cunning exercise in Western moral imperialism.

The cultural challenge to the universality of human rights arises from three distinct sources—from resurgent Islam, from within the West itself, and from East Asia. Each of these challenges is independent of the others, but taken together, they have raised substantial questions about the cross-cultural validity—and hence the legitimacy—of human rights norms.

The challenge from Islam has been there from the beginning. When the Universal Declaration of Human Rights was being drafted in 1947, the Saudi Arabian delegation raised particular objection to Article 16, relating to free marriage choice, and Article 18, relating to freedom of religion. On the question of marriage, the Saudi delegate to the committee examining the draft of the declaration made an argument that has resonated ever since in Islamic encounters with Western human rights, saying that

> the authors of the draft declaration had, for the most part, taken into consideration only the standards recognized by Western civilization and had ignored more ancient civilizations which were past the experimental stage, and the institutions of which, for example, marriage, had proved their wisdom through the centuries. It was not for the Committee to proclaim the superiority of one civilization over all others or to establish uniform standards for all the countries of the world.

This was a defense of both the Islamic faith and patriarchal authority. The Saudi delegate in effect argued that the exchange and control of women is the very raison d'être of traditional cultures, and that the restriction of female choice in marriage is central to the maintenance of patriarchal property relations. On the basis of these objections to Articles 16 and 18, the Saudi delegation refused to ratify the declaration. There have been recurrent attempts, including Islamic declarations of human rights, to reconcile Islamic and Western traditions by putting more emphasis on family duty and religious devotion and by drawing on distinctively Islamic traditions of religious and ethnic tolerance. But these attempts at fusion between the Islamic world and the West have never been entirely successful: agreement by the parties actually trades away what is vital to each side. The resulting consensus is bland and unconvincing.

Since the 1970s the relation of Islam to human rights has grown more hostile. When the Islamic Revolution in Iran rose up against the tyrannical modernization imposed by the shah, Islamic figures began to question the universal writ of Western human rights norms. They have pointed out that the Western separation of church and state, of secular and religious authority, is alien to the jurisprudence and political thought of the Islamic tradition. And they are correct. The freedoms articulated in the Universal Declaration of Human Rights make no sense within the theocratic bias of Islamic political thought. The right to marry and establish a family, to freely choose one's partner, is a direct challenge to the authorities in Islamic society that enforce the family choice of spouse, polygamy, and other restrictions on women's freedom. In Islamic eyes, universalizing rights discourse implies a sovereign and discrete individual, which is blasphemous from the perspective of the Koran.

In responding to this challenge, the West has made the mistake of assuming that fundamentalism and Islam are synonymous. But in fact Islam speaks in many voices, some more anti-Western or theocratic than others. National contexts may be more important in defining local Islamic reactions to Western values than are broad theological principles in the religion as a whole. Where Islamic societies have managed to modernize, create a middle class, and enter the global economy—Egypt and Tunisia being examples—a constituency in favor of basic human rights can emerge. Egypt, for instance, is now in the process of passing legislation to give women the right to divorce, and although dialogue with Egypt's religious authorities has been difficult, women's rights will be substantially enhanced by the new legislation. In Algeria, a secular human rights culture is more embattled. The governing elite, which rode to power after a bloody anticolonial revolution failed to modernize the country, faces an opposition, led by Islamic militants, that has taken an anti-Western, anti-human rights stance. And in Afghanistan, where the state itself has collapsed and foreign arms transfers have aggravated the nation's decline, the Taliban explicitly rejects all Western human rights standards. In these instances, the critical variant is not Islam itself but the fateful course of Western policy and economic globalization.

A second challenge to the universality of human rights comes from within the West itself. For the last 20 years, an influential current in Western political opinion has been maintaining, in the words of the radical scholars Adamantia Pollis and Peter Schwab, that human rights are a "Western construct of limited applicability," a twentieth-century fiction dependent on the rights traditions of the United States, the United Kingdom, and France and therefore inapplicable in cultures that do not share this historical matrix of liberal individualism.

This current of thought has complicated intellectual origins: the Marxist critique of the rights of man, the anthropological critique of the arrogance of late-nineteenth-century bourgeois imperialism, and the postmodernist critique of the universalizing pretensions of Enlightenment thought. All of these tendencies have come together in a critique of Western intellectual hegemony as expressed in the language of human rights. Human rights are seen as an exercise in the cunning of Western reason: no longer able to dominate the world through direct imperial rule, the West now masks its own will to power in the impartial, universalizing language of human rights and seeks to impose its own narrow agenda on a plethora of world cultures that do not actually share the West's conception of individuality, selfhood, agency, or freedom. This postmodernist relativism began as an intellectual fashion on Western university campuses, but it has seeped slowly into Western human rights practice, causing all activists to pause and consider the intellectual warrant for the universality they once took for granted.

This challenge within has been amplified by a challenge from without: the critique of Western human rights standards by some political leaders in the rising economies of East Asia. Whereas the Islamic challenge to human rights can be explained in part by the failure of Islamic societies to benefit from the global economy, the Asian challenge is a consequence of the region's staggering economic success. Because of Malaysia's robust economic growth, for example, its leaders feel confident enough to reject Western ideas of democracy and individual rights in favor of an Asian route to development and prosperity—a route that depends on authoritarian government and authoritarian family structures.

The same can be said about Singapore, which successfully synthesized political authoritarianism with market capitalism. Singapore's Senior Minister Lee Kuan Yew has been quoted as saying that Asians have "little doubt that a society with communitarian values where the interests of society take precedence over that of the individual suits them better than the individualism of America." Singaporeans often cite rising divorce and crime rates in the West to illustrate that Western individualism is detrimental to the order necessary for the enjoyment of rights themselves.

An "Asian model" supposedly puts community and family ahead of individual rights and order ahead of democracy and individual freedom. In reality, of course, there is no single Asian model: each of these societies has modernized in different ways, within different political traditions, and with differing degrees of political and market freedom. Yet it has proven useful for Asian authoritarians to argue that they represent a civilizational challenge to the hegemony of Western models.

## Trades and Compromises

Let it be conceded at once that these three separate challenges to the universality of human rights discourse—two from without and one from within the Western tradition—have had a productive impact. They have forced human rights activists to question their assumptions, to rethink the history of their commitments, and to realize just how complicated intercultural dialogue on rights questions becomes when all cultures participate as equals.

But at the same time, Western defenders of human rights have traded too much away. In the desire to find common ground with Islamic and Asian positions and to purge their own discourse of the imperial legacies uncovered by the postmodernist critique, Western defenders of human rights norms risk compromising the very universality they ought to be defending. They also risk rewriting their own history.

Many traditions, not just Western ones, were represented at the drafting of the Universal Declaration of Human Rights—for example, the Chinese, Middle Eastern Christian, Marxist, Hindu, Latin American, and Islamic. The members of the drafting committee saw their task not as a simple ratification of Western convictions but as an attempt to delimit a range of moral universals from within their very different religious, political, ethnic, and philosophical backgrounds. This fact helps to explain why the document makes no reference to God in its preamble. The communist delegations would have vetoed any such reference, and the competing religious traditions could not have agreed on words that would make human rights derive from human beings' common existence as God's creatures. Hence the secular ground of the document is not a sign of European cultural domination so much as a pragmatic common denominator designed to make agreement possible across the range of divergent cultural and political viewpoints.

It remains true, of course, that Western inspirations—and Western drafters—played the predominant role in the drafting of the document. Even so, the drafters' mood in 1947 was anything but triumphalist. They were aware, first of all, that the age of colonial emancipation was at hand: Indian independence was proclaimed while the language of the declaration was being finalized. Although the declaration does not specifically endorse self-determination, its drafters clearly foresaw the coming tide of struggles for national independence. Because it does proclaim the right of people to self-government and freedom of speech and religion, it also concedes the right of colonial peoples to construe moral universals in a language rooted in their own traditions. Whatever failings the drafters of the declaration may be accused of, unexamined Western triumphalism is not one of them. Key drafters such as René Cassin of France and John Humphrey of Canada knew the knell had sounded on two centuries of Western colonialism.

They also knew that the declaration was not so much a proclamation of the superiority of European civilization as an attempt to salvage the remains of its Enlightenment heritage from the barbarism of a world war just concluded. The declaration was written in full awareness of Auschwitz and dawning awareness of Kolyma. A consciousness of European savagery is built into the very language of the declaration's preamble: "Whereas disregard and contempt for human rights have resulted in barbarous acts which have outraged the conscience of mankind . . ."

The declaration may still be a child of the Enlightenment, but it was written when faith in the Enlightenment faced its deepest crisis. In this sense, human rights norms are not so much a declaration of the superiority of European civilization as a warning by Europeans that the rest of the world should not reproduce their mistakes. The chief of these was the idolatry of the nation-state, causing individuals to forget the higher law commanding them to disobey unjust orders. The abandonment of this moral heritage of natural law and the surrender of individualism to collectivism, the drafters believed, led to the catastrophes of Nazi and Stalinist oppression. Unless the disastrous heritage of European collectivism is kept in mind as the framing experience in the drafting of the declaration, its individualism will appear to be nothing more than the ratification of Western bourgeois capitalist prejudice. In fact, it was much more: a studied attempt to reinvent the European natural law tradition in order to safeguard individual agency against the totalitarian state.

# The Power of One

It remains true, therefore, that the core of the declaration is the moral individualism for which it is so reproached by non-Western societies. It is this individualism for which Western activists have become most apologetic, believing that it should be tempered by greater emphasis on social duties and responsibilities to the community. Human rights, it is argued, can recover universal appeal only if they soften their individualistic bias and put greater emphasis on the communitarian parts of the declaration, especially Article 29, which says that "everyone has duties to the community in which alone the free and full development of his personality is possible." This desire to water down the individualism of rights discourse is driven by a desire both to make human rights more palatable to less individualistic cultures in the non-Western world and also to respond to disquiet among Western communitarians at the supposedly corrosive impact of individualistic values on Western social cohesion.

But this tack mistakes what rights actually are and misunderstands why they have proven attractive to millions of people raised in non-Western traditions. Rights are meaningful only if they confer entitlements and immunities on individuals; they are worth having only if they can be enforced against institutions such as the family, the state, and the church. This remains true even when the rights in question are collective or group rights. Some of these group rights—such as the right to speak your own language or practice your own religion—are essential preconditions for the exercise of individual rights. The right to speak a language of your choice will not mean very much if the language has died out. For this reason, group rights are needed to protect individual rights. But the ultimate purpose and justification of group rights is not the protection of the group as such but the protection of the individuals who compose it. Group rights to language, for example, must not be used to prevent an individual from learning a second language. Group rights to practice religion should not cancel the right of individuals to leave a religious community if they choose.

Rights are inescapably political because they tacitly imply a conflict between a rights holder and a rights "withholder," some authority against which the rights holder can make justified claims. To confuse rights with aspirations, and rights conventions with syncretic syntheses of world values, is to wish away the conflicts that define the very content of rights. Individuals and groups will always be in conflict, and rights exist to protect individuals. Rights language cannot be parsed or translated into a nonindividualistic, communitarian framework; it presumes moral individualism and is nonsensical outside that assumption.

Moreover, it is precisely this individualism that renders human rights attractive to non-Western peoples and explains why the fight for those rights has become a global movement. The language of human rights is the only universally available moral vernacular that validates the claims of women and children against the oppression they experience in patriarchal and tribal societies; it is the only vernacular that enables dependent persons to perceive themselves as moral agents and to act against practices—arranged marriages, purdah, civic disenfranchisement, genital mutilation, domestic slavery, and so on—that are ratified by the weight and authority of their cultures. These agents seek out human rights protection precisely because it legitimizes their protests against oppression.

If this is so, then it is necessary to rethink what it means when one says that rights are universal. Rights doctrines arouse powerful opposition because they challenge powerful religions, family structures, authoritarian states, and tribes. It would be a hopeless task to attempt to persuade these holders of power of the universal validity of rights doctrines, since if these doctrines prevailed, their exercise of authority would necessarily be abridged and constrained. Thus universality cannot imply universal assent, since in a world of unequal power, the only propositions that the powerful and powerless would agree on would be entirely toothless and anodyne. Rights are universal because they define the universal interests of the powerless—namely, that power be exercised over them in ways that respect their autonomy as agents. In this sense, human rights represent a revolutionary creed, since they make a radical demand of all human groups that they serve the interests of the individuals who compose them. This, then, implies that human groups should be, insofar as possible, consensual, or at least that they should respect an individual's right to exit when the constraints of the group become unbearable.

The idea that groups should respect an individual's right of exit is not easy to reconcile with what groups actually are. Most human groups—the family, for example—are blood groups, based on inherited kinship or ethnic ties. People do not choose to be born into them and do not leave them easily, since these collectivities provide the frame of meaning within which individual life makes sense. This is as true in modern secular societies as it is in religious or traditional ones. Group rights doctrines exist to safeguard the collective rights—for example, to language—that make individual agency meaningful and valuable. But individual and group interests inevitably conflict. Human rights exist to adjudicate these conflicts, to define the irreducible minimum beyond which group and collective claims must not go in constraining the lives of individuals.

## Culture Shock

Adopting the values of individual agency does not necessarily entail adopting Western ways of life. Believing in your right not to be tortured or abused need not mean adopting Western dress, speaking Western languages, or approving of the Western lifestyle. To seek human rights protection is not to change your civilization; it is merely to avail yourself of the protections of what the philosopher Isaiah Berlin called "negative liberty": to be free from oppression, bondage, and gross physical harm.

Human rights do not, and should not, delegitimize traditional culture as a whole. The women in Kabul who come to human rights agencies seeking protection from the Taliban do not want to cease being Muslim wives and mothers; they want to combine their traditions with education and professional health care provided by a woman. And they hope the agencies will defend them against being beaten and persecuted for claiming such rights.

The legitimacy of such claims is reinforced by the fact that the people who make them are not foreign human rights activists or employees of international organizations but the victims themselves. In Pakistan, for example, it is poor rural women who are criticizing the grotesque distortion of Islamic teaching that claims to justify "honor killings"—in which women are burned alive when they disobey their husbands. Human rights have gone global by going local, empowering the powerless, giving voice to the voiceless.

It is simply not the case, as Islamic and Asian critics contend, that human rights force the Western way of life on their societies. For all its individualism, human rights rhetoric does not require adherents to jettison their other cultural attachments. As the philosopher Jack Donnelly argues, human rights assume "that people probably are best suited, and in any case are entitled, to choose the good life for themselves." What the declaration does mandate is the right to choose, and specifically the right to exit a group when choice is denied. The global diffusion of rights language would never have occurred had these not been authentically attractive propositions to millions of people, especially women, in theocratic, traditional, or patriarchal societies.

Critics of this view would argue that it is too "voluntaristic"; it implies that individuals in traditional societies are free to choose the manner of their insertion into the global economy and free to choose which Western values to adopt and which to reject. In reality, these critics argue, people are not free to choose. Economic globalization steamrolls local economies, and moral globalization—human rights—follows behind as the legitimizing ideology of global capitalism. "Given the class interest of the internationalist class carrying out this agenda," law professor Kenneth Anderson writes, "the claim to universalism is a sham. Universalism is mere globalism and a globalism, moreover, whose key terms are established by capital."

This idea that human rights represent the moral arm of global capitalism falsifies the insurgent nature of the relationship between human rights activism and the global corporation. The activists of nongovernmental organizations (NGOs) who devote their lives to challenging the labor practices of global giants such as Nike and Royal Dutch/Shell would be astonished to discover that their human rights agenda has been serving the interests of global capital all along. Anderson conflates globalism and internationalism and mixes up two classes, the free market globalists and the human rights internationalists, whose interests and values are in conflict.

Although free markets do encourage the emergence of assertively self-interested individuals, these individuals seek human rights in order to protect themselves from the indignities and indecencies of the market. Moreover, the dignity such individuals seek to protect is not necessarily derived from Western models. Anderson writes as if human rights were always imposed from the top down by an international elite bent on "saving the world." He ignores the extent to which the demand for human rights comes from the bottom up.

Indeed, what makes human rights demands legitimate is that they emanate from the bottom, from the powerless. Instead of apologizing for the individualism of Western human rights standards, activists need to attend to another problem, which is how to create conditions in which individuals on the bottom are free to avail themselves of such rights. Increasing the freedom of people to exercise their rights depends on close cultural understanding of the frameworks that often constrain choice.

The much debated issue of female circumcision illustrates this point. What may appear as mutilation in Western eyes is, in some cultures, simply the price of tribal and family belonging for women. Accordingly, if they fail to submit to the ritual, they lose their place in that world. Choosing to exercise their rights, therefore, may result in social ostracism, leaving them no option but to leave their tribe and make for the city. Human rights advocates should be aware of what it really means for a woman to abandon traditional practices under such circumstances. And activists have an equal duty to inform women of the medical costs and consequences of these practices and to seek, as a first step, to make them less dangerous for those who choose to undergo them.

As for the final decision, it is for women themselves to decide how to adjudicate between tribal and Western wisdom. The criteria of informed consent that regulate medical patients' choices in

Western societies are equally applicable in non-Western settings, and human rights activists must respect the autonomy and dignity of agents. An activist's proper role is not to make the choices for the women in question but to enlarge those women's knowledge of what the choices entail. In traditional societies, harmful practices can be abandoned only when the whole community decides to do so. Otherwise, individuals who decide on their own face ostracism and worse. Consent in these cases means collective or group consent. Yet even group consent must be built on consultation with the individuals involved.

Sensitivity to the real constraints that limit individual freedom in different cultures is not the same thing as deferring to these cultures. It does not mean abandoning universality. It simply means facing up to a demanding intercultural dialogue in which all parties come to the table under common expectations of being treated as moral equals. Traditional society is oppressive for individuals within it, not because it fails to afford them a Western way of life, but because it does not accord them a right to speak and be heard. Western activists have no right to overturn traditional cultural practice, provided that such practice continues to receive the assent of its members. Human rights are universal not as a vernacular of cultural prescription but as a language of moral empowerment. Their role is not in defining the content of culture but in trying to enfranchise all agents so that they can freely shape that content.

The best way to face the cultural challenges to human rights coming from Asia, Islam, and Western postmodernism is to admit their truth: rights discourse is individualistic. But that is precisely why it has proven an effective remedy against tyranny, and why it has proven attractive to people from very different cultures. The other advantage of liberal individualism is that it is a distinctly "thin" theory of the human good: it defines and proscribes the "negative"—that is, those restraints and injustices that make any human life, however conceived, impossible; at the same time, it does not prescribe the "positive" range of good lives that human beings can lead. The doctrine of human rights is morally universal because it says that all human beings need certain specific freedoms "from"; it does not go on to define what their freedom "to" should comprise.[1] In this sense, it is a less prescriptive universalism than the world's religions: it articulates standards of human decency without violating rights of cultural autonomy.

## The West Against Itself

In the moral dispute between the "West" and the "rest," both sides make the mistake of assuming that the other speaks with one voice. When the non-Western world looks at human rights, it assumes—rightly—that the discourse originates in a matrix of historical traditions shared by all the major Western countries. But these Western nations interpret the core principles of their own rights tradition very differently. A common tradition does not necessarily result in common points of view on rights. All of the formative rights cultures of the West—the English, the French, and the

---

[1] These distinctions—negative liberty, positive liberty, freedom from, freedom to—are suggested by Isaiah Berlin, "Two Concepts of Liberty," in *The Proper Study of Mankind*, ed. Henry Hardy (London: Chatto and Windus, 1997), pp. 191–243; on "thin" theories of the good, see John Rawls, *A Theory of Justice* (Cambridge: Harvard University Press, 1970).

American—give a different account of such issues as privacy, free speech, incitement, the right to bear arms, and the right to life.

In the 50 years since the promulgation of the Universal Declaration of Human Rights, these disagreements have become more salient. Indeed, the moral unanimity of the West—always a myth more persuasive from the outside than from the inside—is breaking up and revealing its unalterable heterogeneity. American rights discourse once belonged to the common European natural law tradition and to British common law. But this awareness of a common anchorage now competes with a growing sense of American moral and legal exceptionalism.

American human rights policy in the last 20 years has been increasingly distinctive and paradoxical: it is the product of a nation with a great national rights tradition that leads the world in denouncing the human rights violations of others but refuses to ratify key international rights conventions itself. The most important resistance to the domestic application of international rights norms comes not from rogue states outside the Western tradition or from Islamic and Asian societies. It comes, in fact, from within the heart of the Western rights tradition itself, from a nation that, in linking rights to popular sovereignty, opposes international human rights oversight as an infringement on its democracy. Of all the ironies in the history of human rights since the signing of the Universal Declaration of Human Rights, the one that would most astonish Eleanor Roosevelt is the degree to which her own country is now the odd one out.

In the next 50 years, the moral consensus that sustained the declaration in 1948 will continue to splinter. For all the rhetoric about common values, the distance between the United States and Europe on issues such as abortion and capital punishment may grow, just as the distance between the West and the rest may also increase. There is no reason to believe that economic globalization entails moral globalization. Indeed, there is some reason to think that as economies have unified their business practices, ownership, languages, and networks of communication, a countermovement has developed to safeguard the integrity of national communities, national cultures, religions, and indigenous and religious ways of life.

This is a prophecy not of the end of the human rights movement but of its belated coming of age, its recognition that we live in a world of plural cultures that have a right to equal consideration in the argument about what we can and cannot, should and should not, do to human beings. Indeed, this may be the central historical importance of human rights in the history of human progress: it has abolished the hierarchy of civilizations and cultures. As late as 1945, it was common to think of European civilization as inherently superior to the civilizations it ruled. Today many Europeans continue to believe this, but they know that they have no right to do so. More to the point, many non-Western peoples also took the civilizational superiority of their rulers for granted. They no longer have any reason to continue believing this. One reason for that is the global diffusion of human rights talk—the language that most consistently articulates the moral equality of all the individuals on the face of the earth. But to the degree that it does this, it simultaneously increases the level of conflict over the meaning, application, and legitimacy of rights claims.

Rights language states that all human beings belong at the table in the essential conversation about how we should treat each other. But once this universal right to speak and be heard is granted, there is bound to be tumult. There is bound to be discord. Why? Because the European voices that once took it upon themselves to silence the babble with a peremptory ruling no longer take it as their privilege to do so, and those who sit with them at the table no longer grant them the right to do so. All this counts as progress, as a step toward a world imagined for millennia in different cultures and religions: a world of genuine moral equality among human beings. But a world of moral equality is a world of conflict, deliberation, argument, and contention.

We need to stop thinking of human rights as trumps and begin thinking of them as part of a language that creates the basis for deliberation. In this argument, the ground we share may actually be quite limited—not much more than the basic intuition that what is pain and humiliation for you is bound to be pain and humiliation for me. But this is already something. In such a future, shared among equals, rights are not the universal credo of a global society, not a secular religion, but something much more limited and yet just as valuable: the shared vocabulary from which our arguments can begin, and the bare human minimum from which differing ideas of human flourishing can take root.

# Global Ethics

 Giles Gunn

Global ethics refers to a diverse field of intellectual inquiry devoted to establishing norms, procedures, and practices for addressing issues of conduct, collaboration, and conflict in the global sphere. Such issues can be of consequence either to individuals, communities, states, transnational organizations, or any combination thereof. What makes them global is their sphere of reference and resonance. Do they register on scales of import or significance and consequence that require interpretation within a global as opposed to a national, transnational, regional, or local frame?

From this perspective, there is always both a theoretical and practical dimension to global ethics, but these two dimensions can produce very different forms of inquiry. Those forms concerned with issues already alleged to be global-- environmental degradation, nuclear proliferation, refugee relief, international peace, regulation of multinational corporations, violence against women and children, biomedical questions and protocols--usually tend to focus on the development and implementation of normative guidelines and rules for behavior in specific domains. Those forms concerned instead with the horizon of understanding appropriate for the definition, comprehension, and implications of such issues frequently take a more conceptual direction and seek to elaborate how ethical notions and practices as well as modes of consciousness would have to change if such a perspective were brought to bear. This distinction is reflected in the discipline of ethics in general which is usually divided into applied and foundational branches.

While the application of ethical perspectives and prescriptions to global problems is an immense and always changing project, the emphasis in this essay is on contemporary alternatives for defining a global ethics. Here the intellectual challenge has been twofold: first, to establish what kind of consensus on principles, rights, duties, values, and obligations an ethics of global scope fundamentally requires; and, second, to determine whether any ethics, consensual or not, can address the diversity of need, suffering, inequality, injustice, grievance, and moral confusion that the world in all its particularity actually represents. The first challenge turns on the question of whether there are any ethical universals to which all societies, and the individuals within them, should or can be held accountable. The second challenge proceeds from the fact that, even if certain values are held to be universal, different groups will always disagree about how to construe them, how to interpret their implications and applications, and how to assess and prioritize them.

## Universality of Ethical Values

The argument for the universality of ethical values or norms has often been made with the help of religion, where it is frequently assumed either that all the major religions share an overriding ethical

Gunn, Giles. *Ideas to Live For: Toward a Global Ethics.* pp 190-198, 201-208. © 2015 by the Rector and Visitors of the University of Virginia. Reprinted by permission of the University of Virginia Press.

universal, such as the Golden Rule, or that certain ethical principles such as to love thy neighbor as thyself, carry across many religious communions. But what if the Golden Rule, which is expressed in almost identical terms in the *Analects of Confucius*, the *Mahabharata*, and the *New Testament*, opens up more questions than it resolves? What if what you would do unto others as you would have others do unto you can be described in terms neither you nor they can accept? Is it clear that everyone in the world wants to be treated as everyone else does? Shared ethical assumptions (the importance of law, the dignity of individuals, the importance of honor) have a way of being variously understood and realized in particular cultural traditions.

This has not prevented many from postulating either that the major religions of the world share recurrent themes—the fundamental equality of all human beings, the idea of human vulnerability, the need to alleviate suffering and mitigate harm—or that one can extrapolate from their diverse expressions certain shared principles, such as respect for all life, tolerance and truthfulness, economic justice and solidarity, and equal rights between men and women. But even where the world, so to speak, has stepped forward to condemn "crimes of humanity" such as genocide, where people can be exterminated simply as a punishment for having been born, this prohibition also runs into difficulty when most states that have signed the United Nation's Covenant Against Genocide are nonetheless reluctant to act on it and many people in the world even refuse to acknowledge it.

Some have argued that unanimity of opinion or common agreement on such matters is less important than identifying areas of overlapping consensus, shared dispositions; but here one comes up against the fact that even where there is a measure of mutually reciprocal accord, it may be expressed in languages or terms that are far from being intelligible to or commensurable with one another. Thus, the nomination of specific ethical values as candidates for global support often runs into the problems involved in all cross-cultural understanding. Even where the meanings of values separated by cultural barriers can be sensed and appreciated, there are always two more problems to be negotiated. The first entails translating what is often expressed in the metaphors, narratives, or figures of speech of one tradition into the idioms of another. The second, when such discursive translations can be achieved, involves an act of appropriation in which one must figure out the difference such translations actually make to previous understanding and the internal adjustments that must be made as a consequence. Such negotiations thus depend less on merging or fusing understandings of disparate traditions that may share common assumptions than on enabling different groups to discover through dialogue with one another how they may be traveling separate routes to a similar goal.

For this reason, there has been a growing skepticism on the part of many theorists that it is either possible or desirable to base a global ethics on any unity of opinion about principles, perspectives, or practices. For some, it may be enough that there is disagreement about the same issues, the terms of the disagreement itself thus defining the measure of consensus; for others, the key to developing a global ethics capable of being shared across vast cultural differences has less to do with a shared or shareable sense of the issues at stake than with a shared or shareable sense of the needs, both human and social, to be addressed.

But there is another group of theorists and advocates, numbering in the tens, if not hundreds, of millions of people throughout the world who defend a universalist perspective for global ethics in terms of the absolute and infallible authority of their own traditions. Elements of globalized Islam present perhaps only the most familiar face of this perspective among those who contend that theirs is the only true and righteous system of belief, but a similarly doctrinaire, essentialist stance can be found within various Christian, Hindu, Jewish, and other religious communities and needs to be understood for what it is in the eyes of its followers. The members of these communities of faith, whether militants and jihadist or evangelical and missionary, see themselves as representing an extreme form of ethical universalism that seeks the conversion of the world to its own sacred premises. Whether those premises are associated with the reestablishment of the Islamic Ummah or Hindu restoration of Hindutva, the ultra Orthodox'a reclamation of the Hebrew homeland, or the coming reign of Christ after the victorious battle with the Antichrist at Armageddon, these are to be taken seriously as radical, uncompromising assertions of a global ethical authoritarianism.

## Building Consensus for Mutual Betterment

Short of such universalisms, what do, or can, global ethicists build on to frame a perspective that is not merely trying to define our obligations to others in a world of difference but seeks to outline a better life for individuals as well as societies? Can such an enterprise be anything other than a Western attempt to impose its evolving human rights regime on the rest of the world? Does such an ethics require, as defenders of cosmopolitanism from Immanuel Kant to Jacques Derrida have maintained, a shared system of world governance and jurisprudence that people might be inclined to choose if they were in a position to make such choices? And in what can a global ethics consist if it is not based on a system of belief and value that can be shared in common by the immense variety of cultures and peoples in the world?

The arguments over these questions tend to unfold in predictable patterns. The liberal position holds that even if there aren't any universal goods that all people everywhere recognize and prize, much less espouse, there may be enough common ground among such goods to enable people to cooperate for their mutual betterment. This requires finding areas of convergence, relationship, or interaction among diverse value systems and then developing ways to articulate them in contexts where their connections, however attenuated and unstable, can nonetheless be productively exploited.

The communitarian position is less sanguine than the liberal because it presumes that the only values that are thick, and thus determinative, are associated with individual cultures and societies. Values that seek to stretch across such formations and bind people into larger collective wholes tend to be thin and weak, leading many communitarians to argue that the term *global ethics* is a misnomer because there is no sense of community, actual or hypothetical, on which such values could be based. The main problem with this position is that it fails to perceive that thick communities, like nations, regions, religions, and ethnicities, are at least as much imagined, invented, and constructed as they are actual. We are no more acquainted with all the people who belong to them than we can define the territorial limits or explain the modes of sovereignty and status that they imply. All we know for certain is that they create forms of horizontal comradeship and senses of solidarity for which people are often willing to make ultimate sacrifices, and there is no reason to think that over time the same feelings of belonging and loyalty, the same sense of identification, can and will be (and, for many people throughout the world, already is) projected on a global and even planetary scale. Personal horizons expand as peoples' identifications change, and thus as circumstances force people to relocate themselves on widening maps of experience, whether geopolitical, cultural, social, economic, or technological, so consciousness, albeit more slowly and often with resistance, will also change.

Nowhere is this more evident than in the way the global has come to be felt not simply as opportunity or burden but also as threat. People now live in societies of increasing risk whose dangers no longer possess a local habitation or a name. Climate change, water pollution, desertification, international criminal cartels, financial meltdowns, wars of legitimacy, failing states, health pandemics are hazards that are manufactured rather than natural (or, as they are sometimes called," external") and thus are by-products of modernization itself. In addition to focusing attention on the future rather than the past, these risks have turned modernization itself in a more reflexive direction, where many of the people producing them have simultaneously had to acknowledge that they have been exposed to them. Just as these risks traverse the boundaries of state, nationality, ethnicity, class, race, and gender, so they widen human consciousness about what is potentially shared if not suffered by various societies. The phrase "community of fate" now refers not only to groups of people who suddenly find their futures mutually implicated in the resolution of some temporary social emergency, such as the severe acute respiratory syndrome (SARS) that broke out in Hong Kong in 2003, but global populations, such as those living in low-lying countries or on coastal plains, that could easily be threatened within only a matter of decades by the continuing melting of polar ice caused by the international inability or reluctance to reduce carbon emissions.

These dangers, many of which are not sequestered or containable within any of the categories by which we usually map human experience, have foregrounded the importance of cross-cultural dialogue in the formation of ethical guidelines and strategies for addressing such problems. Among those who have pushed this dialogic alternative, there is some difference of opinion as to whether a global ethics would be substantive or merely procedural. Is it possible to develop any consensus about norms, values, and methods for establishing a global ethical order, or is that order itself to be found in the debates about it, which produce, at the very least, a broadened sphere of public discourse where values can be critiqued and reformed. Some, indeed, feel that this capacity for self-reflection and self-revision—"fallibilism" as it is called by pragmatists—may be all that is left of the moral universalism once aimed at in the European Enlightenment, but proponents of the dialogic position still argue that such communicative logics are not to be discounted because they enable people from very different traditions to keep talking with one another, and if they continue talking with one another, perhaps they can learn from one another.

If this sounds like a minimalist ethical position, it should be remembered that learning from one another need not be restricted to learning more about one another. The key to self-critique and self-revision in a dialogic model of communication is recognizing not only what the so-called Other reveals about itself, important as this may be, but also what undetected aspects of oneself are revealed in exchanges with that Other. Such revelations are, from a pragmatist point of view, the source of most of those changes that deepen dialogue even where it does not yield complete accord.

The object, in any case, is not to settle all disputes or resolve all dilemmas but to keep the discussion going and to make it more salient.

Such discursive tactics may well prove more significant as a result of what other theorists are learning about the human and the nature of moral reasoning. Two of the most promising contributions are coming from capabilities theorists and experiential social psychologists. Capability theorists argue that the human cannot be defined simply in terms of what is necessary to sustain a recognizably human life—food, shelter, clothing, health--but must also include what is required to make such a life functional. This includes such abilities as feeling, thinking, reasoning, and imagining, which enables all human beings not genetically damaged to achieve through education the possibility of self-expression and the power to make choices. The realization of these capabilities is also often thought to require a number of other goods--such as a measure of freedom to select sexual partners, to make friends, to have children, to obtain work, to share in social decisions, to pursue a meaningful life—and the avoidance of certain evils--bodily harm, unnecessary suffering, social humiliation, and other ills.

This is a tall order, but it outlines what might be thought of as universals of condition that do, in fact, possess considerable support throughout much of the world. The existence of such human universals has received some confirmation because of what experimental psychologists have discovered about the moral sentiments. Thus far, they have identified as many as six modes of response to situations identified as moral, but whether they are distinct or interrelated, whether they conflict or cooperate in producing moral feelings, is still an open question. The mere fact that they can be isolated at all is an achievement of some consequence because it suggests that the human mind has over time become hardwired to respond naturally to certain situations: prevention or mitigation of harm, fairness and reciprocity, purity and pollution, hierarchy and respect, in-group versus out-group, and awe and elevation. But the same scientists who have made these claims by no means agree that there is any correlation between the responses human beings make to moral issues and the rationales they give for their actions. Global ethics is thus left with a recurrent dilemma: how to turn the asymmetry between the moral sentiments all human beings may potentially be endowed with, and the diverse and often conflicting justifications they provide for acting on them, into an opportunity for dialogue and self-reflection rather than defiance and self-righteousness.

# CHAPTER SIXTEEN

## *New Geographies of Violence and Terror*

It is reasonable to ask why globalization, which is purported to have brought people into closer relations across many of the territories of human experience, should have produced such extreme forms of violence against so many people. It is generally assumed that the neoliberal economic and political policies of the 1990s opened borders, reduced trade restrictions, encouraged entrepreneurship, and paved the way for new forms of international cooperation. But this new capitalism has also privatized finance, weakened job security, crippled the welfare state, and threatened meaningful life narratives and skill sets. Its collateral damage was competition, uncertainty, and, because of rapid advances in technology and automation, the increasing specter of irrelevance and uselessness.

However, there have also been significant changes in the nature of global violence itself. The mass slaughter of two global hot wars and one global cold war led to the collapse of traditional alliances (East vs. West) and traditional enemies (Communists vs. Capitalists) or (Socialists versus Imperialists). The loss of these old coherences and protections forced many people to turn to their own kind for protection, but this was to produce several new kinds of major violence. The first were pathologies in what Arjun Appadurai has referred to as "the sacred ideologies of nationhood." The second was the mega-violence that fuels the new terrorism that has broken out around the world. The first is based on the quest for certainty and is associated with the totalized worldview or cosmology of the nation state. The quest for certainty creates a politics that is either vivisectionist, as in genocide, or purificatory, as in ethnic cleansing. The second of these two forms of violence is based on the quest for religious conformity and is associated with militant jihadism. It sees whole peoples as worthy of destruction not because of who they are but because of what they believe. Each of these forms of violence require two lethal elements. The first is a Manichean division of the world into good and evil, and the second is a set of images to represent that distinction.

The language of terror has thus produced a new geography of anger. This geography is based on uncertainty about the enemy within and anxiety about the enemy without. While that anger can feed on a number of targets from the global markets to international hegemons, it is fueled most frequently by what Appadurai calls "the narcissism of minor differences." The target of this predatory narcissism is the elimination of so-called "others," whether they be minorities or infidels. The goal for both of these forms of terror is a world without enemies or threats, a world, in other words, recreated in the image of oneself.

Terrorism is, of course, by no means a recent phenomenon. As a tactic, it has been used for thousands of years to create fear and panic among populations for the purpose of coercing and intimidating them. The key to its success has always depended on making violence visible, spectacular, and dramatic, and it has been employed as often by states as by non-state actors. From the French Revolution of the eighteenth century, to the colonialist regimes of the nineteenth and twentieth centuries, to the totalitarianisms associated with the Fascists, the Soviets, and the Chinese in the long middle of the twentieth century, and on to the twenty-first century, when the U.S. used what it described as tactics of "shock and awe" to overwhelm Saddam Hussein's forces and bring the Iraqi people to heel, terror has been used by states to pursue their own interests. But to many thoughtful commentators, the megaterrorism of the sort that exploded on 9/11 somehow seemed to change the game. Though it had clear antecedents in the 1993 attack on the World Trade Towers in New York, the Aum Shinrikyo sarin gas subway attack on Tokyo in 1995, the attack on American embassies in Kenya and Tanzania in 1998, and the bombing of the U.S.S Cole in Yemen in 2000, the Al Qaeda assault on the World Trade Towers and the U.S. Pentagon in 2001 sought significant levels of symbolic and substantive harm on a scale more usually identified with state-sponsored attacks. This not only made it difficult to strike back at an enemy that was seemingly invisible; it also encouraged the United States and its allies to declare a "War on Terror" from which they have yet to extricate themselves.

Part of what made this attack so extraordinary is that the whole world was watching in real time and, thanks to the new communications revolution, could continue to watch and re-watch it endlessly. And what made that terror so spectacularly frightening is not simply because of its destructive power and number of casualties but because of its targets. Those targets, horrendous as they were, were not limited to people alone but were rather very self-consciously extended to symbols both of America—its wealth, its military power, and its global leadership—and of the world itself. There were people of nearly 100 nationalities who worked in the Twin Towers and lost their lives that day, and the towers themselves were a symbol of the trade that does in fact interlink the entire world with itself.

But the attackers themselves were more than mere zealots in the service of an extreme cause or ideology; they were also supporting players in a much larger drama that the United States had helped set in motion itself. That drama had its origins in the 1980s when, in response to the Russian invasion of Afghanistan, the United States encouraged the Saudis to create a series of ultra orthodox madrassas or religious schools for the purpose of creating a cadre of religious extremists to fight the Soviets in the Middle East. Those extremists were referred to as mujahideen or holy warriors that the United States then set about training and arming for the sake of resisting Soviet expansionism. But when the American subsequently stationed American forces in Saudi Arabia, the official birthplace and home of Islam, one group of the Mujahideen known as Al Qaeda under the leadership of Osama bin Ladin and others turned against their distant sponsor for violating the sanctity of their religion. Little wonder, then, that the French philosopher, Jacques Derrida, subsequently described the terror attacks on 9/11 as the response of America's own autoimmune syndrome. The United States was in effect assaulted by forces allied with its own military defense system, or rather, to put it in medical terms, by antibodies it created to protect itself which then turned on their host. But Derrida also perceived with great foresight, this time borrowing a metaphor from nanotechnology rather than from medicine, that this autoimmune syndrome might well set off in turn cycles of revenge and reprisals that could become endless. And so they have, with the two wars in Iraq and Afghanistan, the creation of ISIS, the attacks in Europe and elsewhere, the destabilization of the entire Middle East, the discrediting of the United States, and, most tragically, the continuing violence suffered by Muslims almost everywhere.

The degree to which this terrorism was—and remains—fundamentally religious has been pursued by a number of scholars throughout the world, but none more carefully and thoroughly than Mark Juergensmeyer. The author of *Terror in the Mind of God: The Global Rise of Religious Violence*, Juergensmeyer believes that there are a number of radical religious movements around the world that have emerged from cultures of violence—Islamic, Christian, Hindu, Sikh, Jewish, even Buddhist-- that have several things in common. They reject compromises with liberal values and secular institutions, resist the boundaries that secular society has set around religion, and insist on being true, as they understand it, to the origins of their faiths. This has raised the question about whether radical religion has become the cause or the unwilling servant of their militancy. From Jurgensmeyer's perspective, the problem is not with religion itself but rather with the way it can be involved in public life. While the grievances that propel these movements are not themselves religious, religion can become the medium through which they expressed. And this process has become still more prominent because of the failures of secular nationalism that in so many states was supposed to take the place of religion.

Does this make the failures of secular nationalism the real source or cause of the new jihadism? While many experts think it does, Juergensmeyer believes instead that the real cause of contemporary terrorism is associated with the loss of identity and control in the modern world. This problem is caused by a secular social order that marginalizes religious identities, values, and practices, leaving religion to become an ideology of resistance. Religion then provides vehicles of social mobilization and justifications for violence that challenge the state's monopoly on it. It also does so through providing images of cosmic war that simultaneously absolutize the conflict and demonize the enemy. But Juergensmeyer is convinced that religious symbols and rituals can diffuse violence as well as incite it, which paradoxically makes religion for Juergensmeyer as much the solution to violence as the cause of it.

In the second selection in this chapter, Ashis Nandy, one of the leading public intellectuals from the global South, asserts that the new geographies of violence in the contemporary world are generated by the rage of those who feel shortchanged by, and at the same time blocked out of, global systems themselves. What those systems produce is what Nandy calls "regimes of narcissism and despair." These regimes create a kind of free-floating rage looking for targets. They also create "dyadic bonds," as he terms them, that bind both sides in a kind of lethally mutual hatred. This creates a link not so much between terror and religion as more broadly between terror and culture. On the one hand, there are cultural stereotypes defining the social script that thwart the possibility of intercultural understanding, much less of friendship or of considerate behavior toward others. On the other, there is the natural political self-interest of cultures that, whether religious or not, is inherently protective. When these two interests come together, they can produce the view that the use of terror is always justified because it is always, in fact, a form of counter-terror and attempting to fight terror in any other way is absurd. The fear of "other" cultures often breeds panic as well as suspicion, while all rights to different versions of the future are subverted and ridiculed by the globally dominant knowledge systems.

The acuteness of Nandy's analysis is due to the fact that along with Frantz Fanon and several others, he is one of the comparatively few global cultural theorists, much less students of global terror, who takes the psychological dimensions of group behavior seriously. There is a widespread but very debilitating prejudice against psychological analysis in global political thinking which assumes, as Nandy has frequently noted, that looking within ideology for the psychological dimensions of rationalization is somehow weak or soft. Such myopia or shortsightedness that views the psyche as somehow secondary or epiphenomenal to the understanding of global processes not only reduces interpretation to the culture associated with the dominant social system but also overlooks the continuity between victors and victims. It fails to link such violence and oppression to the way of life of the oppressors and thus to humanity as such.

Nandy is courageous enough to ask if the world as such may require some kind of clean sweep to begin over. Do we need new normative systems if the rich and powerful inevitably welcome the collapse of more traditional ones as a pathway to a freer, more permissive, and predictable future? Can we engage with experiences of dispossession and hopelessness to combat ideologies that encourage terrorism and the entrenchment of privilege? What, under such circumstances, does "engage" actually mean? Does it merely involve the acquisition of more knowledge or rather a call for direct action? If a call to action, then what is to be done in the face of the despair that narcissistic regimes always bring to those outside the walls of their own self-regard and self-protection?

# Terror in the Name of God

 MARK JUERGENSMEYER

Perhaps the first question that came to mind on September 11 when the horrific images of the aerial assaults on the World Trade Center and the Pentagon were conveyed around the world was: Why would anyone want to do such a thing? As the twin towers crumbled in clouds of dust and the identities and motives of the perpetrators began to emerge, a second question arose: Why would anyone want to do such a thing in the name of God?

These are the questions that have arisen frequently in the post–cold war world. Religion seems to be connected with violence everywhere—from the World Trade Center bombings to suicide attacks in Israel and the Palestinian Authority; assassinations in India, Israel, Egypt, and Algeria; nerve gas in the Tokyo subways; unending battles in Northern Ireland; abortion-clinic killings in Florida; and the bombing of Oklahoma City's federal building.

What does religion have to do with this virtually global rise of religious violence? In one sense, very little. If the activists involved in the World Trade Center bombing are associated with Osama bin Laden's al Qaeda, they are a small network at the extreme end of a subculture of dissatisfied Muslims who are in turn a small minority within the world of Islam. Osama bin Laden is no more representative of Islam than Timothy McVeigh is of Christianity, or Japan's Shoko Asahara is of Buddhism.

Still, one cannot deny that the ideals and ideas of these vicious activists are permeated with religion. The authority of religion has given bin Laden's cadres what they believe is the moral standing to employ violence in their assault on the very symbol of global economic power. It has also provided the metaphor of cosmic war, an image of spiritual struggle that every religion has within its repository of symbols: the fight between good and bad, truth and evil. In this sense, the attack on the World Trade Center was very religious. It was meant to be catastrophic, an act of biblical proportions.

What is striking about the World Trade Center assault and many other recent acts of religious terrorism is that they have no obvious military goal. These are acts meant for television. They are a kind of perverse performance of power meant to ennoble the perpetrators' views of the world and to draw us into their notions of cosmic war.

The recent attacks in New York City and Washington, D.C.—although unusual in the scale of the assault—are remarkably similar to many other acts of religious terrorism around the world. In my recent comparative study of religious terrorism, *Terror in the Mind of God*, I have found a strikingly

Mark Juergensmeyer is the author of *Terror in the Mind of God: The Global Rise of Religious Violence* (Berkeley: University of California Press, 2000), from which portions of this essay have been adapted. He is a professor of sociology and director of global and international studies at the University of California at Santa Barbara.

familiar pattern. In each case, concepts of cosmic war are accompanied by strong claims of moral justification and an enduring absolutism that transforms worldly struggles into sacred battles. It is not so much that religion has become politicized but that politics has become religionized. Worldly struggles have been lifted onto the high proscenium of sacred battle.

This is what makes religious terrorism so difficult to combat. Its enemies have become satanized: one cannot negotiate with them or easily compromise. The rewards for those who fight for the cause are transtemporal, and the time lines of their struggles are vast. Most social and political struggles look for conclusions within the lifetimes of their participants, but religious struggles can take generations to succeed. When I pointed out to political leaders of the Hamas movement in the Palestinian Authority that Israel's military force was such that a Palestinian military effort could never succeed, I was told that "Palestine was occupied before, for two hundred years." The Hamas official assured me that he and his Palestinian comrades "can wait again—at least that long," for the struggles of God can endure for eons. Ultimately, however, Hamas members "knew" they would succeed.

In such battles, waged in divine time and with heaven's rewards, there is no need to compromise one's goals. No need, also, to contend with society's laws and limitations when one is obeying a higher authority. In spiritualizing violence, religion gives terrorism a remarkable power.

Ironically, the reverse is also true: terrorism can give religion power as well. Although sporadic acts of terrorism do not lead to the establishment of new religious states, they make the political potency of religious ideology impossible to ignore. Terrorism not only gives individuals the illusion of empowerment, it also gives religious organizations and ideas a public attention and importance that they have not enjoyed for many years. In modern America and Europe it has given religion a prominence in public life that it has not held since before the Enlightenment over two centuries ago.

## Empowering Religion

The radical religious movements that have emerged from cultures of violence around the world have three elements in common. First, they reject the compromises with liberal values and secular institutions that most mainstream religion has made, be it Christian, Muslim, Jewish, Hindu, Sikh, or Buddhist. Second, radical religious movements refuse to observe the boundaries that secular society has set around religion—keeping it private rather than allowing it to intrude into public spaces. And third, these radical movements try to create a new form of religiosity that rejects what they regard as weak, modern substitutes for the more vibrant and demanding forms of religion that they imagine to be essential to their religion's origins.

One of the men accused of bombing the World Trade Center in 1993 told me in a prison interview that the critical moment in his religious life came when he realized that he could not compromise his Islamic integrity with the easy vices offered by modern society. The convicted terrorist, Mahmud Abouhalima, claimed that the early part of his life was spent running away from himself. Although involved in radical Egyptian Islamic movements since his college years in Alexandria, he felt there was no place where he could settle down. He told me that the low point came when he was in Germany, trying to live the way that he imagined Europeans and Americans did: a life where the superficial comforts of sex and inebriates masked an internal emptiness and despair. Abouhalima said his return to Islam as the center of his life carried with it a renewed sense of obligation to make Islamic society truly Islamic—to "struggle against oppression and injustice" wherever it existed. What was now constant, Abouhalima said, was his family and his faith. Islam was both a "rock and a pillar of mercy." But it was not the Islam of liberal, modern Muslims—they, he felt, had compromised the tough and disciplined life the faith demanded.

In Abouhalima's case, he wanted his religion to be hard, not soft like the humiliating, mind-numbing comforts of secular modernity. Activists such as Abouhalima—and Osama bin Laden—imagine themselves defenders of ancient faiths. But in fact they have created new forms of religiosity: like many present-day religious leaders they have used the language of traditional religion to build bulwarks around aspects of modernity that have threatened them, and to suggest ways out of the mindless humiliation of modern life. Vital to their image of religion, however, was that it be perceived as ancient.

The need for religion—a "hard" religion as Abouhalima called it—was a response to the soft treachery they had observed in the new societies around them. The modern secular world that Abouhalima and the others inhabited was a chaotic and violent sea for which religion offered an anchor in a harbor of calm. At some deep and almost transcendent level of their consciousnesses, they sensed their lives slipping out of control, and they felt both responsible for the disarray and a victim of it. To be abandoned by religion in such a world would mean a loss of their own individual locations and identities. In fashioning a "traditional religion" of their own making, they exposed their concerns not so much with their religious, ethnic, or national communities, but with their own personal, perilous selves.

## Assaults on Secularism

These intimate concerns have been prompted by the perceived failures of public institutions. As the French sociologist Pierre Bourdieu has observed, social structures never have a disembodied reality; they are always negotiated by individuals in their own strategies for maintaining self-identity and success in life. Such institutions are legitimized by the "symbolic capital" they accrue through the collective trust of many individuals. When that symbolic capital is devalued, when political and religious institutions undergo what German philosopher Jurgen Habermas has called a "crisis of legitimacy," the devaluation of authority is experienced not only as a political problem but as an intensely personal one, as a loss of agency.

This sense of a personal loss of power in the face of chaotic political and religious authorities is common, and I believe critical, to Osama bin Laden's al Qaeda group and most other movements for Christian, Muslim, Jewish, Sikh, Buddhist, and Hindu nationalism around the world. The syndrome begins with the perception that the public world has gone awry, and the suspicion that behind this social confusion lies a great spiritual and moral conflict, a cosmic battle between the forces of order and chaos, good and evil. Such a conflict is understandably violent, a violence that is often felt by the victimized activist as powerlessness, either individually or in association with others of his gender, race, or ethnicity. The government—already delegitimized—

is perceived to be in league with the forces of chaos and evil.

One of the reasons why secular government is easily labeled as the enemy of religion is that to some degree it is. By its nature, the secular state is opposed to the idea that religion should have a role in public life. From the time that modern secular nationalism emerged in the eighteenth century as a product of the European Enlightenment's political values, it did so with a distinctly antireligious, or at least anticlerical, posture. The ideas of John Locke about the origins of a civil community and the "social contract" theories of Jean Jacques Rousseau required very little commitment to religious belief. Although they allowed for a divine order that made the rights of humans possible, their ideas had the effect of taking religion—at least church religion—out of public life. At the time, religious "Enemies of the Enlightenment"—as the historian Darrin McMahon describes them in a new book with this title—protested religion's public demise. But their views were submerged in a wave of approval for a new view of social order in which secular nationalism was thought to be virtually a natural law, universally applicable and morally right.

Post-Enlightenment modernity proclaimed the death of religion. Modernity signaled not only the demise of the church's institutional authority and clerical control, but also the loosening of religion's ideological and intellectual grip on society. Scientific reasoning and the moral claims of the secular social contract replaced theology and the church as the bases for truth and social identity. The result of religion's devaluation has been a "general crisis of religious belief," as Bourdieu has put it.

In countering this disintegration, resurgent religious activists have proclaimed the death of secularism. They have dismissed the efforts of secular culture and its forms of nationalism to replace religion. They have challenged the idea that secular society and the modern nation-state are able to provide the moral fiber that unites national communities or give the ideological strength to sustain states buffeted by ethical, economic, and military failures. Their message has been easy to believe and has been widely received because the failures of the secular state have been so real.

## Antiglobalism

The moral leadership of the secular state was increasingly challenged in the last decade of the twentieth century following the end of the cold war and the rise of a global economy. The cold war provided contesting models of moral politics—communism and democracy—that were replaced with a global market that weakened national sovereignty and was conspicuously devoid of political ideals. The global economy became controlled by transnational businesses accountable to no single governmental authority and with no clear ideological or moral standards of behavior. But while both Christian and Enlightenment values were left behind, transnational commerce transported aspects of Westernized popular culture to the rest of the world. American and European music, videos, and films were beamed across national boundaries, where they threatened to obliterate local and traditional forms of artistic expression.

Added to this social confusion were convulsive shifts in political power that followed the breakup of the Soviet Union and the collapse of Asian economies at the end of the twentieth century. The public sense of insecurity that came in the wake of these cataclysmic global changes was felt not only in the societies of those nations that were economically devastated by them—especially countries in the former Soviet Union—but also in economically stronger industrialized societies. The United States, for example, saw a remarkable degree of disaffection with its political leaders and witnessed the rise of right-wing religious movements that fed on the public's perception of the inherent immorality of government.

Is the rise of religious terrorism related to these global changes? We know that some groups associated with violence in industrialized societies have had an antimodernist political agenda. At the extreme end of this religious rejection in the United States were members of the American anti-abortion group Defensive Action; the Christian militia and Christian Identity movement; and isolated groups such as the Branch Davidian sect in Waco, Texas. Similar attitudes toward secular government emerged in Israel—the religious nationalist ideology of the Kach party was an extreme example—and in Japan with the Aum Shinrikyo movement. Like the United States, contentious groups within these countries were disillusioned about the ability of secular leaders to guide their countries' destinies. They identified government as the enemy.

The global shifts that have given rise to antimodernist movements have also affected less-developed nations. India's Jawaharlal Nehru, Egypt's Gamal Abdel Nasser, and Iran's Riza Shah Pahlavi once were committed to creating versions of America—or a kind of cross between America and the Soviet Union—in their own countries. But new generations of leaders no longer believed in the Westernized visions of Nehru, Nasser, or the Shah. Rather, they were eager to complete the process of decolonization and build new, indigenous nationalisms.

When activists in Algeria who demonstrated against the crackdown against the Islamic Salvation Front in 1991 proclaimed that they were continuing the war of liberation against French colonialism, they had the ideological rather than political reach of European influence in mind. Religious activists such as the Algerian leaders; the Ayatollah Khomeini in Iran; Sheikh Ahmed Yassin in the Palestinian Authority; Maulana Abu al-Ala Mawdudi in Pakistan; Sayyid Qutb and his disciple, Sheik Omar Abdul Rahman, in Egypt; L. K. Advani in India; and Sant Jarnail Singh Bhindranwale in India's Punjab have asserted the legitimacy of a postcolonial national identity based on traditional culture.

The result of this disaffection with the values of the modern West has been what I described in my earlier book, *The New Cold War?*, as a "loss of faith" in the ideological form of that culture, secular nationalism. Although a few years ago it would have been a startling notion, the idea has now become virtually commonplace that secular nationalism—the idea that the nation is rooted in a secular compact rather than religious or ethnic identity—is in crisis. In many parts of the world it is seen as an alien cultural construction, one closely linked with what has been called-the "project of modernity." In such cases, religious alter natives to secular ideologies have had extraordinary appeal.

This uncertainty about what constitutes a valid basis for national identity is a political form of postmodernism. In Iran it has resulted in the rejection of a modern Western political regime and the creation of a successful religious state. Increasingly, even secular scholars in the West have recognized that religious ideologies might offer an alternative to modernity in the political sphere. Yet, what lies beyond modernity is not necessarily a new form of political order, religious or not. In nations formerly under Soviet control, for example, the specter of the future beyond the socialist form of modernity has been one of cultural anarchism.

The al Qaeda network associated with Osama bin Laden takes religious violence to yet another level. The implicit attack on global economic and political systems that are leveled by religious nationalists from Algeria to Indonesia are made explicit: America is the enemy. Moreover, it is a war waged not on a national plane but a transnational one. Their agenda is not for any specific form of religious nation-state but an inchoate vision of a global rule of religious law. Rather than religious nationalists, transnational activists like bin Laden are guerrilla antiglobalists.

## Postmodern Terror

Bin Laden and his vicious acts have a credibility in some quarters of the world because of the uncertainties of this moment of global history. Both violence and religion historically have appeared when authority is in question, since they are both ways of challenging and replacing authority. One gains its power from force, and the other from its claims to ultimate order. The combination of the two in acts of religious terrorism has been a potent assertion indeed.

Regardless of whether the perpetrators consciously intended them to be political acts, all public acts of violence have political consequences. Insofar as they are attempts to reshape the public order, they are examples of what the sociologist Jose Casanova has called the increasing "deprivatization" of religion. In various parts of the world where defenders of religion have attempted to reclaim the center of public attention and authority, religious terrorism is often the violent face of these attempts.

The postmodern religious rebels such as those who rally to the side of Osama bin Laden have therefore been neither anomalies nor anachronisms. From Algeria to Idaho, their small but potent groups of violent activists have represented masses of supporters, and they have exemplified currents of thinking and cultures of commitment that have risen to counter the prevailing modernism—the ideology of individualism and skepticism—that in the past three centuries emerged from the European Enlightenment and spread throughout the world. They have come to hate secular governments with an almost transcendent passion. They have dreamed of revolutionary changes that would establish a godly social order in the rubble of what the citizens of most secular societies have regarded as modern, egalitarian democracies. Their enemies have seemed to most people to be both benign and banal: symbols of prosperity and authority such as the World Trade Center. The logic of this kind of militant religiosity has therefore been difficult for many people to comprehend. Yet its challenge has been profound, for it has contained a fundamental critique of the world's post-Enlightenment secular culture and politics.

Acts of religious terrorism have thus been attempts to purchase public recognition of the legitimacy of religious world views with the currency of violence. Since religious authority can provide a ready-made replacement for secular leadership, it is no surprise that when secular authority has been deemed to be morally insufficient, the challenges to its legitimacy and the attempts to gain support for its rivals have been based in religion. When the proponents of religion have asserted their claims to be the moral force undergirding public order, they sometimes have done so with the kind of power that a confused society can graphically recognize: the force of terror.

# Terror, Counter-Terror, and Self-Destruction: Living with Regimes of Narcissism and Despair

 Ashis Nandy

That we have dreamed of this event, that everybody without exception has dreamt of it, because everybody must dream of the destruction of any power hegemonic to that degree—this is unacceptable for Western moral conscience. And yet, it is a fact. . . .

It is almost they who did it, but we who wanted it. If one does not take that into account, the event loses all symbolic dimensions to become a pure accident, a purely arbitrary act, the murderous fantasy of a few fanatics, who need then to just be suppressed. But we know very well that this is not the way it is. Thus, all those delirious, counter- phobic exorcisms: because evil is there, everywhere as an obscure object of desire. Without this deep complicity, the event would not have had such repercussions.

This goes much further than hatred for the dominant global power from the disinherited and the exploited, those who fell on the wrong side of the world order. That malignant desire is in the very heart of those who share (this order's) benefits.

–Jean Baudrillard

Interpretations of the events of 11 September 2001, and the diverse political and intellectual responses to them, have oscillated between a concern with the wrath of the disinherited and exploited and the elements of self-destruction built into a hegemonic system. Keeping in mind Baudrillard's warning, I shall nonetheless focus here on the rage of those who feel they have been short-changed by the present global system and have no future within it. This feeling has acquired an ominous edge in recent times and developed close links with the self-destructiveness inherent in any global system. The rage often does not have a specific target, though it is always looking for one; and regimes and movements that latch on to that free-floating rage can go far. Indeed, once in a while, their targets too have the same need to search for and find enemies—to reaffirm their raw power and to recapture the evaporating sense of mission in the managerial ethics of a global system. The two sides then establish a dyadic bond that binds them in lethal mutual hatred?

A decade after 11 September 2001, it is pretty obvious that this time there has been a narrowing of cognitive and emotional range all around. The global culture of common sense has concluded that it is no longer a matter of realpolitik and hard-eyed, calculative interest-based use of terror of the kind favoured by the mainstream culture of international relations and diplomacy—as for instance, the repeated attempts the CIA has made over the last six decades to assassinate recalcitrant rulers presumed hostile to the United States—but a terror that defies rationality and abrogates self-interest, a terror that is deeply and identifiably cultural. Global common sense also seems to insist, to judge by the responses to 11 September 2001, that there are only two ways of looking at this link between terror and culture. One way is to emphasise cultural stereotypes and the way they hamper intercultural and interreligious amity. This way presumes that the West with its freedoms—political and sexual—and its lifestyle, identified in popular imagination with consumerism and individualism, has come to look like a form of Satanism to many millennial movements, particularly those flourishing in Islamic cultures. Multiculturalism and intercultural dialogue are seen as natural, if long-term antidotes to such deadly stereotypes. But, in the short run, the emphasis shifts to 'firm' international policing.

The other way is to locate the problem in the worldview and theology of specific cultures. What look like stereotypes, prejudices, or scapegoating in the first approach are seen as expressions of the 'natural' political self of some cultures in the second. At the moment, Islam looks like the prime carrier of a political self that is inclined to use terror to achieve political ends, though some other cultures are not far behind. The American senator who ridiculed those who wore diapers on their heads, did not have in his mind only the Muslims; nor did the American motorist who, when caught while trying to run over a woman clad in sari, declared that he was only doing his patriotic duty after 11 September 2001.

The first way, because it includes multiculturalism and intercultural dialogue, is of course seen as a soft option, the second as harsh. However, in the short run, the first and second options converge and begin to look a more viable basis for public policy and decisive action. The particular reason of political 'realism' is, however, not new. Terror has been an instrument of statecraft, diplomacy, and political advocacy for centuries. To see it as a new entrant in the global marketplace of politics is to shut one's eyes to the human propensity to hitch terror to organized, ideology-led political praxis. Robespierre said-on behalf of all revolutionaries, one presumes-that without terror, virtue was helpless. Terror, he went on to claim, was virtue itself. When it comes to the serious business of international relations, such connections enjoy intrinsic legitimacy in many cultures of public life that today feign shock and dismay when facing terrorism. Despite recent pretensions, in international politics violence does not have to be justified; non-violence has to be. The mainstream global culture of statecraft insists that the true antidote to terror can only be counter-terror.

In this respect, the killers who struck at New York on 11 September 2001 and the regimes that claim absolute moral superiority over them share some common traits. Both believe that when it comes to Satanic others, all terror is justified as long as it is counter-terror or retributive justice. Both believe that they are chosen and, hence, qualified to deliver life and death in the name of righteous causes. And both are posthumous children of the twentieth century—a century that installed the rights to hone technologies of terror and the capacity to inflict unlimited collateral damage at the centre of public life and public policy. Guernica, Hamburg, Dresden, Nanking Tokyo, Hiroshima, and Nagasaki are all formidable names in the contemporary imagination of permissible political and strategic weapons. So are the attempts to hitch terror to virtue and efficient governance in a wide range of situations—from Jalianwallah Bagh to Lidice, from Sharpeville to My Lai, and from Palestine to Kashmir. The culpable states have sometimes been autocratic, sometimes democratic. Liberal democracy has not often been a good antidote for state terror. Few are now surprised that some of the iconic defenders of democracy, such as Winston Churchill, were as committed to terror as Robespierre was. Not only Churchill was a co-discoverer of the concept of area bombing, as opposed to strategic bombing, he and the armies of the two most powerful democracies in the world did not intercede when supplied with evidence, including aerial photographs, of Nazi death camps. Terror and counterterror are normal statecraft, only saying so is not.

Hence also the widespread tendency to dismiss all ideas of fighting terror without using counter-terror as romantic drivel. Hence also the tacit admiration for garrison states like Israel in 'softer' states like Sri Lanka and India and the attempts of such admirers to use Israeli 'expertise', forgetting that Israel has been fighting terror with terror for decades without noteworthy success. All that Israel can really take credit for is that, in a classic instance of identifying with its past oppressors, it has succeeded in turning terrorism into a chronic ailment within its own boundaries, in the process brutalizing its own polity and turning many of its citizens into fanatics and racists.

Against this backdrop has entered a new kind of terrorists during the last few years in Sri Lanka Palestine, India, Pakistan, and now, the United States and Iraq. The suicide bombers have made their presence felt in roughly twenty countries by now. They come prepared to die and, therefore, are automatically immune to the fear of counter-terrorism. They usually view counter-terrorism—and the reactions to it—as useful means of mobilizing and polarizing communities.

This is one form of political activism that the hedonic, self-interest-based culture of the globalized middle class just cannot handle. It looks like an unwanted war declared by the death-defying on the death-denying. The former thrives on a theology of martyrdom, the latter on a psychology of hard, this-worldly individualism and narcissism, which cannot but wonder what kind of a person one is if one does not want to keep any option open for even glimpsing the future one is fighting for or to care about what might happen to one's family, neighbourhood, or community in the backlash? Living in a hedonic, secularized world, unable to fathom why its secular hedonism seems evil to others, the cultural sensitivities of the globalized middle class, never high, has further narrowed in recent times. To the civilized modern citizen, such suicidal activism look like the negation of civilization, utterly irrational and perhaps even psychotic.

In the nervous, heated discussions that used to take place on the kamikaze sixty years ago, the doomed pilots usually appeared like strange, robotic killers and carriers of collective pathologies, driven by feudal loyalties, unable to distinguish life from death or good from evil. There have been attempts in recent years to view the self-sacrifice as an 'irrationality' imposed by ruthless,, scheming officers of the Japanese army. To that extent, the kamikaze pilots now look less like perpetrators and more like victims. However, while there was ruthlessness and the Japanese army did knowingly push more than 3,000 young men to death, one cannot ignore the atmosphere of desperation and despair that allowed such a scheme to be acceptable to a sizeable section of the Japanese people.

Recent discussions of the suicide bombers of Hamas, Tamil Tigers of Sri Lanka, and Al-Qaeda and sundry terrorist groups in Pakistan and Kashmir are linked to similar imageries and fantasies in the mainstream, global awareness. Hence probably the abortive attempts to rename suicide bombings as homicide bombings. The modern world always seems to be at a loss to figure out how to deter someone who is already determined to die. For most of us, such passions have no place in normal life; it can be only grudgingly accommodated in text books of forensic psychiatry as a combination of criminality and insanity. The expression 'homicide bombing', used as a substitute for 'suicide bombing', is an attempt to endorse this reading. The former sounds more decisively evil, stripped of the touch of ambiguous, insane heroism of the latter. Outside the modern world too, few call it self-sacrifice. For unlike the freedom fighters of India and Ireland, who fasted themselves to death during the colonial period as an act of protest and defiance of their rulers, the self-sacrifice of the suicide bombers also involves sacrificing unwilling, innocent others, what we have now learnt to euphemistically call collateral damage.

Yet, the key cultural-psychological feature of today's suicide bombers and suicide squads, despair, is not unknown to the moderns. In some contexts, the idea of despair has become central to our understanding of contemporary subjectivities and we also admit that it has shaped some of the greatest creative endeavours in arts and some of the most ambitious forays in social thought in our times. Van Gogh, Franz Kafka, or Albert Camus cannot be understood without invoking the idea of despair, nor can be Friedrich Nietzsche or Fyodor Dostoevsky. So powerful has been the explanatory power of the idea of despair that recently Harsha Dehejia, an art historian, has tried to introduce the concept in the Indian classical theory of art, by extending Bharata's theory of *rasas* itself. Dehejia feels that without deploying this construct as a part of Indian theories of art, we just cannot explore contemporary Indian art using Indian categories. One suspects that the desperation one sees in the self-destruction of the new breed of terrorists is the obverse of the same sense of despair that underpins so much of contemporary creativity. 'This despair 'expresses itself in strange and alien ways because it comes from defeated cultures that have remained mostly invisible and inaudible:

Out of eighteen names mentioned as members of the suicide squad that struck on 11 September 2001, fifteen were identified as Saudis. They came from a prosperous society where dissent was taboo, where political conformity and silence were extracted through state terror. Arguably, by underwriting the Saudi regime, which presided over Islam's holiest sites and had acquired undeserved reputation in some circles as an exemplary Islamic state, the United States had identified itself as the major source of the sense of desperation in the killers. The violence of 11 September, Johan Galtung and Dietrich Fischer argue, presumes 'a very high level of dehumanization of the victims in the minds of aggressors: That dehumanization did not come in a day nor can it be explained away as unprovoked. Pervez Hoodbhoy identifies another kind of dehumanization that turns the suicide bombers into drones that are only killing machines-you turn yourself into a weapon for a cause and for a leader who himself never sacrifices his own or his family's life though he routinely sends young recruits to death. That total commitment and blind allegiance not merely become passports to instant salvation, but also the meaning of life. While it is tempting to agree with Hoodbhoy, imputing to hundreds of 'crazed demagogues' such immense persuasive powers and ability to seize control of the minds of worshippers also flies in the face of all psychological knowledge.

Thanks to global news media, we are all too aware of the denominational loyalties of the terrorists who attacked the World Trade Centres. They were Wahhabis, given to an aggressively puritanical form of Islamic revivalism. But all Wahhabis do not tum suicide bombers. Who do?

A part-answer to that question, we may find out in the coming years, lies not in the ethnic, religious, or class connections of terrorism but in the fear of cultures that forces us to deny the desperation that has begun to crystallize outside the peripheries of our known world as a new bonding between terror and culture. This desperation may not be preceded by theocide of the, kind Nietzsche talks about, but it may be prompted by a feeling that God may not be dead but has surely gone deaf and blind. Situations like the Palestinian one is only one part of the story.

For the present global political economy has begun to reward all cultivated ignorance of how the unprecedented prosperity and technological optimism in many countries have as their underside utter penury, collapse of life support systems brought about by ecological devastations, threats to cosmologies, and nonspecific hopelessness. . . .

Clash of cultures and civilizations become a possibility not because some cultures suffer from specific psychological stigmata but when, for whatever reason, sizeable sections in a society develop a heightened fear of 'strange' cultures living with other moral universes. This is not a prerogative of the backwaters of the civilized world. Even in societies resonating to slogans like multiculturalism, such slogans often become only a means of tolerance of cultures that are compatible with the dominant pattern of global common sense—cultures that can be safely consumed in the form of ethnic food, arts museumized artefacts, ethnographies or, as is happening in the case of Buddhism and Hinduism, packaged theories of salvation severed from the ways of life associated with these faiths. That is why the tacit solipsism of Islamic terrorism and its ability to hijack some of Islam's most sacred symbols is matched today by the narcissism of the policy élite in some countries wedded to the idea of their manifest destiny.

The confrontation becomes more serious when, for a large majority of the world, all rights to diverse visions of the future—all utopians thinking and all indigenous visions of a good society—are subverted by the globally dominant knowledge systems and a globally accessible media as instances of maudlin nostalgia, other-worldly delusions or brazen revivalism. The Southern world's future now, by definition, is nothing other than an edited version of contemporary North. What Europe and North America are today, the folklore of the globalized middleclass claims, the rest of the world will become tomorrow. Once the visions of the future are this narrowly defined, the resulting vacuum is sometimes filled by pathological forms of millennialism, the primary concern which is to negate, challenge, or subvert the seemingly unbreakable global consensus on values. Some of these pathological forms are perfectly compatible with the various editions of fundamentalism floating around in the global marketplace of ideas today. In the liminal world of the marginalized and the silenced, desperation embraces millennialism at some corner to redefine violence as a necessary means of exorcizing one's inner ghosts. . . .

# CHAPTER SEVENTEEN

## *Cultural Problematics of the New World Order*

Samuel P. Huntington has provided the subject for this chapter, and indeed for a whole chapter in global discussion, since the publication of his book of 1998 entitled *The Clash of Civilizations and the Making of World Order*. Appearing just three years before the terrorist attack on the twin towers of the World Trade Center in New York and the attack on the Pentagon in Washington, D. C., it seemed to provide an explanation for the outbreak of a new kind of violence sponsored not by state actors but by non-state ideologues. The argument of his book, which is summarized in the first selection of this chapter, is premised on the assumption that cultural factors in the post-Cold War era have become even more influential than economic or even political ones. Huntington explains this by arguing that cultural identities are at the broadest level civilizational in scope, and civilizational identities are now shaping the world's major patterns of cohesion, conflict, and disintegration. While nation- states still remain the most important actors in world affairs, their own interests are now mainly shaped by civilizational beliefs and practices, and they, in turn, are essentially grounded in religious traditions and values.

Huntington is not interested in devising a broader map of the religious origins of the world's civilizations; he is rather interested in explaining what those civilizational systems have to do with the world's continuing violence even after the Soviet Union collapsed. His answer is that for the first time in human history, politics had to become multi-polar and multi-civilizational but without producing, or possessing any hope of producing, either a universal civilization or a Westernization of the rest. While a civilizational world order is emerging, it is unlikely to be any more stable than the one that preceded it. The only difference is that the fault-lines of the world's greatest violence seem to be shifting from the borders between states to the boundaries separating civilizational blocks. The only way of explaining this is to ask what made civilizations so inimical to each other, and the answer that Huntington comes up with is that the religions on which the largest civilizational blocks are based—Christianity, Buddhism, Hinduism, Islam, Judaism, Shintoism, Confucianism, and Taosim—are essentially incompatible with one another. This in turn enables him to lay chief responsibility for global violence in the twentieth, and now twenty-first, century at the door of religious ideologies that have produced the clash of civilizations which defines our new world order.

So convincing was Huntington's argument about the inevitable clash of civilizations globally that he then decided in a later book to apply this thesis to America itself. In *Who are We?: The Challenges to America's National Identity*, Huntington argues that the chief threat to America comes not alone from Muslims bringing their militancy to the American mainland or, somewhat earlier, from European deconstructionism bringing its cultural relativism from the Continent, but now, primarily, from Latinos bringing their alien way of life and thought to America's Anglo-Protestant culture. Normally I would not introduce the discussion of another book by an author selected for inclusion here if in Huntington's case subsequent study was not so pertinent to understanding the power and problems with his clash of civilization thesis. Though I must admit to reservations I have with Huntington's argument in *Who Are We?*, I believe that its discussion is warranted here because it brilliantly captures, in what I regard as its misrepresentations and distortions, the "global" view that many Americans now possess of their culture.

In Huntington's estimation, Anglo-Protestant culture was originally based on a unitary set of core values that America's earliest founding settlers carried with them to the New World and eventually used in the eighteenth and nineteenth centuries to establish what the Swedish economist and sociologist Gunnar Myrdal was the first to call the "American Creed." This creed was based on "principles of liberty, equality, individualism, representative government, and private property." Central to those values were the Christian religion, Protestant morality, the work ethic, the English language, and a series of British traditions "of law, justice, and the limits of government power," along with a European legacy of art and thought. Derived from England's early modern "Tudor Constitution," the religio-cultural and political components embodied in the American Creed thereafter enabled America to be a cohesive society, chiefly because of widespread agreement on the ranking of its values. But that social cohesion, and the identity on which it is based, has now become imperiled, Huntington believes, and the dangers come from several directions. While the chief danger originates from south of the border, it has been augmented by the arrival of the intellectual method and style known as deconstruction from the Continent and, more recently, by militant jihad from the Middle East.

One can obtain some sense of the cast of Huntington's argument from what he says about postmodern European and now American deconstruction. Constantly blurring the lines between its function as an intellectual strategy and method and its effects as, presently, a cultural, even a period, style associated with late modernism or postmodernism, Huntington claims that deconstruction is chiefly responsible for legitimating the multicultural move to redefine America as many people created out of one rather than one people created out of many. Insisting that America was originally composed of many races, ethnicities, and sub-national cultures that eventually became one people sharing common convictions, he believes that the recent deconstruction of America, not the arrival of deconstruction in America, has licensed the development of a host of minority identities that have eroded the idea of American citizenship itself. By the same logic, he argues that all forms of cosmopolitanism risk "merging America," in the language of one of his chapter titles, "with the world." Denationalized elites in business, the media, and the academy are referred to in this book as "dead souls"; diasporan identities of Americans are viewed as inescapably weakening the national sense of self; and the blurring and fading of race produced by intermarriage constitutes a genuine threat to the ethnicity of white Americans.

Such prejudices are no doubt widely shared by many American whites, but one is compelled to ask what such prejudices actually mean in a society where, according to Huntington's own statistics, 75% of African Americans have white ancestors, 22% of American whites are in fact non-white, and marrying out now ranges from 12% for African Americans to as high as 51 to 55% for Asian Americans, at least between the ages of 25 and 34? Huntington's abundance of numbers provide impressive evidence of the increasing diversification of the American population, which is much greater, in fact, than most of its citizens are prepared to acknowledge, even as he maintains, often with little or no substantiation, that this blurring of race and ethnicity is actually eroding the sense of American nationhood.

However, what Huntington most fears is not the intermixing of peoples in America, much as this may dilute the sense of whiteness, but rather their bifurcation, meaning their less than complete integration into the cultural mythos; and here Latino resistance to assimilation represents what he clearly perceives as the gravest internal peril to American identity. Even if the American Creed does not by itself constitute the nation, the integrity of the nation, he insists, has been placed in jeopardy by policies and practices that permit Hispanics as well as other people from identifying wholly with the nation.

This internal danger is now exacerbated, Huntington believes, by the external threat posed by a resurgent, hostile Islam, a threat which consequently leaves Christian America with only three options: either cosmopolitanism, imperialism, or nationalism. In the first, America is reshaped by the world, despite the fact that it possesses strong cosmopolitan traditions of its own (as Huntington seems to forget) deriving from those same Enlightenment beliefs and ideals that he assumes to be essential cornerstones of the American Creed. In the second, the world is supposedly reshaped by America itself, even though, as Huntington acknowledges, the world contains other powers and superpowers whose cooperation America requires to fulfill its global ambitions. In the third, America needs to play its nationalist card because this is the only alternative that prevents it from being swallowed up either by the universalism implicit in cosmopolitanism or by the illusory sense of strength implicit in any unilateral imperialism—and, at the same time, it justifies America's exceptionalism in terms of its historic religiosity.

Huntington's views would not deserve this much attention if they were not so widely shared by a significant number of Americans. While he acknowledges that American Protestantism is, or at least was, a dissenting tradition, he treats it in its current evangelical form as almost exclusively an instrument of moral and theological consensus. Never acknowledging that elements of the American Creed have often been in conflict with one another, he in addition ignores the evidence that ideological consensus about the meaning of America has only been very imperfectly realized in American history except in times of war. He also makes the mistake of restricting support of multiculturalism chiefly to white elites, as though minority populations could not, or have not, often at great cost, spoken for themselves and been emphatic that as U.S. citizens what they want is mainly the right, wholly consistent with democratic principles, to participate with others in determining the

American future. Huntington's belief that white ethnicity, which he wants to preserve, is somehow more American than other kinds of identity sounds merely like *nativism redivivus*. Still more troubling, Huntington frequently gives a spin to the statistical information he has gathered that leads to the stereotyping of 40 million Americans of Hispanic descent who clearly do not all think, much less believe, alike but are, in various ways, seeking to join, to be sure in their own ways, what can only be called the American mainstream.

The second selection in this chapter by the Nobel Prize-winning economist and ethicist, Amartya Sen, challenges Huntington from another direction. Sen wants to consider further the appeals of Huntington's civilizational approach before turning to a discussion of its liabilities and denials. It's appeals include its utilization of the richness of history, which gives political analysis a new gravity and depth; its reflection of common beliefs about different peoples and cultures that are simplistic and uninformed; its misleading claims that global violence rarely occurs within and across civilizations as well as between them; and its resort again to an essentially bi-polar model of the world as now divided not between East and West but rather between a single Western world and a non-Western many.

But the liabilities of Huntington's civilizational approach are also numerous, Sen insists. Not only does it assume that civilizations are fundamentally different but almost inevitably clash; it also assumes that within themselves civilizations are generally unified and coherent as a result of their religious basis and that therefore human beings can never belong to, or share genuine sympathies with, more than one civilization at a time. What such assumptions typically overlook or discount, according to Sen, is that human diversity is almost universal and human identity partially a matter of choice. Moreover, they seem blind to the fact that global identities often cut across one another, and not least because the borders between civilizations, like those between cultures, are so often unstable and porous. Finally, and for Sen most important, the clash thesis recurrently and almost unavoidably plays to the habit of "othering," which further contributes to, and deepens, the serious confrontations and divides that the clash thesis insists are essentially simply civilizational.

As the final selection in this chapter, the essay by Giles Gunn seeks to challenge the ways cultural and other differences are absolutized by clash of civilizations proponents like Samuel P. Huntington. Building on the insights of globalists like Amartya Sen, his aim is to defend the importance of the kind of cosmopolitanism that Huntington disparages and many others in the world discount by exploring three interrelated questions: what is meant by a global world how is it different from what is meant by an international one; what does culture have to do with defining the world as global and why is culture so powerful and potentially volatile a force; and what makes cross- and inter-cultural understanding—what is meant by cosmopolitanism--so crucial to undertake but so difficult to achieve? Gunn's answer depends on reconceiving cosmopolitanism as more of a practice or perspective than an ideology or set of beliefs, one that is distinguished by the ability from time to time to put ourselves in the place of others even if we can never see or feel exactly as they do. What we can do, however, is to learn how we would feel and think if that place were ours instead and this may help us overcome the temptation to believe that our perspective on things is the only one. If such gestures do no more than broaden and deepen our sense of the geography of what counts as human, it may also encourage us to try to become more fully accountable to it, to become what in a global world might be called "other-wise."

# The New Era in World Politics

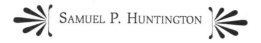 Samuel P. Huntington

## Introduction: Flags and Cultural Identity

On January 3, 1992 a meeting of Russian and American scholars took place in the auditorium of a government building in Moscow. Two weeks earlier the Soviet Union had ceased to exist and the Russian Federation had become an independent country. As a result, the statue of Lenin which previously graced the stage of the auditorium had disappeared and instead the flag of the Russian Federation was now displayed on the front wall. The only problem, one American observed, was that the flag had been hung upside down. After this was pointed out to the Russian hosts, they quickly and quietly corrected the error during the first intermission.

The years after the Cold War witnessed the beginnings of dramatic changes in peoples' identities and the symbols of those identities. Global politics began to be reconfigured along cultural lines. Upside-down flags were a sign of the transition, but more and more the flags are flying high and true, and Russians and other peoples are mobilizing and marching behind these and other symbols of their new cultural identities.

On April 18, 1994 two thousand people rallied in Sarajevo waving the flags of Saudi Arabia and Turkey. By flying those banners, instead of U.N., NATO, or American flags, these Sarajevans identified themselves with their fellow Muslims and told the world who were their real and not-so-real friends.

On October 16, 1994 in Los Angeles 70,000 people marched beneath "a sea of Mexican flags" protesting Proposition 187, a referendum measure which would deny many state benefits to illegal immigrants and their children. Why are they "walking down the street with a Mexican flag and demanding that this country give them a free education?" observers asked. "They should be waving the American flag." Two weeks later more protestors did march down the street carrying an American flag—upside down. These flag displays ensured victory for Proposition 187, which was approved by 59 percent of California voters.

In the post–Cold War world flags count and so do other symbols of cultural identity, including crosses, crescents, and even head coverings, because culture counts, and cultural identity is what is most meaningful to most people. People are discovering new but often old identities and marching under new but often old flags which lead to wars with new but often old enemies.

One grim *Weltanschauung* for this new era was well expressed by the Venetian nationalist demagogue in Michael Dibdin's novel, Dead Lagoon: "There can be no true friends without true enemies. Unless we hate what we are not, we cannot love what we are. These are the old truths we are painfully rediscovering after a century and more of sentimental cant. Those who deny them deny their family, their heritage, their culture, their birthright, their very selves! They will not lightly be forgiven." The unfortunate truth in these old truths cannot be ignored by statesmen and scholars. For peoples seeking identity and reinventing ethnicity, enemies are essential, and the potentially most dangerous enmities occur across the fault lines between the world's major civilizations.

The central theme of this book is that culture and cultural identities, which at the broadest level are civilization identities, are shaping the patterns of cohesion, disintegration, and conflict in the post–Cold War world. The five parts of this book elaborate corollaries to this main proposition.

*Part I:* For the first time in history global politics is both multipolar and multicivilizational, modernization is distinct from Westernization and is producing neither a universal civilization in any meaningful sense nor the Westernization of non-Western societies.

*Part II:* The balance of power among civilizations is shifting: the West is declining in relative influence; Asian civilizations are expanding their economic, military, and political strength; Islam is exploding demographically with destabilizing consequences for Muslim countries and their neighbors; and non-Western civilizations generally are reaffirming the value of their own cultures.

*Part III:* A civilization-based world order is emerging: societies sharing cultural affinities cooperate with each other; efforts to shift societies from one civilization to another are unsuccessful; and countries group themselves around the lead or core states of their civilization.

*Part IV:* The West's universalist pretensions increasingly bring it into conflict with other civilizations, most seriously with Islam and China; at the local level fault line wars, largely between Muslims and non-Muslims, generate "kin-country rallying," the threat of broader escalation, and hence efforts by core states to halt these wars.

*Part V:* The survival of the West depends on Americans reaffirming their Western identity and Westerners accepting their civilization as unique not universal and uniting to renew and preserve it against challenges from non-Western societies. Avoidance of a global war of civilizations depends on world leaders accepting and cooperating to maintain the multicivilizational character of global politics.

## A Multipolar, Multicivilizational World

In the post–Cold War world, for the first time in history, global politics has become multipolar and multicivilizational. During most of human existence, contacts between civilizations were intermittent or nonexistent. Then, with the beginning of the modem era, about A.D. 1500, global politics assumed two dimensions. For over four hundred years, the nation states of the West—Britain, France, Spain, Austria, Prussia, Germany, the United States, and others—constituted a multipolar international system within Western civilization and interacted, competed, and fought wars with each other. At the same time, Western nations also expanded, conquered, colonized, or decisively influenced every other civilization. During the Cold War global politics became bipolar and the world was divided into three parts. A group of mostly wealthy and democratic-societies, led by the United States, was engaged in a pervasive ideological, political, economic, and, at times, military competition with a group of somewhat poorer communist societies associated with and led by the Soviet Union. Much of this conflict occurred in the Third World outside these two camps, composed of countries which often were poor, lacked political stability, were recently independent, and claimed to be nonaligned.

In the late 1980s the communist world collapsed, and the Cold War international system became history. In the post–Cold War world, the most important distinctions among peoples are not ideological, political, or economic. They are cultural: Peoples and nations are attempting to answer the most basic question humans can face: Who are we? And they are answering that question in the traditional way human beings have answered it, by reference to the things that mean most to them. People define themselves in terms of ancestry, religion, language, history, values, customs, and institutions. They identify with cultural groups: tribes, ethnic groups, religious communities, nations, and, at the broadest level, civilizations. People use politics not just to advance their interests but also to define their identity. We know who we are only when we know who we are not and often only when we know whom we are against.

Nation states remain the principal actors in world affairs. Their behavior is shaped as in the past by the pursuit of power and wealth, but it is also shaped by cultural preferences, commonalities, and differences. The most important groupings of states are no longer the three blocs of the Cold War but rather the world's seven or eight major civilizations. Non-Western societies, particularly in East Asia, are developing their economic wealth and creating the basis for enhanced military power and political influence. As their power and self-confidence increase, non-Western societies increasingly assert their own cultural values and reject those "imposed" on them by the West. The "international system of the twenty-first century," Henry Kissinger has noted, ". . . will contain at least six major powers—the United States, Europe, China, Japan, Russia, and probably India—as well as a multiplicity of medium-sized and smaller countries."[1] Kissinger's six major powers belong to five very different civilizations, and in addition there are important Islamic states whose strategic locations, large populations, and/or oil resources make them influential in world affairs. In this new world, local politics is the politics of ethnicity; global politics is the politics of civilizations. The rivalry of the superpowers is replaced by the clash of civilizations.

In this new world the most pervasive, important, and dangerous conflicts will not be between social classes, rich and poor, or other economically defined groups, but between peoples belonging to different cultural entities. Tribal wars and ethnic conflicts will occur within civilizations. Violence between states and groups from different civilizations. however, carries with it the potential for escalation as other states and groups from these civilizations rally to the support of their "kin countries."[2] The bloody clash of clans in Somalia poses no threat of broader conflict. The bloody clash of tribes in Rwanda has consequences for Uganda, Zaire, and Burundi but not much further. The bloody clashes of civilizations in Bosnia, the Caucasus, Central Asia, or Kashmir could become bigger wars. In the Yugoslav conflicts, Russia provided diplomatic support to the Serbs, and Saudi Arabia, Turkey, Iran, and Libya provided funds and arms to the Bosnians, not for reasons of ideology or power politics or economic interest but because of cultural kinship. "Cultural conflicts," Vaclav

Havel has observed, "are increasing and are more dangerous today than at any time in history," and Jacques Delors agreed that "future conflicts will be sparked by cultural factors rather than economics or ideology."[3] And the most dangerous cultural conflicts are those along the fault lines between civilizations.

In the post–Cold War world, culture is both a divisive and a unifying force. People separated by ideology but united by culture come together, as the two Germanys did and as the two Koreas and the several Chinas are beginning to. Societies united by ideology or historical circumstance but divided by civilization either come apart, as did the Soviet Union, Yugoslavia, and Bosnia, or are subjected to intense strain, as is the case with Ukraine, Nigeria, Sudan, India, Sri Lanka, and many others. Countries with cultural affinities cooperate economically and politically. International organizations based on states with cultural commonality, such as the European Union, are far more successful than those that attempt to transcend cultures. For forty-five years the Iron Curtain was the central dividing line in Europe. That line has moved several hundred miles east. It is now the line separating the peoples of Western Christianity, on the one hand, from Muslim and Orthodox peoples on the other.

The philosophical assumptions, underlying values, social relations, customs, and overall outlooks on life differ significantly among civilizations. The revitalization of religion throughout much of the world is reinforcing these cultural differences. Cultures can change, and the nature of their impact on politics and economics can vary from one period to another. Yet the major differences in political and economic development among civilizations are clearly rooted in their different cultures. East Asian economic success has its source in East Asian culture, as do the difficulties East Asian societies have had in achieving stable democratic political systems. Islamic culture explains in large part the failure of democracy to emerge in much of the Muslim world. Developments in the postcommunist societies of Eastern Europe and the former Soviet Union are shaped by their civilizational identities. Those with Western Christian heritages are making progress toward economic development and democratic politics; the prospects for economic and political development in the Orthodox countries are uncertain; the prospects in the Muslim republics are bleak.

The West is and will remain for years to come the most powerful civilization. Yet its power relative to that of other civilizations is declining. As the West attempts to assert its values and to protect its interests, non-Western societies confront a choice. Some attempt to emulate the West and to join or to "bandwagon" with the West. Other Confucian and Islamic societies attempt to expand their own economic and military power to resist and to "balance" against the West. A central axis of post–Cold War world politics is thus the interaction of Western power and culture with the power and culture of non-Western civilizations.

In sum, the post–Cold War world is a world of seven or eight major civilizations. Cultural commonalities and differences shape the interests, antagonisms, and associations of states. The most important countries in the world come overwhelmingly from different civilizations. The local conflicts most likely to escalate into broader wars are those between groups and states from different civilizations. The predominant patterns of political and economic development differ from civilization to civilization. The key issues on the international agenda involve differences among civilizations. Power is shifting from the long predominant West to non-Western civilizations. Global politics has become multipolar and multicivilizational.

# Endnotes

1. Henry A. Kissinger, *Diplomacy* (New York: Simon & Schuster, 1994), pp. 23–24.
2. H. D. S. Greenway's phrase, *Boston Globe*, 3 December 1992, p. 19.
3. Vaclav Havel, "The New Measure of Man," New York Times, 8 July 1994, p. A27; Jacques Delors, "Questions Concerning European Security," Address, International Institute for Strategic Studies, Brussels, 10 September 1993, p. 2.

# Civilizational Imprisonments:
# How to Misunderstand Everybody in the World

 Amartya Sen

## I.

Conflict between civilizations has been a popular topic for a long time—well before the dreadful events of September 11 ushered in a period of open confrontation and pervasive distrust in the world. Yet these terrible happenings have had the effect of magnifying the ongoing interest in the so-called "clash of civilizations," of which the classic statement can be found in Samuel Huntington's famous and ambitiously impressive book *The Clash of Civilizations and the Remaking of World Order,* which appeared five years before the World Trade Center was targeted. Indeed, many leading commentators have tended to see a firm connection between global conflicts and civilizational confrontations—most notably, between "Western" and "Islamic" civilizations. The intellectual basis of that thesis and related ideas requires a close examination, both for its obvious epistemic interest and—more immediately—for its far-reaching relevance to practical politics in the contemporary world. The need for that critical scrutiny is now greater than it has ever been.

The thesis of a civilizational clash can be ideologically linked with a more general idea that provides the methodological foundation of the "clash thesis." This concerns the program of categorizing people of the world according to some single—and allegedly commanding—system of classification. To see any person wholly, or even primarily, as a member of a so-called civilization (in Huntington's categorization, as a member of "the Western world," "the Islamic world," "the Hindu world," or "the Buddhist world") is already to reduce people into this one dimension. The deficiency of the clash thesis, I would argue, begins well before we get to the point of asking whether the disparate civilizations (among which the population of the world is forcefully partitioned out) must necessarily—or even typically—clash. No matter what answer we give to this question, by even pursuing the question in this restrictive form we implicitly give credibility to the allegedly unique importance of one categorization over all the other ways in which people of the world may be classified.

Opponents of the "clash theory" can actually contribute to its intellectual foundation if they accept the same singular classification of the world population. The same impoverished vision of the world—divided into boxes of civilizations—is shared by those who preach amity among discrete and disjunctive civilizations and those who see them as clashing. In disputing the obtuse and gross generalization that members of the Islamic civilization have an essentially belligerent culture, for example, it is common enough to argue that they actually share a culture of peace. But this simply replaces one stereotype with another; and it involves accepting an implicit presumption that people who happen to be Muslim by religion would be much the same in other ways as well.

Aside from all the difficulties in defining civilizational categories as disparate units (on which more presently), the arguments on both sides suffer from a shared faith in the presumption that seeing people exclusively, or primarily, in terms of religion-based civilizations to which they are assumed to belong is a good way of understanding human beings. Civili-zational partitioning is a pervasively intrusive phenomenon in social analysis (stifling other ways of seeing people) even without its being supplemented by the incendiary belief in the particular thesis of a civilizational clash.

If "the clash of civilizations" is the grand thesis about the divisions of the contemporary world, there are lesser but still influential claims that relate contrasts of cultures and identities to the conflicts—and the profusion of atrocities—that we see in different parts of the world today. Instead of one majestically momentous partition, as in Huntington's world, that splits the world's population into contending civilizations, the lesser variants of the approach view local populations as being respectively split into clashing groups, with divergent cultures and disparate histories that tend, in an almost "natural" way, to breed enmity toward each other. Conflicts involving Hutus and Tutis in Rwanda, and Serbs and Albanians in the former Yugoslavia, and Hindus and Muslims in the subcontinent, and so on, are then re-interpreted in lofty historical terms, reading into them much more than contemporary politics. Modern conflicts that call for analysis in terms of contemporary events and machinations are then interpreted as ancient feuds—real or imagined—that place today's players in pre-ordained roles in an allegedly ancestral play. The "civilizational" approach to contemporary conflicts (in grander or lesser versions) serves as a major obstacle to focusing more fully on the actual prevailing politics and the dynamics of contemporary events.

It is not hard to understand why the civilizational approach is so appealing to so many people. It invokes the richness of history, and it seems to call upon the depth and the gravity of cultural analysis, seeking profundity of understanding in a way that an immediate political analysis of the "here and now" would seem to lack. If I am disputing the civilizational approach, it is not because I do not see its attractions and intellectual temptations. Indeed, I am reminded of an event nearly fifty years ago, shortly after I first arrived in England from India as a student at Cambridge. A kindly fellow student took me to see the recently released film Rear Window, in which I encountered James Stewart looking at some very suspicious events in the house opposite his own. Like the James Stewart character, I too, in my naïve way, became convinced that a gruesome murder had been committed in the apartment across the courtyard; but my intellectual friend went on explaining to me (amid whispered requests from neighbors urging him to shut up) that he was quite certain that there was no murder at all, no basis in reality for James Stewart's (and my own) suspicion, and that the whole film was really an indictment of McCarthyism in America, which encouraged everyone to watch the activities of other people with great suspicion. "This film is a critique," my friend informed the novice from the Third World, "of the growing Western culture of snooping." Such a film, I had to agree, would have been in many ways a much more penetrating and solemn work, but I kept wondering whether it was, in fact, the film that we were watching. What must be similarly asked is whether what we are watching in the world in which we live is actually a clash of civilizations, or something much more mundane that merely looks like a civilizational clash to determined seekers of profundity.

The depth that civilizational analysis seeks is not exclusive, though, to the high road of intellectual analysis. In some ways, civilizational analysis mirrors and magnifies common beliefs that flourish in not particularly intellectual circles. The invoking of, say, "Western" values against "non-Western" values is rather commonplace in public discussions, and it makes regular headlines in tabloids as well as figuring in political rhetoric and anti-immigrant oratory (from the United States and Canada to Germany, France, and the Netherlands). In the aftermath of September 11, the stereotyping of Muslims came often enough from people who are no great specialists in civilizational categories (to say the least). But theories of civilizational clash have often provided allegedly dispassionate and sophisticated foundations for coarse popular beliefs. Complicated theory can sometimes bolster uncomplicated bigotry and can make the world a much more flammable place than it needs to be.

# II.

What, then, are the difficulties of civilizational analysis? I shall begin by discussing a little more the problem that I claimed was its most basic weakness: the presumption that a person can be regarded preeminently not as an individual with many affiliations, nor as a member of many different groups, but as a member merely of one particular group, which gives her a uniquely important identity. The implicit belief in the over-arching power of a singular classification is not only gross, it is also grossly confrontational in form and in implication. Such a divisive view goes not only against the old-fashioned belief (which tends to be ridiculed these days as much too soft-headed) that "we are all basically just human beings," but also against the important understanding that we are *diversely* different. Indeed, I would argue that the main hope of harmony in the contemporary world lies in the plurality of our identities, which cut across each other and work against sharp divisions around one single hardened line of impenetrable identity. Our shared humanity gets savagely challenged when the confrontation is unified into a solitary—and allegedly dominant—system of classification; this is much more divisive than the universe of plural and diverse categorizations that shape the world in which we actually live.

The realization that we each have multiple identities may sound like a much grander idea than it is. Indeed, it is a very elementary recognition. In our normal lives, we see ourselves as members of a variety of group's: we belong to all of them. The same person can be an American citizen of Malaysian origin with Chinese racial characteristics, a Christian, a libertarian, a political activist, a woman, a poet, a vegetarian, an asthmatic, a historian, a schoolteacher, a bird-watcher, a baseball fan, a lover of jazz, a heterosexual, a supporter of gay and lesbian rights, and a person deeply committed to the view that creatures from outer space regularly visit Earth in colorful vehicles and sing tantalizing songs. Each of these collectivities, to all of which this individual belongs, gives her a particular identity, which—depending on the context—can be quite important; but none of them has a unique and pre-ordained role in defining this person.

The relative importance of the different groups to which any person belongs can vary, depending on the context and the person's priorities. Being a teetotaler, for example, can be a more important identity when one is invited to a wine-tasting party than the same person's identity as, say, a poet or an American or a Protestant. It need not cause any problem for action choice, either, especially when the demands associated with different identities do not, in fact, conflict. In many contexts, however, the different components of one's identity may well compete in one's decision regarding what to do. One may have to choose the relative importance to attach to one's activism as a citizen over one's love of baseball if a citizens' meeting clashes with a promising game. One has to decide how to deal with alternative claims on one's attention and loyalties that compete with one another.

Identity, then, cannot be only a matter of "discovery" (as communitarian philosophers often claim); it is a matter of choice as well. It is possible that the often-repeated belief that identity is a matter of "discovery" is encouraged by the fact that the choices we can make are constrained by feasibility, and sometimes the constraints are very exacting. The feasibilities will certainly depend on particular circumstances. The constraints maybe especially strict in defining the extent to which we can persuade others to take us to be different from what they take us to be. A Jewish person in Nazi Germany could not easily choose a different identity from the one with which others marked him or her. The freedom in choosing the importance to attach to our different identities is always constrained, and in some cases very sharply so.

This point is not in dispute. The fact that we always choose within particular constraints is a standard feature of every choice. As any theorist of choice knows, choices of all kinds are always made within particular feasibility restrictions. As students of elementary economics all have to learn, the theory of consumer choice does not deny the existence of a budget that restrains the consumer's purchasing ability. The presence of the budget constraint does not imply that there is no choice to be made, but only that the choice has to be made within that constraint. What is true in elementary economics is also true in complex political and social decisions. While the Jewish person in Nazi Germany may have had difficulty in paying attention to her other identities, there are many other contexts that give more room for effective choice, in which the competing claims of other affiliations (varying from nationality, language, and literature to profession and political belief) will demand serious attention and require a reflective resolution.

There is also the ethical issue regarding the status of identity-based claims of any kind vis-à-vis arguments that do not turn on any identity whatsoever. Our duty to other human beings may not necessarily be linked only to the fact that we share a common human identity, but rather to our sense of concern for them irrespective of any sharing of identity. Moreover, the reach of our concern may apply to other species as well, despite the lack of a shared human identity and the non-invoking of any other identity that would try to translate a general ethical argument into a specialized identity-centered morality. (I have discussed these distinctions in these pages in "Other People," December 18, 2000.)

While religious categories have received much airing in recent years, they cannot be presumed to obliterate other distinctions and other concerns, and even less be taken to be the only relevant system of classifying people across the globe. It is the plurality of our identities, and our right to choose how we see ourselves (with what emphases and what priorities), that the civilizational classifications tend to overlook, in a largely implicit—rather than transparent—way.

The civilizational classifications have often closely followed religious divisions. Huntington contrasts "Western civilization" with "Islamic civilization," "Hindu civilization," "Buddhist civilization," and so on; and while hybrid categories are accommodated (such as "Sinic civilization" or "Japanese civilization"), the alleged battle-fronts of religious differences are incorporated into a carpentered vision of one dominant and hardened divisiveness. By categorizing all people into those belonging to "the Islamic world," "the Christian world," "the Hindu world," "the Buddhist world," and so on, the divisive power of classificatory priority is implicitly used to place people firmly inside a unique set of rigid boxes. Other divisions (say, between the rich and the poor, between members of different classes and occupations, between people of different politics, between distinct nationalities and residential locations, between language groups, and so on) are all submerged by this allegedly preeminent way of seeing the differences between people.

The belief in a unique categorization is both a serious descriptive mistake and an ethical and political hazard. People do see themselves in very many different ways. A Bangladeshi Muslim is not only a Muslim but also a Bengali and a Bangladeshi, possibly quite proud of Bengali literature. The separation of Bangladesh from Pakistan was driven not by religion, but by language, literature, and politics. A Nepalese Hindu is not only a Hindu, but also has political and ethnic characteristics that have their own relevance, and that allow Nepal to be, unlike India, an officially Hindu state (indeed, the only one in the world). Poverty, too, can be a great source of solidarity across other boundaries. The kind of division highlighted by the so-called "anti-globalization" protesters (one of the most globalized movements in the world) tries to unite the underdogs of the world economy, cutting across religious or national or civilizational lines of division. The multiplicity of categories works against rigid separation and its ignitable implications.

# III.

Aside from being morally and politically destructive, the epistemic content of the classification according to so-called civilizations is highly dubious. It could not but be so, since in focusing on one exclusive way of dividing the people of the world, the approach has to cut many corners. In describing India as a "Hindu civilization," for example, Huntington's exposition of the alleged "clash of civilizations" has to downplay the fact that India has more Muslims than any other country in the world, with the exception of Indonesia and marginally Pakistan. India may or may not be placed within the arbitrary definition of "the Muslim world," but it is still the case that India (with its 125 million Muslims—more than the entire populations of Britain and France put together) has a great many more Muslims than nearly every country in the so-called "Muslim world."

It is impossible to think of "Indian civilization" without taking note of the major role of Muslims in the history of India Indeed, it is futile to try to have an understanding of the nature and the range of Indian art, literature, music, or food without seeing the extensive interactions that were not deterred by barriers of religious communities. And Muslims are not, of course, the only non-Hindu group that helps to constitute India. The Sikhs are a major presence, as are the Jains. Not only is India the country of origin of Buddhism, but Buddhism was the dominant religion of India for more than a millennium. Atheistic schools of thought—the Charvaka and the Lokayata—have also flourished in the country from at least the sixth century B.C.E. to the present day. There have been Christian communities in India from the fourth century C.E.—two hundred years before there were Christian communities in Britain. Jews came to India shortly after the fall of Jerusalem; Parsees started coming in the eighth century.

Given all this, Huntington's description of India as a "Hindu civilization" is an epistemic and historical absurdity. It is also politically combustible. It tends to add a superficial and highly deceptive credibility to the extraordinary neglect of history—and of present realities—that some Hindu fundamentalists have tried to champion, most recently in an exceptionally barbaric way in Gujarat. Even though these political groups seem to be trying their best to overturn Indian secularism, the secular constitution of India as well as the large majority of Indians who are committed to secularism would make it hard to achieve this. The fact that the poison of sectarian violence so far has not spread beyond the limits of one state—Gujarat, with a ruling government that is at best grossly incompetent but most likely a great deal worse—is perhaps ground for some cautious optimism about the future of India. But the human costs of violent extremism have been truly monumental.

The portrayal of India as a Hindu civilization may be a simple-minded mistake, but crudity of one kind or another is present in the characterizations of other civilizations as well. Consider what is called "Western civilization." Indeed, the champions of "the clash of civilizations," in line with their belief in the profundity of this singular line of division, tend to see tolerance as a special and perennial feature of Western civilization, extending way back into history. Huntington insists that the "West was West long before it was modern," and cites (among other allegedly special features such as "social pluralism") "a sense of individualism and a tradition of individual rights and liberties unique among civilized societies." This, too, is at best a gross oversimplification.

Tolerance and liberty are certainly among the important achievements of modern Europe (leaving out aberrations such as Nazi Germany or the intolerant governance of British or French or Portuguese empires in Asia and Africa). But to see a unique line of historical division there— going back over the millennia—is quite fanciful. The championing of political liberty and religious tolerance, in its full contemporary form, is not an old historical feature in any country or any civilization in the world. Plato and Aquinas were not less authoritarian in their thinking than was Confucius. This is not to deny that there were champions of tolerance in classical European thought, but if this is taken to give credit to the whole Western world (from the ancient Greeks to the Ostrogoths and the Visigoths), there are similar examples in other cultures.

The Indian emperor Ashoka's dedicated championing of religious and other kinds of tolerance in the third century B.C.E. (arguing that "the sects of other people all deserve reverence for one reason or another") is certainly among the earliest political defenses of tolerance anywhere. The recent Bollywood movie *Ashoka* (made, as it happens, by a Muslim director) may or may not be accurate in all its details, but it rightly emphasizes the importance of secularism in Ashoka's thinking two and a half millennia ago and indicates its continuing relevance in contemporary India. While a later Indian emperor, Akbar, the Great Mughal, was making similar pronouncements on religious tolerance in Agra at the end of the sixteenth century ("No one should be interfered with on account of religion, and anyone is to be allowed to go over to a religion that pleases him"), the Inquisitions were active in Europe and Giordano Bruno was being burned in the Campo dei Fiori in Rome.

Similarly, what is often called "Western science" draws on a world heritage. There is a chain of intellectual relations that links Western mathematics and science to a collection of distinctly non-Western practitioners. Even today, when a modern mathematician at, say, Princeton invokes an "algorithm" to solve a difficult computational problem, she helps to commemorate the contributions of the ninth-century Arab mathematician Al-Khwarizmi, from whose name the term "algorithm" is derived. (The term "algebra" comes from his book *Al-Jabr wa-al-Muqabilah*.) The decimal system, which evolved in India in the early centuries of the first millennium, arrived in Europe at the end of that millennium, transmitted by the Arabs. A large group of contributors from different non-Western societies—Chinese, Arab, Iranian, Indian, and others—influenced the science, the mathematics, and the philosophy that played a major part in the European Renaissance and, later, in the European Enlightenment.

In his *Critical and Miscellaneous Essays*, Thomas Carlyle claimed that "the three great elements of modern civilization" are "Gunpowder, Printing, and the Protestant Religion." While the Chinese cannot be held responsible for Protestantism, their contribution to Carlyle's list of civilizational ingredients is not insignificant, though it is less total than it is in the case of Francis Bacon's earlier list, in *Novum Organum*, of "printing, gunpowder, and the magnet." The West must get full credit for the remarkable achievements that occurred in Europe during the Renaissance, the Enlightenment, and the Industrial Revolution, but the idea of an immaculate Western conception would require a genuinely miraculous devotion to parochialism.

Not only is the flowering of global science and technology not an exclusively West-led phenomenon, there were major global advances in the world that took the form of international encounters far away from Europe. Consider printing, which features in Carlyle's list, and which Bacon put among the developments that "have changed the whole face and state of things throughout the world." The technology of printing was a great Chinese achievement, but the use to which the Chinese put this new method was not confined merely to local or parochial pursuits. Indeed, the first printed book was a Sanskrit treatise in Buddhist philosophy, *Vajracchedika-prajnaparamita Sutra* (sometimes referred to as the "Diamond Sutra"), translated into Chinese from Sanskrit in the early fifth century and printed four centuries later in 868 C.E. The translator of the Diamond Sutra, Kumarajiva, was half Indian and half Turkish. He lived in a part of eastern Turkistan called Kucha, traveled extensively in India, and later moved to China, where he headed the newly established institute of foreign languages in Xi'an in the early fifth century. The West figured not at all in the first stirring of what came to be a mainstay of Western civilization.

## IV.

The narrowness of the civilizational mode of thinking has many far-reaching effects. It fuels alienation among people from different parts of the world, and it encourages a distanced and possibly confrontational view of others. Even the resistance to so-called "Westernization" by non-Western activists frequently takes the form of shunning "Western" (or what some Western spokesmen have claimed to be exclusively "Western") objects, even though they are among the historical products of diverse global interactions.

Indeed, in a West-dominated world, many non-Western people tend to think of themselves quintessentially as "the other," in contra-distinction to the West. (This phenomenon has been beautifully analyzed by Akeel Bilgrami in an essay called "What Is a Muslim?" in *Identities*, edited by Kwame Anthony Appiah and Henry Louis Gates Jr.) The political force of this phenomenon makes the effects of Western expropriation of a global heritage even more disastrous. It plays a regressive role in the self-identification of the colonial and postcolonial world, and in parts of the "anti-globalization" movement. It takes a heavy toll by inciting parochial tendencies and needless confrontations; it tends to undermine the possibility of objectivity in science and knowledge; and it deflects attention from the real issues to be faced in contemporary globalization (including the ways and means of reducing massive inequality of opportunities without losing the technological and economic rewards of global interaction).

To focus just on the grand religious classification, in its civilizational garb, is not only to miss many significant concerns and ideas that can move people. Such a focus also has the effect of lessening the importance of other priorities by artificially magnifying the voice of religious authority. The clerics are then treated as the *ex officio* spokesmen for the so-called "Islamic world," even though a great many Muslims have profound differences with what is proposed by one mullah or another. The same would apply to other religious leaders' being seen as the spokespeople for their "flocks." The singular classification not only makes one distinction among many into a uniquely inflexible barrier, it also gives a commanding voice to the "establishment" figures in the respective religious and sectarian hierarchy, while other voices are muffled.

A person's religious or civilizational identity may well be very important for her, but it is one membership among many. The question we have to ask is not, say, whether Islam (or Hinduism or Christianity) is a peace-loving religion or a combative one, but how a religious Muslim (or Hindu or Christian) may combine his or her religious beliefs or practices with other commitments and values, with other features of personal identity. To see one's religious—or civilizational—affiliation as an all-engulfing identity would be a deeply problematic diagnosis. There have been fierce warriors as well as great champions of peace among devoted members of each religion; and rather than asking which one is the "true believer" and which one a "mere imposter," we should accept that our religious faith does not in itself resolve all the decisions that we must make in our lives, including those concerning our political and social priorities and the corresponding issues of conduct and action. Both the proponents of peace and tolerance and the patrons of war and intolerance can belong to the same religion (and may be, in their own ways, true believers) without this being seen as a contradiction. The domain of one's religious identity does not vanquish all other aspects of one's understanding and affiliation.

The increasing use of a religion-based singular civilizational classification also makes the Western response to global terrorism and conflict oddly counterproductive. Respect for other civilizations is shown by praising the religious books of "other people," rather than by taking note of the many-sided involvements and achievements of different peoples in a globally interactive world. As Britain goes down the slippery slope of intensifying faith-based schools (Islamic and Sikh schools are already established, and Hindu ones may come soon), the focus is on what divides people rather than what unites them. The cultivation of analytical and critical reasoning, which Western chauvinists usurp as being quintessentially Western, has to take a back seat to religious education, in which the children of new immigrants are expected to find their "own culture." The sad effect of narrowing the intellectual horizon of young children is further compounded by the gross confusion of civilization with religion.

There is no historical reason, for example, why the championing of the Arab or Muslim heritage has to concentrate only on religion and not also on science and mathematics, to which Arab and Muslim scholars have contributed so much in the past. But crude civilizational classifications have tended to put the latter in the basket of "Western science," leaving other civilizations to mine their pride only in religious depths. The non-Western activists, then, focus on those issues that divide them from the West (religious beliefs, local customs, and cultural specificities) rather than on those things that reflect global interactions (science, mathematics, literature, and so on). The dialectics of the "negation of negation" then extracts a heavy price in fomenting more confrontations in the world.

Moreover, the chosen method of giving each "community" its "own culture" makes the respective religious and theological authorities much more powerful in the schooling of immigrants to Britain, when they are sent to the "faith-based" schools. Religion-based divisions are intensified not only by the efforts of anti-Western religious fundamentalists, but also by the West's own arrangements related to seeing "other people" simply in terms of religion, ignoring the many-sided civilizations from which the immigrants come.

## V.

The reliance on civilizational partitioning fails badly, then, for a number of distinct reasons. First, the classifications are often based on an extraordinary epistemic crudeness and an extreme historical innocence. The diversity of traditions *within* distinct civilizations is effectively ignored, and major global interactions in science, technology, mathematics, and literature over millennia are made to disappear so as to construct a parochial view of the uniqueness of Western civilization.

Second, there is a basic methodological problem involved in the implicit presumption that a civilizational partitioning is the uniquely relevant distinction, and must swamp other ways of identifying people. It is bad enough that those who foment global confrontations or local sectarian violence try to impose a pre-chosen unitary and divisive identity on people who are to be recruited as the "foot soldiers" of political brutality, but that task gets indirectly yet significantly aided by the implicit support that the warriors get from theories of singular categorization of the people of the world.

Third, there is a remarkable neglect of the role of choice and reasoning in decisions regarding what importance to attach to the membership of any particular group, or to any particular identity (among many others). By adopting a unique and allegedly predominant way of categorizing people, civilizational partitioning can materially contribute to the conflicts in the world. To deny choice when it does exist is not only an epistemic failure (a misunderstanding of what the world is like); it is also an ethical delinquency and a political dereliction of responsibility. There is a critical need to recognize the plurality of our identities, and also to acknowledge the fact that, as responsible human beings, we have to choose (rather than inertly "discover") what priorities to give to our diverse associations and affiliations. In contrast, the theorists of inescapable "clashes" try to deny strenuously—or to ignore implicitly—the multiplicity of classifications that compete with each other, and the related need for us all to take decisional responsibilities about our priorities. People are seen as belonging to rigid prisons of allegedly decisive identities.

In a well-known interview, Peter Sellers once remarked: "There used to be a 'me,' but I had it surgically removed." In their respective attempts to impose a single and unique identity on us, the surgical removal of the actual "me" is done by others—the religious fundamentalist, the nationalist extremist, the Western chauvinist, the sectarian provocateur. We have to resist such an imprisonment. We must insist upon the liberty to see ourselves as we would choose to see ourselves, deciding on the relative importance that we would like to attach to our membership in the different groups to which we belong. The central issue, in sum, is freedom. To make our identity into a prison is not social wisdom. It is intellectual surrender.

# Cosmopolitanism in an Era of Globalized Absolutisms

 Giles Gunn

What is the utility of a cosmopolitan perspective in a globalized world? This is a world many of whose most serious challenges arise not just from geopolitical, social, and economic disputes between and across nation-states but also from intercultural and cross-cultural misunderstandings and conflicts going on around and within them. By "cosmopolitan" most people mean "worldly," "universalist," "tolerant," or "civilized," but there are in fact almost as many versions of cosmopolitanism as there are brands of dry cereal. Cosmopolitanism not only comes in various kinds—political, social, economic, cultural—but also in various forms—"vernacular," "situated," "realistic," "patriotic," "Eurocentric," "emancipatory," "transgressive," "minoritarian," "subaltern," "partial," "thick," and "thin."

Some associate cosmopolitanism with the Stoic affirmation of a moral community of humankind where each person is a citizen and every citizen owes a duty to every other. Others identify it with the universal human community to which Immanuel Kant first referred in which all members have a right to represent themselves through the free and uncoerced use of their reason by virtue of their common possession of the earth's surface. Still others associate cosmopolitanism with specific values, such as the recognition of human dignity or the right to human freedom, or believe that it can be expressed in specific policies that deal with everything from governance, security, and the regulation of the economy to the protection of the environment. Yet still others refer to cosmopolitanism as a process going on all around us beyond the container of national spaces that is creating new forms of global risk—nuclear proliferation, carbon emissions, health pandemics, income disparities, food shortages, water crises, failing states, digital degradation—or new victims of global displacement—migrants, refugees, exiles, the jobless, the homeless.

A far cry from what is sometimes ridiculed as the class consciousness of world travelers, cosmopolitanism seems in all such cases to refer to the fact that the boundaries of peoples' lives throughout the world are being re-thematized by global processes that have not only expanded the horizons of their own world but altered their consciousness of its meanings. As a consequence, people rendered vulnerable by these processes have grown increasingly desperate for certainty—or at least for a greater measure of clarity and reassurance—in a world now become strange and frightening, tempting them to seek refuge in almost any doctrine or creed that offers itself as an antidote to the new pathologies of cultural conflict and chaos that surround them. But convictions, as Frederick Nietzsche fatefully warned, can sometimes pose a greater threat to truth than lies. As fear and frustration have expanded into more bellicose convictions and creeds, they have threatened to drown much thinking about the world and its various challenges in a sea of fixed ideas.

There is no doubt that religions and sectarianisms of all kinds have played their part in heightening the recourse to extreme, inflexible, often authoritarian, thinking worldwide, but

Gunn, Giles. *Ideas to Live For: Toward a Global Ethics.* pp 190-198, 201-208. © 2015 by the Rector and Visitors of the University of Virginia. Reprinted by permission of the University of Virginia Press.

its expansion has had as much to do with the decoupling of religion and culture as with their recoupling. The new relationship between ideas and the public world is being reshaped by the process known as deterritorialization, which enables religious and other ideas to circulate in what might be called non-bounded spaces that are dissociated from specific locations or grievances and disconnected from any particular societal or cultural articulation of their meaning. Floating free of any particular interpretive frame of reference, these ideas in effect spread outside or beyond the circuits of inherited knowledge. Hence the communities and crises that once shaped their formation and determined their applications now have less and less relation to their expression or authority. Their efficacy and power derive rather from their ability to operate almost as free floating signifiers that can be attached to any cause or concern, representing themselves as universalist, totalizing remedies to a world turned incomprehensible and hostile because of everything from the collapse of former cultural coherencies, increasing social, economic, and political inequalities, vast demographic movements, accelerated technological change, the normalization of heightened violence and terror, irreversible man-made damage to the ecosphere, and the increasing "narcissism of minor differences." Faced with such disturbing and divisive prospects, absolutisms of almost any kind—right, center, or left; reactionary, traditional, or revolutionary; political, economic, social, or religious—offer both the illusion of sanctuary and security and of retribution and possible revenge.

The proliferation and resilience of this absolutist mentality prompts one to ask again, then, whether any chances remain for the survival of a view of human beings such as cosmopolitanism projects, one where human beings are potentially capable together, even across immense gulfs of difference, misunderstanding, grievance, and injury, of world-making and extending rather than world-rendering and disordering, of what Jacques Derrida called *mondialization*. I am convinced that such a possibility exists but that its realization depends on reversing our usual way of putting this question. The challenge isn't to bring others around to this way of thinking but to cultivate the ability to understand what inhibits it. And this requires learning how to think not as and how others think but how and as we might think if, as of course we cannot fully, we could put ourselves in what is possible to understand about their place. The point is that we know, and can know, a good deal more about people we define as "other," "strange," "different," or "odd, or "alien" than is assumed either by many of our postmodern epistemologies or by our own lethargy or indifference. But real task is not to figure out simply what such knowledge amounts to but what can be learned from it, and this depends far less on making others in their strangeness more like us, or even making ourselves in our strangeness more like them, than on using those contrasting strangenesses as an opportunity to confront and possibly revise our own.

To pursue this further, I propose to take up three interrelated sets of questions. First, what do we mean by a global world, and what differentiates it from an international one? Second, what does culture have to do with it, and why is culture so potent and potentially explosive a force? And, third, what makes understanding across and between cultures—what I have called "the cosmopolitan challenge"—so difficult to achieve but so crucial to undertake? If we can find an acceptable answer to these three questions, I believe that we will move much closer to addressing the issue with which I began: how an outlook or disposition as seemingly "soft" as cosmopolitanism can survive in a global world whose lines of relation and difference are increasingly being hardened by the politics of dogmatism and extremism?

# Global

The term "global" refers to the increasingly interconnected world around us that is not simply local, regional, national, or even transnational or civilizational, but interactive, and on numerous levels of experience simultaneously. This is the world we think we've known ever since we laid our hands on a cell phone, a world many of whose parts, at least whose virtual parts, we can access, thanks to YouTube, Facebook, Twitter, Flickr, Instagram, LinkdIn, CafeMom, and all the hundreds of thousands of other apps that are available to us, with what appears almost to be the speed of light.

But access is not the same thing as understanding. The technological wizardry that has brought the people of the world into closer proximity with one another, into what represents itself, at least in the palm of one's hand, like a "global village" has also increased still more drastically the problems of how to make sense of that world, and what, more importantly, to make of each other. It's one thing to discover that time and space can be miraculously compressed with a few simple keystrokes on one's iphone or android, that "Siri" can answer any number of one's ultimately least important questions. It's quite another to realize that we are now living in a world where our future may be dependent on, and possibly even be determined by, people, problems, and perplexities of whom, or of which, we have little or no knowledge, a world whose widening and deepening and speeding up has left us frequently feeling far behind. While we should not forget that there are still vigorous disputes with very large consequences about just when globalization began, or how it is best conceptualized, or what makes it function, or whether it has or has not been good for the world and its citizens, the one thing most people do accept is that globalization refers as much to a set of interactive processes that affect everything from energy crises and surveillance regimes to social relations and subjective frames of mind as it does to the systematic properties and interplay of relations among individual nation-states.

To some this may appear to be a contradiction of sorts. What could be more interconnected than the international world of nation-states whose founding goes back, at least in the West, to the Peace of Westphalia in 1648, and whose spread slowly knit the world into a world order that continues in large part to govern, or at any rate to control, international affairs? The answer is to be found in the fact that the articulations of the state system were never themselves simply state-driven. They were instead the result of numerous other developments in everything from economics, industrialization, transportation, communications, and armaments to nationalism and civil society that were by no means exclusively political even when they served state purposes. And what these developments have subsequently revealed, and continue to demonstrate, is that what has occurred above and below nation states, as well as beyond them, has become every bit as consequential for world order as what as gone on because of them.

# Culture

But this, then, raises a second question about what culture has to do with such developments and why it is so volatile and unpredictable to begin with. While many people may think of culture as the frosting on the cake of life, or as a kind of "Super Reality" (religion, ideology, or law) which provides the recipe for that cake, or as the brute patterns of collective behavior that, to continue the metaphor, constitute the ingredients of that cake, or as the "Hearts and Minds" one needs to share in order to, as it were, to enjoy that cake, we would be better advised to think of culture, in the language of the contemporary moment, both as a kind of operating system and as an assemblage of software programs to make it work. To be sure, neither the operating system, which is composed of networks of meanings inherited from the past or available in the present, nor the software programs, which are comprised of interpretive technologies for employing them, come built in, or, as we say, "bundled." Instead, they have to be learned with the help of older systems and technologies that our societies have already made available to us. Furthermore, these newer operating systems and technologies, just like their older forbears but now at much higher velocities, are always changing and being revised or--as our computer, notepad, or cell phone periodically tell us—in need of "updating." And though it is also true (and has always been true) that for a variety of reasons some of us are better than others at using such tools, or at least at using them in specific settings--business, finance, sports, politics, mathematics, interior design, cooking--none of us can escape our dependence on many of them to negotiate our way through life. They furnish us with the instrumentalities by which we, like others, make sense of the cultural signs, symbols, gestures, scripts, representations, rituals, and practices through which we express ourselves and interact with others.

But what makes these cultural instrumentalities so unstable and inflammable, so sensitive and potentially combustible? Among the many reasons that could be advanced, two seem to stand out. The first has to do with the way these instrumentalities provision and empower us, both personally and collectively, by enabling us to acquire over time a sense of ourselves as actors who eventually come to possess what is called an "identity." But the more this "identity" assists us in functioning effectually, or at least half-way coherently and consistently, in a world of others, the more we are likely to protect and defend it against all threats, whether real or imagined. Culture thus functions as no mere ornament of behavior but rather as its precondition and the source of its power. What it supplies us with are at once the terms and the means to articulate and enact ourselves in a world of competing forms of self-assertion and force.

The second reason culture is combustible has to do with the fact that the cultural universe operates much more like a marketplace than a museum. Composed, as it is, of meanings defined in part by their import or significance—meanings, in other words, that possess value and can, in that sense, can be thought of as a kind of currency or "asset" which can be bartered and traded—the cultural universe functions as much as a medium of exchange as a repository of wealth. And if its resources constitute a form of "capital" that can be accumulated, sold, or lost, then people can—and no doubt will—struggle over the resources that cultures represent, whether those resources can literally be purchased for money or merely swapped for the power they lend to those who control their meanings. Either way, such struggles can frequently lead to "culture wars" fought over nothing more than "symbolic capital."

Such wars over essentially symbolic as opposed to material or territorial treasure have occurred throughout the entirety of human history, but their virulence often seems to intensify in direct proportion to the degree that the terms in dispute are not merely material or empirical but also metaphorical, figurative, tropological. What is being contested is the valuation of things that are no less real or actual for being defined by images, perceptions, and feelings. But this in turn has transformed, as it is now referred to, the realm of the imaginary into one of the central factors in the formation not only of human identity but also of human history.

To some this claim might sound like a category mistake. How can culture, now viewed as a kind of imaginary universe composed of meanings that assist human beings in negotiating the region between, say, the unavoidable, the potential, and the possible be so determinative of the construction and reconstruction of the global world itself? How, indeed, can forms of expression so often associated with narratives, dreams, paintings, poems, myths, monuments, ceremonies, ritual, and spectacle, with entertainment, fantasy, transport, and escape, have so profoundly helped determine over time the kinds of lives that people have sought to live both with, and for, themselves and also with, or at the expense of, others?

The answer to these questions can be found in the nature of the social, political and economic formations all around us. For example, we now think of nations, which are based on collective senses of identity, as opposed to states, which are based on specific forms of governance, not simply as large bodies of people inhabiting a particular territory or country and united by anything from language, descent, history, or tradition not only as political communities but also as "imagined" ones because the definitive markers of their existence possess only the most minimal correspondence with social and legal fact. Just as their members remain for the most part invisible and thus unknown to one another except statistically, so the boundaries that delimit them and the senses of sovereignty that define them are impossible to represent except through abstractions, and the convictions of solidarity that bind them are based on little more than feelings of horizontal comradeship. Still more dramatically, the Cold War now appears to us in retrospect as a conflict that was conducted not only between opposing world powers but also by differing imaginations and mindsets which were themselves the result of exaggerated intelligence reports, bad guesses, and fictitious aspirations. Still the same could be said of the second Iraq War which the U.S. fought as much in behalf of mythic constructs, delusionary ideals, and outright lies as of policy goals based on accurate intelligence and historical intelligence. But perhaps nothing better reveals the ubiquity of the presence of the imaginary in modern life than the role played in the global economic collapse of 2008 by fictitious financial instruments like securities, derivatives, credit default swaps, hedge funds, short sales, and leverage.

In each of these examples, the logics of the cultural imaginary determine the way that other logics of life—in this case, the geopolitical logics of national identity, the ideological and military logics of superpower rivalry, and the economic and financial logics of the global market—can be read or interpreted. This is not to say that the logics of culture always displace other logics of, say, national identity, international affairs, or commerce, but rather to suggest how cultural logics so often influence, if not determine, the way those other logics can construed and employed.

# Cross-cultural Understanding

This bring us to the third question of what to make of the differences that define a globalized world and how to bridge them, or, at any rate, how to turn them to constructive uses. For many people in the world, such differences, at least the Big Differences, are not bridgeable at all, either because their own values and traditions are held to be pure and inviolate—a common assumption among fundamentalists of one kind or another—or because all civilizational norms are assumed to be incompatible or incommensurable—the presumption of the "clash of civilization" proponents. Such claims are often supported by the notion that cultures, like civilizations, are anchored in religions whose boundaries are defined chiefly by their principal orthodoxies.

But this is to confuse the beliefs of their adherents with the behavior of such systems. Religions have always been heterodox both because of being constructed out of the components of other religions and spiritual practices and also because of being bordered by alternative and competing forms of more archaic, tribal, clannish, pagan, vernacular, and parodistic faiths. Except in their "official" versions of themselves, religions are much more fluid and porous than the clashers concede and much more diverse and hybrid than the fundamentalists admit. What gives the lie to both these prejudices about religious and other cultural formations is that most people belong to more than one civilizational or cultural complex at a time; that most such complexes are constructed out of materials from other complexes both like and unlike their own; that all such complexes are undergoing rapid re-description and repositioning; and that the relations and tensions between and among them operate at all sorts of oblique angles and frequently combine in unpredictable ways.

Yet complexity in a self, or society, or culture is one thing, especially if it is experienced as the result of a series of developments that in retrospect feel consistent and possibly inevitable; change that threatens the loss of sense of self is quite another. It is comparatively easy for the first to be read by a self, or society, or culture as an expression of its own building out and self-actualization. It is difficult, on the other hand, for the second to be read by a self, society, or culture as anything other than a diminishment of its own power and self-worth, and this diminishment can easily produce anger and resentment.

Hence the potentially symbiotic relationship between the prospect of serious change to one's constituted sense of identity and feelings of aggression. And if those feelings are widely shared, they can be quickly socialized and politicized into collective forms of violence where the community is preserved by realigning itself around the repudiation of a common enemy or victim. Such victim or enemy is often found through the psychological practice of scapegoating where we project onto others things we fear or loath in ourselves. Scapegoating turns the appeal to group loyalty into the need for group sacrifice, and here the scapegoat provides the perfect instrument not merely for compensating for such loss, or the threat of it, but also for containing it. But this may underestimate the therapeutics of scapegoating, which are not simply vivisectionist—amputating the diseased member or limb—but also purgative—santizing the remaining body. Hence the ritual technology of scapegoating can do more than protect the community from the threat of further pollution and injury; it can also cleanse and purify it, thereby making ritual sacrifice, even perpetual violence, in the extreme case unending war, the key both to social survival and to spiritual redemption.

Part of the challenge for cross-cultural understanding, then, is how to reduce, if not divert, this potential for violence, a task which can only be accomplished by reminding ourselves that notions of "self" and "other," like "identity" and "difference," are not given with nature but constructed by culture. Far from representing ontological categories, "self" and "other" are symbolic classifications that are frequently constructed as opposites or at least as contraries. But as oppositions or contraries, such categories frequently reveal at least as much about those who construct them as about those they construct. As conceptual creations rather than ontological givens, they mirror back to those who employ them hidden, or at least unrecognized, aspects of themselves. Hence the moral challenge presented by this knowledge is not only to figure out how it might transform our view others but also how it might alter our understanding of ourselves. We are like one another precisely to the extent we are both partial strangers to ourselves. We differ from one another depending on our ability to acknowledge this sense of fundamental kinship with one another.

Such recognitions of kinship across immense divides of every other kind of difference would not be possible if we were not such inter-subjective creatures. Selves, like societies and cultures, develop at all only because of their ability to see in part from the perspective of others. But seeing from the perspective of others, whether of cultures or of selves, is not the same thing as seeing as—or what—others see. Rather, it is a matter of imagining what might be seen if—as, of course, we cannot—we could put ourselves in, so to speak, their place. But putting ourselves in their place, insofar as that "place" can be reconstructed through observation, study, and empathy, is not the same thing as putting ourselves in their skin or seeing with their eyes, much less of adopting their beliefs or sharing their feelings. It is instead a way of determining what we would see if that place were now ours, if, in other words, we could place the essential coordinates of their experience on the map of ours. Though this moral cartography can be extraordinarily difficult to produce because of the infinite variety of inequities it must encompass, it is by no means an empty or futile exercise. Such cosmopolitan gestures are the only means by which to broaden and deepen the geography of what counts as human, much less learn what it might mean to try to become more fully accountable to it. Cosmopolitanism does not presume to legislate what forms that accountability must always take—recognition, generosity, justice, mercy, unconditional hospitality, love—but merely what such accountability entails. It entails being other-wise even at the expense of one's inward ease.

# CHAPTER EIGHTEEN

# Climate Change and Planetary Peril

In Chapters 15 and 17, we have discussed issues of consequence associated with global norms and cosmopolitan ideals, respectively, but what if the horizons for this kind of normative reflection were suddenly to narrow or darken irreversibly? Indeed, what if the conceptual scaffolding that supports them—and thus helps us differentiate between the known, the probable, the possible, the impossible, the unknown, and the unknowable—were suddenly to weaken or collapse? These are far from idle questions, and this is not the first time in recent history that we have been forced to contemplate them. The most unforgettable occasion in modern memory is associated with the Arms Race of the Cold War era, when the world was faced with the possibility of nuclear war and the endless winter that would follow its devastations. Whether the threat of nuclear annihilation has receded, if only perhaps from public consciousness, it has in any case been followed since 9/11 by the prospect of terrorism unchecked, which has sowed panic in the wake of its destructions because of its capacity to spread, as it were, rhizomatically, just as underground bamboo shoots burst through the surface at seemingly random and unpredictable locations.

Neither of these risks to global security is likely to be reduced for a number of decades, and both contain the power to shrink irretrievably the horizon of normative thinking worldwide. But there is yet another hazard stalking the world and its peoples whose operations may be less spectacular but whose catastrophic results in the long run are even more assured. This is the threat posed by carbon emissions and their associations with climate change which will, within a much shorter timeframe than was originally projected as late as 2013, have catastrophic impacts on everything from weather patterns, ocean levels, food production, water supply, energy, health, and institutions to urban populations, coastal cities and regions, and island nations across the globe. New scientific data reveals that because of the much more rapid melting of the Arctic, Antarctic, and Greenland ice sheets, due to ocean water warmed by increased acidity levels, the tipping point for increasing ocean levels may have already been reached and could add as much as another three to seven or more feet to previous estimates for the present century.

At this point, such forecasts may still seem too remote or unimaginable for many people in the world to take seriously, but it is no accident that every nation in the world but the United States has signed the Paris Agreement on Climate Change, and long before such projected scenarios actually play themselves out and become the norm, it could feel to many of the world's people like they were experiencing something on the order of a new Copernican revolution that has shattered their expectations about the permanence, not to say the survival, of life itself. Remove global confidence in the viability of the whole human, if not planetary, project, and long before such still-inconceivable events transpire, the environment for normative thinking could change far more drastically than it ever has since the arrival of modernity itself. Such prospects, especially when coupled with the continuing global danger of nuclear events and clashing ideologies, have already begun to place immense pressure on many of the more familiar terms in which we currently do our normative thinking—national sovereignty, rule of law, international community, civilizational values, religious traditions, and human rights. Since none of these terms have produced a credible global framework for normative reflection that is at once free of the exclusions of cultural bias or capable of grappling with this order of the unimaginable, our best hope for the furtherance of ethical reflection worldwide may lie in the direction of a new "cosmopolitanism to come" that can help cultures and the people within them begin, however tentatively but persistently, to see one another as potential allies rather than adversaries in the quest for the better life to be led. Absent this possibility, and the return to more militant religious, ideological, and ethical universalisms worldwide is likely to accelerate exponentially.

In the first selection in this chapter, geographer, biologist, ecologist, and anthropologist Jared Diamond connects the problems associated with the rise in carbon emissions and climate change to other environmental problems that societies have faced in the past and the present. He groups these harmful problems into several sets. The first set includes various problems that were already apparent in the past, involving the loss or destruction of natural resources, such as natural habitats, food sources, biological diversity, and soil, and other problems that have appeared more recently, such as energy, the photosynthetic ceiling, and atmospheric changes. The second set is defined by problems that human beings have either created, like toxic chemicals and atmospheric gases, or transferred from one domain, where they were native, to another domain, where like smallpox, or the AIDs virus, or numerous plant pathogens, they are alien and become lethal. Still a third set of problems is composed of those associated with population growth and its uneven impacts and unsustainability. As evidence of the latter, Diamond offers a painful reminder that while people in the Third World, by which he principally means the global South, yearn to attain the living standards of the First, by which he means the global North, there is no way that this can occur without overstressing an infinite number of global resources.

The question this raises is whether there are any grounds for hope that the world can avoid being overwhelmed by these problems. Diamond's answer is that there are if we remember that most of these problems are ones that human beings have generated and thus that human beings can decide to prevent. And most of them are not dependent on the creation of new technologies but instead on the creation of a new political will. If the history of past societies is any guide, there are two kinds of choices that will determine the difference between failure and success. The first choice involves a willingness to undertake long-term planning to address these problems. The second choice, still more difficult but also still more critical, is a normative one and requires that we develop the courage to make painful choices among core values. This will be easier, Diamond is confident, if we are prepared to seize the opportunity that past or distant societies never possessed, which is to learn from the mistakes that other societies made in behalf of creating a better future for our own.

If, on the other hand, we do not—if, say, the nations of the West won't take Jared Diamond's set of warnings with enough seriousness—then we might face the prospect in the second selection of this chapter that historian of science Naomi Oreskes and historian of science and technology Erik M. Conway explore in their book alarmingly entitled *The Collapse of Western Civilization*. This, to be sure, is work of fiction, science fiction to be precise, and their technique is to write a story set roughly 75 years in the future when a historian looks back to consider what led to the demise of the West. That demise could most probably have been avoided if the citizens of the West, descendants all of the European Enlightenment, had responded to the evidence they had been given about the existence of climate change and the events that would ensue if nothing were done to resist them. To avoid the coming of a new Dark Age that was predicted, what was called for was robust and decisive action, but what resulted was denial and self-deception on the part of economic, political, and scientific elites. The culprits, as Oreskes and Conway imagine them, were an over-reliance on the economic ability of free markets to correct themselves and an overreluctance by the scientific community to take a stand in the face of threats that according to the most exacting standards could not be absolutely substantiated in advance.

As recounted by the narrator of this story, who is depicted as having moved to China during the great migration of 2073-2093, the people of the West knew what was coming for their civilization but were unwilling to face it, much less prevent it. Despite overwhelming evidence of the effect of carbon emissions and greenhouse gases on the atmosphere, which had led to the intensification of extreme weather effects like forest fires, hurricanes, floods, winter storms, heat waves, and drought, climate deniers either hardened their opposition to the existence of climate change or found other ways to dismiss its significance. Meanwhile, the craven inability of the scientific community to coalesce around this global threat only opened the door further for multinational corporations and other political players to discredit the practice of science itself.

By contrast, the Chinese in this fictive scenario had supposedly seen what was coming by the mid-twentieth century and took drastic steps to deal with it. To face the new Penumbral Age that was otherwise already on its way involved much more than a conversion of China's economy from carbon-based sources of energy to natural ones. It also required the re-education of China's entire population to cope with these otherwise inexorable developments before it was too late. While such efforts on the part of the Chinese government only reinforced the Western view that China was too autocratic to be taken seriously, the West's lack of any political resolve to address this crisis in the first place only insured its own ruin.

*The Collapse of Western Civilization* is, of course, only a fictive projection of the possible consequences of disregarding climate change, but it carries with it a sober warning that many nations, whether or not they will all act on it, have in fact have heard. The Paris Climate Agreement, supported by all the nations of the world but the United States, was signed in 2016. The world as we know it is now in real peril, and time is currently running out to take the necessary, and hopefully efficacious, precautions.

# The World as a Polder: What Does It All Mean to Us Today?

 JARED DIAMOND

It seems to me that the most serious environmental problems facing past and present societies fall into a dozen groups. Eight of the 12 were significant already in the past, while four (numbers 5, 7, 8, and 10: energy, the photosynthetic ceiling, toxic chemicals, and atmospheric changes) became serious only recently. The first four of the 12 consist of destruction or losses of natural resources; the next three involve ceilings on natural resources; the three after that consist of harmful things that we produce or move around; and the last two are population issues. Let's begin with the natural resources that we are destroying or losing: natural habitats, wild food sources, biological diversity, and soil.

**1.** At an accelerating rate, we are destroying natural habitats or else converting them to human-made habitats, such as cities and villages, farmlands and pastures, roads, and golf courses. The natural habitats whose losses have provoked the most discussion are forests, wetlands, coral reefs, and the ocean bottom. As I mentioned in the preceding chapter, more than half of the world's original area of forest has already been converted to other uses, and at present conversion rates one-quarter of the forests that remain will become converted within the next half-century. Those losses of forests represent losses for us humans, especially because forests provide us with timber and other raw materials, and because they provide us with so-called ecosystem services such as protecting our watersheds, protecting soil against erosion, constituting essential steps in the water cycle that generates much of our rainfall, and providing habitat for most terrestrial plant and animal species. Deforestation was a or the major factor in all the collapses of past societies described in this book. In addition, as discussed in Chapter 1 in connection with Montana, issues of concern to us are not only forest destruction and conversion, but also changes in the structure of wooded habitats that do remain. Among other things, that changed structure results in changed fire regimes that put forests, chaparral woodlands, and savannahs at greater risk of infrequent but catastrophic fires.

Other valuable natural habitats besides forests are also being destroyed. An even larger fraction of the world's original wetlands than of its forests has already been destroyed, damaged, or converted. Consequences for us arise from wetlands' importance in maintaining the quality of our water supplies and the existence of commercially important freshwater fisheries, while even ocean fisheries depend on mangrove wetlands to provide habitat for the juvenile phase of many fish species. About one-third of the world's coral reefs—the oceanic equivalent of tropical rainforests, because they are home to a disproportionate fraction of the ocean's species—have already been severely damaged. If current trends continue, about half of the remaining reefs would be lost by the year 2030. That damage and destruction result from the growing use of dynamite as a fishing method, reef overgrowth by algae ("seaweeds") when the large herbivorous fish that normally graze on the algae become fished out, effects of sediment runoff and pollutants from adjacent lands cleared or converted to agriculture, and coral bleaching due to rising ocean water temperatures. It has recently become appreciated that fishing by trawling is destroying much or most of the shallow ocean bottom and the species dependent on it.

**2.** Wild foods, especially fish and to a lesser extent shellfish, contribute a large fraction of the protein consumed by humans. In effect, this is protein that we obtain for free (other than the cost of catching and transporting the fish), and that reduces our needs for animal protein that we have to grow ourselves in the form of domestic livestock. About two billion people, most of them poor, depend on the oceans for protein. If wild fish stocks were managed appropriately, the stock levels could be maintained, and they could be harvested perpetually. Unfortunately, the problem known as the tragedy of the commons (Chapter 14) has regularly undone efforts to manage fisheries sustainably, and the great majority of valuable fisheries already either have collapsed or are in steep decline (Chapter 15). Past societies that overfished included Easter Island, Mangareva, and Henderson.

Increasingly, fish and shrimp are being grown by aquaculture, which in principle has a promising future as the cheapest way to produce animal protein. In several respects, though, aquaculture as commonly practiced today is making the problem of declining wild fisheries worse rather than better. Fish grown by aquaculture are mostly fed wild-caught fish and thereby usually consume more wild fish meat (up to 20 times more) than they yield in meat of their own They contain higher toxin levels than do wild-caught fish. Cultured fish regularly escape, interbreed with wild fish, and thereby harm wild fish stocks genetically, because cultured fish strains have been selected for rapid growth at the expense of poor survival in the wild (50 times worse survival for cultured salmon than for wild salmon). Aquaculture runoff causes pollution and eutrophication. The lower costs of aquaculture than of fishing, by driving down fish prices, initially drive fishermen to exploit wild fish stocks even more heavily in order to maintain their incomes constant when they are receiving less money per pound of fish.

**3.** A significant fraction of wild species, populations, and genetic diversity has already been lost, and at present rates a large fraction of what remains will be lost within the next half-century. Some species, such as big edible animals, or plants with edible fruits or good timber, are of obvious value to us. Among the many past societies that harmed themselves by exterminating such species were the Easter and Henderson Islanders whom we have discussed.

But biodiversity losses of small inedible species often provoke the response, "Who cares? Do you really care less for humans than for some lousy useless little fish or weed, like the snail darter or Furbish lousewort?" This response misses the point that the entire natural world is made up of wild species providing us for free with services that can be very expensive, and in many cases impossible, for us to supply ourselves. Elimination of lots of lousy little species regularly causes big harmful consequences for humans, just as does randomly knocking out many of the lousy little rivets holding together an airplane. The literally innumerable examples include: the role of earthworms in regenerating soil and maintaining its texture (one of the reasons that oxygen levels dropped inside the Biosphere 2 enclosure, harming its human inhabitants and crippling a colleague of mine, was a lack of appropriate earthworms, contributing to altered soil/atmosphere gas exchange); soil bacteria that fix the essential crop nutrient nitrogen, which otherwise we have to spend money to supply in fertilizers; bees and other insect pollinators (they pollinate our crops for free, whereas it's expensive for us to pollinate every crop flower by hand); birds and mammals that disperse wild fruits (foresters still haven't figured out how to grow from seed the most important commercial tree species of the Solomon Islands, whose seeds are naturally dispersed by fruit bats, which are becoming hunted out); elimination of whales, sharks, bears, wolves, and other top predators in the seas and on the land, changing the whole food chain beneath them; and wild plants and animals that decompose wastes and recycle nutrients, ultimately providing us with clean water and air.

**4.** Soils of farmlands used for growing crops are being carried away by water and wind erosion at rates between 10 and 40 times the rates of soil formation, and between 500 and 10,000 times soil erosion rates on forested land. Because those soil erosion rates are so much higher than soil formation rates, that means a net loss of soil. For instance, about half of the top-soil of Iowa, the state whose agriculture productivity is among the highest in the U.S., has been eroded in the last 150 years. On my most recent visit to Iowa, my hosts showed me a churchyard offering a dramatically visible example of those soil losses. A church was built there in the middle of farmland during the 19th century and has been maintained continuously as a church ever since, while the land around it was being farmed. As a result of soil being eroded much more rapidly from fields than from the churchyard, the yard now stands like a little island raised 10 feet above the surrounding sea of farmland.

Other types of soil damage caused by human agricultural practices include salinization, as discussed for Montana, China, and Australia in Chapters 1, 12, and 13; losses of soil fertility, because farming removes nutrients much more rapidly than they are restored by weathering of the underlying rock; and soil acidification in some areas, or its converse, alkalinization, in other areas. All of these types of harmful impacts have resulted in a fraction of the world's farmland variously estimated at between 20% and 80% having become severely damaged, during an era in which increasing human population has caused us to need more farmland rather than less farmland. Like deforestation, soil problems contributed to the collapses of all past societies discussed in this book.

The next three problems involve ceilings—on energy, freshwater, and photosynthetic capacity. In each case the ceiling is not hard and fixed but soft: we can obtain more of the needed resource, but at increasing costs.

**5.** The world's major energy sources, especially for industrial societies, are fossil fuels: oil, natural gas, and coal. While there has been much discussion about how many big oil and gas fields remain to be discovered, and while coal reserves are believed to be large, the prevalent view is that known and likely reserves of readily accessible oil and natural gas will last for a few more decades. This view should not be misinterpreted to mean that all of the oil and natural gas within the Earth will have been used up by then. Instead, further reserves will be deeper underground, dirtier, increasingly expensive to extract or process, or will involve higher environmental costs. Of course, fossil fuels are not our sole energy sources, and I shall consider problems raised by the alternatives below.

**6.** Most of the world's freshwater in rivers and lakes is already being utilized for irrigation, domestic and industrial water, and in situ uses such as boat transportation corridors, fisheries, and recreation. Rivers and lakes that are not already utilized are mostly far from major population centers and likely users, such as in Northwestern Australia, Siberia, and Iceland. Throughout the world, freshwater underground aquifers are being depleted at rates faster than they are being naturally replenished, so that they will eventually dwindle. Of course, freshwater can be made by desalinization of seawater, but that costs money and energy, as does pumping the resulting desalinized water inland for use. Hence desalinization, while it is useful locally, is too expensive to solve most of the world's water shortages. The Anasazi and Maya were among the past societies to be undone by water problems, while today over a billion people lack access to reliable safe drinking water.

**7.** It might at first seem that the supply of sunlight is infinite, so one might reason that the Earth's capacity to grow crops and wild plants is also infinite. Within the last 20 years, it has been appreciated that that is not the case, and that's not only because plants grow poorly in the world's Arctic regions and deserts unless one goes to the expense of supplying heat or water. More generally, the amount of solar energy fixed per acre by plant photosynthesis, hence plant growth per acre, depends on temperature and rainfall. At any given temperature and rainfall the plant growth that can be supported by the sunlight falling on an acre is limited by the geometry and biochemistry of plants, even if they take up the sunlight so efficiently that not a single photon of light passes through the plants unabsorbed to reach the ground. The first calculation of this photosynthetic ceiling, carried out in 1986, estimated that humans then already used (e.g., for crops, tree plantations, and golf courses) or diverted or wasted (e.g., light falling on concrete roads and buildings) about half of the Earth's photosynthetic capacity. Given the rate of increase of human population, and especially of population impact (see point 12 below), since 1986, we are projected to be utilizing most of the world's terrestrial photosynthetic capacity by the middle of this century. That is, most energy fixed from sunlight will be used for human purposes, and little will be left over to support the growth of natural plant communities, such as natural forests.

The next three problems involve harmful things that we generate or move around: toxic chemicals, alien species, and atmospheric gases.

**8.** The chemical industry and many other industries manufacture or release into the air, soil, oceans, lakes, and rivers many toxic chemicals, some of them "unnatural" and synthesized only by humans, others present naturally in tiny concentrations (e.g., mercury) or else synthesized by living things but synthesized and released by humans in quantities much larger than natural ones (e.g., hormones). The first of these toxic chemicals to achieve wide notice were insecticides, pesticides, and herbicides, whose effects on birds, fish, and other animals were publicized by Rachel Carson's 1962 book *Silent Spring*. Since then, it has been appreciated that the toxic effects of even greater significance for us humans are those on ourselves. The culprits include not only insecticides, pesticides, and herbicides, but also mercury and other metals, fire-retardant chemicals, refrigerator coolants, detergents, and components of plastics. We swallow them in our food and water, breathe them in our air, and absorb them through our skin. Often in very low concentrations, they variously cause birth defects, mental retardation, and temporary or permanent damage to our immune and reproductive systems. Some of them act as endocrine disruptors, i.e., they interfere with our reproductive systems by mimicking or blocking effects of our own sex hormones. They probably make the major contribution to the steep decline in sperm count in many human populations over the last several decades, and to the apparently increasing frequency with which couples are unable to conceive, even when one takes into account the increasing average age of marriage in many societies. In addition, deaths in the U.S. from air pollution alone (without considering soil and water pollution) are conservatively estimated at over 130,000 per year.

Many of these toxic chemicals are broken down in the environment only slowly (e.g., DDT and PCBs) or not at all (mercury), and they persist in the environment for long times before being washed out. Thus, cleanup costs of many polluted sites in the U.S. are measured in the billions of dollars (e.g., Love Canal, the Hudson River, Chesapeake Bay, the *Exxon Valdez* oil spill, and Montana copper mines). But pollution at those worst sites in the U.S. is mild compared to that in the former Soviet Union, China, and many Third World mines, whose cleanup costs no one even dares to think about.

**9.** The term "alien species" refers to species that we transfer, intentionally or inadvertently, from a place where they are native to another place where they are not native. Some alien species are obviously valuable to us as crops, domestic animals, and landscaping. But others devastate populations of native species with which they come in contact, either by preying on, parasitizing, infecting, or outcompeting them. The aliens cause these big effects because the native species with which they come in contact had no previous evolutionary experience of them and are unable to resist them (like human populations newly exposed to smallpox or AIDS). There are by now literally hundreds of cases in which alien species have caused one-time or annually recurring damages of hundreds of millions of dollars or even billions of dollars. Modern examples include Australia's rabbits and foxes, agricultural weeds like Spotted Knapweed and Leafy Spurge (Chapter 1), pests and pathogens of trees and crops and livestock (like the blights that wiped out American chestnut trees and devasted American elms), the water hyacinth that chokes waterways, the zebra mussels that choke power plants, and the lampreys that devastated the former commercial fisheries of the North American Great Lakes (Plates 30, 31). Ancient examples include the introduced rats that contributed to the extinction of Easter Island's palm tree by gnawing its nuts, and that ate the eggs and chicks of nesting birds on Easter, Henderson, and all other Pacific islands previously without rats.

**10.** Human activities produce gases that escape into the atmosphere, where they either damage the protective ozone layer (as do formerly widespread refrigerator coolants) or else act as greenhouse gases that absorb sunlight and thereby lead to global warming. The gases contributing to global warming include carbon dioxide from combustion and respiration, and methane from fermentation in the intestines of ruminant animals. Of course, there have always been natural fires and animal respiration producing carbon dioxide, and wild ruminant animals producing methane, but our burning of firewood and of fossil fuels has greatly increased the former, and our herds of cattle and of sheep have greatly increased the latter.

For many years, scientists debated the reality, cause, and extent of global warming: are world temperatures really historically high now, and, if so, by how much, and are humans the leading cause? Most knowledgeable scientists now agree that, despite year-to-year ups and downs of temperature that necessitate complicated analyses to extract warming trends, the atmosphere really has been undergoing an unusually rapid rise in temperature recently, and that human activities are the or a major cause. The remaining uncertainties mainly concern the future expected magnitude of the effect: e.g., whether average global temperatures will increase by "just" 1.5 degrees Centigrade or by 5 degrees Centigrade over the next century. Those numbers may not sound like a big deal, until one reflects that average global temperatures were "only" 5 degrees cooler at the height of the last Ice Age.

While one might at first think that we should welcome global warming on the grounds that warmer temperatures mean faster plant growth, it turns out that global warming will produce both winners and losers. Crop yields in cool areas with temperatures marginal for agriculture may indeed increase, while crop yields in already warm or dry areas may decrease. In Montana, California, and many other dry climates, the disappearance of mountain snowpacks will decrease the water available for domestic uses, and for irrigation that actually limits crop yields in those areas. The rise in global sea levels as a result of snow and ice melting poses dangers of flooding and coastal erosion for densely populated low-lying coastal plains and river deltas already barely above or even below sea level. The areas thereby threatened include much of the Netherlands, Bangladesh, and the seaboard of the eastern U.S., many low-lying Pacific islands, the deltas of the Nile and Mekong Rivers, and coastal and riverbank cities of the United Kingdom (e.g., London), India, Japan, and the Philippines. Global warming will also produce big secondary effects that are difficult to predict exactly in advance and that are likely to cause huge problems, such as further climate changes resulting from changes in ocean circulation resulting in turn from melting of the Arctic ice cap.

The remaining two problems involve the increase in human population:

**11.** The world's human population is growing. More people require more food, space, water, energy, and other resources. Rates and even the direction of human population change vary greatly around the world, with the highest rates of population growth (4% per year or higher) in some Third World countries, low rates of growth (1% per year or less) in some First World countries such as Italy and Japan, and negative rates of growth (i.e., decreasing populations) in countries facing major public health crises, such as Russia and AIDS-affected African countries. Everybody agrees that the world population is increasing, but that its annual percentage rate of increase is not as high as it was a decade or two ago. However, there is still disagreement about whether the world's population will stabilize at some value above its present level (double the present population?), and (if so) how many years (30 years? 50 years?) it will take for population to reach that level, or whether population will continue to grow.

There is long built-in momentum to human population growth because of what is termed the "demographic bulge" or "population momentum," i.e., a disproportionate number of children and young reproductive-age people in today's population, as a result of recent population growth. That is, suppose that every couple in the world decided tonight to limit themselves to two children, approximately the correct number of children to yield an unchanging population in the long run by exactly replacing their two parents who will eventually die (actually, 2.1 children when one considers childless couples and children who won't marry). The world's population would nevertheless continue to increase for about 70 years, because more people today are of reproductive age or entering reproductive age than are old and post-reproductive. The problem of human population growth has received much attention in recent decades and has given rise to movements such as Zero Population Growth, which aim to slow or halt the increase in the world's population.

**12.** What really counts is not the number of people alone, but their impact on the environment. If most of the world's 6 billion people today were in cryogenic storage and neither eating, breathing, nor metabolizing, that large population would cause no environmental problems. Instead, our numbers pose problems insofar as we consume resources and generate wastes. That per-capita impact—the resources consumed, and the wastes put out, by each person—varies greatly around the world, being highest in the First World and lowest in the Third World. On the average, each citizen of the U.S., western Europe, and Japan consumes 32 times more resources such as fossil fuels, and puts out 32 times more wastes, than do inhabitants of the Third World (Plate 35).

But low-impact people are becoming high-impact people for two reasons: rises in living standards in Third World countries whose inhabitants see and covet First World lifestyles; and immigration, both legal and illegal, of individual Third World inhabitants into the First World, driven by political, economic, and social problems at home. Immigration from low-impact countries is now the main contributor to the increasing populations of the U.S. and Europe. By the same token, the overwhelmingly most important human population problem for the world as a whole is not the high rate of population increase in Kenya, Rwanda, and some other poor Third World countries, although that certainly does pose a problem for Kenya and Rwanda themselves, and although that is the population problem most discussed. Instead, the biggest problem is the increase in total human impact, as the result of rising Third World living standards, and of Third World individuals moving to the First World and adopting First World living standards.

There are many "optimists" who argue that the world could support double its human population, and who consider only the increase in human numbers and not the average increase in per-capita impact. But I have not met anyone who seriously argues that the world could support 12 times its current impact, although an increase of that factor would result from all Third World inhabitants adopting First World living standards. (That factor of 12 is less than the factor of 32 that I mentioned in the preceding paragraph, because there are already First World inhabitants with high-impact lifestyles, although they are greatly outnumbered by Third World inhabitants.) Even if the people of China alone achieved a First World living standard while everyone else's living standard remained constant, that would double our human impact on the world (Chapter 12).

People in the Third World aspire to First World living standards. They develop that aspiration through watching television, seeing advertisements for First World consumer products sold in their countries, and observing First World visitors to their countries. Even in the most remote villages and refugee camps today, people know about the outside world. Third World citizens are encouraged in that aspiration by First World and United Nations development agencies, which hold out to them the prospect of achieving their dream if they will only adopt the right policies, like balancing their national budgets, investing in education and infrastructure, and so on.

But no one at the U.N. or in First World governments is willing to acknowledge the dream's impossibility: the unsustainability of a world in which the Third World's large population were to reach and maintain current First World living standards. It is impossible for the First World to resolve that dilemma by blocking the Third World's efforts to catch up: South Korea, Malaysia, Singapore, Hong Kong, Taiwan, and Mauritius have already succeeded or are close to success; China and India are progressing rapidly by their own efforts; and the 15 rich Western European countries making up the European Union have just extended Union membership to 10 poorer countries of Eastern Europe, in effect thereby pledging to help those 10 countries catch up. Even if the human populations of the Third World did not exist, it would be impossible for the First World alone to maintain its present course, because it is not in a steady state but is depleting its own resources as well as those imported from the Third World. At present, it is untenable politically for First World leaders to propose to their own citizens that they lower their living standards, as measured by lower resource consumption and waste production rates. What will happen when it finally dawns on all those people in the Third World that current First World standards are unreachable for them, and that the First World refuses to abandon those standards for itself? Life is full of agonizing choices based on tradeoffs, but that's the crudest trade-off that we shall have to resolve: encouraging and helping all people to achieve a higher standard of living, without thereby undermining that standard through overstressing global resources.

I introduced this section by acknowledging that there are important differences between the ancient world and the modern world. The differences that I then went on to mention—today's larger population and more potent destructive technology, and today's interconnectedness posing the risk of a global rather than a local collapse—may seem to suggest a pessimistic outlook. If the Easter Islanders couldn't solve their milder local problems in the past, how can the modern world hope to solve its big global problems?

People who get depressed at such thoughts often then ask me, "Jared, are you optimistic or pessimistic about the world's future?" I answer, "I'm a cautious optimist." By that, I mean that, on the one hand, I acknowledge the seriousness of the problems facing us. If we don't make a determined effort to solve them, and if we don't succeed at that effort, the world as a whole within the next few decades will face a declining standard of living, or perhaps something worse. That's the reason why I decided to devote most of my career efforts at this stage of my life to convincing people that our problems have to be taken seriously and won't go away otherwise. On the other hand, we shall be able to solve our problems—if we choose to do so. That's why my wife and I did decide to have children 17 years ago: because we did see grounds for hope.

One basis for hope is that, realistically, we are not beset by insoluble problems. While we do face big risks, the most serious ones are not ones beyond our control, like a possible collision with an asteroid of a size that hits the Earth every hundred million years or so. Instead, they are ones that we are generating ourselves. Because we are the cause of our environmental problems, we are the ones in control of them, and we can choose or not choose to stop causing them and start solving them. The future is up for grabs, lying in our own hands. We don't need new technologies to solve our problems; while new technologies can make some contribution, for the most part we "just" need the political will to apply solutions already available. Of course, that's a big "just." But many societies did find the necessary political will in the past. Our modern societies have already found the will to solve some of our problems, and to achieve partial solutions to others.

Another basis for hope is the increasing diffusion of environmental thinking among the public around the world. While such thinking has been with us for a long time, its spread has accelerated, especially since the 1962 publication of *Silent Spring*. The environmental movement has been gaining adherents at an increasing rate, and they act through a growing diversity of increasingly effective organizations, not only in the United States and Europe but also in the Dominican Republic and other developing countries. At the same time as the environmental movement is gaining strength at an increasing rate, so too are the threats to our environment. That's why I referred earlier in this book to our situation as that of being in an exponentially accelerating horse race of unknown outcome. It's neither impossible, nor is it assured, that our preferred horse will win the race.

What are the choices that we must make if we are now to succeed, and not to fail? There are many specific choices, of which I discuss examples in the Further Readings section, that any of us can make as individuals. For our society as a whole, the past societies that we have examined in this book suggest broader lessons. Two types of choices seem to me to have been crucial in tipping their outcomes towards success or failure: long-term planning, and willingness to reconsider core values. On reflection, we can also recognize the crucial role of these same two choices for the outcomes of our individual lives.

One of those choices has depended on the courage to practice long-term thinking, and to make bold, courageous, anticipatory decisions at a time when problems have become perceptible but before they have reached crisis proportions. This type of decision-making is the opposite of the short-term reactive decision-making that too often characterizes our elected politicians—the thinking that my politically well-connected friend decried as "90-day thinking," i.e., focusing only on issues likely to blow up in a crisis within the next 90 days. Set against the many depressing bad examples of such short-term decision-making are the encouraging examples of courageous long-term thinking in the past, and in the contemporary world of NGOs, business, and government. Among past societies faced with the prospect of ruinous deforestation, Easter Island and Mangareva chiefs succumbed to their immediate concerns, but Tokugawa shoguns, Inca emperors, New Guinea highlanders, and 16th-century German landowners adopted a long view and reafforested. China's leaders similarly promoted reafforestation in recent decades and banned logging of native forests in 1998. Today, many NGOs exist specifically for the purpose of promoting sane long-term environmental policies. In the business world the American corporations that remain successful for long times (e.g., Procter and Gamble) are ones that don't wait for a crisis to force them to reexamine their policies, but that instead look for problems on the horizon and act before there is a crisis. I already mentioned Royal Dutch Shell Oil Company as having an office devoted just to envisioning scenarios decades off in the future.

Courageous, successful, long-term planning also characterizes some governments and some political leaders, some of the time. Over the last 30 years a sustained effort by the U.S. government has reduced levels of the six major air pollutants nationally by 25%, even though our energy consumption and population increased by 40% and our vehicle miles driven increased by 150% during those same decades. The governments of Malaysia, Singapore, Taiwan, and Mauritius all recognized that their long-term economic well-being required big investments in public health to prevent tropical diseases from sapping their economies; those investments proved to be a key to those countries' spectacular recent economic growth. Of the former two halves of the overpopulated nation of Pakistan, the eastern half (independent since 1971 as Bangladesh) adopted effective family planning measures to reduce its rate of population growth, while the western half (still known as Pakistan) did not and is now the world's sixth most populous country. Indonesia's former environmental minister Emil Salim, and the Dominican Republic's former president Joaquín Balaguer, exemplify government leaders whose concern about chronic environmental dangers made a big impact on their countries. All of these examples of courageous long-term thinking in both the public sector and the private sector contribute to my hope.

The other crucial choice illuminated by the past involves the courage to make painful decisions about values. Which of the values that formerly served a society well can continue to be maintained under new changed circumstances? Which of those treasured values must instead be jettisoned and replaced with different approaches? The Greenland Norse refused to jettison part of their identity as a European, Christian, pastoral society, and they died as a result. In contrast, Tikopia Islanders did have the courage to eliminate their ecologically destructive pigs, even though pigs are the sole large domestic animal and a principal status symbol of Melanesian societies. Australia is now in the process of reappraising its identity as a British agricultural society. The Icelanders and many traditional caste societies of India in the past, and Montana ranchers dependent on irrigation in recent times, did reach agreement to subordinate their individual rights to group interests. They thereby succeeded in managing shared resources and avoiding the tragedy of the commons that has befallen so many other groups. The government of China restricted the traditional freedom of individual reproductive choice, rather than let population problems spiral out of control. The people of Finland, faced with an ultimatum by their vastly more powerful Russian neighbor in 1939, chose to value their freedom over their lives, fought with a courage that astonished the world, and won their gamble, even while losing the war. While I was living in Britain from 1958 to 1962, the British people were coming to terms with the outdatedness of cherished long-held values based on Britain's former role as the world's dominant political, economic, and naval power. The French, Germans, and other European countries have advanced even further in subordinating to the European Union their national sovereignties for which they used to fight so dearly.

All of these past and recent reappraisals of values that I have just mentioned were achieved despite being agonizingly difficult. Hence they also contribute to my hope. They may inspire modern First World citizens with the courage to make the most fundamental reappraisal now facing us: how much of our traditional consumer values and First World living standard can we afford to retain? I already mentioned the seeming political impossibility of inducing First World citizens to lower their impact on the world. But the alternative, of continuing our current impact, is more impossible. This dilemma reminds me of Winston Churchill's response to criticisms of democracy: "It has been said that Democracy is the worst form of government except all those other forms that have been tried from time to time." In that spirit, a lower-impact society is the most impossible scenario for our future—except for all other conceivable scenarios.

Actually, while it won't be easier to reduce our impact, it won't be impossible either. Remember that impact is the product of two factors: population, multiplied times impact per person. As for the first of those two factors, population growth has recently declined drastically in all First World countries, and in many Third World countries as well—including China, Indonesia, and Bangladesh, with the world's largest, fourth largest, and ninth largest populations respectively. Intrinsic population growth in Japan and Italy is already below the replacement rate, such that their existing populations (i.e., not counting immigrants) will soon begin shrinking. As for impact per person, the world would not even have to decrease its current consumption rates of timber products or of seafood: those rates could be sustained or even increased, if the world's forests and fisheries were properly managed.

My remaining cause for hope is another consequence of the globalized modern world's interconnectedness. Past societies lacked archaeologists and television. While the Easter Islanders were busy deforesting the highlands of their overpopulated island for agricultural plantations in the

1400s, they had no way of knowing that, thousands of miles to the east and west at the same time, Greenland Norse society and the Khmer Empire were simultaneously in terminal decline, while the Anasazi had collapsed a few centuries earlier, Classic Maya society a few more centuries before that, and Mycenean Greece 2,000 years before that. Today, though, we turn on our television sets or radios or pick up our newspapers, and we see, hear, or read about what happened in Somalia or Afghanistan a few hours earlier. Our television documentaries and books show us in graphic detail why the Easter Islanders, Classic Maya, and other past societies collapsed. Thus, we have the opportunity to learn from the mistakes of distant peoples and past peoples. That's an opportunity that no past society enjoyed to such a degree. My hope in writing this book has been that enough people will choose to profit from that opportunity to make a difference.

# Introduction and the Coming of the Penumbral Age

 Naomi Oreskes and Erik M. Conway

## Introduction

*Science fiction writers construct an imaginary future; historians attempt to reconstruct the past. Ultimately, both are seeking to understand the present. In this essay, we blend the two genres to imagine a future historian looking back on a past that is our present and (possible) future. The occasion is the tercentenary of the end of Western culture (1540–2093); the dilemma being addressed is how we—the children of the Enlightenment—failed to act on robust information about climate change and knowledge of the damaging events that were about to unfold. Our historian concludes that a second Dark Age had fallen on Western civilization, in which denial and self-deception, rooted in an ideological fixation on "free" markets, disabled the world's powerful nations in the face of tragedy. Moreover, the scientists who best understood the problem were hamstrung by their own cultural practices, which demanded an excessively stringent standard for accepting claims of any kind—even those involving imminent threats. Here, our future historian, living in the Second People's Republic of China, recounts the events of the Period of the Penumbra (1988–2093) that led to the Great Collapse and Mass Migration (2073–2093).*

## 1

## The Coming of the Penumbral Age

In the prehistory of "civilization," many societies rose and fell, but few left as clear and extensive an account of what happened to them and why as the twenty-first-century nation-states that referred to themselves as *Western civilization*. Even today, two millennia after the collapse of the Roman and Mayan empires and one millennium after the end of the Byzantine and Inca empires, historians, archaeologists, and synthetic-failure paleoanalysts have been unable to agree on the primary causes of those societies' loss of population, power, stability, and identity. The case of Western civilization is different because the consequences of its actions were not only predictable, but predicted. Moreover, this technologically transitional society left extensive records both in twentieth-century-style paper and in twenty-first-century electronic formats, permitting us to reconstruct what happened in extraordinarily clear detail. While analysts differ on the exact circumstances, virtually all agree that the people of Western civilization knew what was happening to them but were unable to stop it. Indeed, the most startling aspect of this story is just how much these people knew, and how unable they were to act upon what they knew. Knowledge did not translate into power.

For more than one hundred years before its fall, the Western world knew that carbon dioxide ($CO_2$) and water vapor absorbed heat in the planetary atmosphere. A three-phase Industrial Revolution led to massive release of additional $CO_2$, initially in the United Kingdom (1750–1850); then in Germany, the United States, the rest of Europe, and Japan (1850–1980); and finally in China, India, and Brazil (1980–2050). (Throughout this essay, I will use the nation-state terms of the era; for the reader not familiar with the political geography of Earth prior to the Great Collapse, the remains of the United Kingdom can be found in present-day Cambria; Germany in the Nordo-Scandinavian Union; and the United States and Canada in the United States of North America.) At the start of the final phase, in the mid-twentieth century, some physical scientists—named as such due to the archaic Western convention of studying the physical world in isolation from social systems—recognized that the anthropogenic increment of $CO_2$ could theoretically warm the planet. Few were concerned; total emissions were still quite low, and in any case, most scientists viewed the atmosphere as an essentially unlimited sink. Through the 1960s, it was often said that "the solution to pollution is dilution."

Things began to change as planetary sinks approached saturation and "dilution" was shown to be insufficient. Some chemical agents had extremely powerful effects even at very low concentrations, such as organochlorine insecticides (most famously the pesticide dichlorodiphenyltrichloroethane, or DDT) and chlorinated fluorocarbons (CFCs). The former were shown in the 1960s to disrupt reproductive function in fish, birds, and mammals; scientists correctly predicted in the 1970s that the latter would deplete the stratospheric ozone layer. Other saturation effects occurred because of the huge volume of materials being released into the planetary environment. These materials included sulfates from coal combustion, as well as $CO_2$ and methane ($CH_4$) from a host of sources including fossil fuel combustion, concrete manufacture, deforestation, and then-prevalent agricultural techniques, such as growing rice in paddy fields and producing cattle as a primary protein source.

In the 1970s, scientists began to recognize that human activities were changing the physical and biological functions of the planet in consequential ways—giving rise to the Anthropocene Period of geological history. None of the scientists who made these early discoveries was particularly visionary: many of the relevant studies were by-products of nuclear weapons testing and development. It was the rare man—in those days, sex discrimination was still widespread—who understood that he was in fact studying the limits of planetary sinks. A notable exception was the futurist Paul Ehrlich, whose book *The Population Bomb* was widely read in the late 1960s but was considered to have been discredited by the 1990s.

Nonetheless, enough research accumulated to provoke some response. Major research programs were launched and new institutions created to acknowledge and investigate the issue. Culturally, celebrating the planet was encouraged on an annual Earth Day (as if every day were not an Earth day!), and in the United States, the establishment of the Environmental Protection Agency formalized the concept of *environmental protection*. By the late 1980s, scientists had recognized that concentrations of $CO_2$ and other greenhouse gases were having discernible effects on planetary climate, ocean chemistry, and biological systems, threatening grave consequences if not rapidly controlled. Various groups and individuals began to argue for the need to limit greenhouse gas emissions and begin a transition to a non-carbon-based energy system.

Historians view 1988 as the start of the Penumbral Period. In that year, world scientific and political leaders created a new, hybrid scientific-governmental organization, the Intergovernmental Panel on Climate Change (IPCC), to communicate relevant science and form the foundation for international governance to protect the planet and its denizens. A year later, the Montreal Protocol to Control Substances that Deplete the Ozone Layer became a model for international governance to protect the atmosphere, and in 1992, based on that model, world nations signed the United Nations Framework Convention on Climate Change (UNFCCC) to prevent "dangerous anthropogenic interference" in the climate system. The world seemed to recognize the crisis at hand, and was taking steps to negotiate and implement a solution.

But before the movement to change could really take hold, there was backlash. Critics claimed that the scientific uncertainties were too great to justify the expense and inconvenience of eliminating greenhouse gas emissions, and that any attempt to solve the problem would cost more than it was worth. At first, just a handful of people made this argument, almost all of them from the United States. (In hindsight, the self-justificatory aspects of the U.S. position are obvious, but they were not apparent to many at the time.) Some countries tried but failed to force the United States into international cooperation. Other nations used inertia in the United States to excuse their own patterns of destructive development.

By the end of the millennium, climate change denial had spread widely. In the United States, political leaders—including the president, members of Congress, and members of state legislatures—took denialist positions. In Europe, Australia, and Canada, the message of "uncertainty" was promoted by industrialists, bankers, and some political leaders. Meanwhile, a different version of denial emerged in non-industrialized nations, which argued that the threat of climate change was being used to prevent their development. (These claims had much less environmental impact, though, because these countries produced few greenhouse gas emissions and generally had little international clout.)

There were notable exceptions. China, for instance, took steps to control its population and convert its economy to non-carbon-based energy sources. These efforts were little noticed and less emulated in the West, in part because Westerners viewed Chinese population control efforts as immoral, and in part because the country's exceptionally fast economic expansion led to a dramatic increase in greenhouse gas emissions, masking the impact of renewable energy. By 2050, this impact became clear as China's emissions began to fall rapidly. Had other nations followed China's lead, the history recounted here might have been very different.

But as it was, by the early 2000s, dangerous anthropogenic interference in the climate system was under way. Fires, floods, hurricanes, and heat waves began to intensify. Still, these effects were discounted. Those in what we might call *active denial* insisted that the extreme weather events reflected natural variability, despite a lack of evidence to support that claim. Those in *passive denial* continued life as they had been living it, unconvinced that a compelling justification existed for broad changes in industry and infrastructure. The physical scientists studying these steadily increasing disasters did not help quell this denial, and instead became entangled in arcane arguments about the "attribution" of singular events. Of course the threat to civilization inhered not in any individual flood, heat wave, or hurricane, but in the overall shifting climate pattern, its impact on the cryosphere, and the increasing acidification of the world ocean. But scientists, trained as specialists focused on specific aspects of the atmosphere, hydrosphere, cryosphere, or biosphere, found it difficult to articulate and convey this broad pattern.

The year 2009 is viewed as the "last best chance" the Western world had to save itself, as leaders met in Copenhagen, Denmark, to try, for the fifteenth time since the UNFCCC was written, to agree on a binding, international law to prevent disruptive climate change. Two years before, scientists involved in the IPCC had declared anthropogenic warming to be "unequivocal," and public opinion polls showed that a majority of people—even in the recalcitrant United States—believed that action was warranted. But shortly before the meeting, a massive campaign was launched to discredit the scientists whose research underpinned the IPCC's conclusion. This campaign was funded primarily by fossil fuel corporations, whose annual profits at that time exceeded the GDPs of most countries. (At the time, most countries still used the archaic concept of a *gross domestic product*, a measure of consumption, rather than the Bhutanian concept of gross domestic happiness to evaluate well-being in a state.) Public support for action evaporated; even the president of the United States felt unable to move his nation forward.

Meanwhile, climate change was intensifying. In 2010, record-breaking summer heat and fires killed more than 50,000 people in Russia and resulted in more than $15 billion (in 2009 USD) in damages. The following year, massive floods in Australia affected more than 250,000 people. In 2012, which became known in the United States as the "year without a winter," winter temperature records, including for the highest overnight lows, were shattered— something that should have been an obvious cause for concern. A summer of unprecedented heat waves and loss of livestock and agriculture followed. The "year without a winter" moniker was misleading, as the warm winter was largely restricted to the United States, but in 2023, the infamous "year of perpetual summer" lived up to its name, taking 500,000 lives worldwide and costing nearly $500 billion in losses due to fires, crop failure, and the deaths of livestock and companion animals.

The loss of pet cats and dogs garnered particular attention among wealthy Westerners, but what was anomalous in 2023 soon became the new normal. Even then, political, business, and religious leaders refused to accept that what lay behind the increasing destructiveness of these disasters was the burning of fossil fuels. More heat in the atmosphere meant more energy had to be dissipated, manifesting as more powerful storms, bigger deluges, deeper droughts. It was that simple. But a shadow of ignorance and denial had fallen over people who considered themselves children of the Enlightenment. It is for this reason that we now know this era as the Period of the Penumbra.

It is clear that in the early twenty-first century, immediate steps should have been taken to begin a transition to a zero-net-carbon world. Staggeringly, the opposite occurred. At the very time that the urgent need for an energy transition became palpable, world production of greenhouse gases *increased*. This fact is so hard to understand that it calls for a closer look at what we know about this crucial juncture.